The
Bible Knowledge
Commentary

MAJOR PROPHETS

The
Bible Knowledge
Commentary

MAJOR PROPHETS

John F. Walvoord and Roy B. Zuck
GENERAL EDITORS

DAVID C COOK

transforming lives together

THE BIBLE KNOWLEDGE COMMENTARY: MAJOR PROPHETS
Published by David C Cook
4050 Lee Vance Drive
Colorado Springs, CO 80918 U.S.A.

David C Cook U.K., Kingsway Communications
Eastbourne, East Sussex BN23 6NT, England

The graphic circle C logo is a registered trademark of David C Cook.

LCCN 2017955604
ISBN 978-0-8307-7265-0
eISBN 978-0-8307-7292-6

© 1984, 2018 John F. Walvoord and Roy B. Zuck
Previously published as part of *The Bible Knowledge Commentary:
Old Testament*, ISBN 978-0-9714100-1-5.

Cover Design: Nick Lee
Cover Photo: Getty Images

Printed in the United States of America
First Edition 2018

1 2 3 4 5 6 7 8 9 10

010818

CONTENTS

PREFACE

The Bible Knowledge Commentary series is an exposition of the Scriptures written and edited solely by Dallas Seminary faculty members. It is designed for pastors, laypersons, Bible teachers, serious Bible students, and others who want a comprehensive but brief and reliable commentary on the entire Bible.

Why another Bible commentary when so many commentaries are already available? Several features make this series a distinctive Bible study tool.

The Bible Knowledge Commentary series is written by faculty members of one school: Dallas Theological Seminary. This commentary interprets the Scriptures consistently from the grammatical-historical approach and from the pretribulational, premillennial perspective, for which Dallas Seminary is well known. At the same time, the authors often present various views of passages where differences of opinion exist within evangelical scholarship.

Additionally, this commentary has features that not all commentaries include. (a) In their comments on the biblical text, the writers discuss how the purpose of the book unfolds, how each part fits with the whole and with what precedes and follows it. This helps readers see why the biblical authors chose the material they did as their words were guided by the Holy Spirit's inspiration. (b) Problem passages, puzzling Bible-time customs, and alleged contradictions are carefully considered and discussed. (c) Insights from modern conservative biblical scholarship are incorporated in this series. (d) Many Hebrew, Aramaic, and Greek words, important to the understanding of certain passages, are discussed. These words are transliterated for the benefit of readers not proficient in the biblical languages. Yet those who do know these languages will also appreciate these comments. (e) Throughout the series, dozens of maps, charts, and diagrams are included; they are placed conveniently with the Bible passages being discussed, not at the end of each book. (f) Numerous cross references to related or parallel passages are included with the discussions on many passages.

The material on each Bible book includes an *Introduction* (discussion of items such as authorship, date, purpose, unity, style, unique features), *Outline, Commentary,* and *Bibliography.* In the *Commentary* section, summaries of entire sections of the text are given, followed by detailed comments on the passage verse by verse and often phrase by phrase. All words quoted from the New International Version of the Bible appear in boldface type, as do the verse numbers at the beginning of paragraphs. The *Bibliography* entries, suggested for further study, are not all endorsed in their entirety by the authors and editors. The writers and editors have listed both works they have consulted and others which would be useful to readers.

Personal pronouns referring to Deity are capitalized, which often helps make it clear that the commentator is writing about a Member of the Trinity. The word LORD is the English translation of the Hebrew YHWH, often rendered *Yahweh* in English. *Lord* translates *'Ăḏōnāy.* When the two names stand together as a compound name of God, they are rendered "Sovereign LORD," as in the NIV.

The consulting editors—Dr. Kenneth L. Barker and Dr. Eugene H. Merrill on the Old Testament, and Dr. Stanley D. Toussaint on the New Testament—have added to the quality of this commentary by reading the manuscripts and offering helpful suggestions. Their work is greatly appreciated. We also express thanks to Lloyd Cory, Victor Books Reference Editor, to Barbara Williams, whose careful editing enhanced the material appreciably, to Production Coordinator Myrna Jean Hasse, to Jan Arroyo, and other people in the text editing department at Scripture

Press, who spent many long hours keyboarding and preparing pages for typesetting, and to the several manuscript typists at Dallas Theological Seminary for their diligence.

This commentary series is an exposition of the Bible, an explanation of the text of Scripture, based on careful exegesis. It is not primarily a devotional commentary, or an exegetical work giving details of lexicology, grammar, and syntax with extensive discussion of critical matters pertaining to textual and background data. May this commentary deepen your insight into the Scriptures, as you seek to have "the eyes of your heart ... enlightened" (Eph. 1:18) by the teaching ministry of the Holy Spirit.

This book is designed to enrich your understanding and appreciation of the Scriptures, God's inspired, inerrant Word, and to motivate you "not merely [to] listen to the Word" but also to "do what it says" (James 1:22) and "also ... to teach others" (2 Tim. 2:2).

John F. Walvoord
Roy B. Zuck

Editors

John F. Walvoord, B.A., M.A., TH.M., Th.D., D.D., Litt.D.
Chancellor Emeritus
Professor Emeritus of Systematic Theology

Roy B. Zuck, A.B., Th.M., Th.D.
Senior Professor Emeritus of Bible Exposition
Editor, *Bibliotheca Sacra*

Consulting Editors

Old Testament
Kenneth L. Barker, B.A., Th.M., Ph.D.
Writer, Lewisville, Texas

Eugene H. Merrill, B.A., M.A., M.Phil., Ph.D.
Distinguished Professor of Old Testament Studies

New Testament
Stanley D. Toussaint, B.A., Th.M., Th.D.
Senior Professor Emeritus of Bible Exposition

Series Contributing Authors

Walter L. Baker, B.A., Th.M., D.D.
Associate Professor Emeritus of World
Missions and Intercultural Studies
Obadiah

Craig Blaising, B.S. Th.M., Th.D., Ph.D.
Professor of Christian Theology Southern
Baptist Theological Seminary Louisville,
Kentucky
Malachi

J. Ronald Blue, B.A., Th.M.
President Emeritus CAM International
Dallas, Texas
Habakkuk

Sid S. Buzzell, B.S., Th.M., Ph.D.
Professor of Bible Exposition Colorado
Christian University Lakewood,
Colorado
Proverbs

Donald K. Campbell, B.A., Th.M., Th.D.
President Emeritus
Professor Emeritus of Bible Exposition
Joshua

Robert B. Chisholm, Jr., B.A., M. Div., Th.M., Th.D.
Professor of Old Testament Studies
Hosea, Joel

Thomas L. Constable, B.A., Th.M., Th.D.
Chairman and Senior Professor of Bible
Exposition
1 and 2 Kings

Jack S. Deere, B.A., Th.M., Th.D.
Associate Senior Pastor Trinity
Fellowship Church Amarillo, Texas
Deuteronomy, Song of Songs

Charles H. Dyer, B.A., Th.M., Th.D.
Provost and Senior Vice-President of
Education
Moody Bible Institute Chicago, Illinois
Jeremiah, Lamentations, Ezekiel

Gene A. Getz, B.A., M.A., Ph.D.
Senior Pastor
Fellowship Bible Church, North Plano,
Texas
Nehemiah

Donald R. Glenn, B.S., M.A., Th.M.
Chairman and Senior Professor of Old Testament Studies
Ecclesiastes

John D. Hannah, B.S., Th.M., Th.D.
Chairman and Distinguished Professor of Historical Theology
Exodus, Jonah, Zephaniah

Elliott E. Johnson, B.S., Th.M., Th.D.
Senior Professor of Bible Exposition
Nahum

F. Duane Lindsey, B.A., B.D., Th.M., Th.D.
Former Registrar, Research Librarian, and Assistant Professor of Systematic Theology
Leviticus, Judges, Haggai, Zechariah

John A. Martin, B.A., Th.M., Th.D.
Provost
Robert Wesleyan College
Rochester, New York
Ezra, Esther, Isaiah, Micah

Eugene H. Merrill, B.A., M.A., M.Phil., Ph.D.
Distinguished Professor of Old Testament Studies
Numbers, 1 and 2 Samuel, 1 and 2 Chronicles

J. Dwight Pentecost, B.A., Th.M., Th.D.
Distinguished Professor Emeritus of Bible Exposition
Daniel

John W. Reed, B.A., M.A., M.Div., Ph.D.
Director of D.Min. Studies
Senior Professor Emeritus of Pastoral Ministries
Ruth

Allen P. Ross, B.A., M.A., M.Div., Ph.D.
Professor of Old Testament Studies
Trinity Evangelical Episcopal Seminary
Ambridge, Pennsylvania
Genesis, Psalms

Donald R. Sunukjian, B.A., Th.M., Th.D., Ph.D.
Professor of Christian Ministry and Leadership
Talbot School of Theology La Mirada, California
Amos

Roy B. Zuck, B.A., Th.M., Th.D.
Editor, Bibliotheca Sacra
Senior Professor of Bible Exposition
Job

*Authorial information based on original edition of the Bible Knowledge Commentary set. At the time of the commentary's first printing, each author was a faculty member of Dallas Theological Seminary.

Abbreviations

A. General

act.	active	n., nn.	note(s)
Akk.	Akkadian	n.d.	no date
Apoc.	Apocrypha	neut.	neuter
Aram.	Aramaic	n.p.	no publisher, no place of
ca.	*circa*, about		publication
cf.	*confer*, compare	no.	number
chap., chaps.	chapter(s)	NT	New Testament
comp.	compiled, compilation,	OT	Old Testament
	compiler	p., pp.	page(s)
ed.	edited, edition, editor	par., pars.	paragraph(s)
eds.	editors	part.	participle
e.g.	*exempli gratia*, for example	pass.	passive
Eng.	English	perf.	perfect
et al.	*et alii*, and others	pl.	plural
fem.	feminine	pres.	present
Gr.	Greek	q.v.	*quod vide*, which see
Heb.	Hebrew	Sem.	Semitic
ibid.	*ibidem*, in the same place	sing.	singular
i.e.	*id est*, that is	s.v.	*sub verbo*, under the word
imper.	imperative	trans.	translation, translator,
imperf.	imperfect		translated
lit.	literal, literally	viz.	*videlicet*, namely
LXX	Septuagint	vol., vols.	volume(s)
marg.	margin, marginal reading	v., vv.	verse(s)
masc.	masculine	vs.	versus
ms., mss.	manuscript(s)	Vul.	Vulgate
MT	Masoretic text		

B. Abbreviations of Books of the Bible

Gen.	Ruth	Job	Lam.	Jonah
Ex.	1, 2 Sam.	Ps., Pss. (pl.)	Ezek.	Micah
Lev.	1, 2 Kings	Prov.	Dan.	Nahum
Num.	1, 2 Chron.	Ecc.	Hosea	Hab.
Deut.	Ezra	Song	Joel	Zeph.
Josh.	Neh.	Isa.	Amos	Hag.
Jud.	Es.	Jer.	Obad.	Zech.
				Mal.

Matt.	Acts	Eph.	1, 2 Tim.	James
Mark	Rom.	Phil.	Titus	1, 2 Peter
Luke	1, 2 Cor.	Col.	Phile.	1, 2, 3 John
John	Gal.	1, 2 Thes.	Heb.	Jude
				Rev.

C. Abbreviations of Bible Versions, Translations, and Paraphrases

ASV	American Standard Version
JB	Jerusalem Bible
KJV	King James Version
NASB	New American Standard Bible
NEB	New English Bible
NIV	New International Version
RSV	Revised Standard Version

Transliterations

Hebrew

Consonants

א – '	ד – $\underline{d}$	י – y	ס – s	ר – r
ב – b	ה – h	כ – k	ע – '	שׂ – ś
ב – $\underline{b}$	ו – w	כ – $\underline{k}$	פ – p	שׁ – š
ג – g	ז – z	ל – l	פ – $\underline{p}$	ת – t
ג – $\underline{g}$	ח – ḥ	מ – m	צ – ṣ	ת – $\underline{t}$
ד – d	ט – ṭ	נ – n	ק – q	

Daghesh forte is represented by doubling the letter.

Vocalization

בָה – bâh	בָ – bā	בֹ – bo[1]	בְ – bĕ
בֹ – bô	בֹ – bō	בֻ – bu[1]	בֵ – b
בוּ – bû	בוּ – bū	בֶ – be	בָה – bāh
בֵי – bê	בֵ – bē	בִ – bi[1]	בָא – bā'
בֶ – bè	בִי – bī	בַ – bă	בֶה – bĕh
בִי – bî	בַ – ba	בֹ – bŏ	בֶה – beh

[1] In closed syllables

Greek

α, ᾳ – a		ξ – x		γγ – ng	
β – b		ο – o		γκ – nk	
γ – g		π – p		γξ – nx	
δ – d		ρ – r		γχ – nch	
ε – e		σ, ς – s		αἰ – ai	
ζ – z		τ – t		αὐ – au	
η, ῃ – ē		υ – y		εἰ – ei	
θ – th		φ – ph		εὐ – eu	
ι – i		χ – ch		ηὐ – ēu	
κ – k		ψ – ps		οἰ – oi	
λ – l		ω, ῳ – ō		οὐ – ou	
μ – m		ῥ – rh		υἱ – hui	
ν – n		῾ – h			

An Overview of Old Testament History

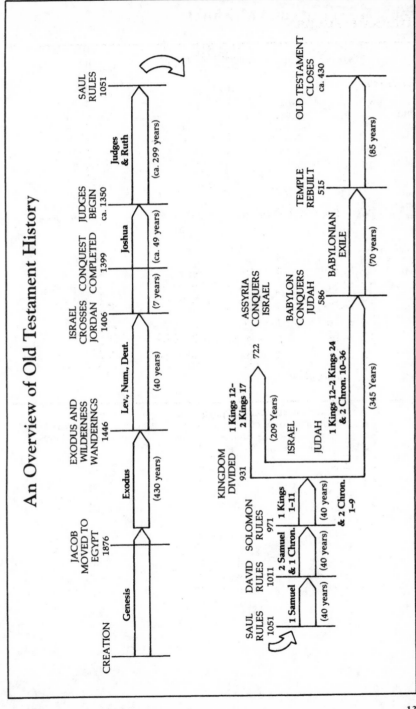

CREATION

Genesis

JACOB MOVED TO EGYPT 1876

Exodus (430 years)

EXODUS AND WILDERNESS WANDERINGS 1446

Lev., Num., Deut. (40 years)

ISRAEL CROSSES JORDAN 1406

(7 years)

CONQUEST COMPLETED 1399

Joshua (ca. 49 years)

JUDGES BEGIN ca. 1350

Judges & Ruth (ca. 299 years)

SAUL RULES 1051

SAUL RULES 1051

1 Samuel (40 years)

DAVID RULES 1011

2 Samuel & 1 Chron. (40 years)

SOLOMON RULES 971

1 Kings 1–11 & 2 Chron. 1–9 (40 years)

KINGDOM DIVIDED 931

1 Kings 12– 2 Kings 17

ISRAEL (209 Years)

JUDAH **1 Kings 12–2 Kings 24 & 2 Chron. 10–36** (345 Years)

ASSYRIA CONQUERS ISRAEL 722

BABYLON CONQUERS JUDAH 586

Babylonian Exile (70 years)

TEMPLE REBUILT 515

(85 years)

OLD TESTAMENT CLOSES ca. 430

13

Biblical Weights and Measures

BIBLICAL UNIT		AMERICAN EQUIVALENT	METRIC EQUIVALENT
WEIGHT			
talent	*(60 minas)*	75 pounds	34 kilograms
mina	*(50 shekels)*	1 1/4 pounds	0.6 kilogram
shekel	*(2 bekas)*	2/5 ounce	11.5 grams
pim	*(2/3 shekel)*	1/3 ounce	7.6 grams
beka	*(10 gerahs)*	1/5 ounce	6 grams
gerah		1/50 ounce	0.6 gram
LENGTH			
cubit		18 inches	0.5 meter
span		9 inches	23 centimeters
handbreadth		3 inches	7 centimeters
CAPACITY			
Dry Measure			
cor [homer]	*(10 ephahs)*	6 bushels	220 liters
lethech	*(5 ephahs)*	3 bushels	110 liters
ephah	*(10 omers)*	1/2 bushel	22 liters
seah	*(1/3 ephah)*	7 quarts	7.3 liters
omer	*(1/10 ephah)*	2 quarts	2 liters
cab	*(1/18 ephah)*	1/2 pint	0.3 liter
Liquid Measure			
bath	*(1 ephah)*	6 gallons	22 liters
hin	*(1/6 bath)*	4 quarts	4 liters
log	*(1/72 bath)*	1/3 quart	0.3 liter

The information in this chart, while not being mathematically precise, gives approximate amounts and distances. The figures are calculated on the basis of a shekel equaling 11.5 grams, a cubit equaling 18 inches, and an ephah equaling 22 liters.

Prophets to Judah, Israel, Edom, and Assyria

Prophets to Judah	Prophets to Israel	Prophet to Edom	Prophets to Assyria
Before the Exile—In Judah			
Joel		Obadiah	Jonah
Isaiah	Hosea		
Micah	Amos		
Jeremiah			Nahum
Habakkuk			
Zephaniah			
During the Exile—In Babylon			
Ezekiel			
Daniel			
After the Exile—In Jerusalem			
Haggai			
Zechariah			
Malachi			

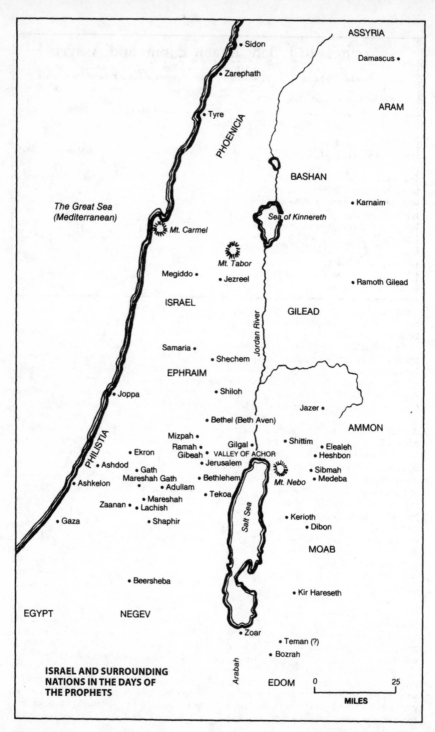

ISRAEL AND SURROUNDING
NATIONS IN THE DAYS OF
THE PROPHETS

16

ISAIAH

John A. Martin

INTRODUCTION

The Book of Isaiah is one of the most-loved books of the Bible; it is perhaps the best known of the prophetic books. It contains several passages that are well known among Bible students (e.g., 1:18; 7:14; 9:6-7; 26:8; 40:3, 31; 53). It has great literary merit and contains beautiful descriptive terminology.

Isaiah also contains much factual material about the society of Israel around 700 B.C. Besides pointing out the shortcomings of the people the prophet noted that God always has a remnant of believers through whom He works.

Isaiah spoke more than any other prophet of the great kingdom into which Israel would enter at the Second Advent of the Messiah. Isaiah discussed the depths of Israel's sin and the heights of God's glory and His coming kingdom.

Author and Date. The author of this book was Isaiah the son of Amoz (Isa. 1:1). The name "Isaiah" means "Yahweh is salvation." Though more is known about Isaiah than most of the other writing prophets, the information on him is still scanty. Probably Isaiah resided in Jerusalem and had access to the royal court. According to tradition he was a cousin of King Uzziah but no firm evidence exists to support this. He did have personal contact with at least two of Judah's kings who were David's descendants (7:3; 38:1; 39:3).

Isaiah was married (8:3). He had two sons, Shear-Jashub (7:3) and Maher-Shalal-Hash-Baz (8:3). Some have supposed from Isaiah's commissioning (chap. 6) that he was a priest, but no evidence in the book supports this.

The year of Isaiah's death is unknown but it was probably after Hezekiah's death in 686 B.C. (and therefore probably in Manasseh's sole reign, 686–642) because Isaiah wrote a biography of King Hezekiah (2 Chron. 32:32). Isaiah's death would have occurred after Sennacherib's death (Isa. 37:38), which was in 681 B.C. Since the prophet's ministry began sometime in Uzziah's reign (790–739 B.C.) Isaiah ministered for at least 58 years (from at least 739, when Uzziah died [6:1], to 681, when Sennacherib died).

According to tradition dating from the second century A.D., Isaiah was martyred by King Manasseh. Justin Martyr (ca. A.D. 100–165) wrote that Isaiah was sawed asunder with a saw (cf. Heb. 11:37).

As is true of all other prophetic books in the Old Testament (except Lam.), the Book of Isaiah bears the name of its author (Isa. 1:1). Many modern scholars divide the book into two or more parts and say that each part had a different author. However, according to strong Jewish and Christian tradition the book had only one author. No doubt was cast on the Isaian authorship until the 18th century when critics began to attack a number of Old Testament books and to question their authorship and internal unity. (See the next section on "Unity.")

Isaiah prophesied in the reigns of Uzziah, Jotham, Ahaz, and Hezekiah, all kings of Judah (1:1). The reigns of these kings (including coregencies) were: Uzziah (790–739), Jotham (750–732), Ahaz (735–715), and Hezekiah (715–686). (See the chart "Kings of Judah and Israel and the Preexilic Prophets," near 1 Kings 12:25-33.)

These years in Israel's history were a time of great struggle both politically and spiritually. The Northern Kingdom of Israel was deteriorating politically, spiritually, and militarily and finally fell to the Assyrian Empire in 722 B.C. The Southern Kingdom of Judah looked as though it too would collapse and fall to Assyria, but it withstood the attack. In this political struggle and spiritual decline Isaiah rose to deliver a message to the people in Judah. His message was that they should trust in the God who had promised them a glorious kingdom through Moses and David. Isaiah urged the nation not to rely on Egypt or any other foreign power to protect them for the Lord was the only protection they would need.

Hosea and Micah were Isaiah's contemporaries. Many have noted several parallels between the messages and vocabularies of Isaiah and Micah (see the *Introduction* to the Book of Micah).

The Book of Isaiah is the first of the 17 Old Testament prophetic books not because it is the oldest but because it is the most comprehensive in content.

Unity. Many scholars question the unity of the book, holding that it was originally two books (with chaps. 40–66 written by "Deutero-Isaiah," who supposedly lived during or after the Babylonian Captivity) or even three (chaps. 1–39; 40–55; 56–66 with the last division written by "Trito-Isaiah"). Many conservative scholars have answered liberal scholars' arguments against the unity of the book. The evidence for its unity is both external (evidence outside the Bible and in other books of the Bible) and internal (evidence within the book itself).

1. External evidence. As already stated, Jewish tradition has uniformly ascribed the entire book to Isaiah. The Dead Sea Scrolls include a complete copy of the Book of Isaiah, thus pointing to its acceptance as one book by the Qumran community in the second century B.C. The Septuagint, the Greek translation of the Hebrew Old Testament in the second century B.C., gives no indication that the Book of Isaiah was anything other than a single book.

Christian tradition has uniformly assumed that Isaiah was a single work until the 18th century when liberals began to challenge that position.

The New Testament writers assumed that Isaiah was the author of the entire book. In the New Testament all the major sections of Isaiah are quoted under the title Isaiah. For example, John 12:38 ascribes Isaiah 53:1 to Isaiah, and John 12:39-40 ascribes Isaiah 6:10 to Isaiah. Several portions of Isaiah 40–66, which are quoted in the New Testament, are ascribed to Isaiah (Isa. 40:3 in Matt. 3:3; Mark 1:2-3; John 1:23; Isa. 40:3-5 in Luke 3:4-6; Isa. 42:1-4 in Matt. 12:17-21; Isa. 53:1 in Rom. 10:16; Isa. 53:4 in Matt. 8:17; Isa. 53:7-8 in Acts 8:32-33; Isa. 65:1 in Rom. 10:20). Interestingly Isaiah is mentioned by name 22 times in the New Testament, more than any other Old Testament prophet.

Jesus Christ assumed that Isaiah was the author of the whole book. Jesus was given the "scroll of the Prophet Isaiah" (Luke 4:17-19) which He unrolled and from which he read Isaiah 61:1-2.

2. Internal evidence. Some of the same terms occur throughout the whole book. For example, "the Holy One of Israel" a title for God, occurs 12 times in chapters 1–39 and 14 times in chapters 40–66. This title is used only 6 times elsewhere in the entire Old Testament (2 Kings 19:22; Pss. 71:22; 78:41; 89:18; Jer. 50:29; 51:5).

The "highway" motif occurs in several parts of the book (Isa. 11:16; 19:23; 35:8; 40:3; 62:10). The "remnant" theme occurs in 10:20-22; 11:11, 16; 28:5; 37:4, 31; 37:32 and also in 46:3 (KJV).

The establishment of justice is a theme in the first division of the book (9:7; 11:4; 16:5; 28:6; 32:16; 33:5) and in the second division (42:1, 3-4; 51:5). And "peace" is mentioned 11 times in chapters 1–39 and 15 times in chapters 40–66. "Joy" occurs 13 times in chapters 1–39 and 19 times in chapters 40–66. Also the Hebrew word *na'ăṣûṣ* ("thornbush") occurs in the Old Testament only in Isaiah 7:19 and 55:13 ("thornbushes" in 33:12 translates a different Heb. word).

Similar passages occur in both parts of the book:

1:15	59:3, 7
1:29	57:4-5
2:3	51:4
10:1-2	59:4-9
28:5	62:3
29:18	42:7
29:23	60:21
30:26	60:19
33:24	45:25
35:6	41:18

The theological unity of the book argues for a single author. This theological factor is strong evidence for persons who believe that the Bible is the Word of God. Chapters 40–55 emphasize the fact that

God would deliver His people from captivity in Babylon. Through Isaiah God predicted that Cyrus would appear on the scene (44:28–45:1) and deliver Judah from captivity. In chapters 40–55 (esp. 43:5-6, 16, 19) the theological point is made that God was telling His people about the return from the Exile beforehand so that they would believe in Him when that event came to pass. In this way He differed greatly from the surrounding nations' gods. As the sovereign God He can foretell events; this ability proves His uniqueness in contrast with false gods.

However, liberal scholars, denying the predictive element in Old Testament prophecy, say that the references to Cyrus mean that chapters 40–55 must have been written after Cyrus ruled Persia (559–530 B.C.). But if those chapters were written *after* the time of Cyrus this means that the God of Israel did not foretell that event and is no different from the gods of the surrounding nations. Therefore to say that chapters 40–55 were written after Cyrus' time strips those chapters of theological validity and makes them almost meaningless.

Purpose. Isaiah's primary purpose was to remind his readers of the special relationship they had with God as members of the nation of Israel, His special covenant community.

Like the other writing prophets, Isaiah knew of the Abrahamic Covenant (Gen. 12:2-3; 15:18-21; 17:3-8, 19) in which God promised that Israel would (a) enjoy a special relationship with Him, (b) possess the land of Canaan, and (c) be a blessing to others.

Isaiah was also aware of the Mosaic Covenant, given Israel at the time of the Exodus from Egypt and repeated by Moses to the generation of Israelites who were about to enter Palestine. Throughout the Book of Deuteronomy God through Moses had promised the people that as members of the covenant community they would be blessed by Him if they lived according to the Mosaic Covenant (e.g., Deut. 28:1-14). But He also warned them that if they did not obey His commands and decrees they would experience the curses (punishments) spelled out in the covenant (Deut. 28:15-68) including exile from the land (see the

chart "The Covenant Chastenings," near Amos 4:6).

However, because of the Abrahamic Covenant in which God promised blessing on Israel and the world, Moses could confidently affirm that even after the people had been exiled from the land the Lord would someday bring them back to the land of promise and establish them in His kingdom.

So Isaiah was calling the people of Judah back to a proper covenantal relationship with God. He was reminding his generation of the sinful condition in which they were living and of its consequences. God would judge the nation, but He would also eventually restore them to the land (cf. Deut. 30:1-5) with full kingdom blessings because of His promises to Abraham.

Isaiah was aware (from Deut. 28:49-50, 64-67) that Judah was destined for exile as had recently befallen the Northern Kingdom. His book, then, was directed to two groups of people: (a) those of his generation, who had strayed from the covenantal obligations given them in the Mosaic Law, and (b) those of a future generation who would be in exile. Isaiah was calling the first group back to holiness and obedience, and he was comforting the second group with the assurance that God would restore the nation to their land and would establish His kingdom of peace and prosperity. The theme of "comfort" is dominant in Isaiah 40–66 ("comfort" occurs in 40:1 [twice]; 51:3, 19; 57:18; 61:2; 66:13; "comforted" occurs in 52:9; 54:11; 66:13; and "comforts" is used in 49:13; 51:12; 66:13)—13 times compared with only 1 occurrence of "comforted" (12:1) in chapters 1–39.

Themes and Theology. Some difficulty exists in determining a central theme for Isaiah around which all the other material in the book revolves. Some have suggested that the book has two themes, one for chapters 1–39 and another for chapters 40–66. Judgment seems to be the emphasis in the first part, and salvation and comfort are prominent in the second. Since Isaiah followed the theology of Deuteronomy (punishment must come for failure to live according to the Mosaic Covenant before a time of blessing can come), the two parts of Isaiah can be reconciled. Chapters 1–39 point out the nation's problem of sin which must be rectified before a proper relationship with the covenant God can be restored. Judgment, emphasized in chapters 1–39, is the purifying force that leads to the forgiveness and pardoning of sins emphasized in chapters 40–66 (cf. 27:9). Ultimately redemption for Israel must come from the "ideal Servant," the Messiah, who will accomplish what the servant-nation cannot do. This accounts for the so-called "Servant Songs" in the second major division of Isaiah (42:1-9; 49:1-13; 50:4-11; 52:13–53:12).

But chapters 40–66 emphasize more than redemption from sin. Those chapters go beyond that to speak of a change in the cosmos, of the Lord's restoration of His created order. In chapters 1–39 judgment on sin is stressed; in chapters 40–66 atonement for that sin *and* the resulting change in people and the world system are discussed. Judgment, then, must come before blessing can follow.

Isaiah had a lofty view of God. The Lord is seen as the Initiator of events in history. He is apart from and greater than His Creation; yet He is involved in the affairs of that Creation.

In the ancient Near East names were more meaningful than they are today. A person's name was an indication of his or her character. The Book of Isaiah is no exception, for in this book the meanings of God's names play an important role in several prophetic utterances. Isaiah used the name "the LORD" (*Yahweh*) by itself more than 300 times, making it by far the most prominent name for Deity Isaiah used. Since this name is the covenant name for God, it is natural that Isaiah used it often. He also frequently used the name "God" (*ĕlōhîm*) in both parts of the book. It is noteworthy that "God" occurs six times in chapter 40 (vv. 1, 3, 8-9, 27-28; "God" in v. 18, however, translates the shorter form *'ēl*), which introduces the section on comfort for the covenant people. As the one supreme Deity, God can give comfort to His people. (See earlier comments on the theme of "comfort" in Isa.) *'Ēl* seems to be used as a polemic against the other gods, for a number of its occurrences appear in the section in which the Lord was speaking of His sovereignty over false gods (chaps. 40–48). Four times God affirmed, "I am God (*'ēl*)—43:12; 45:22; 46:9 (twice). "Lord"

(*'ădōnāy* or the shortened form *'ādôn*) suggests God's dominance over His Creation and is used numerous times in Isaiah, many of them in chapters 1–39. "The LORD Almighty" (*Yahweh ṣᵉbā'ôt*; KJV, "the LORD of hosts"), the most common compound name for God in the Book of Isaiah, appears 46 times in chapters 1–39 and 6 times in the remainder of the book. This compound title links the covenant name of God (*Yahweh*) with His sovereignty over all heavenly powers.

God is also called "the Lord, the LORD Almighty" (*'ădōnāy Yahweh ṣᵉbā'ôt*) 10 times. He is referred to as "the God of Israel" 12 times, and "the Holy One of Israel" 25 times. "Redeemer" is used of God 13 times, all in chapters 41–63, which stress God's redeeming work for Israel, and only one other time in the rest of the Old Testament. Certainly Isaiah centered his theology and his book on God and the work that He was doing and would continue to do in the world.

OUTLINE

COMMENTARY

I. The Retribution of God (chaps. 1–39)

In this first major division of the book, Isaiah wrote much about the judgment that was to come on Judah because of her failure to follow the Mosaic Covenant. God's punishment would prove to the nation that He fulfills His Word. This section also speaks of judgment which is to come on the whole world (chaps. 13–23). All nations of the earth stand guilty before the Holy One of Israel.

In this section on judgment Isaiah also emphasized blessing which will come to the nation because of her covenantal relationship with the Lord. For example, in the Lord's indictment of Judah (chaps. 1–6) 1:24-31 refers to the nation's restoration, 4:2-6 speaks of a remnant of survivors, and 6:13 refers to a "holy seed" or a remnant. In the prophecies on deliverance (chaps. 7–12) Judah, Isaiah wrote, would be delivered from the Aram-Israel alliance (7:3-9; 8:1-15; 9:7–10:4). But also God's glorious empire, the millennial kingdom (Rev. 20:1-6) will rise (Isa. 11) and the regathered people will sing a song of salvation (chap. 12).

In chapters 13–23, on God's judgment on the nations, the prophet wrote that Israel will be restored to the land and will rule over the peoples who have oppressed her (14:1-2). Moab will go to Israel for protection and the establishment of justice and order (16:1-5). The worship of the true God will signal peace on earth (19:19-25).

In the section on punishment and kingdom blessing (chaps. 24–27) much is said about restoration. God will preserve His people (chap. 25) and will be praised by the restored ones (chap. 26). Evil will be judged (27:1) and the remnant restored (27:2-6). Judgment will have a refining effect (27:7-13).

In the section on the woes (chaps. 28–33) a word of comfort is included at the end of each of three portions of these chapters. Judgment will purge the people (28:23-29), a remnant will glorify the Lord (29:17-24), and the Lord will bless and protect His people (30:23-26; 31:4-9). The King will reign in justice and righteousness (chaps. 32–33).

Even in the vengeance section (chaps. 34–35) Isaiah mentioned that a remnant will be gathered together (34:16-17) and the land will be freed from the curse and the remnant will live in joy (chap. 35).

In beautiful and varied language Isaiah made the point that sin must be rooted out of the nation and the world. Eventually, in the Millennium, righteousness will be enforced and the nation will dwell in prosperity and peace because of her renewed relationship with the Lord.

A. The Lord's indictment of the nation (chaps. 1–6)

1. THE HEADING FOR THE BOOK (1:1)

1:1. Isaiah's prophecies focus on **Judah and Jerusalem.** His book is called a **vision,** which suggests that the prophet "saw" (cf. 2:1) mentally and spiritually as well as heard what God communicated to him. This word "vision" also introduces the books of Obadiah, Micah, and Nahum.

Isaiah was familiar with the city of Jerusalem and its temple and royal court. By this time the Northern Kingdom (Israel) was in its final years. The Northern Kingdom fell in 722 B.C. to the Assyrians who were seeking to conquer the entire Syro-Palestine area. Isaiah wrote specifically for the Southern Kingdom (Judah),

which would fall to Babylon a little more than 100 years later in 586 B.C.

For comments on Isaiah **son of Amoz** and the time of Isaiah's ministry (in **the reigns of Uzziah, Jotham, Ahaz, and Hezekiah**) see "Author and Date" in the *Introduction.*

2. THE LORD'S LAWSUIT AGAINST THE NATION (1:2-31)

These verses are in the form of a covenant lawsuit against Judah. In effect, it is a microcosm of chapters 1–39. The Lord, through His messenger Isaiah, indicted His covenant nation for her breach of the Mosaic Covenant, and offered His complete forgiveness to those who would repent but judgment to those who continued to rebel. In 6:9-13 God pointed out to Isaiah that most of the nation, however, would not repent.

a. The Lord's accusation that His people broke the covenant (1:2-9)

1:2a. Isaiah, speaking for the Lord, invoked the **heavens** and the **earth** to **hear** the following accusation against the people. Calling on the heavens and the earth was a way of informing the nation that all creation would agree with what God was about to say.

1:2b-3. In this type of lawsuit the accuser first established his own innocence in the matter. The LORD, like a parent, did this by noting that the people of Judah, His **children** (cf. v. 4), had **rebelled** (cf. "rebels" in v. 28) **against** Him, who was innocent in the matter. The Hebrew word rendered "rebelled" (*pāša'*) was used in treaties to speak of a vassal state's disobedience to the covenant made with it by the suzerain nation. *Pāša'* also occurs in 66:24, the final verse in the book.

Even animals know their masters, but the nation Israel did **not know** and did **not understand** God, her **Master.** (Israel, though often referring to the Northern Kingdom, is sometimes, as here, used of the nation of 12 tribes as a whole, and thus includes Judah.) An **ox** is unusually submissive; in Bible times a **donkey** was known for its stupidity. Therefore to say Israel was less knowledgeable than these domestic animals was an amazingly strong affirmation of her stupidity. These animals were more aware of their owners and the source of sustenance (**manger** was a feeding trough for animals) from their owners than were God's people. Israel did not know God or realize that He was her Provider. By being rebellious (1:2b) the nation failed to carry out God's commands, which proved they did not really "understand" God.

1:4. In His lawsuit God elaborated on the **sinful** condition of the **nation.** This idea that the nation was sinful (*ḥāṭā'*) occurs a number of times in the book (e.g., cf. "sinned" in 42:24; 43:27 and "continued to sin" in 64:5).

Isaiah spoke of the "sins" (*ḥāṭā'îm*) of the people (1:18) and noted that the Suffering Servant came to remove "the sin (*ḥēṭ'*) of many" in the nation (53:12). Because of their sin, the **people** stood guilty before God (cf. Rom. 3:9, 19, KJV). Because they were evildoers, they were corrupt (cf. Rom. 3:10-18 and the word "corrupt" in Gen. 6:12). Their deliberately defiant attitude against God is indicated by the words **forsaken . . . spurned,** and **turned their backs.**

As stated in the *Introduction,* the words **the Holy One of Israel** are used by Isaiah 25 times. This title appropriately contrasts the people's sin with God's holiness.

Though the people had turned their backs on God, in the future He will turn His back on Israel's sin by forgiving her. After Hezekiah was raised from his sickbed, he praised the Lord for placing his sins behind God's back (Isa. 38:17).

1:5-7. When the covenant people turned their backs on God (v. 4) certain consequences followed (cf. Deut. 28:15-68). Isaiah recounted what was happening to them to help them understand that their difficult times had come because of their disobedience. Isaiah first used the figure of a person who had been **beaten** and was bruised over his entire body (Isa. 1:5-6). Though these untreated **wounds . . . welts, and open sores** characterized the nation's spiritual condition, Isaiah was also speaking of her condition militarily. They were beset on all sides by hostile forces and were losing some of their territory to foreign nations (v. 7). They should have realized that these terrible problems had come because of their spiritual condition. Whether Isaiah was describing the soon-coming situation in the Northern Kingdom to be brought

about by the Assyrian invasion (in 722 B.C.) or whether he was speaking prophetically of the coming destruction of Judah (586 B.C.) is open to conjecture though it more likely refers to Judah. His words **desolate . . . burned,** and **stripped** were written as if the devastation had already happened. Thus he emphasized its certainty.

1:8-9. Isaiah then pictured Jerusalem's inhabitants (**the Daughter of Zion;** cf. Jer. 4:31; Lam. 1:6; 2:13; Micah 1:13; 4:8; Zech. 9:9; and see comments on Lam. 2:1; Zech. 8:3) as being **like a shelter in a vineyard** or **a hut in a** melon **field.** Those were temporary structures built to shade from the sun persons who guarded the crops against thieves and animals. Such huts were usually "alone" and easily attacked. Judah **would have** been **like Sodom** and **Gomorrah,** totally devastated, if it had not been for God's grace in leaving **some survivors.** (Centuries later Paul quoted this verse in Rom. 9:29.) In fact Judah *was* like those two wicked cities in her sin. (Cf. the mention of both cities in Isa. 1:10, and of Sodom in 3:9; Ezek. 16:46, 48-49; 55:56.) Isaiah's reference to those two cities no doubt reminded some Judahites of the Lord's reference to them in Deuteronomy 29:23.

b. The Lord's instructions on how the nation should deal with her guilt (1:10-20)

1:10. Building on his reference to **Sodom** and **Gomorrah** in verse 9, Isaiah likened the **rulers** and **people** of Judah to those evil cities. Both the leaders and the populace—those in all levels of society—were to **hear** (cf. v. 2) God's **word.**

1:11-15. The Lord rejected the people's appeal to several aspects of religious ritual—including animal **sacrifices** (v. 11), **incense** (v. 13a), festivals and feasts (vv. 12, 13b-14), and prayers (v. 15)—as compensation for their iniquity.

Some people have mistakenly said (from v. 11) that God had not established the sacrificial system. But this is wrong. Isaiah's point is that the people assumed that merely by offering sacrifices at the altar they would be made ceremonially clean before God. Even multiple sacrifices are **meaningless** (v. 13) and therefore do not please God when the "worshiper" does not bring his life into conformity with God's standards. Also the careful observance of monthly **offerings**

(New Moons; cf. Num. 28:11-14) and Sabbaths (weekly as well as annual Sabbaths on the Day of Atonement and the Feast of Tabernacles, Lev. 16:31; 23:34, 39) were meaningless to God when they were not done with the proper attitude. The same was true of their assemblies on the Sabbath (Lev. 23:3), and the festivals and feasts including the Passover (Lev. 23:4-7), the Feast of Weeks (Lev. 23:15-21), the Feast of Trumpets (Lev. 23:24), the Day of Atonement (Lev. 23:26-27), and the Feast of Tabernacles (Lev. 23:34).

Such observances God called evil because they were carried out hypocritically, with sinful hearts (cf. Isa. 1:4). Therefore those national gatherings, rather than pleasing God, were an obnoxious burden to Him (v. 14).

In addition, the people's many prayers were ineffective because of their guilt (v. 15). The words spread out your hands denoted asking for help (cf. 1 Kings 8:22; Lam. 1:17). Those hands, however, were full of blood (Isa. 1:15). By treating the needy unfairly (cf. vv. 16-17), the people were like a murderer spreading out his bloodstained hands to God in prayer. This spiritual condition made Judah's religious ritual ludicrous. Obviously God would never listen to (i.e., answer) such prayers! (cf. Ps. 66:18) Inward righteousness must accompany outward ritual for that ritual to mean anything to God.

1:16-20. The Lord offered complete forgiveness to the repentant, but promised judgment on the rebels who continued to reject Him. The people had the mistaken idea that they could live any way they pleased so long as they made restitution in the sacrificial system. But instead of trusting in religious ritual (vv. 10-15) the people were to obey God and have the right attitudes toward Him and the right actions toward others.

The people needed to be clean inwardly (like a murderer washing his bloodstained hands). And they needed to replace their evil (cf. v. 13) deeds with right actions. As stipulated in the Mosaic Covenant they needed to evidence their trust in and obedience to the Lord by helping needy people—the oppressed . . . the fatherless, and the widow (cf. v. 23; 10:1-2; Deut. 24:17, 19-21; 26:12; 27:19).

God then invited the sinful people to come to their senses (Isa. 1:18) and admit they had been wrong in their attitudes and practices. The invitation Come now, let us reason together was more than a call for negotiations between the people and God. The word "reason" (yākaḥ) is a law term used of arguing, convincing, or deciding a case in court. The people were to be convinced by their argumentation with God that He was right and they were wrong about their condition. (Other court terms in this chapter are justice . . . defend, and plead, v. 17.) If they acknowledged the depth of their sins—that their iniquities were like blood-colored stains on their souls (scarlet, a red dye made from a worm, and crimson, red-colored cloth)—then God in His grace would cleanse them, making them spiritually white like snow or wool. Acknowledgment of sin was to precede God's cleansing. And the same is true today.

The obedient (v. 19) would eat the best from the land, that is, they would have bountiful crops as promised in the Mosaic Covenant (Deut. 28:3-6, 11). By contrast, those who refused to turn to God (rebels; cf. Isa. 1:23, 28) would be defeated by enemies (devoured by the sword, v. 20; Deut. 28:45-57). This was certain for the . . . Lord has spoken (cf. Isa. 40:5; 58:14).

c. The Lord's lament over Jerusalem (1:21-23)

1:21. The contrast between the original condition of Jerusalem under David and the early years of Solomon's reign with the condition of the people in Isaiah's day is detailed. At one time Jerusalem was considered faithful like a devoted wife. Now, however, the city was a harlot. The imagery of prostitution is common in the prophetic books (esp. Jer. and Hosea). This figure is based on the fact that in marriage, as in the relationship between God and Israel, a covenant was made. When a person becomes a prostitute he or she mars the marriage covenant. In the same way when a person left the true God for idols he marred his covenant with the Lord.

Jerusalem had been known for executive justice and upholding righteousness. "Justice" refers to proper judicial procedures, and "righteousness" is the behavior of those who sought this standard. (Cf. these two in Prov. 8:20; Isa.

5:7; 28:17; Amos 5:7.) **But now** instead of righteousness "living," **murderers** were present. "Murderers" may refer to those who took advantage of the needy (cf. Isa. 1:23 and comments on v. 15).

1:22-23. Their **silver** and **wine,** which used to be valuable, had become worthless: **dross** metal and watered-down wine. Dross is the residue left in the smelting process after pure silver is removed. Like worthless dross, the nation would be "thrown away." The people would be exiled if they would not repent and turn to the Lord.

The rebellious **rulers** in the city were leading the people into ruin by theft, bribery, and injustice to the helpless (cf. comments on v. 17). **The fatherless** and **widows** could not even get hearings because they had no money for bribing the rulers. This situation was especially abhorrent to God because His covenant people were bound to Him and therefore to each other. But now they had no concern for each other's property and needs.

d. The Lord's declaration of the sentence (1:24-31)

God's lawsuit ended with His pronouncing judgment on the guilty nation. In this chapter God is pictured not only as one of the parties in the litigation but also as the Judge who will decide what will happen to the guilty party. Those who were obstinate, refusing to repent, would be judged, but the repentant would be redeemed.

1:24-26. God's judging will bring Him **relief from** the displeasure caused by His **foes (enemies** within the covenant community). It will be like a purging agent, getting rid of the **dross** (v. 25; cf. v. 22), leaving only the pure silver. Vengeance was not for the purpose of "getting even" with unfaithful people. Its purpose was to turn the nation back to a proper relationship to God. The Lord **will** see that the right kind of **judges** are in office **as in** former times (David's and Solomon's empires), and Jerusalem **will** once again **be called the City of Righteousness** and **the Faithful City** (v. 26). References to "the faithful city" (vv. 21, 26) serve as a literary device called an *inclusio* to tie these two verses together.

1:27-31. The contrast between the fate of the remnant and the wicked is detailed in these verses. The remnant will dwell in the new **redeemed** city of Jerusalem (**Zion;** cf. v. 8) where God's **justice** will be present (cf. v. 26). **Rebels** (cf. vv. 20, 23) **will perish,** after being embarrassed that they were ever involved in idol worship near **sacred** oak trees (cf. 57:5) and in **gardens** (cf. 65:3; 66:17). Whereas they once enjoyed worshiping idols (probably including Baal), in those pleasant surroundings they would become like fading **oak** trees and a dry **garden.** Though once strong (like a **mighty man**) in defying God the unrighteous **and his work . . . will burn.** This unquenchable burning probably refers to the destruction by the Babylonian army *as well as* eternal judgment.

3. AN AFFIRMATION OF RESTORATION (2:1-5)

Immediately after the stinging indictment (in the form of a lawsuit) of the nation's sinful practices (1:2-31) Isaiah introduced a concept which was to be a hallmark of his prophecy. A time will come when Jerusalem will have the primary position in the world. Micah 4:1-3 is almost identical to Isaiah 2:1-4.

2:1-2a. The message recorded in these verses **is what Isaiah . . . saw concerning Judah and Jerusalem** (cf. 1:1). The prophets in Israel had at one time been called "seers" because of their divinely given power to "see" or foretell what would happen (1 Sam. 9:9). Here Isaiah was foretelling the future of Jerusalem and Judah. In the prophecies of restoration which are prominent in Isaiah's book, he was not specific as to the exact time when they would be fulfilled (perhaps he did not know; cf. 1 Peter 1:10-11). Here he simply said **in the last days.** Other Bible passages make it clear that these predictions will be fulfilled in the Millennium, Christ's 1,000-year reign on the earth. Because of God's covenant promises to Abraham, Moses, and David, Isaiah knew that Israel will again be in the land and will again have a superior position among the nations.

The mountain of the Lord's temple refers to the mount where the temple was built (and where the millennial temple will be built, Ezek. 40–43). Often in the Scriptures **mountains** denote governmental authorities (Dan. 2:35; Amos 4:1). Here God's rule from the temple will be preeminent (**chief**). The theme of the prominence of the temple mount in Jerusalem is repeated often in Isaiah's prophecies all the way to the end of the book (Isa. 11:9; 25:6-7; 27:13; 30:29; 56:7; 57:13; 65:11, 25; 66:20). Isaiah clearly wanted his readers to be aware that God will protect His covenant nation despite their spiritual insensitivity and even though they would go into captivity.

2:2b-3. When these events take place many **nations will** be attracted to Jerusalem (cf. 14:1; 27:13; 66:23; Zech. 8:23; 14:16) and to God's **house** (the temple, Isa. 2:2a). The attraction will be the Lord's **ways . . . paths . . . Law,** and **Word** which will be made known from that place. In fact **the LORD** Himself will give forth the Law (51:4). (**Zion,** referred to dozens of times by Isaiah, more than by any other author of Scripture, is here a synonym of **Jerusalem;** cf. 4:3; 40:9, 52:1; 62:1. See comments on Zech. 8:3.) In the Millennium, people everywhere will realize that God's revelation is foundational to their lives. They will want to know it (**He will teach us**) and to live according to it (**walk in it**).

2:4. This is one of the more familiar verses in the Book of Isaiah. God will have a worldwide ministry of judging and settling disputes. **He will** require **nations** and **peoples** everywhere to abstain from warfare. Universal peace, with no military conflict or training, will prevail because the implements of warfare (**swords** and **spears**) will be turned into implements of agriculture (**plowshares** and **hooks**; cf. Joel 3:10). At this time of worldwide peace the nations will go to Jerusalem to learn from God (Isa. 2:2). Peace will come not by human achievement but because of God's presence and work in Jerusalem. At that time Israel will be filled with God's Spirit (Ezek. 36:24-30) and her sins will be forgiven (Jer. 31:31-34).

2:5. Isaiah closed this short section with an exhortation for his readers to **walk** (live) **in the light of the LORD.** The prophet called Israel the **house of Jacob,** a reference to Jacob's descendants. Isaiah used this term eight times (vv. 5-6; 8:17; 10:20; 14:1; 29:22; 46:3; 48:1) whereas it is used only nine times by all the other prophets. When great truths about the future are given in the Scriptures, readers are often reminded of how they should live in the present (e.g., 1 Thes. 4:13-18; 5:1-8; 2 Peter 3:10-14;

1 John 3:2-3). In view of the fact that in the Millennium all nations will stream to Jerusalem to learn God's Word, it would be sensible for Israel, already knowing that Law, to follow it (walking in its "light") until the Lord sets up His glorious kingdom.

4. THE PRESENT CONDITION AND FUTURE CONSEQUENCES (2:6–4:1)

Judah's present condition (2:6-11) and its consequences (2:12–4:1) contrast with the glorious kingdom Isaiah had just described (2:1-5). As was true throughout much of Israel's history, the people were not obeying the Lord and therefore had to be disciplined by Him.

a. Judah's likeness to pagan peoples (2:6-11)

2:6-9. God had **abandoned** His **people** (on **the house of Jacob** see comments on v. 5) not because He no longer loved them but because they had become like the **pagans** around them. The people of Judah were as superstitious as the people in **the East,** that is, they were following the practices of the Assyrian Empire, which at that time was encroaching on the entire Syro-Palestinian area. (Or perhaps the people of "the East" were Arameans; cf. 9:12.) At the same time Judahites were engaging in **divination like the Philistines.** The Philistines occupied the southwestern part of Canaan and had sought to control Israel. So Israel was influenced by pagan practices from several sources. That Philistines were involved in divination is evident from 1 Samuel 6:2; 2 Kings 1:2. Divination (from '$\bar{a}nan$, "to practice sorcery"; cf. Lev. 19:26; Deut. 18:10, 14; 2 Kings 21:6; Micah 5:12, "cast spells") was the attempt to control people or circumstances or to seek to know the future through power given by evil spirits (demons).

Isaiah's irony here is strong, for Judah should have known what her future would be because of the Word of God; yet she was trying to discern the future by pagan means. No wonder Isaiah asked God **not** to **forgive** her (Isa. 2:9). Judah had great material wealth (**silver and gold**) and military strength (**horses** and **chariots,** v. 7) which they no doubt mistakenly thought came to them because of their worshiping **idols.** This probably led to pride and self-confidence because God said they would **be brought** low and **humbled** (v. 9; cf. vv. 11-12, 17). Their sinful condition made judgment a necessity.

2:10-11. Ultimately only one Person will be **exalted**. That One will be **the LORD alone** (v. 11; cf. v. 17). When the Lord comes to judge, people will seek to escape His judgment by hiding in caves (cf. vv. 19, 21; Rev. 6:16). They will fear His **splendor** (cf. Isa. 2:19, 21), realizing that their arrogance (v. 11; cf. v. 17) and wealth (vv. 7-8) cannot save them. Throughout this section (2:6–4:1) and many others in the Book of Isaiah, there is an interesting interplay between the judgment which the Lord will inflict on the nation by the Assyrian and Babylonian Captivities and the judgment which will come on Israel and the whole world in the "last days" just before the Millennium. Probably Isaiah and the other prophets had no idea of the lengthy time span that would intervene between those exiles and this later time of judgment. Though many of the predictions in 2:10-21 happened when Assyria and Babylon attacked Israel and Judah, the passage looks ahead to a cataclysmic judgment on the whole world ("when He rises to shake the earth," vv. 19, 21).

b. The Lord's day of reckoning (2:12-22)

When the Lord comes to establish justice on the earth human values will be reversed. Things that people had considered important will be considered unimportant and some things that people thought were insignificant will be highly valued.

2:12-18. God **has a day** (cf. "day" in v. 17) **in store,** a scheduled time of reckoning for sinners. **The LORD Almighty** (*Yahweh ṣᵉbā'ôt*) is an appellation used of God 62 times in Isaiah's book; 52 times alone and 10 times in the title "the Lord ('*ăḏōnāy*), the LORD Almighty." It denotes His military might and strength. When this Almighty One comes nothing will be able to stand in His way. **Proud** people **will be humbled** (cf. vv. 9, 11, 17), and even the great cedar trees in the forests **of Lebanon,** north of Israel, and oak trees (cf. 1:29) in **Bashan** (meaning "fertile plain"), east of the Sea of Kinnereth (later named Galilee), will be no match for the Lord. **Mountains,** perhaps suggesting governmental authorities (cf. comments on 2:3), and their military defenses repre-

sented by towers and **fortified** walls, cannot oppose Him (vv. 14-15). He will also demolish man's trade efforts typified by the merchant ships, the hub of which existed in the city of Tyre, north of Israel (v. 16). Everything that seemed to **man** in his **arrogance** to be permanent and secure will be swept away. The LORD **alone will be exalted** (cf. v. 11) when He demolishes Judah's **idols** (cf. v. 8). This may refer to the time when the Babylonians captured Judah in 586, but the ultimate judgment will be in the future at Christ's Second Advent.

2:19-22. When the Lord's vengeance comes, people will try to escape by fleeing into **caves** (cf. vv. 10, 21). They will be terrified because God will **shake the earth** (see comments on Hag. 2:6-7). Carrying their **idols** made with **silver** and **gold** (cf. Isa. 2:7) will hinder their escape, so the people will toss them aside to **rodents and bats** (v. 20). Once again Isaiah's sense of irony is strong: things highly valued will be thrown aside to detestable creatures that people hate. In verse 21 Isaiah again spoke of people hiding in caves away from God's terror (cf. vv. 10, 19a) when **He** will **shake the earth** (cf. v. 19b).

Then the prophet called on Judah to **stop trusting in man** (v. 22; cf. Ps. 118:8-9). Man is merely like a vapor. His **breath** can be snuffed out quickly. Therefore to trust in him is nonsensical, for man is easily removed (Isa. 2:9, 11-12, 17). In view of God's coming judgment Judah should begin to turn to Him in the present. God's glory should cause them to live righteous, holy lives and thus escape His severe judgment.

c. Judgment on Judah for her actions (3:1-15)

Having affirmed in broad terms (2:9-21) that judgment would come, Isaiah gave examples of present sins in the nation that needed to be judged by God.

3:1-7. God would **take** away **from . . . Judah** any semblance of good government and replace it with a sense of futility. Because of her sin **the LORD** would take away all the supplies and people on which she relied: **food** and **water** (v. 1), soldiers (v. 2), civil (**judge**) and religious (**prophet**) leaders (v. 2), wise people (v. 2), military leaders (v. 3a), and skilled workers (v. 3b). The fact that Isaiah included **the soothsayer** (v. 2) and the **clever enchanter** (v. 3) in this list does not mean he was endorsing them. He was merely noting those on whom the nation was depending for survival and security. The Mosiac Covenant prohibited involvement in soothsaying and enchanting (Deut. 18:10-14). Isaiah himself wrote about Babylon trusting in this kind of activity (Isa. 47:12).

In contrast with these people who were considered wise and mighty the Lord would raise up foolish, weak leadership. Inexperienced **boys** and **children** (3:4; cf. Ecc. 10:16, NIV marg.) would be unable to stop oppression and conflict (Isa. 3:5). Anybody who could be grabbed would be placed in charge of the people, his only qualification (v. 6) being that he owned a **cloak. But** the only thing over which he would rule anyway would be a **heap** of **ruins.** The leaders would have no solution to the problem shortages the people would face (v. 7). Isaiah was speaking of the coming devastation of Judah by the Babylonian army.

3:8-9. The reason such destruction would come on on **Judah** (v. 1) is that everything the nation said and did was **against** her covenant God. The people defied God and were open about **their sin** much **like** the people of **Sodom** (cf. Gen. 18:20; 19:1-11; see comments on Isa. 1:9-10). Therefore the coming **disaster** was **brought** on by **themselves. Woe** ('ôy) is an interjection of distress or of a threat voiced in the face of present or coming disaster. Isaiah's book includes 22 occurrences of that word or its companion word hôy, more than in any other prophetic book.

3:10-12. When God judges, **the righteous** need not fear; they will be justly rewarded for **their deeds.** But **the wicked will be** recompensed (**paid back) for . . . their** deeds (cf. comments on Rom. 3:7-11). God's judgment is always fair. Wicked people often think that sinful living is the way to get ahead in life. Isaiah noted, however, that it is far better for a person to live righteously. The leaders (**guides**) were turning the nation away **from the** proper **path** (Isa. 3:12). **Youths** may refer to minors in age or to adults who were naive like the young. The reference to **women** may mean that wives were influencing their husbands who were rulers, or that the male leaders lacked vigor.

3:13-15. Isaiah pictured **the** LORD seated in a courtroom ready to judge **the people** and especially the **leaders.** By stating that **He rises to judge** Isaiah meant that God, having the authority to judge, was about to do so. Two charges were leveled against the leaders. The first is that they had **ruined** God's **vineyard** (v. 14), that is, God's people (5:1, 7; cf. Ps. 80:8-18; Jer. 2:21; 12:10; Ezek. 15:6-8; Hosea 10:1). Like husbandmen caring for a vineyard, the leaders were to care for the people. But they had ruined the **people** by oppressing (**crushing,** Isa. 3:15a) them. The second charge is that they had taken advantage of **the poor** (vv. 14b, 15b) by plundering them (stealing what little they had) and **grinding** their **faces.** This violated the commands in the Book of Deuteronomy not to oppress others, especially widows, orphans, and the poor. Concern for the poor is also encouraged and illustrated in the New Testament (Acts 9:36; 10:4, 31; 24:17; James 1:27; 2:1-9). A materialistic, oppressive spirit was symptomatic of the leaders' self-centeredness. Rather than seeing their leadership positions as service opportunities they saw them as means of making money at the expense of others.

d. Judah's fall after her pride (3:16–4:1)

Judah's proud condition was illustrated by Jerusalem's society women. Isaiah contrasted what they looked like then with what they will look like after God's judgment comes on them.

3:16. The **haughty** wealthy **women of Zion** (Jerusalem) were trying to attract attention by the way they walked (proudly, **with outstretched necks),** flirted, minced along, and dressed. Isaiah may have implied that the entire nation was proud.

3:17–4:1. In contrast with their pride, wealth, and beauty, the **women of Zion** (cf. 3:16) would be in deep distress. They would have **sores on** their **heads** and would be **bald.** This baldness may refer to their shaving their heads, either in mourning or for medical reasons, because of their head sores. Being in deep distress they would not care how they looked. In fact **the** LORD would cause the Babylonian soldiers to take **away** all the women's fine jewelry and wardrobes (vv. 19-23). **Instead of fragrance** they would have an awful odor (v. 24) perhaps from their head sores (v. 17). Taken captive by the Babylonians, the women would be pulled by **a rope** and would wear **sack-cloth**, black coarse cloth made from goats' hair and symbolizing mourning (cf. Gen. 37:34; 1 Kings 21:27; Neh. 9:1; Es. 4:1; Isa. 15:3; 22:12; 32:11; 37:1-2; Lam. 2:10; Ezek. 27:31; Dan. 9:3). Their **beauty** would be replaced by painful **branding** by their captors. The women would mourn because their **men** (husbands, brothers, and male friends) would be dying **in battle** (Isa. 3:25). The city would be so **destitute** of men and the women would be so disgraced that they would compete to gain a husband (4:1). Isaiah's picture of the Jerusalem socialites and their plight might be humorous if it were not so pathetic and realistic. Years later Jeremiah wrote that the women resorted to eating their own children during the siege (Lam. 2:20; 4:10; cf. Lev. 26:27-29; Deut. 28:53-57; Jer. 19:9).

5. THE HOLY SURVIVORS (4:2-6)

After God's original indictment or "lawsuit" (1:2-31) He gave a promise of restoration (2:1-5). Now at the close of the stinging reiteration of judgment (2:6–4:1) is another section on comfort (4:2-6). In spite of the terrible blow facing the nation because of its sin, some people would survive. Isaiah's initial audience might have thought he was speaking of those who would survive the Exile. However, in the light of Matthew 24:4-30 he was referring to the people who will survive the difficulties in the Great Tribulation just before the Lord Jesus Christ returns to set up His kingdom.

4:2. In spite of the coming severe judgment, divine blessing would eventually come. Sometimes the phrase **in that day** refers to the Babylonian attack on Jerusalem (e.g., 3:7, 18; 4:1), but here (see the statements in vv. 2, 5) as in 2:11-12, 17 it means the millennial reign of Christ.

Some interpreters say **the Branch of the LORD,** who is **beautiful and glorious,** refers to the believing remnant. It seems better, however, to take the "Branch" as a reference to the Messiah since this is its meaning in Jeremiah 23:5; 33:15; Zechariah 3:8. The term "Branch" is a fitting figure for the Messiah because He "sprouted" from David's line (Jer. 33:15) and will bear fruit. Just as people delight in fruit from their land so **the survivors**

will delight in the Messiah, **the Fruit of the land.** The Branch is suggestive of Jesus' words that He is the Vine (John 15:1).

4:3-4. The mark of distinction for surviving Israel will be holiness, not wealth or prestige. Their sins will be forgiven. Speaking again of **the women of Zion** (cf. 3:16–4:1) Isaiah noted that they, representing the nation, **will** be cleansed **by a spirit of judgment and a spirit of fire,** as the judging will be like fire that will burn **away** the nation's undesirable **filth** (sin). Only the sovereign work of **the Lord,** not human effort, will be able to **cleanse** (cf. 1:25) the nation (cf. Zech. 13:1). John the Baptist said that Jesus would "baptize . . . with fire" (Matt. 3:11), that is, purify the nation by an act of judging (cf. Mal. 3:2-5).

4:5-6. In this yet-future time of blessing for redeemed Israel **the glory** of God will be evident in Jerusalem (**Mount Zion**). As God's glory was visible to Israel in the Exodus from Egypt in a **cloud . . . by day** and **fire by night** (Ex. 13:21-22; 40:34-38; cf. 16:10), so also will His glory be visible when the redeemed nation will be in her land of promise. God's glory, like a tent, will provide safety and peace.

6. THE WORTHLESS VINEYARD (5:1-7)

In the first stanza (vv. 1-2) of this song which Isaiah composed he sang about God's care for His vineyard and the condition of the vineyard. The second stanza (vv. 3-6) details what God said in view of her condition. In the third stanza (v. 7) the vineyard in the figure is identified. Elsewhere God referred to Israel as a vineyard (3:14; Ps. 80:8-18; Jer. 2:21; 12:10; Ezek. 15:6-8; Hosea 10:1).

5:1-2. In his **song** Isaiah pictured his **loved One** (i.e., God), planting **a vineyard on a fertile hillside,** removing the **stones** (of which there are many in Israel!) and planting only the best **vines. He built a watchtower,** a stone structure from which to guard the vineyard (cf. "shelter," 1:8). And He made **a winepress** in anticipation of producing good wine. However, only poor **grapes** grew on His vines.

5:3-6. The words in these verses in the song are "spoken" by God. He asked the people **of Judah** to **judge** the situation. They were to tell whether the **bad**

grapes were the fault of the **vineyard** Owner. Though God could have done nothing **more** to make the **vineyard** productive (v. 4) there was one thing He would now **do**: He would let it be destroyed (vv. 5-6). By removing the protective **hedge . . . its wall** (probably of stone) around it, He would allow animals (including foxes, Song 2:15) to enter and destroy it. Without cultivating the vines, thornbushes would **grow** up and smother them. Nor would God let **rain** fall on the vineyard. Because of the nation's sinful actions (their bad fruit), destruction would come. Without God's protection Judah would be ruined.

5:7. The **vineyard** in this song is identified as **Israel** and **Judah.** As elsewhere in Isaiah, "Israel" is sometimes a synonym for the Southern Kingdom (Neh. 1:6; 13:3). Delighting in His people, God wanted good fruit, that is, **justice** and **righteousness** (cf. comments on Isa. 1:21). Instead He **saw** only **bloodshed** (cf. 1:15) and **heard cries of distress.** Because of its "bad grapes" (injustice) most people would be killed or taken into captivity. Isaiah used two interesting cases of assonance (similarity in word sounds) to stress the contrast between what God expected in His people and what happened to them. "Justice" (*mišpāṭ*) was replaced with "bloodshed" (*mišpoḥ*), and instead of "righteousness" (*ṣᵉdāqâh*) there was "distress" (*ṣᵉʿāqâh*).

7. AN INDICTMENT ON SIN (5:8-30)

Though verses 8-30 are not a part of the song in verses 1-7, they fit into Isaiah's train of thought nicely because their six indictments ("woes") are against the "bad fruit" the nation had been producing. Between the second and third woes God referred to the consequences of Judah's sins (vv. 13-17); after the sixth woe He did a similar thing (vv. 24-30).

a. Woe to materialists (5:8-10)

5:8-10. Each of the six indictments is introduced by **Woe** (*hôy*; see comments on 3:9). Some people were acquiring much **land** at the expense of their fellow countrymen (cf. Micah 2:1-2). Selling houses permanently in a walled city was allowed under the Law, but selling houses in unwalled cities and fields was allowed only until the Year of Jubilee when the houses would revert back to

their former owners. Because God had given the people the land they were not to get rich at others' expense. Because of this sin the big **houses** and **mansions** the people once enjoyed would be empty, for many people would be killed and, as noted in the Mosaic Covenant (Deut. 28:20-24), their crops would fail. Normally a large **vineyard** would **produce** many gallons of **wine,** but here the amount would be a mere six gallons (**a bath**). And six bushels (**a homer**) **of** seed would normally yield scores of bushels of **grain,** but ironically the grain would be only one-half a bushel (**an ephah**), just 1/12 the amount of seed sown!

b. Woe to drunkards (5:11-12)

5:11-12. Apparently heavy consumption of wine was prevalent in Isaiah's day for this sin is mentioned in two of the six woes (cf. v. 22). People were so addicted to wine that, unlike most drunkards, they rose **early in the morning** to drink. They also stayed **up late at night.** In their revelry they enjoyed music **at their banquets,** but cared nothing **for the deeds of the** LORD. Their lack of **respect for the work of His hands** meant they abused other people made in the image of God. Caring only for their own pleasures, they had no concern for the Lord or for others.

c. Results of Judah's lifestyle (5:13-17)

5:13-17. Because of Judah's lifestyle she would experience several results, the worst being **exile.** Included in that experience would be death by **hunger** and **thirst** (v. 13). Many would **die,** both **nobles and masses,** since death has no respect for rank (v. 14). The carousing drunkards (**brawlers and revelers**) of whom Isaiah had just spoken (vv. 11-12) would also die (v. 14). All proud people would be humiliated (cf. 2:11-12, 17) regardless of their previous stations in life (5:15). With the houses of the wealthy ruined (cf. vv. 8-9) and desolate, **lambs** would easily **graze** there (v. 17). This destruction of the nation would lead to a display of God's **justice** and holiness (v. 16). This does not mean that He delights in revenge. Rather, He keeps His word as spoken in the covenant. His discipline of the nation would show that He still loved her and would someday bring her back into a favored position.

d. Woe to the doubters of God (5:18-19)

5:18-19. Perhaps Isaiah referred here to people who were genuinely questioning whether God was in control of the nation. Though attached to sin and **wickedness** by **cords** and **ropes** (i.e., deeply involved in sin) they wondered if God could save their nation. Apparently they wanted **God** to deliver them even though they did not want to give up their sinful practices. They wanted to **see** God act **(let Him hasten His work)** without any spiritual change on their part. However, deliverance, both personal and national, does not work that way. A spiritual change must be made before God will save His people from destruction.

e. Woe to those calling evil good (5:20)

5:20. Some people lead others astray by their perverted values. **Evil**—for example, adultery, idolatry, materialism, murder, and many other sins forbidden in the Scriptures—is often held up as being **good.** Those who say such things are under the threat **(woe)** of God's judgment.

f. Woe to conceited ones (5:21)

5:21. Thinking themselves **wise** and **clever,** some people were not relying on God's power to deliver the nation. They thought they could protect themselves.

g. Woe to the drunken bribe-takers (5:22-23)

5:22-23. Rather than being **heroes** and good government authorities, many leaders were known for their heavy **drinking.** They were ready to be bribed, not caring for the people they were ruling. They were more concerned for their own pleasure than for the rights of **the innocent.** Therefore *they* (those leaders) would be judged.

h. Further results of Judah's lifestyle (5:24-30)

Isaiah had already mentioned a number of the judgments to come on the people because of their sins (vv. 13-17). Now he spoke again of the consequences of disobeying the covenant stipulations.

5:24-25. These people Isaiah had been writing about would be burned like **straw** and **dry grass** and their **flowers** blown **away like dust.** This was because they had deliberately disobeyed God's Word (on the LORD **Almighty** see com-ments on 1:9; on **the Holy One of Israel** see comments on 1:4). Because of **the** LORD's **anger** many would die **in the streets** of Jerusalem. **His** raised **hand** (cf. 14:27) suggests His executing punishment; **the mountains** shaking from an earthquake speaks of His awesome presence (cf. Ex. 19:18; 1 Kings 19:11; Jer. 4:24; Hab. 3:10).

5:26-30. When God's judgment would come on Judah, the **nations** of Egypt and Assyria (7:18), and later Babylon would respond as if God had raised **a banner** as a signal for war. Those nations would seemingly come from **the ends of the earth,** a phrase Isaiah used frequently to suggest people everywhere (5:26; 24:16; 40:28; 41:5, 9; 42:10; 43:6; 45:22; 48:20; 49:6; 52:10; 62:11). The soldiers, responding **speedily,** would be vigorous (5:27) and well armed. Their chariots would be fast (v. 28). Ferocious like **lions** (v. 29) they would completely devastate Judah (v. 30). They would cover Judah like a **sea** and blot out the sun like **the clouds,** a picture of **distress** and gloom.

8. ISAIAH'S COMMISSION (CHAP. 6)

Though this is one of the better-known chapters in the Book of Isaiah, at least three problems in it have caused debate among Bible students.

The first problem concerns the chronological relationship of chapter 6, which records God's call of Isaiah, to the preceding five chapters on judgment and deliverance. Did Isaiah minister for a period of time before being commissioned, or is this chapter out of order chronologically but in order logically? Some have argued that since the vision occurred "in the year that King Uzziah died" (v. 1) Isaiah must have had some previous ministry (chaps. 1–5) since he is said to have ministered *during* the reign of Uzziah (1:1). It can be countered, however, that Isaiah saw this vision anytime up to 12 months before the king's death. In that sense then his vision *was* "in" Uzziah's reign.

It is possible, as some suggest, that Isaiah, seeing the sinful condition of the nation (chaps. 1–5), set himself apart from that nation until he saw the vision of God and then realized that he too was part of the sin problem. He also was "a man of unclean lips" (6:5).

On the other hand it is possible that

the vision and commissioning of chapter 6 came *before* he delivered the messages in chapters 1–5 and that he recorded this experience here as a fitting logical climax to the stinging indictment in those chapters. Chapter 6 emphasizes the extreme depravity of the nation, contrasting it with God's holiness. Here Isaiah also emphasized that the people lacked spiritual insight and would not turn from their sinful condition.

A second problem pertains to whom Isaiah saw. Isaiah "saw the LORD" (v. 1), whom he called "the LORD Almighty" (v. 3) and "the King, the LORD Almighty" (v. 5). Because the Apostle John wrote that Isaiah "saw Jesus' glory" (John 12:41), Isaiah may have seen the preincarnate Christ, who because of His deity is the Lord. The prophet did not see the very essence of God for no man can see Him (Ex. 33:18; John 1:18; 1 Tim. 6:16; 1 John 4:12) since He is invisible (1 Tim. 1:17). But there was no problem in Isaiah's seeing God in a vision or a theophany, much as did Ezekiel (Ezek. 1:3-28), Daniel (Dan. 7:2, 9-10), and others.

A third problem is related to the fact that Isaiah's vision was in the temple (Isa. 6:1). Was Isaiah there because he was a priest? Jeremiah was the son of a priest (Jer. 1:1) and Ezekiel was a priest (Ezek. 1:3), but the Book of Isaiah says nothing about Isaiah being of priestly lineage. If he were not carrying out priestly duties he may have been a worshiper there when he saw the heavenly vision. Or perhaps he, like Ezekiel (Ezek. 8:1-4), was not physically in the temple but was transported there in a vision.

a. *Isaiah's vision of the Lord (6:1-4)*

6:1. Since Isaiah ministered during **King** Uzziah's reign (1:1) Isaiah's vision of God **in the year . . . Uzziah died** would have occurred within the 12 calendar months before or after the king's death in 739 B.C. If the vision occurred *before* Isaiah began his ministry then obviously the vision was before the king's death. However, if the vision came sometime *after* the prophet's ministry started—see comments earlier under "B. Isaiah's commission (chap. 6)"—then Isaiah could have seen the vision within the calendar year (739 B.C.) either shortly before or shortly after the king died.

This time notation points to a contrast between the human king and the divine King (v. 5), God Himself and to some contrasts between Uzziah and Isaiah. In Uzziah's long (52-year), prosperous reign (2 Chron. 26:1-15) many people were away from the Lord and involved in sin (2 Kings 15:1-4; **Uzziah** is also called Azariah). By contrast, God is holy (Isa. 6:3). In pride, Uzziah disobediently entered the temple (insensitive to the sin involved) and was struck with leprosy which made him ceremonially unclean (2 Chron. 26:16-20). Isaiah, however, was sensitive to sin, for he stated that he and his people were spiritually unclean (Isa. 6:5). Though Uzziah was excluded from the temple (2 Chron. 26:21) Isaiah was not.

Three things struck Isaiah about God: He was **seated on a throne,** He was **high and exalted,** and **the train of His robe filled the temple.** In the most holy place of the temple in Jerusalem, God's glory was evident between the cherubim on the atonement cover over the ark of the covenant. Therefore some Israelites may have erroneously thought that God was fairly small. However, Solomon, in his dedicatory prayer for the new temple, had stated that no temple could contain God and that in fact even the heavens could not contain Him (1 Kings 8:27). Therefore Isaiah did not see God on the ark of the covenant, but on a throne. Almost 150 years later Ezekiel had a similar experience. He envisioned God being borne along on a great chariot throne by living creatures called cherubim (Ezek. 1). To Isaiah, the throne emphasized that **the Lord** is indeed the true King of Israel.

God's being "high and exalted" symbolized His position before the nation. The people were wanting God to work on their behalf (Isa. 5:19) but He *was* doing so, as evidenced by His lofty position among them.

The Lord's long robe speaks of His royalty and majesty. His being in the temple suggests that though He hates mere religiosity (1:11-15) He still wanted the nation to be involved in the temple worship. The temple and the temple sacrifices pictured the righteous dealings of the sovereign God with His covenant people.

6:2-4. Seraphs, angelic beings who were **above** the Lord, are referred to in the Scriptures only here. "Seraphs" is from *śārap*, which means "to burn," possibly suggesting that they were ardent in their zeal for the Lord. It is also noteworthy that one of the seraphs took a *burning* coal to Isaiah (v. 6). They had six wings (the four living creatures Ezekiel saw each had four wings, Ezek. 1:5, 11). Covering their faces with two wings indicates their humility before God. Their covering their feet with two other wings may denote service to God, and their flying may speak of their ongoing activity in proclaiming God's holiness and glory.

In calling to one another the seraphs, whose number is not given, were proclaiming that the LORD Almighty is holy. The threefold repetition of the word holy suggests supreme or complete holiness. This threefold occurrence does not suggest the Trinity, as some have supposed. The Trinity is supported in other ways (e.g., see comments on Isa. 6:8). Repeating a word three times for emphasis is common in the Old Testament (e.g., Jer. 22:29; Ezek. 21:27). The seraphs also proclaimed that His glory fills the earth (cf. Num. 14:21) much as His robe filled the temple. By contrast the people of Judah were unholy (cf. Isa. 5; 6:5) though they were supposed to be a holy people (Ex. 22:31; Deut. 7:6).

As the seraphs cried out, Isaiah saw the temple shake and then it was filled with smoke (Isa. 6:4). The thresholds (cf. Amos 9:1) were large foundation stones on which the doorposts stood. The shaking (cf. Ex. 19:18) suggested the awesome presence and power of God. The smoke was probably the cloud of glory which Isaiah's ancestors had seen in the wilderness (Ex. 13:21; 16:10) and which the priests in Solomon's day had viewed in the dedicated temple (1 Kings 8:10-13).

b. Isaiah's response to the vision (6:5)

6:5. This vision of God's majesty, holiness, and glory made Isaiah realize that he was a sinner. When Ezekiel saw God's glory he too responded with humility. (Cf. the responses of Job, Job 42:5-6; Peter, Luke 5:8; and the Apostle John, Rev. 1:17.) Isaiah had pronounced woes (threats of judgment) on the nation (Isa. 5:8-23), but now by saying **Woe to me!** (cf. 24:16) he realized *he* was subject to judgment. This was because he was unclean. When seen next to the purity of God's holiness, the impurity of human

sin is all the more evident. The prophet's **unclean lips** probably symbolized his attitudes and actions as well as his words, for a person's words reflect his thinking and relate to his actions. Interestingly Isaiah identified with his people who also were sinful (**a people of unclean lips**).

c. Isaiah's cleansing and message (6:6-13)

6:6-7. Realizing his impurity, Isaiah was cleansed by God, through the intermediary work of **one of the seraphs.** It is fitting that a seraph (perhaps meaning a "burning one") **touched** Isaiah's **lips** with a hot **coal . . . from the altar,** either the altar of burnt offering, on which a fire was always burning (Lev. 6:12), or the altar of incense where incense was burned each morning and evening (Ex. 30:1, 7-8). This symbolic action signified the removal of the prophet's **guilt** and his **sin.** Of course this is what the entire nation needed. The Judahites needed to respond as Isaiah did, acknowledging their need of cleansing from sin. But unlike the prophet, most members of the nation refused to admit they had a spiritual need. Though they, through the priests, burned sacrifices at the temple, their lives needed the purifying action of God's "fire" of cleansing.

6:8. The rest of this chapter deals with the message Isaiah was to preach to Judah. Significantly he was not called to service till he had been cleansed. After hearing the seraph's words (vv. 3, 7) he then **heard the** Lord's **voice.**

God asked, **Whom shall I send? And who will go for Us?** The word "Us" in reference to God hints at the Trinity (cf. "Us" in Gen. 1:26; 11:7). This doctrine, though not explicit in the Old Testament, is implicit for God is the same God in both Testaments.

The question "Who will go?" does not mean God did not know or that He only *hoped* someone would respond. He asked the question to give Isaiah, now cleansed, an opportunity for service. The prophet knew that the entire nation needed the same kind of awareness of God and cleansing of sin he had received. So he responded that he would willingly serve **the Lord** (**Here am I**).

6:9-10. Probably Isaiah, responding as he did in verse 8, thought that his serving the Lord would result in the nation's cleansing. However, the Lord told him his message would *not* result in much spiritual response. The people had not listened before and they would not listen now. The Lord did not delight in judging His people, but discipline was necessary because of their disobedience. In fact the **people**, on hearing Isaiah's message, would become even more hardened against the Lord. Interestingly six of the seven lines in verse 10 are in a chiasm: **heart . . . ears . . . eyes** are mentioned in lines 1-3, and in lines 4-6 they are reversed: **eyes . . . ears . . . hearts**. This is a common arrangement of material in the Old Testament. Possibly this pattern emphasizes the "eyes," mentioned in the middle. Jesus quoted part of this verse to explain that Israel in His day *could* not believe because they *would* not believe (see comments on John 12:40).

6:11-13. Isaiah's response to the message implies that he was ready to speak whatever God wanted him to say. Yet he wondered **how long** he would have to go on delivering a message of judgment to which the people would be callous. The **Lord** answered that Isaiah was to proclaim the message **until** His judgment came, that is, till the Babylonian Exile actually occurred and the people were deported from **the land** (v. 12), thus leaving their ruined **cities** and **fields** (v. 11). Though Isaiah did not live that long, God meant he should keep on preaching even if he did live to see Judah's downfall. The **tenth** that remained **in the land** (v. 13) refers to the poor who were left in Judah by Nebuchadnezzar (2 Kings 24:14). But most of them were laid waste (Jer. 41:10-18; 43:4-7).

Isaiah, perhaps discouraged by such a negative response and terrible results, was then assured by **the LORD** that not all was lost. A remnant would be left. God compared that remnant to **stumps** of **terebinth and oak** trees. From this stump or **holy seed** of a believing remnant would come others who would believe. Though Judah's population would be almost totally wiped out or exiled, God promised to preserve a small number of believers **in the land**.

B. Prophecies of deliverance (chaps. 7–12)

In these chapters the prophet focused on the deliverance God would bring the nation. Judah's deliverance from the Aram-Israel alliance (7:1-4) pictures her ultimate deliverance. And the fall of the Assyrian Empire (10:5-19), resulting in "deliverance" for Judah, pictures the fall of all nations who oppose God and His people. Isaiah did not say that these deliverances would bring about the glorious kingdom. But he did indicate that the glorious kingdom, the Millennium, eventually will come (chap. 11). It will be greater than any previous kingdom. In that kingdom "the holy seed" (6:13), the believing remnant (10:20-21), will sing a song of thanksgiving (chap. 12).

1. THE BIRTH OF IMMANUEL (CHAP. 7)

Isaiah prophesied about a Child to be born who in some way would relate to the nation's deliverance. The birth of the Baby, to be named Immanuel, has great significance for the line of David.

a. The historical situation (7:1-2)

7:1-2. Rezin, king **of Aram**, northeast of Israel, **and Pekah . . . king of Israel** (752–732) had made an alliance. Rezin may have usurped the throne of Aram, and Pekah was a usurper. Rezin was Aram's last king, and Pekah was Israel's next-to-last king. After Jeroboam II (793–753) of Israel died, the Northern Kingdom became increasingly weak. Rezin convinced Pekah to join him against Pekah's southern neighbor Judah (2 Kings 15:37; 16:5). They threatened to replace Judah's King **Ahaz** with a puppet king, "the son of Tabeel" (Isa. 7:6). Perhaps Tabeel was a district or a person in Aram. The prospect of such formidable enemies as Aram and Israel caused the people of Judah to be afraid. **The house of David** (v. 2) refers to King Ahaz who was of that kingly line. Hearing of the **Aram**-Israel alliance **Ahaz** was terrified. **Ephraim**, Israel's largest tribe, represented the entire nation, as is also the case in the Book of Hosea (see, e.g., Hosea 4:17; 5:3, 5, 9-14). This was in the year 734 B.C. Perhaps Ahaz thought he could call on the Assyrian King Tiglath-Pileser III (745–727) to come to his aid and attack the Aram-Israel confederacy.

b. The assurance that Judah would not be destroyed (7:3-9)

7:3. God told **Isaiah** to go with his **son . . . to meet** King **Ahaz at the end of**

the aqueduct of the Upper Pool. This pool was a reservoir that held water from the Gihon Spring near Jerusalem. (Isa. 22:9 refers to a Lower Pool.) Perhaps Ahaz was there to inspect the city's water supply in anticipation of an attack by Aram and Israel. The aqueduct was near the road to the Washerman's Field, just outside Jerusalem's city walls. This was the place where, about 33 years later, Sennacherib's spokesman would hurl his challenge to the Jerusalemites (36:2). The name of Isaiah's son, Shear-Jashub (which means "a remnant will return"; cf. 10:21) illustrated the prophet's message. The nation of Judah would not be destroyed by the Aram-Israel alliance.

7:4-6. Isaiah told Ahaz not to be afraid of Rezin and Pekah, for they were mere smoldering stubs of firewood. Their lives would soon end; like firewood they would be burned up and gone. Both men died two years later in 732 B.C. Aram and Israel threatened to invade Judah, split it between the two conquering nations, and set up a puppet king.

7:7-9. In response to the Aram-Israel threat the Sovereign LORD had an answer: It (the attack) would not take place; it would not happen. The reason was that both of those nations were headed by mere (only, vv. 8-9) men. Ironically Isaiah referred to Pekah by name only once (v. 1). Four other times he called him "the son of Remaliah" or Remaliah's son (vv. 4-5, 9; 8:6). He and Rezin could not thwart God's plans.

In fact Isaiah made the startling prophecy that within 65 years Israel would no longer even be a people because they would be so shattered (7:8). Isaiah gave this prophecy in 734 B.C., so 65 years later was 669. When Assyria conquered Israel in 722, many Israelites were deported to other lands by Assyria and foreigners were brought into Samaria (2 Kings 17:24). However, in 669 many more foreigners were transferred to Samaria by Ashurbanipal (Ezra 4:10), king of Assyria (669–626). This "shattered" Israel, making it impossible for her to unite as a nation ("a people").

The second sentence in Isaiah 7:9 has been translated in various ways. But it challenged Ahaz to believe what Isaiah was telling him. Obviously Ahaz was not alive 65 years later. But he could have faith that God would fulfill both predic-

tions: that Israel would be shattered 65 years later and that in his day the northern confederacy (Aram and Israel) would not overpower Judah. If he did not believe those predictions he too would fall.

c. Ahaz's rejection of a sign (7:10-12)

7:10-12. As a means of strengthening his faith Ahaz was told to ask the LORD . . . for a sign, an attesting miracle that would confirm God's word. The king could choose any miraculous work he wished, from the deepest depths to the highest heights. This was a figure of speech, a merism, that mentioned two extremes with the intention of including all the areas in between them. With a miracle performed simply for the asking, Ahaz would have visible confirmation that Isaiah's words (vv. 7-9) were truly from the Lord. Ahaz could count on the fact that the northern alliance would not defeat Judah.

But Ahaz refused to request a sign, saying he would not . . . test God (cf. Deut. 6:16). This answer sounded pious but probably the way he said it showed he was not believing Isaiah. Perhaps he did not want to believe Isaiah, who had been prophesying about the eventual destruction of Judah if her people did not return to the LORD.

d. The Lord's response (7:13-25)

7:13. Ahaz, by rejecting the offer of a sign from God's messenger, was in effect rejecting the One who sent the prophet. The house of David (cf. v. 2) refers not to all David's descendants, but to Ahaz and those kings of Judah who would descend from him. Ahaz's answer was impious. He said he did not want to test the Lord, but by refusing to follow God's directive to ask for a confirming miracle, he was testing the Lord's patience (as well as man's patience).

7:14-16. Though Ahaz refused to request a sign that would have confirmed the truth of Isaiah's message, the prophet said God would give him one anyway. The sign was to be a boy named Immanuel. Three elements pertain to the sign: (1) The boy would be born of a virgin (v. 14). (2) He would be raised in a time of national calamity (v. 15; on the curds and honey see comments on v. 22). (3) While he was still a youth, the two-king alliance would be broken (v. 16).

"Virgin" translates 'almâh, a word used of an unmarried woman of marriageable age. The word refers to one who is sexually mature. It occurs elsewhere in the Old Testament only in Genesis 24:43 ("maiden"); Exodus 2:8 ("girl"); Psalm 68:25 ("maidens"); Proverbs 30:19 ("maiden"); Song of Songs 1:3 ("maidens"); 6:8 ("virgins"). It also occurs in 1 Chronicles 15:20 (alamoth) and in the title of Psalm 46 (alamoth may be a musical term). The child's name Immanuel means "God (is) with us."

Most Bible scholars hold one of three views on the virgin in Isaiah 7:14-16:

(1) The boy of whom Isaiah wrote was conceived shortly after Isaiah spoke this message. A young woman, a virgin, married and then had a baby. Before he would be old enough to tell the difference between good and evil the northern Aram-Israel alliance would be destroyed. According to this view the woman was a virgin when Isaiah spoke his prophecy but was not when the boy was born because he was conceived by sexual relations with her husband. Some say this child was born to Isaiah (8:3-4). They point out that 8:1-4 corresponds in a number of ways to 7:14-17. But this view must be rejected because (a) Isaiah's wife already had a child (Shear-Jashub, v. 3) and so was not a virgin, and (b) the second child born to Isaiah's wife was not named Immanuel (8:3). In this view Ahaz would have known this woman, and hearing of the child's birth and his name Immanuel he would understand that Isaiah's prophecies were correct.

(2) A second view sees the predicted birth as exclusively messianic and the virgin as Mary, Jesus' mother. It is argued that in Isaiah 7:14 the virgin is said to be with child (lit., "the virgin is or will be pregnant"). It is also argued that Matthew, stressing the fact that Joseph and Mary's marriage was not consummated till after Jesus' birth (Matt. 1:18, 25), affirmed that Jesus' birth fulfilled Isaiah's prophecy (Matt. 1:21-23).

Proponents of this view point out that since Isaiah spoke this prophecy to the house of David (Isa. 7:13) and not just to Ahaz himself, the sign was given not just to the king but to the entire kingly line and the entire nation. However, if the fulfillment did not occur until Joseph and Mary's day, how does the prophecy

relate to Isaiah's point that the Aram-Israel confederacy would soon be defeated? And how does the birth of the Lord Jesus relate to the eating of curds and honey (v. 15) and to the breaking of the alliance before the boy was old enough to know good and evil? (v. 16) Proponents of this view answer that the time is similar: the two years of Jesus' babyhood (before He would know between right and wrong) point to the same time segment, two years, within which the Aram-Israel threat would be gone.

(3) A third view, a combination of the first two, sees the prophecy as directed primarily to Ahaz regarding the breaking of the alliance. The 'almâh was a virgin when Isaiah spoke his message, but then she would marry and have a baby. When the Aram-Israel alliance was broken the boy would still be young. Centuries later the Holy Spirit led Matthew to quote Isaiah 7:14 as a statement that was also true of a virgin birth (i.e., a birth to a woman who was still a virgin). This is the first of many prophecies about the Messiah given by Isaiah. (See the chart "Messianic Prophecies in the Book of Isaiah.")

The sign must have had some significance for the historical situation in which it was given. The sign involved not only the birth and the boy's name (Immanuel, "God [is] with us," would assure the people of God's presence), but also a designated length of time: **before the boy knows enough to reject the wrong and choose the right, the land of the two kings . . . will be laid waste.**

Within about three years (nine months for the pregnancy and two or three years until the boy would know the difference between good and evil) the alliance would be broken. It was broken in 732 B.C. when Tiglath-Pileser III destroyed Damascus. After Tiglath-Pileser had defeated Aram and put Rezin to death Ahaz went to Damascus to meet the Assyrian monarch (2 Kings 16:7-10). Ahaz liked an altar he saw in Damascus, and had a sketch of it drawn so a similar altar could be set up in Jerusalem. No wonder Isaiah and God were angry with Ahaz. Even after the alliance had been broken by Tiglath-Pileser Judah had no peace. Though Assyria did not defeat Judah, she had to pay Assyria a heavy tribute. Isaiah foretold the consequences of Ahaz's attitude (Isa. 7:17-25).

Messianic Prophecies in the Book of Isaiah

1. He will be called before His birth to be God's Servant (49:1).

2. He will be born of a virgin (7:14).

3. He will be a Descendant of Jesse and thus in the Davidic line (11:1, 10).

4. He will be empowered by the Holy Spirit (11:2; 42:1).

5. He will be gentle toward the weak (42:3).

6. He will be obedient to the Lord in His mission (50:4-9).

7. He will voluntarily submit to suffering (50:6; 53:7-8).

8. He will be rejected by Israel (49:7; 53:1, 3).

9. He will take on Himself the sins of the world (53:4-6, 10-12).

10. He will triumph over death (53:10).

11. He will be exalted (52:13; 53:12).

12. He will come to comfort Israel and to bring vengeance on the wicked (61:1-3).

13. He will manifest God's glory (49:3).

14. He will restore Israel spiritually to God (49:5) and physically to the land (49:8).

15. He will reign on David's throne (9:7).

16. He will bring joy to Israel (9:2).

17. He will make a New Covenant with Israel (42:6; 49:8-9).

18. He will be a light to the Gentiles (42:6; 49:6).

19. He will restore the nations (11:10).

20. He will be worshiped by Gentiles (49:7, 52:15).

21. He will govern the world (9:6).

22. He will judge in righteousness, justice, and faithfulness (11:3-5; 42:1, 4).

7:17-19. God said He would send **the king of Assyria** to **Judah.** These would be the worst enemy attacks **since** the 10 Northern tribes (here called **Ephraim;** see comments on v. 2) **broke . . . from** the 2 Southern tribes in 931 B.C. From Ahaz's day on, Judah was troubled by the Assyrian Empire, to which it had to pay a large tribute. Ahaz called on Tiglath-Pileser to rescue him from Aram and Israel, which the Assyrian king gladly did. However, Tiglath-Pileser gave Ahaz trouble, not help (2 Chron. 28:20-21). Then in Hezekiah's reign Sennacherib, king of Assyria, invaded Judah, who had asked for help from **Egypt** (Isa. 30:1-5), and was about to take it when, in 701 B.C., God miraculously delivered Jerusalem (chaps. 36–37). God's hand was in all this for He would **whistle for flies from** Egypt (i.e., Egyptian soldiers were as numerous and bothersome as flies) **and for bees from . . . Assyria** (i.e., Assyrian soldiers who were vicious as bees).

7:20-25. Judah would experience deprivation and humiliation. **Assyria,** like **a razor,** would **shave** Judah's **hair.** In the ancient Near East shaving one's hair and beard was a sign of humiliation or deep distress (cf. Job 1:20; Isa. 15:2; Jer. 47:5; 48:37; Ezek. 7:18; Amos 8:10; Micah 1:16). **The abundance of . . . milk** was a distressful factor, not a good one. With many animals dying, a farmer's **young cow and two goats** would have no young to nurse, and so the milk (and **curds** from it) would be plentiful for the people. **Honey** would also be abundant because wild flowers would grow in the desolate fields and bee swarms would be more plentiful. All this would fulfill the sign given Ahaz by Isaiah (Isa. 7:15): he **will eat curds and honey.** Also the farmers would have no crops because of the ruined farmland. The vineyards would be ruined along with the cultivated **land,** and only **briers and thorns** (mentioned three times in vv. 23-25) would grow.

The land would be good only for grazing by **cattle** and **sheep**.

In that day (v. 21) denotes a time of judgment on the nation of Judah. Often this phrase (as in 4:2, e.g.) is used eschatologically to refer to the time of extreme judgment in the Great Tribulation just before the Messiah will return to establish the millennial kingdom. But sometimes as here (7:21) it refers to a judgment to come on the nation soon. The near judgment pictures the extreme judgment to come at the end of the age.

2. THE COMING DELIVERER (8:1–9:7)

This section is closely related to the previous chapter. It concerns the same event, namely, the deliverance from the Aram-Israel alliance and the subsequent Assyrian invasion that would eventually extend to Judah. Chapter 7 included several "negatives"—Ahaz's rejection of God's Word through Isaiah, Ahaz's continued unbelief, and the difficult times that would come to Judah. This section focuses on a positive note: the nation would be delivered and this deliverance would picture another Deliverer, who will bring an even greater deliverance.

a. The coming fall of Israel and Aram (8:1-4)

Isaiah had already prophesied of the fall of the Aram-Israel alliance (7:4-17). Now he gave another prophecy of the same event. As in chapter 7, this prediction also involves the birth of a baby, this time to Isaiah and his wife, a prophetess. Some have suggested that this birth fulfilled the prediction in 7:14. However, the two accounts have several differences. The child in 8:1-4 was not named Immanuel (cf. 7:14). The child in 8:1-4 was born to Isaiah's wife. She was not a virgin because Isaiah already had at least one child (7:3), unless the wife in 8:3 refers to a second wife of Isaiah. This, however, seems unlikely. This birth probably occurred some time after the prediction in 7:14 because according to 8:4 the fall of the alliance would occur fairly soon—before the child was even able to say "my father" or "my mother." Most children can say those words before or soon after they are one year old. Apparently God graciously allowed this second prediction of the Assyrian destruction of Aram to be given to Judah. This prophecy was witnessed by several im-

portant people, to prove to the nation once again that Isaiah was speaking for the Lord and that his words were true.

8:1. Isaiah was to use a visual aid to help secure the prophecy in the minds of his audience. On **a large scroll** Isaiah was to record the name of a son to be born to him soon. The son's name was to be announced even before he was conceived, thus pointing to the certainty of the birth. The name **Maher-Shalal-Hash-Baz,** the longest personal name in the Bible, means "quick to the plunder, swift to the spoil." Soldiers would shout these words to their comrades as they defeated and plundered their foes. Isaiah's listeners, remembering his prophecy of the fall of the Aram-Israel alliance (7:4-17), would have understood the significance of his son's name as they continued to listen to his prediction of impending doom for Aram and Israel.

8:2. God said He would **call in** two **witnesses** (Num. 35:30; Deut. 17:6; 19:15), who could confirm that His words were true. **Uriah the priest** is mentioned later in an unfavorable light (2 Kings 16:10-16) when he complied with Ahaz's order to change the temple worship after the Aram-Israel alliance had been broken. Apparently he was an influential priest. **Zechariah son of Jeberekiah** is nowhere else mentioned by that full title. He may have been a prophet during the time of Uzziah (2 Chron. 26:5) or a Levite who helped cleanse the temple in Hezekiah's day (2 Chron. 29:12-13).

8:3-4. The prophetess, Isaiah's wife, is unnamed. She was called a prophetess either because she was married to a prophet or because she had the God-given ability to prophesy. The latter seems preferable. Isaiah's son, **Maher-Shalal-Hash-Baz,** was a sign of the coming break in the Aram-Israel alliance against Judah. In about a year and nine months (nine months for the pregnancy and one year of the child's life), Assyria would **plunder** both **Damascus** (Aram's capital city) and **Samaria** (Israel's capital). This happened in 732 B.C., which confirms the date of 734 for Isaiah's prophecy. When Damascus and Samaria fell, Judah should have turned to God as Isaiah had told them to. Unfortunately Uriah, one of the two witnesses (v. 2), followed Ahaz's orders after 732 B.C. and changed the temple worship to conform with the pagan worship practiced at Damascus.

b. The coming Assyrian invasion (8:5-8)

8:5-6. **This people** could refer to the Northern Kingdom of Israel since she was the nation that **rejected** Judah in favor of aligning with Aram, under its king **Rezin** (cf. 7:1). **The gently flowing waters of Shiloah,** also called Siloam, then would refer by metonomy to the city of Jerusalem. These waters were a spring that fed a small reservoir within Jerusalem's walls. This gentle pool contrasted with the "mighty floodwaters" (8:7) which would destroy the people. On **the son of Remaliah** see comments on 7:4. Others interpret "this people" to refer to Judah (the house of Ahaz and his people). They had rejected God ("the gentle waters") and therefore the mighty flood (Assyria) would come and engulf them. This of course happened in 701 B.C. when the Assyrians invaded Judah.

8:7-8. Because Israel allied with Aram, she would be swept away by **the mighty floodwaters** from **the River,** a normal designation for the Euphrates River, which ran through the Assyrian Empire. **The king of Assyria** (cf. 7:17) would **sweep** down on the Northern Kingdom like a river in flood stage overflowing **its banks.** Amazingly this "floodwater," that is, Assyria, would continue **on into** the land of **Judah** (701 B.C.). Assyria would cover Judah up **to the neck,** meaning that Judah would be almost but not quite drowned.

Isaiah changed figures of speech and pictured Assyria as a giant bird whose **wings** would **cover** the entire **land,** ready to devour it.

This message was given to **Immanuel** ("God [is] with us"). Isaiah had used that word (7:14) when he told Ahaz that a boy, soon to be born, would be a sign that the nation would not perish at the hands of Aram and Israel. Now the Assyrians would try to "drown" the land of Judah. But the word Immanuel assured the hearers that God had not forgotten His covenant people and would be with them (cf. 8:10). The next verses (vv. 9-15) discuss that fact.

c. The coming victory from God (8:9-15)

Though Judah would be almost defeated by the Assyrian invasion (vv. 1-8), Isaiah noted that Judah should not fear because she would experience victory.

8:9-10. The great truth of chapters 7-9 is that God was with Judah. Isaiah uses the same term Immanuel to close verse 10—**God is with us.** Even though the **nations** would **raise** a **war cry** and **prepare for battle** against Judah, they would not succeed. They would **be shattered,** a fact stated three times in verse 9 for emphasis. Even though they would carefully work out a **strategy** and a **plan** for battle they would not succeed because God was with Judah ("Immanuel" in Heb.; cf. 7:14; 8:8). That great truth separated Judah from all other nations of the world. Because God has promised to be with His people they were to have faith in Him no matter how bad their circumstances. He would not desert them. Thus God and Isaiah were proved right, and Ahaz was rebuked for his lack of faith (cf. 7:9).

8:11-15. The Lord had promised to be with His people (v. 10), but many in both Israel and Judah refused to believe He would keep His promise. The LORD warned Isaiah **not** to be like many of those **people** (v. 11). Again Isaiah emphasized that the people of Judah should not be afraid of the Aram-Israel alliance or of the Assyrian threat looming on the horizon (v. 12). Rather they were to be afraid of **the LORD Almighty. He is the One** they should **fear** and **dread** (v. 13; cf. **fear** and **dread** in v. 12 and see the comments on "fear" in Deut. 4:10). The Lord **will be a sanctuary,** a place of safety, for those who believe in Him, **but for** those who do not believe Him, He will be the means of destruction (**a stone . . . a rock. . . . a trap, and a snare**). Peter quoted part of Isaiah 8:14 (1 Peter 2:8), referring to those who reject Jesus Christ. Isaiah's message follows an emphasis in the Old Testament. God promised that those who believe in and obey the Lord will be blessed but those who refuse to believe in and obey Him will be disciplined.

d. The names that confirm God's coming help (8:16-18)

8:16-18. Having been warned by God "not to follow the way of this people" (v. 11), Isaiah reaffirmed his dependence on God. By binding **the testimony** and sealing **the Law** (cf. v. 20), Isaiah was in effect inscribing it on the hearts of the

Lord's **disciples.** Because Hebrews 2:13 ascribes Isaiah 8:17c-18a to Christ, some interpreters feel that all of Isaiah 8:16-18 was spoken by the Messiah. Certainly the attitude conveyed in these verses was that of the Lord Jesus Christ. But in the context of Isaiah 7–9 these words should be ascribed to Isaiah (with the writer of Heb. applying them to Christ). This was the prophet's attitude in spite of all the opposition he saw around him. Isaiah's confidence is expressed twice in 8:17. **I will wait for the LORD** and **I will put my trust in Him.** The fact that the Lord was **hiding His face** (withholding His blessings) was no surprise to the people of faith. The Lord's withdrawal was because most of the Judahites failed to follow Him. Even so, Isaiah still had confidence in the Lord, knowing that he and his **children** were **signs and symbols** of the Lord's sovereign rule **on Mount Zion** (Jerusalem; cf. 2:3).

In what way were they signs and symbols? Each one had a name that held significance for the nation's future. Isaiah's name, "Yahweh is salvation," was a reminder that God will ultimately deliver His people. Maher-Shalal-Hash-Baz's name reminded the people that the Aram-Israel alliance would be broken by the Assyrians who would plunder those nations. The name Shear-Jashub kept before the people the truth that a believing remnant would return from captivity (cf. 10:21-22).

e. The coming deliverance of Judah by God's Word (8:19-22)

8:19-22. Isaiah again spoke of the people's sinful bent. Most people want to know the future. Even people in Judah were pulled into the pagan practice of consulting **mediums and spiritists,** who specialized in trying, by whispering and muttering, to contact **the dead** (cf. comments on Deut. 18:10-12). Isaiah questioned the rationality of going to the dead to find out the future instead of inquiring of the living **God.** The place to look was in **the Law and . . . the testimony** (cf. Isa. 8:16), which contained everything the nation needed to know about her future. A person's failure to heed God's **Word** means he has **no** spiritual **light** (cf. John 3:19-20). Spiritists and mediums and those who consult them will eventually be judged by God (Isa. 8:21-22). In their distress they will look up to **God** and **curse** Him and **look** to **the earth** where they will face **distress** and then **be thrust into . . . darkness** (cf. 2 Peter 2:17). Ironically those who seek to consult the dead will be forced to join them!

f. The future deliverance of the nation (9:1-7)

In these verses Isaiah spoke of the coming Deliverer who will effect the changes in the nation of which the prophet had been speaking. The Messiah's coming will lead the nation into joy and prosperity, which had been lacking for years. His coming will fulfill the promises to Abraham and David about the prosperous kingdom. The "child" motif again is evident (v. 6; cf. 7:14-16; 8:1-4, 18). The Child will grow up to be the Deliverer (9:7), not a sign (8:18) of deliverance but the Deliverer Himself. He will effect the changes necessary for prosperity and spirituality to come to the nation.

9:1. A time will come when **gloom** and darkness (8:22) will be a thing of **the past.** The gloom on the northern section of Israel came because of discipline. God **humbled . . . Zebulun and . . . Naphtali** for a while. Though Isaiah was probably using these two tribal names to represent the Northern Kingdom, it is striking that Jesus' upbringing and early ministry was mostly in that very area near the Sea of Galilee. His presence certainly "honored" that area. In 732 B.C. this northern portion of Israel became an Assyrian province under Tiglath-Pileser III, thus humbling the people there and putting them in gloom. Under Gentile domination, that area was called **Galilee of the Gentiles.**

The way of the sea describes a major international highway running through this region. This is the only place where the Bible used this phrase, but it appears often in Assyrian and Egyptian records. The invading Assyrian soldiers took that route when they invaded the Northern Kingdom. From that area the Messiah will arise and will wipe away the gloom and darkness brought on by Gentile domination.

9:2. With typical Hebrew parallelism the prophet described the effect of the Messiah on this northern part of Israel. **The people** were **in darkness** (cf. 8:22) and in **the shadow of death.** Then they saw **a great light** and **light . . . dawned on them.** Matthew applied this passage to Jesus, who began His preaching and healing ministry in that region (Matt. 4:15-16).

9:3-5. You probably refers to God the Father, who will lead the people from spiritual darkness into light (v. 2) by sending the Child (v. 6), the Messiah. The light will increase **their joy** like the joy at harvesttime or the joy of winning a battle and **dividing the plunder.** "Joy" is another emphasis of Isaiah's, mentioned more than two dozen times in the book. This will be a supernatural work of God much like the nation's deliverance when Gideon defeated Midian (Jud. 7:1-24; Isa. 10:26). It will be like taking a burden off one's back (9:4). At that time, after the Child-Messiah will come, the implements of warfare will be destroyed (v. 5) because in His reign of universal peace implements of war will not be needed (cf. 2:4).

9:6-7. Here Isaiah recorded five things about the coming Messiah.

1. He was to be born **a Child.** The implication, given in parallel style, is that this Child, **a Son,** was to be born into the nation of Israel (**to us**) as one of the covenant people.

2. He will rule over God's people (cf. Micah 5:2) and the world (Zech. 14:9). **The government will be on His shoulders** figuratively refers to the kingly robe to be worn by the Messiah. As King, He will be responsible to govern the nation. In Isaiah's day Judah's leaders were incompetent in governing the people. But the Messiah will govern properly.

3. He will have four descriptive names that will reveal His character. He will be the nation's **Wonderful** (this could be trans. "exceptional" or "distinguished") **Counselor,** and the people will gladly listen to Him as the authoritative One. In the kingdom many people will be anxious to hear the Messiah teach God's ways (2:3). He is also the **Mighty God** (cf. 10:21). Some have suggested that this simply means "a godlike person" or hero. But Isaiah meant more than that, for he had already spoken of the Messiah doing what no other person had been able to do (e.g., 9:2-5). Isaiah understood that the Messiah was to be God in some sense of the term.

This Deliverer will also be called the **Everlasting Father.** Many people are puzzled by this title because the Messiah, God's Son, is distinguished in the Trinity from God the Father. How can the Son be the Father? Several things must be noted in this regard. First, the Messiah, being the second Person of the Trinity, is in His essence, God. Therefore He has all the attributes of God including eternality. Since God is One (even though He exists in three Persons), the Messiah is God. Second, the title "Everlasting Father" is an idiom used to describe the Messiah's relationship to time, not His relationship to the other Members of the Trinity. He is said to be everlasting, just as God (the Father) is called "the Ancient of Days" (Dan. 7:9). The Messiah will be a "fatherly" Ruler. Third, perhaps Isaiah had in mind the promise to David (2 Sam. 7:16) about the "foreverness" of the kingdom which God promised would come through David's line. The Messiah, a Descendant of David, will fulfill this promise for which the nation had been waiting.

The Messiah is also called the **Prince of Peace,** the One who will bring in and maintain the time of millennial peace when the nation will be properly related to the Lord. Together, these four titles give a beautiful picture of the coming Messiah's character. (Isa. 9:6 includes the first of Isaiah's 25 references to peace.)

4. The Messiah, seated **on David's throne** (Luke 1:32-33), will have an eternal rule of **peace** and **justice.** His rule will have **no end**; it will go on **forever** (cf. Dan. 7:14, 27; Micah 4:7; Luke 1:33; Rev. 11:15). Following the kingdom on earth, He will rule for eternity. He will maintain **righteousness** (cf. Jer. 23:5), as His rule will conform to God's holy character and demands.

5. This will all be accomplished by **the zeal of the LORD Almighty.** The coming of the millennial **kingdom** depends on God, not Israel. The Messiah will rule because God promised it and will zealously see that the kingdom comes. Without His sovereign intervention there would be no kingdom for Israel.

Apparently Isaiah assumed that the messianic Child, Jesus Christ, would establish His reign in one Advent, that when the Child grew up He would rule in triumph. Like the other prophets, Isaiah was not aware of the great time gap between Messiah's *two* Advents (cf. 1 Peter 1:10-12; and see comments on Isa. 61:1-2).

3. EXILE FOR THE NORTHERN KINGDOM (9:8–10:4)

After giving a glorious description of the coming Messiah, who will usher in the kingdom for the nation and whose reign will last forever, Isaiah focused on the nation in his day. Some have questioned why Isaiah placed these verses here. But, characteristic of this great prophetic writer, he alternated the message of judgment with the message of blessing. In contrast with the Messiah's future reign of justice and righteousness (9:6-7; 11:4; 16:5; 28:6, 17; 32:16; 33:5; 42:1, 3-4; 51:5), the nation in Isaiah's day was ruled by leaders who did not care about the people under them (cf. 5:7).

a. Israel judged because of arrogance (9:8-12)

9:8. Though Isaiah was writing to the nation of Judah he often used the Northern Kingdom of **Israel** (also called **Jacob**) as an example of the fact that God judges His sinful people. The **message** was one of coming judgment on the North. When these words were written, the Northern Kingdom was already in some disrepair (v. 10a). The coming **fall** of Israel (in 722 B.C.) should have warned Judah that God is active in the affairs of His people. Judah should have realized that she too would be destroyed if she persisted in the activities that characterized the North.

9:9-12. The coming judgment on Israel would be widely known, but it would not be enough to turn her back to God. **Ephraim,** one of Israel's largest tribes, often represented the entire Northern Kingdom (cf. 7:2, 17). **Samaria** was the Northern Kingdom's capital city. Apparently Israel's inhabitants felt that they would experience only a temporary setback (**the bricks have fallen**) and in proud confidence thought they could **rebuild.** In fact they felt that they would be able to make their nation better than ever. But this was not to be the case. They were going to be squeezed by **Rezin's foes** (Rezin was the king of Aram, 7:1, an ally of Israel). Those foes were **from the east** (other **Arameans;** Rezin was king of part of Aram) **and Philistines from the west** (cf. 2:6). This was the

Lord's doing. But even this judgment did not appease God's wrath because the people continued to refuse to deal with their sin. So God would continue to chasten them. This section (9:8-12) ends with a refrain which is repeated three more times in the following verses: **Yet for all this His anger is not turned away, His hand is still upraised** (vv. 12, 17, 21; 10:4). This repetition heightens the effect of God's intense anger and underscores the certainty of continued judgment.

b. The entire nation judged (9:13-17)

9:13. The prophet lamented that even though the Northern Kingdom had suffered at the hand of God, they still had **not returned to Him.** So their continued refusal would lead to more judgment. Israel was like a child who stubbornly refuses to obey his parents and therefore is punished more severely.

9:14-17. Israel's refusal to turn to God would result in the most severe judgment imaginable. The whole nation, from rich to poor and from old to young, would be cast aside. **Both head and tail** (v. 14, explained in v. 15) is a merism, a figure which gives opposite extremes to include the whole spectrum. **Elders (the head)** and false **prophets (the tail),** guides **and those who are guided,** and **young men . . . the fatherless . . . widows**—these were all **ungodly and wicked** and therefore would be judged by God. On the refrain in verse 17b see comments on verse 12.

c. A description of wickedness (9:18-21)

9:18-21. The people's **wickedness** (cf. v. 17) is pictured as burning them up **like a** huge **fire** with a large **column of smoke.** The judgment would come not only from God (v. 11) and from enemies of the nation (v. 12), but also from within. The nation would destroy itself by its own wicked deeds. **People** would oppose each other (v. 19), **devour** each other (v. 20), and even entire tribes will be in conflict (v. 21). On the refrain in verse 21b see comments on verse 12.

d. Woe to unjust people (10:1-4)

10:1-4. The corrupt leaders in Israel were perverting the cause of justice and righteousness, in contrast with the Messiah's justice and righteousness (9:6-7). So Isaiah pronounced **woe** (see comments on 3:9) on those people. The readers should have realized that this woe would befall them if they followed their leaders' wicked ways. Israel's leaders were guilty of six things: They were (a) making unjust laws and (b) issuing oppressive decrees. These actions were repulsive because the Israelites were supposed to care for each other as members of God's people redeemed from Egyptian slavery by their God. Also they were (c) depriving the poor (dal, "feeble, weak, helpless") of their rights, (d) taking away justice, (e) hurting widows, and (f) robbing the fatherless. These actions, which involved taking advantage of people who could not defend their rights, violated God's Law (Ex. 22:22; 23:6; Deut. 15:7-8; 24:17-18; cf. Isa. 1:17). Because of this behavior, the nation would go into captivity (10:3-4). In disaster . . . from afar (i.e., from Assyria) no one would help them, as they had refused to help those in need. In anger God's judgment would fall (see comments on 9:12).

4. ASSYRIA'S FALL AND THE GREAT KINGDOM'S RISE (10:5–12:6)

In this section Isaiah again contrasted two kingdoms: the Assyrian Empire and God's millennial kingdom. Assyria would fall because it dared to defeat God's people. Even though God used the Assyrian Empire to punish Israel, He did not like the attitude Assyria displayed. (Isaiah picked up that theme again in chaps. 13–23.) God's glorious empire will come after the fall of Assyria though not immediately afterward. Isaiah was merely contrasting the two.

a. The fall of the Assyrian Empire (10:5-34)

(1) Assyria's fulfilling of God's will (10:5-11). Isaiah described Assyria's mission (vv. 5-6) and her motives (vv. 7-11).

10:5-6. God had commissioned Assyria to chasten Israel as the rod of His anger and the club of His wrath. Because Israel was godless and had angered God with her sin, Assyria would plunder her cities and ruthlessly trample her people. God often uses unlikely instruments to accomplish His purposes in the world (cf. His using Babylon against Judah, which puzzled Habakkuk, Hab. 1:6-17). Isaiah was not claiming that Assyria was godly or that the empire even knew that God was using it to do His bidding. In His

sovereignty He directed Assyria to be His tool for vengeance.

10:7-11. Though Assyria was a tool in God's hands (vv. 5-6) God was not pleased with her. She had the wrong attitude in conquering Israel. Discounting the greatness of Israel's God, Assyria assumed that Israel and Judah were like any other nation. Assyria had conquered the Aramean cities of Calno (the same as Calneh, Amos 6:2), Carchemish . . . Hamath . . . Arpad, Damascus, and Israel's capital Samaria. So Assyria thought she could easily take Jerusalem. Since these other conquered cities had greater gods, in the minds of the Assyrians, than did Jerusalem, that city could be taken more easily (cf. the Assyrians' similar boasting in Isa. 36:19-20; 37:12). Though God was using Assyria, her motives were purely political and expansionist.

(2) Assyria's punishment (10:12-19). 10:12-14. After using Assyria to punish Jerusalem, God would then punish Assyria because of the king's willful pride evidenced by his haughty look (cf. Pss. 18:27; 101:5; Prov. 6:17; 30:13). The words of the Assyrian king in Isaiah 10:13-14 express the empire's haughty pride. The king felt that what had been achieved had been done by his strength and wisdom (six times he said I and three times my). He took other nations and their wealth as easily as a person takes eggs from a nest. No one was able to oppose his military might.

10:15-19. Because of Assyria's pride, the Lord said He would judge the king of Assyria and his empire. The instrument (ax or rod or club; cf. vv. 5, 24) is not above the one who uses it. Therefore Assyria, though used by God, was not above Him. The LORD said He would destroy the Assyrian army by disease and fire. God would destroy Assyria's soldiers like trees (cf. v. 33-34) consumed by a forest fire. The remaining trees (soldiers) would be so few that even a child could count them. In 701 B.C. 185,000 Assyrian soldiers surrounding Jerusalem were killed (37:36-37). Then in 609 B.C. the Assyrian Empire fell to Babylon. The fall of the Assyrian Empire is a prototype of the fall of all who oppose God and His plans for His covenant people.

(3) The remnant of Israel. 10:20-23. In spite of judgment on Israel, a remnant will return to the land and trust in

(rely on) the LORD (not on Assyria; cf. Hosea 5:13; 7:11; 8:9). In that day often refers to the last days when the Lord will punish the wicked and set up His righteous kingdom (cf. Isa. 4:2). However, here it seems to refer to the more immediate judgment on the Northern Kingdom by Assyria (cf. 10:27) and the return of a remnant from that empire. Though Israel had many people like . . . sand (cf. Gen. 22:17; 32:12; 2 Sam. 17:11), only a few would return. Destruction, though overwhelming, would be fair (righteous) and would be on the whole land (the Northern Kingdom).

(4) Assyria's yoke to be lifted. 10:24-27. Isaiah then assured his readers that the Assyrian burden would be removed from Judah. They need not be afraid of the Assyrians. After God had used them to accomplish His purpose against Israel, He would turn His anger against Assyria and punish her (cf. 37:36-37). This would be like His destruction of the Midianites by Gideon (Jud. 7:1-24; cf. Isa. 9:4) and the two Midianite leaders at the rock of Oreb (Jud. 7:25). God would destroy Assyria (figuratively called the waters; cf. Isa. 8:7) as He destroyed Egypt. God promised to lift the Assyrian burden and yoke from Judah (cf. 9:4).

(5) Assyria's defeat (10:28-34). 10:28-32. The route the Assyrian invaders would take in trying to defeat Judah in 701 B.C. was from the northern boundary of Judah at Aiath (another name for Ai), about eight miles north of Jerusalem, southward to Nob, about two miles north of Jerusalem. The sites of 8 of the 12 towns are known (all except Gallim . . . Laishah . . . Madmenah, and Gebim).

10:33-34. Assyria would not succeed in its plan to take Jerusalem. The LORD Almighty is the One who cuts down the lofty trees (the Assyrian soldiers and leaders; cf. v. 18). Isaiah had already reminded the people that they need not worry about the Assyrian aggression because He was on their side (vv. 24-27). Even Lebanon, known for its thick forests of cedar trees, would fall before God. Certainly, then, Assyria should not think it could escape.

b. The rise of God's glorious empire (11:1–12:6)

The Assyrian Empire would fall (10:5-34), but another empire would arise. This section about God's empire (11:1–12:6) includes a description of the Messiah, the kingdom itself, and the remnant who will inhabit the kingdom. Besides contrasting this kingdom with the Assyrian kingdom, Isaiah also contrasted it with the sinful actions of Israel in his day.

11:1. The Lord would cut down the forests and the mighty trees (10:33-34), that is, foreign soldiers and leaders, but God's kingdom will arise by a Shoot coming up from the stump of Jesse, David's father (cf. Rev. 22:16). Isaiah undoubtedly was thinking of God's promise to David (2 Sam. 7:16) that a Descendant of David will rule over his kingdom (cf. Isa. 9:7) forever. This Branch, the Messiah (cf. Jer. 23:5), will bear fruit, that is, prosper and benefit others. (He is the Root; cf. Isa. 11:10.) This Hebrew word for branch (nēṣer) differs from the word used for branch in 4:2 (ṣemaḥ). However, the concept is the same. (Yônēq in 53:2 for "tender shoot" is still another word.) He will come directly from the line of David (cf. Matt. 1:1) and will fulfill God's promises in the Davidic Covenant.

11:2-3a. In these verses the character and work of the "Branch" are described. The Spirit of the LORD will rest on Him, that is, the Holy Spirit would empower Him (at Jesus' baptism, Matt. 3:16-17) for His work which would be characterized by wisdom . . . understanding . . . counsel . . . power . . . knowledge, and the fear of the LORD. The attributes of the Holy Spirit would characterize the Messiah. Because of His wisdom, understanding, counsel, and knowledge He is the Wonderful Counselor (Isa. 9:6). Isaiah referred to the Holy Spirit more than did any other Old Testament prophet (11:2 [four times]; 30:1; 32:15; 34:16; 40:13; 42:1; 44:3; 48:16; 59:21; 61:1; 63:10-11, 14).

He is characterized by the fear of the LORD and has delight in it (11:3) just as His people should have. To fear God is to respond to Him in awe, trust, obedience, and worship. (Interestingly all three Persons of the Trinity are suggested in vv. 1-2.) The Messiah constantly seeks to do what God the Father wants Him to do. This contrasted with the religious leaders in Isaiah's day who were unconcerned about following God's Word.

11:3b-5. As world Ruler, the Messiah will judge the world (cf. 2:4). But He will **not** be like an ordinary judge who may be swayed by superficial knowledge. He will **judge** impartially and in **righteousness.** The needy and the poor will not be oppressed by Him as they often are by human leaders (10:1-2). The oppressed will be the beneficiaries of His justice, and the wicked will be slain. His reign will be characterized by **righteousness** (11:5; cf. 9:7; 16:5) and **faithfulness** as if they were integral parts of His clothing, as a **belt** and **sash.**

11:6-9. Isaiah described the righteous kingdom which the Messiah will set up. The curse will be lifted, peace and harmony will be present, and wild animals will again be tame and harmless to domesticated animals and humans. The **wolf . . . leopard . . . lion,** and **bear** are mentioned as examples of wild animals that will dwell safely with farm animals (the **lamb . . . goat . . . calf. . . . cow,** and **ox**). A **little child** will be safe with lions, bears, cobras, and vipers (cf. 65:25). And on the temple mount (God's **holy mountain;** cf. 27:13; 56:7; 57:13; 65:11, 25; 66:20) tranquility will prevail.

Many Bible students interpret these verses nonliterally, because they suppose such changes in the animal world are not possible. However, because the Messiah is "God [is] with us" (7:14) and He will be dwelling with His people, it need not be difficult to envision these changes in nature. Though the curse of sin will be removed to some extent it will not be totally removed until the end of the millennial kingdom when finally death will be abolished (Rev. 20:14).

The reason such tranquility is possible is that all **the earth will be full of the knowledge of the** Lord (Isa. 11:9; cf. Jer. 31:34; Hab. 2:14). This means more than people knowing intellectually about the Lord. The idea is that people everywhere will live according to God's principles and Word. Animals will be affected, as well. This will occur in the Millennium when the Messiah will be reigning (Isa. 9:6-7), Jerusalem will have prominence in the world (2:2), and Judah and Israel will be regathered to the land in belief and will be living according to the New Covenant. The Millennium can hardly be in existence now since these factors do not characterize the present age.

11:10. Israel will have a special place in the kingdom because of the Abrahamic Covenant (Gen. 15:18-21; 17:7-8; 22:17-18), the Davidic Covenant (2 Sam. 7:16), and the New Covenant (Jer. 31:33-34). But people in other nations will also benefit from the kingdom. The Messiah, **the Root of Jesse** (cf. comments on "stump of Jesse," Isa. 11:1), will be a means of rallying for the **nations** (cf. v. 12; Zech. 14:9, 16). Jesus Himself made the same point that many people from outside Israel will have a part in God's kingdom (Luke 13:29). God had promised Abraham that through his line all peoples on the earth would be blessed (Gen. 12:3). The dispensational teaching that Israel has a special place in God's program because of His promises to Abraham does not exclude the Gentiles from also having a special place.

11:11-12. In verses 11-16 Isaiah spoke of the Lord's gathering the **people** of Israel and Judah from all over the world. He compared it to a second "Exodus," like the release from Egypt about 700 years earlier. That first Exodus was one of Israel's most significant events for in only three months after that God gave the Mosaic Covenant, thus marking the beginning of Israel as a nation.

The remnant will be drawn by God from the north (**Hamath**), south (**Egypt** and **Cush**), east (**Assyria . . . Elam . . . Babylonia**) and west (**islands of the sea**)—**from the four quarters of the earth.** Both **Israel** and **Judah** will be regathered (v. 12; cf. Jer. 31:31-34). This was important as the Northern Kingdom would go off into captivity, and Judahites in Isaiah's day might have thought it unlikely that both parts of the nation would ever be united.

11:13-14. In that day of regathering, **Ephraim** (the Northern Kingdom) **will not be jealous of Judah** (the Southern Kingdom) and the South **will** have no hostilities **toward** the North.

Reunited **they** (Israel and Judah) will occupy the land and defeat their enemies. **Philistia** refers to the southwestern edge of Israel along the Mediterranean Sea. **People to the east** may be those in northern Arabia (see comments on Job 1:3) and beyond (see comments on Isa. 11:11). **Edom . . . Moab, and the Ammonites** were south and east of Israel. In the kingdom period Israel will no longer be bothered by these or other enemies (cf. Obad. 19).

11:15-16. When Israel returns to her land at the beginning of the Millennium, God will prepare the way for her. **The Gulf of** Suez will be dried up to enable Israelites to return from Egypt and Cush (cf. v. 11), and **the Euphrates River** will be divided into shallow canals so that the people can return to Israel from the east. This drying of the waters will be reminiscent of the first Exodus when Israel crossed the Red Sea (lit., "Sea of Reeds") on dry land (Ex. 14:21-22). The return **from Assyria** (Isa. 11:16), perhaps representative of all places from which the remnant would come, will be like Israel's "exit" **from Egypt.** Isaiah did not know when this new Exodus would take place; he may have thought it would occur soon.

12:1-3. Chapter 12 stresses that when the remnant is regathered to the land they will rejoice. The two stanzas in this chapter are each introduced by the words "In that day you will say" (vv. 1, 4).

In that day (cf. 10:20; 11:10) refers to the time of deliverance which has been described in 11:1-12:6. When the nation is regathered and the Messiah is reigning the remnant, designated by the word I, will utter these words of praise. The remnant is distinguished from the nations, referred to in verse 4. In verses 1-3 God is praised because His **anger has** been **turned away,** Israel has been **comforted** (v. 1), and **the LORD is** (i.e., is the Source of) **strength . . . salvation,** and **song.** ("Salvation" is mentioned at the beginning and end of v. 2.) Israel's "salvation" will be more than spiritual peace of mind and deliverance; it will also include prosperity. To **draw water from the wells of salvation** (v. 3) pictures living according to God's principles and thus participating **with joy** in the blessings He will provide.

12:4-6. The remnant will thank **the LORD** and will call on each other to let the world know **what** God **has done,** probably meaning what He will have done for Israel and Judah. God's **name** (His revealed character) is to be **exalted** (vindicated) before the world, so that people everywhere will realize that He fulfills His promises. And people will **sing to** Him because of His **glorious** deeds. The remnant also will remind them-

selves of the greatness of God, **the Holy One of Israel** (cf. comments on 1:4). Being reassured that God is **among** them, they will be joyful (cf. 12:3). Chapter 12 is a fitting climax to the contrast between the fall of the Assyrian Empire, which was threatening Judah in Isaiah's day, and the rise of God's glorious kingdom, which will certainly come. Eventually all the world will know of God's truth.

C. Judgment on the nations (chaps. 13-23)

A major break occurs between chapters 12 and 13, but not as major as some interpreters have suggested. Even in chapters 13-23 Isaiah reiterated some of the same themes he voiced earlier: God uses various means to punish sin, and will judge those nations who are arrogant against His covenant people. These messages against nine sinful Gentile nations or cities around Judah were probably not written for *them* to read. The messages were probably to be read by God's covenant people to show that God actually will judge Israel's enemies. This would reassure Judah that God will establish His kingdom.

Isaiah wrote these messages when Assyria was about to attack the Syro-Palestine area. The coming devastation caused by the Assyrians would have a tremendous impact on Israel and also on other nations of the Near East. The culmination of Assyrian attacks came when Sennacherib, king of Assyria, sacked the city of Babylon in 689 B.C., thus showing that Babylon, the greatest city in its day, was not immune to the advancing Assyrians. Many commentators have assumed that Isaiah's message in 13:1-14:27 about the fall of Babylon referred to its fall to Medo-Persia in 539. However, it seems better to see this section as pertaining to the Assyrian attack on Babylon in 689. This ties in better with the Assyrian threat Isaiah had written about in 7:17-8:10, beginning with the attacks under the rule of Tiglath-Pileser III (745-727). (See the chart "Kings of Assyria in the Middle and New Assyrian Kingdoms," near Jonah 1:2.)

Each of the three great writing prophets included prophecies about God's judgment on Gentile nations (Isa. 13-23; Jer. 46-51; Ezek. 25-32). Isaiah and Jeremiah emphasized the destruction of

Babylon (though referring to different destructions) whereas Egypt is singled out for severe judgment in Ezekiel's prophecies.

In his oracles Isaiah moved westward from Babylon to Tyre. These prophecies are some of the most difficult in the entire book and it is not surprising that differing views of interpretation are held. Part of the difficulty is the lack of any extrabiblical written records about the destruction of many of these areas. Isaiah was picturing the final destruction God will bring on all the world (Isa. 13:11; cf. vv. 6, 9). But it seems that he was also picturing the soon-coming destruction from the Assyrians. Assyria's stated purpose was to "destroy . . . many nations" (10:7). The Lord would let the Assyrian Empire do that, but later He would judge it for its pride and haughtiness against Israel and her God (10:12-19).

1. BABYLON (13:1–14:27)

a. Introduction (13:1)

13:1. This section (13:1–14:27) is ascribed to **Isaiah son of Amoz** (cf. 1:1). This is significant in view of the fact that it is clearly prophecy spoken *before* the fall of Babylon. This is important for many believe that Isaiah 40–66 could not have been written by Isaiah son of Amoz because he could not have prophesied about something yet future. The passage in 13:1–14:27 shows that Isaiah's writing about events *before* they happened *was* possible.

This section is **an oracle,** sometimes translated "burden," as it comes from the verb meaning "to be lifted or carried." It was a weighty or burdensome kind of message to deliver. It is a common term in the prophetic writings (13:1; 14:28; 15:1; 17:1; 19:1; 21:1, 11, 13; 22:1; 23:1; 30:6; Jer. 23:33-34, 36, 38; Ezek. 12:10; Nahum 1:1; Hab. 1:1; Zech. 9:1 [see comments there]; 12:1; Mal. 1:1). Isaiah's oracle concerns **Babylon.** Babylon deserved God's wrath, for that city had long been a rallying point of anti-God activity. From its very beginning (Gen. 11:1-9) it had been characterized by rebellion against God. Over the centuries, as various dynasties ruled over that city, it was viewed as a place of hatred against the God of Israel. Even in the Tribulation it will be a center of hatred against God (Rev. 17–18).

b. God's army against Babylon (13:2-18)

(1) The forming of God's army. 13:2-5. The army referred to in these verses is clearly God's because He said He **summoned** His **warriors to carry out** His **wrath** against Babylon; that is, they would do His bidding. This army was **a great multitude. . . . like** an amassing of entire **nations.** Coming **for war** they would assemble **from faraway lands, from the ends of the heavens.** This is not a specific geographical description as much as a way of saying that his great army would include soldiers from many places. Though Isaiah was writing about the military strife in his day, a similar mustering of vast armies will occur just before the millennial kingdom (Rev. 16:12-16).

(2) The nearness of the day of the Lord. 13:6-13. **The day of the** LORD refers to the time of the Lord's judgment on the wicked world and/or deliverance of His people. (See comments on "the day of the LORD" under "Major Interpretive Problems," in the *Introduction* to Joel.) In Isaiah's day that judgment was coming because of the tremendous political turmoil of the next several decades that would culminate with the fall of Babylon to the Assyrians in 689 B.C. That political turmoil was similar to the judgment which will come on the whole world just before God establishes His millennial kingdom on the earth. This judgment **from the Almighty** would cause people to be in extreme distress, in pain **like a** woman's **labor** pains (cf. Isa. 21:3; 26:17; Jer. 4:31; 6:24; 13:21; 22:23; 30:6; 48:41; 49:22, 24; 50:43; Micah 4:9-10). The day of the Lord, expressing His **anger** (Isa. 13:3, 13) against sin, will **destroy . . . sinners** (v. 9) and **punish the world for its evil** and its proud attitude toward God (v. 11; cf. v. 19; 10:6, 12-13). The statements in 13:10 about the heavenly bodies (**stars. . . . sun . . . moon**) no longer functioning may figuratively describe the total turnaround of the political structure of the Near East. The same would be true of **the heavens** trembling **and the earth** shaking (v. 13), figures of speech suggesting all-encompassing destruction. Again, all this is similar to the final judgment to come on the world. On the luminaries not shining, see 34:4; Ezekiel 32:7; Joel 2:10, 30-31; 3:15; Zechariah 14:6-7; Matthew 24:29; and on the final shaking

of the earth see Isaiah 24:18; Joel 2:10; 3:16; Haggai 2:6-7, 21-22. Because so many will die in battle, people will be **scarcer than** the **rare** and valuable **gold of Ophir,** a town probably located on the southwestern coast of Arabia (cf. Job 22:24; 28:16).

(3) The army's unrelenting attack. **13:14-18.** In the day of the Lord, described in verses 6-13, the army formed by God (vv. 1-5) would attack unrelentingly. The people attacked would be utterly powerless to stop the invasion. They would be like **antelope** and **sheep,** defenseless creatures that are easy prey for hunters. People within the Assyrian Empire from other countries would try to escape the coming destruction (they **will flee to** their **native** lands). Terrible things would happen, including death **by the sword** (v. 15), infanticide, plundering, and rape (v. 16). The destruction would be unrelenting in that the invaders would not be dissuaded by money (v. 17) and they will have **no mercy on** babies (cf. v. 16) or **children** (v. 18).

The statement **I will stir up against them the Medes** (v. 17) has caused much discussion among Bible students. Many interpreters, because of the mention of the fall of Babylon (v. 19), assume that Isaiah was (in vv. 17-18) prophesying Babylon's fall in 539 (cf. Dan. 5:30-31) to the Medes and Persians. However, that view has some difficulties. In the Medo-Persian takeover in 539 there was very little change in the city; it was not destroyed so it continued on much as it had been. But Isaiah 13:19-22 speaks of the *destruction* of Babylon. Also the word "them," against whom the Medes were stirred up (v. 17), were the Assyrians (referred to in vv. 14-16), not the Babylonians. It seems better, then, to understand this section as dealing with events pertaining to the Assyrians' sack of Babylon in December 689 B.C. As Seth Erlandsson has noted, "The histories of the Medes, Elamites, and Babylonians converge around the year 700 in the struggle against the Assyrian world power and . . . Babylon assumes a particularly central position in that great historical drama from the latter years of the 8th century down to the fall of Babylon in 689" (*The Burden of Babylon: A Study of Isaiah 13:2-14:23.* Lund, Sweden: C.W.K. Glerrup, 1970, pp. 91-2).

c. *God's soon-coming destruction of Babylon (13:19-22)*

13:19-22. The recipient of this destruction is **Babylon** the city, not the entire empire. Because of her **pride** (cf. v. 11) and godless idolatry Babylon would **be overthrown by God.** The overthrow, as already stated, was done by the Assyrians, God's instrument of wrath under King Sennacherib. Just as God overthrew the wicked cities of **Sodom and Gomorrah** (Gen. 19:24-25), so He would overthrow the wicked city of Babylon. The destruction would be extensive, which was true of Sennacherib's sack of the city. Isaiah's description of the devastation of Babylon—no inhabitants for **generations** and no tents or flocks, but instead **jackals . . . owls . . . wild goats,** and **hyenas**—is typical of the way ancient Near Eastern cultures described the desolate condition of demolished cities (Erlandsson, *The Burden of Babylon,* p. 118). The Hebrew in Isaiah 13:20a can be translated, "She will not be inhabited for a long time and she will not be lived in for generation after generation." A few years after this destruction, Babylon was rebuilt by Sennacherib's son Esarhaddon (681–669 B.C.). All this preceded the rise of the Neo-Babylonian Empire in 626 and its fall to Medo-Persia in 539. Ultimately Babylon will again be rebuilt and then destroyed by God a final time (Rev. 18; cf. comments on Jer. 50:1–51:58). Isaiah was convinced that the destruction he wrote about would come quickly (**her time is at hand**). It came in 689 B.C. (see comments on Isa. 14:3-4a).

d. *God's compassion on Israel (14:1-2)*

14:1-2. The fall of Babylon (and of other nations, 14:24–21:17; 23) would assure God's people that He would work on their behalf. In spite of the destruction to come on the nation Israel, God **will** again **have compassion.** This contrasts with 9:17, where Isaiah said God in punishing His nation would *not* have compassion ("pity" translates the same word as "compassion" in 14:1). **Once again He will choose** the nation to be His people, as He had done at Mount Sinai. **Jacob** and **Israel** here probably refer to all 12 tribes, as they do in Exodus 19:3. God's choosing of Israel (and of Judah, Jerusalem, David, and Solomon) is an important Old Testament theme (cf. Deut. 7:6), especially in 1 and 2 Chronicles and the Psalms (1 Chron. 16:13; 28:4-5, 10; 29:1; 2 Chron. 6:6, 34, 38; 7:12; 12:13; 33:7; Pss. 33:12; 47:4; 78:68, 70; 89:3; 105:6, 43; 106:5; 132:13; 135:4). The fact that non-Israelites (aliens) will join Israel is also a recurring theme in Scripture (Isa. 56:6; 60:10; 61:5). Israel's role will be reversed (14:2): rather than Israel being exiled as captives in other nations, other nations will serve Israel. Israel will be prominent.

e. A taunt against Babylon (14:3-21)

(1) The defeat of the tyrant (14:3-8). **14:3-4a.** Verses 3-21 record a song or a **taunt** that will be sung by people freed from the fear of **the king of Babylon.** The song's overall message is that people will be amazed that this great king is cast down like the monarchs of other cities. People will rejoice in his demise for they had lived in fear of him.

Who is this king of Babylon? Many expositors hold the view that he is Satan, the ultimate personification of pride. Tertullian (ca. A.D. 160–230) and Gregory the Great (ca. 540–604) were the first to present this view, now widely accepted. Though verses 12-14 seem to support the view, little else in the chapter does. Though many hold that verses 12-14 refer to the entrance of sin into the cosmos by Satan's fall, that subject seems a bit forced in this chapter. (However, Ezek. 28:12-19 *does* refer to Satan's fall; see comments there.)

It seems more natural to view this proud tyrant as Sennacherib (705–681). There are interesting parallels between the description of the tyrant in Isaiah 14 and the curse against Sennacherib in 37:21-29. But wasn't Sennacherib king of Assyria rather than Babylon? He was king of both because Babylon was a vassal of Assyria from the end of the 10th century B.C. Occasionally the vassal ruler over Babylon revolted against Assyria, but in 728 Tiglath-Pileser III, Assyria's aggressive ruler from 745 to 727, was crowned king of Babylon. Nineveh was Assyria's capital, but Babylon became the center of its cultural life. Because of this assimilation, the worship of Babylon's god Marduk gained popularity in Assyria. Sargon II (722–705) and Sennacherib (705–681), later Assyrian monarchs, also called themselves kings of Babylon. After Sargon II died in 705 there was much

rebellion in the Assyrian Empire. The Elamites put Mushezib-Marduk over Babylon (692–689); he made an alliance with several nations including the Medes. To subdue the rebellion in Babylon, Sennacherib marched there in 689 and destroyed it. He even released over the city's ruins huge volumes of water to attempt to devastate the city (Erlandsson, *The Burden of Babylon,* p. 91). However, a few years later the city was rebuilt by Sennacherib's son and successor Esar-haddon.

Sennacherib's death by assassination (2 Kings 19:37) eight years after he destroyed Babylon would give great joy and comfort to the surrounding nations, especially Judah. (Sennacherib was the king who had failed in his attempt 12 years earlier, 701 B.C., to capture Jerusalem, Isa. 37; 2 Kings 18:13–19:36.)

14:4b-8. The one whose **fury** (v. 4; cf. v. 6) would **end** is **the oppressor** who had **struck down peoples** and aggressively **subdued nations.** His death would bring **rest . . . peace** and joy (**singing**) to the entire region. This rest is pictured symbolically by the great cedar trees **of Lebanon** saying that they were then safe. No longer would they be in danger of being **cut . . . down** to provide tribute to Sennacherib.

(2) The death of the tyrant. **14:9-11.** The grave ($\check{s}^e\hat{o}l$) is pictured as a great throne room where the **leaders** and **kings** of the earth go when they die. **Spirits of the departed** translates $r^e\bar{p}\bar{a}\hat{i}m$, which is rendered "departed spirits" in 26:14 and "dead" in 26:19; Job 26:5 (see comments on Job 26:5). This tyrant (Sennacherib) is envisioned as having died and as being met by the kings already in the grave. Amazed at the fate of this glorious king, whose splendor had surpassed theirs, they were **all astir.** His coming would even make **them rise from their thrones** (as if they sat on thrones in the grave) to greet him. They would act amazed that he had **become weak** and dead **like** them. Though he had lived in **pomp** with music (**harps**) he would now lie in corruption. **Maggots** and **worms** would decompose his body in the grave.

(3) The arrogance and fate of the tyrant. **14:12-15.** In his military might this great king had **laid low the nations,** including Phoenicia, Philistia, Egypt, Moab, Edom, Cilicia, much of Judah, and

northern Arabia. But he would fall like a **morning star.** The brilliance of a star in the early **dawn** suddenly vanishes when the sun rises. Sennacherib, because of his great power, thought himself godlike, but now by startling contrast he would be in the grave. In the ancient Near East, kings had supreme power; many were deified by their subjects. The people taunting this tyrant pictured him ascribing godlike characteristics to himself. Ascending **to heaven . . . above the stars** and being **enthroned on . . . the sacred mountain** recalls the belief of several Semitic peoples that the gods lived on Mount Zaphon. "Sacred mountain" translates ṣāpôn (lit., "the north"). By ascending the mountain **above . . . the clouds,** he was seeking to make himself **like** God, **the Most High.** (The language used here, of course, is hyperbolical.) Yet he would be **brought** low **to the grave** (**pit** is a synonym for grave). Nothing could save him from death and from decay in the grave.

(4) A lesson to be learned from the defeat of the tyrant. **14:16-21.** One lesson to be learned from the death of this great one is that all kings, no matter how invincible they may seem, will pass from the scene. People would **ponder** Sennacherib's **fate,** finding it hard to believe he was the same one **who** had **made** everyone **tremble** in fear by devastating **cities** and taking so many people **captives** (vv. 16-17). In his death he was not even given a decent burial as are most **kings** who **lie in state** (v. 18). He would be cut off completely, killed **by the sword** and **trampled underfoot** (v. 19). He was assassinated by his sons Adrammelech and Sharezer, who were then unable to rule in his place (**they** would **not rise to inherit the land,** v. 21) because they had to run for their lives (2 Kings 19:37).

f. Babylon's destruction by Assyria (14:22-23)

14:22-23. After the people's taunt song (vv. 4-21) **the Lord Almighty** affirmed that the people of **Babylon** would be destroyed (v. 22). Ruined by Assyria (689 B.C.) the city of Babylon would be a desolate **place for owls** (cf. 13:20-22). In fact Sennacherib described Babylon in similar words after he destroyed it. Again, this destruction, rather than the

takeover by Medo-Persia in 539 B.C., is probably referred to here (see comments on 14:3-4a), because the latter attack did not demolish the city.

g. Assyria's defeat (14:24-27)

14:24-27. Many interpreters feel that these verses are a separate section. But it seems preferable to see them as part of the oracle beginning in 13:1. Though the Lord was using the Assyrian Empire for his purposes He would eventually judge that empire harshly (10:5-19). Assyria's plan to destroy Jerusalem was thwarted (10:7), but God's plans would be carried out (14:24). He would **crush the Assyrian in** His **land, on** His **mountains** (v. 25). This probably refers to the great slaughter of the Assyrian army when it surrounded Jerusalem (37:36-37). Because of God's sovereign control **over all nations** nothing can thwart His plans by turning back **His** hand (14:27).

2. PHILISTIA (14:28-32)

14:28-32. This oracle, though written about Philistia, was for Judah's benefit (cf. v. 32). Isaiah received **this oracle** (cf. comments on 13:1; Zech. 9:1) from God **in the year** in which **King Ahaz died** (cf. Isa. 6:1, "in the year that King Uzziah died"), 715 B.C. God condemned the Philistine cities for thinking they were safe from destruction. They were rejoicing **that the rod that struck** them was **broken.** This probably does not refer to Israel, or to Judah's King Ahaz, but to Assyria. Ashdod, the Philistine city, and Judah revolted against Assyria; but in 711 B.C., only four years after this oracle, Assyria defeated Ashdod and made Philistia an Assyrian province. This happened under Assyria's ruler Sargon II (722-705; cf. 20:1). Therefore Philistia had felt secure (**in safety,** 14:30) but it would suffer defeat **by famine** and the sword. Philistia should **wail** since Assyria was coming like an uncontrollable **cloud of smoke.** However, **Zion** (Jerusalem) need not fear for it would not fall till much later (to Babylon in 586).

3. MOAB (CHAPS. 15-16)

A major question pertaining to this prophecy is when the oracle was written. In the final paragraph (16:13-14) God said that judgment would come on Moab "within three years." For the views as to what this refers to, see the comments on those verses.

For centuries Moab, east of the Dead Sea, had been an enemy of Israel. In Israel's wilderness wanderings, Moabite women seduced Israel's men (Num. 31:15-17). In the time of the Judges Israel was oppressed by Moab for 18 years (Jud. 3:12-14). Saul fought Moab (1 Sam. 14:47) and David defeated Moab (2 Sam. 8:2, 12). Solomon was influenced by his wives to build an altar to Moab's god Chemosh (1 Kings 11:7-8). Mesha, Moab's king, had to pay tribute to Ahab, king of Israel (2 Kings 3:4). After Ahab died (in 853 B.C.) Mesha rebelled against Joram (also called Jehoram) but was defeated (2 Kings 3:5-27). The destruction of Moab described in Isaiah 15–16 caused the Moabites, under Assyrian attack, to flee south to Edom.

a. The defeat of Moab (chap. 15)

(1) Lament over Moab. **15:1-4.** In chapters 15–16 Isaiah mentioned the names of several Moabite cities and towns. Ar and Kir had been **destroyed** before Isaiah recorded this oracle. These unlocated towns may have been near the southern end of the Dead Sea. **Dibon** (modern-day Dhiban) was one of Moab's main cities. **Nebo,** not to be confused with Mount Nebo, is either present-day Khirbet Ayn Musa or Khirbet el Mukkayet. **Medeba** is modern-day Madaba. Shaving one's head (cf. Job. 1:20; Jer. 47:5; Ezek. 7:18; Amos 8:10; Micah 1:16) and cutting off one's beard were signs of humiliation (Isa. 7:20; Jer. 48:37). Wearing **sackcloth,** coarse dark cloth, pictured one's dejected inward state of mourning (see comments on Isa. 3:24). Here the Moabites were bewailing the last of their cities. People in **Heshbon and Elealeh** (cf. 16:9), in northern Moab, wailed. Even Moab's soldiers wailed because of their inability to protect their cities.

(2) Moab's flight from the enemy. **15:5-9.** Isaiah's heart was emotionally disturbed by Moab's distress (cf. his similar heart tugs in 21:3-4; 22:4). The Moabites, fleeing the invading Assyrians, went south into Edom. **Zoar** was the northernmost Edomite city, directly south of the Dead Sea. **Eglath Shelishiyah** has not been discovered, but it was probably in the desert region. **Luhith** is unidentified but it is linked in parallel structure to **Horonaim** (cf. Jer. 48:34), which was in southern Moab.

The waters of Nimrim (Isa. 15:6) probably refer to the Wadi en-Numeirah, in southern Moab. Since it was **dried up,** the refugees went farther south to **the Ravine of the Poplars,** possibly near the Dead Sea's southern tip. The wailing extended to **Eglaim** and **Beer Elim,** sites presently unknown, but perhaps near Moab's southern border. Perhaps **Dimon** (v. 9) is Dibon (cf. NIV marg.). The water supply there was bloody, indicating much death and destruction had occurred there. But the bloodshed was not over. More terror was to come. It was as if the survivors were being chased relentlessly by **a lion.**

b. Protection for Israel (16:1-5)

16:1-5. In the midst of the devastation coming on Moab, protection was to be found in Israel. The Moabites had now fled all the way south to strongholds in Edom such as **Sela,** about 50 miles south of Moab's southern border. If they really wanted to be safe they should have joined themselves to Jerusalem (**the Daughter of Zion;** cf. 1:8), sending **lambs** on ahead **as tribute.** Isaiah could suggest this because he had already prophesied that Jerusalem would be spared from destruction by Assyria (10:24-34). Frustrated **like . . . birds . . . the women of Moab** were begging for protection and help (16:2-4a). But, as God promised, eventually **the destroyer**—also called **the oppressor** and **the aggressor**—would himself by destroyed (cf. 14:4-5). God **in** His **love** (ḥeseḏ, "loyalty") will see that **the One from the house of David,** the Messiah, **will sit on** David's **throne** (2 Sam. 7:16) and judge the world fairly (in **justice** and **righteousness,** a frequent topic in Isaiah's book; cf. Isa. 9:7; 11:4; 28:6; 32:16; 33:5; 42:1, 3-4; 51:5). Only through Judah could this be accomplished; the forces of Moab were obviously inadequate.

c. The pride of Moab (16:6-12)

16:6-12. Isaiah exposed the **pride and conceit** of Moab (cf. Assyria's pride, 13:11). The people of Moab should have realized their impotence before the Assyrians and turned to God through their neighbor Israel, but they refused to do so. Because of their pride, confident that they did not need God, the fruitfulness and productivity of their land would be stopped (16:7-10). Several words indicated that the fruit to be lost was grapes: **raisin cakes** (a delicacy; cf. 1 Chron. 12:40; Hosea 3:1) **of Kir Hareseth** (cf. Isa. 16:11), another city in Moab, possibly the same as Kir (15:1), **vines of Sibmah** (16:8-9), **choicest vines. . . . vineyards** (vv. 8, 10), **wine . . . presses. Harvests** (v. 9) and **orchards** (v. 10) suggest other fruits too. (On **Heshbon** and **Elealeh** in v. 9 see 15:4.) The invading army and the drought which would accompany it would wipe out Moab's chances for survival. Isaiah felt deeply **for Moab** (16:11; cf. 15:5); his **heart** responded to her calamities as the strings of **a harp** respond when played. Moab's religious ritual of sacrificing **at her high place** and praying at **her shrine** would not help alleviate God's judgment (16:12).

d. The destruction of Moab (16:13-14)

16:13-14. Moab had already suffered greatly. Now the prophet announced that there would be further destruction **within three years.** And it would be *precisely* that period of time, just **as a servant . . . would count** the years till his servitude would end. This is similar to chapter 7 in which Isaiah told Ahaz that the Aram-Israel alliance would break up in a few years. Possibly this oracle against Moab was written about the same time, picturing Tiglath-Pileser's coming invasion of Moab in 732 (after he invaded Aram). Or perhaps Isaiah was saying that Moab would be attacked in three years (701) by Sennacherib, in the year he invaded Judah. Isaiah's contemporaries could have watched current events to see if **the LORD** really was prophesying through him. When they saw that his words came true, they could be assured that his message of salvation for Judah (16:5) would also come true.

4. DAMASCUS (17:1-11)

17:1-3. The **oracle** (cf. comments on 13:1) in 17:1-11 was directed against **Damascus,** the capital city of Aram. The Northern Kingdom of Israel had allied with Aram (7:2) against the Assyrian threat. Here (17:1-11) Isaiah was again noting that Aram and Israel would be defeated by the Assyrians (cf. 8:4). **Damascus** would **become a heap of**

ruins, no longer **a city.** Since Aroer was a city in Moab, the words **the cities of Aroer** are difficult to understand. Some Septuagint (Greek) manuscripts read that Damascus and her cities will be "abandoned forever." With the cities around Damascus deserted, animals will make the ruins their home (17:2). Both **Ephraim,** representing Israel, and **Damascus,** representing Aram (cf. 7:8), would be defeated (17:3). Assyria defeated **Aram** in 732 and Israel in 722.

17:4-6. This is the first of three sections beginning with the phrase **in that day.** The others are verses 7-8 and verses 9-11. This refers to the time of God's wrath on His enemies followed by His blessings showered on His people. In some passages, it has eschatological implications (referring to the Tribulation and the Millennium), but in others it refers only to the current situation. In verses 4, 7, 9 the phrase "in that day" refers to the situation mentioned repeatedly throughout the first portion of Isaiah—the invasion of Aram and Israel by the Assyrian army. Because of that invasion Israel would face difficulties, compared to **the fat of** one's **body** wasting **away** (v. 4), and to the barren appearance of a field (v. 5) and **an olive tree** (v. 6) after harvest. **The Valley of Rephaim** (cf. Josh. 15:8; 18:16) was a fertile area west of Jerusalem where David had twice defeated the Philistines (2 Sam. 5:18-20, 22-25). As a few **olives** are left on an olive tree's higher **branches,** so a few people would be left, but most of them would be slaughtered.

17:7-8. When Israel would be invaded by the Assyrians, God's people would **look to their Maker** to see **the Holy One of Israel** (cf. comments on 1:4). When faced with the terror and distress of warfare they would realize the inadequacy of worshiping idols. **The altars** were those set up to idolatrous gods, not to the true God. **The Asherah poles** were wooden symbols of Asherah, Canaanite fertility goddess and consort of Baal. In the Northern Kingdom of Israel, widely influenced by Baalism, were many Asherah-worshipers. But when under Assyrian attack, Israel would realize that only the Lord could deliver them.

17:9-11. As a result of the judgment **in that day** (see comments on v. 4) Damascus and her **strong cities** would be abandoned and thickets and underbrush would grow. Because of her unfaithfulness to the true God and her having forgotten Him, her efforts at planting vines and getting a harvest (as if she were secure, in a time of peace) would be fruitless. The plants would be diseased and the people would be in pain.

5. THE LAND OF WHIRRING WINGS (17:12–18:7)

17:12-14. Many interpreters place verses 12-14 with the previous section. However, the fact that **Oh** (*hôy;* see comments on 3:9) is the same Hebrew word translated "woe" in 18:1 may indicate that 17:12-14 goes with chapter 18. **The raging . . . nations** (17:12; cf. Ps. 2:1) are said to be **like the roar of surging waters.** These **peoples** were the Assyrians, whom God was using to judge His people. Apparently the "nations" (pl.) means the particular nation which was the dominant power in its day, namely, Assyria. When God would punish (rebuke) **them** (the Assyrians), they would become **like chaff** (cf. Isa. 29:5), the light and useless part of grain which, when winnowed, blows away. How appropriate that though Assyria brought **terror** in **the evening,** the enemy would be **gone** before **morning,** for such was the case with the Assyrian army (37:36-37). Though the Assyrian soldiers had plundered many cities of Judah, 185,000 soldiers were slaughtered overnight.

18:1-2. The message in chapter 18 is directed against **the land of whirring wings,** the nation of **Cush.** (On the word **woe;** see comments on "Oh" in 17:12 and comments on 3:9.) The whirring wings may refer to locusts. Cush included modern-day southern Egypt, Sudan, and northern Ethiopia. Apparently the Cushites sent **envoys** in swift-moving **papyrus boats** (cf. Job 9:26) to suggest that Israel form an alliance with them against the Assyrians. The Cushites, a people who were **tall,** fearsome, and **aggressive,** spoke a language that would have sounded **strange** to Hebrews because it was non-Semitic. Like Egypt, Cush **is divided by rivers** (cf. Isa. 18:7) that is, by branches of the Nile. Nothing is known elsewhere in the Bible or from extrabiblical sources about any contacts of this nation with Israel in a joint venture against Assyria.

18:3. The prophet exhorted the Cushites to go back home and not try to form an alliance because the Lord would defeat the enemy at the proper time. The Cushites represented **all** the **people of the world** who desired to see the Assyrians fall. But the Lord promised through Isaiah that **when** the time would come to fight the Assyrians they would know it and would see the enemy fall.

18:4-6. God's plans would linger much like the summer **heat** and harvest dew. The Lord told Isaiah that He would wait till the proper time to cut off the enemy. Isaiah had already been given the reason for this (10:12, 25, 32). But the Assyrian army first had to complete the task God gave them, to punish the people of Israel by taking them captive. However, once God's purposes had been accomplished He would intervene and **cut** them **off** (18:5) just when they, like grapes, were beginning to ripen, to extend their empire. They would be killed and would **be left** on the mountains as food for wild **birds** in the **summer** and **wild animals** in the **winter.**

18:7. After the Assyrian defeat, **the Lord** would cause the people of Cush (cf. vv. 1-2) to take **gifts** to the Lord at **Mount Zion,** where His **name** dwelt (see comments on Deut. 12:5). Whether this occurred after the fall of Assyria is not known. Possibly Isaiah was speaking of the millennial kingdom when peoples from around the world will worship **the Lord** (cf. Zech. 14:16) because of His gracious acts.

6. EGYPT (CHAPS. 19–20)

Chapter 19 focuses on Egypt; chapter 20 concerns both Egypt and Cush (cf. chap. 18). As in the other oracles the historical situation, the impending Assyrian advance throughout the whole region, serves as a backdrop for the prophecies.

a. Egypt to be punished (19:1-15)

Some people wanted to look to Egypt for protection against the Assyrian threat. But Isaiah pointed out that Egypt would be no help, because she too would be overwhelmed by God's judgment.

(1) Egypt's internal troubles. **19:1-4.** Judgment was coming against **Egypt** from **the Lord.** God is pictured as riding

on a swift cloud (cf. Pss. 68:4, 33; 104:3). In Canaanite mythology this same idea is used of Baal, the god of rain and fertility. However, the Lord, not Baal, is the true Giver of rain (something Egypt would sorely need, Isa. 19:5-10) and fertility. The gods of Egypt—of which there were many (see the chart "The Plagues and the Gods and Goddesses of Egypt," near Ex. 7:14)—would not be able to save their people from coming judgment. Their idols would tremble before Him, which would cause the people to be disheartened and depressed (Isa. 19:1). The coming judgment would cause internal divisions (v. 2) and despair among the people when they would realize that their gods, only mere idols, and their occult practices (cf. mediums and . . . spiritists, 8:19; Lev. 19:31; 20:6) could not save them. Now they would be overtaken by a cruel master and a fierce king, the Assyrian empire's king. Egypt, who centuries before had been a cruel master over Israel (Ex. 1:11-14), would now be the object of cruelty. This Assyrian king was Esarhaddon, who conquered Egypt in 671 B.C. This judgment would come from the Lord, the LORD Almighty (Isa. 19:4), Israel's Master and great covenant-keeping God.

(2) Egypt's lack of fertility. 19:5-10. To show that the judgment really would be from God, Isaiah said that the destruction would affect nature. A drought would ruin the economy and cause the people whose work depended on the Nile to be depressed. The river (v. 5) undoubtedly refers to the Nile, Egypt's "lifeblood," the source of the nation's agricultural growth. Without the Nile, Egypt could not have survived. The annual flooding of the Nile over the fields enriched the soil. With the drying up of the Nile (brought on by God, not by military conquest), papyrus reeds . . . plants, and every sown field would wilt (vv. 6-7). Fishermen using either hooks or nets would not be able to pursue their livelihood (v. 8), and those who derived their income from working with flax (cf. Ex. 9:31; which depended on water for its growth), or linen made from flax, or other cloth, would not be able to ply their trade (Isa. 19:9-10). The entire economy depended on the Nile River.

(3) Egypt's wisdom unable to help. 19:11-15. Egypt was well known in the ancient world for its wisdom writings and its wise men. But Isaiah warned Egypt not to count on her wise men to save the nation from the coming destruction. The officials of Zoan (vv. 11, 13; cf. Zoan, a city in Egypt's Delta, in Num. 13:22; Ps. 78:12, 43; Isa. 30:4; Ezek. 30:14), the wise counselors of Pharaoh (Isa. 19:11), and the leaders of Memphis (v. 13; cf. Jer. 2:16; 44:1; 46:14, 19; Ezek. 30:13, 16; Hosea 9:6) thought their wisdom might save them from their coming judgment. But their wisdom was foolishness compared with the wisdom of the LORD Almighty who was planning the onslaught. No one in Egypt could do anything to avert the destruction; they were like staggering drunkards before the LORD. Neither the leaders (the head and the palm branch) nor the populace (the tail and the reed; cf. Isa. 9:15) could hold back God's judgment. At one time Zoan was Egypt's capital city (ca. 2050-1800). Memphis, on the Nile about 20 miles north of Cairo, was the first capital of united Egypt (ca. 3200 B.C.) and one of the major cities during much of its long history.

b. Israel to control Egypt (19:16-25)

The phrase "in that day" appears five times in this passage (vv. 16, 18-19, 21, 23). As stated earlier (see comments on 17:4, 7, 9) the phrase often refers to judgment followed by blessing. In 19:16-25 Isaiah emphasized the outcome of the judgment on Egypt; eventually Egypt will fear the Lord, realizing that He is the true God.

(1) Judah's control of Egypt. 19:16-17. In contrast with Isaiah's day when Judah was thinking about turning to Egypt for help, a time will come when Egypt will recognize Judah as the dominant force in the world. The Egyptians will be like women, that is, Egypt will be in terror of Judah because they will realize that Judah is under the uplifted hand (strength) of the LORD Almighty. This will be a reversal of the situation in the prophet's time.

(2) Egypt's allegiance to the Lord. 19:18. The five cities in Egypt no doubt represented the rest of the nation. To speak the language of Canaan apparently does not mean that the Egyptians will stop speaking their own language. Rather, because of their new worship (swear-

ing **allegiance to the LORD Almighty**; cf.
vv. 20, 25) in offering sacrifices in Jerusalem, they will have to be fluent enough
in Hebrew to get by (cf. vv. 19, 21; Zech.
14:16-19). The meaning of **the City of
Destruction** (*heres*) has caused much debate. It seems preferable to follow the
reading preserved in the Dead Sea Scrolls
and the Vulgate, namely, "the City of the
Sun" (*heres*), meaning Heliopolis (cf. NIV
marg. and Ezek. 30:17). Heliopolis, one
of the major cities in the south end of
Egypt's Delta, was dedicated to worship
of the sun god. Such a significant change
(i.e., worshiping the Lord instead of the
sun god) will prove to the world and to
Israel that Egypt will be serious in its new
worship.

(3) True worship to be instituted.
19:19-22. In **Egypt an altar** will be built **to
the LORD** along with **a monument . . . at**
Egypt's **border. Egypt** will openly avow
that she is worshiping the God of Israel.
This will be national policy (suggested by
the monument, which **will be a sign and
witness**) and also private worship (suggested by the altar). **Egypt** will be in the
same position as Israel, God's covenant
people, for when the Egyptians will ask
God for help **He will** give it to them (v.
20). They will also be involved in the
sacrificial worship system (v. 21; cf. Zech.
14:16-19; Mal. 1:11), and God will **heal
them** after they repent and ask for help.
This situation was almost unbelievable
for the people of Judah in Isaiah's day.
But it *will* occur. It will take place after
the Messiah has returned and established
His millennial kingdom.

(4) Peace to be established on earth.
19:23-25. The situation described by Isaiah in verses 19-22 will not be limited to
Egypt. **Assyria** and the rest of the earth
will also be recipients of blessing **in that
day,** the Millennium. People will travel
on **a highway from Egypt to Assyria,** and
people in those two nations—enemies in
Isaiah's day!—**will worship together.** In
Isaiah's day Judah was hoping that Egypt
would save her from the **Assyrians.** But
remarkably, in the Millennium these
three powers, **Assyria, Egypt,** and **Israel,**
will have a harmonious, peaceful relationship under God's hand of blessing.
All this, of course, will fulfill part of the
promise to Abraham that "all peoples on
earth will be blessed through" him (Gen.
12:3).

**c. Egypt's inability to help Israel
(chap. 20)**

20:1. Isaiah interposed a narrative
section here to drive home what had
been said in chapter 18 against Cush and
in 19:1-17 against Egypt. Some in Judah
wanted to form an alliance with these
two nations to help stave off the Assyrian
threat. Chapter 20 shows the foolishness
of such a course of action. In 711 B.C.
Ashdod, a Philistine city, was captured
by the **commander**-in-chief of the Assyrian king **Sargon** II (722–705). The capture
of Ashdod was to signal to the Judahites
that they could not count on foreign alliances to protect them, for the Assyrians
believed their advances could not be
stopped.

20:2-6. For three years Isaiah did not
wear his outer garment of **sackcloth** (also
the attire of Elijah, 2 Kings 1:8), or his
sandals. (He was not completely naked.)
This object lesson was to show how the
Egyptians and Cushites would be treated
by the victorious Assyrian forces. When
those nations (**Egypt and Cush**) would
fall to the Assyrians (Isa. 20:4), the
Judahites who thought an alliance with
those countries would help them would
be afraid and ashamed (v. 5). People
would realize that if **Egypt** and **Cush** had
fallen to **Assyria,** then they had no
chance for **escape** (v. 6). Judah, then,
should trust in the **LORD** for protection
rather than in the foreign alliance they
were contemplating.

7. THE DESERT (21:1-10)

Many interpreters assume that since
Elam (v. 2), Media (v. 2), and Babylon (v.
9) are mentioned, Isaiah must have been
referring to the fall of Babylon to the
Medo-Persian Empire in 539 B.C. However, passages referring to the fall of Babylon in 539 indicate that it was something
about which Israel was to rejoice (because
it soon resulted in the return of the Jews
to their homeland), whereas this fall of
Babylon was terrifying, something to be
feared. "The Desert by the Sea" (v. 1)
most likely refers to the area around the
gulf known today as the Persian Gulf, that
is, territory near Babylon.

As already mentioned, in Isaiah's
previous oracles (chaps. 13–20) he wrote
of the Assyrian incursion into other
countries in the ancient world and the
effects it had on the Syro-Palestine re-

gion. In 722 B.C. a Chaldean prince from the Persian Gulf region, named Marduk-apal-iddina (called Merodach-Baladan in 39:1), revolted against Assyria, captured Babylon, and was crowned king of Babylon. Elam, a nation northeast of Babylon, supported his revolt. Not till 710 B.C. was Sargon able to evict Marduk-apal-iddina from Babylon. After the death of Sargon in 705 Marduk-apal-iddina along with Elamite troops revolted against Sennacherib. In 702 Sennacherib finally defeated him (and Elam) and devastated his home area around the Persian Gulf. Undoubtedly Isaiah was prophesying about this situation. Hezekiah, king of Judah, and other members of his royal court felt that Marduk-apal-iddina would be able to break the strength of the Assyrian Empire. But Isaiah was warning them that this would not happen.

21:1. In this **oracle** (see comments on 13:1) Isaiah pictured an invasion of **the Desert by the Sea** (i.e., Babylon by the Persian Gulf) as being like an approaching **desert** storm. The **invader** was probably Marduk-apal-iddina (Merodach-Baladan) who arose suddenly from the desert regions to revolt against Assyria.

21:2. God gave Isaiah a **vision** about the Babylonian uprising against Assyria. The prophet heard the battle cry for **Elam** and **Media** (north of Elam) to attack Babylon and free it from Assyria. It refers to the invader in the vision (see comments on v. 1); he said he would stop **the groaning . . . caused** by **the traitor,** the Assyrian Empire which had caused most nations in the region to "groan" under the devastation caused by her conquests. Apparently Marduk-apal-iddina felt that he would be able to stop the Assyrian advance and thereby liberate the entire region.

21:3-5. Isaiah now contrasted his feelings with the actions of those around him. Because of this prophecy he was about to utter he was in **pain** like that of **a woman in labor,** a simile often used by the prophets (see comments on 13:8 and cf. 26:17). **Bewildered,** he trembled and was in a state of **horror** (cf. 15:5-7; 22:4). By contrast, the people around him were living as if nothing was happening. They continued in a festive attitude (21:5a) not realizing the implications of what was happening. Perhaps Isaiah had in mind the feasting which would be done when Marduk-apal-iddina's (Merodach-Baladan's) men came to Jerusalem (chap. 39). Isaiah realized that Babylon under Marduk-apal-iddina's control could not change what God had ordained. So rather than eating they should have prepared for battle, implied by the words **oil the shields.** Shields made of animal skins needed to be rubbed with olive oil to prevent their cracking.

21:6-10a. God told Isaiah to have someone be on the **lookout** for the battle between Babylon and Assyria. The watchman was to look for anyone who would come his way to **report** on the battle (vv. 6-7). The watchman looked **day after day** till finally someone came with the message that **Babylon** had **fallen** and **its gods** lay **shattered on the ground** (v. 9). The emotional impact of this message on the people of Judah, who were hoping Babylon's revolt would be successful, would be stunning. They had hoped that the alliance Hezekiah made with Bablyon would break the Assyrian domination. But it was not to be. Sennacherib pushed Marduk-apal-iddina out of Babylon and as stated earlier (see comments on chap. 13), the Assyrian king eventually destroyed the city in 689 B.C. Babylon's fall seemed like the last straw. Now no one could stop the Assyrian Empire. So Judah felt **crushed** emotionally like grain **on the threshing floor** (cf. Jer. 51:33).

21:10b. Isaiah reiterated that his message was from **God.** He was only telling what he had **heard from the LORD Almighty** (cf. comments on 1:9). Judah must not rely on the Babylonians to save them. This man from the Desert by the Sea (Marduk-apal-iddina) would not be successful.

8. EDOM (21:11-12)

21:11-12. This brief **oracle** (see comments on 13:1) seems to be against Edom because of the reference to **Seir** (21:11). Seir is an alternate name for Edom because the mountains of Seir were given as a possession to Esau and his descendants (Josh. 24:4). The name **Dumah** may be a wordplay on "Edom" since Dumah means silence or stillness (cf. NIV marg.) and **the watchman** in the oracle saw no activity. More likely, however, Dumah is a transliteration of Udumu or Udumai, the Akkadian designation for Edom. Both Tiglath-Pileser (in 734) and Sargon (in 711) mentioned taking tribute from Udumu. Was there any chance Edom's political situation would change? The answer was no, not immediately. Even though **morning** was **coming**, another **night** would follow. It did not look as if the situation would change soon.

9. ARABIA (21:13-17)

21:13-17. The Assyrian threat is the background of this oracle (see comments on 13:1) too. The **Dedanites** (21:13) were a tribe from southern Arabia. **Tema** (v. 14; cf. Job 6:19; Jer. 25:23) was a well-known oasis in northwestern Arabia, and **Kedar** (Isa. 21:16-17; cf. 42:11) was in northern Arabia. This oracle discusses the difficult times the people of **Arabia** would soon experience at the hands of the Assyrians. **Within one year** Kedar's **pomp** would **end** (Kedar was known for its tents, Ps. 120:5; Song 1:5; also cf. Jer. 49:28-29, which were a beautiful black). **The warriors of Kedar** would experience a great defeat (Isa. 21:16-17). The Arabians would be fugitives, running for their lives from the sword. The oracle would be fulfilled, for **the Lord, the God of Israel,** had **spoken** (v. 17). In 715 Sargon II wrote that he had defeated a number of Arabian tribes and had them deported to Samaria.

10. JERUSALEM (CHAP. 22)

Chapters 13–23 are more than a catalog of judgments against various nations. They also discuss the responses of various peoples to the Assyrian threat in the days of Isaiah. Jerusalem, "the Valley of Vision," was also under God's judgment and needed to respond properly to the Assyrian threat. That Isaiah was speaking of Jerusalem is evident in 22:9-10.

a. Judgment against Jerusalem (22:1-14)

It is not certain which Assyrian invasion Isaiah was speaking of in these verses. Perhaps it was the invasion of Sennacherib, who surrounded Jerusalem in 701 B.C. (chaps. 36–37). From God's perspective the purpose of that invasion was to encourage Judah to turn to Him and repent of her sinful ways. Unfortunately the people did not respond positively to the invasion and used it as a

time for revelry (22:2) and for shoring up the city's defenses (vv. 8-11).

22:1-4. This **oracle** (see comments on 13:1) pertains to **the Valley of Vision** (cf. 22:5). Often Jerusalem is referred to as a mountain (e.g., Mount Zion), but here the city is called a valley. This also fits because a valley—the Kidron—runs between two hills directly east of the city. From this city God was revealing Himself to Isaiah; hence it was called the Valley of Vision. Jerusalem was filled with people (in **commotion** and **tumult;** cf. v. 5) from the surrounding towns and villages in Judah. (Sennacherib wrote that he had captured 46 towns of Judah.) The important people (**leaders**) had escaped but were **captured** (v. 3) by the Assyrians. People still inside the city of Jerusalem went **up on the** flat **housetops** (v. 1) to observe the enemy outside the city walls. Because the Assyrian advance had caused **the destruction of** many of Isaiah's **people** (v. 4), he lamented (cf. his remorse in 15:5-7; 21:3-4).

22:5-8a. Jerusalem was being besieged and the people inside the walls could do nothing about it. The people realized that the enemy's advancing to the very walls of Jerusalem was **a day** of judgment brought on by **the Lord, the Lord Almighty** (cf. vv. 12, 14-15, 25). The attack was not happenstance; it had come because of the people's disobedience (cf. vv. 12-14). In the city people were in **tumult** and **terror** as they saw the enemy camped outside waiting for an opportunity to get inside to sack and burn the city (v. 5). The Hebrew words for "tumult," "trampling," and "terror" sound much alike. They are $m^e h\hat{u}m\hat{a}h$, $m^e b\hat{u}s\hat{a}h$, and $m^e b\hat{u}k\hat{a}h$. Soldiers from **Elam,** east of Assyria with its capital at Susa, and **Kir,** perhaps an Assyrian province (2 Kings 16:9; Amos 1:5; 9:7), joined the Assyrian warriors. Perhaps Isaiah mentioned these two areas of the Assyrian Empire to point out (by a figure of speech known as a merism) that troops from all over the empire were now gathered at Jerusalem's very door. Enemy **chariots** were in the **valleys** around Jerusalem, and **at the city gates** enemy **horsemen** were ready to attack (Isa. 22:7). Since Judah was defenseless, this was certainly a frightening time!

22:8b-11. One would think that in such a precarious position the nation would turn back to God and repent. Obviously the city could not deliver itself (v. 8a). However, in their sinful condition the people still tried to do things their own way. Rather than count on God for protection they wanted to depend on their own strength. So they got out **the weapons** from **the Palace of the Forest,** which Solomon had built (1 Kings 7:2; cf. 1 Kings 10:17, 21). It got its name from the huge cedar columns brought to Jerusalem from Lebanon. Apparently armaments were stored in that building in Isaiah's day.

At the time of Sennacherib's threat Hezekiah took several defense measures: (a) he repaired broken parts of the wall (cf. 2 Chron. 32:5) of **the City of David** (cf. 2 Sam. 5:7, 9); (b) he collected **water in the Lower Pool** (cf. 2 Chron. 32:4); (c) he demolished some **houses** to use their material for repairing **the wall;** and (d) he preserved the city's **water** supply in **a reservoir between the two walls.** The exact location of this reservoir and the meaning of the two walls and of **the Old Pool** are not known. Perhaps the reservoir refers to the Pool of Siloam which Hezekiah connected to the Gihon Spring (2 Chron. 32:30) by his now-famous underground water tunnel, which extends 1,777 feet and was carved out of solid rock. This marvelous feat of engineering was successful. But it could not be a means of the nation's deliverance, for the people refused to look for help to God who had given them the water **long ago.**

22:12-14. When the people saw the enemy they should have repented, realizing they were helpless before the Assyrians. Pulling **out** their **hair** (cf. Ezra 9:3; Neh. 13:25) and wearing **sackcloth** (cf. comments on Isa. 3:24) were signs of mourning. But instead of mourning (22:12) the Jerusalemites "lived it up" in **revelry** (cf. v. 2), banqueting, and wine-**drinking** in the face of their impending death (**tomorrow we die,** v. 13). They did not believe God was powerful enough to save them and to follow through on His promises. Therefore a pronouncement of woe came to the people through Isaiah: this sin of lack of trust in **the LORD would not be atoned for.** Eventually the curses of the Mosaic Covenant (Lev. 26:14-39; Deut. 27:15-26; 28:15-68) would come on the nation of Judah.

b. Judgment against Shebna (22:15-25)

22:15-19. The reason for this section on judgment (vv. 15-25) is not explicitly stated. **Shebna** was a high court official, a **steward,** involved in the negotiations with Sennacherib when he besieged Jerusalem (2 Kings 18:18, 26, 37; 19:2; Isa. 36:3, 11, 22; 37:2). Some think that his position as steward (secretary) **of the palace** gave him a position second only to the king. Why he was to be deposed from this important **position** is not stated. Perhaps he opposed Isaiah's message of impending judgment. He apparently shared the attitudes of the Jerusalemites Isaiah had described (22:2, 11-13).

The impiety of Shebna apparently involved his trying to make a permanent name for himself by fashioning **a grave,** as people did in many of the surrounding nations. Perhaps he thought that by being buried in a prominent **grave** site (**on the height**) his name would live on in spite of the current conditions. However, Isaiah prophesied that Shebna, rather than having a permanent resting place, would be demoted and would **die** in **a large** foreign **country,** probably Assyria. There is no record of what happened to him other than the prophecy given here by Isaiah.

22:20-25. Eliakim, the palace administrator and a godly man, would fill Shebna's important position (vv. 20-21). Eliakim also was involved in the negotiations with Sennacherib (2 Kings 18:18, 26, 37; Isa. 36:3, 11, 22; 37:2). He would be a respected leader (like **a father** to the Judahites) and a faithful administrator who would make wise decisions (22:22). In contrast with Shebna, who was to be cast away, Eliakim was to be **like a** well-driven **peg** (v. 23a), a firm foundation for the nation. He would be an honorable person (v. 23b), and would cause **his family** name to be well known to humble people (figuratively called **lesser vessels**) and to more influential family members (called **bowls** and **jars**). However, Isaiah warned that eventually even this **peg** would come to an end (v. 25), signifying that eventually the kingdom of Judah would be taken away into captivity.

11. TYRE (CHAP. 23)

a. A prophecy of Tyre's fall (23:1-14)

As in the other prophecies (chaps. 13–22) this one about Tyre also pertains to the Assyrian aggression at the end of the eighth century B.C. Though Tyre was not destroyed until some 200 years later, the trade of this great city was cut off between about 700 and 630 B.C.

23:1. This **oracle** (see comments on 13:1) begins with a call to a fleet of merchant ships to **wail** (cf. 23:14) in distress during their trading voyages on the Mediterranean Sea. On **ships of Tarshish** see comments on Ezekiel 27:25 (cf. Isa. 23:14; 60:9). Those ships were docked at the island of **Cyprus**, about 150 miles northwest of **Tyre**, when the news of Tyre's destruction reached them.

23:2-5. Phoenicia, with its chief city ports of **Tyre** (vv. 1, 3, 8, 15, 17) and **Sidon** (vv. 2, 4, 12), depended on seafaring trade for its economy. The Phoenicians greatly benefited by the wares she received in international commerce, and in turn those other countries, including **the island** of Cyprus, were **enriched** by Phoenician trade. **Grain** from Egypt was one of the staples channeled through the Phoenician trading centers of **Tyre** and **Sidon**. Shihor (cf. Josh. 13:3; 1 Chron. 13:5; Jer. 2:18) was in eastern Egypt and may be a branch of the Nile River. **The grain of the Shihor** referred to grain grown in the fertile land watered by that part of the Nile. The wealth of Sidon and Tyre (the **fortress**, mā'ōz, trans. "stronghold" in Pss. 27:1; 37:39; 43:2; 52:7 and "refuge" in Nahum 1:7) did not come from their own efforts. It came by trading with the Mediterranean nations. Thus **the sea,** personified, could say that it had not gone through the **birth** experience; it had produced quick wealth without going through the pain (Isa. 23:4; cf. 66:7-8). But the demise of Tyre was bad not only for Phoenicia; it was also bad for the places from which the trade came, such as **Egypt** (23:5).

23:6-9. People in **Tarshish** were to **wail** too (cf. vv. 1, 5, 14) because of their economic losses. Tarshish was rich in silver (Jer. 10:9), iron, tin, and lead (Ezek. 27:12). Therefore Tarshish was probably in the West Mediterranean where mineral deposits were plentiful. Many scholars identify Tarshish with Tartessus in southwest Spain. The people of that region would be in despair because of the fall of that great trading center, **Tyre,** which was a **city of revelry** (cf. Isa. 23:12) and an ancient **city.** According to He-

rodotus Tyre was founded around 2700 B.C. However, the people of Tarshish needed to realize that their difficulty came directly from the God of Israel. The LORD **Almighty** (v. 9) **planned** the humbling of this great and wealthy city **(the bestower of crowns)**, proud of its **glory** and **renowned** for its commercial enterprise.

23:10-14. Throughout the entire Mediterranean region—from **Tarshish** in the northwest to the **Nile** River in the southeast, and to Cyprus in the northeast (vv. 10, 12)—people would mourn and weep for the fall of **Phoenicia** (v. 11). The Phoenicians would have no more protection than did **the Babylonians** who were defeated by **the Assyrians** (v. 13; cf. 21:1-10). **Reveling** would end in **Sidon,** probably along with the revelry in Tyre (cf. 23:7). (On the words **Virgin Daughter** see the comments on 47:1.) To escape **to Cyprus** would not help. The trading **ships of Tarshish** were advised by Isaiah to **wail** because the Mediterranean world's great trading center would be gone (v. 14; cf. v. 1).

b. A prophecy of Tyre's future (23:15-18)

23:15-18. The **70 years** mentioned by Isaiah (v. 15) were probably from about 700 to 630 B.C. when Phoenicia's trading was greatly restricted by the Assyrians. In 701 Assyria installed Tubu'alu (Éthbaal III) over **Tyre.** But around 630 Assyria declined in power, enabling Tyre to regain its autonomy and restore its trade.

This 70-year span is called **the span of a king's life** (cf. Ps. 90:10). **But after 70 years . . .** Tyre would again become a trading center, like a **prostitute** (Isa. 23:15-17) who was **forgotten** but who returned to her illicit practice, singing to attract lovers to her again. Tyre would again **ply her trade with** various nations. But this time the profits from her trading would somehow benefit those who feared **the LORD** (v. 18). It is difficult to know exactly what Isaiah was referring to. Some have suggested that the 70 years referred not to the time from about 700 to 630 but to the coming Babylonian Captivity of Judah (605–536 B.C.) and that at the end of those years materials from Tyre were used in construction of the temple complex in Jerusalem which was built by the postexilic community. But Tyre's trading was not restricted during those years (except for Nebuchadnezzar's 13-year siege of the city from 587 to 574).

D. Punishment and kingdom blessing (chaps. 24–27)

God's judgment on the nations through the Assyrian invasions (chaps. 13–23) forms a backdrop for the Lord's eventual judgment on the whole world (24:1, 4). Known as "Isaiah's apocalypse," chapters 24–27 describe the earth's devastation and people's intense suffering during the coming Tribulation and the blessings to follow in the millennial kingdom.

1. A TIME OF JUDGMENT (CHAP. 24)

24:1-3. The coming desolation and ruin of the whole **earth** ("earth" is mentioned 16 times in this chap.) will be by the direct intervention of **the LORD,** and will level all of society. No advantage will come from having a high rather than a low position, for all will come under God's hand of judgment (v. 2). The world will be **laid waste and totally plundered** (v. 3; cf. Rev. 6; 8–9; 15–16). This is certain because **the LORD** said so.

24:4. In this worldwide judgment, **the earth** will wither (dry up). Even important people (**the exalted**) will **languish.** No one will be spared from this eschatological judgment.

24:5. The reason such devastation will come is that the **people,** not living as they should, will have **defiled** the **earth.** In creating the world God said it was "very good" (Gen. 1:31). But people in their sin defiled the good earth, by disobeying God's **laws,** violating His **statutes,** and breaking His **everlasting covenant.** "The everlasting covenant" probably refers not to the Abrahamic or Mosaic Covenants but to the covenant people implicitly had with God to obey His Word. Right from the very beginning mankind refused to live according to God's Word (Gen. 2:16-17; 3:1-6; cf. Hosea 6:7). And throughout history people have refused to obey God's revelation.

24:6-13. Because people have "defiled" the earth by their sins (v. 5), judgment will come. They must **bear** the consequences of their **guilt.** God's judgment is likened to a burning fire that consumes all but a **few** on the earth (v. 6). In the earth's devastation vineyards will wither and music (with **tambourines** and harps) and parties (vv. 7-9, 11) will stop. The fruit of the vine is often associated in the Bible with joy (e.g., 16:9; Zech. 10:7). **The . . . city** (Isa. 24:10; cf. 25:2), representative of **the** whole **earth** (24:13), will be in **ruins** with all its houses uninhabited. When God pours out His wrath on the unbelieving world in the Tribulation, all will be **desolate** and gloomy. Little will be left, as after the harvesting of olives (cf. 17:6) or grapes.

24:14-16a. The word **they** probably refers to the righteous who will be left after God's judgment on the earth. Though few in number (v. 6) they will delight in the fact that the earth is cleansed from people's sin. They will **raise their voices** and **shout** to proclaim **glory to the LORD . . . the God of Israel.** Everywhere—in **the west** (v. 14), **the east** (v. 15), **the islands of the sea** (v. 15), and **the ends of the earth** (v. 16; cf. comments on 5:26)—the same song is proclaimed: **Glory** to God, **the Righteous One.** The believing remnant will view the earth's desolation as a righteous act by the righteous God. It will not be viewed in the way the Assyrian advance was viewed—as a cruel, unfair punishment.

24:16b. In contrast with the future joyful song of glory to the God of Israel (v. 16a), the distress in Isaiah's day caused him to pronounce **woe** on himself (cf. 6:5). All around him were **treacherous,** unfaithful people on whom judgment must fall.

24:17-20. Because of the people's treachery (v. 16) and their other sins, they would suffer. They would **fall into a pit** used to capture animals or **be caught** by **a snare** (trap). Trying to escape one danger they will be overcome by another calamity. God's judgment will be like a great rainstorm and earthquake. The earthquake will cause great crevices to open in the earth and swallow up people. In the earthquake **the earth** will reel **like a drunkard** and will sway **like a** temporary unsturdy **hut** in a field, blowing **in the wind.** (This Heb. word for "hut" is used in the OT only here and in 1:8.) Judgment will come because of **guilt** (cf. 24:6), the guilt of the whole world in rebelling against God.

24:21-23. Isaiah again (cf. v. 1) stated that the coming judgment will be God's direct intervention: **the LORD will pun-**

ish. Natural disasters will occur only because the Lord will cause them to happen. **The powers in the heavens** may refer to spiritual forces opposed to God (cf. Rev. 19:20; 20:2). **The kings on the earth below** undoubtedly refer to political forces that will be banished. Those powers in the heavens and on the earth will become like cattle when the Lord herds them **together** and places them **like prisoners . . . in a dungeon.** Their punishment **after many days** refers to the great white throne judgment after the Millennium when all the unrighteous will have to stand before God and be judged for their evil deeds and lack of faith in Him (Rev. 20:11-15). When this judgment takes place **the LORD,** the Messiah, will be reigning **on Mount Zion** (Isa. 24:23; see comments on 1:8) **and in Jerusalem.** He will reign **gloriously,** that is, His glory will be manifest (cf. 24:15-16). In the 1,000-year kingdom the Messiah **will reign** as King over the earth (Zech. 14:9) from Jerusalem, God's "centerpiece" (Isa. 2:2-4; Micah 4:1-5). After the Millennium and the great white throne judgment God will reign for eternity from the New Jerusalem (Rev. 21:2, 10), which will be filled with the glory of God and therefore will not need the light of **the moon** or **the sun** (Isa. 24:23; cf. Rev. 21:23).

2. A TIME OF BLESSING IN THE KINGDOM (CHAPS. 25–27)

a. The Lord's preserving of His people (chap. 25)

This chapter is a praise psalm extolling the Lord's deliverance of His people. Soon after God in His judgment will wipe out sinful people (chap. 24) the Messiah's glorious kingdom will begin. In poetry Isaiah described the praise that will be ascribed to the Lord in the Millennium for His marvelous work.

(1) Praise to the Lord for the coming kingdom. **25:1-5.** Speaking in the first person Isaiah described the situation which will exist when the kingdom is established on the earth. The prophet ascribed **praise** to the Lord's **name** (His revealed character) for His **marvelous** acts of judgment (vv. 2-3) and deliverance (vv. 4-5). God's judgment on **the city,** representative of the world (cf. 24:12-13), will cause **peoples** from **ruthless nations** to **honor** and **revere** God.

This will fulfill the promise given Abraham that all the world's nations will be blessed through Israel (Gen. 12:3). The theme of Gentiles knowing and worshiping God in the kingdom is common in the prophets (see, e.g., Isa. 2:3; 11:9; 49:7; 56:6; 66:20-21; Zech. 14:16-19; Mal. 1:11).

When the Lord will establish His kingdom on the earth, a reversal of fortunes will occur (Isa. 25:4-5). **The poor** (*dal,* "feeble, weak, helpless") and **the needy** (*'eḇyôn,* "oppressed") will be rescued and **the ruthless** will be **stilled.** God's care for the poor and the needy is mentioned many times in the Old and New Testaments. The reversal of fortunes, in which those who depend on God are helped and those who depend on themselves are judged, is a major theme of Scripture (e.g., 1 Sam. 2:1-10; James 5:1-6). **The ruthless** in their harsh treatment of others are **like a storm** and the oppressive desert **heat.** But God's judgment on them will be like **a cloud** that suddenly covers the sun, thus limiting its heat.

(2) Effects of the coming kingdom (25:6-12). The deliverance that the Lord will bring will include the wiping away of death (vv. 6-8), the rejoicing of His people (v. 9), and judgment on His enemies (vv. 10-12).

25:6. God's deliverance of His people in the kingdom is pictured as a banquet **feast** on the **mountain** of **the LORD Almighty.** Mountains are often symbols of governmental authority (e.g., Dan. 2:44-45) but here the mountain probably refers to Jerusalem (Mount Zion) from which the Messiah will rule in the kingdom. **Food** will be provided **for all peoples,** which fact once again stresses the worldwide extent of God's kingdom over those who believe. This does not mean that everyone who lives in the Millennium will be saved (though only redeemed people will enter the Millennium at its beginning); instead it means that people in all areas of the world will be saved. **The best of meats and the finest of wines** picture God's ability to supply the needs of His people during that time. Some Bible interpreters say this refers symbolically to God's care for His people in the present age. However, Isaiah was speaking of a future time when (after God's worldwide judgment) His people in Israel and other nations will feast together in peace and prosperity. This is the 1,000-year reign of Christ.

25:7-8. Death, pictured as a **shroud** and a **sheet**, the covering placed over a dead body, will be swallowed up or done away with. This will mean that **tears** of grief caused by the separation of the dead from the living also will be a thing of the past. This removal of death and wiping **away** of **tears** will take place at the end of the 1,000-year reign of Christ (Rev. 21:4), when death, Satan, and hell will be thrown into the lake of fire (Rev. 20:14) and the new heavens and new earth established (Rev. 21:1-3). Since God's future kingdom includes both the Messiah's millennial reign and the eternal state, Isaiah telescoped them together (cf. Isa. 65:17-25). Elsewhere the first and second comings of Christ are seen together (9:6-7; 61:1-3). The certainty of future prosperity and joy and absence of death would encourage Judah in Isaiah's day to trust in the LORD and not lose heart.

25:9. **In that day** (cf. 24:21), the day when the believing remnant will be delivered, **they** (the saved ones) **will** affirm their trust **in** the Lord, who **saved** them. In response they will say **let us rejoice and be glad in** the **salvation** He provided. Meanwhile, in Isaiah's day, believers in Judah were to rejoice in the Lord's salvation.

25:10-12. Isaiah referred to Moab as representing those who oppose God and will be judged by Him. Moab was east of Israel across the Dead Sea. Israel and Judah had many altercations with Moab, that was known for her **pride** (v. 11; cf. 16:6). She felt that the works of her **hands** and her **cleverness** would protect her, but it would not. Moab—and all God's enemies—will be totally destroyed, **trampled,** and brought **down . . . low** (cf. 26:5) **to the very dust.** Only God's people, in Israel and in other nations, will enjoy God's time of prosperity and blessing.

b. The redeemed to praise the Lord (chap. 26)

The prophet wrote a song that will be sung by the redeemed when the Messiah will establish the millennial kingdom. Isaiah was picturing himself standing in the redeemed land with the remnant listening to the people express

their thanks to and confidence in God.

(1) The humble to be exalted (26:1-6). **26:1. This song,** to **be sung in . . . Judah,** first emphasizes the reversal of fortunes (cf. 25:1-5): the humble will be exalted and the oppressors vanquished. In contrast with "the city" that will be destroyed (24:12-13; 25:2), the redeemed will **have a strong city.** Throughout the world the redeemed will live in cities and towns, but the strong city (Jerusalem) where the Messiah will reign pictures the security of the world's redeemed inhabitants. Because of the Messiah's presence there, that city is figuratively said to have **salvation** for **its walls and ramparts.**

26:2-4. This city will be opened for **the righteous nation,** a reference to the remnant of Israel. Other nations will have places in the kingdom, but believers in Israel will have special positions.

People who **trust in the LORD** enjoy **perfect** (i.e., complete, genuine) **peace** (cf. Phil. 4:7), now as well as in the Millennium. This availability of inner tranquility encourages believers to continue trusting **the LORD** (Isa. 26:4) because He is firm like a **Rock** (cf. 17:10; 44:8; see comments on Ps. 18:2) and He is **eternal.**

26:5-6. In contrast with the righteous who enter this special city of God, people who try to dwell in the **lofty city** (i.e., who persist in their pride) will be abased (cf. 25:12) because they did not trust in Him (26:3-4). **The oppressed** and **the poor** will **trample** those wicked people (v. 6). This was a reversal of fortunes, an act of God's justice against the proud who had taken advantage of the poor. Isaiah was not implying that some special merit was given the poor. He was reflecting the scriptural principle that God has special concern for the poor who seek Him (see, e.g., 25:4).

(2) Deliverance to come from God (26:7-21). The song continues by expressing the certainty that deliverance has come to the remnant, not because of their own efforts, but because of God's work on their behalf. Therefore they will continue to trust in Him.

26:7-9. In a confession of trust the prophet affirmed that it is good for people to live righteously, because God smooths out their **path.** That does not mean righteous people never have any problems. Isaiah was reflecting the truth that certain consequences follow one's actions so that if a person lives according to God's rules he will have favorable consequences, but if he disregards God's Word he will experience dire consequences. The remnant walk according to Scripture (God's **laws,** v. 8a) and yearn for God (vv. 8b-9a). Those who refuse to heed God's ways **learn** of God's **righteousness** when they are eventually judged.

26:10-11. Many **wicked** people **do not learn righteousness** when God bestows His **grace** (v. 10); they learn it only when He judges them (cf. v. 9). Living where the righteousness of God is revealed **(in a land of uprightness,** i.e., Judah), many people still did not live righteously. A favorable environment is not enough; there must be a change of heart.

Though chapter 26 is a song of the redeemed, verses 10-11 indicate that Isaiah was writing for the people of his day, many of whom were spiritually insensitive, unconcerned about God's **majesty** and works (His **hand).** Isaiah asked the Lord to **put** them **to shame** (v. 11) and to take vengeance on them. In this way God's character would be vindicated. Isaiah was not asking this for his own sake but for the sake of God who desires that His people lead holy lives.

26:12-15. In the kingdom believers will enjoy the **peace** God gives and will recognize God's work on their behalf (v. 12). They will affirm that they remained true to God **(Your name** [character] **alone do we honor)** even though they will have been under the domination of others (v. 13). Those who will seek to dominate the remnant will be **dead,** under God's judgment. **Departed spirits** translates $r^e p \bar{a}' \hat{i} m$, also used in the last line of v. 19 (see comments on 14:9). In contrast the remnant will endure in **the land** God promised the patriarchs and their descendants (26:15).

26:16-18. The Lord's discipline on His people will not be easy to bear; it will be a time of great distress, a time when they will **barely whisper a prayer** either because of thirst or because of terror. Isaiah then compared their distress to the painful experience of childbirth (cf. comments on 13:8). Childbirth, once it begins, must continue until it is finished. However, the nation of Israel will seem to give **birth to wind,** that is, her travail

will continue but will avail nothing; it will not result in deliverance. Unbelievers in Israel will be judged and will not enter the Millennium.

26:19. Even though Israel's travail will not be efficacious, Isaiah was confident that her believing **dead will** be resurrected. This resurrection of Old Testament saints will occur at Christ's second coming (Dan. 12:2). When they **wake up** (i.e., when **their bodies** are resurrected) they will **shout for joy.** They will be refreshed in the way morning **dew** refreshes the grass (cf. Hosea 14:5), that is, they will experience God's blessings in the Millennium.

26:20-21. Isaiah wrote that the future remnant should **hide** during the time of distress (God's **wrath** in the Tribulation), knowing that deliverance from the Lord will come. Eventually the Lord will set matters right by punishing **people . . . for their sins.** All sins will be made known **(the earth will disclose the blood shed upon her),** whether they have been done in secret or in public. These words would have encouraged the remnant in Isaiah's day to remain true to **the LORD,** knowing that He will eventually judge sin. After that judgment is accomplished, believers will be able to sing the song recorded in chapter 26.

c. Salvation for Israel and Judah (chap. 27)

This chapter may be divided into three sections each beginning with the phrase "in that day" (v. 1, vv. 2-11, vv. 12-13).

(1) The culmination of judgment. **27:1.** This verse, referring to the culmination of God's judgment on the world, ties in with the judgment mentioned in 26:21. With a **sword** the LORD will cut up a great serpent called **Leviathan.** This **gliding . . . coiling serpent** is the many-headed sea dragon mentioned in Psalm 74:13-14. In Ugaritic literature (of Ugarit, a city-state in North Syria) reference is made to a similar seven-headed creature. Isaiah, though not believing this ancient Semitic myth, simply referred to Leviathan to convey his point (cf. Job 3:8). Leviathan, the twisting **monster of the sea,** was viewed in Ugaritic literature as an enemy of order in Creation. But the Lord can stop this chaotic state and establish order on the earth and in people's

hearts. When God's judgment comes in that day, when He slays the wicked at the end of the Tribulation, it will be like His slaying the chaotic dragon Leviathan.

(2) The song of the vineyard. 27:2-6. The vineyard symbolizes Israel (see comments on 5:7). In the song of the vineyard in 5:1-7 destruction was emphasized; in the song of the vineyard in 27:2-6 the promise of protection is the major theme. In the first song the vineyard was to be made a wasteland because of the people's sinful condition. In the second song the vineyard (Israel) is to be made fruitful. After God judges Israel (v. 1), the nation will be spiritually fruitful. This fruitfulness comes because of the Lord's constant protection and care (v. 3). If the vineyard (Israel) does not please the Lord, He must judge it (v. 4), but He much prefers that they turn to Him in repentance as their Refuge (v. 5). This desire that Israel be in the proper covenant relationship with Him is borne out by the repetition of let them make peace with Me. When the Kingdom Age arrives, Jacob (a synonym for Israel) will be productive again (cf. 35:1-3, 6-7; Amos 9:13-14; Zech. 14:8) and will be the nation through which God will bless the world (cf. Gen. 12:3).

(3) The coming judgment (27:7-11). 27:7-8. Because the Lord cares for His people He will judge them and purify them so they can be fruitful. Isaiah foretold that judgment would come on Israel. But He will not treat her the way He treats her enemies (v. 7). He will judge her by warfare and exile (v. 8; cf. Deut. 28:64-68). The east wind, strong in the Middle East, may refer figuratively to Babylon, east of Israel, which took Judah into captivity. The Exile would help purify Judah so that she would not worship foreign gods and goddesses.

27:9-11. The sin of the nation had to be atoned for. Of course atonement for all sin is through the death of Jesus Christ. But in view of Israel's covenant relationship with God, she had to be driven out of the land because of her disobedience to the Law (Deut. 28:49-52, 64). Evidence of that atonement would be her pulverizing her altar stones dedicated to idolatrous gods, and removing the Asherah poles, wooden symbols of the Canaanite pagan goddess of fertility.

Because of Judah's sin, her city (i.e., Jerusalem) would be destroyed and its people removed. Jerusalem was destroyed by the Babylonians in 586 B.C. and was left desolate. Isaiah said calves would graze in Jerusalem's ruins and being hungry would strip tree branches of their bark. Women then would cut off the branches and use them for firewood. In judging His senseless people, God, their Maker and Creator, temporarily withdrew His compassion on them.

(4) The regathering of Israel. 27:12-13. The Lord promised that in that day (cf. vv. 1-2) He will thresh (i.e., judge) a large area from the . . . Euphrates to the Wadi of Egypt. In other words the Lord will judge this large area of land for the purpose of bringing His people back to Jerusalem and its environs. The Wadi of Egypt may be the stream that marks the southwest border of Canaan (Num. 34:4-5; 1 Kings 8:65). Or perhaps it refers to the Nile, since the point of Isaiah 27:13 is that the Lord will regather His people from both Assyria and Egypt, two great enemies of Israel in most of her history up to Assyria's fall in 609 B.C. The people will be regathered to the holy mountain in Jerusalem, that is, the temple mount where the Messiah will reign (cf. 24:23). In God's kingdom on earth Israel will dwell in the land of Palestine as believers.

E. The woes (chaps. 28–33)

Isaiah continued his theme of judgment with a series of "woes" against various groups who were opposing his words. Here he was attacking primarily the rulers of the Northern and Southern Kingdoms for their failure to heed God's Word and for looking to other means for protection. They were trusting in their wealth (chap. 28) and foreign alliances (chaps. 30–31). But neither of these, Isaiah said, could help them. Only the coming Deliverer could save them from the enemies around them (chaps. 32–33). God's plans cannot be thwarted by the obstinate refusal of people to believe in Him. He will sovereignly provide peace and security for the remnant through the messianic Deliverer.

1. WOE TO EPHRAIM AND JUDAH (CHAP. 28)

The strong pronouncements in this chapter are directed against the Northern

Kingdom (vv. 1-13) and the Southern Kingdom (vv. 14-29). Before long the Northern Kingdom would fall to the Assyrians (722 B.C.). Writing to the people of the South, Isaiah was encouraging them not to be like their Northern brothers and sisters. God's judgment was designed to bring the people to repentance before Him (vv. 23-29), not to "get even" with them.

a. Woe to Ephraim (28:1-13)

(1) The state of the Northern Kingdom (28:1-8). **28:1.** In this first **woe** (*hôy*, an interjection suggestive of impending doom or grief; cf. comments on 5:8), Ephraim, a prominent tribe representative of the Northern Kingdom, is likened to a drunkard. The area of the North was **fertile** at that time. Samaria, the capital city built by Omri (1 Kings 16:24), overlooked a fruitful **valley** (cf. Isa. 28:4). Because of Samaria's **beauty** it was called a **wreath** (cf. v. 3). The possibility of material prosperity was great. However, the Northern Kingdom was throwing away the blessings of God as a drunkard throws away his money in the pursuit of **wine.** Apparently drunkenness was a problem in both the Northern and Southern Kingdoms, so the figure of a drunkard is apt.

28:2-4. Isaiah predicted that Assyria, **like a** strong **hailstorm and** windstorm, would go against the 10 Northern tribes. Samaria, like an ornamental **wreath** (cf. v. 1), would **be trampled underfoot** by Assyria with no regard for its worth. Samaria, the **beauty** of Israel overlooking **a fertile valley** (cf. v. 1), would become **like a** ripened **fig,** which is eaten by a stranger before it can be harvested. Early figs were considered a delicacy (cf. Hosea 9:10; Micah 7:1). The Northern Kingdom would have no safety; she would be taken into exile.

28:5-6. Though Samaria, the capital of Ephraim, has twice been described as a wreath (vv. 1, 3), now **the** LORD **Almighty** is said to be like **a beautiful wreath.** He, not a prosperous beautiful city, should be honored. **In that day,** when the Lord establishes the Millennium, **the remnant** will be honored by the Lord and will be under the One **who sits in judgment.** Even in the Assyrian siege of Samaria the Lord gave **strength to** the Israelite soldiers, enabling them to hold

off the siege for three years.

28:7-8. Returning again to the picture of the Northern Kingdom as a drunkard (cf. v. 1), Isaiah referred to the people and their leaders (**priests and prophets**) being drunk at a banquet where **the tables are covered with vomit.** They were intoxicated even **when** supposedly **seeing visions** (the false prophets) or **when rendering decisions** (the false priests). No wonder the nation was ripe for judgment!

(2) Ephraim's refusal to believe (28:9-13). **28:9-10.** The speakers in verse 9 are probably the priests and prophets mentioned in verses 7-8. They were angry that Isaiah was treating them as if they were young **children.** They felt they were adults who could think for themselves; they had no need for someone to tell them what to do or think. So they mimicked Isaiah as if he were speaking "baby talk" to them (v. 10). **Do and do, do and do, rule on rule, rule on rule** (cf. v. 13) is a series of sounds in Hebrew (*ṣaw lāṣāw, ṣaw lāṣāw, qaw lāqāw, qaw lāqāw*). Mocking Isaiah's messages, the leaders were acting as if he were an adult "lecturing" a little child. **A little here, a little there** was a method used in teaching children, inculcating a little at a time. In other words they were refusing to take Isaiah's words seriously. They wanted nothing to do with his message or his ministry.

28:11-13. Following up on the leaders' mimicking, Isaiah said that if they did not want to listen to his "lecturing" then they would be "lectured" by another people who had a difficult and different speech. **Foreign lips** would deliver the message of judgment on them. Isaiah was referring to the Assyrians who were advancing on Israel and would soon conquer it. Though God had offered Israel **rest** and **repose** they refused to **listen** to Him and His messenger. Therefore **the** LORD would turn their mocking back on them and they would **be injured . . . snared, and captured** by a people whose language they did not understand.

b. Woe to Judah (28:14-29)

The message to Israel of destruction by foreign invaders was also for Judah. Though she would not be completely destroyed, because Jerusalem would not be taken, Judah would face much suffering. The people of the Southern Kingdom had much the same attitude as their Northern brothers. They too were scoffing at God's revelation through Isaiah.

28:14-22. The people of Judah should not think they were guiltless before God. The leaders of **Jerusalem,** like their counterparts in the North, were responsible to guide and lead the people toward godliness. But they scoffed, boasting of several things. They said since they had made **a covenant with death,** the scourge could not **touch** them, and **a lie** and a **falsehood** were their **hiding place** (vv. 14-15). Why would the rulers of Jerusalem say such a thing? It seems that Isaiah was using imagery rich in the symbolism of Semitic mythology. For example, in the Ugaritic pantheon death was personified as the god of the underworld. The Jerusalem leaders were trusting in other gods to save them from the coming scourge, the Assyrian invasion. However, to trust in false gods was futile. The LORD sets the **stone** and the **sure foundation,** that is, only He is the basis for physical and spiritual salvation (v. 16). Whether Isaiah thought of the **cornerstone** as the Messiah or simply as genuine belief in the Lord is not clear. In other passages the cornerstone refers to Christ (Zech. 10:4; Eph. 2:20; 1 Peter 2:6).

The Lord responded to each of these boasts. Their **covenant with death** would **be annulled** (Isa. 28:18), their **lie** would be swept **away** (v. 17), and they would be defeated by the **scourge** (v. 18) that would continue **day** after day (v. 19). **This message** of judgment would **bring sheer terror** (v. 19) as the people realized its implications. To seek protection from false gods would be as inadequate as lying in a **bed** that **is too short** or trying to cover oneself with a **blanket** that is **too** small. The destruction would sweep down into Judah (**Mount Perazim** and **the Valley of Gibeon,** 1 Chron. 14:11, 16, are near Jerusalem, where David defeated the Philistines). Therefore they should **stop** . . . **mocking** Isaiah's message given by **the LORD Almighty.**

28:23-29. Isaiah then inserted a word of comfort into this message of woe and judgment. The judgment would last for only a short while as it was designed to purge the people. A **farmer** must crush his crops to get the desired results. For example, **caraway** and **cummin,** aromatic herbs, are **beaten out with a rod** or stick,

not **threshed,** because their seeds are so small. **Grain** is **ground** by millstone, after the wheat stalks are threshed. Various crops must be treated differently so no one step (plowing, harrowing, **planting,** or **threshing**) is done continuously.

Similarly God would bring about judgment but not forever. He is the Master "Farmer," who knows how to handle each "crop." Therefore the Southern Kingdom should submit to Him because He is **wonderful in counsel** (cf. 9:6) **and magnificent in wisdom** (cf. 11:2).

2. WOE TO JERUSALEM (CHAP. 29)

a. Judgment coming on Jerusalem (29:1-4)

29:1-4. In this second of five "woes" in chapters 28–33 Isaiah continues with the theme of the last part of the first woe (28:14-29). Judgment was coming on Jerusalem and on Judah, and its purpose was to get the nation to return to God. Unlike the judgment that would sweep away the Northern Kingdom, this judgment on Jerusalem, though very severe, would be averted by the Lord. Jerusalem would not fall into the hands of the Assyrians.

Ariel undoubtedly refers to Jerusalem as can be concluded by the parallel phrase **the city where David settled** (cf. 2 Sam. 5:7, 9, 13). Many interpreters say **Ariel** means "lion of God," in which case the city is seen as a strong, lionlike city. Ariel may also be translated "altar hearth," as in Isaiah 29:2; Ezekiel 43:15-16. Jerusalem is the place where the altar of burnt offering was located in the temple.

Though Jerusalem is where **festivals** were celebrated before God (Isa. 29:1), the city would be besieged and fighting and bloodshed would turn it into a virtual **altar hearth.**

Though the Assyrians under Sennacherib surrounded Jerusalem in 701 B.C. it was as if God had done so (**I.** . . . **I** . . . **I** . . . **My,** vv. 2-3). Being humiliated (**brought low**), Jerusalem spoke softly rather than in loud tones. Though Jerusalem would be surrounded it would not be taken at this time. This assurance should have encouraged the people to trust God and to worship Him properly.

b. Deliverance coming for Jerusalem (29:5-8)

29:5-8. Jerusalem's protection described in these verses refers to her deliverance from Assyria, recorded in chapter 37. It would have seemed impossible to hope that the Assyrians would not take the city. Only by God's sovereign intervention was Jerusalem spared. Though 29:5-8 refers to the Assyrian soldiers becoming **like . . . dust** and **chaff** when they were slaughtered, these verses also seem to have eschatological overtones. At the end of the Tribulation when **nations** (vv. 7-8) will **attack** Jerusalem (Zech. 14:1-3), **the LORD Almighty will come** and destroy each attacking nation. The threat of those **nations** will vanish like **a dream**. When the Assyrian soldiers were destroyed in Isaiah's day, no doubt the people of Jerusalem were delirious with joy. But shortly the difficulty of that situation subsided in their thinking, and life returned to normal. Rather than turning back to God the nation got more deeply involved in sin.

c. Jerusalem's understanding of God's revelation (29:9-24)

In this section a contrast is drawn between the people's present spiritual insensitivity and their future spiritual understanding.

29:9-12. The Jerusalemites' spiritual insensitivity was in itself a judgment from God. The people were told to **blind** themselves (v. 9) but the **LORD** also caused the blindness (v. 10). The fact that **the prophets** and **the seers** did not see and understand clearly was part of God's judgment. They did not understand God's revelation about His judgment on the Assyrians that Isaiah recorded on **a scroll** (vv. 11-12). No one, either people **who** could **read** or those who couldn't, could understand this truth.

29:13-14. The **people** of Jerusalem, professing to know God, were formally involved in acts of **worship** but they did not worship God from **their hearts.** They were more concerned with man-made legalistic **rules** than with God's Law, which promotes mercy, justice, and equity. Because of that, God would judge them; their **wisdom** would **vanish.**

29:15-16. God pronounced **woe** on those who thought He did not see their actions. They attempted **to hide their plans from** God by doing things at night. They were not thinking clearly, for God can hide things from man (vv. 10-12) but not vice versa. Such thinking twisted

the facts and confused **the potter** with **the clay.** A jar, however, cannot deny that the potter made it, or say that **the potter** is ignorant (cf. 45:9; 64:8). Actually the *people* knew **nothing** of what was going on, but *God* always knows everything.

29:17-21. However, things in the future will be different. The phrase **in a very short time** refers to the coming millennial kingdom. Some think it refers to the time when the Assyrian army was slaughtered (37:36), but the conditions described in 29:20-21 seem to nullify that interpretation. **Lebanon,** which was then occupied by Assyrian troops, will eventually be productive (**fertile**) again. The second occurrence of the words **fertile field** may refer to Mount Carmel. When the Millennium comes **the deaf** and **the blind . . . will hear** and see (cf. 32:3; 35:5). This contrasts with 29:10-12, which referred to the nation's impaired sight. **The needy will rejoice** in the **LORD** because of what He will do for them, and conversely **the ruthless** who deprived **the innocent of justice** will be punished (vv. 20-21; cf. v. 5).

29:22-24. The attitude of the people of Jerusalem and Judah will completely change. They will **no longer . . . be ashamed** (v. 22) or brought low (v. 4) by foreign domination and their own sin (cf. 1:29). As **their children** grow up in safety they will realize that God has protected them and will worship (**stand in awe of**) Him. The Lord's delivering them from Sennacherib was a foretaste of the ultimate deliverance they will experience. People **who are wayward** and **who complain** will change and **will accept instruction.** No longer will blindness prevail; then they will know God's ways (cf. 29:18).

3. WOE TO THE OBSTINATE CHILDREN (CHAP. 30)

This oracle (chap. 30) and the next one (chap. 31) center on the folly of attempting to make an alliance with Egypt to ward off the Assyrian threat. At this time Egypt was waning as a world power and could be of no real assistance to Israel and Judah in their fight against the strong Assyrian Empire. But a strong faction in Judah, rather than turning to God for protection, wanted to seek aid from Egypt.

a. The woe pronounced (30:1-5)

30:1. This **woe** (see comments on 3:9) was pronounced against those in Judah who wanted to form **an alliance.** The prophet spoke to those people as if they were children, and **obstinate children** at that. Like children, they did not have the proper perspective to know what was best for them. Floundering in their desire to save themselves and their nation, they were forming **plans** but not God's plans. Actually their plans were sinful because they were not what God wanted them to do.

30:2-5. An alliance with **Egypt,** made **without consulting** the Lord, would **put** Judah **to shame** (vv. 3, 5 [twice]). The Jews even sent a delegation to two Egyptian cities—**Zoan** and **Hanes** —to talk about an alliance, but the talks were doomed to fail. The **officials in** Zoan were incapable of helping (see comments on 19:11). The location of Hanes is unknown, but it may have been in the Egyptian Delta near Zoan. The Lord had already said many times through Isaiah that He would use Assyria to wipe out the Northern Kingdom and to punish the Southern Kingdom. So to look to a crumbling empire for help was useless and could only result in **disgrace** (vv. 3, 5).

b. The oracle about the Negev (30:6-17)

30:6-7. As the **envoys** (cf. v. 4) traveled to Egypt they had to pass through **the Negev,** a desolate, dangerous area with wild **animals (lions** and **snakes).** The delegation from Judah took expensive gifts to Egypt on the **backs** of donkeys and **camels.** Judah's people were so desperate for help that they were willing to risk **hardship** and go to great expense. But Isaiah called Egypt—a nation unable to **help—Rahab the Do-Nothing.** In Ugaritic literature Rahab was the name of a female sea monster associated with Leviathan (see comments on 27:1; cf. Job 9:13; 26:12). Perhaps the hippopotamus, an animal that often sits in the water of the Nile doing nothing, represents that mythical water beast. Understandably Rahab came to be a poetic synonym for Egypt (and also for a demon behind Egypt) when God overpowered the Egyptian soldiers in the sea at the Exodus (cf. Isa. 51:9; Pss. 87:4; 89:10). So **Egypt,** Isaiah wrote, was good for nothing; she could not assist Judah in any way.

30:8-11. The people did not want to listen to God's instructions through Isaiah. So God told him to **write** down his message so that they could not claim they had never heard it. In the future, the **scroll** on which the message was written would **witness** against them. They were like **rebellious . . . children** (cf. v. 1), **unwilling to listen to** the Lord, to receive messages from His **prophets.** They did not want to be confronted with the truth from God, **the Holy One of Israel** (cf. v. 12 and see comments on 1:4).

30:12-17. Immediately after they said they did not want to be confronted by the Holy One of Israel (v. 11) ironically Isaiah **did** confront them with more words from **the Holy One of Israel** (cf. v. 15). Rejecting Isaiah's **message** (vv. 9-11) and relying **on oppression** (i.e., fraud, or plans to avoid God's counsel) and **deceit** (which Egypt would practice on them), they would undergo judgment.

That judgment would come suddenly—like a cracked **wall** that would collapse on them (v. 13). And it would be severe—like a pot so **shattered** that the **pieces** cannot be used for anything (v. 14). Though the Lord had called for **repentance** and **trust** so that the Judahites might have **salvation** and **strength** (v. 15) they did not want any of it. Instead they depended on military might (v. 16). But if they were to rely **on horses** (cf. 31:1), God said they would be forced to **flee** (30:16-17), being easily alarmed by the enemy. They would stand alone **like a banner on a hill** as a warning to others not to count on military strength.

c. The Lord's graciousness to His people (30:18-33)

30:18-22. Though the people had turned from **the Lord,** He longed **to be gracious** and compassionate **to** them (v. 18; cf. v. 19) for they were in a covenant relationship with Him. He is also the **God of justice,** giving blessings to those **who** depend on **Him.** In the Millennium Israel will again be faithful to **the Lord.** And when she calls on Him (not on some other nation) for help, **He will answer.** Though she experienced difficulties (e.g., having only **bread** to eat and **water** to drink in times of calamity), eventually God will bless her. The Israelites will readily listen to their spiritual guides (**teachers**) such as the prophets and priests (in contrast with rejecting them, v. 10); no longer will the teachers need to hide for safety. The people will be sensitive to God's Word, as if He were saying, **This is the way, walk in it.** They will be conscious of God's leading at all times. When they heed His instructions they will then get rid of their **idols** (cf. 31:7; Hosea 14:3b; Micah 5:13-14), things that are defiled and morally dirty.

30:23-26. Isaiah then described what times will be like when the people live according to God's Word and are obedient to Him. In the Millennium God will **send . . . rain,** and crops will be **plentiful** (cf. Deut. 28:1-14). Even the animals will have plenty to eat (Isa. 30:23-24). **The day of great slaughter** may refer to the Battle of Armageddon (cf. Rev. 16:16; 19:17-21). After Israel's and God's enemies are defeated, Israel will enjoy great peace and an abundance of **water** in the land (Isa. 30:25).

Also light will be increased, for **the moon will be like the sun** and the sun **will be seven times brighter** than normal. Perhaps this is figurative language but it is difficult to know for sure. At that time the Lord will heal His people of **the wounds** (cf. 1:5) **He inflicted,** that is, He will restore them to the place of blessing.

30:27-33. Isaiah now spoke again of the present situation, prophesying that the Assyrian army (v. 31), which was surrounding Jerusalem, would be defeated (37:36). This occurred in 701 B.C. God in His **anger** would rush against His enemies. Like **dense clouds . . . a fire,** and a **torrent** (cf. v. 30) His **wrath** would overtake the enemy. **He shakes the nations in a sieve,** like a farmer shaking grain to clear it of small pebbles (cf. Amos 9:9). This defeat of Assyria would cause Judah to **rejoice** much as they did in their three annual festivals (Ex. 23:14-17) when they went to the temple on Mount Zion, **the mountain of the LORD** (cf. Isa. 11:9; 27:13; 56:7; 65:25; 66:20), who is the nation's **Rock** (cf. 17:10; 26:4; 44:8; cf. comments on Ps. 18:2), its source of security.

Merely by a command (**voice,** Isa. 30:30-31) of **anger** (cf. vv. 27-28) God would **shatter** Assyria **with His scepter and rod.** This would cause Judah to rejoice (cf. v. 29) with music from **tambourines and harps** (cf. 24:8). The Assyrian army would be destroyed like a pile of **wood** or a sacrifice in **Topheth,** an area in the Valley of Hinnom south of Jerusalem where children were sometimes sacrificed to the false Ammonite god Molech (2 Kings 23:10; Jer. 7:31; cf. Jer. 7:32; 19:6, 11-14). This fire was **for the king,** perhaps Hezekiah, as if he were to use it in destroying his enemy. By God's **breath** (cf. Isa. 30:28) He would figuratively kindle the fire by which He would consume the bodies of the Assyrian soldiers. His breath would be like **sulfur,** which burns with great intensity (cf. Gen. 19:24; Job 18:15; Ps. 11:6; Ezek. 38:22; Rev. 9:17-18). This speaks of the eternal torment of the wicked in "the lake of fire" (KJV; Rev. 19:20; 20:10; 21:8).

4. WOE TO THE EGYPTIAN ALLIANCE (CHAPS. 31–32)

Like the previous woe (chap. 30) this one was directed against the Egyptian alliance which some people of Judah wanted to make (chap. 31). But this oracle also speaks about the messianic King who will someday deliver His people (chap. 32).

a. The woe pronounced (31:1-3)

31:1-3. This **woe** (see comments on 3:9) was pronounced on those who went **to Egypt for help** (cf. 30:1-2), and who relied on Egyptian **horses** (cf. 30:16) and **chariots** instead of on God. Both actions —going to Egypt and acquiring horses— violated God's stipulations in the Deuteronomic Covenant (Deut. 17:16). Since God **does not** go **back** on **His words,** He would judge the nation for her disobedience. **The Egyptians** could not help Judah (cf. 30:3, 5, 7) for they were weak **men.** Only **God** could ultimately protect them from their enemies. If Judah persisted in seeking an alliance with Egypt, **both** countries would meet disaster.

b. The Lord's protection (31:4-9)

31:4-5. God assured the people that His greatness would protect them from the terrifying Assyrian threat. **As a lion** meets up with a flock of sheep and is unafraid of a number of **shepherds, so the LORD** was not afraid of the Assyrians. He promised **to do battle on Mount Zion,** and **like birds** flying **overhead** He would **shield Jerusalem** and not let it fall into the enemy's hands.

31:6-7. Since Judah would be rescued by God (v. 5), Isaiah called on the nation to turn back to Him. Eventually they would throw their idols away (cf. 30:22) in favor of the true God. Therefore Judah ought to throw them away now. Their future hope in the kingdom should change their present behavior. The future reality should have an ethical impact on their lives.

31:8-9. Isaiah affirmed again (cf. 30:31) that **Assyria** would **fall,** but only because of God's work (by **a sword that is not of man**). The Assyrian **commanders,** seeing Judah's **battle standard** and their soldiers being slaughtered (by the Angel of the Lord; cf. 37:36), would be terrified. The **fire** may refer to the fire of the altar of burnt offering that burned continually, and the **furnace** is literally a baking oven. By protecting Judah, God would see that the fire on the altar continued to burn.

c. A time of justice and righteousness (32:1-8)

Because the Lord would protect Jerusalem, He will also bring about a time when righteousness will abound.

32:1-2. In the Millennium the **King** (cf. comments on 33:17), that is, the Messiah, **will reign in righteousness** (11:1-5; cf. Jer. 23:5), and **rulers** under Him (cf. 2 Tim. 2:2; Rev. 5:10; 20:6; 22:5) **will** be just. In fact every person entering the Millennium will be a believer. **Each** one will be protective of others **like a shelter from the wind** and will refresh others **like . . . water in the desert** and a **rock** that gives shade from the desert heat.

32:3-8. In the Kingdom Age, people will **see** and **hear** spiritual things clearly (cf. 29:18; 35:5; 42:7) in contrast with Judah's spiritual insensitivity (29:10-12). People will **understand** God's Word and will speak the truth clearly (32:4). Fools and scoundrels will no longer be **respected.** As in the Book of Proverbs **the fool** (*nāḇāl,* "senseless") is one who is **evil** (Isa. 32:6). He teaches falsehood and disregards the needs of others. In contrast with the scoundrel who wickedly plots to take advantage of **the poor** and **the needy. . . . the noble** person **plans** to do good to others. Because he is righteous **he stands**; he will continue to live.

d. Future judgment and blessing (32:9-20)

32:9-14. This message addressed to the **women** is reminiscent of 3:16-26. The women of Judah should not complacently think that God's judgment would not come, for the devastation would begin soon, in **little more than a year.** Probably this refers to Assyria's final push into Judah in 701 b.c., but it cannot be proved. The first evidence of the judgment would be the failing of the **harvest** of grapes and other **fruit,** perhaps because the Assyrians would overrun the fields. Therefore because of the ravaging of **the land** the **women** would mourn. (On sackcloth see comments on 3:24.) If **the noisy city** to be **deserted** (32:14) refers to Jerusalem then Isaiah meant that the Assyrian attack was the beginning of the end for Jerusalem, which fell to the Babylonians 115 years later (in 586 b.c.). In that case Isaiah was not saying (v. 10) that the judgment would be completed in about a year but that it would *begin* in about a year. However, perhaps "the noisy city" refers to any one of the 46 Judean cities Sennacherib king of Assyria claimed to have defeated. The desolation (whether by Assyria or Babylon) would come on the land **forever** (*'ôlām*). This Hebrew word does not always carry the same force as the English word "forever." From verse 15 it is obvious that Isaiah saw a day when the desolation would cease. So it is better to understand *'ôlām* here as meaning "for a long indeterminable time."

32:15a. After speaking of desolation on Judah (vv. 9-14) Isaiah described a time of future blessing on the land and the people (vv. 15-20). That great time—the Millennium—will come about after **the** Holy **Spirit is poured** out (cf. 44:3) on Israel (**us**) **from on high.** Other prophets also spoke of this outpouring of the Holy Spirit, including Ezekiel (Ezek. 36:26-27; 37:14), Joel (Joel 2:28-29), and Zechariah (Zech. 12:10, NIV marg.). As the redeemed of Israel enter the millennial kingdom they will have the same benefit of the indwelling presence of the Holy Spirit as do believers in the Church Age today. Therefore they will have an inward compulsion to do the will of God (Ezek. 36:27).

32:15b-20. Along with the outpouring of the Spirit will be fertility, justice, and security. Israel's deserts will be **fertile** (cf. 35:1-2), and with **justice** and **righteousness** (cf. 9:7; 11:4; 16:5; 33:5) will come **peace** and **quietness** (32:17) and security for the redeemed (cf. Amos 9:15; Micah 4:4; Zech. 3:10; 14:11). Under the Deuteronomic Covenant if the people obeyed God the land would be productive. Similarly in the kingdom, righteous living will result in fertility. In contrast with the destruction that would come in Isaiah's day (Isa. 32:19), the redeemed nation is assured that they will be **blessed** with agricultural productivity (cf. Ezek. 36:30) and with no rivalry over each other's grazing land.

5. WOE TO THE DESTROYERS (CHAP. 33)

This final woe describes the greatness of God's judgment on those who live unrighteously (vv. 1-12) and the wonder of His blessings on the redeemed in the kingdom (vv. 13-24).

a. Woe to the enemies of God's people (33:1-12)

33:1. Verses 1-12 discuss the **woe** (see comments on 3:9) of judgment to come on people who live unrighteously, who are traitors to the truth. The **destroyer** was the Assyrian enemy, and the **traitor** probably refers to those within Judah who wanted to form alliances either with Egypt or with other powers to protect them from Assyria. None of them would succeed in their efforts, for the destroyer would **be destroyed** and the traitor **betrayed.**

33:2-4. The words in these verses seem to be those of the righteous remnant waiting for the LORD to deliver them. They will long for His grace (cf. 30:18-19) and the Lord Himself. Longing for His **strength** and **salvation** (deliverance) they were confident that He would **scatter** the **nations** who opposed Israel. Then speaking to the nations who will be judged, the remnant will say that the **plunder** which those **nations** had taken from others will be taken from them. That plundering will be as complete and irreversible as **locusts** destroying everything in their path.

33:5-6. Speaking now to the remnant, Isaiah said that the **exalted** Lord (cf. 6:1) will eventually **fill Zion with justice and righteousness** (cf. 9:7; 11:4; 16:5; 32:16) when the kingdom is established. But in order to have these things, including **salvation . . . wisdom, and knowledge** they must **fear . . . the LORD** (cf. Prov. 1:7; 15:33). Fearing God does not

mean being terrified of Him (except for those who are being or will be judged). It means to recognize and respect Him and His authority and righteous demands, which in turn results in godly living, worshiping, trusting, serving, and obeying Him. Those who fear Him find Him to be their **sure Foundation,** their Source of inner security and peace (cf. "Rock," Isa. 26:4).

33:7-12. Those in Judah who thought they could achieve **peace** through an alliance (cf. **envoys** in 30:4, 6) would **weep bitterly.** Assyrian terror would be everywhere and people would be unable to travel **the roads** because of lurking danger. **Lebanon,** north of Israel and well known for its cedar forests, would wither. **Sharon** was the coastal plain south of Mount Carmel extending inland to the hill country of Ephraim. A fertile area, Sharon would become a desert **like the Arabah** (which means "arid" or "dry"), the desolate rift valley extending from the Dead Sea south to the Gulf of Aqabah. **Bashan** ("fertile plain"), east of the Sea of Kinnereth (later named the Sea of Galilee), was productive agriculturally (cf. Jer. 50:19) and known for its oak trees (Isa. 2:13; Ezek. 27:6; Micah 7:14; Zech. 11:2). **Carmel** ("fruitful land") was a mountain range thickly forested and well watered at that time. This destruction would show that the people could not save themselves. When **the** LORD would use the Assyrians against Judah, Judah's plans for peace would come to nothing. It was as if the people gave **birth** like a mother to nothing but **chaff** and **straw,** which can easily **be burned** up.

b. The deliverance of the righteous (33:13-24)

In contrast with the destruction of the destroyer and traitor, the righteous will live. Isaiah noted the kind of people who will be saved (vv. 13-16) and then described the land in which they will live (vv. 17-24).

33:13-16. God called on people everywhere (**far away** and **near,** v. 13) to **acknowledge** His righteous actions and His **power. Sinners** asked **who** can endure God's awesome judgment (a **consuming fire**), and the prophet responded that those who **can dwell with** God walk **righteously** and speak **what is right** (v.

15). They do not extort or take **bribes.** They refuse to be involved in **plots of murder** and other sins (cf. Ps. 15). These people will be safe and will enjoy God's blessings (Isa. 33:16). Therefore the people should live by God's standards even though the nation as a whole would be judged by Him.

33:17-24. The prophet then described the fruitful land in which these redeemed individuals (vv. 15-16) will dwell. This is the kingdom of Israel where righteousness and peace will flourish in the **land. The King** (cf. 32:1; 33:22; 43:15; Micah 2:13; Zeph. 3:15; Zech. 14:9), the Messiah, will be there (Isa. 33:17), and the people **will see** Him. They will think back on their **former** times (vv. 18-19) and realize that those who did not live righteously will be with them no longer. No foreign invader will be among them, including the Assyrians, **those arrogant people,** who spoke an **incomprehensible** language (v. 19; cf. 28:11). **Jerusalem** will be **peaceful** and secure (33:20), and **no** warships will attack the nation Israel (v. 21). Being properly related to **the LORD,** the people will acknowledge Him as their **Judge . . . Lawgiver . . . King** (cf. v. 17), and Savior (v. 22).

Assyria's defeat will be like a shipwreck, after which the many **spoils** on the ship **will be divided** among the Israelites. So much **plunder** will be there that plenty will be left by the time **even . . . lame** people get there. Illness will be wiped away (cf. 57:18-19; 58:8; Jer. 33:6) and **the sins of** the redeemed remnant **will be forgiven** (Isa. 33:24; cf. Jer. 31:34; 33:8; 36:3; 50:20). Peace, prosperity, and salvation will come by God's sovereign work not by foreign alliances or human cunning.

F. Vengeance and blessing (chaps. 34–35)

These two chapters form a fitting climax to the judgment and salvation motifs which have been spoken of extensively by Isaiah. Chapters 36–39 record the historical fulfillment of many of the prophecies in the first half of the book. Discussion of the judgment on Assyria (30:27-33; 31:8-9; 33:1, 18-19) naturally led to a discussion of God's judgment on the whole world in the Tribulation. God's vengeance on the world will be followed by millennial blessing on His covenant people, Israel.

1. THE LORD'S DAY OF VENGEANCE (CHAP. 34)

This chapter includes an invitation to the nations (v. 1), God's coming judgment on the nations (vv. 2-4), and an announcement of judgment on Edom (vv. 5-17), a representative of all nations hostile to Israel.

a. An invitation to hear (34:1)

34:1. The Lord invited all **nations** and **peoples** to **hear** the announcement He was about to make (cf. 1:2).

b. Judgment on the whole world (34:2-4)

34:2-4. In God's judgment of **wrath** against the **armies** of **all nations** the **dead bodies** will rot on the ground. Also **the stars . . . will be dissolved.** Catastrophic events in the **sky** will accompany the Messiah's return to the earth to establish His millennial reign (cf. Joel 2:10, 30-31; 3:15; Zech. 14:6-7; Matt. 24:29). However, Isaiah 34:4 may refer to the judgment of the sixth seal in the Tribulation (Rev. 6:12-13), or to the eternal state, after the Millennium, when the sun will not be needed (Rev. 21:1). Or perhaps Isaiah was speaking figuratively of a change in the whole power structure in the Millennium when human kings will be done away with and God alone will be in control.

c. Judgment on Edom (34:5-17)

Isaiah used Edom as an example of God's judgment against the world. The Edomites were descendants of Esau, Jacob's older brother. Their father Isaac told Esau he would live in an infertile area (Gen. 27:39-40). Because Edom became a perpetual enemy of Israel (cf. comments on Ezek. 35; 36:5), she was an appropriate example of what the Lord will do to all nations that fight against His people.

34:5-8. God's slaughter of **Edom** by His **sword** is pictured as a great **sacrifice in Bozrah** (cf. 63:1), modern-day Buseirah about 25 miles southeast of the Dead Sea, where various animals were slaughtered for sacrifice. God's reason for judging Edom is that He must **uphold Zion's cause** (34:8). (On the **day of vengeance;** see 61:2; 63:4.) Having promised to bless His Chosen People, He must fulfill His promises. Therefore when they are attacked He goes to their aid.

34:9-17. As a result of God's sword of judgment on Edom, **her land will** seem to be ablaze (cf. Obad. 18) with **sulfur** (see comments on Isa. 30:33) and burning **pitch,** a tar-like substance seemingly unquenchable. The land **will lie desolate** for many generations (34:10; cf. v. 11). Edom's cities and territories will be inhabited by wild birds and animals, which do not normally inhabit populated villages and towns. **Owls** (vv. 11, 13), ravens (v. 11), **jackals** (v. 13), **hyenas . . . wild goats** (v. 14), **falcons** (v. 15), and other **desert creatures** (v. 14) will thrive because no people will be there (v. 12). Edom's defenses will be overgrown with thornbushes (v. 13). The wild creatures will live in Edom **from generation to generation** (v. 17; cf. v. 10) because God's **Spirit will** so direct them (v. 16).

2. THE LORD'S DAY OF BLESSING (CHAP. 35)

The description in this chapter of the land and the people is a highlight of the first half of the book. This is the desired millennial state for which the nation has longed since God first promised it to Abraham. This is the state that mankind constantly longs for—a utopia in which peace and fertility prevail. This condition will not come, however, till after God's judgment on the world (chap. 34). This emphasis in Isaiah rules out postmillennialism, which teaches that the world will get increasingly better thus bringing in the kingdom which will be *followed* by the Messiah's return. The amillennial teaching that there will be no earthly kingdom at all because the Old Testament promises to Israel are being fulfilled in the church today is also foreign to Isaiah's thought. Isaiah taught that the Lord will regather believing Israel, Abraham's physical descendants, and will establish God's long-awaited kingdom on earth. That promised restoration is not being fulfilled in the church today in any sense.

35:1-2. In the Millennium **the parched land will** become rich agricultural land (cf. 32:15). The dry areas of the nation will become fertile (figuratively expressed as being **glad**) and will **blossom.** Apparently God will bring about climatic changes that will result in more rain in those areas. **Lebanon . . . Carmel, and**

Sharon, which were becoming barren (see 33:9 and comments there), will once again become fruitful areas of agriculture. People in those areas **will see the** Lord's **glory,** that is, they will see the fruitfulness that comes because of righteousness; they will see Him who will be dwelling in their midst as King (cf. comments on 33:17).

35:3-4. Isaiah now spoke again to the people in his day. He encouraged the believing remnant to live according to God's covenantal stipulations. They should encourage the depressed (those with **feeble hands**), the terrified (those whose **knees . . . give way**), and the **fearful,** for **God** in **divine retribution will . . . save** (deliver) them.

35:5-7. Changes will occur in the people and the land. Because of God's healing power (cf. 33:24) those who are **blind** will see, those who are **deaf** will hear (cf. 32:3; 42:7) those who are **lame** will **leap** (cf. 33:23), and those who cannot talk will **shout.** The Messiah will bring this about.

The land will change from dryness to a well-watered condition (cf. 35:1-2; 41:18; 43:19-20; 44:3-4). **Water will** be plentiful, helping **grass . . . reeds, and papyus . . . grow,** all of which require much water. Though some interpreters take these statements as figurative of spiritual blessings, it seems preferable to take them as literal statements, especially in view of the covenant promises (Deut. 28:1-14). With the Lord living among His people and with righteousness being practiced by them, the Lord will provide physical healing and agricultural fecundity.

35:8-10. Righteous pilgrims will once again travel to Jerusalem. They will go on **a highway** known as **the Way of Holiness,** for it will lead to God's city where His ways will be followed. It will **not** be traveled by **the unclean** or wicked **fools.** No ferocious animals will hinder the travel of **the redeemed** on that highway. In the millennial kingdom God's people will once again be involved in certain aspects of Old Testament formal worship (Zech. 14:16-19; Ezek. 40–44). Since righteousness and a desire to do the will of God will be esteemed, the people will willingly follow His instructions for worship. Also the redeemed will be indwelt by the Holy Spirit (Ezek.

36:24-28). **The ransomed of the** LORD will have **everlasting joy,** with no **sorrow,** for they will realize what God has done for them. They will rejoice that He will have saved them from destruction and brought them to peace and prosperity, in fulfillment of His promises.

G. Historical interlude: Judah to be in captivity (chaps. 36–39)

The historical material in these chapters concerns two events which are foundational to a proper understanding of Isaiah's theology and Judah's history. The first event (chaps. 36–37) concerns the Assyrian threat which God miraculously dissipated. This event climaxes Isaiah's argument in chapters 1–35. In those chapters he had argued that God brought the Assyrians into Judah as a punishment for Judah's sins and as a catalyst to turn them back to Him. However, he had prophesied that Jerusalem would not fall to the Assyrians and that God would miraculously destroy the Assyrian army because of their pride.

The second event (chaps. 38–39) concerned Hezekiah's breach of the covenant when he was delivered by God from death but then allowed pride to enter his heart. This event serves as a foundation for chapters 40–66 which speak of the deliverance from the Babylonian Captivity prophesied in 39:5-8.

1. GOD'S SUPERIORITY TO ASSYRIA (CHAPS. 36–37)

Probably these chapters were written before the similar accounts in 2 Kings 18–19 and 2 Chronicles 32:1-23. Isaiah wanted to portray Hezekiah as one who believed in God and who was miraculously delivered from the Assyrian threat by a sovereign act of God. The point of these chapters is that God can and does fulfill His Word to His people. He had told them on a number of occasions that the Assyrians would be defeated; now that promise was fulfilled.

a. Sennacherib's threatening of Jerusalem (36:1–37:4)

The Assyrians were convinced that they were invincible and that the God of Israel was no different from any other gods they had overcome on their westward march. So in 36:1–37:4 Isaiah stressed the pride of the Assyrians, and

that their arrogance would result in God's judging them (cf. 10:15-19).

(1) The setting. **36:1-3.** This attack occurred in 701 B.C. This was **the 14th year of . . . Hezekiah's** sole **reign** (cf. 2 Kings 18:13), which began in 715. Some scholars have proposed that **Sennacherib** (705–681) made several attacks against Jerusalem, but extrabiblical evidence does not seem to support that view. Sennacherib boasted of taking 46 walled villages in **Judah.** He went from the north along the coast defeating (among others) the towns of Aphek, Timnah, Ekron, and **Lachish.** Lachish was then his staging area for attacking a number of other towns. From Lachish he sent **a large army** against **Jerusalem** to surround it and to demand its surrender.

The Assyrian **commander stopped at the aqueduct of the Upper Pool, on the road to the Washerman's Field.** Besides setting the stage geographically, that information has theological significance. Ahaz had faced the Aram-Israel challenge at that same place (Isa. 7:3). Isaiah had told Ahaz that he would not fall to his enemy, that the Lord would deliver him. But Ahaz had refused to believe the man of God. Now **Hezekiah** was also confronted with a message of deliverance from the same man of God. The geographic notation heightened the tension over the question of whether Hezekiah would respond positively to the Word of God. **Eliakim . . . Shebna . . . and Joah** (cf. 22:20; 36:11, 22; 37:2) were chosen to negotiate with the Assyrians. These men, in important positions, were trusted by Hezekiah.

(2) The commander's mockery (36:4-10). **36:4-7.** The **field commander** was the main Assyrian spokesman. According to 2 Kings 18:17 two other leading officials were with him. (The KJV and NASB translate "field commander" by "Rabshekah," as if the word were a proper name. This, however, is probably not correct.) As a representative of the Assyrian Empire, his words of mockery characterized the whole empire. In speaking for the Assyrian **king** the field commander asked the Jerusalemites **whom** they were **depending** on for victory (Isa. 36:4-5). To depend **on Egypt** would be like leaning on a **splintered reed**—it would do no good and would even be harmful. Amazingly this was

what Isaiah had been saying about Egypt. The odds were overwhelmingly against the people of Jerusalem who had no means of escape for thousands of enemy troops were surrounding them. The commander then said that it would be foolish to depend on **God** (v. 7). Apparently this commander had heard of Hezekiah's partial reforms (2 Kings 18; 2 Chron. 31) in which he had **removed** the **high places,** sites of worship on hills throughout **Judah.** The commander did not really understand the situation for he may have thought that Hezekiah was no longer depending on God since he had removed many **altars** from the land, leaving only one **altar** in **Jerusalem.**

36:8-10. To the commander, Jerusalem's only reasonable action was to surrender. Mockingly he even offered to **give** the Jews **2,000 horses if** they could find **riders** for them to fight against him. But he claimed that even 2,000 could not fight off *one* Assyrian low-ranking **officer.** Finalizing his argument, the commander said that **the LORD** had ordered him to **destroy** Judah. This was meant to terrorize the people by making them think that God had actually turned against them. Of course Isaiah had said that Jerusalem would not fall to the Assyrians, so the commander was wrong.

(3) **The commander's challenge** (36:11-20). **36:11-12.** Realizing the seriousness of their situation the three Judahite negotiators (cf. v. 3) requested that the negotiations be carried on **in Aramaic** rather than **Hebrew.** Aramaic, a major diplomatic language in that day, is similar to Hebrew. But it is different enough that many of the common people would have had difficulty understanding negotiations spoken in it. The three leaders were concerned that panic would spread throughout the city if **the people** heard the Assyrian's demands in Hebrew. However, the commander refused because he said he was sent to speak to every Jew in earshot, not just to these three. Confident of an Assyrian victory, he said the Jerusalemites would be forced to **eat** and **drink their own** body waste to survive in the siege.

36:13-20. Calling **out** to the people **in Hebrew,** the Assyrian **commander** urged them **not** to **let Hezekiah deceive** them into thinking the **LORD** would de-

liver them (vv. 13-15). Then the commander told the people that Sennacherib promised them prosperity in another **land** (vv. 16-17). Again the commander exhorted the people not to be deceived by **Hezekiah** (cf. vv. 13-15) for **the gods** of other nations had not been able to deliver them (vv. 18-20).

Hamath and Arpad were in Aram. The location of **Sepharvaim** is uncertain but it may be near Hamath and Arpad. Hamath and Sepharvaim were two of the cities from which people were brought to repopulate Samaria after its fall (2 Kings 17:24). The commander also boasted that since **Samaria** was not helped by its god (it had fallen to Assyria 21 years earlier, 722 B.C.), why should the people of **Jerusalem** count on their God to protect them?

(4) The people's response. **36:21-22.** Though no doubt terrified, **the people** followed Hezekiah's instructions not to answer the Assyrian spokesman's taunts. **Eliakim . . . Shebna,** and **Joah** (cf. vv. 3, 11) **told** Hezekiah **what the . . . commander had said.** They had **torn** their **clothes,** a sign of distress and/or mourning (cf. 37:1; Gen. 37:29; Josh. 7:6; 2 Kings 11:14; 19:1; 22:11; Es. 4:1; Job 1:20; 2:12).

(5) Hezekiah's faith (37:1-4). **37:1-2.** Like the envoys, **Hezekiah** in distress **tore his clothes.** He was disturbed because of the Assyrian threat and also because the name of the Lord had been profaned. Putting **on sackcloth** was another act of mourning (see comments on 3:24). In trust and dependence on God Hezekiah **went into the temple of the LORD,** showing symbolically that the nation now could do nothing on their own—their destiny was completely up to God. He also sent his top leaders **Eliakim** and **Shebna** along with **the leading priests . . . to . . . Isaiah.** Why Joah (cf. 36:3, 11, 22) is not mentioned is not known.

37:3-4. The men informed Isaiah of the situation, asked for a word from **the LORD** to **rebuke** the Assyrians, and then asked the prophet to **pray** for them. **Hezekiah** was thereby acknowledging that the Lord spoke through Isaiah. This contrasts with Ahaz's attitude (chap. 7) when he was confronted by a national calamity 33 years earlier, 734 B.C. In the leaders' report to Isaiah they picked up

ISAIAH

his imagery of distress (from 26:17-18) about a woman who is about to deliver a baby but has no strength and would die in the process.

b. Isaiah's response from the Lord (37:5-7)

37:5-7. In Isaiah's brief word to the messengers from the LORD he first told them not to be afraid of the Assyrians. God had heard that they had blasphemed Him (cf. v. 4). Then the prophet said that the Assyrian king would return home and would be killed there (the fulfillment of this is recorded in vv. 36-38).

c. God's defeat of Assyria (37:8-38)

37:8-13. Sennacherib had left Lachish and was at Libnah, about five miles north of Lachish. Word had come that Tirhakah was coming to assist Judah in her fight against Assyria. Tirhakah was called the Cushite king of Egypt. He was from Cush, south of Egypt, and ruled Egypt at that time. In 701 Tirhakah was an army commander; he actually did not become king of Cush until 690; but since he was king when Isaiah wrote this account, Isaiah called him the king.

Again Sennacherib told Hezekiah that other nations' gods had not been able to help them against the Assyrian advance (cf. 36:18-20). Gozan, a city on the Habor River, was conquered about 100 years earlier by the Assyrians. Haran, a city in Aram, was at that time an Assyrian stronghold. Rezeph, also an Aramean city, was captured about 100 years earlier by the Assyrians. Eden was probably in northern Mesopotamia, and may refer to a territory in which Tel Assar was a city. (See comments on Hamath . . . Arpad, and Sepharvaim in 36:19.) The location of Hena is not known. The site of Ivvah is also unknown but it may have been in the Babylonian region.

37:14-20. Receiving the communication (a letter) from Sennacherib, Hezekiah prayed a great prayer of faith in the temple (cf. v. 1). By placing the matter in God's hands (v. 14), he was calling God's attention to it (though of course he believed that God already knew). The king began his prayer with praise (vv. 15-16). Referring to Him as the God of Israel, the king recalled the special covenant position Israel had with the LORD. God's being enthroned between the cherubim refers to His presence in the Jerusalem temple and thus with His people (1 Kings 8:10-13). (On the cherubim see comments on 1 Kings 6:23.) Besides being the God of Israel, the LORD is also over all the kingdoms of the earth, including Assyria! Hezekiah also stated that God is the Creator.

Then Hezekiah asked God to intervene for His glory, so that the other nations would know that He, the LORD of Israel, is the true God (Isa. 37:17-20). Hezekiah requested deliverance from the Assyrians so that nations everywhere would acknowledge God's sovereignty.

37:21-35. Responding to Hezekiah's prayer, the Lord sent a message to him through Isaiah that Assyria would be defeated (cf. God's first reply, vv. 6-7). That message included three parts.

First, the Assyrians would be driven back (vv. 21-29). Deliverance would come to Jerusalem (the Virgin Daughter of Zion; see comments on 1:8; 47:1) for Assyria would flee (cf. 37:7). The tables would be turned and Zion would mock Assyria (v. 22). This would come about as an answer to Hezekiah's prayer (v. 21) and as punishment on the Assyrians for their blasphemy (vv. 23-24; cf. 36:20; 37:4, 17) and pride (I and my occur seven times in vv. 24-25). Sennacherib claimed to have felled the choicest tall cedars and pines in the heights (mountains and hills) of Lebanon (cf. 10:34). This may refer to his overrunning Lebanon or it may be a figurative way of saying he conquered leading nations. He also claimed to have conquered Egypt though it is questionable that he ever entered Egypt. However, he did defeat the Egyptians in Philistia. Those successes came only because the Lord allowed them, for He ordained them all. The nations Sennacherib conquered were weak and like grass on flat housetops (cf. Ps. 129:6) readily scorched by the sun. But now the Lord, knowing Sennacherib's rage, would cause him to go back to his land as if he were being led like an animal (Isa. 37:29), that is, in disgrace. This is fitting because the Assyrians were known for leading their captives by hooks in their noses.

Second, God assured Hezekiah that a remnant would remain (vv. 30-32) and that life would go on as usual. For the next two years life would be difficult as they sought to get their crops back to

76

normal, **but in the third year** (the normal time it takes for a vineyard to begin producing grapes) there would be a bountiful harvest. **The LORD** would do this because of his **zeal** for Judah.

Third, the message again addressed **the king of Assyria** (vv. 33-35). God told him that he would **not** set foot inside the **city** of Jerusalem or even **build a siege ramp against** its walls. He would have to **return** home because God Himself would **defend** the **city** of David.

37:36-38. The account of the destruction of the Assyrian army (predicted by Isaiah in 30:27-33; 31:8-9; 33:1, 18-19) is almost anticlimactic, occupying only three verses. The overnight slaughter did not come from the hand of an enemy but by **the Angel of the LORD,** who killed **185,000** soldiers. This angel may have been the preincarnate Christ (see comments on Gen. 16:7) though not all scholars agree on this. **Sennacherib** was assassinated 20 years later (681 B.C.) by two of **his sons.**

2. JUDAH'S CAPTIVITY IN BABYLON
(CHAPS. 38-39)

These chapters concern an interesting event in Hezekiah's life. Though God miraculously healed the king, his pride led to national calamity. In chapters 36-37, Hezekiah was a man of faith, but here he was a man of pride. This account is also recorded in 2 Kings 20.

a. Hezekiah's healing from his illness (38:1-8)

(1) Isaiah's prophecy that Hezekiah would die. **38:1.** From verse 6 it is clear that Hezekiah's illness preceded Sennacherib's surrounding of Jerusalem, recorded in chapters 36-37. Merodach-Baladan, mentioned in 39:1, ruled from 721 to 710 and nine months in 703–702 B.C. (he ruled before Sennacherib's invasion of Judah in 701). Though chapters 38-39 precede chapters 36-37 chronologically they follow them here because Hezekiah's folly led to the prophecy of the Babylonian Captivity, and because chapters 38-39, as stated earlier, prepare the way for chapters 40-66. Hezekiah's illness included a boil (38:21). **Isaiah** told him he would **die.**

(2) Hezekiah's prayer for a longer life. **38:2-3.** Hezekiah's prayer does not explicitly state a request to live longer,

but it is implied. Many have criticized Hezekiah for this request. However, self-preservation characterizes nearly everyone. **Hezekiah** asked the LORD to **remember** the good things he had done as king (cf. 2 Kings 18:5-8).

(3) God's answer to Hezekiah. **38:4-6.** In response to the king's **prayer** God said through **Isaiah** that He would grant the king **15** more **years.** Since **Hezekiah** died in 686 B.C. this illness would have been in 701 (see the chart "Kings of Judah and Israel and the Preexilic Prophets," near 1 Kings 12:25-33). In addition, God would not allow the Assyrians to take Jerusalem. These facts would have been a great comfort to Hezekiah.

(4) God's sign. **38:7-8.** God confirmed His promise to Hezekiah by a **sign** (cf. comments on v. 22). Apparently a special **stairway** had been built as a time device, a kind of sundial. As **the sun** went down in the west, a **shadow** would move upward on the staircase so that people could ascertain the time of the day. Interestingly **Ahaz** had rejected a sign from **the LORD** (7:10-12) but now on a staircase named for him his son Hezekiah was given a sign. How this miracle of the reversal of the sun's shadow occurred is not known. Perhaps the earth's rotation was reversed or perhaps the sun's rays were somehow refracted.

b. Hezekiah's song of thanksgiving (38:9-20)

(1) Hezekiah's statement about his condition. **38:9-15.** After he was healed **Hezekiah** wrote a song to express his thanks to God. His **illness** came, he said, **in the prime** of his **life. Death** was referred to figuratively as having **gates** through which a person entered (cf. Job 38:17; Pss. 9:13; 107:18). His statement that in death he would **not . . . see the LORD** does not mean he had no hope of heaven. It probably means that he would no longer have the benefit of enjoying God's blessings in this life. He would be without friends (Isa. 38:11) as his **house** (his body) was dismantled. By death he would be **cut . . . off** like a cloth being cut from a weaver's **loom.** He had hoped he would get well (v. 13) but he got worse (vv. 13-14). His illness was as if God were **a lion** breaking all his **bones,** a figure of speech depicting his deep inner anguish. In some way his cries of pain were like the sound of a bird and his

mourning like the doleful sound of a **dove** (cf. 59:11; Nahum 2:7). Hezekiah realized that this experience should humble him because God had brought on this illness.

(2) Hezekiah's affirmation that God was his strength. **38:16-20.** Hezekiah was grateful that God **restored** him **to health.** After the experience he could see that **it was** really **for** his **benefit** that it happened (v. 17; cf. Rom. 8:28). He sensed for one thing that God's **love** was with him and that God did not punish him in accord with what his **sins** deserved. When he said that those who are dead **cannot praise** the LORD (Isa. 38:18) he was not denying life after death. He was simply noting that in death one's activities on earth are stopped and that one's service on earth for God terminates (Ps. 30:9). However, Hezekiah affirmed that while he was still alive he would proclaim the Lord's **faithfulnesss** (Isa. 38:19). Because **the** LORD healed him, the king said he would sing to the Lord **in the temple.**

c. Hezekiah's healing (38:21-22)

38:21-22. In the parallel account in 2 Kings these two verses in Isaiah precede the giving of the sign (see 2 Kings 20:7-9). **A poultice of** dried **figs,** a common treatment for boils and ulcers in those days, applied **to the boil** (possibly an inflamed ulceration), was used by God medicinally to promote the healing. This is an example of healing occurring because of a combination of prayer, medicine, and God's work. Hezekiah's question, **What will be the sign. . . ?** did not evidence lack of faith. In fact it was the opposite. Believing that he would be healed, he asked God for confirmation of His word.

d. Isaiah's prophecy of captivity (chap. 39)

39:1. Merodach-Baladan . . . sent envoys from Babylon to **Hezekiah** with **letters and a gift.** Seemingly they went to congratulate the king on his **recovery.** But there was probably more to it than that. Merodach-Baladan was Marduk-apal-iddina, the invader (see comments on 21:1-10). Twice he had tried to break away from the Assyrian Empire, and once had succeeded in taking the city of Babylon. After his second reign (of nine

months in 703–702 B.C.) he was deposed by Sennacherib and went to Elam. While there (and while still known as **the king of Babylon)** he actively tried to form an alliance with other nations to throw off the Assyrian yoke. Undoubtedly his friendly visit after Hezekiah's illness was intended to persuade the king of Judah to join the rebel alliance in the fight against Assyria. This made Hezekiah's indiscretion all the worse in view of Isaiah's words that God was using Assyria to punish the whole region (chap. 10). The visit was also God's test of Hezekiah's heart (2 Chron. 32:31). Merodach-Baladan's visit preceded Sennacherib's attack on Jerusalem in 701 (since some of the wealth there had not yet been given to Sennacherib as tribute, 2 Kings 18:16). Therefore it seems as if all three events occurred in 701, in this order: Hezekiah's illness, Merodach-Baladan's visit, Sennacherib's attack.

39:2. In pride **Hezekiah . . . showed** the Babylonian **envoys** everything of value **in his storehouses. . . . palace,** and **kingdom.** Apparently Hezekiah was acting as if those riches all belonged to him and not to God. Undoubtedly **Hezekiah** thought he could impress the Babylonian emissaries, but they probably were thinking more of his ability to pay great sums of money to aid in the fight against Assyria.

39:3-7. When **Isaiah** heard of the foreigners' visit, he asked **Hezekiah . . . what** they said and **where** they came **from.** The king answered the second question but not the first one. When the prophet learned that **Hezekiah** had shown him all his **treasures. . . . Isaiah** gave him a two-part prophecy of judgment. First, the king's wealth would **be carried off to Babylon.** That was an astounding statement at that time because the great threat then was Assyria, not Babylon. The Babylonian envoys had come from a rebel force that was on the run and that had been defeated repeatedly. Second, **some of** the king's **descendants** would be forced to serve in the royal court of **Babylon.** The beginning of this was fulfilled in 605 B.C. when Daniel and a number of other royal sons were taken into the king's service in Babylon (Dan. 1:1-7). (On **eunuchs,** *sārîs,* see comments on "officials," Dan. 1:3.)

39:8. Hezekiah felt glad that **there**

would **be peace and security** during his days.

II. The Restoration by God (chaps. 40–66)

Whereas the first portion of the book (chaps. 1–39) is filled with messages of judgment, this portion emphasizes restoration and deliverance. This section divides into three parts of nine chapters each (chaps. 40–48; 49–57; 58–66). The first two parts each conclude with the statement, "There is no peace . . . for the wicked" (48:22; 57:21). These prophecies of deliverance center around three events: (1) Deliverance from captivity in Babylon (already prophesied by Isaiah, 39:7). This is the main subject of chapters 40–48 and the chief deliverer is Cyrus, mentioned near the middle of the section (44:28–45:1). (2) The rejection and restoration of the Suffering Servant. This is discussed in 52:13–53:12, near the middle of chapters 49–57. (3) The consummation of God's restoration of Israel and the world. At the heart of this third section (chaps. 58–66) is the coming of the Messiah (chaps. 61–63).

When Isaiah wrote these prophecies of restoration Judah still had over 100 years of difficulty ahead of her before she fell to Babylon, and then she faced 70 years of captivity. Anticipating the future Captivity and God's restoration, Isaiah wrote to encourage the Judahites to live righteously in the present, despite forthcoming difficult circumstances.

For support for the view that all the Book of Isaiah, including chapters 40–66, was written by Isaiah the son of Amoz, see "Unity" in the *Introduction*.

A. Deliverance of God's people (chaps. 40–48)

In these chapters the prophet reminded the people of their coming deliverance because of the Lord's greatness and their unique relationship with Him. He is majestic (chap. 40), and He protects Israel and not the world's pagan nations (chap. 41). Though Israel had been unworthy (chap. 42) the Lord had promised to regather her (43:1–44:5). Because He, the only God (44:6–45:25), was superior to Babylon He would make Babylon fall (chaps. 46–47). Therefore Isaiah exhorted the Israelites to live righteously and to flee away from Babylon (chap. 48). Ju-

dah's people are viewed as being in Babylon (43:14; 47:1; 48:20) and Jerusalem in ruins (44:26).

1. THE MAJESTY OF GOD (CHAP 40)

a. Words of comfort: Deliverance is coming (40:1-11)

40:1-2. These words of comfort in verses 1-11 begin with **God** saying to His people (through Isaiah) that their time of trial was almost over. The repetition of the word **comfort** is for emphasis. Looking ahead to the Exile, Isaiah wanted the covenant nation (**My people**) to be comforted. As stated in the *Introduction* the words "comfort," "comforted," "comforts" occur 13 times in chapters 40–66.

Jerusalem was to be addressed **tenderly** (lit., "to the heart," i.e., in gentle, encouraging words; cf. Hosea 2:14) as a mother would speak to her child. The 70-year Captivity was seen as almost over. **Hard service** translates the Hebrew word for "warfare" and "time of enlistment in war." Judah's captivity was like the hardships of war. That time of trial had come because of **her sin.** But now her sin had **been paid for** so that God's blessings could begin. As stated in the Mosaic Covenant, God would bless His people if they lived according to His Word. However, if they disobeyed Him, He would curse them and eventually cast them out of the land of Israel (Deut. 28:15-68, esp. vv. 49-52, 64). Now that cursing was seen as almost accomplished, Israel could have a new start. To receive **double for all her sins** does not mean to be punished beyond what she deserves but in keeping with what she deserves. The point is that she has now received "full" or "sufficient" punishment for all her sins (cf. "double" in Isa. 51:19; 61:7).

40:3-5. A voice (probably Isaiah's, different from the voice in v. 6) called out to the people to **prepare the way for the Lord** (v. 3) and His **glory** (v. 5). True prophets were "voices," for their messages were from God. They were calling the nation to get back into a proper relationship with Him. Each Gospel writer applied Isaiah 40:3 to John the Baptist (Matt. 3:1-4; Mark 1:1-4; Luke 1:76-78; John 1:23). John was a **desert** prophet who prepared the way for Jesus Christ, and who **in the wilderness** made **a high-**

way for Him (cf. Matt. 3:3). However, here in Isaiah the entire nation was in a spiritual wilderness, and each Israelite needed to get ready spiritually for the appearing of the Lord.

Raising the valleys and lowering the mountains refer in hyperbole to workmen leveling or smoothing out the roads on which a dignitary would travel when he came to visit an area. Today an equivalent is, "roll out the red carpet." In Isaiah's day he was calling Israel to be "smoothed out" so that the Lord could come to the nation and rule. This was emphasized by all the prophets—ethically the nation must be righteous. Eventually the nation will be "smoothed out" spiritually when the glory of the LORD is revealed (Isa. 40:5). Isaiah was thinking of the millennial kingdom when the Lord will be revealed in His glory, that is, when His unique splendor will be evident everywhere. As Isaiah wrote elsewhere, the Messiah would suffer and would also appear in glory. However, apparently he was not aware of the time interval that would elapse between these two aspects. Though the disciples saw Jesus' glory (John 1:14), all mankind has not yet seen it, but they will see it in the Millennium. This coming glory is certain for the . . . LORD has spoken it (cf. Isa. 1:20; 58:14). The word of the Lord is sure and cannot be broken.

40:6-8. A second voice (cf. v. 3) spoke. This voice, probably God's, gave the command, probably to Isaiah, to cry out. The voice told him to contrast the difference between people and God. People are temporary and they change. They are like wild grass and flowers that come up in the springtime only to fade and fail when the weather gets hot (cf. Pss. 37:2; 102:11; 103:15-16). By contrast, God never fails for His Word endures forever. This fact would greatly comfort and encourage the people in exile who read these words. Because God's Word stands, His prophecy that the people would be restored to their land was sure to be fulfilled.

40:9-11. Perhaps the one who was to take good tidings to Jerusalem was someone who was passing on Isaiah's message. The messenger was to tell loudly to the towns of Judah that God was coming (v. 9) to Jerusalem, restoring His people from exile. Presumably Isaiah

envisioned the return from exile as leading immediately into the Millennium, though of course Bible passages written later indicate an extensive time gap between the two events. God was described first as the Sovereign LORD who is a powerful, conquering King (v. 10). He not only rules in power, but He also brings booty (His reward, i.e., blessings) with Him. Arm suggests strength, a concept Isaiah frequently mentioned (40:10; 51:5 [twice], 9; 52:10; 53:1; 59:1, 16; 60:4; 62:8; 63:5, 12). God was also pictured as a tender Shepherd (cf. Pss. 23:1; 80:1; John 10:11, 14; Heb. 13:20; 1 Peter 2:25; 5:4), who carefully carries and leads the weak and helpless members of His flock (cf. Jer. 13:17, 20; Micah 4:8; 5:4; 7:14; Zech. 10:3). These two aspects of the Lord's character are emphasized throughout this second portion of Isaiah's book.

b. Additional words of comfort: God is majestic (40:12-26)

The various aspects of God's majesty discussed in these verses are repeated often by Isaiah throughout the next eight chapters. For example, God's knowledge and creative power are stressed in 44:24–45:8, and His uniqueness is emphasized in 44:6-23.

(1) God's incomparable knowledge (40:12-17). 40:12-14. By five rhetorical questions Isaiah emphasized that God, in creating the universe (v. 12), did not need anyone to assist Him (vv. 13-14). He is such a great Creator that all the waters of the globe were held, as it were, in His hand. Figuratively, He can measure the vast starry universe with the breadth of His hand. Also all the earth's dust could be put in a basket of His; and the mountains and hills, though vast, are so small compared with Him that He, figuratively speaking, could weigh them all on small scales. Though the immensity of Creation is awe-inspiring, no one on earth is God's equal.

In verses 13-14 Isaiah spoke of the infinite knowledge and skill the LORD possesses. No one on earth can claim to have taught the LORD anything. He did not need to consult anyone. Isaiah was probably thinking of the Creation account (Gen. 1) in which God spoke and Creation came into being. In irony God had also pointed out to Job by numerous questions that his knowledge was nothing compared with God's (Job 38:2–39:30).

40:15-17. Since God's Creation is so grandiose, the people of **the nations are as nothing** before Him (like a mere **drop** of water or **dust** particles on **scales**). All the wood and the animals in fertile, wooded **Lebanon,** north of Israel, would be inadequate for sacrifices that would be significant before the great God. **The nations** who do not know the Lord are **worthless and less than nothing** before Him.

(2) God's uniqueness compared with idols. **40:18-20.** With irony Isaiah wrote about two idols—one made of metal by a **craftsman** and then overlaid **with gold** and decorated with **silver** ornaments, and another selected by a **poor** man from **wood** and fashioned so that it **will not** fall over. (Other passages denouncing idols are 41:7; 44:9-20; 45:16, 20; 46:1-2, 6-7; Pss. 115:4-7; 135:15-18; Jer. 10:8-16; Hab. 2:19.) Both of these idol-makers used materials God created, and skills that God gave them! God, however, is unlike any idol. He is the Creator of **all** things including people. God is unique.

(3) God's sovereign control over the world (40:21-26). **40:21-22.** From His sovereign position in heaven God watches over His created universe. **You** (used four times in v. 21) refers to people in general. The force of the first question, for example, is "Doesn't everyone know this?" (cf. v. 28) The Lord is like a king sitting **enthroned above the circle** (*ḥûg,* "horizon," which is circular; cf. Job 26:10; Prov. 8:27) **of the earth** and over His **people** who by comparison seem **like** mere **grasshoppers. The heavens** (the sky) are pictured as spread **out like a tent** for Him to live in (cf. Ps. 104:2). Isaiah was not presenting a detailed idea of God's abode. He was merely using imagery that his readers would easily understand.

40:23-24. In controlling history God establishes **rulers** and removes them (cf. Dan. 2:21). This truth would have been comforting to Isaiah's original readers who were living under the threat of the Assyrian Empire and who heard his prophecy that the Babylonian Empire would take them into captivity.

40:25-26. God, who cannot be compared to anyone or anything (cf. v. 18; 46:5) knows everything about His Cre-

ation and sustains it. In His **strength** He created and also controls and sustains millions upon millions of stars, **each** one of which He, amazingly, has named (cf. Ps. 147:4). In Isaiah 40–66, God is frequently referred to as Creator and Maker, probably as a polemic against the lifeless idols of Babylon. He created the heavens, the earth, people, Israel, and darkness, and will create the new heavens and new earth.

c. Further words of comfort: God watches over His people (40:27-31)

Isaiah's readers were under the threat of Assyria. Years later Isaiah's readers during the Babylonian Captivity were under the domination of a godless empire. So Isaiah encouraged the people to remember that God never relaxes; He is always watching His people.

40:27. God's people should never think He has forgotten them. **Jacob** and **Israel** are synonyms for all 12 tribes. In chapters 40–49, Isaiah used these two words together 16 times (40:27; 41:8, 14; 42:24; 43:1, 22, 28; 44:1, 5, 21, 23; 45:4; 46:3; 48:1; 49:5-6). Though the people of the Northern Kingdom were already exiled to Assyria, **God** was still watching over the few believers who remained true to Him. His covenant people should never think God did not see or remember them.

40:28-31. On the question **Do you not know?** see comments on verse 21. Since **God,** who unlike pagan idols is eternal and **the Creator,** never grows **weary** (v. 28) **He** can give **strength to** those who are **weary** or weak (vv. 29-31). Among Isaiah's original readers **those who hope in the LORD** were believers who remained faithful to God. They were the ones who would be restored. For his readers in captivity Isaiah was probably speaking of a national refreshing when the captives would be released and would return to their land. Even though in captivity they were **weary** the LORD would help them endure and **soar . . . like eagles,** to be uplifted emotionally and spiritually.

2. A CHALLENGE TO THE NATIONS (CHAP. 41)

This challenge from the Lord to the nations stemmed from His special relationship with Israel. He would sovereignly protect Israel but the other nations would not enjoy that protection.

a. God's confrontation of the nations (41:1-7)

41:1. The Lord confronted **the nations** and **the islands** (the remotest places where humans live) face to face in **judgment.** Of the 15 occurrences of "islands" in the Old Testament, 14 are in Isaiah. Together the islands and nations suggest all the world's peoples. In suggesting that they **meet together,** God was not asking that they negotiate; instead He was asking that they come together and realize the truth of His words.

41:2-4. God now told the nations that because He controls history, they in the final analysis really have no control over their future. For example, He **stirred up** a leader **from the east** (cf. v. 25 about God stirring up one from the north). This one from the east who would serve God's purpose was called **in righteousness.** This did not mean that warrior was righteous, but that he would carry out God's righteous plan on the earth. He would fulfill God's will even if he was unaware of it. God would hand **nations over to him** and subdue **kings before him,** that is, the conqueror could not be stopped in his conquests (turning enemies **to dust** and **chaff**).

Who was this conqueror? Because he would follow a **path his feet** had **not traveled before,** he could not be an Assyrian king (Assyria had invaded the west on several occasions). Since Isaiah was writing in advance for people who would be enslaved in Babylon, he must have been referring to that great Persian ruler Cyrus, whom he mentioned by name in 44:28 and 45:1. The Lord had planned this and would carry it out (41:4). In emphatic terms the LORD affirmed that **He** is the One who brings events to pass.

41:5-7. Mockingly Isaiah noted that alliances between the nations would not help them withstand the advance of Cyrus and the Persians as they carried out God's will. In **fear** the nations everywhere would be driven to help and encourage **each . . . other** (v. 6). (On **islands** see comments on v. 1; and on the **ends of the earth** see comments on 5:26.) Rather than turn to the true God, these idolatrous people would get more and more involved in **idol**-worship (41:7). The idols, which Isaiah had already mocked (see comments on 40:19-20), would not help them offset Cyrus' conquests.

b. God's protection of Israel (41:8-20)

41:8-10. God sovereignly chose **Israel** (also called **Jacob** and **Abraham's descendants**) to be His servants (cf. 43:10) and to do His will. Unfortunately she often failed to be a faithful **servant** so God had to punish her. Taking the nation **from the ends of the earth** (see comments on 5:26) probably refers to God's regathering Israel after the Babylonian Captivity, rather than His leading Abraham from Ur of the Chaldees. Israel's being **chosen** by God is a frequent theme in the second major division of the Book of Isaiah (41:8-9; 42:1; 43:10, 20; 44:1-2; 45:4; 49:7; 65:9, 15, 22). Even though Israel was exiled because of sin and unbelief, she still was **not rejected** by God. Since the covenant the Lord made with Abraham was unconditional (Gen. 15), his descendants need **not fear.** The Lord remains their **God** (cf. Isa. 43:3) so He will continue to be with them (cf. 43:5) and **strengthen** (cf. 40:31), **help** (cf. 41:13-14), and **uphold** them.

41:11-16. In contrast with God's choosing and helping **Israel,** He will not protect nations **who oppose** her. They will perish (vv. 11-12). With the Lord's help Israel will defeat the nations as if she were **threshing** and winnowing grain (vv. 15-16). This, however, will not be by her own power because she is a **worm** and is **little** (v. 14). Israel should not be **afraid** (cf. v. 10; 43:5; 44:2, 8; 54:4). God is her **Redeemer,** a title Isaiah used of God 13 times (41:14; 43:14; 44:6, 24; 47:4; 48:17; 49:7, 26; 54:5, 8; 59:20; 60:16; 63:16), 5 of them with the title **the Holy One of Israel** (41:14; 43:14; 48:17; 49:7; 54:5). This help from God will cause Israel to **rejoice in** Him (41:16).

41:17-20. In God's care for Israel He will see that extremely thirsty persons will encounter **rivers . . . springs,** and **pools of water** in the desert (vv. 17-18; cf. 35:1-2, 6-7; 43:19-20; 44:3-4). In many places in the Middle East water is scarce, so this figure is most apt. God will also cause trees (seven kinds are mentioned) to grow **in the desert** whereas normally most of those trees grow only in fertile areas. In the Millennium the climate of the land of Israel will be changed so that the land will be well-watered and fertile. **People** will **know** that God, **the Holy One of Israel** (cf. 41:14, 16), **has done this.**

c. God's knowledge of the future (41:21-29)

41:21-24. With the information the nations have received in verses 1-20, they are now challenged to use their idols to recall past events and predict the **future.** By doing **something** the nations might then cause others to **fear.** But their inability to tell the future shows that their gods are ineffective and **worthless.** Someone who would choose such a nation would be **detestable.**

41:25-29. In contrast with idols (vv. 21-24), which are man-made and unable to help people, God can and does tell the future. God predicted that a strong leader would come **from the north** and **from the east (the rising sun)** who would easily destroy many nations. This was Cyrus (see comments on v. 2). He was from the east (Persia was east of Israel) and also from the north as his conquests extended to the north of Israel. Only God could predict such a thing; **no one** else could even hint at it. Only He could **tell Zion** and **Jerusalem** that **a messenger** would give them **good** news about the Jews being released by Cyrus (cf. 40:1-5, 9-11). This proves that the Lord is the true God and **all** idols are **false** gods amounting **to nothing.** Those who believe in such idols have an empty faith; those **images** offer no more help than the **wind** and they confuse people's minds.

3. THE INDIVIDUAL SERVANT CONTRASTED WITH THE SERVANT NATION (CHAP. 42)

Verses 1-17 in this chapter are the first of Isaiah's "Servant Songs" referring to the Messiah. Israel is called the servant of the Lord (41:8; 42:19; 43:10; 44:1-2, 21; 45:4; 48:20). And the Messiah, on whom God has placed His Spirit (42:1; cf. 11:2), is also called the Servant (cf. 49:3, 5-7; 50:10; 52:13; 53:11). Which servant Isaiah was referring to in each passage must be determined by the context and the characteristics assigned to the servant. Israel as God's servant was supposed to help bring the world to a knowledge of God, but she failed. So the Messiah, the Lord's Servant, who epitomizes the nation of Israel, will fulfill God's will.

a. The Servant and His work (42:1-17)

42:1-4. Some Bible students say **My Servant** here refers to Israel, which is clearly the case in verse 19. True, Israel was upheld and **chosen** by the Lord, and was His **delight.** However, the statements in verses 1b-4 suggest that here the Servant is the Messiah. This **One** has the **Spirit** of God **on** Him (cf. 11:2), **and He will bring justice to the nations** (cf. 9:7; 11:3-4; 16:5). He will be gentle (42:2-3a)—most people would break a weak, useless **reed,** but **He will not** do so—and He will be faithful (v. 3b) and **not . . . discouraged** (v. 4). He gave the **Law** in which **the islands** (i.e., people in remote parts; cf. 41:1) **will . . . hope.** Matthew 12:18-21 quotes Isaiah 42:1-4 with some minor variations, relating it to Jesus and His ministry in Israel. As God's Servant, Jesus did what Israel could never do. He perfectly carried out the will of the Father so that people everywhere may believe in the Holy One of Israel.

42:5-7. The LORD promised to assist the Servant in His mission, which **God** can do because He is the Creator (cf. 40:12-14, 26). He **created the** immense **heavens** and **the earth** (cf. 44:24; 45:12, 18; 48:13; 51:13, 16) and life in it, including man, giving him **breath.** Speaking to His Servant (42:6-7) God assured Him that He had been **called** to perform the will of God. To be **called . . . in righteousness** (as Cyrus also would be, 41:2), meant to be responsible to do God's righteous will. Of course the Messiah, unlike Cyrus, lived a righteous life (for He is God). Because **the** LORD would **take hold of** the Servant's **hand** the Messiah would have the power to carry out God's will.

Also the Servant was assured that He would **be a covenant for the people** (cf. 49:8). He would fulfill God's covenant promises to Israel, and would also be **a light** (cf. 42:16; Luke 1:79) **for the Gentiles** (cf. Isa. 49:6). Spiritually unredeemed Israel and the Gentiles are **blind,** and they are **captives . . . in darkness.** Though Cyrus would be the servant to release Jewish captives from exile, the Messiah gives spiritual **release** (cf. 61:1; John 8:32; Col. 1:13), sight (cf. John 9:39-41), and light (cf. John 8:12) to those who trust Him. (On **eyes** being opened; cf.

Isa. 32:3; 35:5.) This spiritual salvation to both Jews and Gentiles will eventuate in the glorious messianic kingdom.

42:8-9. The LORD, Israel's covenant-keeping God, had given the prophecy recorded in verses 6-7 and He **will not** let **idols** take credit for it (cf. comments on 41:21-24). In view of all that God had already done for Israel (**the former things**) these **new things** (cf. 48:6) of which He had been speaking would certainly happen. No other god can foretell such things. If, as some scholars argue, someone other than Isaiah wrote chapters 40–66 *after* the Jewish captives were released by Cyrus, then Isaiah's point in 42:9 and elsewhere is destroyed. Isaiah was affirming that God, unlike idols, *can* tell the future. And this divine ability adds to His glory (v. 8).

42:10-17. People everywhere (in **the ends of earth**; cf. 41:5 and see comments on 5:26) should **sing** this **song** of **praise** to **the LORD.** These should include (a) people who make their living by **sea** commerce, (b) those who **live** in **the islands** (cf. 41:1, 5), and (c) those in **the desert** regions and **towns. Kedar** (cf. 21:16-17) is an area in Northern Arabia, and **Sela** was a city in Edom. People everywhere should **sing** and **shout. . . . to the LORD** because of His victory **over His enemies** at the Messiah's second coming.

God, seemingly **silent** for **a long time,** will act in judgment though, humanly speaking, it will be painful for Him (42:14). He will **dry up** the places where people do not revere Him (v. 15). But He will **guide** those who trust in Him, giving them **light** (cf. v. 7) and smoothing their **paths** (v. 16). However, pagans **who trust in idols** will be ashamed (v. 17; cf. 44:9, 11; 45:16).

b. Israel's current condition (42:18-25)

42:18-20. Later when Jews in the Babylonian Exile would read this chapter in Isaiah, they might wonder why they were experiencing such difficulties. Isaiah answered this implied question by pointing out that though the LORD said He would lead them they were being punished because spiritually they had been **deaf** and **blind** (cf. v. 16). Now God told them to **hear . . . look,** and **see.** The **blind** and **deaf . . . servant** (v. 19) refers to Israel, not the Messiah. They *should* have been a light to the Gentiles (v. 6),

helping others come to know God. But they failed. Though they saw and heard certain events they disregarded them (cf. 43:8; 48:8).

42:21-22. The Mosaic **Law** stipulated that if Israelites lived according to God's righteous standards He would bless them. In that sense the Law was **great and glorious.** Living by it would reveal to others **His righteousness. But** if Israel did not keep His stipulations they would be driven out of the land (Deut. 28:49-53). Their cities would be **looted** (cf. Isa. 42:24) and the people put **in prisons** (in exile). **No one** could **rescue them** except of course the Lord.

42:23-25. Why would Israel be plundered? (cf. v. 22) Was it because **the LORD** could not protect them? No, it was because the Lord was punishing them for disobeying the **Law** (cf. v. 21). Though God in His **anger** against their sin would destroy Jerusalem **in flames** and lead them into captivity, they still would be blind to their sin and His ways (cf. vv. 19-20). That is why the Lord would send His Servant to open their eyes.

4. A PROMISE TO REGATHER THE UNWORTHY SERVANT (43:1–44:5)

Judah's exile was pictured as drawing to a close (40:2) for the Lord was raising up a leader who would release them (41:2-4, 25). God would also raise up a Servant, the Messiah, to give them spiritual release (42:1-17). However, the nation was still in spiritual captivity (42:18-25). Now the Lord exhorted the nation not to fear (43:1-7) for their condition would show the world that He is truly the only God (43:8-13). He would restore them from Babylon, bringing them back home in a new "Exodus" (43:14-28). Therefore He said again they were not to fear (44:1-5).

a. Israel exhorted not to fear (43:1-7)

43:1-2. Jacob (also called **Israel;** see comments on 40:27) need have no **fear** in her captivity because God had **created** (cf. v. 7) and **formed** her (cf. vv. 7, 21; 44:2, 24) and had **redeemed** her from bondage in Egypt. "Redeemed" translates *gā'al,* "to buy out of slavery" (cf. comments on "Redeemer" in 41:14 and note "redeemed" in 44:22-23; 48:20; 52:9; 63:9). Reference to this Exodus was fitting in view of what Isaiah wrote in

43:14-28 about a new "Exodus" in which God would bring the people back to their homeland from Babylon. To be **called** (cf. 48:12) **by name** points up Israel's special relationship with the LORD as His covenant people. This is similar to a shepherd calling his sheep by name in his personal care for them. Because of God's past work in creating, redeeming, and caring for Israel, He would continue to protect her. Therefore in difficult times, pictured as floodwaters and **fire,** Israel should not give up and fear, for God would **be with** her and protect her.

43:3-4. A second reason Israel need not fear is that God loves her. This special love is not because of something the nation did or some quality she possesses. It is because of His choosing. As a **ransom** or reward for releasing the Jewish captives, Persia was enabled by God to conquer **Egypt . . . Cush** (modern-day southern Egypt, all of Sudan, and northern Ethiopia), and **Seba,** possibly the same as Sheba in southern Arabia (cf. 60:6; Job 6:19; 1 Kings 10:1-13) where the Sabeans lived (cf. Job 1:15; Isa. 45:14; Ezek. 23:42; Joel 3:8). In contrast with non-Israelites (represented by these three nations), Israel is **precious** and **honored** because of God's **love.**

43:5-7. A third reason Israel need not fear (**do not be afraid;** cf. 41:10, 14; 44:2, 8; 54:4) is that God, who was **with** them (cf. 41:10), promised to **bring** them back to their land. Though Isaiah was referring primarily to the restoration from Babylon (2 Chron 36:22-23; Ezra 1:1-4), he was also speaking of a wider regathering. At the second coming of Christ Israel will be regathered to her land (Matt. 24:31) from around the world —**from the east . . . west** (Isa. 43:5), **north,** and **south** (v. 6), and even from **the ends of the earth** (see comments on 5:26). These regathered ones who will be **called by** God's **name** and are those He **created** (cf. 43:1) and **formed** (cf. vv. 1, 21; 44:2, 24) **for** His **glory** (cf. 44:23); they will display His attributes.

b. Israel to be a witness to the world (43:8-13)

43:8-10. God invited Israel, still spiritually **blind** and **deaf** (cf. 42:20; 48:8), to be brought before **the nations.** God challenged the nations to **bring . . . witnesses to** try **to prove** that they could predict

the future (cf. 41:21-23). Then He said that the Israelites, as His **witnesses** (cf. 43:12; 44:8) and His chosen servant (cf. 41:8-9), demonstrate that **He** is the only God (43:10). He existed **before** any **god** was made, and He will continue to exist long **after** the last idol perishes.

43:11-13. The Lord's deliverance of Israel also shows that He is the true God. He is her only **Savior** and no one can oppose His plans. "Savior" is another title of God that Isaiah used frequently (cf. 17:10; 43:3; 45:15, 21; 49:26; 60:16; 62:11; 63:8). God's revealing His plans and saving His people could not be duplicated by any **foreign god.** Israel's existence **witnesses** to His sovereignty and eternity. No one can **reverse** what **God** puts into action or thwart His plans (cf. Job 42:2).

c. Israel promised deliverance from Babylon (43:14-21)

43:14-15. Verses 14 and 16 are introduced by the statement, **This is what the LORD says,** a statement used frequently by Isaiah in the second major division of his book (43:14, 16; 44:2, 6, 24; 45:1, 11, 14; 48:17; 49:7-8; 50:1; 52:4; 56:1, 4; 65:8, 13; 66:1, 12) to stress the divine authority behind his words. The Lord calls Himself Israel's **Redeemer** (cf. comments on 41:14), **the Holy One of Israel** (cf. comments on 1:4), **the LORD,** the **Holy One, Israel's Creator** and **King** (cf. comments on 33:17). He said He would change **the Babylonians** from conquerors to the conquered. Babylon's **ships** may have been the trading vessels she used on the Euphrates River and the Persian Gulf.

43:16-21. God, who in the first Exodus brought Israel out of Egypt and drowned the Egyptian **army,** would do an even greater thing. Therefore forgetting **the past** (v. 18), Israel should realize God would do **a new** work. In this new "Exodus," the return from the Exile, the Jews would be going through desolate **desert** land where God would **provide water** and **streams** in abundance (cf. 35:6-7; 41:18; 44:3-4). Therefore His **Chosen** People (cf. comments on 41:8-9), whom He created (**formed;** cf. 43:21; 44:2, 24), would **praise** Him (cf. 42:10-13). Still a third and more glorious "Exodus" will take place when the Messiah returns to regather His people (cf. 43:5-6) and establish His millennial reign on earth.

d. Israel's deliverance to be by God's grace (43:22-28)

43:22-25. The future "Exodus" from Babylon would not come as the result of Israel's religious acts, including prayers, **offerings . . . sacrifices . . . incense,** or **calamus** (possibly sweet cane; cf. Song 4:14; Jer. 6:20; Ezek. 27:19). They had not bothered (**wearied,** Isa. 43:22) themselves in the sacrificial system, **but** their **sins** had wearied **God!** (cf. Mal. 2:17) Without the Jerusalem temple the exiles were obviously unable to take **sacrifices** to the altar. So with no **offerings their unforgiven sins** piled up! However, God would forgive them because of His grace, **for** His **own sake.**

43:26-28. Though the Lord would forgive Israel (v. 25), He still needed to discipline them. Suggesting that they **state** their **case** (v. 26), the Lord then stated *His* case against them. Their **first father**—either Adam (cf. Hosea 6:7) or Abraham (cf. Gen. 12:18)—had sinned as had their **spokesmen,** the prophets and priests. Therefore God would punish Israel with **disgrace . . . destruction,** and **scorn** (Isa. 43:28), which He did in the Babylonian Captivity.

e. Israel again exhorted not to fear (44:1-5)

44:1-2. Again the prophet emphasized God's choosing (see comments on 41:8-9) and forming (cf. 43:1, 7, 21; 44:24) Israel. (On the word **listen,** see comments on 46:3.) Since God promised to **help** her, she need **not be afraid** (cf. 41:10, 14; 43:5; 44:8; 54:4). (On Jacob as God's **servant** see comments on 41:8.) **Jeshurun,** meaning "the upright one," is a poetic synonym for Israel, used elsewhere only in Deuteronomy 32:15; 33:5, 26.

44:3-5. The Lord will revive Israel physically and spiritually. He will **pour water on the . . . land,** making it well watered (cf. 35:6-7; 41:18; 43:19-20) and He **will pour** His Holy **Spirit** (cf. 32:15) **on** their **descendants.** This outpouring of the Spirit will occur when the people have returned in belief to the land (cf. Ezek. 36:24, 27; Joel 2:25-29) just after the Messiah's second coming to establish the Millennium. Redeemed **Israel** will prosper numerically **like grass** and **poplar trees,** and they will want to be known as righteous individuals (Isa. 44:5), un-

ashamed of Him and their nation.

5. THE LORD'S UNIQUENESS AS THE ONLY GOD (44:6–45:25)

This section emphasizes that the Lord is the only God and that therefore idol-worship is illogical and absurd. His uniqueness and sovereignty are (a) contrasted with the idols (44:6-23), (b) revealed by His prophesying the coming of Cyrus (44:24–45:8), (c) shown by His having created everything (45:9-13), and (d) demonstrated by the fact that eventually Gentiles will proclaim Him to be the Lord (45:14-25). Addressed primarily to Gentiles, 44:6–45:25 would also have encouraged the covenant people, especially those in captivity, as they would read that their captors would someday acknowledge the true God of Israel.

a. God's sovereignty over nonexistent idols (44:6-23)

(1) The uniqueness of God. **44:6-8.** Several titles stress God's sovereignty: **Israel's King** (cf. 43:15), **Redeemer** (cf. 43:14; see comments on 41:14), **the LORD Almighty** God, and **the First** and **the Last** (i.e., the eternal One; cf. 48:12; Rev. 1:17; 2:8; 22:13). The Lord argued for His uniqueness (**apart from Me there is no God;** cf. Isa. 43:11; 44:6; 46:9) by challenging anyone to tell of the past and the future (44:7; cf. 41:22-23). Since His knowledge of the future (from **long ago**) proves His uniqueness, His people should **not be afraid** (cf. 41:10, 14; 43:5; 44:2; 54:4). They themselves are **witnesses** (cf. 43:10, 12) to His uniqueness, strength, and stability (**Rock;** cf. 17:10; 26:4; 30:29).

(2) The unprofitableness of idols. **44:9.** Idol-worship does **nothing** for those who practice it; it only shows them up as being spiritually **blind** and **ignorant.** Pagans view their worship of idols as meritorious, but it will ultimately bring them **shame** (cf. v. 11; 42:17; 45:16).

(3) The weakness of idol-makers. **44:10-14.** People who make idols **will** experience **shame** (cf. v. 9) and disrepute. The fact that **craftsmen are nothing but men** (cf. 40:19) epitomizes the foolishness of idol-worship. A **blacksmith** who **gets hungry** while making **an idol** from metal, and a **carpenter** who has to **outline** his idol on wood, do not inspire confidence in their idols. The gods themselves have

no life for they are made from metals or from **trees** which ironically the true God **made**.

(4) The material nature of idols. **44:15-20.** From the same piece of **wood** a workman **makes an idol** and **bakes bread.** What folly to bow down to wood, part of which is used to cook one's food and to keep **himself . . . warm!** People who pray that an **idol**—mere wood— would **save** them (v. 17) are ignorant and have no spiritual sight or comprehension (v. 18; cf. 6:10). Having **their eyes . . . plastered over** may refer to a religious rite in which mud was applied to worshipers' eyes. Idolaters do not **think** of the incongruity of using part of a piece of wood **for fuel** for baking and roasting and making an idol (sarcastically called by Isaiah **a detestable thing**) **from what is left.** To worship wood is to feed on ashes (cf. Ps. 102:9), that is, to trust in something totally worthless, something that deceives.

(5) The joy of the Lord's redeemed. **44:21-23.** The contrast between **Israel** and deluded people who make and worship idols (vv. 9-20) is striking. Believers in Israel were redeemed but idol-makers were deceived. Israel was to **remember** that God can foretell the future (vv. 6-8) and that idols are really nothing (vv. 9-20). Therefore she should worship the Lord who has forgiven her sins (cf. 43:25) and **redeemed** her. Some, however, think **these things** refer to what follows and that Israel was to remember she had been redeemed. In either case the nation was to **sing.** In fact all nature is personified as being asked to sing (cf. the **mountains** in 49:13) about Him who **redeemed Jacob** and who **displays His glory in Israel** (cf. 43:7). In contrast with the other nations' spiritual darkness, Israel will live in the light of God's glory.

b. God's prophecies about Cyrus (44:24–45:8)

The fact that God predicted more than 150 years in advance that a man named Cyrus would release the Jewish exiles points to God's uniqueness. To approach the Bible with an antisupernaturalistic bias and say that the references to Cyrus were added later, *after* he released the captives, causes the passage, as stated earlier, to lose its emphasis on God's uniqueness in predicting the

future. This would mean that God is no different from idols—the very point Isaiah is disproving!

44:24-28. The LORD, Israel's **Redeemer** (see comments on 43:14), **who formed** her (cf. 43:1, 7, 21; 44:2), is the Creator of **all things** including **the heavens** and **the earth** (cf. 42:5; 45:12, 18; 48:13; 51:13, 16) and the One who makes **false prophets . . . diviners,** and supposedly **wise** people look foolish. Those who said God could not release His people from Babylon would be proved false when God's **predictions** were fulfilled. Through the prophets, **His messengers,** He said **Jerusalem** would again have people living in it. **Cyrus** would allow the exiles to go back and rebuild their capital city **Jerusalem** (cf. 45:13) and **the temple.** In 586 B.C. Nebuchadnezzar and his forces broke through Jerusalem's walls, burned the houses and the temple, and carried many captives into exile. Cyrus, founder of the Persian Empire, first came to the throne of Anshan in Eastern Elam in 559. In 549 he conquered the Medes and became the ruler of the combined Persian and Median Empire. In 539 he conquered Babylon (Dan. 5:30) and the very next year issued a decree that the Jews could return to Jerusalem and rebuild the temple (2 Chron. 36:22-23; Ezra 1:1-4). In doing this Cyrus was serving God's purposes as if he were God's **shepherd.** Those returnees built the temple, completing it in 515 B.C., and years later (in 444 B.C.) Nehemiah went to Jerusalem to rebuild the city walls (see comments on Neh. 1–2; Dan. 9:25).

45:1-4. Besides issuing a decree permitting the captives to return home, **Cyrus** also avenged God's wrath on the **nations.** Amazingly the Lord called Cyrus **His anointed.** The word "anointed" referred to the relationship Israel's first two kings, Saul and David, had with God (1 Sam. 10:1; 16:6). Since Israel in exile had no king, Cyrus functioned in a sense as her king (the anointed one) to bring about blessing. Like the Messiah (lit., "the Anointed One") who would come after him, Cyrus would have a twofold mission: to free the people, and to bring God's judgment on unbelievers.

Cyrus would easily conquer other nations (Isa. 45:1b), with God's help (v. 2), and would receive wealth from the nations he overcame (v. 3). This he did in conquering Lydia and Babylon. All this would be **for the sake of Jacob,** God's **Chosen** People (see comments on 41:8-9). And even though Cyrus would enjoy a special relationship with God (God called him **by name;** cf. 43:1) and was honored by God, he still was not a believer for he did **not acknowledge** the Lord as the true God.

45:5-7. Again the uniqueness of **God** is stressed. The fact that **there is no other** is stated in verses 5-6, 14, 18, 21-22 (also see 43:11; 44:6; 46:9). In Cyrus' day the Lord was not universally acknowledged, but eventually He will be (cf. Phil. 2:10-11). People will realize that all that happens—**light** (life), **darkness** (death), **prosperity,** and **disaster** (not "evil" as in the KJV; cf. Amos 3:6)—comes from God. As the sovereign LORD of the universe He can **do** everything.

45:8. When the millennial kingdom is established on the earth the **heavens,** figuratively speaking, will **rain down righteousness** (God's standards will be followed). And **salvation,** like a great harvest, will **spring up.** That is, people everywhere will know **the LORD** (cf. v. 6; 11:9; Hab. 2:14).

c. God's sovereignty in Creation (45:9-13)

45:9-13. The Lord can work sovereignly over individuals on **the earth** because He **created** it. When someone who is created voices disapproval of the Creator's work he risks receiving a pronouncement of impending doom (**woe,** vv. 9-10; cf. comments on 3:9) from **the LORD. A potsherd,** a broken, discarded piece of pottery, has no right to question **the potter.** Nor does a child have the right to question why his parents **brought** him into the world. In the same way **Israel** has no right to question God her **Maker** (45:9, 11), the world's Creator (v. 12), in His plans to **raise up Cyrus** (v. 13). Cyrus' task was again stated: to allow freed **exiles** to rebuild God's **city,** Jerusalem (cf. 44:28).

d. Gentile submission to God (45:14-19)

45:14-17. In the Millennium Gentiles will realize that Israel's **God is** the only God. People from **Egypt** and **Cush** and the **Sabeans** (see comments on 43:3) will be subservient to **Israel** and will admit that **there is no other god** (cf. 45:6, 18, 21-22; also note Zech. 14:16-19; Mal. 1:11).

Though at times it seems as if the Lord is hiding, He really is the **Savior of Israel** (see comments on Isa. 43:11). Whereas people who persist in idol-worship will be ashamed (cf. 42:17; 44:9, 11; 45:24) believing Israelites **will never** be ashamed (cf. 54:4; Rom. 9:33; 10:11; 1 Peter 2:6) for they will enjoy God's salvation forever.

45:18-19. Again God's creative power (cf. 42:5; 44:24; 45:12; 48:13; 51:13, 16) is proof that what He predicted about Cyrus is true. Another proof is the very nature of God's word. He speaks only what is true. In captivity the Jews could count on the fact that the Lord would deliver them from exile by Cyrus.

e. The Lord's appeal to the Gentiles (45:20-25)

45:20-25. The Lord appealed to the Gentiles to turn from wooden **idols** and **be saved** from coming destruction. They were to note the prophecies **God** had given and to acknowledge His uniqueness as the only **God** (vv. 21-22; cf. vv. 5-6, 14, 18) and to **turn to** Him because eventually everyone will acknowledge His sovereignty (cf. v. 14; Mal. 1:1; Rom. 14:11; Phil. 2:10-11). Even so, some Gentiles will be saved, recognizing that only in Him is **righteousness** available. But many will continue to rage **against Him** (Isa. 45:24). However, **Israel,** God's covenant people, **will be** justified (**found righteous**) in the LORD, and in that they **will** rejoice (**exult**).

6. THE LORD'S SUPERIORITY OVER BABYLON (CHAPS. 46-47)

Babylon would be used by God to judge Judah, but she in turn would be destroyed by God. Her gods, mere idols, would not be able to save her from defeat (chap. 46), and Babylon would fall in spite of her sorceries and wisdom (chap. 47).

a. The Lord's superiority over Babylon's gods (chap. 46)

46:1-2. The Babylonian gods would not be able to save Babylon from being conquered. **Bel,** not to be confused with the Canaanite Baal, was another name for Marduk (cf. Jer. 50:2), god of the sun. **Nebo,** son of Marduk, was the god of learning, writing, and astronomy. Large **images** of those gods, **carried about** on Babylon's New Year's Day festival, were heavy and **burdensome**. So those idols could not help relieve the Babylonians' **burden**. In striking contrast, the God of Israel sustains and carries His people (Isa. 46:3-4).

46:3-4. God's admonition to His people to **listen** to Him is frequent in Isaiah's prophecies (44:1; 46:3, 12; 47:8; 48:1, 12, 14, 16; 51:4; 52:8; 55:2). Besides caring for and carrying His people (see comments on 46:1-2), God also sustains them throughout their lives. From the time of conception (v. 3) to **old age** (v. 4) the Lord watches over His own and rescues them from trouble.

46:5-7. Gods of **gold** and **silver** (cf. 40:19) cannot **be compared** (cf. 40:18, 25) to the true God because such gods are incapable of action. Pagans hired craftsmen **to make** heavy gods out of precious metals and then had to **carry** them to their resting places, from which they could not **move**. This is one of several times Isaiah belittled idols (cf. 40:18-20; 41:7; 44:9-20; 45:16, 20; 46:1-2). Unlike the false gods, the true God can **answer** peoples' prayers and **save** them.

46:8-11. The **rebels**, people of Babylon (cf. v. 12), were to **remember** that **God** is the only God; He is unique (v. 9; cf. 43:11; 44:6; 45:5-6, 14, 18, 21-22). Proofs of God's uniqueness include His knowledge and control of the future (cf. 45:21) and His abililty to bring Cyrus **from the east** (cf. 41:2) like a quick **bird of prey** to accomplish His plans.

46:12-13. The **stubborn-hearted** and those **far from righteousness** were the Babylonians (cf. rebels, v. 8), who would be defeated by the Persian Empire. God would bring against the unrighteous Babylonians His **righteousness,** that is, Cyrus, who would carry out God's righteous will. This would result in **salvation** for **Zion,** deliverance from exile for Jerusalem, which would mean Israel would again display God's **splendor** or glory (cf. 44:23).

b. The Lord's assurance of Babylon's fall (chap. 47)

Isaiah described Babylon's fall to the Persians in 539 B.C., more than 150 years before the event took place. The Babylonians, Judah's captors, would become captives.

47:1-3. When conquered, **Babylon** would become a humbled servant, sitting in the dust, an act depicting great mourning (cf. Jonah 3:6). The words **Virgin Daughter** personify the people of a city as a young, innocent girl (cf. Isa. 23:12; 37:22), probably meaning that the city's walls had never been breached. The people would **no** longer be **tender** and **delicate** like a virgin because of the hardships they would face. As servants of the conquerors, they would have to **grind** the **flour,** unable to worry about their clothing or modesty. Some of them would have to flee across **streams.** Many of them would be raped and abused (47:3).

47:4. This verse records the response of Israel when they would sense the relief coming to them because of Babylon's defeat. Seeing God's vengeance on their captors (v. 3b), they would praise the Lord for they would recognize that release from exile would come from God, not themselves. So they would call God their **Redeemer** (cf. comments on 43:14), **the LORD Almighty,** and **the Holy One of Israel** (cf. comments on 1:4).

47:5-7. The Lord had used Babylon to judge Judah, but that ruthless nation, like Assyria (cf. Isa. 10), had abused its power (cf. Hab. 1:6-11). So God's sentence was pronounced on Babylon: **no** longer would she be . . . **queen of kingdoms** (cf. "eternal queen" in Isa. 47:7). Babylon was considered nearly impregnable.

Babylon had been able to conquer Judah, God's **inheritance** (see comments on Deut. 4:20), only because God allowed it (Isa. 47:6). Merciless, **the Babylonians** even treated **the aged** Jewish captives harshly. Therefore God would treat everyone in Babylon harshly (v. 3b). The Babylonians never considered the possibility that they would not be in a position of power **forever** (v. 7). Babylon thought she was **the eternal queen** (cf. v. 5).

47:8-11. Babylon thought that she could never be defeated (v. 8). But the Lord said that she would lose her **children** and become **a widow. . . . on a single day,** speaking figuratively of her desolation from defeat (cf. Jerusalem as a widow, Lam. 1:1). Though Babylon thought she was unique—**I am, and there is none besides me** (Isa. 47:8, 10)—she was wrong; *God* is the One who is unique, as Isaiah had stated repeatedly (43:11; 44:6; 45:5-6, 14, 18, 21-22; 46:9).

Babylon prided herself in her sorcerers who supposedly "told the future" and cast **spells** to influence others (cf. 47:12). **Sorceries** (vv. 9, 12) translates *kešāp̄îm,* a word used in the Old Testament only here and in 2 Kings 9:22; Micah 5:12; Nahum 3:4. It suggests seeking information about the future by means of demonic forces. Such supposed **knowledge,** however, was unreliable, for the sorcerers could not foresee Babylon's forthcoming **calamity** and would not be able to **conjure it away.**

47:12-15. The Lord mockingly urged the Babylonians to **keep on** in their **spells** and **sorceries** (cf. v. 9), which the city had been involved in **since childhood** (cf. v. 15), that is, since the nation was founded. In sarcasm He suggested the **astrologers** and **stargazers . . . save** them. Astrology was common in Babylon (cf. Dan. 2:2, 4-5). But their work was worthless, **like** mere **stubble,** the dried stalks of grain that burn quickly. Those religious leaders could not **save** even **themselves,** let alone Babylon. Yet they persisted in their **error.**

7. AN EXHORTATION FOR ISRAEL (CHAP. 48)

a. An exhortation to remember God's prophecies (48:1-11)

48:1-5. The LORD reminded His people—called the **house of Jacob . . . Israel,** and **the line of Judah**—of their hypocrisy. They took **oaths,** invoking God's **name,** but they were **not** righteous. They thought that being **citizens of** Jerusalem **(the holy city;** cf. 52:1), though they were not living there, and claiming to **rely on . . . the LORD,** were adequate. Comfortable in the Babylonian Empire (and later the Persian Empire), they considered it unimportant to go back to Jerusalem. The LORD said He had prophesied what would happen (48:3), apparently referring to the coming Captivity. But knowing of the coming Exile, the people were **stubborn** (v. 4), refusing to change their ways. Again one reason God made those predictions was to point up His superiority to **idols.**

48:6-8. Israel had disregarded the previous prophecies, so God would give her **new** prophecies (v. 6), predictions that God's wrath would be delayed (cf. v. 9) and that she would be freed from captivity. Those plans were **created now,** not that God had never thought of them before, but that they would be put into effect at that time. From Deuteronomy 30:1-5, Israel knew she would be brought back to the land after captivity, and her dwelling in the land was assured by the Abrahamic Covenant (Gen. 15:18-21). But until Isaiah's prophecies were given she did not know *how* God would deliver her. This was so the people would not feel smug (Isa. 48:7b), thinking their own cunning had set them free. They actually were spiritually insensitive (v. 8; cf. 42:20; 43:8) because they were **treacherous** and rebellious. So their physical and spiritual deliverance would come not from their goodness or their own plans, but from God's grace.

48:9-11. The Lord would **delay** His **wrath,** that is, withhold it so His people could return to Judah. This would be for His **sake** primarily (vv. 9, 11; cf. 43:25). The Exile was to refine them so they would return to the land in belief. That refining, however, was **not** with **silver.** This means either that the refining was not accomplished with money, or that the process could not be compared to silver, or that unlike silver which becomes pure, the nation would not. Whatever the meaning, the Captivity was like being in a **furnace,** to test them, not destroy them. If God would go back on His word about the return, His reputation would be **defamed.**

b. An exhortation to note God's sovereignty (48:12-19)

48:12-15. Urging the nation to **listen** to Him (cf. comments on 46:3), God once again spoke of His unique position as the only God. (On **the First** and **the Last** see comments on 44:6.) Isaiah repeatedly wrote about two proofs of His uniqueness: (a) His creative power (cf. 42:5; 44:24; 45:12, 18; 51:13, 16) and (b) His ability to foretell the future, in this case, the fall of **Babylon** by means of Cyrus, God's **chosen ally** (cf. "shepherd" and "anointed," 44:28; 45:1). God **called him** and would help him **succeed.** No other god could have predicted this.

48:16. The LORD, who is speaking, said He had not been secretive about Cyrus' defeat of Babylon. Suggestions on who is speaking in the second part of verse 16, beginning with the words **And now,** include Cyrus, Israel, Isaiah, and the Messiah. Probably the Messiah,

God's Servant, is intended because of His association (as in 42:1; also note 11:1-2) **with the Spirit.** Just as Cyrus would not fail in his mission (48:15), so the Messiah-Servant, sent by God with the Holy Spirit on Him, will not fail in His mission.

48:17-19. The LORD, Israel's Redeemer (cf. comments on 41:14) and **Holy One,** had constantly been teaching and guiding **Israel** through the Law. But they **had** not **paid attention to** His **commands.** Had they done so, they would have experienced not the Exile but **peace** and **righteousness,** and none of their **children** would have been killed.

c. An exhortation to flee Babylon (48:20-21)

48:20-21. With Cyrus' edict (2 Chron. 36:22-23; Ezra 1:1-4) allowing the Jews to return home, God urged His people to **leave Babylon** quickly **(flee).** Because this return was like being **redeemed** (gā'al, "to buy out of slavery"; cf. 43:1)—this time from Babylon, not Egypt —the people could rejoice. After the Egyptian Exodus God provided water in **the deserts** and **from the rock** (cf. Ex. 17:1-7). Here too, it is implied, God would provide for them in their second "Exodus."

d. The absence of peace for the wicked (48:22)

48:22. In contrast with joy (v. 20) for those who obey the Lord **there is no peace . . . for the wicked,** either in the nation Israel or among Gentile nations. This brief statement is repeated in 57:21.

B. Restoration by the Suffering Servant (chaps. 49–57)

The previous nine-chapter section (chaps. 40–48) dealt mainly with Cyrus and his mission in the Jews' restoration. These nine chapters (49–57) deal primarily with the Servant-Messiah fulfilling His ministry of restoring the covenant people to the land just before the Millennium will begin. Neither person would fail in his mission. Because of the similarity of their missions, several of the same expressions and figures of speech are used in the two nine-chapter sections.

Chapters 49–57 may be divided into four parts: (1) The Servant, being rejected by His people, will take salvation to the Gentiles (chaps. 49–50). (2) The believing remnant will be exalted (51:1–52:12). (3) The Servant, however, will be abased and then exalted (52:13–53:12). (4) Salvation through the Servant will come to Jews and Gentiles in the Millennium (chaps. 54–57).

1. THE SERVANT TO BE REJECTED (CHAPS. 49–50)

a. The Servant's mission (49:1-13)

(1) The Servant's ministry to the Gentiles (49:1-6). **49:1-3.** God's **Servant** (vv. 3, 5-6) is the speaker in verses 1-5; God addressed Him in verse 6. Like the LORD, He called on the **islands** (see comments on 41:1) and the **nations** to **listen** (see comments on 46:3) to Him because of His special "calling" from the Lord. His **mouth** was **like a sharpened sword,** that is, it was a weapon to destroy the disobedient (cf. 1:20; also note Heb. 4:12; Rev. 1:16; 19:15). He was also likened to a sharp **arrow.** The Servant was to **display** God's **splendor** (Isa. 49:3; cf. 60:21; 61:3).

Why is the Servant here called **Israel?** This cannot refer to the nation because the Servant is to draw that nation back to God. The Messiah is called Israel because He fulfills what Israel should have done. In His person and work He epitomizes the nation.

49:4. The Servant saw little visible reward for His service. No change was evident in the nation by which the Servant could claim He had accomplished what He set out to do (cf. John 1:11). However, this did not bother Him for He trusted that in due time **God** would **reward** Him.

49:5-6. Formed . . . in the womb as God's Servant (cf. v. 1), the Messiah's commission is to restore **Jacob** and **Israel** (see comments on 40:27) to **the LORD.** With **God** as His **strength,** He would also be **a light for the Gentiles** (cf. 42:6; Luke 1:79) so that **salvation** from the Lord would extend to people in **the ends of the earth** (see comments on Isa. 5:26).

(2) The Lord's promise to the Servant. **49:7. The LORD** assured the Servant—**despised and abhorred by** His people—that He would succeed in His ministry to the Gentiles. **Kings** and **princes** will bow down to Him because He has been **chosen** by the **LORD.** In His first coming Jesus Christ was rejected by His own people (John 1:10-11), but at His

second coming all will **bow** before Him (Phil. 2:10-11).

(3) Israel's restoration. **49:8-12.** In the Millennium, here called **the time of God's favor** and **the day of salvation,** the Lord will enable the Servant **to be a covenant for the people** (cf. 42:6; i.e., to fulfill God's covenant promises to Israel; see comments on Jer. 31:31-34 on the New Covenant).

When **the land** is restored **the captives** will return to the Promised Land from various places around the world (Isa. 49:9; cf. v. 12). The land will be fertile with **pasture** (v. 9) and **water** (v. 10) and **mountains** and valleys will be changed (v. 11). As in 40:3-4, this may signify a change in the people's lives. The location of **Sinim** is uncertain, but many think it is the Aswan region of Egypt (NIV marg.).

(4) The prophet's response. **49:13.** As the prophet spoke, he called on nature, personified, to **rejoice** (on the **mountains** rejoicing see 44:23). The reason for rejoicing is that **the LORD comforts** and has **compassion** (cf. 49:10) on those who need help, including Gentiles.

b. Israel assured of the return (49:14-26)

49:14-16. In verses 14-21 the prophet recorded a dialogue between Israel and God. **Zion** (i.e., the people in Jerusalem) felt as if God had **forgotten** her (v. 14). But God replied that He certainly had **not** forgotten Israel. He could not possibly do so because He is like **a mother** to the nation. Furthermore, the nation was inscribed, as it were, on His **palms.** Therefore whenever He, figuratively speaking, lifts up His hands He sees the nation's name which reminds Him of her.

49:17-21. Judah's captors will **depart** (v. 17) and **be far away** (v. 19) and Judah's **sons** will begin to return (vv. 17-18). This will brighten up the nation as a **bride** enjoys **ornaments.** This return will be so great that the land (personified by **you** and **your,** vv. 19-21) will not be large enough for all the inhabitants, called its **children.**

But when the people returned from the Babylonian Captivity they were a comparatively small, struggling band. The return mentioned in verses 19-21 seems to be much larger and therefore probably refers to Israel's return at the beginning of the Millennium.

49:22-26. When Israel returns to the land in the future **the Gentiles** will worship before **the LORD** and will be friendly toward Israel. In fact the Gentiles will even help transport Israelites to Palestine. Gentile leaders will be subservient to Israel, which will cause her to realize that **the LORD** really is in control of the world (v. 23). It is unusual for **captives** to be **rescued,** but God will see that it is done for Israel. Israel's enemies will be destroyed, which will cause the whole world to acknowledge that **the LORD** is Israel's God and her **Savior** (cf. comments on 42:11), **Redeemer** (cf. comments on 41:14), and **the Mighty One of Jacob** (cf. 60:16).

c. Israel exhorted to walk by faith (chap. 50)

The statements about Israel's future were to evoke an ethical response. Israel was rebellious but the prophet pleaded for her to trust in the Lord, not in her own devices.

(1) The Lord's "divorce" of Zion. **50:1-3.** The LORD declared that He was temporarily "divorcing" Zion because she had rejected Him without cause. He explained to Zion's children that He temporarily **sent away** their **mother** because she sinned. In the Mosaic Law a husband could give his wife a divorce certificate detailing her fault(s) and she would be required to leave the home (Deut. 24:1). Israel's captivity was like a wife having to leave her husband **because of . . . sins.** Isaiah also pictured Israel's exile as being like sons **sold** into indentured servitude because of a great debt. Yet Israel's rejection of Him was unreasonable (Isa. 50:2). Did they think God could not **ransom** or **rescue** them? Of course He could. He is the One who can withhold rain and **dry up . . . rivers** (cf. Deut. 28:23-24).

(2) The Servant's growth by experience (50:4-9). **50:4-6.** In verses 4-9 the Servant was speaking, for He addresses God as **the Sovereign LORD** (vv. 4-5, 7, 9). As the Lord taught the Servant daily how to comfort **the weary** (v. 4), the Servant did **not** rebel against that instruction (v. 5). In fact He even gave His body to those who persecuted Him (v. 6). Jesus, before He was crucified, was beaten, mocked, and spit on (Mark 14:65; 15:16-20). In extremely difficult circumstances, more difficult than what Isaiah's original readers were facing, the Servant was obe-

dient and submissive (cf. 1 Peter 2:22-23).

50:7-9. The Servant was convinced that He will be vindicated by the **Sovereign Lord who helps** Him (vv. 7, 9). Even if it did not seem as if He were winning a battle, He was convinced that He was doing God's will. The Servant was aware that those who falsely accused Him will eventually **face** Him as their Judge and will come to nothing. Like moth-eaten garments, they will perish (cf. 51:8).

(3) The prophet's exhortation. **50:10-11.** Isaiah exhorted the Servant's followers—those who fear the LORD and obey His **Word,** but who are **in the dark** (i.e., living in difficult times when the Servant was rejected, v. 6)—to walk by faith, trusting **in the . . .** LORD. If they insist on walking by their own **light** they will suffer the fate of those who reject Him. They **will lie down in torment** (cf. Luke 16:23, 28; also note Rev. 20:13-15; 21:8). This admonition was directed to those living in Isaiah's day. But all who refuse to **trust** the Lord will suffer eternal damnation.

2. THE REMNANT TO BE EXALTED (51:1–52:12)

a. The Lord's comfort of the remnant (51:1-16)

(1) The remnant's origin in the covenant. **51:1-3.** Here the LORD is speaking to those **who pursue righteousness** (cf. Matt. 5:6) and **seek** Him. The believing remnant in Israel is to think back on their background. **The rock from which** they **were cut,** figuratively speaking, is explained in verse 2 as **Abraham** and **Sarah,** the "founders" of the nation. God **made him many,** that is, gave the patriarch many descendants as He had promised (Gen. 12:2; 15:5; 17:6; 22:17). For many years Abraham and Sarah had no children, but they believed God (Gen. 15:6). These people too are to believe Him. Though they have not yet seen the fruition of God's promises about Israel being a nation in the land (Gen. 15:18-21) they do have His sure word that God's kingdom will be established on the earth. Because of the Lord's **compassion** (cf. Isa. 49:10, 15) the land will someday be fruitful **like Eden . . . the garden of the** LORD. Because of this, **joy** (cf. 51:11) will abound among the remnant.

(2) The Lord's justice to extend over the world. **51:4-8.** God's **Law** will be known (cf. 2:3) and **justice** and **righ-**teousness (see comments on 1:21) will be established for **the nations** and **the islands** (see comments on 41:1) by His **arm** (i.e., His power; cf. 51:9 and see comments on 40:10). **The heavens** and **the earth** will pass away (**vanish like smoke** and **wear out like a garment;** cf. Heb. 1:11), **but** the Lord's work (**salvation**) and standards (**righteousness**) will continue **forever** (Isa. 51:8). Therefore, knowing this fact, the remnant with God's **Law** (v. 4) within them and eternal hope before them, should take courage and not be disheartened by their enemies' **insults** (cf. vv. 12-13; also note the **Suffering** Servant's response in 50:6). Those enemies will perish **like a** moth-eaten **garment,** a metaphor the Servant used earlier (50:9).

(3) The remnant's prayer for another "Exodus." **51:9-11.** These verses could be taken as a prayer of the righteous remnant (though some scholars say they record the prophet's words as he reflected on what would happen to that remnant). The plea is that God in His power (**arm;** cf. v. 5) would rise again (**Awake;** cf. v. 17) and save His people as He did in the Exodus (**as in the days gone by**). The question **Was it not you?** (vv. 9-10) was a way of affirming that the LORD did these things for their forefathers. (On **Rahab,** a mythical sea **monster** representing Egypt, see comments on 30:7.) When Israel escaped from Egypt the Egyptian army was drowned in **the sea.** The Israelites crossed over the Red (Reed) Sea on dry ground (Ex. 14:21-31). In the same way **the** LORD by His strength will allow Israel to **return** in a new "Exodus" to her homeland (**Zion**) with **joy** (cf. Isa. 51:3).

(4) The Lord's promise and power. **51:12-16.** The Lord now spoke to the remnant that was living in **fear** of destruction. He gave comfort reminding them that the ones they feared were only **men** (like **grass;** cf. 40:6-8) and that God is the all-powerful Creator (cf. 42:5; 44:24; 45:12, 18; 48:13; 51:16). The imprisoned remnant would soon be freed to return to the Promised Land in another "Exodus" (v. 14) because the LORD, the Creator God (vv. 15-16) is **their** God. He is intimate with them and protects them with His **hand** because they belong to Him in a unique relationship as His people (cf. Hosea 2:1, 23).

b. The Lord's comfort of Jerusalem (51:17–52:10)

(1) Jerusalem to be freed. (51:17–52:6). **51:17-23.** The remnant (or the prophet) had asked God to awaken (be alert; cf. v. 9) and do something. Now God asked **Jerusalem** to be **awake** (cf. 52:1) because He is doing something—their calamity was coming to an end. In their exile the Jerusalemites had **drunk** (i.e., experienced; cf v. 21) God's wrath fully—all the way to the bottom of **the cup** (cf. v. 22). In the terrible destruction of Jerusalem many young men (**sons**) had died (v. 18). **Ruin . . . destruction, famine, and sword** spoke of the awful plight of the city (v. 19). The destruction was so terrible that the city experienced **double** calamities. Young men, objects of God's **wrath,** had been killed (cf. v. 20) in Jerusalem's streets.

However, the Lord pronounced that the time of judgment was over (v. 22). Now the judgment, again pictured as a **cup** to be **drunk,** would be given to her **tormentors** who had walked on the dead bodies in Jerusalem (v. 23). The Babylonians, who had destroyed Jerusalem, would in turn suffer God's wrath.

52:1-6. **Jerusalem** was to **awake** not only because her exile was almost ended (v. 1) but also because she would be freshly adorned with new clothes, that is, she would be rebuilt. Jerusalem's pagan conquerors—**the uncircumcised and defiled**—would never again invade and pollute **the holy city** (cf. 48:2). This no doubt refers to the time when the Messiah will establish God's kingdom on earth, for only then will pagans never again trample the city. To **shake off . . . dust** means to stop mourning (dust on one's head was a sign of mourning, Job 2:12). **Jerusalem** will be freed from her **chains,** never again to be enslaved. She had been **sold** because of her sins (cf. Isa. 50:1) but now she would be **redeemed** (*gā'al*, "to purchase out of slavery"). However, God did not *have* to buy them. He will graciously bring them back to Him and they will pay **nothing.**

Then God briefly reviewed the history of the nation in slavery. They had been slaves in **Egypt** and more recently **Assyria** had conquered the Northern Kingdom and also exacted tribute from Judah (52:4). Now another power, Babylon, would take **away** Judah and **mock**

them (v. 5) and blaspheme God. Through all this the Lord's power to bring them back each time should show the people that He is the only unique God. Eventually when they return in belief they will **know** Him.

(2) The Lord to return to Zion. **52:7-8.** The prophet exulted in the **good news** to be proclaimed when the time of blessing (spoken of in 51:17–52:6) will begin. Though Israel experienced great joy at the return from Babylon in 536 b.c., the joy Isaiah wrote about in 52:7-8 will be when Israel's Messiah **returns to Zion** to reign. His reign will be one of **peace.**

(3) The remnant to be joyful. **52:9-10.** When the LORD returns, the righteous remnant will sing joyfully because He will have **comforted** and **redeemed** His **people.** This work of grace on their behalf will show **all the nations** His power (**arm;** see comments on 40:10) and **the salvation** He provides. (On **the ends of the earth** see comments on 5:26.)

c. The Lord's exhortation to return (52:11-12)

52:11-12. As in the Exodus out of Egypt and the Exodus away from Babylon, so in Israel's yet-future return, the righteous remnant is exhorted to get away from the evil places where they will be living: **Depart, depart. . . . come out.** However, there will be a difference: they **will not** have to **leave in haste** (cf. 48:20). Since **the** LORD will be with them and will protect them they need have no fear.

3. THE SERVANT TO BE EXALTED (52:13–53:12)

This is perhaps the best-known section in the Book of Isaiah. Several parts of this passage are quoted in the New Testament: Isaiah 52:15 in Romans 15:21; Isaiah 53:1 in John 12:38 and Romans 10:16; Isaiah 53:4 in Matthew 8:17; Isaiah 53:7-8 in Acts 8:32-33; Isaiah 53:9 in 1 Peter 2:22; and Isaiah 53:12 in Luke 22:37.

Most of this vivid passage concerns the suffering and rejection of the Servant, but the main point (in Isa. 52:13; 53:11-12) is that His suffering will lead to exaltation and glory. True, the suffering is important, but His glory, which will be revealed, is equally important for it will show that the Servant did the will of God voluntarily.

The Servant was rejected (chaps.

49–50), and then the remnant was exalted (51:1–52:12). Now the Servant is to be exalted (52:13–53:12).

a. The reaction of the nations (52:13-15)

52:13. Two important points are made in this verse: the **Servant will act wisely,** doing what the Lord wants Him to do, and He **will be . . . highly exalted.** His being **lifted up** refers not to the kind of death He died on the cross, but to His being exalted at God's right hand (Phil. 2:9; Col. 3:1; Heb. 1:3; 8:1; 10:12; 12:2; 1 Peter 3:22).

52:14. **Many** will be **appalled** (this could also be trans. "awestruck or astonished") **at** the Servant. But who are the "many"? They are probably the people in "many nations" and their "kings" (v. 15). By human standards Jesus was not attractive when He was on the earth (53:3). But when people see Him at His second coming those who did not consider Him important will be absolutely astounded. They will see Him from a new perspective.

52:15. The Servant will **sprinkle** people in **many nations.** "Sprinkle" is associated with cleansing by the priest under the Mosaic Law (Lev. 4:6; 8:11; 14:7). This Servant, whom many have not considered important at all, will actually provide the most important thing for nations and their **kings,** namely, cleansing from sin (cf. John 1:29; Heb. 10:14). That is why they **will shut their mouths.** They will be appalled that they had miscalculated the situation so badly. Realizing their great mistake, they will have nothing to say. Eventually, when they see Him exalted in His Second Advent, **they will** finally **understand** and **see** clearly.

b. The report of the death of the Servant (53:1-12)

This report on the death of the Servant will be given by enlightened Israel after they realize the significance of His death on their behalf. Like the nations, they badly miscalculated the Servant's importance to them.

(1) Israel's confession regarding her rejection of the Servant (53:1-3). Isaiah wrote that Israel will confess that she did not value the Servant. She would reject Him because He was considered an ordinary person.

53:1. The Jewish remnant will lament the fact that so few people will believe their **message** about the Servant, and that so few will acknowledge their message as coming from God and His strength (**arm;** see comments on 40:10).

53:2. Though lamenting the fact that few people will believe (v. 1), the remnant will realize that **nothing** about the Servant's **appearance** would automatically attract a large following (cf. v. 3). He **grew . . . before** God as **a tender shoot** (i.e., coming from David's line; cf. 11:1), and as **a root out of dry ground,** that is, from an arid area (spiritually speaking) where one would not expect a large plant to grow. In His appearance He did not look like a royal person (in **beauty** and **majesty**). The remnant was not excusing people for rejecting the Servant; it was merely explaining why the nation rejected Him.

53:3. The nation Israel **despised and rejected** the Servant who experienced **sorrows** (mak'ōḇ, "anguish or grief," also used in v. 4) **and . . . suffering** (ḥŏlî, see comments on "infirmities" in v. 4). He was the kind of individual people do not normally want to look at; they were repulsed by Him. For these reasons the nation did **not** esteem **Him;** they did not think He was important. Yet He was and is the most important Person in the world, for He is the Servant of the Lord.

(2) Israel's realization about the Servant's substitutionary death (53:4-6).
53:4. Though not realizing it at the time, the nation will realize that the Servant bore the consequences of their sin. His taking **our infirmities and . . . sorrows** (mak'ōḇ, see comments on v. 3) speaks of the consequences of sin. The verb **took up,** rendered "bore" in verse 12, translates nāśā', "to carry." His bearing "infirmities" (ḥŏlî, lit., "sickness," the same word trans. "suffering" in v. 3) refers to illnesses of the soul. His healing many people's physical illnesses (though not all of them) in His earthly ministry anticipated His greater work on the Cross. Though He does heal physical ailments today (though not all of them) His greater work is healing souls, giving salvation from sin. That this is the subject of Isaiah 53 is clear from the words "transgressions" (v. 5), "iniquities" (vv. 5, 11), "iniquity" (v. 6), "transgressions" (v. 8), "wicked" (v. 9), "transgressors" (v. 12

[twice]), and "sin" (v. 12). The Servant vicariously took on Himself all the sins (and spiritual anguish caused by sin) of the nation (and the whole world) and **carried** (*sābal*, "to carry as a burden"; cf. 46:4, 7) them on Himself (cf. 1 Peter 2:24; 3:18). When Jesus was crucified, Israel thought His hardships (being **stricken . . . smitten,** and **afflicted;** cf. Isa. 53:7) were deserved for His supposedly having blasphemed God. Actually He was bearing the judgment that *their* sin required.

53:5. Pierced . . . crushed . . . punishment . . . wounds are words that describe what the remnant will note about the Servant's condition on their behalf and because of their **transgressions** (*peša'*, "rebellion"; cf. v. 8; 1:2) and **iniquities.** As a result those who believe in Him have inner **peace** rather than inner anguish or grief (see comments on "infirmities" in 53:4) and **are healed** spiritually. Ironically His wounds, inflicted by the soldiers' scourging and which were followed by His death, are the means of healing believers' spiritual wounds in salvation. Jesus' physical agony in the Crucifixion was great and intense. But His obedience to the Father was what counted (cf. Phil. 2:8). His death satisfied the wrath of God against sin and allows Him to "overlook" the sins of the nation (and of others who believe) because they have been paid for by the Servant's substitutionary death.

53:6. The redeemed remnant (and others) will acknowledge that they were guilty and that the Lord made the Servant the object of His wrath in order to take away their guilt. **Sheep** tend to travel together, so if the leading sheep turns aside from the path for grass or some other purpose, usually all the sheep do so. They tend to follow the lead sheep which is often dangerous. Similarly all Israel had turned aside (cf. 1 Peter 2:25) from following the Lord, from keeping His commandments. The essence of sin is going one's **own** way, rather than God's way. That **iniquity** had to be punished, so **the LORD . . . laid** the punishment for that iniquity (cf. Isa. 53:11) not on the "sheep" (Israel and other sinners) that deserved it, but on the Servant who died in their place.

(3) Israel's account about the Servant's death (53:7-9). The Servant died willingly (v. 7) and for others' transgressions (v. 8), even though He is righteous (v. 9).

53:7. As noted, the tendency of sheep is to follow others (v. 6), even to their destruction. In verse 7 the quiet, gentle nature of sheep is stressed. Seeing many **sheep** sheared for their wool or killed as sacrifices, Israelites were well aware of the submissive nature of sheep. Jesus, as the **Lamb** of God (John 1:29), quietly submitted to His death. He did not try to stop those who opposed Him; He remained **silent** rather than defend Himself (Matt. 26:63a; 27:14; 1 Peter 2:23). He was willingly **led** to death because He knew it would benefit those who would believe.

53:8. After His **oppression** (being arrested and bound, John 18:12, 24) **and judgment** (sentenced to die, John 19:16) Jesus was led to His death. He died not because of any sins of His own (for He, the Son of God, was sinless, 2 Cor. 5:21; Heb. 4:15; 1 John 3:5) but because of **(for) the** sins (**transgression,** *peša'*; cf. Isa. 53:5) of others. To be **taken away** means to be **taken** to death. It is parallel to being **cut off from the land of the living,** an obvious reference to death, and **stricken.** The words **and who can speak of His descendants?** mean He was cut off in the prime of life and left no descendants. Those words, however, could also be translated, "and who of His generation considered" (cf. NIV marg.) meaning that few of those who lived then considered His death important. Some verbs in this verse ("was cut off, was stricken"), like those in verse 4 ("smitten, afflicted") and verse 5 ("was crushed"), indicate by their passive voice that these actions were done to Him by God the Father (cf. v. 10; 2 Cor. 5:21, "God made Him . . . to be sin for us").

53:9. The soldiers who crucified Jesus apparently intended to bury Him **with the wicked** like the two criminals (John 19:31). However, He was buried **with the rich,** in the **grave** of a rich man named Joseph (Matt. 27:57-60).

(4) The Lord's promise about the blessing of the Servant (53:10-12). **53:10.** The suffering and death of the Servant was clearly **the LORD's will.** In that sense He was "slain from the Creation of the world" (Rev. 13:8). The statement, **the LORD made the Servant's life a**

guilt offering, does not mean that Jesus' *life* satisfied the wrath of God but that His life which culminated in His *death* was the sacrifice for sins. As indicated in Isaiah 53:7-8 He had to die to satisfy the righteous demands of God. The word for "guilt offering" is *'āšām,* used in Leviticus 5:15; 6:5; 19:21 and elsewhere of an offering to atone for sin.

His death and burial appeared to end His existence (He was "cut off," Isa. 53:8), but in actuality because of His resurrection Jesus **will see His offspring** (those who by believing in Him become children of God, John 1:12) **and He will prolong His days** (live on forever as the Son of God). He will be blessed (**prosper;** cf. Isa. 53:12a) because of His obedience to **the will** (plan) **of the LORD.**

53:11. His **suffering,** which included His death, led to **life** (His resurrection). **Satisfied** that His substitutionary work was completed ("It is finished," John 19:30), He now can **justify** (declare righteous those who believe; see comments on Rom. 1:17; 3:24) **many** (cf. Isa. 53:12). **By His knowledge** could be translated "by knowledge of Him" as in the NIV margin. **He** bore the punishment (cf. vv. 4, 6), for **their iniquities** (cf. v. 6), so that many people would not have to die. Because He died, they live.

53:12. Having willingly followed God's plan, the Servant is exalted (cf. 52:13). To have **a portion** and **divide the spoils** pictures a general, after winning a battle, sharing goods taken from the enemy (cf. Ps. 68:18; Eph. 4:7-8). Because He **was numbered with the transgressors,** that is, was considered a sinner (cf. Matt. 27:38) and **bore the sin** (cf. Isa. 53:6) **of many,** that is, everyone, He is exalted and allows believers to share in the benefits of that exaltation. And because He is alive (cf. v. 10), He now intercedes (prays; cf. Rom. 8:34; Heb. 7:25) **for . . . transgressors** (related to the word *pešaʿ,* "transgression[s]," in Isa. 53:5, 8).

This great passage gives a tremendously complete picture of what the death of Jesus Christ accomplished on behalf of Israel (John 11:49-51) and the whole world (1 John 2:2). His death satisfied God's righteous demands for judgment against sin, thus opening the way for everyone to come to God in faith for salvation from sin.

4. SALVATION TO COME FROM THE SERVANT (CHAPS. 54–57)

These chapters speak of the great salvation which will come to Israel (chap. 54) and proselytes (55:1–56:8) on the basis of the work of the Servant, and of the condemnation which will come on the wicked (56:9–57:21). Ultimately the Servant will establish the millennial kingdom. Unlike Israel, He will not fail in His mission.

a. Salvation for Israel (chap. 54)

(1) Israel's numerical growth. **54:1-3.** In Israel a **barren woman** was disgraced, for children aided in family chores and helped the parents in their old age. Fertility on every level was a sign of God's blessing. For example, when Hannah was not able to have children she was devastated, but when the Lord allowed her to have a son she sang for joy (1 Sam. 1:1–2:10). Israel was like a woman who had no children and was therefore in a continual state of mourning. But by God's sovereignty and grace He will enable her to have many **children.** So she will break **into song** and **shout for joy.** Jerusalem, once desolate and mourning (Lam. 1:1-5), will be revitalized and teeming with people. Also like a nomad who has so many children he has to **enlarge** his **tent** to accommodate them all, Israel's **descendants will** increase and even **settle in the cities** of foreign **nations** because there will not be enough room for them in their homeland.

(2) Israel's regathering. **54:4-8.** The LORD will regather Israel the way a man would take back his **wife.** The nation need have no **fear** (cf. 41:10, 14; 43:5; 44:2, 8) of **disgrace,** for she will no longer be desolate and helpless like a widow. **God,** like a **husband** (cf. Jer. 3:14; 31:32; Hosea 2:16), will take **back** Israel, His **wife.** He is **the LORD Almighty . . . the Holy One of Israel,** her **Redeemer** (cf. Isa. 54:8; see comments on 41:14), and in His uniqueness He is **the God of all the earth,** that is, its Creator and Sustainer. The Lord had **deserted** His people for a short while (**a brief moment**). Though not stated here, Isaiah had given the reason for it several times: because of the nation's sins (cf. 50:1) and God's commitment to His word. But because of His **compassion** (54:7) and **kindness** (*ḥeseḏ,*

"loyal love," v. 8, trans. "unfailing love" in v. 10), He will restore the nation to Himself. The short **moment** during which God **hid** His face (i.e., abandoned Israel because of His **anger** against her sin) contrasts with the **everlasting** nature of His covenant loyalty.

(3) Israel's security. **54:9-10.** After the Flood, in which God executed His anger against the world's depravity, He promised **never again** to devastate **the earth** in the same way (Gen. 9:11). Similarly God promised that the day is coming when He will **never . . . rebuke** Israel **again.** Statements like this show that Isaiah was speaking of the millennial kingdom rather than the return from the Babylonian Captivity, for the nation has suffered God's anger many times since the postexilic return. Even if the world could be punished again as in the Flood, God's **love** (ḥeseḏ; cf. v. 8) and **compassion** will never cease. The **covenant of peace** (also mentioned in Ezek. 34:25; 37:26) refers to this promise which God had just made. God will give His people lasting peace (cf. Isa. 9:7; 32:17-18; 54:13; 55:12; 66:12; Jer. 30:10; 33:6, 9; 46:27).

(4) Israel's peaceful future (54:11-17). **54:11-12.** Jerusalem, the **afflicted city,** had been through many troubles, called **storms,** and no one had **comforted** her (cf. Lam. 1:2, 9, 15-17, 21). However, the Lord will **build** up the city **with stones** made of **precious** gems, symbolic of His care and esteem for the value of the city.

54:13-14. Israelites always considered the training of their children a high priority. Many wanted them to be true to the Lord and not guided by the pagan world around them. In the Millennium, the children **will be taught by the Lord** Himself and will enjoy His **peace** (cf. comments on v. 10). **Righteousness** will prevail (cf. 33:5; 46:13; 58:8; 62:1-2) and Jerusalemites will no longer **fear** for the Lord will protect her from **tyranny.**

54:15-17. In the millennial kingdom no nation will be allowed to defeat Israel because the Lord has so decreed. Nations rise and fall on the basis of His word. In the past He allowed **the destroyer** (Babylon) to overcome His people, but this will never again occur. Peace and safety are **the heritage** of those who trust in **the Lord.**

b. Salvation for the Gentiles (chap. 55)

(1) An invitation to come to the Lord. **55:1-2.** God invites people in need to **come** (this word occurs four times in v. 1) to Him. By coming they indicate that they are trusting in and relying on Him for salvation and are agreeing to obey His commandments. The blessings God gives them are available **without cost.** Salvation is a free gift of God, whether it refers to spiritual redemption or physical deliverance. Probably both are intended here. The Lord asked the people how they could be interested in other things besides Himself as He is the only One who can bring genuine satisfaction. Throughout all history people have tried to find satisfaction through many things other than God.

(2) An everlasting covenant. **55:3.** By coming to the Lord people will have life and the benefits of God's **everlasting covenant** with **David** (2 Sam. 7:11b-16) in which the Lord **promised** that David's line would continue forever. **Kindnesses** renders the word ḥeseḏ (here in the pl.), God's covenantal "loyal love," which relates to His loyal covenant with David (see ḥeseḏ, "love," in 2 Sam. 7:15). Some interpreters say the "everlasting covenant" refers to the New Covenant (Jer. 32:40; Heb. 13:20). That is possible but the reference to David points to the Davidic Covenant, which also is said to last forever (2 Sam. 7:16). Just as God promised to keep His good hand on David, so He assured those who come to Him that He will never remove His good hand (His blessings) from them. He will always be with them and consider them His people.

(3) Nations to be under Messiah's leadership. **55:4-5.** The word **Him** refers not to Israel, but to the Messiah (David's "Son"; cf. Matt. 1:1) for He will be the world's **Leader and Commander.** The word **you** (Isa. 55:5) probably refers to Israel, to whom many nations will go to worship **the Lord.** They will recognize the Lord's **splendor** ("glory"; cf. 35:2; 46:13; 49:3; 60:9, 21; 61:3; 62:3).

(4) Salvation available to all (55:6-13). **55:6-7.** The wicked (v. 7) are commanded to **seek** and **call on** the Lord (v. 6), and to do so **while He may be found,** because when His judgment comes it will be too late. Such seeking and calling means that an individual will **turn** from

his former evil **way** and **thoughts.** Turning to the Lord one receives **mercy** and **pardon.** In every dispensation the Lord has required the same thing for salvation: trust in Him. Israelites, though God's covenant people, were saved only by believing in **the LORD.**

55:8-9. God's compassion on those who turn to Him (vv. 6-7) comes because His **thoughts** and **ways** are far superior to human **thoughts** and **ways,** which in fact are evil (cf. v. 7). God's plan is something people would have never dreamed of.

55:10-11. Having spoken of the future time of blessing (the Millennium) and the salvation which leads to it, the Lord then assured believers that His **Word . . . will accomplish what** He says it will. His word is like **rain** and **snow** that water **the earth** and help give it abundant vegetation. In the Near East dry hard ground can seemingly overnight sprout with vegetation after the first rains of the rainy season. Similarly when God speaks His Word, it brings forth spiritual life, thus accomplishing His **purpose.**

55:12-13. Because of salvation the effects of sin will be reversed in the Millennium, including the provision of inner **joy** and **peace** (see comments on 54:10) and changes in the physical creation. After Adam and Eve sinned in the Garden of Eden thorns and thistles began to choke out the good vegetation and Adam's work to grow good crops was increased (Gen. 3:17-19). But in the future even nature will be joyful (Isa. 55:12b). **The trees** personified as clapping with **hands** (branches moving in the wind) suggests the joy people will have because of the changes in nature. Various kinds of trees will grow **instead of the thornbush** and **briers.** Fertility on the earth will be a sign that God is in control. Many interpreters say this imagery (v. 13a) symbolizes what God does in a person's heart at salvation. True, God does change individuals. But the earth will indeed be unusually fertile during the whole Millennium (cf. 35:1-2, 41:18-19; 44:3a).

c. Gentiles included in Israel's blessings (56:1-8)

(1) A command to be righteous. **56:1-2.** People are urged to **do what is right** (cf. 1:17) because God's **salvation** (spiritual deliverance and physical protection) will come soon. Again Isaiah linked present behavior with future salvation and blessings. Because the Lord will bring salvation to those who believe, they should act justly in the present.

In Isaiah's day a righteous person (a believer who does what is right, 56:1) lived according to God's Law, an expression of His righteous standards. Keeping **the Sabbath** was important under the Law (Ex. 20:8-11), for a person by not engaging in agricultural or business pursuits on that day thereby acknowledged that he believed God would take care of him and bless him. Since the Sabbath was a sign of Israel's covenant with God, keeping the Sabbath signified that a person believed in the covenant and the Lord. Such a person also turned **from doing . . . evil** (cf. Isa. 55:7).

(2) A promise that believing foreigners will be blessed (56:3-8). **56:3-5.** Gentiles, people outside the covenant community, who followed **the LORD** were not to think they would have no salvation or part in the millennial kingdom. Even foreigners (cf. 14:1) and **eunuchs** who join themselves to the Lord are welcome. This contrasts with the exclusion of eunuchs under the Mosaic Law (Deut. 23:1). Keeping the **Sabbaths** and obeying God's **covenant** stipulations (cf. Isa. 56:6) would demonstrate their loyalty to **the LORD** (cf. vv. 1-2). In fact they will be memorialized forever (v. 5). This is striking because a **eunuch,** unable to sire children, has no way of passing on his name through **sons.**

56:6-8. Foreigners who love . . . **the LORD** are acceptable to God and will be regathered along with believing Israelites. Redeemed Gentiles, though not in the covenantal family of Israel, can still receive God's blessings. They show their devotion to **the LORD** by their service, worship, and obedience (keeping **the Sabbath** and God's **covenant** stipulations; cf. v. 4). As God promised Abraham, through him all peoples of the world will be blessed (Gen. 12:3). These Gentiles will be gathered to Zion (His **holy mountain;** see comments on Isa. 11:9) along with **Israel,** where they too will worship the Lord in **prayer** and **offerings.**

d. Condemnation of the wicked (56:9–57:21)

Throughout most of this second nine-chapter division of Isaiah (chaps. 49–57) the emphasis has been on the future glorious state of the redeemed remnant in the kingdom to be established by the Messiah. Now in 56:9–57:21, which concludes these nine chapters, Isaiah reflected on the spiritual situation in his day. In view of their glorious future, one would suppose that his people would want to obey the Lord in anticipation of that kingdom. But this was not true in Isaiah's time.

(1) The call to Gentiles to destroy Israel. 56:9-12. The Lord called for the beasts (Gentile powers, probably Babylon) to devour (punish) Israel because she was spiritually insensitive. The watchmen (cf. Jer. 6:17; Ezek. 33:7), priests and religious leaders, were blind and ignorant and were like dogs who like to sleep and eat. Good shepherds know the best grazing ground for their flocks. But these leaders were ignorant (cf. Isa. 56:10) shepherds going their own way like their sheep! (cf. 53:6) They were more interested in their own gain than in their people's welfare. Concerned only with their own pleasure, they failed to consider that judgment will come (56:12).

(2) The righteous to die. 57:1-2. The society then was so bad that the righteous people in Israel (also called devout and those who walk uprightly) had to die in order to find peace. Observing the evil all around apparently frustrated them. They could do nothing to turn the nation back to the Lord. The only way the righteous could be spared from such frustration was to die.

(3) Israel's involvement in false religions (57:3-10). 57:3-4. In contrast with the righteous people mentioned in verses 1-2, the rest of the Israelites were engaged in false religious practices picked up from pagans around them, including sorcery (from 'ānan; see comments on 2:6) and religious prostitution (cf. Hosea 4:14). In fertility religions "worshipers" engaged in sexual relations with prostitutes, supposedly identifying in that way with gods and goddesses to help guarantee fertility in crops, animals, and families. Such people in Israel were mocking the righteous while they were involved in shameful deeds. By such actions they

were rebels against God.

57:5-8. Worship centers were set up on hillsides, probably so that the people could imagine themselves closer to their gods. Often such centers were in lush forest areas to picture the fertility being sought by the worshipers. Thus the people, as Isaiah wrote, would lust among the oaks (cf. 1:29). Sometimes the people were also involved in child sacrifice in attempts to appease the wrath of various gods (cf. Ezek. 20:31; Hosea 13:2). They were in the habit of giving offerings to their idols and sacrificing to foreign gods on the high hills where they also were involved in adultery (Isa. 57:6-7). Their homes were supposed to be centers of learning about the Lord, but the people had made them places of idol worship and adultery (v. 8). (Cf. the use of pagan symbols with God's command in Deut. 6:9.) Beds and nakedness may refer to sexual perversity involved in such worship or they may symbolize idolatry (which was sometimes likened to spiritual adultery).

57:9-10. The worship of Molech, an Ammonite god, was sometimes accompanied by child sacrifice (2 Kings 23:10; Jer. 32:35), but sending representatives to Ammon to worship their god sometimes resulted in death (you descended to the grave). Yet in the face of these difficulties the people still refused to give up their sinful ways. They simply renewed their strength and continued on in sin.

(4) Israel's forgetfulness of God. 57:11-13. Most of the Israelites had forgotten the true God, apparently because He had seemingly been silent. So in irony the Lord said He would expose their righteousness and . . . works. Their alleged righteous works, when exposed, would be shown for what they really were, and as a result their deeds would be of no help to them before the Lord. When in trouble, God said sarcastically, they should cry out to their gods. But they would find that God will blow . . . away their idols. In contrast those Israelites who trust the Lord will inherit the land (cf. Pss. 25:12-13; 37:9, 11, 22, 29; 69:35-36), that is, they will enjoy physical blessings, including the temple mount (God's holy mountain; see comments on Isa. 11:9) again belonging to Israel.

(5) The Lord's promise of forgiveness. 57:14-21. The exhortation to pre-

pare a road for the people of faith recalls 40:3-5 which speaks of a road being prepared for the Lord. Now the faithful are walking to the Lord. Even though He is majestic (**high and lofty**; cf. 6:1), eternal, and **holy** (cf. 6:3), He fellowships (**lives**) with those who are **contrite and lowly in spirit** (cf. 66:2). His accusations and anger do not last **forever,** because of His grace. In the past He had to be harsh with His people because of their **greed** and independence. But when they repent He forgives them, giving healing, guidance, and **comfort**. The forgiven ones enjoy **peace.** . . . **but the wicked** have no **rest** and **no peace** (cf. 48:22). They are doomed for punishment because they refuse to turn to the Lord.

C. Restoration realized and completed (chaps. 58–66)

In this final nine-chapter section of the book, Isaiah looked to the present and the future. In his day most of the people were not righteous (chap. 58). Because of their depravity the restoration of the nation must be God's initiative (chap. 59). Eventually peace and prosperity will come to Israel and the whole world (chap. 60). Isaiah wrote of the coming of the Messiah and of the Father (61:1–63:6) and of the nation's prayer and the Lord's response (63:7–65:25). In conclusion the prophet wrote again that God will fulfill His promises to Israel as well as the entire world (chap. 66).

1. THE RESTORATION TO COME BY GOD'S INITIATIVE (CHAPS. 58–60)

a. Obedience required (chap. 58)

(1) The reminder of the people's sins. **58:1-2.** God called for heralds to go about telling the nation of **their rebellion** (*peša'*, "transgressions," from *pāša'*, "to transgress"; see comments in 1:2; also cf. 1:5; 53:5, 8; 59:13) and **sins. Like a trumpet** used to get people's attention, the heralds were to **shout**. Outwardly the people seemed **eager** to want **to know** God and for **God to** be **near them.**

(2) The concern of the people. **58:3a.** The people voiced their concern that they were in difficulty though they seemed to be doing what the Law required. They **fasted** and **humbled** themselves, but they feared that God had not **seen it** or **noticed**. Apparently they thought that by

going through the "motions" of religion (without any inward reality of faith) they would be blessed.

(3) The response of the Lord (58:3b-14). The Lord responded by pointing out that He was more interested in their obedience than their rituals. Unfortunately they, like many people, had confused rituals with relationship, outward acts with true obedience. **58:3b-5.** Their fasts did not alter their poor relationship with others. They were disregarding other peoples' needs by exploiting their employees (cf. Deut. 24:14-15; James 5:1-6) and by **quarreling** and fighting. Therefore their prayers would not **be heard,** for their kind of **fasting** was not what the Lord accepted. Their hearts, not just their **heads,** needed to bow before **the Lord.**

58:6-7. Fasting was to encourage a person to respond positively to God's commands. In the Old Testament only one fast was commanded—the annual Day of Atonement (Lev. 16:29, 31). Only after the fall of Jerusalem were fast days instituted (Zech. 7:3, 5; 8:19). Ironically on the other hand many *specific* commands were *not* being followed. So the Lord reminded the people that they should be just (Isa. 58:6) and openhanded with those in need—**the hungry** (cf. v. 10), **the poor** . . . **the naked** (v. 7). The Israelites were to consider themselves members of one family who at one time had been slaves in Egypt. Therefore they were not to neglect each other. When someone shared with one in need, it was a reminder that everything he owned belonged to the Lord.

58:8-12. If the people had inner **righteousness** (revealed in outward acts of justice and mercy, vv. 6-7), **then . . . the Lord** would bless them (cf. Deut. 28:1-14) with **light** (often a picture of blessing; cf. Isa. 58:10), **healing** (spiritual restoration), righteousness (high standards), protection from trouble, and answered prayer (vv. 8-9a). If they would **do away with** . . . **oppression** and gossip and would help others in need (cf. v. 7), then the Lord would bless them (give them **light;** cf. v. 8). He would give guidance, satisfaction, strength, fertility (**like a spring**), and physical restoration (rebuilding the **ruins**).

58:13-14. Sabbath observance was a barometer of one's faithfulness to the

Mosaic Covenant (cf. comments on 56:4-6). By following the rules for the Sabbath a person acknowledged the importance of worshiping God and showed that he depended on God to bless him materially for that time he took off from work. By putting God first and not seeking to do as he wished, a person would have joy, not only in spiritual salvation (ride on the heights) but also in prosperity (feast on the inheritance). All this was certain because the LORD has spoken (cf. 1:20; 40:5).

b. Salvation to come by God's initiative (chap. 59)

Because of the depravity of the nation, national salvation and prosperity would have to come from God's initiative. In chapter 59 the Lord again spoke of the people's sins and His provision of salvation because of the Abrahamic Covenant.

(1) The Lord's ability to save. 59:1. The prophet reminded the nation that the LORD could save them in spite of their difficult circumstances. He is powerful enough—His arm (cf. v. 16; see comments on 40:10) is not . . . short. And He is caring enough—He is not dull of hearing. This implies that Israel simply needed to call out to God and He would come to her rescue.

(2) Israel's spiritual depravity (59:2-15a). 59:2-8. However, though the Lord could save them, the nation's sins had separated them from the Lord (cf. Ps. 66:18; Prov. 28:9). Though He could hear them (Isa. 59:1) He chose not to (v. 2). Sin prevents prayer from being answered (cf. Ps. 66:18). Those sins included murder, lying, injustice (cf. Isa. 59:9, 11, 14-15), and planning evil (vv. 3-4). Their actions were like those of deadly poisonous snakes (vipers and an adder), for they were harming each other. Just as people can see through cobwebs, which therefore are inappropriate for clothing (v. 6), so God could see through the evil deeds of these people and judge them. In a hurry to do evil things, they were bringing ruin to others (v. 7) and were constantly traveling down evil paths. As a result they knew no peace (cf. 48:22; 57:20-21).

59:9-15a. Here the prophet, using first-person plural pronouns (us. . . . we. . . . our), identified with the people (cf.

6:5). Israel was so corrupt spiritually, without justice (cf. 59:4, 11, 14-15) and righteousness, that it was as if they were in darkness and were blind and dead. As a result, the oppressed were angry like growling bears and moaned like doves. They wanted justice and help but found none (v. 11). Isaiah confessed that the people were noted for their many . . . sins, deliberate rebellion (cf. 1:5; 58:1) against the LORD, lying, injustice, and dishonesty (59:12-15a).

(3) The Lord's promise to help Israel (59:15b-21). 59:15b-16a. Because of her depraved condition (vv. 2-15a), no one but the LORD could save the nation. Being displeased with her injustice (cf. vv. 4, 9, 11, 14), He realized there was no one to intercede on her behalf. Isaiah was not saying that the Lord did not want to get involved, but that Israel was totally incapable of helping herself. Only God could help her. This is true of salvation in any era. No one can save himself. Only God can forgive sin and change a person's heart.

59:16b-20. In His power (by His . . . arm; cf. v. 1 and comments on 40:10) God provided salvation, both spiritual and physical, for him (i.e., for Israel personified as a man). Like a warrior God goes forth to fight for His people. Righteousness is His breastplate and salvation is His helmet (cf. Paul's use of this imagery in Eph. 6:14, 17). God's other garments are vengeance and zeal. This verse (Isa. 59:17) means that God supplies righteousness and salvation (cf. v. 16) for His people as He zealously executes vengeance on His enemies (v. 18). Because of this, people everywhere will acknowledge His glory, overpowering majesty, and strength (like a pent-up flood let loose). When the LORD executes judgment on His enemies (at Christ's second coming), the Messiah will go to Zion. He will be the Redeemer (see comments on 41:14) of those Israelites who turn to Him in repentance (59:20). Showing their future hope, the nation was being encouraged to repent.

59:21. When the Messiah returns in judgment (v. 18), He will inaugurate His covenant (elsewhere called the New Covenant, Jer. 31:31), pouring His Spirit on believing Israelites (cf. Ezek. 36:27a; Joel 2:29) and instilling His words within them (Jer. 31:33-34; Ezek. 36:27b).

c. *Peace and prosperity to come (chap. 60)*

(1) God's glory to come to Israel. **60:1-3.** Because of the Lord's redeeming work (59:19a, 20-21), **light** (blessing) will fall on Israel, who in turn is to **shine** forth, as a spiritual light to the **nations,** revealing God's Word and **glory** to them. In that way, she will be instrumental in removing the spiritual **darkness** that pervades the world (cf. 29:18; John 12:35; Acts 26:18; Rom. 2:19; Col. 1:13; 1 Peter 2:9). When **the LORD** returns to live among His people (Isa. 60:2) the nations will be attracted to the light of **His glory** (cf. vv. 19-20) and will flock to Israel for the **light** (the blessings of salvation from spiritual darkness). This will occur in the Millennium. Though everyone entering the Millennium will be saved, people will be born during that 1,000-year period of time. Many of them will come to salvation because of God's work on Israel's behalf.

(2) The nations' wealth to come to Israel. **60:4-9.** At the beginning of the Millennium when Israel will be regathered to her land, her **sons** will **come from** great distances (cf. v. 9). Also Israel will rejoice because redeemed people from **the nations** (v. 5; the "sheep" of Matt. 25:31-46) will want to join Israel in her worship in Jerusalem (cf. Zech. 14:16-19). Those people will bring **wealth** to Israel (cf. Isa. 60:11; 61:6; Hag. 2:7-8; Zech. 14:14). Examples of the kinds of wealth to be brought are **gold** . . . **incense.** . . . **flocks** . . . **rams** and **silver** (Isa. 60:6-7, 9). Examples of the nations that will bring those riches are: (a) **Midian,** south of the Dead Sea; (b) **Ephah,** a branch of the Midianites as Midian was Ephah's father (Gen. 25:4; 1 Chron. 1:33); (c) **She-ba,** probably the Sabeans in southwest Arabia (see comments on Seba in Isa. 43:3); (d) **Kedar** in northern Arabia; (e) **Nebaioth,** apparently an Arabian tribe (Nebaioth was Ishmael's eldest son, Gen. 25:13; and (f) **Tarshish** (probably in southwestern Spain; see comments on Isa. 23:1), whose **ships** will bring not only riches but also Israelites. Some of this wealth will be used **as offerings** (60:7; cf. 56:6-7) and some will be used to **adorn** the **temple** (cf. 60:13), undoubtedly the millennial temple (Ezek. 40–43). This wealth, brought in haste (Isa. 60:8), will all be to **honor** . . . **the LORD,** who

will have manifested His **splendor** (glory) in Israel (cf. v. 21; 35:2; 46:13; 49:3; 55:5; 61:3; 62:3).

(3) The nations to acknowledge Israel. **60:10-14.** Israel will occupy the foremost position in the world's political, economic, religious, and social structures. **Foreigners** and **kings** (cf. vv. 3, 11) will assist in rebuilding Jerusalem's **walls,** evidence of God's **favor** and **compassion** in contrast with His **anger** (cf. 57:16-18). The flow of **wealth** into Jerusalem will be steady (60:11). And any **nation** that might try to rise up against Israel will be defeated by God (v. 12).

Even wood will be brought from **Lebanon** for the temple construction, thus again making it a place of beauty for the Lord (cf. v. 7). God called the temple His **sanctuary** and **the place of** His **feet.** People from the nations that formerly despised Israel will recognize that Jerusalem or **Zion,** is God's chosen **city,** the place where He dwells.

(4) Righteousness to come to Israel (60:15-22). **60:15-16.** During this time of blessing righteousness will be evident throughout the land. In contrast with Israel's having been **forsaken and hated** (cf. v. 14), God **will** cause others to take **pride** in her. Much as a nursing child gets sustenance from its mother, so Israel will be sustained by the wealth of the **nations** (v. 16; cf. vv. 5, 11; 61:6). This blessing will cause Israel to recognize all the more that **the LORD** really is the unique God of the world, her **Savior** (see comments on 43:11), **Redeemer** (see comments on 41:14), and her **Mighty One** (cf. 49:26).

60:17-22. Wealth to be brought to Jerusalem (cf. vv. 5-9) will include not only **gold** and **silver** (already mentioned in v. 9), but also **bronze** and **iron.** The city will be peaceful and joyful. Also the Lord will protect her as her **Light** and **Glory** (v. 19; cf. vv. 1-2). Her **people** will **be righteous,** displaying God's **splendor** (v. 21; cf. comments on v. 9), and they will be numerous (v. 22). The Millennium will be a utopia for which many people have longed.

2. THE COMING OF THE MESSIAH AND THE COMING OF THE FATHER (61:1–63:6)

a. *The coming of the Messiah (chap. 61)*

61:1-3. In verse 1 all three Persons of the Trinity are mentioned: the **Spirit** . . .

the Sovereign LORD, and the Messiah. Three factors indicate that Me refers to the Messiah: (1) The association of the Holy Spirit with the anointing points to Jesus Christ. After being anointed with oil, Israel's first two kings, Saul and David, were blessed with the Spirit's ministry (1 Sam. 10:1, 10; 16:13). Similarly Christ was anointed by the Holy Spirit (Matt. 3:16-17) to be Israel's King. The Hebrew word for Messiah (*māšîaḥ*) means "the Anointed One," and Christ (*christos*, from *chriō*, "to anoint") is the Greek equivalent of *māšîaḥ*. (2) Part of this passage (Isa. 61:1-2a) was read by Jesus (Luke 4:18-19) in reference to Himself. (3) The mission of this Anointed One was Jesus' ministry: to **preach good news**, to heal and free (Isa. 61:1; cf. 42:7), **to proclaim . . . favor and . . . vengeance** (61:2), and **to comfort** (vv. 2-3). When Jesus read from this passage He stopped in the middle of the sentence, after the word "favor" (Luke 4:18-19). By doing this He was showing that His work would be divided into two advents. In His First Advent He did the things mentioned in Isaiah 61:1-2a; in His Second Advent He will do the things in verses 2b-3. When He returns He will bring judgment on unbelievers (Micah 5:15; Rev. 19:15-20); this will be **the day of** God's "vengeance" (cf. Isa. 34:8; 35:4; 63:4). But the Messiah will also "comfort" Israel, for she will have undergone great persecution, the Great Tribulation, in the preceding years (cf. Dan. 7:21, 24-25; Rev. 12:13-17).

When the Messiah comes He will change believing Israelites' sadness to joy, a truth Isaiah mentioned frequently. In place **of ashes**, put on one's head as a sign of mourning (cf. 2 Sam. 13:19; Es. 4:1; Dan 9:3), they will wear **a crown.** Light olive **oil**, when applied to one's face and hair, would soothe him and brighten his spirits (cf. Pss. 23:5; 45:7; 104:15; Ecc. 9:8; Matt. 6:17; Heb. 1:9), thus dispelling **mourning.** Another sign of joy is a bright **garment** (cf. Ecc. 9:7-8). Israel will be righteous (cf. Isa. 54:14; 58:8; 60:21; 62:1-2) and like stalwart oak trees will **display** God's **splendor** (cf. 35:2; 46:13; 49:3; 55:5; 60:9, 21; 62:3).

61:4-9. After the Messiah's Second Advent Israel **will rebuild** her **ruined cities,** even those that had been destroyed many years before. Israel will be so re-vered that Gentiles (**aliens and foreigners**) will join her (cf. 14:1; 60:10) in her farming and shepherding. As a nation of **priests** each one will know **the LORD,** and have access to Him, and mediate on behalf of others, as did the Levitical priests. This was to be one of Israel's functions in the world (Ex. 19:6), but unfortunately she will not fully carry out that responsibility till in the Millennium. **Nations** will bring their **wealth** to Israel (see comments on Isa. 60:5, 11). The **double portion** refers to the inheritance the eldest son in a family would receive from his father's estate (Deut. 21:17). The eldest son was given special honor. Similarly Israel, like the Lord's firstborn (Ex. 4:22), will be honored. Because of these blessings and God's giving Israel **an everlasting covenant** (the New Covenant; cf. Jer. 32:40; Ezek. 16:60; 37:26; Heb. 13:20), people everywhere **will acknowledge that** she is indeed God's special **people.**

61:10-11. In these verses the prophet seems to be speaking for the redeemed remnant who will rejoice (cf. comments on 9:3) in response to God's blessings mentioned in 61:1-9. **Salvation** and **righteousness** are pictured as clothes worn by the people (cf. God's "clothes," 59:17). In other words the Israelites are characterized by salvation (God's redeemed people) and righteousness (those who are living by God's standards; cf. 58:8; 60:21). To picture their joy and blessing **a bridegroom** wore a fancy headgear, like a priest's turban, and the **bride** wore costly jewelry. God will cause Israel's **righteousness** to **spring up** in (be known by) other **nations** (cf. 61:11; 62:1-2) much **as the soil** sustains the growth of plants.

b. Preparation for the coming of the Lord (chap. 62)

Much of this chapter speaks of preparation being made for the coming of the Lord and for the restoration of His people, thus expanding the thoughts in 40:3-5, 9.

62:1-5. Is the speaker in these verses the Messiah, the Lord (God the Father), or the prophet? Since "I" in verse 6 seems to be the Father, verses 1-5 may also be spoken by Him. The Lord announced that He will continue to work on **Jerusalem's** behalf until her **righteousness . . . salvation,** and **glory** are observed by the rest of the world (cf.

61:10-11) and the city is **called by a new name.** That name is not stated here but several names are given later, in 62:4, 12 (cf. 60:14). In the ancient Near East names often signified one's anticipated or present character. So Jerusalem's having a new name means it will have a new righteous character. Like **a crown** or **diadem** (a large metal ring worn on the head) adorning one's head so Jerusalem will be an adornment to **the LORD.** She will display His **splendor** (cf. 35:2; 46:13; 49:3; 55:5; 60:9, 21; 61:3), that is, her inhabitants will manifest His character in their conduct.

The city's new relationship with God is compared to the happiness of a marriage. Rather than being called **Deserted** (cf. 62:12) or **Desolate,** previous characteristics of the city, Jerusalem will be named **Hephzibah** ("My delight is in her") and **Beulah** ("Married one"). The words **so will your sons marry you** (Jerusalem) imply that people again will live in Jerusalem and **God** will be happy about the wonderful state of affairs.

62:6-9. In the ancient world **watchmen** were stationed **on** city **walls** (often in towers) to watch for any approaching enemy. While on guard they were never to sleep. Righteous Israelites, like watchmen, were to be alert on Jerusalem's behalf. They were to **give** themselves and God **(Him) no rest till He establishes Jerusalem,** that is, they were constantly to ask God that the city become **the praise of the earth,** so blessed by God that people everywhere would extol her (cf. 60:15; 61:11).

The "watchmen" were to hold God to His promises, knowing that is what He desires. God's people should pray for things even when they know God has promised them. Jesus made this clear when He taught His disciples to pray that the kingdom will come (Matt. 6:10). When Jerusalem is restored, it will **never again** fall to its enemies (Isa. 62:8-9). God has assured it by oath **(sworn by His right hand) and by His** power **(arm;** see comments on 40:10).

62:10-12. Verses 10-12 were written as if the Lord were on His way, so His people should be ready. The repeated commands, **Pass through, pass through** and **build up, build up,** convey a sense of urgency; quickly **the people** are to pre-

pare themselves spiritually for His coming (see comments on 40:3-5, 9). To **raise a banner** was a way of announcing something. **The nations** are to be informed that **the LORD** is coming to Jerusalem. When He arrives word is to be given throughout the world (on **the ends of the earth** see comments on 5:26) that He, Israel's **Savior** (see comments on 43:11), has come to **reward** Jerusalemites with His blessings. Giving the people of the city new names **(The Holy People, The Redeemed of the LORD,** and **Sought After)** speaks of the new character Israel will have. Because of God's redemption the people will be holy (Ex. 19:6; Deut. 7:6), and Gentiles will visit **the city. No longer** will it be **deserted** (Isa. 62:12; cf. v. 4; 60:15; Zech. 14:11).

c. The coming of the Lord (63:1-6)

63:1. When the Lord returns two questions will be asked of Him: **Who is this?** (twice in v. 1) and "Why are Your garments red?" (v. 2) He will be **coming from Edom** (cf. 34:5-9), the wicked nation southeast of Israel that often opposed God's people and therefore is under God's wrath (Mal. 1:4), and **from Bozrah,** a city (modern-day Buseirah) in Edom. Coming from there God's **garments** will be **crimson** (Isa. 63:1) and red (v. 2) because they are **stained** with blood (v. 3) from slaughtering His enemies (the nations, vv. 3, 6) in Edom. **Robed in splendor** signifies His power and glory as He will stride **forward** toward Israel **to save** (deliver) her (cf. Rom. 11:26).

63:2-6. The Lord's **garments** spattered with blood will appear **red** as if He had been in a **winepress.** "Red" ('*ādōm* is a wordplay on "Edom" ('*ĕdôm*). A **winepress** was usually a shallow pit with a hole on the side leading out to a container. As individuals trampled on grapes in the press, the juice flowed through the hole into the container. Obviously some juice would also splatter on the workers' clothes. As the Lord will fight and defeat **the nations** (cf. 34:2) in the Battle of Armageddon (cf. Zech. 14:3; Rev. 16:16; 19:15-19), He will take **vengeance** on them (cf. Isa. 34:8; 35:4; 61:2) in His **anger** and **wrath.** God's **wrath** is also pictured as being like a winepress in Revelation 14:19-20. Though that day will bring doom to the Lord's enemies, it will mean deliverance **(redemption** and **salvation,**

Isa. 63:4-5) for those of His covenant people who turn to Him.

3. THE NATION'S PRAYER AND THE LORD'S RESPONSE (63:7-65:25)

This section records a pathetic prayer of the Jewish remnant and the Lord's appropriate response. Isaiah was writing for the exiles in Babylon who would view their situation as somewhat hopeless. They would not be able to sense how God could possibly help them in their distress. However, they would remember the way the Lord had helped His people in bringing them out of bondage in Egypt. This would encourage them to pray for release from *their* bondage. In responding to their prayer, the Lord explained that their sin caused their distress and promised that He would deliver them and bring them into the promised kingdom.

a. The prayer of the nation (63:7–64:12)

63:7-9. Before stating their two requests—that God be compassionate toward them (vv. 15-19) and that He punish their enemies (64:1-7)—the righteous remnant said it would recite (**tell of**) the Lord's goodness in the past. (The word **I** refers to Isaiah, representing the nation.) Because of their distress, recalling God's past help in the nation's Exodus would reassure them of the Lord's concern. His actions on their behalf (**for us**) would be **kindnesses** (pl. of *ḥeseḏ*, meaning expressions of His covenantal "loyal love"), extended to **Israel** because of **His compassion** (63:7), **love, and mercy** (v. 9). As His people and His **sons,** they would know God as **their Savior** (see comments on 43:11). Seeing their ancestors in **distress** in Egypt (cf. Ex. 2:23-25; 3:7), God **redeemed** (*gāʾal*, "to buy out of slavery"; cf. Isa. 43:1) **them. The angel of His presence** is probably the Angel of the Lord, the Lord Himself (cf. Ex. 33:14; see comments on Gen. 16:10).

63:10. In spite of all God did for Israel, she **rebelled** against Him. "Rebelled" is not from *pāšaʾ*, "to revolt or rebel against a covenant stipulation," but *mārâh*, "to be contentious, to be rebellious" (cf. Ps. 78:8; Jer. 5:23). From almost the beginning of the wilderness experience Israel rebelled against God (Ex. 17:1-7). This **grieved** the **Holy Spirit** (cf. Eph. 4:30), the only place in the Old Testament where this statement is made. (Cf. references to the Spirit in Isa. 63:11, 14; see comments on 11:2.) Because of this rebellion God **fought against them,** bringing troubles, distresses, and enemies to discipline them.

63:11-14. At various times in her history Israel, when disciplined by God, would recall how in the great Exodus He used **Moses** like a **shepherd** to bring them out of Egypt by His . . . **arm** (v. 12; see comments on 40:10) **of power,** leading them **through the sea** (63:11; cf. Ex. 14:16), also referred to as **the waters** (Isa. 63:12) and **the depths** (v. 13). Being freed from Egypt was like giving **a horse** free rein **in open country** or like letting **cattle** graze on a wide **plain.** As God gave them **rest** and guidance, His reputation was made known.

63:15-19. The remnant would beg God to **look down** on them and remember their plight in the same way He had remembered the distress of their forefathers in Egypt (cf. v. 9). They would long for a display of both His strength and His love. Though they had not been following in the tradition of **Abraham** or **Israel** (i.e., Jacob), God was still their **Father** (cf. 64:8) and **Redeemer** (see comments on 41:14). Penitently the remnant would ask that God sovereignly **return** them, His **servants,** to Him, reminding Him that the temple (**Your sanctuary**) was destroyed (63:17-18). (This is one of many places in chaps. 40–66 which shows that Isaiah, living more than 100 years before the Babylonian Captivity, wrote prophetically to prepare that future generation of exiles for it.) Though the nation had belonged to God for centuries (**from of old**), it had been a long time since the people were in a proper relationship with God and His theocratic rule **over them.**

64:1-7. The second plea of the remnant is recorded in these verses (the first is in 63:15-19). Realizing their uncleanness (64:5-7), they would ask God to smite their **enemies** (vv. 1-4). They would pray that the Lord would **rend the heavens** (the sky is pictured as a piece of cloth He would tear), **come down** (vv. 1-2; cf. "look down," 63:15), and execute judgment on **the nations. Fire** and boiling **water** picture judgment (cf. Jer. 1:13-14; Mal 4:1, 5). The **awesome things** (Isa. 64:3) probably refer to the phenomena of fire, darkness (Deut. 4:11-13), and earthquake (Ex. 19:16-19) when God gave the Mosaic Law. This revealing God—the only God (Isa. 64:4; cf. 1 Cor. 2:10)—acts on behalf of those who believe in Him and who therefore willingly do what is right. Recalling this, the remnant would ask that God work on *their* behalf. They would confess their sin (Isa. 64:5b), spiritual uncleanness (v. 6a), weakness (v. 6b, like a shriveled leaf), and lack of prayer (v. 7). However, they would not blame God for their dreadful condition; they would know that their wasting away was because of their sins. Therefore they would have to count on God's faithfulness and promises.

64:8-12. This final part of this beautiful prayer by the righteous remnant is a confession of trust in the LORD. The remnant would address God as their Father (cf. 63:16) and as the Potter. Israel was to be like obedient children and as submissive as clay (cf. 29:16; 45:9). Therefore the remnant would obediently and submissively ask the Lord to withhold His anger and to look on them (cf. 63:15) as His own. The remnant would remind God that Israel's cities including Jerusalem had been destroyed and that even the temple had been burned. The nation would urge God to do something about the situation (64:12), thereby breaking His silence (cf. 62:1; 65:6) and withholding His punishment on her.

b. The response of the Lord (chap. 65)

In several ways the Lord's response to the remnant's prayer sums up the message of the entire Book of Isaiah. The Lord said that though He had constantly been presenting His love to Israel, they had rejected Him which made judgment necessary (vv. 1-7). However, in that judgment, a remnant will be preserved (vv. 8-12). The consequences of righteous living differ from those of wicked living (vv. 13-16). The Lord will establish a glorious kingdom in which peace and righteousness will flourish (vv. 17-25). Throughout the chapter, as well as throughout the book, the prophet implicitly pleaded for the people to place their trust in the Lord, their covenant God, and to live righteously.

65:1-7. Constantly reaching out to Israel, God revealed Himself to those who did not even ask for that revelation. Only because of His grace did He do so,

even calling out to them, Here am I. Yet they did not respond. He was always ready to help them (holding out His hands; Paul quotes vv. 1-2 in Rom. 10:20-21), but they continued to be stubborn, independent, and evil. They provoked God by (a) worshiping in pagan gardens (cf. Isa. 1:29; 66:17); (b) being involved in necromancy (supposedly consulting the dead, while sitting among the graves, 65:4; cf. 8:19); (c) disregarding His dietary laws (65:4b; cf. 66:3, 17; Lev. 11:7); and (d) being religiously arrogant till they became as repulsive and irritating to Him as smoke in a person's nose. Because of their sins, the LORD would judge them. The Assyrian threat (Isa. 1–37) and the Babylonian Exile (chaps. 38–66) were two of the ways the Lord disciplined His people. The consequences of sin had to be faced; God would pay them back in judgment for their idolatrous worship in high places (cf. 57:7).

65:8-12. Though judgment was addressed to the whole nation (vv. 6-7), it will not be total. As a few grapes are left when vineyards are gleaned (Deut. 24:21), so a remnant will be left who will return to the land (possess My mountains) and cultivate it, and pasture their flocks there again. Sharon, the coastal plain south of Mount Carmel, is excellent land for agriculture, and the Valley of Achor (cf. Hosea 2:15) west of Jericho was known for its sheep-herding.

On the other hand people are destined for slaughter if they do not trust the LORD, and if they disregard the temple (on God's holy mountain; see comments on Isa. 11:9). Fortune and Destiny were names of gods Israel worshiped in her attempts to know the future. Food and drink were set before those idols to seek to please them. Such people, God said, are doomed to die by the sword, for they refused to listen to Him and deliberately chose to go on sinning (cf. 66:4).

65:13-16. Contrasts between people who are the Lord's servants and those who have departed from Him are dramatically presented in these verses. His servants will eat . . . drink, and rejoice, while the rejectors will be hungry . . . thirsty, and shamed. God's servants will sing for joy whereas the rejectors will wail, be cursed, and put . . . to death. God's servants . . . will receive another name, that is, will be given a new character (cf. 62:2), so that they will take oaths honestly (**by the God of truth**; cf. Ps. 31:5). God will forget their previous difficulties and sins because of His grace.

65:17-25. In these verses the Lord described the millennial kingdom, which is seemingly identified here with the eternal state (**new heavens and a new earth**). In Revelation, however, the new heavens and new earth (Rev. 21:1) *follow* the Millennium (Rev. 20:4). Most likely Isaiah did not distinguish between these two aspects of God's rule; he saw them together as one. After all, the Millennium, though 1,000 years in duration, will be a mere pinpoint of time compared with the eternal state.

The need for new heavens and a new earth is suggested in Isaiah 51:6. During the Millennium Jerusalem will be a place of **joy** (65:18). Also the Lord Himself **will rejoice over** it, for sorrow will be vanished (v. 19). Though death will still be present, life spans will be extended (v. 20) and people will **enjoy** safety and the produce of their **vineyards** (vv. 21-22). God's blessing will be on their work and families (v. 23) and He will speedily **answer** their prayers (v. 24). Wild animals will lose their ferocity (cf. 11:6-8; Hosea 2:18) and harmony and safety will prevail under God's good hand (Isa. 65:25). (On God's **holy mountain** see comments on 11:9.)

4. THE LORD'S FULFILLMENT OF HIS
   PROMISES (CHAP. 66)

As the climax to the book, this chapter fittingly describes the Millennium, the time toward which history has been looking, which was promised to Abraham.

a. The Lord to esteem the humble
   (66:1-2)

66:1-2. God is pictured figuratively as sitting on a **throne** (cf. 6:1) with **the earth** as His **footstool** (cf. Acts 7:49). Because of His majesty no one can **build** a **house** for Him to dwell in (1 Kings 8:27); *He* is the Creator. Yet what He values above His inanimate Creation are people who are **humble and contrite** (cf. Isa. 57:15) and who follow His **word.** In one way or another, this has been Isaiah's message throughout this book. God wants His people to follow the truth He has revealed to them. For Israel that was primarily the Mosaic Covenant. Pointing the people back to the Word of God, Isaiah was indicating that they needed to obey it if they were to enjoy His blessings.

b. The Lord to judge (66:3-6)

66:3-6. The strange comparisons in verse 3 indicate that the people's religious **sacrifices** and offerings were only external ritual. In their hearts the people were murderers, perverters of God's dietary laws (cf. 65:4; Lev. 11:7), and idolaters. In reality they were going **their own ways** (cf. Isa. 53:6) rather than the Lord's way. Therefore **harsh** judgment would come. (The last four lines of 66:4 are almost identical with 65:12; see comments there.) People in Israel who professed to know **the LORD** but **who** actually hated and discriminated against God's people would be shamed by His discipline when **the temple** would be destroyed by the Babylonians.

c. The Lord to give birth to His
   nation (66:7-21)

66:7-11. Israel's return to the land will be so remarkably quick that it will be like a woman giving **birth** to **a son** before (v. 7) or as soon as (v. 8) she has any **labor . . . pains**! God does not start something and leave it unfinished. As surely as a woman's **womb** opens, not closes, for **delivery,** so God will do for **Jerusalem** what He has set out to do. This then is cause for rejoicing. The people of Israel will **delight in** Jerusalem as an infant delights in her mother's sustenance.

66:12-13. As stated many times in the Book of Isaiah, **peace** will come to **Jerusalem** (cf., e.g., 48:18; 55:12) and the nations' **wealth** will flow to her (cf. 60:5, 11; 61:6). In 66:11-12 Jerusalem is compared to a mother; in verse 13 God is compared to **a mother** who **comforts her child.**

66:14-18. When God restores His people to Jerusalem (vv. 10-13) in the Millennium, they **will rejoice** and prosper, but on His and her enemies He will swoop down in judgment like a **fire** (cf. 2 Thes. 1:7-9) and a **whirlwind** to slay them. This **judgment** will be fair because of their abominations: worshiping in idolatrous **gardens** (cf. Isa. 1:29; 65:3) and eating ceremonially unclean animals such as **pigs** (cf. 65:4; 66:3; Lev. 11:7) **and**

rats (cf. Lev. 11:29). When the Messiah returns, His judgment will be on **all nations** (cf. Zech. 14:3; Rev. 19:17-18) and because of that judgment the world will **see His glory.**
66:19-21. People outside Israel will turn to Him and worship Him. The remnant of believing Israelites will travel as missionaries to other parts of the world, to tell Gentiles about God's **glory.** Those places and peoples will include **Tarshish,** probably in southwestern Spain (cf. 23:1, 6, 10, 14; 60:9), **Libyans** in northern Africa, **Lydians** in western Asia Minor, **Tubal** in northeastern Asia Minor, **Greece,** and **distant islands.** These and other peoples will be converted and will travel to **Jerusalem** to worship in **the temple** (cf. 2:2; Zech. 8:23). **Some of them** will even be selected as **priests and Levites,** thus showing that all the nations will in fact be blessed through Israel (cf. Gen. 12:3).

d. *The Lord to establish new heavens and new earth (66:22-24)*

66:22-24. Israel will be as enduring **as the new heavens and the new earth** (see comments on 65:17). **All mankind** (i.e., people from all nations) **will** worship **the LORD,** bowing **down before** Him. As Isaiah had frequently written, these righteous ones will contrast greatly with **those who rebelled** (*pāšaʿ*; see comments on 1:2) **against** the LORD. They will suffer eternal torment (cf. Mark 9:48). This awesome way in which the majestic Book of Isaiah concludes points to the need for unrepentant people to turn to the Lord, the only God, the Holy One of Israel.

BIBLIOGRAPHY

Alexander, Joseph A. *Commentaries on the Prophecies of Isaiah*. 1865. Reprint (2 vols. in 1). Grand Rapids: Zondervan Publishing House, 1980.

Allis, Oswald T. *The Unity of Isaiah: A Study in Prophecy*. Nutley, N.J.: Presbyterian and Reformed Publishing Co., 1952.

Barnes, Albert. *Notes on the Old Testament, Explanatory and Practical: Isaiah*. 2 vols. Reprint. Grand Rapids: Baker Book House, 1950.

Bultema, Harry. *Commentary on Isaiah*. Translated by Cornelius Lambregtse. Grand Rapids: Kregel Publications, 1981.

Delitzsch, Franz. "Isaiah." In *Commentary on the Old Testament in Ten Volumes*. Vol. 7. Reprint (25 vols. in 10). Grand Rapids: Wm. B. Eerdmans Publishing Co., 1982.

Gray, George B. *A Critical and Exegetical Commentary on the Book of Isaiah*. Vol. 1: *Introduction and Commentary on I–XXVII*. The International Critical Commentary. Edinburgh: T. & T. Clark, 1912.

Herbert, A.S. *The Book of the Prophet Isaiah: Chapters I–XXXIX*. Cambridge: Cambridge University Press, 1973.

Jennings, F.C. *Studies in Isaiah*. New York: Loizeaux Brothers, 1935.

Kaiser, Otto. *Isaiah 1–12: A Commentary*. Philadelphia: Westminster Press, 1972.

_____. *Isaiah 13–39: A Commentary*. Philadelphia: Westminster Press, 1974.

Leupold, H.C. *Exposition of Isaiah*. 2 vols. Grand Rapids: Baker Book House, 1968.

MacRae, Allan A. *The Gospel of Isaiah*. Chicago: Moody Press, 1977.

Martin, Alfred. *Isaiah: The Salvation of Jehovah*. Chicago: Moody Press, 1967.

Martin, Alfred, and Martin, John A. *Isaiah: The Glory of the Messiah*. Chicago: Moody Press, 1983.

Mauchline, John. *Isaiah 1–39*. London: S.C.M. Press, 1962.

Orelli, C. von. *The Prophecies of Isaiah*. Translated by J.S. Banks. Edinburgh: T. & T. Clark, 1889.

Westermann, Claus. *Isaiah 40–66: A Commentary*. Philadelphia: Westminster Press, 1969.

Wright, G. Ernest. *The Book of Isaiah*. The Layman's Bible Commentary. Richmond, Va.: John Knox Press, 1964.

Young, Edward. *The Book of Isaiah*. 3 vols. The New International Commentary on the Old Testament. Grand Rapids: Wm. B. Eerdmans Publishing Co., 1965, 1969, 1972.

_____. *Studies in Isaiah*. Grand Rapids: Wm. B. Eerdmans Publishing Co., 1954.

_____. *Who Wrote Isaiah?* Grand Rapids: Wm. B. Eerdmans Publishing Co., 1958.

JEREMIAH

Charles H. Dyer

INTRODUCTION

Jeremiah was the premier prophet of Judah during the dark days leading to her destruction. Though the light of other prophets, such as Habakkuk and Zephaniah, flickered in Judah at that time Jeremiah was the blazing torch who, along with Ezekiel in Babylon, exposed the darkness of Judah's sin with the piercing brightness of God's Word. He was a weeping prophet to a wayward people.

Authorship and Date. The author of the book is "Jeremiah son of Hilkiah" (1:1). The exact meaning of Jeremiah's name (*yirmᵉyāhû* or *yirmᵉyâh*) is disputed. Suggested meanings include "Yahweh establishes," "Yahweh exalts," and "Yahweh hurls down." Jeremiah's father, Hilkiah, was a member of the Levitical priesthood and lived in Anathoth, a small village about three miles northeast of Jerusalem (see the map "The World of Jeremiah and Ezekiel"). This city was one of those given to the descendants of Aaron the priest by Joshua (cf. Josh. 21:15-19). Probably this Hilkiah is not the same as his contemporary by the same name who discovered the Law in the temple during the reign of Josiah (cf. 2 Kings 22:3-14). Like Ezekiel (Ezek. 1:3) and Zechariah (Zech. 1:1; cf. Neh. 12:1, 4, 16), Jeremiah was from the priestly line. However, no evidence indicates that he ever entered the priesthood in Jerusalem.

Jeremiah's ministry extended from "the 13th year of the reign of Josiah" (Jer. 1:2) until the Exile of the Jerusalemites (1:3). Thus he prophesied from about 627 B.C. till at least 586 B.C. In fact Jeremiah 40-44 indicates that Jeremiah's ministry continued beyond the fall of Jerusalem to at least 582 B.C. In his book Jeremiah included a large number of chronological references that help date many of his prophecies.

A major difficulty is trying to determine how the various prophecies in the Book of Jeremiah were compiled. Many scholars feel that the book is an anthology of selected sayings from Jeremiah (or his disciples) that were later collected and arranged, often rather haphazardly. Some deny that a purposeful order can be (or should be) determined in the text.

The chart "The Dating of Jeremiah's Prophecies" shows how his prophecies are arranged chronologically. Three observations may be made.

(1) Obviously there is no chronological consistency. Unlike Ezekiel, whose prophecies are arranged in chronological order, Jeremiah often placed prophecies together that are dated years apart.

(2) Jeremiah's messages were given during times of stress, upheaval, and need. Chapters 1–6 and 11–12 correspond roughly to the time of King Josiah's reforms. The next major burst of prophetic activity (chaps. 7–10; 14–20; 22:1-19; 26) came when Nebuchadnezzar rose to power. The rest of Jeremiah's prophecies came at the time of the first deportation to Babylon, the second deportation to Babylon, the secret plot to rebel against Babylon, and the final siege and deportation to Babylon. Chapter 52 was written at a later date.

(3) The book itself gives evidence of multiple stages of growth. That is, Jeremiah, at different stages of his ministry, collected his prophecies and rearranged them in a definite pattern (cf. 25:13; 30:2; 36:2, 32). Jeremiah could have completed the final form of chapters 1–51 after he was taken hostage to Egypt (cf. 51:64). But what about chapter 52? Jeremiah 52, nearly identical to 2 Kings 24:18–25:30, was written sometime after 561 B.C. when King Jehoiachin was released from prison in Babylon (Jer. 52:31). Apparently this last chapter was appended to Jeremiah's prophecies by the same writer who compiled the Book of Kings. The chapter

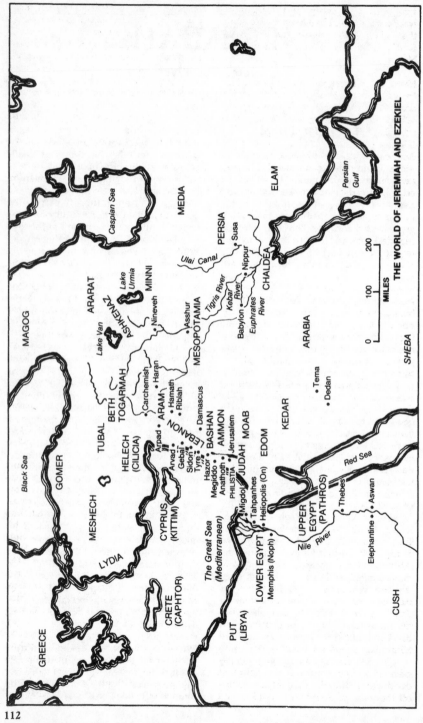

THE WORLD OF JEREMIAH AND EZEKIEL

was added to show that Jeremiah's words of judgment had been fulfilled and that Jehoiachin's release foreshadowed God's promises of restoration and blessing.

Historical Background. Jeremiah's ministry spanned the final five decades of Judah's history. His call to service came in 627 B.C. in the 13th year of King Josiah (cf. 1:2), Judah's last good king. Josiah's reign was the final ray of light before the darkness of idolatry and foreign intrigue settled over the Davidic throne. Josiah came to the throne when he was eight years old, and provided 31 years of relative stability for Judah.

Internally the nation of Judah was gripped by the idolatry that King Manasseh had promoted during his 55-year reign (2 Kings 21:1-9). In 622 B.C. (Josiah's 18th year) Judah experienced her final spiritual renewal (cf. 2 Kings 22:3–23:25). Prompted by the rediscovery of a copy of the Mosaic Law in the temple, Josiah embarked on a diligent effort to rid the nation of idolatry. He succeeded in removing the outward forms, but his efforts did not reach into his subjects' hearts. After Josiah's untimely death, the people returned to their wicked ways.

Internationally the Assyrian Empire, which had dominated the ancient Near East for centuries, was on the brink of collapse. The capital city, Nineveh, had been destroyed in 612 B.C., and in 609 the retreating Assyrian army was defeated at Haran. The beleaguered remains of the once-great Assyrian Empire staggered to Carchemish just across the Euphrates River (see the map "The World of Jeremiah and Ezekiel").

This collapse of Assyria was caused largely by the rise of another power—Babylon. In October 626 the Chaldean prince Nabopolassar had defeated the Assyrian army outside Babylon and claimed the throne in Babylon. The kingdom he founded came to be known as the Neo-Babylonian Empire. He consolidated his empire, and by 616 he was on the march to expand his territory. The combined army of the Babylonians and Medes destroyed Nineveh in 612.

Babylon's rise and Assyria's collapse created a realignment of power throughout the area. Judah, under Josiah, threw off the yoke of Assyrian dominion and enjoyed a brief period of national independence. This independence was shattered, however, by events in 609 B.C.

Egypt sensed an opportunity for expansion in Assyria's collapse. If a weakened Assyria could be maintained as a buffer state to halt Babylon's westward advances, Egypt would be free to reclaim much of western Palestine (including Judah) which she had lost to Assyria earlier.

Though Egypt had always feared a powerful Assyria, she now feared the prospect of a powerful Babylon even more. So Egypt entered the conflict between Assyria and Babylon on Assyria's side. In 609 Pharaoh Neco II marched with a large Egyptian army toward Haran to support the remaining Assyrian forces in a last attempt to retake their lost territory.

King Josiah knew what the consequences would be for Judah if Egypt were successful. He did not want Egypt to replace Assyria as Judah's taskmaster. So Josiah mobilized his army to stop the Egyptian advance. A battle took place on the plain of Megiddo—and Judah lost. Josiah was killed in battle and the Egyptian army continued on toward Haran (2 Chron. 35:20-24).

Whether Josiah's attack had an effect on the battle's outcome is not known, but possibly he delayed the Egyptian army from arriving in time to provide the assistance Assyria needed. Assyria failed in its bid to recapture the land, and it ceased to be a major force in history.

The city of Carchemish then became the line of demarcation, and the powers facing each other were Egypt and Babylon. After the defeat of Judah, Egypt assumed control of Palestine. Judah had appointed Jehoahaz king in place of his father Josiah; but after a reign of only three months he was deposed by Neco and taken to Egypt. (See the chart "The Last Five Kings of Judah," near 2 Kings 23:31-32.) Neco then plundered the treasuries of Judah and appointed Jehoiakim, another son of Josiah, as his vassal king (2 Kings 23:34-35).

In 605 B.C. another major shift occurred in the balance of power. For four years the Egyptians and Babylonians had faced each other at Carchemish with neither side able to gain the upper hand. Then in 605 crown prince Nebuchadnez-

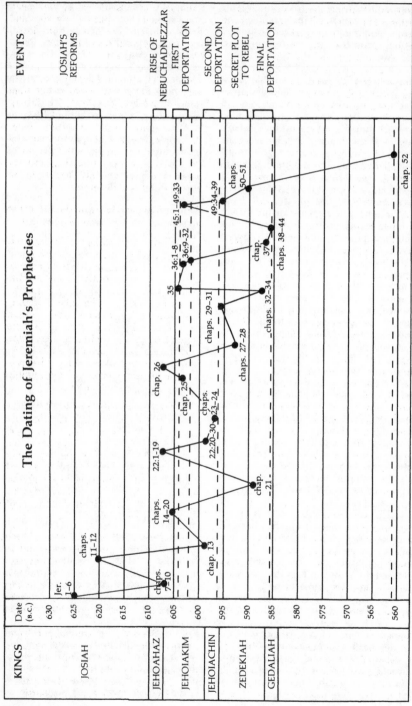

The Dating of Jeremiah's Prophecies

zar led the Babylonian forces to a decisive victory. The army of Babylonia smashed through the Egyptian defenses at Carchemish and pursued the forces to Egypt. Two other events in 605 B.C. influenced Judah's history. First, King Jehoiakim switched allegiance to Babylon after the Battle of Carchemish and agreed to serve as a vassal king for Nebuchadnezzar (2 Kings 24:1). Second, on August 15, 605 Nabopolassar, the king of Babylon, died. Nebuchadnezzar returned to Babylon to claim the throne.

Nebuchadnezzar solidified his rule over this territory by appointing kings and taking "hostages" to assure continued loyalty. During this campaign he took Daniel captive (Dan. 1:1-6).

Judah remained a vassal state until late in 601 B.C. At that time Nebuchadnezzar made another advance through Palestine. His objective was Egypt, but his goal was not achieved. The army of Babylon suffered a major defeat and was forced to retreat.

Jehoiakim was a political chameleon. He had switched allegiance from Egypt to Babylon in 605 when Nebuchadnezzar had defeated Egypt. After Babylon's defeat in 601, however, he again changed sides and supported Egypt (cf. 2 Kings 24:1). This was a fatal mistake.

By December 598 Nebuchadnezzar's army was prepared for an attack. His chief objective was to take Jerusalem to teach it (and no doubt other vassal nations too) the awful consequences of rebelling against Babylon. Jehoiakim died during the time of Babylon's attack, and was followed to the throne by his son, Jehoiachin. Jehoiachin saw the folly in opposing Babylon, and Jerusalem surrendered in March 597.

Nebuchadnezzar replaced the new king, looted the city, and removed the chief individuals. Jehoiachin, after a three-month reign, was deported to Babylon, and his uncle, Zedekiah, was installed as Judah's vassal king.

Along with Jehoiachin, Nebuchadnezzar also deported 10,000 of the leaders, skilled laborers, and soldiers of Jerusalem (cf. 2 Kings 24:12-16). This was probably when Ezekiel was taken to Babylon. Five years later he began his prophetic ministry in Babylon.

Because Judah's new king, Zedekiah, was weak and vacillating, Judah eventually collapsed. His 11-year reign was marred by spiritual decline and political instability. Rather than learning from the mistakes of the past, Zedekiah repeated them.

With the enthronement of another Pharaoh (Hophra) in Egypt in 588, Judah was once again enticed to revolt from Babylon (2 Kings 24:20–25:1; Jer. 52:3-4). A coalition of vassal states (Judah, Tyre, and Ammon) refused to remain under Babylon's control. Nebuchadnezzar's response was swift and harsh. The army of Babylon surrounded Jerusalem and began a long siege. In July-August 586 the city fell and was destroyed.

Structure and Style. Four characteristics are evident in the Book of Jeremiah.

1. Lack of chronological arrangement. As noted earlier under "Authorship and Date" the book has no chronological progression. Jeremiah compiled his prophecies in stages, but not chronologically. For example, many of Jeremiah's prophecies against the nations were written early in his ministry (cf. 25:1, 13). Yet the content of these prophecies is recorded near the end of the book (cf. 46:1–49:33). Thus one must look for some other reason for the arrangement of the prophecies in their present order.

2. Autobiographical nature. Writing an intensely personal book, Jeremiah revealed the nation's response to his ministry and his personal feelings about his messages. He wept over the impending destruction (9:1; 13:17; 14:17) and complained about the ridicule he was forced to endure (20:7-10). He also recorded his self-doubt (1:7-8) and his doubts about God's justice (12:1-2).

3. Different literary materials. Three types of literary materials are found in the Book of Jeremiah: poetic discourses, prose discourses, and prose narratives. The arrangement of these materials can provide a key to the underlying structure of Jeremiah. They are in the book as follows:

Chapters 1–25 Mixture of poetic and prose discourse with occasional narrative

Chapters 26–29 Mixture of prose discourse and narrative

Chapters 30–31 Poetic discourse

Chapters 32–33 Prose discourse

Chapters 34–36 Mixture of prose discourse and narrative

Chapters 37–45 Narrative in chronological order

Chapters 46–51 Poetic discourse

Chapter 52 Narrative in chronological order

These literary materials seem to offer major breaks in the content of the book. The significance of these divisions will be discussed next.

4. *Logical arrangement of material.* If Jeremiah did not arrange his book chronologically, how *did* he arrange it? The best answer seems to be that he used a broad logical arrangement of his material to convey an overall message to the people. That is, as Jeremiah compiled his subsequent collections of his prophecies, he rearranged them in a logical pattern. The arrangement developed his theme of God's judgment. Chapters 2–45 focused on God's judgment on Judah and chapters 46–51 focused on God's judgment on the Gentile nations.

The various literary materials provide additional keys for dividing Jeremiah's book. Thus chapters 2–25 (mixture of poetic and prose discourse) contain Jeremiah's 13 messages of judgment on Judah. These were followed by chapters 26–29 (mixture of prose discourse and narrative) which indicated how the people responded to Jeremiah and his message. The Jews' rejection assured this judgment. However, before the judgment began, Jeremiah pointed ahead to Judah's future hope (chaps. 30–31, poetic discourse; and chaps. 32–33, prose discourse). Chapters 34–36 (mixture of prose discourse and narrative) continue the theme of rejection from chapters 26–29. Judah's destruction was inevitable because she had rejected the Word of God. Jeremiah sketched the events that occurred before, during, and after the fall of Jerusalem in chapters 37–45 (narrative in chronological order). God accomplished His judgment on the nation because of her sin. And yet if God's Chosen People were judged for their sin, how could the rest of the world hope to escape? In chapters 46–51 (poetic discourse) Jeremiah turned to these other nations and foretold their judgment. The different literary materials were used by Jeremiah to mold and shape his message.

OUTLINE

I. Introduction (chap. 1)
   A. The prophet's background (1:1-3)
   B. The prophet's call (1:4-10)
   C. The prophet's confirming visions (1:11-16)
      1. The blossoming almond branch (1:11-12)
      2. The boiling pot (1:13-16)
   D. The prophet's challenge (1:17-19)
II. Prophecies concerning Judah (chaps. 2–45)
   A. Divine judgment on Judah (chaps. 2–25)
      1. Jeremiah's nine general prophecies of judgment (chaps. 2–20)
      2. Jeremiah's four specific prophecies of judgment (chaps. 21–25)
   B. Personal conflict with Judah (chaps. 26–29)
      1. Conflict with the people (chap. 26)
      2. Conflict with the false prophets in Jerusalem (chaps. 27–28)
      3. Conflict with the false prophets in exile (chap. 29)
   C. Future comfort for Israel and Judah (chaps. 30–33)
      1. The restoration of Israel and Judah declared (chaps. 30–31)
      2. The restoration of Israel and Judah illustrated (chap. 32)
      3. The restoration of Israel and Judah reaffirmed (chap. 33)
   D. Present catastrophe of Judah (chaps. 34–45)
      1. Before the fall (chaps. 34–36)
      2. During the fall (chaps. 37–39)
      3. After the fall (chaps. 40–45)
III. Prophecies concerning the Nations (chaps. 46–51)
   A. Prophecy against Egypt (chap. 46)
      1. Egypt to be defeated at Carchemish (46:1-12)
      2. Egypt to be invaded and exiled (46:13-26)
      3. Israel to be regathered (46:27-28)
   B. Prophecy against Philistia (chap. 47)

COMMENTARY

I. Introduction (chap. 1)

The Book of Jeremiah opens by introducing its readers to the prophet. His background and call into the prophetic ministry set the stage for the rest of his book.

A. The prophet's background (1:1-3)

1:1. **Jeremiah** gives information on his family background (v. 1) during the time he ministered (vv. 2-3). He was **one of the priests,** descended from the priestly line of Aaron. His father, **Hilkiah,** was probably not the high priest Hilkiah who discovered the copy of the Law during the time of Josiah (2 Kings 22:2-14). The name "Hilkiah" was evidently a common name given to several men in the Old Testament who were priests or Levites (1 Chron. 6:45-46; 26:10-11; 2 Chron. 34:9-22; Neh. 12:7; Jer. 1:1).

Jeremiah's hometown was **Anathoth** which was **in the territory of Benjamin.** The village of Anathoth was about three miles northeast of Jerusalem. The territory of Benjamin bordered the territory of Judah, and the dividing line extended roughly east to west and passed beside Jerusalem (cf. Josh. 18:15-16). Anathoth was a city allocated by Joshua to the priests (Josh. 21:15-19). Solomon exiled Abiathar the priest to Anathoth for supporting Adonijah as David's successor (1 Kings 1:7; 2:26-27).

1:2-3. Jeremiah was born a priest, but began functioning as a prophet when he received **the word of the LORD.** A prophet was one through whom God spoke directly to His people. God's call of Jeremiah came **in the 13th year of the reign of Josiah.** Josiah became king of Judah in 640 B.C., so his 13th year was 627 B.C. Josiah was the last righteous king of Judah. After his untimely death in 609 B.C., every king who ascended Judah's throne was unworthy of the task. Jeremiah continued as God's spokesman **down to the fifth month of the 11th year of Zedekiah.** That date was July-August 586 B.C. Thus Jeremiah's ministry lasted at least 41 years. However, this verse probably refers to Jeremiah's ministry to the nation of Judah until **the people of Jerusalem went into exile** because 39:11–44:30 records events of Jeremiah's ministry that occurred *after* August 586.

B. The prophet's call (1:4-10)

1:4-5. God's call of Jeremiah as a prophet, though brief, contained a message designed to motivate him for his task. God revealed that His selection of Jeremiah as a prophet had occurred **before** he had even been **formed . . . in the womb.** The word **knew** (*yāḏaʿ*) means far more than intellectual knowledge. It was used of the intimate relations experienced by a husband and wife ("lay," Gen. 4:1) and conveyed the sense of a close personal relationship ("chosen," Amos 3:2) and protection ("watches over," Ps. 1:6). Before Jeremiah was conceived God had singled him out to be His spokesman to Israel.

Jeremiah had been **set . . . apart** for this ministry. The verb translated "set apart" (*qāḏaš*) means setting something or someone apart for a specific use. Individuals or objects "set apart" (or sanctified or made holy) for use by God included the Sabbath Day (Ex. 16:23; 20:8), the tabernacle and its furnishings (Ex. 29:44; 40:9), and the priests (Ex. 29:1; 30:30). God had marked Jeremiah from conception and reserved him for a special task. He was appointed to be **a prophet to the nations.** Though Jeremiah proclaimed God's Word to Judah (chaps. 2–45), his ministry as God's spokesman extended beyond Judah to Gentile nations (chaps. 46–51).

1:6. Jeremiah responded to God's appointment with a measure of self-doubt. He first objected that he did **not know how to speak.** Jeremiah was not claiming that he was physically unable to talk. He was claiming a lack of eloquence and speaking ability required for such a public ministry.

He also objected that he was **only a child** (*naʿar*). This word was used of infants (Ex. 2:6; 1 Sam. 4:21) and of young men (Gen. 14:24). Jeremiah's age is not given, but possibly he was in his late teens or early 20s at this time. By using the term "child" Jeremiah was emphasizing his lack of experience. He felt ill-prepared to be God's ambassador to the nations.

1:7-10. God gave three answers to Jeremiah's objections. First, He stressed the authority under which Jeremiah was to act. Jeremiah should not use inexperience as an excuse for evading his task. He would have no choice in the selection of his audience or his message. Rather, he was to **go to everyone** to whom God sent him and **say whatever** God commanded. Jeremiah did not have to be an eloquent elder stateman—he was simply to be a faithful messenger.

Second, God stressed that He would protect the future prophet. Evidently Jeremiah was afraid for his personal safety. Certainly his fears were based on his awareness of the times because the people did try to get rid of him (cf. 11:18-23; 12:6; 20:1-2; 26:11; 37:15-16; 38:4-6). Yet God told Jeremiah **not** to **be afraid of them,** because He would be on his side. The people would try to kill Jeremiah, but God promised to **rescue** him.

Third, God showed Jeremiah the source of his message. Jeremiah's call must have come in the form of a vision (cf. Ezek. 1:1) because he noted that **the LORD reached out His hand** to touch Jeremiah's **mouth.** This visible manifestation of God was His object lesson to tell Jeremiah that the Lord Himself would **put** His **words in** Jeremiah's **mouth.** Jeremiah need not worry what to say; God would provide the very words he would speak.

God then summarized the content of Jeremiah's message (Jer. 1:10). It would be a message of both judgment and blessing to **nations and kingdoms.** God used two metaphors to describe Jeremiah's mission (cf. 31:28 for a later use of the same two metaphors). Comparing Jeremiah to a farmer, God said he would **uproot** (announce judgment) **and . . . plant** (announce blessing). Comparing Jeremiah to an architect, God said he would **tear down . . . destroy, and overthrow** (pronounce judgment) and **build** (pronounce blessing).

C. The prophet's confirming visions (1:11-16)

God confirmed His call to Jeremiah by giving him two visions. The first (vv. 11-12) focused on the nature of the message Jeremiah would deliver and the second (vv. 13-16) pointed out the content of that message.

1. THE BLOSSOMING ALMOND BRANCH (1:11-12)

1:11. God's first confirming vision caused Jeremiah to **see the branch of an almond tree.** The Hebrew word for "almond tree" is *šāqēḏ*, from the word "to watch or to wake" (*šāqaḏ*). The almond tree was named the "awake tree" because in Palestine it is the first tree in the year to bud and bear fruit. Its blooms precede its leaves, as the tree bursts into blossom in late January.

1:12. The branch represented God who was **watching to see that His word is fulfilled.** God used a play on words to associate the almond branch with His activity. The word for "watching" is *šōqēḏ,* related to the Hebrew noun for "almond tree." Jeremiah's vision of the "awake tree" reminded him that God was awake and watching over His word to make sure it came to pass.

2. THE BOILING POT (1:13-16)

1:13. God's second confirming vision caused Jeremiah to **see a boiling pot.** The pot was a large kettle that was evidently sitting on a fire because it was "boiling" (lit., "blown upon," *nāpûaḥ,* indicating a wind or draft blowing on the fire to help bring the cauldron's contents to a boil). The pot was **tilting away from the north** indicating that its contents were about to be spilled out toward the south.

1:14-16. The tilting pot represented **disaster that will be poured out on** those **who live in** Judah. The direction from which the pot was facing represented **the peoples of the northern kingdoms** whom God was summoning to punish the nation **of Judah.** Some scholars feel that God was referring to a Scythian invasion, but it seems better to understand His message as a reference to the coming invasion by Babylon and her allies (cf. 25:8-9). Though Babylon was located to the *east* geographically, the invading armies followed the trade routes along the Euphrates River in their march to Judah. Thus those armies did approach from the *north* (cf. 4:6; 6:1, 22; 10:22; 13:20; 15:12; 16:15; 23:8; 25:9, 26; 31:8; 46:24; 47:2; 50:3, 9, 41). They would **set up their thrones in the entrance of the gates of Jerusalem,** indicating that the city would fall to them. Jeremiah recorded the fulfillment of this prophecy in 39:2-3 after the Babylonians captured Jerusalem.

Judah's fall to Babylon would be God's judgment for her idolatry. **In forsaking** God and **worshiping what their hands** had **made** the people of Judah had violated their covenant with God (cf. Deut. 28). The sin of Judah brought about her downfall.

D. The prophet's challenge (1:17-19)

1:17-19. After explaining the task, God charged Jeremiah to take up the challenge. **Get yourself ready!** is literally, "gird up your loins" (cf. Ex. 12:11; 2 Kings 4:29; 9:1; Luke 12:35; Eph. 6:14; 1 Peter 1:13). God gave him the needed strength to **stand** against the people of Judah. Through God's enablement Jeremiah would be as strong as **a fortified city, an iron pillar, and a bronze wall.** God's strength to withstand attack would be needed because all the people would oppose Jeremiah's message. They would **fight against** Jeremiah, but God assured him that they would **not overcome** him.

II. Prophecies concerning Judah (chaps. 2–45)

This section begins with Jeremiah recording 13 oracles of divine judgment against the nation of Judah (chaps. 2–25). He then indicated the personal conflicts that ensued as the people rejected his messages (chaps. 26–29). The judgment of Judah was now sealed; but before he chronicled the execution of that judgment, Jeremiah inserted God's message of future comfort for Israel and Judah (chaps. 30–33). Though Judah would go into captivity, God would not abandon His people. After this message of future hope, Jeremiah recorded the fall of Judah to Babylon (chaps. 34–45). Then the word of judgment he had pronounced was fulfilled.

A. Divine judgment on Judah (chaps. 2–25)

These 13 messages of judgment include nine general prophecies of judgment (chaps. 2–20) and four specific prophecies of judgment (chaps. 21–25).

1. JEREMIAH'S NINE GENERAL PROPHECIES OF JUDGMENT (CHAPS. 2–20)

a. Jerusalem's faithlessness (2:1–3:5)

2:1-3. Jeremiah's first message confronted **Jerusalem** with her waywardness. To emphasize this Jeremiah contrasted Judah's former devotion (vv. 1-3) with her present departure from God (v. 4–3:5). At the time of the Exodus Israel **loved** God and **followed** Him **through the desert.** Israel had her lapses of faith when she murmured against God in the wilderness wanderings, but God in His grace and "forbearance" (Rom. 3:25) passed over her. Yet for the most part she had remained faithful as a nation.

Israel had been set apart as **holy to the LORD** (cf. Ex. 19:6; 22:31). Just as **the firstfruits** of **the harvest** belonged to God (cf. Lev. 23:9-14), so Israel had been chosen as the first nation to worship the Lord. Those **who devoured her** were as guilty as those who ate of the firstfruits dedicated to God, and God would bring **disaster** on them (cf. Gen. 12:3).

2:4-8. Israel's faithfulness to God, however, did not last. **Jacob** (a synonym for **Israel,** v. 4) **followed worthless idols** (v. 5; cf. vv. 8, 11; 8:19; 10:8, 14-15; 14:22; 16:19; 18:15; 51:17-18) forgetting that **the LORD** had **led** them **through the** desert (2:6) **into a fertile land.** And the people **defiled** the **land** with their idolatry (v. 7).

Jeremiah singled out the three groups charged with leading the nation and exposed their lack of obedience (v. 8). **The priests** who were to instruct the people in the ways of God **did not know** God, that is, they themselves did not have an intimate relationship with the One about whom they were teaching (see comments on "knew" in 1:5).

The leaders (rō'îm, lit., "shepherds") were the political and civil leaders appointed by God to guide and protect the nation. In the early history of Israel this function was fulfilled by judges, but later the duty was assigned to kings. Ironically the ones who were to lead Judah were themselves in need of correction. They **rebelled against** the One who had appointed them to their task.

The prophets were the third group charged with leading the nation. But instead of declaring God's words of rebuke and correction, they **prophesied by Baal** and urged the people to follow **worthless idols** (cf. comments on 2:5). Baal was a Canaanite god of fertility whose worship was a constant thorn in Israel's side (cf. 1 Kings 18:18-40; 2 Kings 10:18-28; 21:1-3).

2:9-12. Having clearly shown the faithlessness of the people, Jeremiah used the image of a court case to focus on the seriousness of Israel's sin. God would **bring charges** (rîb, a legal term for filing a court case or lawsuit; cf. Micah 6:1-2). Jeremiah asked the people to go on a "field trip" to observe the faithfulness of the Gentiles. But whether they went **to the coasts of Kittim** (Cyprus) in the west or **to Kedar** (north Arabian desert tribes) in the east, the results would always be the same: no pagan society had **ever changed its gods.** The idolatrous nations surrounding Israel were more faithful to their false gods than Israel had been to the true God of the universe.

2:13. Israel had **committed two sins.** The first was one of omission: she had **forsaken** her God. Her second sin was one of commission: she had replaced her true God with false idols. Man's heart, like nature, abhors a vacuum. Using imagery that those residing in Judah would understand, Jeremiah compared the nation's actions to someone abandoning a **spring of living** (running) **water** for **broken cisterns.** The most reliable and refreshing sources of water in Israel were her natural springs. This water was dependable; and its clear, cool consistency was satisfying. In contrast, the most unreliable source of water was cisterns. Cisterns were large pits dug into the rock and covered with plaster. These pits were used to gather rainwater. This water was brackish; and if the rains were below normal, it could run out. Worse yet, if a cistern developed a crack it would not **hold the water.** To turn from a dependable, pure stream of running water to a broken, brackish cistern was idiotic. Yet that is what Judah did when she turned from God to idols.

2:14-16. Judah's apostasy brought severe repercussions. Her **land** was **laid waste** by foreign invaders (compared to **lions**) and her **towns** were **burned and deserted.** The reference to **Memphis** (cf. Ezek. 30:13, 16) **and Tahpanhes** (cf. Ezek. 30:18), cities in Egypt, could refer to Pharaoh Shishak's invasion of Judah in 925 B.C. (1 Kings 14:25-26) or to Pharaoh Neco's killing King Josiah in 609 (2 Kings 23:29-30). In both instances Egypt triumphed over Judah and **shaved the crown of** Judah's **head.**

2:17-19. In addition to **forsaking the LORD** (v. 13) for false gods, Judah had also forsaken **the LORD** for false alliances.

The nation vainly went from **Egypt** to **Assyria** trying to forge treaties that would guarantee her safety (cf. v. 36; Ezek. 23; Hosea 7:11). **Shihor** is a branch of the Nile River (NIV marg.; cf. Josh. 13:3; 1 Chron. 13:5; Isa. 23:3). No alliance could protect Judah from her sin. Only after she received her judgment would she realize how **evil and bitter it** was to **forsake the** LORD.

2:20. Judah's spiritual apostasy was matched by her spiritual adultery. By describing Judah as a spiritual nymphomaniac Jeremiah pictured her insatiable lust for false gods. Jeremiah painted four verbal pictures (vv. 20-28) of Judah to describe her wayward state. The first picture was an animal that had broken its yoke. Judah **broke off** her **yoke** that had bound her to the Lord and followed after the gods of her heathen neighbors (cf. 5:5). She set up worship centers **on every high hill** (frequently called "high places") to serve these gods (cf. 3:2; Ezek. 6:1-7, 13). Spiritually Judah was acting like **a prostitute,** though Jeremiah's words could also refer to the sexual perversions that accompanied the worship of Baal (cf. Hosea 4:10-14).

2:21. Jeremiah's second picture of Judah is one of **a choice vine** from **reliable stock** that God **had planted** and nurtured. Judah is often pictured as God's vine in the Old Testament (cf. Isa. 5:1-7; Ezek. 15) and in the Gospels (cf. Matt. 21:33-46). God did all He could. for the nation, but in spite of His care she became **a corrupt, wild vine,** incapable of producing any good fruit.

2:22. The third picture of Judah was of someone with a **stain** that could not be washed off. Her sin was so ingrained that even **soda** (lye, a strong mineral alkali) and **soap** (a strong vegetable alkali) could not remove the stain.

2:23-25. Jeremiah's fourth picture of Judah is of a wild animal in **heat.** Like **a swift** female camel Judah vigorously pursued her false gods (on the word **Baals** in the pl., see comments on Jud. 2:11; also cf. Jer. 9:14); like **a wild donkey** she could not be restrained in her lust for those **foreign gods.**

2:26-28. Judah's pursuit of false gods caused her to be **disgraced.** Though she was ascribing her very existence to idols of **wood** and stone, yet when **trouble** came she had the audacity to ask God to

come and save her. Her false **gods** were impotent, yet **Judah** had **as many gods as** she had **towns** (cf. 11:13)—showing the multiplication of her idolatry.

2:29-30. Judah had become spiritually irresponsible. In spite of her sin she felt she could **bring charges against** God. This is an ironic reversal of verse 9 where God brought charges against Judah. Judah was charging God with harassment, but God's judgment was deserved because the people had **all rebelled against** Him. God had **punished the people,** but His chastisement was intended to bring **correction.** Yet the people refused to **respond,** and even murdered God's messengers, the **prophets.**

2:31-33. Judah's irresponsibility showed up most clearly in her forgetfulness of God's past dealings. The **people** thought they were **free,** independent of God. **A bride** would never forget **her wedding ornaments** that identified her as a married woman, but Judah had **forgotten** her God who had adorned her and set her apart from the other nations of the world. And she had done this **days without number.** Jeremiah sarcastically concluded that Judah had become so **skilled** in the art of **pursuing** illicit **love** that even the **worst of women** could learn new secrets of seduction by observing her perverse ways.

2:34-35. Another indication of her irresponsibility was her involvement in the shedding of innocent blood. Her clothes were covered with **the lifeblood of the innocent poor.** Had these people been caught **breaking in,** that is, caught in burglary and were killed, then the one responsible for the death was considered guiltless (Ex. 22:2). But those Judah killed were not killed for crimes they had committed; they were "innocent." Yet Judah continued to claim, **I am innocent. . . . I have not sinned.** She would therefore experience God's **judgment.**

2:36-37. A fourth indication of Judah's irresponsibility was her fickle foreign policy. She was constantly **changing** her **ways** in her dealings with other nations (cf. v. 18; Ezek. 23). Yet she would find that any new alliance with **Egypt** would be just as disappointing as her past alliance with **Assyria** (cf. 2 Kings 16:7-9; Isa. 7:13-25). The LORD had **rejected** these nations so Judah could **not be helped by them.**

3:1-5. Jeremiah ended his first message by exposing the spiritual harlotry of Judah. If a couple divorced and the wife married another man, she was prohibited by Law from ever being reunited with her first husband (Deut. 24:1-4). Yet Judah had separated from her Husband, Yahweh, and had lived as a prostitute (cf. Jer. 2:20) with many lovers. Such actions were defiling (on defiled, cf. 3:2, 9 and see comments on 23:11). There was the possibility that God would not take His people back. Obviously this would be a temporary rejection because Jeremiah later recorded God's promise of Israel's national restoration under a New Covenant (cf. 3:18; 31:31-33).

Israel's spiritual harlotry was obvious. It was hard to find a place where she had not been ravished in her spiritual union with false gods (cf. 3:9 and comments on 2:20). Her eager wait by the roadside . . . for lovers was the type of activity commonly employed by cult prostitutes (cf. Gen. 38:13-14, 20-21). Judah's desire for idolatrous lovers was as keen as a marauding nomad in the desert who waited for passing caravans to plunder.

God judged Judah by withholding showers and spring rains (cf. Deut. 28:23-24; Jer. 14). Yet Judah refused to blush with shame. Though she called out to God, My Father, my Friend from my youth, and asked Him to stop being angry, her words were hollow cries designed merely to manipulate God. Her talk was of friendship, but her actions never changed. She continued to do all the evil she could.

b. Repentance in light of coming judgment (3:6–6:30)

Jeremiah's second message is a distinct prophecy that was probably given at a different time from the first message. Yet the content of this prophecy is logically related to 2:1–3:5 and forms a fitting conclusion to the first message. In light of Judah's sin God summoned the nation to repent. The prophecy is dated generally "during the reign of King Josiah." Perhaps it can be placed sometime between the beginning of Jeremiah's ministry in 627 B.C. and the discovery of the Law in 621 B.C. (cf. 11:1-8).

(1) The summons to repentance (3:6–4:4). **3:6-11.** God revealed to Jeremi-

ah the story of two sisters—Israel and Judah (cf. Ezek. 23). The Northern Kingdom of Israel committed adultery on all the high places of the land, a reference to her extensive idol worship. God in His patience waited for her to return to Him, but Israel refused and continued in her idolatry. Moreover, her unfaithful sister Judah was watching Israel sin. God's response was to give Israel a certificate of divorce and to send her away (cf. comments on Hosea 2:2). Jeremiah was referring to the destruction of the Northern Kingdom of Israel by Assyria in 722 B.C. (cf. 2 Kings 17:5-20).

Unfortunately Judah did not learn from Israel's fall. Instead she also . . . committed adultery. Indeed Judah added hypocrisy to the sin of Israel because Judah committed the same sins while making a pretense of returning to the LORD. Thus Israel in spite of her sin was still more righteous than unfaithful Judah.

3:12-18. Jeremiah paused in his condemnation of sin to offer a message of repentance and hope to the Northern Kingdom. If Israel would return to her God (cf. 7:3; 26:13), He would frown on her no longer and extend His mercy. But the people needed to acknowledge their guilt of rebellion and idolatry.

God promised to gather a remnant (one . . . from every town and two from every clan) and bring them up to Jerusalem (Zion; see comments on Lam. 1:4 and Zech. 8:3). This remnant would have shepherds (leaders; cf. Jer. 10:21; 22:22; 23:1-2, 4) who would provide the leadership intended by God, and their numbers would increase greatly—a sign of God's blessing (Deut. 30:5, 9).

The ark of the covenant, which was lost after Babylon destroyed Judah in 586 B.C., would not be missed, and another ark would not be made. In place of the ark will be The Throne of the LORD, a title by which the city of Jerusalem will be known. It is significant that Ezekiel (cf. Ezek. 43:7) also pictured the millennial temple as a place where God's throne will be. Evidently Christ will rule from the temple during the millennial period. God's rule from Jerusalem will extend over all nations who will go to Jerusalem to worship Him (cf. Zech. 14:16-19).

In addition to spiritual renewal Judah and Israel will also experience physical restoration. **The house of Judah** and **the house of Israel** will reunite as a nation (cf. Jer. 31:31-33; Ezek. 37:15-28). They will return from their captivity to **the land** God had promised to their **forefathers as an inheritance.** Israel and Judah divided as a nation in 931 B.C., and have never reunited as a nation under God. The fulfillment of this promise awaits the return of Christ.

3:19-20. God's desire was to bless His people. He wanted to **treat** them **like sons** and to restore their **inheritance, but** the nation was **like a woman** who was **unfaithful to her husband.** The roadblock to restoration was **Israel,** not God.

3:21-25. It is possible that in these verses Jeremiah was painting an idealistic picture for **the people of Israel.** The people mourn for their condition (v. 21), God offers repentance (v. 22a), and the people feel abject and heartfelt remorse for their sin (vv. 22b-25). But the Book of Jeremiah leads one to believe that the **people** did not follow this example. It still awaits the future repentance of the nation when Christ returns as King (Zech. 12:10–13:1).

The section opens with the people **weeping and pleading.** Their cry was prompted because of their transgressions **(they had perverted their ways)** and because they had **forgotten . . . their God.** In Jeremiah's ideal picture of repentance the nation finally realized the depth of the pit into which she had fallen. God responded to the nation's cry by offering to help her if she would **return.**

Israel's response is a model of true repentance. She consciously determined to **come to . . . God** because of who He is. Admitting that her **idolatrous commotion** which had been rampant in the land was **a deception,** the nation acknowledged that only in **God is there salvation for Israel.** The **shame** and **disgrace** of her past actions forced her to admit that she had **sinned against the** LORD.

4:1-2. God promised to respond positively if **Israel** and **Judah** would indeed **return to** Him. However, the repentance had to be genuine. The **detestable idols** had to be removed from God's **sight,** and the people could **no longer go astray** after their false gods. Yet if **the nations** of Israel and Judah did repent, they would **be blessed by** God.

4:3-4. Jeremiah then used two metaphors to show the need for repentance.

The first metaphor pertained to farming. Just as a farmer does not sow his seed on unplowed ground, so God does **not sow** His seed of blessing in unrepentant hearts. **The men of Judah and . . . Jerusalem** needed to **break up** the **unplowed ground** of their hearts through repentance. The second metaphor came from the Jewish practice of circumcision. Circumcision was a sign of being under God's covenant with Israel (cf. Gen. 17:9-14). The men, though circumcised physically, needed to **circumcise** their **hearts** so that their inward condition matched their outward profession (cf. Deut. 10:16; 30:6; Jer. 9:25-26; Rom. 2:28-29).

Unless Judah did exercise true repentance—not just outward profession—God's **wrath** would be released and would **burn like fire** against the **people.** And once God's wrath was released **no one** could **quench it.**

(2) The warning of coming judgment (4:5-31). **4:5-9.** Lest the people wonder what form God's wrath might take, Jeremiah described the coming judgment as the unleashing of Judah's enemies to the north. The command would go out to **sound the trumpet,** which would **signal** the approach of the enemies' armies (cf. Hosea 5:8; Joel 2:1; Amos 3:6). In response, those living in the countryside would **flee for safety** to Jerusalem **(Zion)** to escape the **disaster from the north** that was bringing **destruction.**

The approaching army of Babylon in its ferocity was like **a lion** that had **come out of his lair** to attack the **land** of Judah. The invasion would leave the **towns** of Judah **in ruins without inhabitant.** Realization of the coming destruction would cause the people to **lament** and to wear **sackcloth,** rough, coarse material, symbolizing mourning (cf. Jer. 6:26; 48:37; 49:3; Gen. 37:34; 1 Kings 21:27; Neh. 9:1; Pss. 30:11; 35:13; 69:11; Lam. 2:10; Dan. 9:3) because God's **fierce anger** had **not** been **turned away** (cf. Jer. 4:4).

The day of God's judgment would hold special dread for Judah's leaders. **The king and the officials** along with **the priests** and **the prophets** would be paralyzed by fear as they watched the annihilation of their country. Yet the destruction came in part because of their failure to provide the leadership Judah needed (cf. 2:8).

4:10. This verse, Jeremiah's response

to God, is one of the most difficult verses in the book to interpret. The prophet claimed that God had **deceived the people** by promising they would **have peace when** in fact God had brought His **sword** of judgment to their **throats.** Had God misled His people by lying to them about their fate? This interpretation must be rejected because it is out of character with the nature of God (cf. Num. 23:19). In fact God's true prophets had been predicting judgment, not peace (cf. Jer. 1:14-16; Micah 3:9-12; Hab. 1:5-11; Zeph. 1:4-13). Only the false prophets had been proclaiming peace (cf. Jer. 6:14; 14:13-14; 23:16-17). Therefore it is better to see Jeremiah complaining that God had allowed these false prophets to proclaim their message.

4:11-12. Jeremiah returned to God's announcement of the coming invasion of Judah. God compared the armies to **a scorching wind** that blows in from **the desert.** Wind affected the lives of everyone in Palestine. The refreshing breezes from the Mediterranean Sea helped the farmers in winnowing grain, and also brought the life-sustaining dew which nourished the land during the summer. However, the hot, dry, east **wind,** the sirocco, that blows in from the desert causes serious difficulties. It is **not** used **to winnow** because it is **too strong.** Instead, the sirocco could wither vegetation (Gen. 41:6) and cause extreme discomfort for those who had to endure it (Jonah 4:8). Also Ezekiel compared Babylon's invasion to the coming of the east wind (Ezek. 17:10; 19:12).

4:13-14. Using a different illustration, God compared the advance of Babylon's army to an approaching storm. The soldiers were sweeping into Judah **like the clouds,** and their **chariots** swirled along **like a whirlwind.** In light of Judah's certain destruction God again graciously called the people to repentance. If they were to **wash the evil from** their **heart** they would **be saved** (delivered) from their impending doom.

4:15-18. The approach of Babylon's soldiers would be signaled by messengers **from Dan** in the extreme north of Israel and **from the hills of Ephraim** 30-40 miles north of **Jerusalem.** The word brought by these heralds was that **a besieging army** was coming . . . **against the cities of Judah.**

God sent this force to punish Judah **because** the nation had **rebelled against** Him. Judah herself was responsible for the calamity. It was her **own conduct and actions** that **brought this . . . punishment** from God.

4:19-22. Jeremiah responded to the news of the coming invasion by crying out in **anguish.** His **heart** pounded and he could not **keep silent** as he thought of the approaching **battle** and the **disaster** it would bring Judah. Jeremiah concluded by admitting that the **people** of Judah were **fools** (*ĕwîl*, a person lacking sense and morally corrupt). They were like **children** and had **no understanding** of the way of righteousness which they should have been following. In an ironic reversal of Proverbs 1:2-3 the people were **skilled** (*ḥăkāmîm*, "wise") **in doing evil,** but ignorant in knowing **how to do good.**

4:23-28. Jeremiah pictured God's coming judgment as a cosmic catastrophe—an undoing of Creation. Using imagery from the Creation account (Gen. 1) Jeremiah indicated that no aspect of life would remain untouched. God would make Judah **formless and empty** (*tōhû wāḇōhû*), a phrase used to describe the chaos that preceded God's works in Creation (cf. Gen. 1:2). The **light** that had pierced into the darkness during Creation (cf. Gen. 1:3-5) **was** now **gone. The mountains** and **hills,** which had been separated from the waters (cf. Gen. 1:9-10), were now **quaking** and **swaying** at the judgment of God. The **people** along with **every bird. . . . and the fruitful land** were again removed. The land became as barren as it had been before the creation of life (Gen. 1:11-13, 20-26).

God's imagery was so awesome that some might have thought He would totally destroy the land of Israel. To guard against this misunderstanding, God qualified His statement (Jer. 4:27). Though **the whole land** would **be ruined** as He judged the people, He still promised that He would **not destroy it completely** (cf. 5:18). Nevertheless **the earth** would **mourn;** judgment would come (4:28).

4:29-31. As the armies approached Judah people in **every town** fled to avoid being killed. The people hid in **the thickets** and **among the rocks,** hoping not to be apprehended by the soldiers. By contrast the Jerusalemites tried to **dress** themselves **in scarlet** with **jewels of gold** and **eyes** that were shaded **with paint** (to make them appear larger). They tried to dress like a harlot to allure the Babylonians away from their attack (cf. Ezek. 16:26-29; 23:40-41). But the ruse would not work because Jerusalem's former **lovers** now sought her **life.**

As the Babylonians pressed their attack, Jeremiah pictured **the Daughter of Zion** (Jerusalem) crying out in agony like **a woman in labor** (cf. Isa. 13:8; 21:3; 26:17; Jer. 6:24; 13:21; 22:23; 30:6; 48:41; 49:22, 24; 50:43; Micah 4:9-10). She stretched out **her hands** for assistance which never materialized as her **life** ebbed out before her **murderers.**

(3) The reasons for coming judgment (chap. 5). **5:1-3.** Judah was to be judged because of her corruption. God sent Jeremiah on a divine scavenger hunt in **Jerusalem.** He had to **find** only **one person** who dealt **honestly** with his fellow Israelites or who was actively seeking **the truth.** If he could find just **one,** God would **forgive this city.** Unfortunately Jeremiah's search was less fruitful than the one made at Sodom (cf. Gen. 18:22-23). The people **refused correction** and their **faces** were **harder than stone,** indicating their stubborn refusal **to repent.**

5:4-6. Jeremiah assumed that those he encountered were **only the poor**—the uneducated masses who were uninstructed in the **requirements of** the righteous **God.** Surely, he thought, if he went **to the leaders . . . they** would **know the way of the LORD. But** Jeremiah's visit brought only disappointment (cf. 2:8). The leaders had joined the people and **had broken off the yoke** of service to God (cf. 2:20).

So **God** would judge leaders and followers alike for their sin. Jeremiah referred to three wild animals to picture the coming punishment. By breaking away from her Master's yoke, Judah had opened herself up to attack from marauding beasts. The **lion,** the **wolf,** and the **leopard** symbolized the ravages of Babylon's **attack** on Judah.

5:7-9. God asked Judah two rhetorical questions. First, He asked why He **should . . . forgive** Judah (v. 7). Second, He asked why He **should . . . not punish** Judah for her sin (v. 9). Between the two questions God described Judah's character in a way that made the answers obvious. He could not forgive Judah because she had **forsaken** Him and **sworn by** false gods. Though God had provided for them, the people, acting like **lusty stallions,** went after each others' wives. God would punish Judah for her idolatry and adultery.

5:10-19. Judah, God's choice vine, had become a wild vine (2:21), so God called His invaders to **go through** Judah's **vineyards** and prune off the dead **branches.** Though the nation would **not** be destroyed **completely,** those individuals who did **not belong to the LORD** would be removed in judgment.

The people refused to believe that God would ever destroy Jerusalem. Instead they announced that **He** would **do nothing. The prophets**—Jeremiah, Ezekiel, and others who were predicting doom—were, the people said, just full of **wind. God** therefore told Jeremiah that His **words** would be **fire** that would consume the **people.** God would bring **a distant nation** (Babylon) **against** Judah—a nation **whose language** the Judeans did **not know.** These **warriors** would **devour** the crops, **herds,** and children of the Judeans; and they would **destroy the** mighty **fortified cities** which Judah trusted for protection.

God again emphasized that He would **not destroy** Judah **completely** (cf. 4:27). He would preserve a remnant. When these captives asked **why** they had been defeated, **God** told Jeremiah to say that they had **forsaken** God to serve **foreign** gods in their **own** land. Therefore God would have them **serve foreigners** (the Babylonians) **in a** foreign **land.** His punishment fit their sin.

5:20-31. Judah had become willfully ignorant of God. Though she had **eyes** and **ears,** she did **not see** or **hear** (i.e., comprehend) the true character of God (cf. Ezek. 12:2). She refused to **fear,** or reverence, God (cf. Prov. 1:7). Though even **the sea** remains within its **everlasting barrier** (cf. Job 38:10; Ps. 104:9), the **people** of Judah refused to stay within God's covenant limits. Instead they **turned aside** and went **away.** They refused to see God's gracious hand at work, providing them the **fall and spring rains** which assured the **. . . harvest.**

Jeremiah then specified some of the

people's **sins. Wicked** people, who were **rich and powerful,** were waiting to **snare** the poor. They refused to help the downtrodden (**the fatherless** and **the poor**). **The prophets,** who were to proclaim God's word of truth, were prophesying **lies;** and **the priests,** who were to instruct the people in the ways of God, were instead ruling **by their own authority** (cf. 2:8). Yet these aberrations of righteousness were condoned by the **people** who loved it that way. All the elements of society preferred wickedness to righteousness.

(4) The certainty of coming judgment (chap. 6). **6:1-3.** Jeremiah again used the symbol of an alarm being sounded to announce an impending invasion (cf. 4:5-6), to signal Babylon's coming attack. The **people of Benjamin** (cf. 1:1), just north of Jerusalem, were to **flee for safety.** But instead of stopping at the capital city, they were to **flee from Jerusalem** and continue heading south. The **trumpet** would be sounded at **Tekoa,** about 11 miles southeast of Jerusalem (cf. Amos 1:1). And the **signal** fires at **Beth Hakkerem,** a vantage point midway between Jerusalem and Bethlehem, would be lit to warn the inhabitants of the land to flee. God threatened to **destroy** Jerusalem so completely that **shepherds** would **pitch their tents** and graze their herds on its site. This extensive destruction is confirmed by Nehemiah (cf. Neh. 1:3; 2:3, 11-17).

6:4-6a. As the enemy massed **against Jerusalem** they were eager to attack. They hoped to **attack at noon;** but before the preparations were completed **the shadows of evening** had begun to stretch through the valleys around the city. Most armies would wait till the next day to begin, but the Babylonians decided to begin their **attack** that **night.** God directed the soldiers of Babylon as they built **siege ramps** to breach the city's defenses (cf. Ezek. 4:1-2).

6:6b-9. Jerusalem had to **be punished** because of her **oppression.** Her **wickedness** was so profuse it poured forth like **water** from a well. Unless she would **take warning** and repent, she would become **desolate.** God would have Babylon **glean** Jerusalem **as thoroughly as** one gleans **a vine** when **gathering grapes.**

6:10-15. Jeremiah responded in amazement to Judah's unbelief. But no one would **listen to** him as he tried to warn them of the coming calamity. This is the first of more than three dozen times in Jeremiah where the people did not listen to (i.e., they disobeyed) God's **Word.** Indeed **their ears** were **closed** (lit., "uncircumcised"), and they found God's Word to be offensive. But Jeremiah had to speak God's word of judgment; he could not **hold it in** (cf. 20:9).

God's wrath was to be poured out on all elements of society—from the **children** to **the old** (and everyone in between). The people would lose **their houses** along with **their fields and their wives** to the coming invaders. Such action would occur because all sections of society were corrupt. Both the **prophets** and the **priests** practiced **deceit,** and the nation was injured. **The wound** refers to the people's spiritual malady and its spiritual and physical effects (cf. 8:11, 22; 10:19; 14:17; 15:18; 30:12, 15; cf. "wounds" in 19:8; 30:17; 49:17; 50:13). The prophets and priests were proclaiming **peace** (cf. 8:11; 23:17) though God had not given them that message. These charlatans had **no shame** about lying to the people. In fact they were so hardened in their ways that **they** did **not even know how to blush** when their sin was exposed. God promised that these false leaders would **fall** when the city was destroyed (cf. 8:12).

6:16-21. Judah was in danger of destruction because she had strayed from **the ancient paths** of God's righteousness. Yet though God urged her to **walk in the good way** where she would **find rest,** Judah refused. Prophets were like **watchmen** (men assigned to watch for and warn a city of impending danger), but the nation refused to **listen.**

Judah **rejected** God's **Law,** thinking she could substitute rituals for obedience. God responded by showing His disdain for **incense** that had been imported **from Sheba** in southwest Arabia (cf. 1 Kings 10:1-13; Ezek. 27:22) and for **sweet calamus** (possibly sweet cane, Ex. 30:23; also cf. Song 4:14; Isa. 43:24) **from a distant land.** The elaborate **burnt offerings** and **sacrifices,** divorced from a genuine love for God, did **not please** Him. Instead of accepting this hypocritical worship, God vowed to **put obstacles** in the way of the **people** so they would stumble. The nature of the obstacles is not given, but it is likely that God was again referring to the Babylonians (cf. Jer. 6:22).

6:22-26. Jeremiah concluded his second message by again pointing to the foe **from . . . the North** (cf. 1:13-15; 4:5-6; 6:1). The coming army was **cruel** and would **show no mercy** to those it captured, an apt description of the Babylonians (cf. Hab. 1:6-11). As they came **in battle formation** their goal was **to attack** Jerusalem.

The report of Babylon's advance would bring **anguish** to those in Judah, like a woman's labor pains (cf. comments on Jer. 4:31). The people would be afraid of leaving their cities because of **a sword** which would strike them down. Instead they would **put on sackcloth,** a dark, rough cloth worn at times of mourning (Gen. 37:34; 2 Sam. 3:31; 1 Kings 21:27; Es. 4:1-4) and penitence (Neh. 9:1; Dan. 9:3; Matt. 11:21). The sadness experienced by Jerusalem would be similar to that experienced by one who had lost **an only son.**

6:27-30. God appointed Jeremiah as a **tester of metals,** or an assayer, and the **people** of Judah were **the ore.** As Jeremiah observed the nation, he concluded **they** were **all hardened rebels.** God tried to refine them through judgment, **but the refining** efforts were useless. The wicked had **not** been **purged out** in the refining process so the nation was like **rejected silver.** God's attempts to reform the nation had failed, so judgment was inevitable.

c. False religion and its punishment (chaps. 7–10)

These chapters, often known as Jeremiah's temple address, focus on God's punishment of the people because of their false religion. The people believed that God's punishment would never extend to Jerusalem or to them (cf. 5:12-13) because of the presence of God's temple and because of their outward display of religion (cf. 6:20). Jeremiah's temple address destroyed this false hope and exposed the festering sore of idolatry that was producing spiritual gangrene in the people. The events described in chapter 26 probably indicate the people's response to this message.

(1) The temple sermon and Judah's false worship (7:1–8:3). **7:1-8.** God summoned Jeremiah to **stand at the** entrance to the temple and announce His **message** to those coming there **to worship.** The message was similar to that just recorded: the people had to **reform** their **ways** (cf. 3:12; 26:13) if they wanted to continue living there.

Jeremiah answered the objection voiced by the people to his message. They believed judgment would not come because in Jerusalem was located **the temple of the Lord** (repeated three times to emphasize their belief in its protecting power). The people of Judah viewed the temple as a talisman or good luck charm that could ward off any attack.

But **God** did not value buildings over obedience. God's protection would remain only if the people would **change** their ways (7:5; cf. v. 3). Jeremiah listed three examples to illustrate the change God wanted. The first two related to actions toward fellow Israelites, and the third related to actions toward God. (1) The people were **not** to **oppress** the helpless in society—people who could not easily protect themselves if wronged (cf. Deut. 14:29; 16:11; 24:19; Ps. 94:6). (2) They were **not** to **shed innocent blood** (cf. Deut. 19:10-13; 21:1-9). (3) And they were **not** to **follow other gods.** If these evidences of faithfulness to God's covenant were observed, God would allow the nation to **live . . . in the land.** But for the people to trust in the temple building rather than in obedience to the covenant for their protection was to put their faith **in deceptive words that** were **worthless.**

7:9-15. Judah felt so secure because of the presence of God's temple that she believed it was **safe to do all** kinds of **detestable things.** Her vileness had actually turned the temple into **a den of robbers** (cf. Matt. 21:12-13). What she failed to realize was that God had **been watching** and was aware of her deeds.

Jeremiah pointed to Israel's past to expose the fallacy of believing that the mere presence of God's temple would avert disaster. He asked the crowd to remember **the place in Shiloh** where the tabernacle of God had first dwelt (Josh. 18:1; Jud. 18:31; 1 Sam. 1:3; 4:3-4). They were to observe what God **did to it because of** Israel's **wickedness.** The Bible is silent on the fate of Shiloh; but after the

Philistines captured the ark of the covenant (1 Sam. 4:10-11) the priests evidently fled to Nob (1 Sam. 22:11) and Shiloh was abandoned as Israel's central worship center (cf. Ps. 78:56-61). Archeological studies also indicate that the village of Shiloh was destroyed about 1050 B.C., probably by the Philistines.

The point of Jeremiah's message was that what God did to Shiloh He would also do to the . . . temple. If Judah did not change her ways God would thrust her from His presence just as He had done with the Northern Kingdom (Ephraim) in 722 B.C. (2 Kings 17:5-20, esp. v. 20). The temple bore God's name (Jer. 7:10, 12, 14; cf. v. 30) in the sense that it was a symbol of God's presence (His "name" refers to His revealed attributes).

7:16-20. God prohibited Jeremiah from interceding for Judah because He would not listen (cf. 11:14; 14:11-12). The nation's sin had progressed to the point where Jeremiah's pleas were futile. To illustrate how degraded Judah had become God highlighted one aspect of her idolatrous worship. Throughout Judah, families were uniting to prepare cakes of bread (flat cakes possibly formed into the image of the goddess; cf. 44:19) for the Queen of Heaven (probably Ishtar, the Babylonian goddess of love and fertility). The families were also offering drink offerings (usually wine) to other gods. Yet such idolatrous rituals were only harming those who participated in them; their false worship did not damage God. For the people would bear the consequences of their actions when God's anger and wrath would be poured out on all Judah.

7:21-29. The people of Judah offered all the correct sacrifices, but they failed to realize that God had given another command at Sinai. He had called on Israel to obey Him and to walk in all the ways He established for them. Unfortunately Israel refused to listen or pay attention to this command of God. Though God continually sent His prophets to warn the people, they refused to pay attention (cf. 25:4-7).

Jeremiah was not to expect the response of people in his day to be any different from people's response in the past. Indeed God told Jeremiah that the nation would not listen to him. So Jeremiah was to cut off his hair, a sign of

deep mourning (cf. Job 1:20; Isa. 15:2-3; Jer. 48:37; Ezek. 7:18), and take up a lament (qînâh, "funeral dirge") for the nation. The time of mourning could commence because the destruction of Judah was assured. God had already abandoned that generation to His wrath.

7:30-34. God continued to elaborate on the sin of Judah which brought her judgment. The people had set up . . . idols in the temple itself so that even the house of God was defiled (cf. Ezek. 8:3-18). Outside the city they had built the high places of Topheth (cf. Jer. 19:6, 11-14) which were located in the Valley of Ben Hinnom (cf. 19:2, 6; 32:35; also called simply the Valley of Hinnom). Here they practiced child sacrifice, burning their sons and daughters in the fire (cf. 2 Kings 21:6; 2 Chron. 33:6; Jer. 19:5). The origin of the word "Topheth" (tōpet) is uncertain, but possibly it came from a word for "cookstove" or "oven." The change in vowels was deliberate; the vowels from the word bōšet ("shame") were transferred to the other word to emphasize the shameful character of the practices there. This "high place of shame" was located in the Valley of Hinnom, immediately south and west of the city. In this valley the refuse from the city was burned. In Greek the Valley of Hinnom (Heb., gê'-hinnōm) became known as Gehenna (geenna) to picture the fiery corruption of hell (cf. Matt. 5:22, 29-30; 2 Peter 2:4). God vowed that the name of this place would be changed to the Valley of Slaughter because of the great number of dead bodies that would be burned after the destruction of Jerusalem. The prediction about birds and beasts eating the carcasses affirms the Mosaic Covenant because of the people's disobedience (Deut. 28:26). Joy will be gone (cf. Jer. 16:9; 25:10) when the city would become desolate.

8:1-3. Even the dead would not escape God's judgment. The bones of all the officials who had worshiped false gods but who had died before the fall of Jerusalem would be removed from their graves and exposed to the elements they had once worshiped. They would remain as refuse . . . on the ground (cf. 25:33). Those who survived the fall of Jerusalem would be banished, and their lives would be so terrible that they would prefer death to life.

(2) God's retribution on the people (8:4–10:25). **8:4-7.** God asked a series of questions to expose Judah's stubborn refusal to turn back to Him. When people **fall down** they try to **get up** again. If someone **turns away** from the right path he tries to **return** as quickly as possible. But though most **people** learn from their mistakes, Judah refused **to return.** Failing to acknowledge any wrongdoing, she pursued her **own** ways with determination **like a horse charging into battle. Even** migratory birds **observe the time of their migration, but** Judah did **not** realize that it was time to return to her God. She had even less wisdom than a bird!

8:8-13. Judah felt superior in her wisdom to other nations because she had **the Law of the** LORD. Unfortunately that Law was being **handled . . . falsely** by **the scribes.** Their rejection of God's Law would bring judgment (cf. Deut. 28:30-45). This attitude encompassed all the people **from the least to the greatest.** The leaders were treating the nation's sin lightly—they would **dress** (or bandage) **the wound** (cf. Jer. 8:22 and comments on 6:14), assuming the injury was **not** serious when in fact it was terminal. Jeremiah 8:10b-12 repeats the message the prophet had given in 6:12-15 (cf. comments there). The truth was repeated for emphasis. God would punish the nation by taking **from them** the blessings of the **harvest** that He had earlier **given them.**

8:14-17. Jeremiah pictured the panic that would ensue when God's judgment began. The people would **flee to the fortified cities** knowing that **God** had **doomed** them **to perish** there. Their hopes **for peace** were dashed and the **terror** of the Babylonians filled the land. As the sound **of the enemy's horses** echoed southward **from Dan** in the north, the **land** trembled as it waited in dread for the army to **come to devour.** God compared the Babylonians to **venomous snakes** that would **bite** the Judeans.

8:18–9:2. Jeremiah responded to Judah's plight by making a heartfelt cry to God. He asked God to **listen to the cry of the people** who had been deported to **a land far away.** Those captured by the Babylonians wondered how their city could have fallen since God's temple was there. In anguish they questioned if Judah's **King,** Yahweh, was **no longer there.** God responded by indicating that

Jerusalem's destruction was brought about by their sin, not by His absence. God brought the army of Babylon because Judah had **provoked** Him **to anger with their . . . idols.**

God gave Judah every opportunity to repent, but she continued to rebel. Jeremiah 8:20 recorded the mournful cry of those who learned the consequences of sin too late. **The harvest,** representing God's opportunities to repent, was **past.** By not taking advantage of God's provision for deliverance from judgment when it had been available, the people were now without hope (**we are not saved**).

Jeremiah's reaction to Judah's fate mixed sadness and despair. He so identified with his people that he was **crushed** by the fact of their destruction. In vain he sought for **balm** from **Gilead** to heal **the wound of** his **people** (cf. v. 11 and comments on 6:14). "Balm" was the resin of the storax tree that was used medicinally. Gilead, east of the Jordan River, was famous for its healing balm (cf. Gen. 37:25; Jer. 46:11; 51:8; Ezek. 27:17). The grief caused Jeremiah to wish his **eyes** would become **a fountain of tears** so he could **weep** continually (**day and night**) for those who had been **slain.** This heartfelt empathy with his people's suffering earned Jeremiah the nickname, "the weeping prophet" (cf. Jer. 13:17; 14:17). Yet his empathy for their suffering was balanced by his revulsion at their sin. An isolated **lodging place in the desert** was preferable to living with the **unfaithful people** of Judah.

9:3-6. A person used his **tongue** as an archer would use **a bow**—it became a weapon **to shoot lies.** Honesty was not being practiced by those living in Judah. One had to watch his **friends,** and no one could **trust** his **brothers.** As the very fabric of society unraveled, **no one** would speak the truth. Jeremiah (**you** is sing.) lived in a nation that was full of **deception** and refused **to acknowledge** God.

9:7-9. God responded to Judah's deception by seeking to **refine and test** her **because of** her **sin** (cf. 6:28-30; Ezek. 22:18-22). God would place Judah in the crucible of judgment and deal with her **deceit.** God rhetorically asked Jeremiah if He should **not** indeed **avenge** Himself **on** the **nation** because of her sin.

9:10-16. Jeremiah began to **weep and wail** over the land of **Judah** because the

Babylonian invasion and deportation made it **desolate and untraveled.** God responded by indicating He would **make Jerusalem a heap of ruins** that would be inhabited only by wild **jackals** (cf. 10:22; 49:33; 51:37). He asked the **wise** men of Judah to explain **why the land** was **ruined and laid waste.** Before anyone could answer, God stated the obvious. The destruction came **because** the people had turned from God's **Law** and had **followed the Baals** (cf. 2:23 and see comments on Jud. 2:11). **This** was why God would **scatter them among** the **nations** and why many in Judah would be killed by **the sword** (cf. Ezek. 5:2, 12).

9:17-24. Jeremiah listed three separate pronouncements from **the LORD** (vv. 17-21, 22, 23-24) each beginning with a similar phrase. In the first section (vv. 17-21) God called for **the wailing women,** professional mourners, to lament for Jerusalem. These mourners were then to **teach** their **daughters . . . another . . . lament.** This funeral dirge was over the **death** of **the children** and **the young men** who were killed when the Babylonians broke into the city.

In the second section (v. 22) God pictured the severity of the massacre by Babylon. **The dead bodies** would resemble the **cut grain** left **behind the reaper** in a field. But there would be **no one** left to **gather** this gruesome "harvest."

The third pronouncement (vv. 23-24) summarized the response God expected from the people. The people were not to **boast** in their human **wisdom** or **strength** or **riches** for these would not last. Instead a person should **boast** only to the extent **that he understands and knows** God. Again the word "know" (*yādaʿ*) pictured an intimate knowledge of God (see comments on 1:5). God wanted the people to be intimately acquainted with His **kindness, justice, and righteousness.** "Kindness" (*hesed*) refers to God's loyal love (cf. 31:3; 33:11; Lam. 3:22). God would stand by His commitment to His people. "Justice" (*mišpot*) is a broad term that pointed to governing justly. God would vindicate the innocent and punish the guilty. "Righteousness" (*sedāqâh*) conveys the idea of conforming to a standard or norm. God's standards of conduct were supposed to be Israel's norm.

9:25-26. If personal achievement or ability would not please God (v. 23), nei- ther would outward conformity to religious rituals. God would **punish** those **circumcised only in the flesh** whether they were near or far. Judah's faith in her covenant sign was a misplaced faith because people in some other nations also practiced this ritual—and they were not under God's covenant. Judah's actions exposed the fact that the nation was **really uncircumcised . . . in heart** (cf. 4:4).

10:1-5. The first 16 verses of chapter 10 are parenthetical. Before continuing his discussion of the coming Exile, Jeremiah focused on the nature of the God who would bring this judgment. God addressed the entire **house of Israel,** which included the Northern Kingdom already in exile, and explained the foolishness of idols. Israel was **not** supposed to **learn the ways of** idolatry practiced by **the nations** around her, nor was she to **be terrified by signs in the sky.** These "signs" were most likely unusual occurrences such as eclipses or comets which were thought to be signs of coming events given by the gods.

Such idolatrous practices were **worthless** (*hebel,* "breath"; cf. comments on *hebel* in Ecc. 1:2) because the "gods" being honored were created by their worshipers (cf. Isa. 40:18-20). A person would chop down **a tree,** give the wood to a **craftsman** who fashioned it to the desired shape. This "god" was then covered **with silver and gold** and fastened to a base so that it would **not totter.** Once the god was made by man it had to **be carried** to its destination. It was as lifeless as **a scarecrow in a melon patch.** Certainly such a "god" could not **speak** to impart knowledge to its followers. So God exhorted His people **not** to **fear** those false idols. The idols had **no** power to **harm** those who disregarded them or power to **do any good** for those who followed them.

10:6-16. Jeremiah responded to God's description of idols by affirming that the LORD truly is unique. There is **no one . . . like** Him (vv. 6a, 7b; cf. Isa. 40:18, 25). The **worthless wooden idols** (cf. Jer. 10:15 and comments on 2:5), were decorated with **silver . . . from Tarshish and gold from Uphaz.** Tarshish was a city probably in southern Spain, or was a technical term for a "mineral-bearing land." Uphaz is either a location (now unknown), or a textual variant for

Ophir, a land in Arabia known for its gold (cf. 1 Kings 9:28; 10:11; 22:48; Job 22:24; 28:16; Ps. 45:9; Isa. 13:12), or a technical term for "refined gold." Jeremiah described the LORD as the true (genuine) God in contrast with the false idols. He is alive but they were lifeless; and He is eternal whereas they came into existence through the work of craftsmen and were subject to decay.

Jeremiah 10:11 is the only verse in this book written in Aramaic instead of Hebrew. Aramaic was the trade language of the day. Probably this verse is in Aramaic because it was directed to the pagan idolaters surrounding Israel. God spoke in a language they would be sure to understand. His message to these idolaters was that their false gods, who had no part in creating the universe, would themselves ultimately perish from God's universe.

In contrast with the false idols the Lord was responsible for Creation (vv. 12-13). He made the earth and stretched out the heavens. (Vv. 12-16 are virtually the same as 51:15-19.) Only He has the power and wisdom to have accomplished such a feat. This power of the Lord was mirrored in His continuing revelation in nature. By focusing on the awesomeness of a thunderstorm with clouds . . . lightning . . . rain, and wind, Jeremiah illustrated the continuing power of God (on storehouses; cf. comments on Job 38:22; also cf. Pss. 33:7; 135:7; Jer. 51:16).

When God's grandeur would finally be manifested, those who had made worthless idols (cf. 10:8 and comments on 2:5) would be shamed at the objects of mockery they had once worshiped. In contrast God would be known as the Portion of Jacob (cf. 51:19). A "portion" (ḥēleq, "share") usually referred to something allotted to an individual (cf. Gen. 14:24; Lev. 6:17; 1 Sam. 1:5). God, in a real sense, belonged to Israel. But at the same time Israel belonged to God. She was His inheritance (see comments on Deut. 4:20). God is also the Maker of all things (cf. Job 4:17; 32:22; 35:10; Pss. 115:15; 121:2; Ecc. 11:5) in contrast with the lifeless idols who can make nothing! Jeremiah ended this parenthetical portion (Jer. 10:1-16) by identifying this true God who was inseparably bound to His people. His name is the LORD Almighty.

10:17-22. After discussing the superiority of God to idols (vv. 1-16), Jeremiah continued his temple address by describing the coming destruction and Exile. The people of Jerusalem were to gather up their meager belongings to leave the land (cf. Ezek. 12:3-16). God vowed to hurl out those living in the land so they would be captured and carried into captivity.

Jerusalem responded in anguish to the Captivity. The wound she had suffered was incurable (see comments on Jer. 6:14). The city was also pictured as a tent that had collapsed. Her sons were deported, and the shepherds (rō'îm, "leaders"; cf. 2:8) who were to guide the flock had allowed the flock to be scattered (cf. 23:1-2; Ezek. 34:1-10). The attack from . . . the north would decimate Judah so that her towns would be desolate (cf. Jer. 9:11).

10:23-25. Jeremiah concluded his temple address with a prayer to the LORD. The prophet admitted that a person's life cannot be considered his own as though he is free to direct his own steps. God is in control, and only those who let God direct their ways will be truly blessed (cf. Prov. 3:5-6; 16:9; 20:24). Because Judah's judgment was inevitable, Jeremiah pleaded that it might come only with God's justice and not with His anger. That is, Jeremiah was asking for God's patience and leniency in dispersing judgment lest the nation be reduced to nothing. By using the word me Jeremiah was identifying with and representing Judah. Then Jeremiah asked that God's judgment of Judah be accompanied by His judgment on the nations. They refused to call on God's name, and they had devoured and destroyed God's covenant people.

d. The broken covenant (chaps. 11–12)

Jeremiah's fourth message focused on Judah's broken covenant with her God. Though the message itself is undated, several markers help date the passage to 621 B.C., six years after Jeremiah began his ministry. That year the temple was being repaired as part of King Josiah's reforms, and a copy of the Law was discovered in the renovation (cf. 2 Chron. 34:14-33). Several of Jeremiah's references seem to allude to this discovery of God's Law and the realization of the broken covenant (cf. Jer. 11:3-5). Jeremiah called on the people to heed the words of the covenant that Josiah read to them (11:6; 2 Chron. 34:19-32).

(1) The violation of the covenant (11:1-17). **11:1-5.** God told **Jeremiah** to **listen to** the stipulations of His **covenant** and to relate those terms **to the people of Judah** and . . . **Jerusalem.** The specific portion of the covenant God mentioned were **the terms** that regarded obedience and disobedience to His Law (cf. Deut. 28). On Canaan as **a land flowing with milk and honey** see comments on Exodus 3:8.

11:6-8. As Jeremiah called out to the people to **follow** the **words** of the **covenant,** he also reminded them of the nation's past failure. Though God had repeatedly **warned** the nation to **obey** Him, they refused to **pay attention.** Because of this God **brought on them all the curses of the covenant.** Israel's history was one of rebellion and correction.

11:9-13. Though King Josiah forced an outer conformity to **the covenant,** his reform did not penetrate the hearts of the people in a lasting way. After Josiah died the people returned to their idolatrous ways. **Among the people** was **a conspiracy** to abandon the covenant. Instead of heeding the warning of Jeremiah (vv. 2-8) they **returned to the sins of their** ancestors **to serve** false gods. **Both** the Northern Kingdom (**Israel**) and the Southern Kingdom (**Judah**) followed this wayward path.

Judah's deliberate decision to follow after idols assured her doom. God vowed to send **a disaster** from which the nation could not **escape.** In that hour of distress the people would **cry out to** God, and also to their idols, but neither would **help them at all.** Judah's abundance of **gods** and **altars** (cf. 2:28) would be her downfall, not her deliverance. Though Josiah tried to rid the land of idolatry (2 Chron. 34:33), the number of **incense** altars devoted to the **shameful god Baal** (cf. Jer. 11:17) were still as numerous **as the streets of Jerusalem.**

11:14-17. The people's sin was so pervasive that God again commanded Jeremiah **not to pray for** them because He would **not listen** to their prayers for deliverance in **their** coming **time of** . . . **distress** (cf. 7:16; 14:11). Jeremiah 11:15 has caused much concern for translators.

Apparently the thought is this: the **beloved** were the people of Judah who were in God's **temple** (lit., "house"). Evidently some people came to the temple to offer **consecrated meat** as a sacrifice, believing that this ritual would **avert** . . . **punishment.** Yet they never ceased to **engage in** their **wickedness.**

God then pictured their judgment like an **olive tree** being **set** . . . **on fire,** probably by lightning, in **a mighty storm.** God had **planted** . . . **Judah** as His people, and He would now uproot them because they had **provoked** Him **to anger** by their idolatry.

(2) The consequences of violating the covenant (11:18–12:17). **11:18-23.** The people responded to Jeremiah's rebuke by trying to kill him. This is the first episode in their continuing opposition to his ministry (cf. 1:8, 17-19). However, God **revealed their plot to** Jeremiah. These enemies planned to **cut** Jeremiah **off from the land of the living,** that is, to kill him. His response was to ask God to execute His **vengeance** on these conspirators.

God responded by assuring Jeremiah of His swift judgment. The plot against Jeremiah was formulated by **the men of Anathoth,** Jeremiah's own hometown (1:1), who ordered him **not** to **prophesy** or he would **die by** their **hands.** God promised to **punish** these rebels with **the sword** and with **famine. Anathoth** would suffer **disaster** because of her opposition to God's message and messenger.

12:1-6. Jeremiah responded to God's revelation of the plot against his life by complaining about the prosperity of the wicked. Though admitting that God was **righteous** whenever he brought **a case** (*rîḇ*; cf. 2:9, 29) **before** Him, still Jeremiah wanted to question God about His **justice.** Specifically he wanted to know **why** . . . **the way of the wicked** seemed to **prosper** if God was indeed angry with their sin (cf. Job 21:7; Pss. 73:3-5, 12; 94:3). In fact it seemed to Jeremiah as if God Himself had **planted them** because **they** had **taken root** and were bearing **fruit** materially.

Jeremiah asked God to judge the unrighteous (cf. Jer. 11:20). He hoped that God would **drag them off like sheep to be butchered** (cf. their having treated him like "a gentle lamb led to the slaughter," 11:19). Just as Jeremiah was "set apart" by God for his task (1:5) so he wished that God would set . . . apart the wicked for their day of slaughter!

God had judged the nation because of the sins of the wicked, but the righteous also suffered in this judgment. In 12:4 Jeremiah was not contradicting what he had just said about the prosperity of the wicked (v. 1). The thought is probably that even in times of difficulty the wicked seemed to come through better than the righteous. God had sent a drought to judge the nation (cf. 14:1-6; Lev. 26:19-20; Deut. 28:22-24) so that the land was parched and the grass was withered. Yet the people refused to acknowledge God's hand of judgment. They believed that God was indifferent to their sin as they claimed that He would not see what happens to them (cf. Pss. 73:11; 94:7).

God's answer to Jeremiah's question was something of a surprise. God indicated that if Jeremiah found his present circumstances difficult, his future situation would be even worse (Jer. 12:5). God used two metaphors to make this point— a race and a cross-country walk. If Jeremiah had raced with men on foot and was complaining about being worn . . . out, how could he compete later with horses? Or if Jeremiah would stumble (bāṭaḥ, should be trans. "trust"; cf. NIV marg.) in safe country, how could he manage if he were thrust into the thickets by the Jordan? "Thickets" were the dense growth along the Jordan River. The idea of this second question could possibly be paraphrased: If Jeremiah could trust in God only in a time of peace, how would he manage when the going got tough?

God continued His response to Jeremiah by indicating that even his own family had betrayed him. Evidently they had joined the plot against Jeremiah at Anathoth. So God warned Jeremiah not to trust them in spite of their outward words of praise.

12:7-13. God continued His pronouncement of judgment that was interrupted in 11:18 by the explanation of the plot against Jeremiah's life. God would forsake and abandon Judah and turn her over to her enemies. By describing the nation as His house, His inheritance (cf. 10:16 and comments on Deut. 4:20), and

the one He loved, God was indicating that the judgment was not coming from the hardened heart of a capricious king. Though He wanted to do just the opposite, God was forced to judge because of the people's sin. The nation had become like a lion who had raised her voice (roars) in opposition to Him.

The nation had changed so much that she had become . . . like a speckled bird of prey. A "speckled" (colored) bird was one whose markings were different from the other birds of prey. Consequently those other birds would surround and attack this strange bird. Judah had become so different that the other nations of the world would attack her.

The devastation coming on Jerusalem was compared to shepherds and their flocks entering a vineyard and ruining it by trampling it down. God's once-productive nation would become a wasteland as the sword of the LORD (i.e., the Babylonians' swords wielded as God's instruments) killed its inhabitants. Those who had sown wheat would reap only thorns (because of the devastation of war) and would be forced to bear the shame of their harvest of judgment.

12:14-17. Jeremiah closed his fourth message by giving God's promise/threat to the nations. Those wicked neighbors who had seized Israel's inheritance (cf. vv. 7-9) would themselves be uprooted from their lands (cf. 25:12-14, 27-29; 46–51). In contrast God would later uproot the house of Judah from these Gentile nations where they had been scattered and would restore them to their land (cf. 31:7-11; Ezek. 37:1-14).

Though God will judge these Gentile nations, He will later have compassion on them and restore them to their own lands. This will happen when Christ returns to establish His millennial kingdom on earth. Those nations that learn well the ways of God's people and swear by His name will be blessed and established. However, any nation that rebels will be destroyed (cf. Zech. 14:9, 16-19).

e. The linen belt and the wineskins (chap. 13)

The people were not responding to Jeremiah's message, so God had him perform a symbolic act to get their attention (vv. 1-11). Jeremiah also began using parables to gain their interest (vv. 12-14). These unusual means of communication were designed to arouse the curiosity and interest of his unresponsive audience. Later Ezekiel was commanded to use similar techniques in his ministry in Babylon (cf. Ezek. 4:1–5:4).

(1) The illustration of the linen belt (13:1-11). **13:1-7.** God commanded Jeremiah to **buy a linen belt** and wear it **around** his waist. He was **not to let it touch water.** Some scholars have felt that verses 1-7 describe a vision Jeremiah had. But nothing in the text indicates that the event did not actually occur. In fact verse 2 says that Jeremiah actually carried out the assignment. A **belt** (*'ēzôr*) was a sash or cloth tied around one's **waist** (cf. 2 Kings 1:8; Isa. 5:27). The fact that the belt was made of "linen," the material used for the priestly raiment (cf. Lev. 16:4), would have held some significance for those observing Jeremiah's actions.

After wearing the belt for a time, God told him to **take** it **to Perath and hide it** . . . **in a crevice in the rocks.** Perath (*p^erāṯ*) is usually translated "Euphrates" (cf. Jer. 51:63); many have felt that Jeremiah walked to the Euphrates River, a round-trip journey of about 700 miles, to bury this sash. However, another possibility is that Jeremiah traveled to the village of Parah (*pārâh*) about three miles northeast of Anathoth in the tribe of Benjamin (cf. Josh. 18:21, 23). A deep wadi in this area, known today as 'Ain Farah, fits the description of a place with crevices and rocks. In Hebrew the spelling for "to Parah" and "to Euphrates" are identical (both are *p^erāṯāh*; cf. Jer. 13:4-7). By using a location so close to home the people were able to observe Jeremiah's symbolic actions, and the similarity of name would remind the nation of the army from the Euphrates that was coming to destroy them.

Many days later God told Jeremiah to retrieve **the belt** he had buried. (Another round-trip walk of 700 miles would have been necessary if Perath is the Euphrates! This adds further support to the view that the place where Jeremiah was sent was the nearby village of Parah.) As he **dug up the** sash he found that its exposure to the elements had made it **completely useless.** The garment had rotted.

13:8-11. God interpreted Jeremiah's symbolic actions. The message was one of judgment on the **wicked people** who

refused **to listen to** God's **words.** The belt **bound around** Jeremiah's **waist** represented **Israel** and **Judah.** As long as it remained around his waist it occupied a position of **renown and praise and honor.** However, when it was removed from his waist and buried it became **completely useless.** So Israel and Judah had become ruined by departing from their God to serve false gods.

(2) The parable of the wineskins. **13:12-14.** Jeremiah announced what seemed to be a self-evident parable to the people. He declared, **Every wineskin should be filled with wine.** "Wineskin" (*nēḇel*) can refer to an animal-skin bottle (1 Sam. 10:3; cf. Luke 5:37) or to an earthen jar or pitcher (Jer. 48:12; Lam. 4:2). Because the containers were to be smashed together (Jer. 13:14), they were probably jars.

The people scoffed at Jeremiah's self-evident proverb. Of course **every** wine jar **should be filled with wine.** Then Jeremiah drove home the point of the parable. The empty jars represented **all** who lived **in the land** including the leaders and the people. God would **fill** them **with drunkenness**—a symbol of judgment (cf. Isa. 49:26; 63:6; Jer. 25:15-25; 51:7, 39). He would then **smash** the people like jars, **one against the other.** Nothing would prohibit God **from destroying them.**

(3) The message on sin and its results (13:15-27). **13:15-17.** Because of the approaching **darkness** of judgment Jeremiah warned the **arrogant** people of Judah to acknowledge their sin and to **give glory to** . . . **God.** "Darkness" and dark clouds often picture impending doom (cf. Ezek. 30:3, 18; 32:7-8; 34:12; Joel 2:2; Amos 5:18-20; Zeph. 1:15). If they refused to **listen** . . . **because of** their **pride** Jeremiah would **weep bitterly** (Jer. 14:17) to himself **because** they would surely **be taken captive.**

13:18-19. Jeremiah turned from the multitudes to address **the king and** . . . **the queen mother.** They are not identified here, but probably the king was Jehoiachin (also known as Jeconiah) and the queen mother was Nehushta—the widow of Jehoiakim (cf. 29:2; 2 Kings 24:8, 12, 15). Jeremiah exhorted them to humble themselves in light of the coming Exile. Since they went into captivity in 597 B.C. after his reign of just three months (2 Kings 24:8) this prophecy must have been penned during that three-month period.

Jeremiah called on the king and queen mother to come down from their thrones in humility because their crowns would soon fall off when Nebuchadnezzar removed them from office. Their deportation to Babylon was a foretaste of Judah's judgment because the whole nation would be carried into exile.

13:20-27. Jeremiah urged the leaders to look at the armies coming from the north (1:14; 4:6; 6:1, 22; 10:22) who would remove the flock (cf. 10:21; 13:17) that had been entrusted to them. Those with whom Judah had once tried to be aligned as her allies would become her cruel taskmasters (cf. Isa. 39:1-7; Ezek. 23:14-27). As a result, Judah would be in pain like a woman in labor (cf. comments on Jer. 4:31).

If, when the judgment came, the people asked why, God let them know in advance that it was because of their many sins. Judah was as incapable of reforming herself as a dark-skinned Ethiopian was of changing his skin pigmentation or as a leopard was of removing its spots. Her sin was so ingrained that she was accustomed to doing only evil.

God would scatter the people in exile like chaff that was blown in every direction by the desert wind (cf. 4:11-12). This judgment was not accidental. It was the portion . . . decreed for Judah by God because of her trust in false gods.

Using language to match Judah's lewd conduct God declared that He would pull up her skirts to expose her to the nations. The nations would see her adulteries and her lustful neighings (like wild animals; cf. 2:23-24) that characterized her shameless prostitution. Her detestable acts of idolatry had been seen by God, and she would suffer the consequences.

f. The drought and prayer (chaps. 14–15)

(1) The plight because of the drought (14:1-6). **14:1-4.** One of the covenant curses God threatened to send on the disobedient nation was drought (cf. Lev. 26:18-19; Deut. 28:22-24). Jeremiah had already mentioned God's use of drought (Jer. 3:3; 12:4), though it is uncertain whether he was pointing to one major drought or to a series of droughts

that came during Judah's final years.

The severity of the drought produced a cry of distress from Jerusalem. The rainfall had ceased and the stored water was running out. Though nobles sent their servants to the cisterns for water, they returned with their jars unfilled. Those who had rejected the Living Water of life for false cisterns (2:13) now found their physical water supply matching the spiritual water supply to which they had turned. The ground began to crack from a lack of rain, and the farmers became dismayed (cf. 14:3) as they watched their crops wither away. Jeremiah recorded that both the people in the city and the farmers in the country would cover their heads, a sign of grief or shame (cf. 2 Sam. 15:30).

14:5-6. The drought also affected the animals of the field. For example, the normally protective doe was forced to abandon her newborn fawn because of lack of grass. Wild donkeys were also on the barren heights panting for water (cf. Ps. 42:1) like jackals. Their usually good eyesight now failed them as they looked in vain for any pasture in which to graze.

(2) The pleading because of the drought (14:7–15:4). **14:7-9.** The severity of the drought forced the people to cry to God for deliverance. While admitting their sins and their backsliding, they asked God to intervene and supply rain. By calling God the Hope of Israel (cf. 17:13) and the Savior, the people acknowledged God's unique position as the only One who could deliver their nation from its current crisis.

Though God had the power to help, He did not answer the people's pleas for rain. He was acting like a stranger or traveler who had no real concern for the country through which He was traveling. God's failure to act reminded them of a man taken by surprise (one who had been ambushed and overcome before he could offer any resistance) or a warrior who was powerless. Because of God's lack of action the people pleaded with Him not to forsake them.

14:10-12. At first God's reply seems rather startling. Instead of accepting the people's confession, He upbraided them for their waywardness. God knew that their confession was only superficial. They claimed God as their Lord, but they refused to restrain their feet from following evil. Because of their continuing bent toward sin, God said He would **not accept** their superficial confession. Instead He would **punish them for their sins.** God again told Jeremiah **not to pray for the . . . people** (cf. 7:16; 11:14). Their feeble efforts to manipulate God took several forms. **They** would **fast** and **offer burnt offerings,** hoping to appease the LORD and avert His wrath. But God cannot be bought off. He vowed to **destroy** the rebels **with the sword, famine, and plague**—the three hammerblows of divine judgment (cf. Lev. 26:23-26; Jer. 21:6-7, 9; 24:10; 27:8, 13; 29:17-18; 32:24, 36; 34:17; 38:2; Ezek. 5:12; 6:11; 7:15; 12:16; Rev. 6:8; also note Jer. 42:17, 22; 44:13).

14:13-16. Jeremiah interrupted God by reminding Him that the false **prophets** were contradicting His message. Instead of the **sword** or **famine,** they were announcing that God would give **lasting peace** to Jerusalem (cf. 5:12-13; 6:13-14; 7:4, 9-10; 27:16; 28:2-4).

God answered Jeremiah by explaining that the messages of these false prophets were **lies** because they had not been **appointed** by Him. Their messages were **delusions of their own minds.** God would judge them for their lies by destroying both the false **prophets** and those who listened to them. They would all **perish by sword and famine** (cf. 14:13, 18).

14:17-18. Jeremiah's sorrow burst forth at the thought of Jerusalem's judgment. His **eyes** welled up **with tears** as he cried continually (**night and day**) over Jerusalem's fall (cf. 9:1, 18; 13:17; Lam. 3:48-51). For some reason he pictured the city as a **virgin daughter,** who had **suffered a** mortal **wound** (cf. comments on Jer. 6:14) and Jeremiah was grieving over her loss. In the **country** (the countryside surrounding Jerusalem) lay the corpses of **those slain by the sword.** Those who escaped to **the city** were slowly falling to **the ravages of famine.** Prophets and priests, who should have set the people aright, were deported to Babylon.

14:19-22. The people again addressed God and pleaded for His intervention. They were puzzled as to why God would **despise** them and **why** He **afflicted** them (cf. "why" in vv. 8-9). Though they **hoped for peace,** they experienced **only terror.** This concern

prompted them again to **acknowledge** their **wickedness** (cf. v. 7) and **guilt** and to ask God to help them.

Their appeal for God's help was based on His personal character (**for the sake of Your name**; cf. v. 7), His temple (**His glorious throne**; cf. 3:17; 17:12), and His **covenant** (cf. 11:2-5). The people were quick to remind God of His obligations to the nation, but failed to remember their own obligations to Him. They finally admitted that the **worthless idols** (cf. comments on 2:5) they had worshiped could not **bring rain** to quench the drought. **God** was **the** only **One** who could do **all this** (cf. 1 Kings 17:1; 18:18-46).

15:1-4. The chapter break between 14 and 15 should be disregarded. The first 4 verses of chapter 15 are God's answer to the apparent "confession" in 14:19-22. The nation's sin was so ingrained (cf. 13:23) that judgment was inevitable. **Even** the intercessory prayer of **Moses** or **Samuel** could not stop God's judgment. Mention of these two men was significant because Moses had interceded for the nation to turn away God's wrath (Ex. 32:9-14; Num. 14:11-20; Deut. 9:18-20, 25-29), and Samuel had interceded to defeat the nation's enemies and turn away God's wrath (1 Sam. 7:5-11; 12:19-25).

The fate of the people was sealed. **Four** options had been selected by God. Some were **destined** to **death**—probably meaning death by plague (cf. Jer. 14:12). Others would be cut down with **the sword,** while others would die from **starvation.** However, those not appointed to God's triad of terror (plague, sword, famine; cf. comments on 14:12) would escape death but would be taken into **captivity.** The scene of carnage continued (15:3) as Jeremiah pictured **dogs . . . birds,** and wild **beasts** devouring and destroying those who had been slain (cf. 16:4).

Judah had passed "the point of no return" in her dealings with God. That line was crossed through the actions of **Manasseh son of Hezekiah** (cf. 2 Kings 21:1-18; 2 Chron. 33:1-20). Manasseh so polluted **Jerusalem** with idolatry that her destruction was inevitable (2 Kings 21:10-15). Even Josiah's reforms could only postpone her certain destruction (2 Kings 22:16-20).

(3) The fate of Jerusalem (15:5-9). **15:5-7.** God asked **Jerusalem. . . . who**

would **pity** her or **mourn** for her when she was judged. The only One who had ever cared for her was God, but she had **rejected** Him. Therefore God vowed to **destroy** her without **compassion.** He would **winnow** her as a farmer winnowed his grain to remove the unbelievers who were like chaff.

15:8-9. The awesome effects of judgment touched all the people. **Widows** would become **more numerous than . . . sand** as the men were slaughtered by the Babylonians. Even **the mothers** would not escape. To be a **mother of seven** young men symbolized a zenith of happiness and security. But even seven ablebodied defenders would not be able to deflect the blow of God's judgment. That mother would **breathe her last** breath as the invading soldiers entered the city to kill **the survivors** of the siege. Though this "mother" could mean a physical mother, it is possible that Jeremiah was also picturing Jerusalem as a mother who felt secure. In either case, Babylon would shatter her security by destroying the city and those who lived in it.

(4) Jeremiah's complaint (15:10-21). **15:10-11.** Jeremiah lamented his own condition in life as he pictured **the whole land** against him. Though he had not **lent** or **borrowed,** actions which could cause tensions and conflicts (cf. Neh. 5:1-13; Prov. 22:7), Jeremiah was still being cursed by the people. God answered by assuring Jeremiah of vindication. Those who had been his **enemies** would **plead with** him when the **times of distress** finally arrived. This promise was fulfilled specifically in the requests of King Zedekiah to Jeremiah (cf. Jer. 21:1-7; 37:1-10, 17-20; 38:14-18).

15:12-14. God asked a rhetorical question to emphasize the inevitability of judgment. Just as **a man** cannot **break iron** or **bronze** with his bare hands, so the people of Judah would be unable to break the power of the Babylonian attack on their nation. Indeed all their **wealth** would be plundered (cf. 17:3; 20:5) by these invaders. The Babylonians would **enslave** the Judeans and deport them to **a land** they did **not know** (cf. 14:18; 15:2; 16:13; 17:4). This judgment was the result of God's **anger** which burned like **a fire . . . against** the people of Judah.

15:15-18. God had promised ultimately to deliver and vindicate Jeremiah (v. 11); but in light of the coming calamity (vv. 12-14) Jeremiah asked for a speedy settling of accounts. He wanted God to **avenge** him **on** his **persecutors.** Though God was **long-suffering,** Jeremiah hoped for swift justice; he wanted to be vindicated before God would **take** him **away** in death.

Jeremiah could make this request because of his relationship with God. In contrast with the people of Judah who despised God's Word (8:9), Jeremiah accepted (**ate**) it and claimed it as his **joy** and **delight** (cf. Ps. 1:2). Jeremiah refused to associate with **the company of revelers** (cf. Ps. 1:1), choosing instead to sit **alone** and be guided by God's **hand.** He shared God's **indignation** over the people's sin.

Jeremiah ended this address by painfully lamenting his pitiful condition. He wanted to know **why** his **pain** seemed **unending** and his **wound . . . incurable** (see comments on Jer. 6:14). He felt as though God was protracting his suffering. Worse yet, he wondered if the God who claimed to be a spring of Living Water (2:13) had become **like a deceptive brook** or **a spring that fails.** The disappointment of a dry wadi bed that only held water after a heavy rain was a depressing sight to those searching for water (cf. Job 6:15-20). Jeremiah hoped that God would not disappoint him.

15:19-21. God rebuked Jeremiah for his doubt and self-pity. Jeremiah needed to **repent** if he hoped to **serve** God. To be God's **spokesman** he had to **utter worthy, not worthless, words.** He was to remain steadfast before God so the **people** would **turn to** him; in no case was he to **turn to them.** If someone was to move, it was to be the people, not Jeremiah!

God ended His rebuke by restating the promises He made when He commissioned Jeremiah as a prophet (cf. 1:18-19). He would strengthen Jeremiah as a **wall of bronze** so that those opposing him could never **overcome** him. Though opposition would come, God promised to **rescue** Jeremiah **from** those who sought to kill him.

g. Jeremiah's restrictions and Judah's sin (16:1–17:18)

(1) Jeremiah's restrictions (16:1-9). **16:1-4.** God placed several restrictions on Jeremiah's personal life that were intended as object lessons for the people.

The first restriction was the command **not to marry and** raise a family. Jeremiah was denied this normal relationship that was cherished by all Israelites. God's purpose was to show that the coming catastrophe would disrupt all normal relationships. Many spouses and children would **die of deadly diseases.** Those who remained would **perish by sword and famine** (cf. 14:15-16; 15:2). The carnage would be so awesome that those killed would **not** even **be mourned or buried** (cf. 16:6). Instead they would remain **like refuse . . . on the ground** (cf. 25:33)—their lifeless bodies serving as **food for** wild animals (cf. 15:3).

16:5-7. The second restriction placed on Jeremiah was **not** to **enter a house where . . . a funeral meal** was being eaten, or **mourn or show sympathy** (cf. Ezek. 24:15-24). He was not to display the normal emotion of grief or to offer comfort when someone died. There were two purposes in this action. First, it was to show that God had **withdrawn** His **blessing . . . love,** and **pity.** Second, it served as a reminder that those who would **die** during the fall of Jerusalem would **not be buried or mourned** (cf. Jer. 16:4) and that the survivors would find no one **to console them** in their grief. The devastation would simply be too widespread. To **cut** oneself and to **shave** one's **head** were signs of grief (cf. 41:5; 47:5; 48:37) though cutting oneself was forbidden by the Law (Deut. 14:1) because of its pagan associations (cf. 1 Kings 18:28). On shaving one's head see comments on Job 1:20.

16:8-9. The third restriction placed on Jeremiah was **not** to **enter a house where there** was **feasting.** The purpose of this prohibition was to indicate that times of feasting and happiness would soon cease. God vowed to **bring an end to** Judah's **joy** and her present times of happiness (cf. 25:10).

(2) Judah's sin (16:10–17:18). **16:10-13.** As Jeremiah explained his behavior to the people, **they** asked **why** God had **decreed such a great disaster against** them. Naively they asked **what sin** they had **committed** to deserve such judgment. God's answer to these questions underscored the root problem throughout Israel's history. Though the previous generations (**fathers**) had abandoned the true God to follow **other gods,** the present generation **behaved** even **more wickedly.** Instead of profiting from their ancestors' errors, the current generation was going further astray. **Each** person was **following the stubbornness** within **his evil heart** rather than **obeying** God.

Because of the continued rebellion of the people, God vowed to **throw** them **out** of the land. "Throw" (*tûl*) means to cast or hurl an object (cf. 1 Sam. 18:11; 20:33; Jer. 22:26-28). The people would be violently thrust into a country they had not **known** before (cf. 14:18; 15:2, 14; 17:4) where they would **serve other gods** (cf. 5:19). Because they rejected God He would **show** them **no favor** (cf. 16:5).

16:14-15. Once again God paused in His judgment to clarify His message. Lest the people interpret His previous words to mean that Israel would no longer have any place in His covenant program, God clearly indicated that this judgment was not permanent (cf. 4:27; 5:18). Ultimately Israel as a nation will be restored to her land and will enjoy God's blessing. This will happen during the millennial reign of Christ when the nation will experience the benefits of the New Covenant (31:31-34).

God promised that after Judah's coming Captivity there would be a new "Exodus." **No longer** would the people look back to the first Exodus when God **brought the Israelites . . . out of** bondage in **Egypt.** Instead they would point back to the time when God **brought** them from **the land of the north** (i.e., Babylon; cf. comments on 1:14) where they had earlier been **banished.** Thus God reaffirmed His promise ultimately to **restore** Israel to **the land.**

Since 16:14-15 is nearly identical to 23:7-8, some scholars think that 16:14-15 was placed here later by mistake, but such a view is unnecessary. Jeremiah used the same or similar wording in several places throughout his book (cf. 1:18-19 with 15:20; 6:13-15 with 8:10b-12; 7:31-32 with 19:5-6; 15:13-14 with 17:3-4).

16:16-18. After assuring the nation of her final restoration, God continued describing her impending judgment. Restoration could be expected in the future, **but now** the people were facing deportation. God first pictured the Babylonian invaders as **fishermen** who would **catch** the Judeans in their nets. Then he pictured the Babylonians as **hunters** who would hunt . . . down those who had managed to escape and were in hiding. No one could escape because God's **eyes were on all their ways.** Neither the refugees nor **their sin** were ever **concealed** from God. He would hunt the people down and **repay them** for the way they had **defiled** the land (ironically called His land, not theirs) **with their detestable idols.**

16:19-21. Jeremiah affirmed his trust in God as his **Strength . . . Fortress,** and **Refuge** (cf. comments on Ps. 18:2), three words that emphasized the protection God had provided for him. After affirming his trust in God, Jeremiah looked forward to the day when all the world would know God. Though Judah had turned to the false gods of the Gentiles, a time will come when the **nations will come** to the true God of Israel. They will admit that their former objects of worship were **nothing but false gods, worthless idols** (cf. comments on Jer. 2:5). At that **time** God **will teach them** of His **power and might** so they will understand His true character. **They will know** then **that** His **name is the** LORD (cf. Ezek. 36:22-23).

17:1-4. The Gentiles will one day forsake their idols and turn to God. However, in Jeremiah's day the people of Judah were permeated with idolatry. They were so entrenched in their ways that it was as if their **sin** were **engraved** or etched on **their hearts** with **an iron tool** or **a flint point.** Both iron and flint, being extremely hard, were used to chisel words into stone tablets (cf. Job 19:24). The sin of Judah, however, extended beyond their hearts and showed up **on the horns of their** idolatrous **altars.** The "horns" were stone projections at the top of each altar on the four corners.

Idolatry was so pervasive that **even . . . children** participated in worship at the **altars and Asherah poles.** Asherah was the Canaanite goddess of fertility. A carved image of Asherah had been placed in God's temple by Manasseh (2 Kings 21:7; cf. Deut. 16:21) though he later removed it (2 Chron. 33:13, 15). Evidently the image was put back in the temple after he died because Josiah took it out during his reforms and burned it in the Kidron Valley outside the city (2 Kings 23:6). After Josiah's death the people resumed their idolatry, and the

Asherah poles were again set up. Possibly the "idol of jealousy" (Ezek. 8:5) was a carved image of Asherah. These idols were being worshiped by **spreading trees and on the high hills,** traditional places of worship for false gods (cf. Ezek. 6:13).

Because of the people's sin God would **give** the city of Jerusalem (His **mountain in the land)** and the **wealth** of its inhabitants **as plunder** (cf. Jer. 15:13; 20:5) to the invaders. The people of Judah would **lose** the land (their **inheritance)** as God enslaved them to their enemies and deported them to **a land** they did **not know** (cf. 14:18; 15:2, 14; 16:13).

17:5-8. Jeremiah included a short poem contrasting the way of the wicked (vv. 5-6) with the way of the righteous (vv. 7-8). Judah had been turning to false gods and foreign alliances for protection, but God indicated that a person **who trusts in man** for protection is **cursed** because his **heart** has turned **away from** God. Instead of prospering, he will wither away **like a desert bush.** God would make him as unfruitful as the barren **salt land** around the Dead Sea, unable to support life.

A righteous person is **blessed** because his **confidence** (trust) is in God. Unlike the person in verses 5-6, a righteous person will flourish **like a tree planted by the water** (cf. Ps. 1:3). When difficulties (represented figuratively by **heat** and **drought)** come, he will **not fear.** Instead he will continue to prosper like a tree that bears **fruit** and whose **leaves** remain **green.**

17:9-13. If the ways of blessing and cursing are so clear (vv. 5-8), why would anyone choose the path of sin? The cause for such action is in the **heart.** It is so **deceitful** that Jeremiah wondered **who** could even **understand it.** God answered by informing Jeremiah that He can **search the heart and examine the mind.** God knows those innermost thoughts and motives that an individual might hide from all others. Therefore God could justly render to each person what **his deeds deserve.**

The principle of judgment was applied to those who had amassed **riches by** using **unjust means.** If **a partridge** hatched the **eggs** of another bird, the offspring would soon **desert** the mother and fly away. So wealth that had been acquired unjustly would be taken away, and the one who had been hoarding it would be exposed as a fool.

Jeremiah's solution to sin was to focus on the majesty of God. God was enthroned in His sanctuary. Those who chose to forsake God (the Hope of Israel; cf. 14:8) would be written in the dust—a possible reference to their lack of permanence (as opposed to being written in the book of life, Ex. 32:32-33; Ps. 69:28). They deserved such a fate because they had abandoned God, the Spring of Living Water (cf. Jer. 2:13).

17:14-18. Jeremiah concluded his message by calling on God to vindicate him. The message is in the form of an individual lament. Jeremiah contrasted his faithful devotion to God with the unbelief of those persecuting him. They scoffed at his predictions and demanded that those prophecies now be fulfilled if they were true. Yet, in spite of this opposition, Jeremiah had not run away from faithfully serving as God's shepherd. Therefore he asked God to put his persecutors . . . to shame by bringing on them the day of disaster Jeremiah had been predicting. Because they refused to accept his message, he asked God to bring the full measure of judgment against them (double destruction; cf. 16:18).

h. The keeping of the Sabbath (17:19-27)

Jeremiah's previous messages dealt with the general sin and rebellion of the people. In these verses, however, he focused on one specific command in the Mosaic Law to show the nation how far they had departed from God (cf. Ex. 20:8-11). Again there is an explicit offer of repentance. Blessing will follow obedience, but judgment will follow disobedience.

17:19. God told Jeremiah to stand at the gate of the people. Which gate this was is unknown, though it is identified as the gate through which the kings . . . go in and out. The spot was selected because of the large number of people who passed by. Possibly this was the Eastern Gate that led from the temple mount to the Kidron Valley. Ezekiel pictured this gate as a place where Judah's leaders gathered (Ezek. 11:1). Or this may be the Benjamin Gate at the northern end of the city (cf. Jer. 37:13). It too was a place where a king would set up

his throne (38:7). Whatever the gate's location, Jeremiah did not stay there. He was to take his message to all the other gates so that the whole city would hear it.

17:20-24. His message to those who passed through these gates was to keep the Sabbath Day holy. In contrast with their forefathers who disobeyed, they were to honor the day God had set aside by not doing any work on it. This was one visible test of their faithfulness to God's covenant.

17:25-27. Faithfulness to the Law would bring blessing. If the people obeyed God's commandments, Jerusalem would be inhabited forever. People would flock to the city from the north (the territory of Benjamin), from the low, rolling hills of the Shephelah on the west (western foothills), from the rugged mountainous area between Jerusalem and the Jordan Valley and Dead Sea on the east (hill country), and from the semi-arid wilderness in the south (Negev). These people would bring their offerings and sacrifices to the temple. However, if they would not obey God's injunction on the Sabbath, He would kindle a fire of judgment that would consume her fortresses and leave her defenseless (cf. 49:27).

i. The potter and the broken jar (chaps. 18–20)

Jeremiah's ninth message was a series of parables and events that climaxed the first section of the book. The Parable of the Potter (chap. 18) demonstrated God's sovereign dealings with Judah. This was followed by the symbolic breaking of a potter's jar to show God's impending judgment (chap. 19). Chapter 20 serves as a pivot in the book. It is connected chronologically with chapter 19, but it also prepares the reader for the open opposition and specific prophecies of judgment that follow.

(1) The message at the potter's house (chap. 18). 18:1-4. God directed Jeremiah to go down to the potter's house and watch him molding clay into pots on his wheel. As Jeremiah watched, the potter discovered a flaw in the pot he was shaping . . . in his hands. The potter pressed the clay into a lump and formed it into another pot.

18:5-12. God announced that the

potter and the clay illustrated His relationship to His people. They were **like clay in His hand.** God has the right to tear **down** or build **up** a **nation** as He pleases. He had promised the **nation** blessing; but since she continued to do **evil,** He would **reconsider the good** He **had intended** and bring about judgment. However, if **Judah** would **turn from** her **evil ways** God would also revoke the **disaster** He promised to send.

The people of Judah would respond by saying that they were helpless to change (**it's no use**). They would stubbornly **continue** to follow the **plans** of their sinful hearts. The nation refused to turn from her idolatry to follow the LORD.

18:13-17. Judah stood alone **among the nations** in her stubborn refusal to follow her God (cf. 2:10-11). Even the **snow** on the slopes **of Lebanon** and the **cool waters** that **flow** from these majestic mountains were more dependable than fickle Judah. She had turned from God **to** worship **worthless idols** (cf. comments on 2:5) which only caused her to **stumble.** By abandoning **the ancient paths** of obedience to God (cf. 6:16), Judah found herself on **bypaths,** wandering aimlessly over rough **roads.**

God would judge the nation for her sin by having her **land . . . laid waste.** She would become **an object of . . . scorn** to those who were **appalled** at her stupidity in abandoning her God (cf. 19:8; Lam. 2:15). **The** LORD vowed to **scatter** the nation like the **wind from the east** (cf. Jer. 4:11-12; 13:24). They should expect God's judgment (His **back**), **not** His favor (His **face**).

18:18-23. Again the people responded by making **plans against Jeremiah.** They refused to accept his declaration of doom because it conflicted with their belief in the permanence of the then-present order. Their solution was to **attack him with** their **tongues** in an effort to slander and malign his message and also to **pay no attention** to his words, hoping to silence him by ignoring him. Evidently their plans were more sinister because Jeremiah told the LORD that they were plotting to take his life (**they have dug a pit,** vv. 20-21; cf. 11:18-21).

Jeremiah reacted to their threats by calling on God to **listen** to their accusations, to **remember** his (Jeremiah's) faithfulness, and to judge the plotters for their sin. Jeremiah had earlier asked God to **turn** His **wrath away** (18:20; cf. 7:16; 8:20-22), but now he called on God to **deal with them** in His **time of . . . anger** (18:23). They had rejected both God and His messenger; Jeremiah could do no more for them. They would experience **famine** and **the sword** (v. 21).

(2) The message of the broken jar (chap. 19). **19:1-6.** Probably chapter 19 was placed next to chapter 18 because both contained messages based on **a potter** and his wares. Jeremiah bought a narrow-necked pottery flask or vessel for carrying water. The word for **clay jar** is *baqbūq,* an onomatopoetic word suggesting the sound the water made as it was poured out. After gathering a group of **elders** and **priests,** he walked **to the Valley of Ben Hinnom** (see comments on 7:31) just outside **the Potsherd Gate.** The Hinnom Valley ran along the south and west of the city and served as Jerusalem's "community dump." The gate at the south of the city which opened into the valley was called the "Potsherd Gate" because people carried their potsherds (broken pieces of pottery) and other refuse through this gate to throw it in the Hinnom Valley. The Targum identifies the Potsherd Gate with the Dung Gate (cf. Neh. 2:13; 3:13-14). The modern Dung Gate in Jerusalem is also located on the south of the city, but the present walls are several hundred yards north of the walls in Jeremiah's day.

With the Hinnom Valley as a backdrop, Jeremiah delivered his message. God vowed to **bring a disaster on** Jerusalem because of her idolatry. The valley itself was a witness against the people because it contained **the high places of Baal** where people slaughtered **their sons** to offer them as sacrifices **in the fire.** Because of these wicked deeds God again (cf. Jer. 7:32-33) vowed to rename the place **the Valley of Slaughter** as He destroyed the people there.

19:7-9. Jeremiah elaborated on the coming catastrophe. The people would **fall by the sword before** Babylon, and **their carcasses** would serve **as food** for **the birds** and beasts (cf. 7:33; 16:4; 34:20; Deut. 28:26). The **city** itself would become **an object of scorn** (cf. Jer. 18:16) to those who observed her destruction. Those who sought refuge in the city would resort to cannibalism (**eat the flesh of their sons and daughters**) as Babylon's **siege** choked off the supply of food to the inhabitants (cf. Lev. 26:27-29; Deut. 28:53-57; Lam. 2:20; 4:10). All the curses promised by God would overtake the people because of their sin (cf. Lev. 26:14-39; Deut. 28:15-68; Jer. 11:1-8).

19:10-13. To dramatize the message to his audience God commanded Jeremiah to **break the jar** he had carried out to the valley. God said He would **smash** both the **nation** of Judah and the **city** of Jerusalem **just as** Jeremiah **smashed** the **potter's jar.** The **city** itself would become **like Topheth** (cf. comments on 7:31-32); its once-beautiful dwellings would be reduced to rubble and the entire area would **be defiled** with decaying bodies of the slain. The cause for the destruction was the sin of the people in burning **incense . . . to all the starry hosts** and in offering libations **to other gods.**

19:14-15. Returning **from Topheth** to the city Jeremiah went directly to **the** temple **court.** The message given to the leaders (cf. v. 1) was now repeated **to all the people.** God's judgment would come against Jerusalem **and the villages around it . . . because** the people refused **to listen to** His **words.**

(3) The response of Pashhur (20:1-6). **20:1-2.** Jeremiah's message of judgment was rejected by one of the priests, **Pashhur son of Immer.** This Pashhur was not the Pashhur in 21:1. The Pashhur in 20:1 was **the chief officer in the temple** and was probably assigned to maintain order within the temple area (cf. 29:26). He seized Jeremiah and had him **beaten,** or flogged with 40 lashes (cf. Deut. 25:2-3). Then he put Jeremiah **in the stocks** for public ridicule. These stocks were located **at the Upper Gate of Benjamin,** the northern gate of the city. This was the first of several instances of open opposition against Jeremiah's ministry.

20:3-6. When Jeremiah was **released** from his chains **the next day** he refused to change his message. Instead he changed Pashhur's name. God's new **name for Pashhur** was **Magor-Missabib** ("terror on every side"). Because **Pashhur** refused to heed God's message, he would **see** the outpouring of God's judgment. He would watch in terror as his own friends fell **by the sword,** and he

would see **Babylon** carry away **all the wealth of** Jerusalem **as plunder** (cf. 15:13; 17:3). **Pashhur** and his family would be exiled in **Babylon** where they would all **die.** The reason for this judgment was not only that he had Jeremiah beaten. Pashhur also **prophesied lies,** probably by denying the truth of Jeremiah's message. The exact fulfillment of the prophecy was not given, but it is possible that Pashhur was taken to Babylon during the second deportation in 597 B.C. along with the priest, Ezekiel (cf. 2 Kings 24:15-16; Ezek. 1:1-3).

(4) The complaint of Jeremiah (20:7-18). **20:7-10.** Jeremiah opened his heart to God and expressed the depth of his inner emotions. He felt that God had **deceived** him by letting him be **ridiculed** by the people for his message. He had faithfully warned them of the coming **violence and destruction;** but his reward was only their insults. Discouraged, Jeremiah considered withholding God's Word to avoid persecution. But when he did, the **Word** became **like a burning fire** (cf. 23:29) within him so that he was unable to contain it. To feel something in one's **bones** meant to feel it intensely (cf. Job 30:17; 33:19).

Jeremiah wanted to quit his ministry because the people plotted against him. The message of **terror on every side** that he was constantly proclaiming (Jer. 20:3-4; cf. 6:25; 17:18; 46:5; 49:29; Lam. 2:22) was now being hurled back at him (cf. Ps. 31:13). Even his **friends** were watching for him **to slip** up, perhaps by uttering a wrong prediction, so they could **take** their **revenge on him** as a false prophet (cf. Deut. 18:20).

20:11-13. Jeremiah continued his prayer by expressing his trust in God and by calling on God to avenge him (cf. 18:19-23). Though he had felt deceived (20:7), he still realized that God was **with** him **like a mighty warrior.** Since the Lord was fighting on Jeremiah's side, he was confident that those who were persecuting and mocking him would **stumble** and would ultimately be **disgraced.** Jeremiah asked to **see** the **vengeance** of the all-knowing God poured out on his opponents because he had **committed** his **cause** to God.

This assurance of vindication allowed Jeremiah to **sing** and **praise** God for His mighty acts. God could be praised because He would rescue Jeremiah **from . . . the wicked.**

20:14-18. In a sudden change of emotion Jeremiah again plunged from a height of confidence (vv. 11-13) to the depths of despair. Perhaps he realized that the vindication for which he sought could come only through the destruction of the city and nation which he dearly loved. His agony made him wish that the **day** he **was born** would have been **cursed.** By cursing the day of his birth, Jeremiah was wishing that he had never been **born** (cf. 15:10; Job 3:1-19). Had he died **in the womb,** he would not have **come out of the womb** in birth and been subject to the **trouble and sorrow** he was experiencing. Jeremiah's self-pity could not erase the fact that he had been selected "in the womb" for the task he was performing (cf. Jer. 1:5).

2. JEREMIAH'S FOUR SPECIFIC PROPHECIES OF JUDGMENT (CHAPS. 21-25)

The opposition of Pashhur (20:1-6) serves as a pivot or bridge in the Book of Jeremiah. Through a series of nine undated prophecies Jeremiah had denounced Judah's sin, threatened judgment, and offered hope if the people would repent. Though opposition had surfaced (11:18-23; 12:6; 15:10; 17:18; 18:19-23), he had not suffered any physical persecution. With the recording of Pashhur's response, however, Jeremiah's book took on a more personal note. His prophecies were now directed against specific individuals and groups, and Judah's hope of repentance was replaced with the certainty of God's judgment.

a. The rebuke of the kings (21:1–23:8)

The first group singled out by Jeremiah was the kings—those appointed by God to be shepherds of the flock of Judah (cf. 2:8; 10:21; 23:1-8; Ezek. 34:1-10). Jeremiah first rebuked the wicked kings who had ruled Judah (Jer. 21–22). Then he offered hope in the righteous King who would come to restore Judah (23:1-8).

Jeremiah's messages to the wicked kings were arranged in an unusual order. (See the chart "The Last Five Kings of Judah," near 2 Kings 24.) The first king listed was Zedekiah who was the last king chronologically (Jer. 21:1–22:9). The other kings were then arranged chrono-

logically beginning with Shallum (Jehoahaz, 22:10-12), continuing with Jehoiakim (22:13-23), and ending with Coniah (Jehoiachin/Jeconiah, 22:24-30). Why did Jeremiah place Zedekiah out of chronological order, putting him first and Coniah last? Perhaps for two reasons. First, by discussing Zedekiah at the beginning he was able to put the story of "Pashhur son of Malkijah" (21:1) next to the story of "Pashhur son of Immer" (20:1). The fact that these two individuals had the same name provides continuity. The vindication Jeremiah sought because of Pashhur son of Immer's ridicule was realized when Pashhur son of Malkijah was sent to Jeremiah to inquire of the Lord. Second, the accounts were arranged so that the prophecy against Coniah would climax God's judgments against the kings. The line of the wicked kings would be cut off (22:30) because God would raise a righteous Branch to rule the nation (23:1-8). So the arrangement of these prophecies provided both continuity and climax.

(1) The message to Zedekiah (21:1–22:9). **21:1-2.** This message was given some time between 588 B.C. and 586 B.C. **King Zedekiah sent . . . Pashhur son of Malkijah and . . . Zephaniah son of Maaseiah** to Jeremiah with a request. Pashhur, one of the king's officials, later petitioned the king to execute Jeremiah for treason (cf. 38:1-4). Zephaniah succeeded Jehoiada (29:25-26) as a **priest** second in rank to the high priest, Seraiah (52:24). So Zephaniah was the second highest religious leader in Judah. Later, after the fall of Jerusalem (52:24-27), Zephaniah was executed by Nebuchadnezzar.

These officials asked Jeremiah to **inquire . . . of the LORD** regarding Nebuchadnezzar's attack on Jerusalem. Though Jeremiah was to ask God what the outcome would be, they hoped that God would **perform wonders** as He had done **in times past so that Nebuchadnezzar** would **withdraw.** Probably Zedekiah and his advisers were thinking of King Hezekiah's day when the Assyrians had threatened Jerusalem (2 Kings 18:17–19:37; Isa. 36–37). Hezekiah responded to the crisis by sending his chief political and religious advisers to the Prophet Isaiah to ask for his intervention (Isa. 37:2-4). No doubt Zedekiah hoped that God's answer would be similar to that given by Isaiah (Isa. 37:5-7).

21:3-7. Unfortunately for **Zedekiah,** Jeremiah's message was one he did *not* wish to hear. Instead of rescuing Jerusalem, **God** would **turn against** her **the very weapons of war** she had in her **hands.** The armies **outside the wall** who were **besieging** the city would be gathered by God **inside** the **city.** Their siege would be successful. Rather than being Jerusalem's Deliverer, God would **fight against** her **with** His own **outstretched hand.** Those who were huddled for protection in the **city** would **die of a terrible plague**—one of the worst fears of a city under siege (cf. comments on 14:12).

Those who managed to **survive** the siege would not rejoice because God would **hand** them **over** to **Nebuchadnezzar.** They could expect **no mercy or pity or compassion** for he would kill them. This was fulfilled in 586 B.C. after the city fell. King Zedekiah was blinded and taken in chains to Babylon (39:5-7). The other leaders of the city were captured and sent to Riblah where they were executed (52:24-27).

21:8-10. The people had two clear choices: **the way of life and the way of death.** The "way of death" was selected by those who chose to remain in the **city.** They would die. The "way of life" was selected by those who deserted (surrendered) to the enemy besieging Jerusalem. This was the only hope for those still in the **city** because God had **determined** to harm Jerusalem by letting it fall to **Babylon.** The response to this message from Jeremiah is in 38:1-4.

21:11-14. Jeremiah again singled out **the royal house of Judah** and focused on their sin. The king was supposed to **administer justice** and to uphold the rights of those who were oppressed. Since he refused to heed God's warning, God's **wrath** would **burn like** an unquenchable **fire** (cf. 4:4; 17:4).

Evidently the king saw no need to obey God's injunction. He felt so secure in his well-protected city that he boasted, **Who can enter our refuge?** Because of this proud self-reliance, coupled with sinful disobedience, God would **punish** the king and his people. God's **fire** (cf. 21:12) of judgment would **consume everything around** them.

22:1-5. God instructed Jeremiah to go **down** from the temple to the king's **palace.** His message to **the king** and to the **officials** and **people** who were there was for them to **do what is just and right.** The content of this message was similar to 21:12, but certain consequences were attached to the actions. **If** the king would be **careful** to observe God's **commands** he could expect continued blessing. But if he disobeyed those **commands,** God vowed that the royal **palace** would **become a ruin.**

22:6-9. In these verses Jeremiah was referring to the royal **palace.** Both **Gilead** and **Lebanon** were known for their forests (Jud. 9:15; 1 Kings 4:33; 2 Chron. 2:8), and the royal palace in Jerusalem was known as the "Palace of the Forest of Lebanon" (1 Kings 7:2-5; Isa. 22:8). But after God's judgment the palace would be as desolate as **a desert.** The Babylonians would **cut up** the palace's **fine cedar beams** and cast **them into the fire** (cf. Jer. 52:13).

As **people from** other **nations** saw the destruction of this magnificent structure, they would **ask . . . why** God had **done such a thing. The answer** was simple. God had judged the city **because** the people had **forsaken the covenant** and had **worshiped . . . other gods.** God had judged the people with His promised curses because of their disobedience.

(2) *The message to Shallum.* **22:10-12.** **Shallum** was another name for Jehoahaz. He was a **son of Josiah,** and succeeded Josiah to the throne in 609 B.C. after Josiah was killed by Pharaoh Neco II (2 Kings 23:29-33). After a reign of only three months, Shallum was deposed by Pharaoh Neco. Jeremiah penned this prophecy in 609 after Shallum had **gone from** Jerusalem into captivity in Egypt (2 Kings 23:34). Jeremiah predicted that Shallum would **never return** to Jerusalem. Instead, he would **die in the place where** he had been deported as a **captive.**

(3) *The message to Jehoiakim (22:13-23).* **22:13-14.** After being appointed as king by Pharaoh Neco, Jehoiakim acted the part of a typical oriental despot. Judah needed a firm hand to guide the "ship of state," but instead she got a corrupt, petty king who cared only for personal gain. Jehoiakim sought to build a **palace** for himself, and did so at the expense of his subjects. They were forced

to **work for nothing** as Jehoiakim lavished his money on **panels** of **cedar** wood.

22:15-17. Jeremiah contrasted Jehoiakim with his **father,** King Josiah. Josiah had done **what was right and just** and had **defended the . . . poor and needy.** These were actions God expected of the king. As God's shepherd he was expected to nurture the flock, not decimate it. However, Jehoiakim inherited none of his father's godly traits. He cared **only** for **dishonest gain,** bloodshed, **oppression, and extortion.**

22:18-19. Because of Jehoiakim's heavy-handed oppression, the people would **not mourn for him** at his death. Instead of the lavish funeral normally given a monarch, Jehoiakim, Jeremiah predicted, would **have the burial of a donkey.** When an animal died in the city it was simply **dragged away** from the spot where it died and **thrown outside the gates.** Jehoiakim's body would be treated with the same contempt. Jehoiakim died in late 598 B.C. as Nebuchadnezzar was advancing on Jerusalem to punish the city for rebellion. Perhaps, as some suppose, Jehoiakim was assassinated in an attempt to appease Nebuchadnezzar and spare the city. The new king, Jehoiachin, surrendered and was taken to Babylon; but the city was spared (2 Kings 24:1-17).

22:20-23. Because of Jehoiakim's foolishness Jeremiah called on the city of Jerusalem to lament her fate. This passage should probably be dated in late 598 or early 597 B.C. since it focused on the coming invasion of Babylon in retaliation for Jehoiakim's rebellion. Jerusalem's **cry** would be heard throughout the land. From **Lebanon** in the north to **Bashan** in the northeast to **Abarim** (the mountains in Moab; cf. Num. 27:12; Deut. 32:49; Ezek. 39:11) in the southeast the lament would sound as Judah's **allies** would be **crushed** by Babylon.

God had **warned** Jerusalem of the consequences of disobedience **when** she **felt secure,** but she refused to **listen.** Now she could only watch in sorrow as her **shepherds** (kings) were taken **away** and her **allies** (possibly the Egyptians) also faced exile (cf. 2 Kings 24:7). In an ironic twist Jeremiah referred to the inhabitants of Jerusalem as those **who live in "Lebanon."** So much cedar had been

imported to Jerusalem from Lebanon (cf. Jer. 22:6-7, 13-15) that living in Jerusalem was like dwelling among Lebanon's cedars. Yet those living in these majestic **cedar buildings** would **groan** when the **pangs** of God's judgment came on them (on a woman's **labor** pains cf. comments on 4:31).

(4) The message to Jehoiachin (22:24-30). **22:24-27.** Jehoiachin followed his father **Jehoiakim** to the throne. After a three-month reign Jehoiachin surrendered to Nebuchadnezzar and was deported to Babylon where he lived the rest of his life (cf. 52:31-34). God indicated that even if Jehoiachin were as valuable to Him as **a signet ring,** He **would** still **pull** him **off** because of his sins. A signet ring was most valuable because it was used to impress its owner's signature or seal on various documents. **Even if . . . Jehoiachin** were this important to God (and the clear implication is that he was not), God would rather remove him than allow him to continue sinning. (For a reversal of this judgment see the promise to Zerubbabel in Hag. 2:21-23.)

God vowed to **hand** Jehoiachin **over to** the **Babylonians.** He and his **mother** would be cast **into another country** (Babylon) where they **both** would **die.** Jehoiachin's mother was Nehushta, the widow of King Jehoiakim (2 Kings 24:8). This is Jeremiah's second prophecy of their deportation (cf. Jer. 13:18-19).

22:28-30. By a series of questions, Jeremiah indicated that God was responsible for Jehoiachin's judgment. The first question should be answered no. The people did *not* despise Jehoiachin as a **broken,** unwanted **pot.** In fact some hoped he would be restored as king (28:1-4), and some considered him to be the king even after Zedekiah was placed on the throne (cf. comments on Ezek. 7:27). But if Jehoiachin was so popular, **why** would **he and his children be** removed from office and **cast into** a foreign nation? (On the words, **a land they do not know;** cf. Jer. 14:18; 15:2, 14; 16:13; 17:4.) The answer is that God was in control, and He was responsible for Jehoiachin's fall. God called on the **land** (repeated three times for emphasis; cf. 7:4) to **hear** His **word** of judgment. Though King Jehoiachin did have children (22:28; cf. 1 Chron. 3:17), he was to be *considered* **childless** because **none of**

his offspring would be allowed to sit on the throne of David to rule as king of Judah.

This prophecy had both immediate and long-range significance. No offspring of Jehoiachin followed him to the throne. His uncle, Zedekiah, who replaced Jehoiachin, was Judah's last king. God "pruned away" that portion of the line of David from the kingly line. This prophecy also helps explain the genealogies of Christ in Matthew 1 and Luke 3. Matthew presented the legal line of Christ through his stepfather, Joseph. However, Joseph's line came through Shealtiel who was a son of Jehoiachin (Jeconiah, Matt. 1:12; cf. 1 Chron. 3:17). Had Christ been a physical descendant of Joseph and not virgin-born, He would have been disqualified as Israel's King. Luke presented the physical line of Christ through Mary, who was descended from David through the line of his son Nathan (Luke 3:31). In that way Christ was not under the "curse" of Jehoiachin. (For additional information see comments on Matt. 1:2-17; Luke 3:24-38.)

(5) The message concerning the righteous Branch (23:1-8). **23:1-4.** Jeremiah summarized the unrighteous kings as being like **shepherds** who were **destroying and scattering** God's **sheep. The shepherds** deserved **punishment** because of **the evil** they had **done** (cf. Ezek. 34:1-10). But if God removed them, whom would He appoint to regather His sheep? Jeremiah gave a twofold answer. First, God Himself would **gather the remnant** of the people who were dispersed and would **bring them back.** He would assume responsibility for Israel's regathering (cf. Jer. 31:10; Micah 2:12; 5:4; 7:14). Second, God would raise up new **shepherds over them who** would **tend** and care for the people the way God intended.

23:5-6. The branch of David through Jehoiachin had been "cut off." However, God promised to **raise up to David** another King who would be **a righteous Branch,** that is, another member of the Davidic line. Jesus Christ is the fulfillment of this prediction. As **King,** He **will reign wisely** and will **do what is just and right** (in contrast with God's condemnation of Jehoiachin, 22:25). Though Christ offered Himself as Israel's Messiah at His First Advent, the final fulfillment of this prophecy awaits His Second Advent immediately before His millennial reign. At that time the Southern Kingdom (**Judah**) and the Northern Kingdom (**Israel**) will again be delivered (cf. Rom. 11:26) from oppression and reunited as a single nation and will **live in safety** (cf. Ezek. 37:15-28).

The **name** of this coming King will be the LORD **Our Righteousness** (*Yahweh ṣidqēnû*). Unlike Zedekiah (*ṣidqîyāhû*, "my righteousness is Yahweh"), this coming King will live up to His name as Israel's righteous God.

23:7-8. Having already mentioned the future restoration of Judah and Israel (v. 6), Jeremiah now said the restoration will be so dramatic that the **people will no longer** look back to the time when God **brought** them **up out of Egypt.** The first Exodus will pale in comparison with this new Exodus when God will bring **the descendants of Israel . . . out of all the countries where** they have been and will restore them to **their own land** (cf. 16:14-15).

b. The rebuke of the false prophets (23:9-40)

Jeremiah turned from addressing Judah's kings to deliver God's verbal broadside against the prophets. These pseudo-seers opposed Jeremiah's declaration of doom (cf. 6:13-14; 8:10-11; 14:14-16; 28:1-4, 10-11; 29:8-9, 20-23, 31-32) and offered in its place a promise of peace.

(1) The character of the false prophets (23:9-15). **23:9-12.** Jeremiah's **heart** was **broken** and his body became weak when he thought of God's **holy words.** A prophet was God's spokesman, and his life and message reflected on the One who sent him. Thus the false prophets were impugning God's name because they claimed that their message came from Him and that He had authorized them to speak (cf. 28:2, 15-16). God had shown His displeasure on the physical and spiritual adulteries being done in Judah by bringing His **curse** of drought (cf. Deut. 28:23-24) so that the **land** was **parched** and **withered** (cf. Jer. 14:1-6, 22). Yet, instead of calling Judah back to her covenant with God, **the prophets** continued to lead the people on **an evil course,** implying that God was not using the drought to judge people for their sin.

The basic flaw of all Judah's spiritual leaders (**both prophet and priest**) was that they were godless (*ḥānap*). This Hebrew word does not mean that these leaders did not believe in God. On the contrary, they were quite "religious." Rather, it means "to be polluted or profaned." Jeremiah had used the word earlier to describe the "defilement" of the land (cf. 3:1-2, 9). These leaders had such a low view of God's holy character that they would even pollute His temple with their wickedness. Because of their sin God vowed to bring disaster on them.

23:13-15. Jeremiah compared the prophets of Samaria (v. 13) to the prophets of Jerusalem (v. 14). The prophets of the Northern Kingdom of Israel ("Samaria") had prophesied by Baal and led the nation astray (cf. 1 Kings 18:16-40; 2 Kings 10:18-29; 17:16). Because of their wickedness, God destroyed the Northern Kingdom.

The prophets of Judah followed in the same paths of sin. They continued to commit adultery and support evildoers. Their conduct was so repulsive that both they and the people of Jerusalem had become like Sodom and Gomorrah before God. The only alternative available to God was to judge them for their sin. God would make the false prophets eat bitter food (*la'ănâh*, "wormwood"; cf. Jer. 9:15; Lam. 3:15, 19) and drink poisoned water.

(2) The message of the false prophets (23:16-40). **23:16-22.** The message delivered by the false prophets was one of their own making. Their visions came from their own minds (cf. v. 26) instead of from God's mouth. They proclaimed peace (cf. 6:14; 8:11) and no harm, but they did not hear this word from God. God's message was that a whirlwind would destroy those in its path. God said His anger would not turn back until He had finished His judgment. Only then would the people understand . . . clearly that God had not sent these prophets. Had they been from God (cf. council in 23:18) they would have proclaimed His words to turn Judah from her evil deeds.

23:23-32. The false prophets misunderstood the character of God. He was not some localized God from whom a prophet could hide so God could not see him. Indeed, God in His omniscience fills heaven and earth so that no place is outside His realm. He had heard what the prophets said when they spoke lies in His name.

The prophets claimed that God had given them revelation in a dream, but their visions were only delusions of their own minds (cf. v. 16). These dreams were designed to make Judah forget God's name much as earlier prophets did through Baal worship (cf. v. 13). Their "dreams" were as worthless for meeting spiritual needs as was straw for meeting physical hunger. Their words had no force, while God's Word is as penetrating as fire (cf. 20:9) and as effective as a hammer that breaks a rock in pieces. Nothing can prevent God's Word from being fulfilled.

Because God had not spoken to these false prophets they were forced to steal from one another as they pronounced plagiarized prophecies that were supposedly from Him. God set Himself against those prophets because they were leading the people astray with . . . reckless lies, falsely claiming God's authority.

23:33-40. The people of Jerusalem were asking one another, What is the oracle of the LORD? The word "oracle" (*maśśā'*, from the verb *nāśā'*) means "to lift, carry, take" (see comments on Zech. 9:1). The noun referred to the load or burden that someone had to lift or carry (Ex. 23:5; Neh. 13:19). The "burden" the prophet had to carry was the message or oracle "laid on his heart" by God (Isa. 13:1; 14:28; Nahum 1:1; Hab. 1:1). Often the message was one of judgment (cf. Isa. 15:1; 17:1; 19:1; 21:1, 11, 13; 22:1; 23:1).

When the people sought for an oracle from God, Jeremiah was to announce that there was none. It had already been given; and the word from God was that He would forsake them. God said He would punish those who claimed any other oracle. The people were misusing the term so much in claiming divine authority for their own words that God told them not to mention the word again. Its misuse had caused the people to distort the true words of the living God. Those who continued to claim divine oracles would be judged. God vowed to cast them out of His presence along with the rest of Jerusalem. These false prophets faced the threat of unending disgrace and shame for their wicked words.

JEREMIAH

c. The two baskets of figs (chap. 24)

(1) The vision of the two baskets of figs. **24:1-3.** The vision of the two baskets of figs was given Jeremiah **after Jehoiachin** and the other leaders of Jerusalem **were carried into exile** by the Babylonians (cf. 2 Kings 24:8-16). Thus this prophecy can be dated sometime in 597 B.C. at the beginning of the reign of Zedekiah. In the vision Jeremiah saw **two baskets of figs** that had been **placed in front of the temple.** The vision called to mind the offering of the firstfruits in a basket before the LORD (cf. Deut. 26:11). In **one** of the baskets the **figs** were **very good** and resembled **those that ripen early** (cf. Isa. 28:4; Hosea 9:10; Micah 7:1)—those firstfruits that were to be offered to God (Deut. 14:22). The second basket contained **very poor figs** that had deteriorated to the point where **they could not be eaten.** Such offerings were unacceptable to the LORD (cf. Mal. 1:6-9).

(2) The explanation of the good figs. **24:4-7.** God said the **good figs** represented **the exiles from Judah** who had been carried away to Babylon. This was a surprising answer because the people of Jerusalem believed that those in captivity had been taken away from the LORD (cf. Ezek. 11:14-15). Yet God promised to **watch over** the remnant in captivity and **bring them back to** the land (cf. Ezek. 11:16-17). He also promised to **give them a new heart** so they will **know** Him (cf. Jer. 4:22). At that time **they will be** His **people** (cf. comments on 30:22) and **will return to** Him **with all their heart.** Though God did restore a minority of the people to the land after the Babylonian Captivity, they never experienced the full blessings of fellowship promised by God (cf. 31:31-34; Ezek. 36:24-32). This awaits a still-future fulfillment when God again will regather Israel at the beginning of Christ's millennial reign on earth (Matt. 24:29-31).

(3) The explanation of the poor figs. **24:8-10.** The **poor figs** represented **Zedekiah** and the other **survivors** (cf. 29:17-19), including those in Israel and those who fled to **Egypt** (cf. 43:4-7). God vowed to **make them abhorrent . . . to all the kingdoms of the earth.** They would be ridiculed and cursed **wherever** they went. (Several times in the Book of Jer. the prophet predicted that the people would be cursed, ridiculed, and/or re-

proached and that others would be horrified at their desolate condition; cf. 25:9, 18; 26:6; 29:18; 42:18; 44:8, 12, 22. Also note 48:39; 49:13, 17; 51:37, about other countries.) God would send His instruments of judgment (**sword, famine, and plague;** cf. 14:12; 15:2-4) **until they** were all **destroyed.** These survivors had felt blessed of God, but in reality they were cursed.

d. The 70-year Captivity in Babylon (chap. 25)

Jeremiah's 13 messages of judgment (chaps. 2–25) were arranged topically, not chronologically. Chapter 25 was placed last because it served as the capstone for all Jeremiah's previous messages.

(1) Warnings ignored (25:1-7). **25:1-3.** Jeremiah's final message concerned **all the people of Judah.** Because of the significance of the message, the time when it was given was recorded. It was delivered **in the fourth year of Jehoiakim . . . which was the first year of Nebuchadnezzar.** This has caused some confusion because the "first year" of Nebuchadnezzar's reign (after his accession year) would have begun on April 2, 604 B.C., while Jehoiakim's fourth year (using the Nisan [March-April]-to-Nisan dating system that Jeremiah usually employed) would have extended from April 12 (Nisan 1), 605 B.C. to April 2 (Nisan 1), 604 B.C. (not April 11, 604 B.C. because of the lunar calendar). So the two dates (Nebuchadnezzar's first year and Jehoiakim's fourth year) do not seem to occur in the same calendar year.

Two possible solutions have been suggested. First, it is possible that the word "first" (ri'šônî) should be translated "beginning." This word is not the normal word used to describe the first year of a king's reign (cf. Jack Finegan, *Handbook of Bible Chronology.* Princeton, N.J.: Princeton University Press, 1964, p. 202). Thus the "beginning" year of Nebuchadnezzar could be equated with his accession year. This would place Jeremiah's prophecy sometime between September 7, 605 B.C. when Nebuchadnezzar ascended the throne and April 2, 604 B.C. when the first full year of his reign officially began.

Second, possibly Jeremiah was here using a Tishri (September-October)-to-

Tishri dating system for Jehoiakim. Thus Jehoiakim's fourth year extended from October 7 (Tishri 1), 605 B.C. to September 26 (Tishri 1), 604 B.C. (not October 6, 604 B.C. because of the lunar calendar). In this case Jeremiah's prophecy would have been given sometime between April 2, 604 B.C. (the start of Nebuchadnezzar's first full year) and September 25, 604 B.C. (the end of Jehoiakim's fourth year). Either solution allows the text to stand as it is written.

Jeremiah had been prophesying **for 23 years** (cf. 1:2)—a ministry that had spanned the reigns of three kings at the time of this prophecy. But though **Jeremiah** had **spoken to** the people **again and again,** they had **not listened** to his warnings to repent. God had given ample time for them to respond, but they refused.

25:4-7. God had also **sent** other **prophets** who warned the people to **turn** from their **evil ways** and **practices.** Had the people heeded the prophets' warnings, God would have graciously let them **stay in the land** and He would **not** have harmed them. Unfortunately the people **did not listen** to God. They continued in their idolatry and **brought harm to** themselves.

(2) Judgment described (25:8-14). **25:8-11. Because** the people had repeatedly rejected God's warnings, God would **summon** the Babylonians (**the peoples of the north;** cf. comments on 1:14). Their leader, **Nebuchadnezzar,** was called God's **servant** in the sense that he would do God's bidding in coming to destroy Jerusalem. God would use the Babylonians to **completely destroy** both Judah and her allies. **The sounds of joy and gladness** would cease (cf. 7:34; 16:9) in the nation because the **whole country** would **become a desolate wasteland** when **Babylon** was finished. God would deport Judah and the other rebellious people to **Babylon** to **serve** the Babylonians **70 years.**

Why did God predict that the Babylonian Exile would last 70 years? (605–536 B.C.) The answer seems to be that this was the number of years that the people had failed to observe God's Law of a "Sabbath rest" for the land. God had decreed that every seventh year the land was to lie fallow (Lev. 25:3-5). The people were not to sow their fields or prune their vineyards. If the people would fail to follow this command, God would remove them from the land to enforce this "Sabbath rest" (Lev. 26:33-35). The writer of 2 Chronicles indicated that the 70-year Babylonian Captivity promised by Jeremiah allowed the land to enjoy its "Sabbath rest" (2 Chron. 36:20-21). Therefore the Captivity lasted 70 years probably because this was the number of Sabbath rests that had not been observed for the land.

25:12-14. After **the 70 years** were **fulfilled** God would also **punish . . . the Babylonians** because of the **guilt** they had incurred. He would fulfill **all the things . . . written in** Jeremiah's **book** against **Babylon.** The material to which God alluded is in chapters 50–51. Evidently at least part of chapters 50–51 was written about the same time as chapter 25. God would **repay** Babylon **according to** her **deeds.**

(3) Wrath promised (25:15-29). **25:15-26.** Jeremiah had a vision of **the LORD** holding in His **hand a cup.** The cup was **filled** with God's **wrath.** Jeremiah's task was to **make all the nations to whom** he was sent **drink it** (cf. Lam. 4:21; Ezek. 23:31-33; Rev. 16:19; 18:6). The first ones to drink of this bitter brew, God's "grapes of wrath," were **Jerusalem and the towns of Judah.**

Other nations would follow Judah in judgment. (For the locations of many of these nations see the map "The World of Jeremiah and Ezekiel," in the *Introduction.*) These included **Egypt,** whose feeble assistance prompted Judah to rebel against Babylon (cf. Ezek. 29:6-9). The location of **Uz** is somewhat uncertain, but it was probably east of Edom in northern Arabia (cf. comments on Job. 1:1). **The Philistines** occupied the coastal region on the shore of the Mediterranean just west of Judah, while **Edom, Moab, and Ammon** (listed from south to north) were the three nations just east of Judah on the other side of the Jordan River and the Dead Sea. Both **Tyre and Sidon** were north of Judah on the Mediterranean coast. **Dedan, Tema,** and **Buz** were cities in the northern part of the Arabian Peninsula, but the exact location of Buz is unknown. They are associated with **the kings of Arabia** who were bedouins in the desert. The identification of **Zimri** is uncertain, but it is associated with **Elam** and **Media** which were two countries east of the Tigris River. All these nations were conquered by Babylon.

All these nations would be judged at the hand of Babylon; but **after all of them,** God would make **the king of Sheshach . . . drink it too.** Who or what is Sheshach? Most scholars believe that the word is a cryptogram or *atbash* for Babylon. An *atbash* was a code in which the letters of a name counted from the end of the alphabet are substituted for the letters counted from the beginning. For example, in English the letter "z" would replace the letter "a," the letter "y" would replace the letter "b," etc. The word "Abby" as an *atbash* would become "zyyb." If "Sheshach" (*ššk*) is a Hebrew *atbash* the consonants become *bbl*, which is the spelling for Babylon (cf. Jer. 25:1). God would judge Babylon after judging the other nations. Because he had mentioned Babylon's judgment already (cf. vv. 12-14), it is unclear why Jeremiah would put such a message in code. Still this seems to be the best explanation of Sheshach.

25:27-29. The nations who **drink** from the cup of God's wrath will fall. Like a man who has become **drunk,** they will **vomit and fall.** Yet this collapse will be caused by **the sword** rather than strong drink. Some nations might try to **refuse** judgment, but God would make them partake of it. If God would **bring disaster on** His own **city** because of its sin, how could these heathen nations hope to **go unpunished?**

(4) Universal judgment affirmed (25:30-38). **25:30-33.** Switching from prose to poetry, Jeremiah continued the theme of God's judgment on the nations. Like a lion that would **roar mightily** before pouncing on his prey (cf. Amos 1:2; 3:4, 8), so God would shout **from His holy dwelling,** heaven, **against all who live on the earth.** God intended to bring **charges** (*rîḇ;* cf. comments on Jer. 2:9) **against** these **nations.** His **judgment** would extend beyond Judah to **all mankind.** This judgment was pictured as a **mighty storm** that would envelop all nations. In its wake the **slain** would be scattered **everywhere.** Their corpses would be **like refuse lying on the ground** in the same way that Judah's dead had remained unburied (cf. 8:2; 14:16; 16:4-6).

25:34-38. The **leaders of** these many

nations (pictured as **shepherds**) would **weep and wail** and **roll in the dust** (signs of deep grief or mourning; cf. 6:26; Micah 1:10). They were mourning for their own lives because the **time** had **come** for them **to be slaughtered.** By briefly shifting his imagery from shepherds to pottery Jeremiah pictured the total destruction of these **leaders.** They would be **shattered** in pieces **like** a piece of **fine pottery** dropped on the floor. Jeremiah then returned to the pastoral image to complete his picture. The leaders (**shepherds**) would try **to flee,** but would have **no place to escape.** God would destroy **their** land (**pasture**) and would prowl around **like a lion** among the sheep (cf. Jer. 25:30). The **land** of all these nations would **become desolate.**

B. Personal conflict with Judah (chaps. 26–29)

Though Jeremiah did record some opposition to his message (cf. 11:18-23; 15:10; 20:1-6), that was not his main point in chapters 1–25. The focus in those chapters was on God's coming judgment if the people refused to repent. But in chapters 26–29 Jeremiah zeroed in on the people's response to his message. Both he and his message were rejected by the leaders and the people.

1. CONFLICT WITH THE PEOPLE (CHAP. 26)

a. Jeremiah's message (26:1-6)

26:1-3. Jeremiah indicated that this message was delivered **early in the reign of** King **Jehoiakim.** Since Jehoiakim ascended the throne in 609 B.C., a date of 609–608 B.C. for this event seems probable. The message itself should probably be associated with the "temple address" of chapters 7–10. In those chapters Jeremiah focused on the content of the message, while in this chapter he focused on the response to the message. The purpose of the message was to get **the people to listen** to God's threatened judgment so they would each . . . **turn from his evil way.** If the people would repent, God promised that He would **not bring on them the disaster** He **was planning** (cf. 7:3-7).

26:4-6. The content of the message was one of judgment for disobedience. If the people refused to **follow** God's **Law** and to **listen to** God's **servants the prophets** (cf. 7:21-26), God would make the temple (**this house**) as desolate as the tabernacle that once stood at **Shiloh** (cf. 7:14). Also people would curse the **city** of Jerusalem (cf. comments on 24:9).

b. *Jeremiah's arrest and trial (26:7-15)*

26:7-11. In chapters 7–10 Jeremiah did not record the response of the crowds to his message. When **the priests, the prophets, and all the people** who were in the temple courts **heard** Jeremiah's **words,** they **seized him** just as he finished his message and demanded that he **must die** for his words. The charge brought against **Jeremiah** was that he was a false prophet because he had claimed **in the LORD's name that** the temple and the **city** would become **desolate and deserted.** Obviously they believed that such a prophecy could never come from God.

The charges against Jeremiah had to be "tried in court," so Judah's **officials** (*śārîm,* lit., "princes," probably the high officials of the king; cf. 36:11-12) heard the case **at the entrance of the New Gate.** The city gate was where the leaders sat to administer justice and to conduct official business (cf. Deut. 21:18-19; Ruth 4:1-11; Jer. 39:3). The mob charged that Jeremiah **should be sentenced to death.** His crime was that he had **prophesied against** the **city** of Jerusalem.

26:12-15. Jeremiah gave a threefold defense on his own behalf. First, he announced that **the** LORD had **sent** him to deliver the message they had **heard.** He was not a false prophet. Second, he announced that his message was conditional. If the people would **reform** their **ways** (cf. 3:12; 7:3) God promised **not to bring** about the disaster. Thus Jeremiah's message did offer some hope for the city. Third, Jeremiah warned that if they **put** him **to death** they would **bring the guilt of innocent blood on** themselves. They would be guilty in God's sight of murdering an innocent man.

c. *Jeremiah's deliverance (26:16-24)*

26:16-19. After hearing the case **the officials** along with **all the people** sided with Jeremiah against the religious establishment (**the priests and** false **prophets**). They declared that Jeremiah **should not be sentenced to death.** This verdict was supported by some **elders** who quoted from the Prophet **Micah.** By quoting

from Micah 3:12 they indicated that Micah had made similar statements against the city and **the temple** nearly 70 years earlier. Yet instead of seeking to **put** Micah **to death,** King **Hezekiah** listened to Micah's words and sought the **favor** of **the** LORD. In response to Hezekiah's request God **did not bring the disaster** predicted by Micah. Failure to follow Hezekiah's example was **to bring a terrible disaster on** Judah.

26:20-23. Though Jeremiah was spared, other prophets were not so fortunate. Another prophet during this time was **Uriah son of Shemaiah.** Nothing is known about this man apart from his hometown (**Kiriath Jearim**). He **prophesied the same things . . . as Jeremiah;** but when **the king** heard about it, he decided **to put** Uriah **to death. Uriah** was informed of the plot and **fled . . . to Egypt.** The king **sent** a delegation **to Egypt** to extradite him back to Judah. The delegation was led by **Elnathan son of Acbor.** Elnathan was one of the officials who heard the reading of Jeremiah's scroll (cf. 36:11-12), and his father, Acbor, may have been an earlier official of King Josiah (2 Kings 22:12-14). Uriah was convicted of treason and killed by **a sword.** He was given an ignoble burial, **his body** being **thrown into the burial place of the common people** (cf. 2 Kings 23:6).

26:24. Jeremiah had the support of **Ahikam son of Shaphan** who prevented the people from having Jeremiah **put to death.** The family of Shaphan played an important part in the final years of Judah (see the chart "The Line of Shaphan"). Shaphan was King Josiah's secretary who reported the finding of the Law to Josiah (2 Kings 22:3-13). Shaphan had at least four sons—three of whom were mentioned in a positive way by Jeremiah (Ahikam, Gemariah, and Elasah). The fourth son, Jaazaniah, was the "black sheep" of the family; his presence among the idol-worshipers in the temple caught Ezekiel by surprise (Ezek. 8:11). Ahikam's son, Gedaliah, was appointed governor of Judah by Nebuchadnezzar after the fall of Jerusalem in 586 B.C.

2. CONFLICT WITH THE FALSE PROPHETS IN JERUSALEM (CHAPS. 27–28)

a. *Jeremiah's prophecy (chap. 27)*

(1) The message to the ambassadors (27:1-11). **27:1-7.** The events of chapter 27

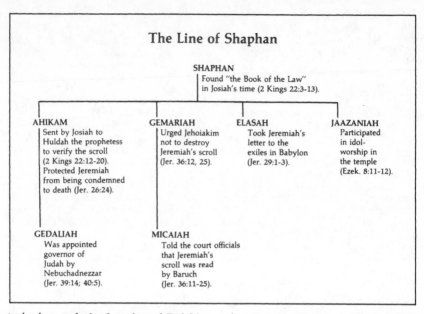

The Line of Shaphan

SHAPHAN
Found "the Book of the Law" in Josiah's time (2 Kings 22:3-13).

AHIKAM
Sent by Josiah to Huldah the prophetess to verify the scroll (2 Kings 22:12-20). Protected Jeremiah from being condemned to death (Jer. 26:24).

GEMARIAH
Urged Jehoiakim not to destroy Jeremiah's scroll (Jer. 36:12, 25).

ELASAH
Took Jeremiah's letter to the exiles in Babylon (Jer. 29:1-3).

JAAZANIAH
Participated in idol-worship in the temple (Ezek. 8:11-12).

GEDALIAH
Was appointed governor of Judah by Nebuchadnezzar (Jer. 39:14; 40:5).

MICAIAH
Told the court officials that Jeremiah's scroll was read by Baruch (Jer. 36:11-25).

took place **early in the reign of Zedekiah.** There is a textual problem here, and most Hebrew manuscripts name Jehoiakim (cf. KJV; NIV marg.) rather than Zedekiah. However, the internal evidence indicates that the chapter was written during the time of Zedekiah instead of Jehoiakim. Zedekiah is named as the king of Judah in verses 3 and 12, and 28:1 indicates that the prophecy of chapter 27 was given while he was king. Why then did most Hebrew manuscripts name Jehoiakim in this verse? No doubt it resulted from a later scribe's error in copying the manuscript. It is possible that a scribe mistakenly recopied 26:1 at the beginning of chapter 27. If so, the Septuagint (which omits 27:1) is preserving the text of the original manuscript. Or possibly a later scribe intentionally changed the king's name in 27:1 to make it conform to 26:1.

God commanded **Jeremiah to make a yoke** like those used to hitch together teams of oxen and to **put it on** his **neck.** Then he sent **word to the . . . envoys who** were in **Jerusalem** to meet with **Zedekiah.** These delegates were from **Edom, Moab,** and **Ammon** to the east of Judah and from **Tyre and Sidon,** Phoenician cities to the north. What were these delegates doing in Jerusalem? Most likely they were there to discuss the possibility

of uniting together in a revolt against Babylon. This meeting occurred sometime between May and August 593 B.C. (cf. 28:1). The Babylonian Chronicle recorded that just over a year earlier a rebellion had occurred in Babylon. Evidently Nebuchadnezzar had to defend himself against an attempted coup. Certainly such unrest within Babylon would cause the various vassal states to evaluate their chances of success for throwing off Babylon's yoke of domination.

Jeremiah's public pronouncement dashed any hope the delegates might have had of keeping their meeting secret. God's message was that He had **made the earth** and all life **on it** so He could **give it to anyone** He pleased. The one selected by God to subdue all nations was **Nebuchadnezzar king of Babylon.** God announced that **all nations** would **serve** Babylon until its **time** to be judged came. Only then would others be able to **subjugate** Babylon.

27:8-11. With the fact of Nebuchadnezzar's divine appointment clearly established, Jeremiah warned the ambassadors not to rebel. **Any nation** that refused to **bow its neck under** Babylon's **yoke** would be punished by **sword, famine, and plague** from God (cf. v. 13, and comments on 14:12). For the first of three times in chapter 27 Jeremiah warned his audience not to listen to the false prophets (cf. vv. 14, 16). Because he was addressing the representatives of heathen nations in verses 8-11, he also warned against listening to the methods of divination they might use to receive an answer. (On the word diviners; cf. 29:8 and see comments on qāsam in Deut. 18:10.) These false religious leaders were speaking lies when they promised a successful rebellion against Babylon because God vowed to remove any nation who rebelled. Only those nations that would submit to the authority of Babylon would be allowed to remain in their own lands.

(2) The message to Zedekiah. 27:12-15. Jeremiah delivered the same message to the king of Judah. Again the prophet's word contained two parts. The first part was God's command to Zedekiah to bow his neck under Babylon's yoke and to continue to serve Babylon as a vassal king. If he refused to serve Babylon, the judgment God had threatened would come on Judah. The second part of Jeremiah's message was a warning not to trust the false prophets. Those predicting victory were prophesying lies because God had not sent them.

(3) The message to the priests and people. 27:16-22. Jeremiah modified his message to the priests and the masses. He cautioned them not to listen to the prophets. These false prophets were predicting that the articles from the LORD's house that had been taken to Babylon (cf. 2 Kings 24:13; Dan. 1:1-2) would soon be brought back. In fact just the opposite would happen. The furnishings still remaining in the house of the LORD (along with those of the king's palace) which had not been removed during the deportation of Jehoiachin would remain in Babylon until God's judgment was complete. Only then would He bring them back (cf. 2 Kings 25:13-17; Ezra 1:7-11).

b. Hananiah's opposition (chap. 28)

(1) Jeremiah's conflict with Hananiah (28:1-11). 28:1-4. Chapter 28 is a continuation of chapter 27. The specific time when Jeremiah gave his message was not given (cf. 27:1), but the exact month and year that his opponent spoke was recorded. It was the fifth month of the fourth year of King Zedekiah. The date was August-September 593 B.C. Jeremiah was careful in noting the date because of the

events that happened later (cf. 28:17).

Jeremiah's message was challenged by Hananiah son of Azzur. Perhaps Hananiah was a brother of "Jaazaniah son of Azzur" who was denounced by Ezekiel (Ezek. 11:1-3). Hananiah was from Gibeon, about six miles northwest of Jerusalem. Gibeon was another town that Joshua had assigned to the priests (cf. Josh. 21:17-18), so perhaps Hananiah, like Jeremiah, was from a priestly family.

Hananiah's message directly contradicted Jeremiah's prophecy. He stated that God promised to break the yoke of Babylonian oppression. So Hananiah was urging Judah and the nations to rebel against Babylon, not to submit to her (cf. Jer. 27:2, 8, 11-12, 17). Hananiah promised that the rebellion would be followed by restoration. Within two years, he said, God promised to bring back to Judah all the articles of the LORD's house (cf. 27:16-22). These would be accompanied by Jehoiachin and all the other exiles.

28:5-11. Two prophets had made conflicting claims, each one attributing his message to God. Though Jeremiah could have wished that the LORD would fulfill the words of Hananiah, nevertheless Hananiah's prophecy was false. The ultimate test for prophets was whether their prophecies were fulfilled. A prophet was known to be sent by God only if his prediction came true (cf. Deut. 18:20-22). Time would tell whether Jeremiah or Hananiah was the false prophet.

As if to convince the people that he was right, Hananiah took the yoke off Jeremiah's neck (cf. Jer. 27:2) and broke it apart. This dramatically visualized his prophecy that God would break the yoke of Nebuchadnezzar . . . within two years. Rather than opposing this open insult from Hananiah, Jeremiah went on his way.

(2) Jeremiah's message to Hananiah (28:12-17). 28:12-14. God's word came to Jeremiah shortly after . . . Hananiah broke Jeremiah's yoke. God's message used Hananiah's actions to show the harshness of the coming judgment. Hananiah had broken a wooden yoke, but God would replace it with a yoke of iron that could not be broken. This iron yoke, figuratively speaking, would be fastened to the necks of all these nations who gathered in Jerusalem (27:3) to force

them to **serve Nebuchadnezzar.**

28:15-17. After answering Hananiah's predictions (vv. 12-14) **Jeremiah** attacked Hananiah's credentials as a **prophet.** God had **not sent** Hananiah as His spokesman, but through his eloquent speech he had **persuaded** the **nation** of Judah **to trust in lies.** As a judgment on **Hananiah** (and as a proof that Jeremiah was the true prophet of God) God said He would **remove** Hananiah **from the face of the earth.** His death would expose him as a false prophet. To emphasize the divine origin of this judgment, Jeremiah indicated that Hananiah's death would happen that **very year.** It was already the fifth month (28:1), so within the next seven months Hananiah would die. This was why Jeremiah took special care to state the exact month in verse 1. God fulfilled His word, and **in the seventh month**—less than two months after Jeremiah's prediction—**Hananiah . . . died.** God vindicated His true prophet, Jeremiah, and judged the false prophet, **Hananiah.**

3. CONFLICT WITH THE FALSE PROPHETS IN EXILE (CHAP. 29)

a. Jeremiah's first letter to the exiles (29:1-23)

(1) The introduction. **29:1-3.** Jeremiah inserted **the text of the letter that** he **sent** to those who had been **carried into exile from Jerusalem.** He identified the deportation as the one associated with the removal of **King Jehoiachin and the queen mother** (cf. 2 Kings 24:8-17; Jer. 13:18; 22:24-27; Dan. 1:1-2). This deportation occurred in 597 B.C., so Jeremiah's letter must have been written after that date.

(2) The announcement of a long exile (29:4-14). **29:4-9.** God's word to the exiles was to prepare for a long stay in **Babylon.** They were to **build houses and settle down.** They were also to **plant gardens** to sustain them during the period. Life was to go on as normal. The people were exhorted to **marry and have sons and daughters.** Instead of hoping for Babylon's quick demise they were encouraged to **seek** its **peace and prosperity.** Jeremiah even told them to **pray . . . for** Babylon! Those **prophets and diviners** (cf. 27:9) who were predicting a soon return to Judah were **prophesying lies.** They were **not sent** by God.

29:10-14. The restoration of the exiles to Judah would happen only **when** God's **70 years** of judgment were **completed** (cf. 25:11-12). Then God would **fulfill** His **gracious promise to** restore the exiles to their land. The 70-year Exile was a part of God's **plans** to give Judah **hope and a future.** The judgment prompted the exiles to **seek** God wholeheartedly (cf. Dan. 9:2-3, 15-19). Once they had turned back to their God He would **gather** them **from all the nations where** they had been **banished** and return them to their land. The larger purpose of the Exile was to force Israel back to her God (cf. Deut. 30:1-10).

(3) The warning against false prophets (29:15-23). **29:15-19.** The people disbelieved Jeremiah's message because it contradicted the message of the false Jewish **prophets . . . in Babylon.** Evidently these prophets were proclaiming the safety of Jerusalem and the swift return of those in captivity (cf. 28:2-4). Jeremiah shattered their optimistic forecasts by announcing that those who had **not** been exiled were destined for **the sword, famine, and plague** (cf. comments on 14:12). He shared with the exiles his vision of the two baskets of figs (cf. 24:1-2). Those remaining in Jerusalem were **like poor figs that** had to be thrown out. God would judge them for refusing to obey His words of warning (cf. 24:8-9). Unfortunately the **exiles** had **not listened** to God's words of warning **either.**

29:20-23. Jeremiah singled out two men who were evidently the ringleaders of the false prophets in Babylon. They were **Ahab son of Koliah and Zedekiah son of Maaseiah.** Nothing else is known about these men, but they were **prophesying lies** (v. 21) to the people and committing **adultery with their neighbors' wives** (v. 23). Such brazen lies and sinful actions would not go unpunished.

God vowed to judge these false prophets by handing **them over to Nebuchadnezzar.** Evidently they were predicting Nebuchadnezzar's and Babylon's downfall (cf. 28:2), and Nebuchadnezzar would hear of their rebellious remarks. He would **put them to death before** the **very eyes** of the exiles, to serve as an object lesson on the danger of fomenting rebellion. They were executed by being **burned** (*qālâh*, lit., "to roast") **in the fire,** a form of punishment often used in Babylon (cf. Dan. 3:6, 11, 15, 17, 19-23). Their death by fire would give rise to a **curse** that would be used by the captives. The curse probably developed as a play on words because the word for "curse" (*qᵉlālâh*) is similar to the word for "burned" (*qālâh*).

b. Jeremiah's second letter to the exiles (29:24-32)

(1) The report of Shemaiah's letter to Jerusalem. **29:24-29.** The sequence of events is somewhat confusing here. Evidently after Jeremiah's first letter to the exiles (vv. 1-23) another prophet in Babylon, Shemaiah, wrote the leaders in Jerusalem urging them to punish Jeremiah (vv. 25-28). However, the letter was read to Jeremiah (v. 29) who then wrote a second letter to the exiles. He quoted the text of Shemaiah's letter (vv. 24-28) and delivered God's word of judgment against the false prophet (vv. 29-32).

Shemaiah sent letters in his own name to Zephaniah son of Maaseiah who had been **appointed** as **the priest** who was **in charge of the** temple. Possibly this Zephaniah was a brother of the false Prophet Zedekiah, who was in Babylon (assuming that Maaseiah, the name of each of their fathers, refers to the same man; cf. v. 21). Shemaiah exhorted **Zephaniah** that as guardian of the temple precincts he was to **put any madman who** was acting **like a prophet** (he was referring to Jeremiah) **into the stocks and neck-irons** (cf. 20:1-3). Shemaiah was upset that Zephaniah had **not reprimanded Jeremiah** for posing **as a prophet.** He cited the contents of Jeremiah's first letter to the exiles as proof that Jeremiah should be disciplined. But instead of attacking Jeremiah, **Zephaniah . . . read the letter** from Shemaiah to him. Evidently Zephaniah at this time accepted Jeremiah's authority as a prophet. He later consulted Jeremiah twice on behalf of King Zedekiah (cf. 21:1; 37:3). Zephaniah was captured and killed by Nebuchadnezzar after the fall of Jerusalem (52:24-27).

(2) The condemnation of Shemaiah. **29:30-32.** Under God's guidance **Jeremiah** sent a second **message to all the exiles** (cf. v. 1). This letter contained God's judgment against **Shemaiah** for claiming to be His prophet. God would **punish** both **Shemaiah . . . and his descendants.** Neither he nor his family would live to **see the good things** God promised

to **do for** His **people.** These "good things" are explained in chapters 30–33. **Shemaiah** forfeited his right to take part in these blessings because, by urging those in Jerusalem to oppose Jeremiah, he had **preached rebellion against** God.

C. Future comfort for Israel and Judah (chaps. 30–33)

God had threatened Judah with judgment for her disobedience, but the nation refused to mend her ways. The stage was set and the curtain was about to rise on the final act of Judah's history as a nation. But before this sad scene of suffering started to unfold, Jeremiah inserted "The Book of Consolation," a collection of prophecies that offered hope in desperate times. These prophecies looked beyond Judah's imminent collapse and pointed to a new age when Israel and Judah would be returned to their land, reunited as a nation, and restored to their God.

1. THE RESTORATION OF ISRAEL AND JUDAH DECLARED (CHAPS. 30–31)

a. The nation's physical deliverance (30:1-11)

(1) The nation's restoration to the land. **30:1-3. God** told **Jeremiah to write** His promises of comfort **in a book** so they would be available to the exiles after Jerusalem fell. This book would declare a note of hope that **the days are coming . . . when** God will **. . . restore** His **people.** Jeremiah's use of "the days" was significant because it described two different periods of time. The first "day" to which Jeremiah pointed was the day of destruction when God would judge Judah for her sin (cf. 5:18; 7:32; 9:25; 19:6). This day was fulfilled when Judah fell to Babylon. However, the second "day" to which Jeremiah pointed was a day of restoration when God will bring the nations of Judah and Israel into a new relationship with Him and when He will set straight His accounts with the Gentile nations (cf. 3:16, 18; 16:14; 23:5, 7, 20; 30:3, 24; 31:27, 29, 31, 33, 38; 33:14-16; 48:12, 47; 49:2, 39; 50:4, 20; 51:47, 52). This day has an eschatological perspective. It is the day when God will fulfill the blessings of restoration promised in Deuteronomy 30:1-10. However, as in all prophetic material one must keep in mind the principle of "foreshortening." That is, though Jeremiah saw all these predic-

tions as one continuous series of events, they were fulfilled over a long period, with intervening gaps of time. Thus, for example, prophecies about the suffering Messiah and the ruling Messiah appear together though they describe two different Advents of Christ (e.g., Isa. 9:6-7; 61:1-2). In the same way Jeremiah described the restoration of Judah after the Babylonian Captivity and the still-future restoration of Judah within some of the same passages. Therefore one should be cautious in interpreting the various parts of Jeremiah's predictions concerning "the coming days."

God's first promise was to **bring** the nations of **Israel and Judah back from captivity.** God promised to **restore them to the land** He had given them (cf. Deut. 30:3-5). This promised return of both the Northern and Southern Kingdoms served as an introduction to these chapters and provided hope to those who would soon be dispossessed from their land.

(2) The nation's distress. **30:4-7.** The return of **Israel and Judah** to the land will be preceded by a time of national distress. **Cries of fear** and **terror** will be **heard** among these captives instead of cries of **peace.** Jeremiah compared the anguish of men clutching themselves in fear to **a woman in labor** (cf. 4:31; 6:24; 13:21; 22:23; 49:24; 50:43). The coming calamity will be so **awful** that **none will be like it** in comparison. Jeremiah characterized it as **a time of trouble.** Yet all will not be lost because God guaranteed that the nation **will be saved out of it.** God will rescue His people in the midst of their distress.

To what "time of trouble" was Jeremiah referring? Some have felt that he was pointing to the coming fall of Judah to Babylon or to the later fall of Babylon to Medo-Persia. However, in both of these periods the Northern Kingdom of Israel was not affected. It had already gone into captivity (in 722 B.C.). A better solution is to see Jeremiah referring to the still-future Tribulation period when the remnant of Israel and Judah will experience a time of unparalleled persecution (Dan. 9:27; 12:1; Matt. 24:15-22). The period will end when Christ appears to rescue His elect (Rom. 11:26) and establish His kingdom (Matt. 24:30-31; 25:31-46; Rev. 19:11-21; 20:4-6).

(3) The Lord's deliverance (30:8-11). **30:8-9.** When God comes to rescue the nation, He **will break the yoke** of bondage He had placed on her neck. This deliverance did not come when the false prophets predicted it would (cf. 28:2, 10-11, 14), but God said it will come eventually **(in that day).** Instead of serving foreign powers the nation **will** once again serve the LORD. The people will also submit to the authority of **David their king** whom God **will raise up for them.** Many scholars view this as a reference to Christ who is from the line of David. However, there is no compelling reason not to take Jeremiah's reference in a literal sense (cf. comments on Ezek. 34:23-24). David is referred to by name elsewhere in passages that look to the future restoration of a united Israel (cf. Ezek. 34:23-24; 37:24-25; Hosea 3:5).

30:10-11. God's promise of restoration was designed to give **Israel** hope. She had no need to **fear** or **be dismayed** because God promised to **save** her **out of a distant place.** No country would be too far away for God to reach and rescue His people. When He brings them back to the land they will have the **peace and security** that was absent in Jeremiah's day (cf. 8:11). God will **completely destroy the nations** where Israel and Judah had been scattered. Though He would **discipline** Israel and Judah, He assured them that He would never **completely destroy** them. Any judgment would be mingled **with justice** (cf. 10:24; 46:28) so that the punishment for His Chosen People would not be overly severe.

b. The nation's spiritual healing (30:12-17)

(1) Israel's sin caused her wounds. **30:12-15.** Israel's condition was critical. Her **wound** appeared **incurable** (cf. comments on 6:14), and **no one** was available to provide a **remedy for** her **sore.** The **allies** in whom the nation had placed such great hope had **forgotten** her. Even God had **struck** her **as an enemy** and **punished** her **because** of her **guilt.**

(2) God would heal Israel's wounds. **30:16-17.** Israel's condition appeared hopeless, but God promised to reverse her misfortunes. Those who were devouring the nation would themselves be **devoured** by God. He would send her **enemies . . . into exile** and **plunder** those who sought to **make spoil of** her.

At the same time God promised to restore Israel to spiritual health. He would intervene for His outcast people.

c. The nation's material blessing (30:18-22)

30:18-22. God's restoration will involve a physical rebuilding. (**Restore** Judah's **fortunes** is mentioned also in 32:44; 33:11, 26; cf. Deut. 30:3.) **The city** of Jerusalem **will be rebuilt on her ruins,** including **the** king's **palace. The** festive **sound of rejoicing** that had been silenced by Babylon (cf. Jer. 7:34; 16:19; 25:10) will once again be heard in the city, and God will increase Judah numerically (cf. Deut. 30:5). The nation **will be** secured and **established before** God, and He **will punish** anyone who tries to **oppress** her.

The **leader** of Israel will again **be one of their own** instead of some foreign despot (cf. Jer. 30:9). This ruler **will come close to** God as **the** Lord brings him into His service. Only at that future date when the city, its inhabitants, and their ruler have been restored to God will someone be able to declare that Israel is God's **people** and that He is her **God.** This ideal relationship between Israel and her God was expressed several times in the Old Testament (cf. Lev. 26:12; Deut. 7:6; 26:16-19; Jer. 7:23; 11:4; 24:7; 31:1, 33; Ezek. 11:20; 14:11; 34:30; 36:28; 37:23, 27; Hosea 2:23; Zech. 8:8; 13:9). Israel will finally experience the relationship with God that He had always intended.

d. The judgment on the wicked (30:23–31:1)

30:23-24. Jeremiah repeated, with minor variations, the same words he had written in 23:19-20. Before God's blessing can be experienced He must judge sin. His **wrath** will **burst out** against **the wicked.** Though these words applied to false prophets in 23:19-20, Jeremiah may have been using them here to refer to God's judgment on the wicked nations who opposed Israel (cf. 30:16-20). God's **fierce anger** that had been poured out on Judah would **not turn back** till it also extended to the other nations of the earth.

31:1. This verse should be linked with the statements in 30:23-24. It explains the results of God's judgment on the earth and also serves to introduce the section on national restoration which follows. God promised that when He will judge the world for its sins He will also restore all **Israel** to Himself. **All the clans,** not just the tribe of Judah, will be known as God's **people** (cf. 30:22).

e. God's national restoration (31:2-40)

(1) The national restoration of Israel (31:2-22). **31:2-6.** God assured the Northern Kingdom that He will restore her. Those who had survived **the sword** (probably Assyria's destruction of **Israel**) will yet experience God's **favor** as He leads them into **the desert** for their new Exodus (cf. 16:14-15; 23:7-8; Hosea 2:14-15). The turmoil of their long years of exile will cease when God intervenes **to give rest to** the nation **Israel.**

The motivation for God's future restoration of the nation is His **everlasting love** (*'ahăḇâh*) which He will freely bestow on His people (cf. Hosea 11:4; 14:4; Zeph. 3:17) and His **loving-kindness** (*ḥeseḏ*; cf. Jer. 9:24; 32:18; Lam. 3:32; Dan. 9:4). God had made a covenant with Abraham (Gen. 15:7-21) and another covenant with the nation Israel (Ex. 19:3-8; Lev. 26; Deut. 28:1–30:10), and He vowed to stay faithful to His commitments. Israel could look forward to experiencing God's blessing.

Jeremiah drew three word-pictures that will characterize God's restoration of Israel. First, it will be a time of renewed joy. Israel will once again **take up** her **tambourines** and **dance with the joyful.** The times of sadness will cease when the Captivity ends (cf. Ps. 137:1-4; Jer. 16:8-9; 25:10-11). Second, it will be a time of peace and prosperity as the people **plant** their **vineyards on the hills of Samaria.** Free from external threats, they will be able to **enjoy their fruit** (cf. Lev. 26:16; Deut. 28:33; Micah 4:4; Zech. 3:9-10). Third, it will be a time of renewed commitment to the Lord. The **watchmen** stationed **on the hills of Ephraim** will summon the people to **go up to Zion** to worship **the** Lord.

31:7-9. God's restoration will be accompanied by songs of **joy** and the **praises** of the people for His deliverance. No one will be too far away for the Lord to restore him; God will **gather** His people **from the ends of the earth.** Also no one will be too insignificant for the Lord to deliver him; God will restore **the blind and the lame** along with **expectant mothers.** As God leads these people on their new Exodus into Israel He will provide for their every need. He will guide the people **beside streams of water** (cf. Ex. 15:22-25; Num. 20:2-13; Ps. 23:2) and they will travel **on a level path** so they **will not stumble.** God will do all this because of His special relationship to Israel. He is **Israel's father** (Deut. 32:6), and **Ephraim** (emphasizing the Northern tribes of Israel) is his **firstborn son** (cf. Ex. 4:22). Jeremiah used the image of a father/son relationship to show God's deep love for His people (cf. Hosea 11:1, 8).

31:10-14. Israel's regathering (like a flock of sheep; cf. 23:3; Micah 2:12; 5:4; 7:14) will be accompanied by a renewal of God's material blessings. Those who will be restored to the land will **rejoice in the bounty of** crops (cf. Jer. 31:5) and **flocks.** Jeremiah compared Israel's material wealth to **a well-watered garden** that was producing in abundance (cf. Deut. 30:5, 9). This outpouring of blessing will produce **gladness . . . comfort, and joy** (cf. Jer. 31:4, 7).

31:15-20. The nation's future hope will contrast sharply with her present misery. The cry from **Ramah** was one of **mourning and great weeping** as Jeremiah pictured **Rachel weeping for her children.** To what was Jeremiah referring? Ramah was a town five miles north of Jerusalem, and Rachel was Joseph and Benjamin's mother. Joseph was the father of Ephraim and Manasseh, who became the two major tribes in the Northern Kingdom of Israel. Thus Jeremiah was picturing the weeping of the women of the Northern Kingdom as they watched their children being carried into exile in 722 B.C. However, Jeremiah could also have had the 586 B.C. deportation of Judah in view because Ramah was the staging point for Nebuchadnezzar's deportation (cf. 40:1). In all likelihood these women were crying because they would never see their **children** again. But as the women of Israel and Judah wept for their exiled children, God offered a word of comfort. There was **hope for** their **future** because their **children** would **return to their own land.** God would bring about a restoration.

In what sense was Herod's slaughter of the babies (Matt. 2:17-18) a "fulfillment" of Jeremiah 31:15? Jeremiah pointed to an Old Testament deportation of children from a town north of Jerusalem;

Matthew used the passage to explain the New Testament slaughter of children in a village south of Jerusalem. The answer to the problem hinges on Matthew's use of the word "fulfilled" (*plēroō*). Though Matthew did use the word to record an actual fulfillment of an Old Testament prediction (cf., e.g., Matt. 21:4-5 with Zech. 9:9), he also used the word to indicate that the full potential of something in the Old Testament had been realized (cf. Matt. 3:15; 5:17). In these latter instances there is no prophetic significance to the word "fulfill," which is how Matthew used the word to associate the slaughter in Bethlehem with the sadness in Ramah. Matthew used Jeremiah 31:15 in his book (Matt. 2:17-18) to explain the sadness of the mothers of Bethlehem. The pain of those mothers in Ramah who watched their sons being carried into exile found its full potential in the cries of the mothers of Bethlehem who cradled their sons' lifeless bodies in their arms.

Jeremiah ended this section by recording Israel's cry of contrition that she will recite when she returns to the land. Though she had **strayed** (Jer. 31:19) she will repent. When she returns to her God she will be **ashamed and humiliated because** of her sin. God in turn will express His **great compassion for** the wayward but returning nation (cf. Hosea 2:16-23).

31:21-22. God called on the captives to **set up road signs** and **guideposts** as they traveled to Babylon and to remember **the road** they would **take.** They would need this information during His promised restoration so they could **return to** their **towns.** This time of promised restoration will be so remarkable that it will be as if God **will create a new thing on earth.** That new event is described proverbially by the clause, **a woman will surround a man.** This is probably the most difficult verse to understand in the Book of Jeremiah. One possible idea is that a woman will seek, or court, a man (NIV marg.). In that culture a woman would not normally court a man, so this would indicate something unusual. The woman here is **Israel** (v. 21). She had been **unfaithful,** but in the future she will finally seek out her God and ask to be united with Him.

(2) The national restoration of Judah. **31:23-26.** When **God** will restore the nation of **Israel,** He will also reverse the

fortunes of **Judah.** Those living in the land of Judah will again invoke a blessing on Jerusalem (God's **righteous dwelling)** and the temple area (**the sacred mountain;** cf. Pss. 2:6; 43:3; Isa. 66:20). The land itself will be repopulated, and God will meet every need.

(3) The establishment of a new relationship with Israel and Judah (31:27-40). The rest of the chapter focuses on the new relationship God will establish with His people. Jeremiah used the same Hebrew phrase to introduce the three sections that form this unit. Each section begins with *hinnēh yāmîm bāʾîm* (lit., "Behold, days are coming," vv. 27, 31, 38; cf. comments on 33:14). In the third occurrence the word for "coming" was omitted, but it is clear that Jeremiah intended for the reader to supply it. Jeremiah used this phrase to introduce three aspects of the Lord's new relationship with His people.

31:27-30. God vowed to provide a new beginning for His covenant people. In this new age God **will plant** the nations of **Israel** and **Judah with the offspring of men and animals.** Jeremiah again used agricultural and architectural metaphors to illustrate God's work (cf. comments on 1:10). God had judged Judah for her sin, but He will reverse that judgment.

God's work for the nation will silence a proverb that was common in Jeremiah's day (cf. comments on Ezek. 18:2-4). Those facing judgment in Jeremiah's day felt they were being unfairly punished by God for their ancestors' sins. Though the **fathers** had **eaten sour grapes,** it was the **children** who experienced the effects of having their **teeth . . . set on edge.** This proverb was false because it implied that God was unrighteous. God's justice will guarantee that each guilty person **will die for his own sin.**

31:31-37. In addition to a new beginning God promised to **make a New Covenant with** His people. This New Covenant was expressly for **the house of Israel** (the Northern Kingdom) and **the house of Judah** (the Southern Kingdom). It would **not be like the covenant** God had **made with** Israel's **forefathers** at the time of the Exodus because that covenant had been broken by the people (cf. 11:1-8). The earlier covenant God referred to

was the Mosaic Covenant contained in the Books of Exodus, Leviticus, Numbers, and Deuteronomy. Twice God had announced a series of punishments or "curses" that would be invoked on those who violated His Law (Lev. 26; Deut. 28). The final judgment would be a physical deportation from the land of Israel. With the destruction of Jerusalem in 586 B.C. this final "curse" was completed. God had set a holy standard of conduct before the people, but because of their sinful hearts they could not keep those standards. A change was needed.

God's New **Covenant** will involve an internalization of His Law. He **will put His Law in their minds** and **on their hearts,** not just on stones (Ex. 34:1). There will be no need to exhort people to **know the** LORD **because they will** already **all know** God (cf. Isa. 11:9; Hab. 2:14). God's New Covenant will give Israel the inner ability to obey His righteous standards and thus to enjoy His blessings. Ezekiel indicated that this change will result from God's bestowal of the Holy Spirit on these believers (cf. Ezek. 36:24-32). In Old Testament times the Holy Spirit did not universally indwell all believers. Thus one different aspect of the New Covenant is the indwelling of the Holy Spirit in all believers (cf. Joel 2:28-32).

A second aspect of the New Covenant will be God's provision for sin. The sins of the people resulted in the curses of the Old Covenant. However, as part of the New Covenant God will **forgive** Israel's **wickedness** and **remember their sins no more.** But how could a holy God overlook sin? The answer is that God did not "overlook" sin—its penalty was paid for by a Substitute (cf. Isa. 53:4-6). In the Upper Room Christ announced that the New Covenant was to be inaugurated through the shedding of His blood (cf. Matt. 26:27-28; Luke 22:20). Forgiveness of sin would be part of the New Covenant only because God provided a Substitute to pay the penalty required of man.

To underscore Israel's permanence because of this New Covenant, God compared her existence to that of the heavens and the earth. As God had appointed **the sun to shine by day** and **the moon and stars to shine by night** (cf. Gen. 1:14-19), so He had appointed Israel as His chosen nation. It would take a feat as fabulous as making **these** natural **decrees vanish from** nature to make Israel . . . **cease to be a nation.** The power God displayed in creating the universe was the power that He exercises in preserving Israel as a nation. Throughout history people have tried in vain to destroy Israel, but none have succeeded—and none ever will.

How is the church related to the New Covenant? Is the New Covenant being fulfilled in the church today? Ultimately the New Covenant will find its complete fulfillment during the Millennium when Israel is restored to her God. The New Covenant was made with Israel (Jer. 31:31, 33) just as the Mosaic Covenant had been (v. 32). One key element of the New Covenant is the preservation of Israel as a nation (vv. 35-37). However, though the ultimate fulfillment of this covenant awaits the millennial reign of Christ, the church today is participating in some of the benefits of that covenant. The covenant was inaugurated at Christ's death (Matt. 26:27-28; Luke 22:20), and the church, by her union with Christ, is sharing in many of the spiritual blessings promised to Israel (cf. Rom. 11:11-27; Eph. 2:11-22) including the New Covenant (2 Cor. 3:6; Heb. 8:6-13; 9:15; 12:22-24). But though the church's participation in the New Covenant is real, it is not the ultimate fulfillment of God's promise. The fact that believers today enjoy the spiritual blessings of the New Covenant (forgiveness of sins and the indwelling Holy Spirit) does *not* mean that spiritual *and* physical blessings will not be realized by Israel. That still awaits the day when Israel will acknowledge her sin and turn to the Messiah for forgiveness (Zech. 12:10–13:1). Some Bible scholars, however, take a slightly different view. They see one covenant (a covenant of grace), which God will apply to Israel in the Millennium and is now applying to the church in this present age. In both views the New Covenant is made possible by the blood of Christ.

31:38-40. The third aspect of God's new relationship will be the establishment of a new city for His people. Jerusalem, the city that symbolizes God's relationship with His people, was destroyed by Babylon. But even before that event took place God promised that the **city will be rebuilt. The Tower of Hananel**

was at the northeast corner of the city (cf. Neh. 3:1; 12:39; Zech. 14:10) and **the Corner Gate** was probably located on the northwest corner of the city (cf. 2 Kings 14:13; 2 Chron. 26:9; Zech. 14:10). Thus the northern wall will be restored. The locations of **the hill of Gareb** and **Goah** are unknown; but since Jeremiah 31:38 described the northern boundary and verse 40 describes the southern and eastern boundaries it may be assumed that Gareb and Goah detail the western boundary of the city. Perhaps Gareb referred to the hill west of the Tyropeon Valley that is today called Mount Zion. The southwestern and southern boundary will be the **valley** in which **dead bodies and ashes are thrown.** This is the Hinnom Valley (cf. 7:30-34; 19:1-6). The eastern boundary is **the terraces out to the Kidron Valley.** This boundary would extend to **the corner of the Horse Gate** on the southeast tip of the city, where the Kidron Valley and Hinnom Valley unite.

God described two characteristics of this new city. First, it **will be holy to the Lord** (cf. Zech. 14:20-21). The city and its inhabitants will be set apart to God who will dwell in her midst (Ezek. 48:35). Second, the city will no more **be uprooted or demolished.** The ravages of war will not be experienced in this new city. These verses were not fulfilled after the Babylonian Captivity ended. Since the postexilic period provides clear evidence that holiness was not a primary characteristic of the people in Jerusalem and Judah (cf. Mal. 1:6-14), so the city was destroyed again in A.D. 70 by the Romans. These promises (Jer. 31:31-40) await their future fulfillment during the Millennium.

2. THE RESTORATION OF ISRAEL AND JUDAH ILLUSTRATED (CHAP. 32)

a. The illustration (32:1-12)

(1) The circumstances (32:1-5). **32:1-2.** Jeremiah recorded the time frame in which this prophecy was given because of its significance to the message. The time was **the 10th year of Zedekiah which was** also **the 18th year of Nebuchadnezzar.** The 10th year of Zedekiah would have ended on October 17, 587 B.C. (using the Judean Tishri-to-Tishri year) while the 18th year of Nebuchadnezzar began on April 23, 587 (using the Babylonian Nisan-to-Nisan year). Thus this prophecy occurred sometime be-

tween April 23 and October 17, 587 B.C. During this time **Babylon** was **besieging Jerusalem**—a siege that lasted from January 15, 588 till July 18, 586—and Jeremiah was under arrest and **confined in the palace courtyard of the guard.**

32:3-5. The reason for Jeremiah's imprisonment is stated here. He had been **imprisoned** by **Zedekiah** for his "treasonous" prophecies. Jeremiah predicted Nebuchadnezzar's **capture** of both Jerusalem and **the king of Judah. Zedekiah** would **be handed over to** Nebuchadnezzar and taken **to Babylon.** Any attempt to oppose the Babylonians would **not succeed.** Such statements were not appreciated by those trying to hold out against Babylon's assault.

(2) The purchase of land (32:6-12).
32:6-9. In this grim time God came to tell **Jeremiah** of an impending visit. Jeremiah's cousin, **Hanamel son of Shallum,** would visit Jeremiah in prison and ask him to **buy** his **field at Anathoth.** Hanamel was following the Mosaic Law which called for a person to redeem (purchase) the property of a relative who was forced to sell so that it would not leave the family (Lev. 25:25-28; Ruth 4:1-6). So **Hanamel** told Jeremiah it was his **right and duty to buy it.** Perhaps Hanamel was trying to sell the land to obtain money for food because of the siege. The village of Anathoth was already under Babylonian control so this purchase would appear to be foolish. Who would buy a parcel of land that had already fallen into enemy hands? Because of this apparent foolishness, God told Jeremiah in advance that Hanamel would come so Jeremiah would recognize God's hand in the request.

When **Hanamel** came, Jeremiah **bought the field** for **17 shekels of silver** (about 7 ounces; cf. NIV marg.). Ordinarily this would have been a small price for a field (cf. Gen. 23:12-16). But the size of the field is unknown and it was not really available at that time.

32:10-12. Following the legal customs of the day, Jeremiah **signed and sealed the deed** and **had it witnessed** before he paid **Hanamel.** Two copies of the **deed of purchase** were made. One was **sealed** by being bound with a piece of string or cord and then having Jeremiah's official seal stamped into a lump of clay placed over the string. The other

copy remained **unsealed** so it could later be examined. Jeremiah handed both copies of the **deed to Baruch,** Jeremiah's scribe and friend (cf. Jer. 36:4, 8, 26).

b. The explanation (32:13-15)

32:13-15. Jeremiah instructed **Baruch** to take both **documents** and **put them in a clay jar** for preservation. The documents had to **last a long time** because it would be many years before the people would be able to return from captivity and claim their land. Yet Jeremiah's purpose in buying the land and preserving the deeds was to show that **houses, fields, and vineyards** would **again be bought** by the people of Israel in the **land.**

c. The prayer of Jeremiah (32:16-25)

(1) His praise for God's greatness (32:16-23). **32:16-19.** Jeremiah began his prayer by focusing on the incomparable greatness and majesty of God's character. God's Creation of **the heavens and the earth** proves that **nothing** is **too hard for** Him (cf. v. 27). He is omnipotent, and He is also a God of love and justice. He shows **love** (*ḥeseḏ*; cf. 9:24; 31:3) to many, but He also punishes sin (cf. Ex. 20:5; 34:7; Num. 14:18; Deut. 5:9-10). In God's omniscience He sees **all the ways of men.** Since nothing escapes His notice He can justly **reward everyone according to his conduct.**

32:20-23. God's character was displayed in His deeds throughout Israel's history. From the time of the Exodus God's **signs and wonders** (cf. Deut. 4:34; 26:8; 29:3; 34:11) had **continued** on Israel's behalf. God displayed His loyal love when He **brought . . . Israel out of Egypt** and **gave them** the **land** He had promised them. Unfortunately when Israel **took possession of** the land she refused to **obey . . . or follow** God's **Law.** She violated her covenant with Him. God was forced to display His power and justice as He **brought** the **disaster** of His curses (which included invasion and deportation) **upon them** (cf. Lev. 26:14-39; Deut. 28:15-68).

(2) His puzzlement over God's promise. **32:24-25.** After reminding God of His mighty character and deeds, Jeremiah expressed his continued perplexity at God's workings. In light of verses 17-23 it seems harsh to believe that Jere-

miah doubted God's ability to restore His people. Probably Jeremiah was expressing in verses 24-25 his bewilderment over *how* God would accomplish this restoration rather than doubting *if* God would accomplish it.

Babylon's **siege ramps** were already erected against Jerusalem, and the city's fate was sealed. Jerusalem would **be handed over to the Babylonians.** (On the **sword, famine, and plague**; cf. v. 36 and see comments on 14:12.) Everything that God had foretold through His prophets had **happened.** Yet as the army of Babylon stood poised to reduce Jerusalem to rubble, God had commanded Jeremiah to **buy a field** that was already under Babylon's control (32:6-12). Jeremiah did not understand how God's promised restoration related to Judah's present calamity.

d. The answer of the Lord (32:26-44)

(1) The city will be destroyed (32:26-35). **32:26-29.** God answered **Jeremiah** by first reminding him of His character. As Jeremiah had said, nothing is **too hard** for God (cf. v. 17). Jeremiah could depend on God's Word even if he did not understand how it would be accomplished. **Nebuchadnezzar** would indeed destroy Jerusalem. He would **set it on fire** and **burn it down** (cf. 21:10; 34:2, 22; 37:8, 10; 38:18, 23) because of the people's idolatry (19:13).

32:30-35. Evil had characterized both **Israel and Judah . . . from their youth**— it was a long-standing problem. All **the people** provoked God with their wicked conduct. Spiritually **they turned their backs** on God and refused to **listen or respond to discipline.** The temple was polluted with **abominable idols** (cf. 7:30; Ezek. 8:3-16), and **the Valley of Ben Hinnom** had become a slaughterhouse where the people would **sacrifice their sons and daughters** (cf. comments on Jer. 7:31-32; 19:5-6) **to Molech.** God would destroy Jerusalem because of her sin.

(2) The city will be restored (32:36-44). **32:36-41.** Jerusalem was **handed over to . . . Babylon** for **the sword, famine, and plague** (cf. v. 24 and see comments on 14:12), **but** that catastrophic event did not signal the end of God's covenant **people. God** offered hope in the midst of despair. First, He promised a regathering (cf. Ezek. 37:1-14). God will **gather** His people **from all the lands where** they had been in exile and will **bring them back to** the land of Israel where they will **live in safety** (cf. Jer. 31:1-17). Second, He promised an everlasting covenant (cf. 31:31-34; Ezek. 36:24-32). Not only will the people of Israel be restored to their land, but also they will be restored to their God. **They will be His people and He will be their God** (see comments on Jer. 30:22). With **singleness of heart** they will follow the Lord as He makes **an everlasting covenant with them.** This "everlasting covenant" is another term for the "New Covenant" (see comments on 31:31-34). It was called "everlasting" (*'ôlām*) to stress its duration. Then God **will never stop doing good to** His people, and **they will never turn away from** Him.

32:42-44. Just as God had been faithful to His word in bringing **great calamity on** Israel because of her sin (Deut. 28:15-68), so He will also be faithful in providing **the prosperity** He had **promised them** (Deut. 30:1-10). Thus Jeremiah's purchase of the field (Jer. 32:1-15) was a symbolic act to show that **fields will again be bought for silver** throughout the land of Israel **because** God **will restore their fortunes** (cf. 30:18; 33:11, 26; Deut. 30:3).

3. THE RESTORATION OF ISRAEL AND JUDAH REAFFIRMED (CHAP. 33)

Chapter 33 concludes "The Book of Consolation." This chapter is structurally and chronologically related to chapter 32. Jeremiah 33:1-13 continued God's promise of blessing as He reaffirmed both the coming destruction and the future restoration of Jerusalem. God then reaffirmed His covenants with David and with the Levitical priests (vv. 14-26).

a. The coming judgment and future restoration (33:1-13)

(1) The judgment (33:1-5). **33:1-3.** Chapter 33 followed closely the message of chapter 32 as **Jeremiah was still confined in the courtyard of the guard** (cf. 32:1-2). God again identified Himself to Jeremiah by stressing both His power and His character. He is the God **who made the earth** (cf. 32:17). By revealing to Jeremiah that **the Lord** (*Yahweh*) **is His name,** God emphasized His covenant-keeping faithfulness on behalf of His people (cf. 32:18; Ex. 3:13-15). Jeremiah did not understand how God could re-

store a nation that was destined for doom (cf. Jer. 32:24-25), so God challenged the prophet to call to Him for understanding. God promised to answer by revealing great and unsearchable things. The word for "unsearchable" (b^eṣūrôṯ) means something that is made inaccessible by fortifying it or enclosing it. It is used to describe heavily fortified cities (cf. Num. 13:28; Deut. 3:5; 28:52; Ezek. 21:20). God's plans for the future are inaccessible to ordinary people. Only God can unlock the secrets of the future, and He offered this knowledge to Jeremiah. God would share with Jeremiah "things" the prophet did not know or understand about Israel's future.

33:4-5. The first revelation focused on Jerusalem's impending fall. As Babylon's siege wore away at Jerusalem's outer defenses, **the houses** of Jerusalem along with **the royal palaces were torn down to** provide wood and stone to strengthen the walls **against the siege ramps.** The object of this frantic effort was to prevent Babylon's soldiers (**the sword**) from making a breach in the walls and entering the city.

God announced that Jerusalem's feeble attempts to shore up her defenses were futile. The partially dismantled houses would **be filled with the dead bodies** of those slain by **the Babylonians.** God would hide His face from the city, refusing to deliver it from this destruction (cf. 18:17; Ezek. 4:1-3). Jerusalem had to be destroyed **because of all its wickedness.**

(2) The restoration (33:6-13). **33:6-9.** The secret to understanding God's seemingly contradictory prophecies of judgment and blessing is to realize that the judgment was to be only temporary. After the time of judgment God will someday **bring health and healing to** His city and **people.** God spoke to Jeremiah about three elements of this blessing. First, the blessing will involve a restoration to the land (cf. 31:8-11; 32:37). God **will bring both Judah and Israel back from captivity.** Second, the blessing will involve a restoration to the Lord (cf. 31:31-34; 32:38-40). God **will cleanse** the people **from all** their **sin** and **forgive** them of their **rebellion.** Third, the blessing will involve a restoration to a special place of honor among the nations (cf. 31:10-14). Jerusalem will **bring . . . renown, joy,**

praise, and honor to God **before all nations.** Those nations **will be in awe and will tremble** as they marvel **at the abundant prosperity and peace** (cf. 33:6) God will lavish on His people.

33:10-13. God elaborated on the contrast between Israel's present judgment and her future blessing by drawing two pictures of the changes that would come. Each picture began with a similar phrase (vv. 10, 12) as God emphasized that **this is what the Lord** (or **Lord Almighty**) **says.** In each picture the scene in Jeremiah's day was similar (cf. vv. 10, 12). Jerusalem was **a desolate waste** that was **without men or animals** (cf. 32:43). Though the siege was still in progress, the fall of Jerusalem was so sure that God pictured it as if it had already happened. At this point the two pictures changed. In 33:10-11 God illustrated the joy and gladness that will again return to Jerusalem and Judah, and in verses 12-13 He illustrated the peace and prosperity that will again characterize Judah.

The streets of Jerusalem that were **deserted** after its destruction by Babylon (cf. Lam. 1:1-4) will again be filled with **the sounds of joy and gladness.** This joyful sound will be typified by **the voices of a bride and bridegroom** in a wedding ceremony (cf. Jer. 7:34; 16:9; 25:10) **and the voices of** worshipers as they **bring thank offerings to the house of the Lord** (cf. Ps. 100:1-2, 4). The song to be sung by the worshipers, recorded by Jeremiah, resembled the refrain of several psalms (cf. Pss. 100:4-5; 106:1; 107:1; 136:1-3). Joy will come when God restores Judah's **fortunes** (cf. Jer. 30:18; 32:44; 33:26; Deut. 30:3).

The **towns** of Judah that were destroyed by Babylon will also experience peace and prosperity. God **will again** provide safe **pastures for flocks.** This peace will extend from Jerusalem to the **hill country** of Judah in the east, **the western foothills** of the Shephelah in the west, **the Negev** in the south, and **the territory of Benjamin** in the north (cf. Jer. 17:26).

Throughout the land **flocks will again pass under the hand of the one who counts them** as a shepherd counts his sheep to be sure none is absent. Possibly Jeremiah was using shepherd and sheep in a metaphorical sense to refer to the leaders of Israel and the people. He had already compared the leaders to shepherds (cf. comments on 3:15) and the restored nation was compared to a regathered flock (cf. 23:3; 31:10). Jeremiah had also used this imagery to introduce his message on the righteous Branch from David (23:1-6), which is the subject of 33:14-26.

b. The covenants with David and the Levitical priests (33:14-26)

(1) The covenants (33:14-18). **33:14-16.** The second section of this chapter is introduced with the phrase **the days are coming** (hinnēh yāmîm bā'îm). Jeremiah used this phrase 16 times in his book. In a negative sense it referred to the coming destruction of Judah and the surrounding nations (cf. 7:32; 9:25; 19:6; 48:12; 49:2; 51:47, 52). However, in its remaining 9 occurrences it pointed to a future period of blessing for Israel when (a) the nation will be restored from captivity (16:14-15; 23:7-8; 30:3), (b) the righteous Branch of David will be ruling over a united monarchy (23:5-6; 33:14-15), (c) the nation will be experiencing peace and prosperity in the land (31:27-28; 33:14, 16), (d) the New Covenant with its cleansing from sin will be in effect ("The time is coming," 31:31-34), and (e) the city of Jerusalem will be rebuilt as a Holy City that will never again be destroyed (31:38-40). These promises transcend anything that Israel has experienced throughout her long history. They will find their ultimate fulfillment only in the Millennial Age when the kingdom of the Messiah is established. This will be when God **will fulfill the gracious promise** He **made to . . . Israel** and **Judah.**

The first aspect of this fulfillment will be the restoration of the monarchy (cf. 23:5). The **righteous Branch** that will **sprout from David's line** will rule as King over the nation. This was a prophecy about Jesus Christ who descended from the line of David and was promised David's throne (cf. Luke 1:31-33).

The second aspect of this fulfillment will be the restoration of **Jerusalem** as God's dwelling place. The city that was about to be destroyed by Babylon (Jer. 33:4-5) will someday **live in safety.** Though this verse is also found in 23:6, Jeremiah made a significant change in this passage to give it a new meaning. In 23:6 Jeremiah pictured the safety of Israel

and Judah through the ministry of the Messiah who was called "The LORD Our Righteousness." However, by changing "Israel" to "Jerusalem" and by changing the preposition "he" to "it" (lāh, lit., "to her") Jeremiah made the title, **The LORD Our Righteousness** apply to the city of Jerusalem instead of to the Messiah. The city will take on the same characteristics as the Lord who will dwell within her (cf. Ezek. 48:35).

It is significant that Jeremiah singled out the royal (Jer. 33:15) and religious (v. 16) aspects of God's restoration. Both were vital to Israel's existence as God's covenant community.

33:17-18. To emphasize the importance of both elements, God reiterated His covenants with the line of David and with the Levitical priests. The first covenant mentioned was God's covenant with David (cf. 2 Sam. 7:8-16; 1 Chron. 17:4-14). God vowed, **David will never fail to have a man to sit on** Israel's **throne.** Some have felt that this promise was incorrect because the throne did cease in 586 B.C. when Jerusalem fell. However, God did not promise an unbroken monarchy but an unbroken line of descendants from David who would be qualified to sit on that throne when it was reestablished. David's line would not fail before the righteous Branch came to claim His throne (cf. Luke 1:31-33). The genealogies of Matthew and Luke show that this promise was fulfilled as Christ was able to trace both His legal line through Joseph and His physical line through Mary back to David (Matt. 1:1-16; Luke 3:23-31).

The second covenant mentioned was God's covenant with **the priests, who are Levites.** This covenant was God's promise that the Levites would never **fail to have a man to stand before** Him **to offer burnt offerings . . . grain offerings,** and **sacrifices.** Again the promise was not that the sacrifices would continue unabated, because they did cease in 586 B.C. and were not resumed till 537 B.C. (cf. Ezra 3:1-6). The promise here was that the Levitical priesthood would not be extinguished. God was referring back to the promise He made to Phinehas (Num. 25:12-13). In other words neither the monarchy nor the priesthood would be abolished.

(2) The confirmation (33:19-26). God

gave two assurances that He would keep His covenant promises. Each assurance began with the same introductory phrase ("The word of the LORD came to Jeremiah," vv. 19, 23); and each used God's "covenant of day and night" to illustrate the permanence of these institutions (vv. 20, 25; cf. 31:35-37).

33:19-22. Only if man could **break God's covenant with the day and . . . the night** (cf. Gen. 1:14-19) could he break God's **covenant with David** and His **covenant with the Levites who are priests.** That is, God's covenants with these groups were as fixed as the natural order of the universe. They could not be overthrown by mere mortals. The word for "covenant" (*bᵉrîṯ*) referred to a treaty or agreement made between individuals or parties by which they bound themselves to a specific relationship or course of action. God had promised to preserve the kingly line of **David** (2 Sam. 7:8-16) and the priestly line of Phinehas (Num. 25:12-13), and He would not break His oath. Indeed, God promised to bless both lines so **the descendants** would become **as countless as the stars** and **the sand.**

33:23-26. God's second assurance (cf. vv. 19-22) to **Jeremiah** came because of external doubt and reproach. The group in question (**these people**) was not specified—they may have been doubting Israelites or Israel's heathen neighbors. Whoever they were, "these people" were claiming that God had so **rejected the two kingdoms** (*mišpāḥôṯ*, lit., "families or clans"; cf. 31:1) that He would **no longer regard them** as a nation. They felt that Israel's and Judah's sin had invalidated all God's covenant promises so that He was no longer obligated to fulfill them.

God responded to this argument by reaffirming His commitment to His covenant promises. The covenants with Abraham and **David** were not conditioned on the people's obedience but on God's character. They were as sure as His **covenant with day and night** and as immutable as **the fixed laws of heaven and earth.** Only if these natural laws could be undone would God **reject** Jacob's and David's **descendants.** The reference to **Abraham, Isaac, and Jacob** called to mind God's covenant promise to these patriarchs regarding His selection of Israel (cf. Gen. 15:7-21; 17:1-8; 26:1-6; 28:10-

15). God was bound to His promises and He would **restore** the nation's **fortunes** (cf. Jer. 30:18; 32:44; 33:11; Deut. 30:3) and **have compassion on** her. The greatest argument for the future restoration of Israel as a nation is the character of God. He made a series of covenants with the patriarchs, David, and the Levites; His character demands that He will ultimately fulfill these promises to their nation.

D. Present catastrophe of Judah (chaps. 34-45)

After describing the future hope of Judah (chaps. 30–33), Jeremiah returned to discuss their present judgment. The collapse of the kingdom that he had been predicting (chaps. 2–29) would now come to pass. Chapters 34–36 continued the theme of rejection that began in 26–29. The judgment was sure because the people rejected God's word of warning. Chapters 37–45, arranged in chronological order, detailed the events that occurred during and after Jerusalem's fall to Babylon.

1. BEFORE THE FALL (CHAPS. 34-36)

a. The inconsistency of the people (chap. 34)

(1) The warning to Zedekiah (34:1-7). **34:1-3.** When **Nebuchadnezzar** and **his army . . . were fighting against Jerusalem** God gave **Jeremiah** a message for King **Zedekiah.** This message was that Zedekiah's rebellion against Babylon would not succeed. **God** had already determined to **hand** the **city over to the** Babylonians, who would **burn it down** (cf. v. 22; 32:29; 37:8, 10; 38:18, 23). Though Zedekiah would try to flee, he would **not escape.** Instead he would be taken to Nebuchadnezzar and be required to meet with him **face to face** and be judged for his rebellion. Zedekiah would be taken captive **to Babylon** as punishment for his rebellion. Everything Jeremiah predicted came to pass (cf. 39:4-7; 52:7-11).

34:4-5. In the midst of judgment God did offer a **promise of** peace. Because of his rebellion **Zedekiah** could have been executed by Nebuchadnezzar, but God promised that he would **not die by the sword.** He would **die peacefully** and would receive a proper funeral befitting a king (in contrast with Jehoiakim; cf. 22:18-19). The **people** would kindle **a funeral fire** to **honor and lament** Zedekiah.

This fire does not refer to cremation because Israel and Judah buried dead bodies rather than cremating them. Instead it referred to the custom of lighting a large bonfire as a tribute to a dead king (cf. 2 Chron. 16:14; 21:19).

34:6-7. Jeremiah delivered his message to King Zedekiah as the army . . . of Babylon relentlessly continued its attack against Jerusalem and the two other fortified cities that remained in Judah—Lachish and Azekah. All the other Judean cities had already fallen. This grim picture of Judah's precarious position was illustrated by a tragic letter inscribed on a clay potsherd that was found in the ruins of Lachish. The letter was written to the commander at Lachish from an outpost that was close enough to Lachish and Azekah to see signal fires from both cities. Evidently Azekah had just fallen because the officer wrote, "And let my lord know that we are watching for the signals of Lachish, according to all the indications which my lord hath given, for we cannot see Azekah" (Lachish Letter No. 4; James B. Pritchard, ed., *Ancient Near Eastern Texts Relating to the Old Testament.* 3rd ed. Princeton, N.J.: Princeton University Press, 1969, p. 322).

(2) The warning to the people (34:8-22). **34:8-11.** Jeremiah raised the curtain of history on many social evils being practiced in his day. One such practice was the enslavement of Israelites by their own people. This violated God's Law (cf. Ex. 21:2-11; Lev. 25:39-55; Deut. 15:12-18). Perhaps in a desperate attempt to win God's favor during Babylon's siege of Jerusalem, the king proclaimed freedom for the slaves, a kind of "Emancipation Proclamation." Everyone was to free his Hebrew slaves in accordance with God's Law.

The slaves' freedom, however, was short-lived. All those who released their slaves changed their minds . . . and enslaved them again. What caused this reversal? Jeremiah placed at the end of the chapter (Jer. 34:21-22) the key that unlocks the puzzle. After the people had made the covenant and released the slaves, the army of Babylon broke off its siege of Jerusalem to repel an attack by the Egyptians (cf. 37:4-13). The people hoped for an Egyptian victory, which would force Babylon from Judah. But after so much destruction slaves would be

needed to rebuild the cities and towns. So the people reneged on their promise to God when it seemed that life would return to normal.

34:12-16. God rebuked the people for their inconsistency by reminding them of the covenant He had made with their forefathers when He freed them from their slavery in Egypt. The Law required that every seventh year all Hebrew slaves were to go free. No Israelite was to be forced into permanent bondage again. Unfortunately the people did not listen to God's Word. But because of Babylon's attack the people finally repented and did what was right by granting freedom to their countrymen. When they rescinded their promise they profaned God's name (His reputation) because the covenant had been made before God in the temple.

34:17-20. God's punishment matched their sin. By revoking their covenant the people had not proclaimed freedom for those Israelites who were wrongfully enslaved. Therefore ironically God would give them freedom to die by the sword, plague, and famine (cf. comments on 14:12).

In making their covenant in the temple (cf. 34:15) the people had slaughtered a calf . . . cut it in two, and walked between its pieces to signify their commitment to the bargain. By walking through the parts of the animal they were symbolizing the judgment that should befall them if they violated the agreement. They were to be hacked to pieces like the calf. Significantly when God made His covenant with Abraham, the patriarch did not pass between the parts of the animal. Only God did; apparently the blazing torch symbolized Him (Gen. 15:4-18, esp. v. 17). The Abrahamic Covenant rested on God's character, not on man's obedience.

God promised to treat those who broke the covenant like the calf they had slaughtered. All who made the agreement would be handed over to their enemies. Like the parts of the calf, their dead bodies would lie on the ground as food for both birds and beasts (cf. Jer. 7:33; 15:3; 16:4; 19:7).

34:21-22. Zedekiah and his officials should have been models of godly leadership, but they were as vacillating as the people. Though the Babylonians had withdrawn from Jerusalem, God would give the order to bring them back. The siege would resume until the Babylonians would take Jerusalem and burn it down (cf. v. 2). The other towns would be devastated too so the whole country would be virtually deserted.

b. *The consistency of the Recabites (chap. 35)*

(1) The fidelity of the Recabites (35:1-11). 35:1-5. This prophecy was given during the reign of Jehoiakim (609–598 B.C.)—at least 11 years (and possibly 20 years) earlier than the prophecies in chapter 34. Jeremiah placed the chapter here to contrast the faithfulness of the Recabite family with the unfaithfulness of the people of Judah. The Recabites were a nomadic clan (35:7-10) descended from Jonadab [or Jehonadab] son of Recab" (v. 6) who assisted Jehu in exterminating Baal worship from Israel (2 Kings 10:15-27). They were related to the Kenites (1 Chron. 2:54-55) who descended from Moses' father-in-law, Jethro (Jud. 1:16). Evidently Jonadab rejected a settled way of life for the life of a nomad, and his lifestyle became the norm for his clan (Jer. 35:6-10). They traveled in the wilderness of the Negev (Jud. 1:16; 1 Sam. 15:6), but were forced to move to Jerusalem when Nebuchadnezzar threatened Judah in 598 B.C. (Jer. 35:11).

Jeremiah invited the Recabites, including Jaazaniah, into one of the side rooms in the temple. These rooms surrounded the temple court and were used for meetings, storage, and as priests' residences (1 Kings 6:5; 1 Chron. 28:12; 2 Chron. 31:11; Neh. 13:7-9). The particular room Jeremiah entered beonged to the sons of Hanan son of Igdaliah. Nothing is known about Igdaliah except that he was a man of God—a term usually used to describe a prophet (cf. 1 Kings 12:22; 2 Kings 1:9-13; 4:21-22). The room occupied a prominent position, next to the room of the officials and over the room of Maaseiah son of Shallum the doorkeeper. Maaseiah was one of three "doorkeepers" for the temple. This was evidently a high position because those holding it were singled out by the Babylonians for judgment along with the chief priests (cf. 2 Kings 25:18-21; Jer. 52:24-27). Into this august company Jeremiah brought the rough, nomadic Recabites.

He set bowls full of wine and some cups before the Recabites and asked them to drink some wine.

35:6-11. The Recabites refused to drink the wine because their forefather Jonadab had prohibited it. The way of life chosen by Jonadab would not allow his descendants . . . ever to drink wine. Nor were they allowed to build houses, sow seed, or plant vineyards, that is, to settle down to a life of farming. Instead they were to live simple lives in tents as nomads.

Jonadab's descendants had obeyed everything he had commanded. They had never drunk wine or built houses to live in, nor had they ever cultivated vineyards, fields, or crops. In fact it was only because Nebuchadnezzar had invaded the land that they had come to Jerusalem.

(2) The example of the Recabites (35:12-17). 35:12-16. Why did Jeremiah bring the Recabites into the temple and offer them wine when he knew they would refuse it? This was to provide a lesson to Judah. The Recabites consistently obeyed their forefather's command. They stood in sharp contrast with the people of Judah who had consistently not obeyed God.

35:17. The Recabites served as a visual reminder of Judah's sin. God vowed to bring on Judah . . . every disaster He had pronounced against them. This "disaster" could refer either to the curses of the covenant (cf. Lev. 26:14-39; Deut. 28:15-68) or, more probably, to the fall of Judah and Jerusalem predicted by Jeremiah (cf. Jer. 4:20; 6:19; 11:11-12; 17:18). Judah would be punished because she did not listen to God's words and did not answer God's summons.

(3) The reward of the Recabites. 35:18-19. In contrast with faithless Judah the Recabites had consistently obeyed the command of their forefather Jonadab. God promised to reward their faithfulness, and assured them that they would never fail to have a man to serve Him. The phrase "serve Me" ('ōmēd l⁰pānay) means literally, "to stand before Me." It was used of those who served the Lord as prophets (1 Kings 17:1; Jer. 15:19), of officials who served Solomon (1 Kings 10:8), and of priests in the temple (Deut. 4:10; 10:8; 2 Chron. 29:11). However, though God might have been

offering the Recabites a special place of service to Him in the covenant community, this interpretation is not required. The same phrase also described the people of Israel who stood before the LORD at the tabernacle and the temple (cf. Lev. 9:5; Deut. 4:10; Jer. 7:10). So God may have promised that the line of the Recabites would always have descendants who would be able to worship the Lord. The promise pointed to a continuing line rather than a specific place of ministry.

c. *Jehoiakim's scroll-burning (chap. 36)*

(1) The writing of the scroll (36:1-7). **36:1-3.** The events of this chapter began **in the fourth year** of King **Jehoiakim** (605–604 B.C.; cf. 25:1). God commanded **Jeremiah** to **write on a scroll all the** prophecies God gave him about **Israel, Judah, and . . . other nations from the time** God **began speaking to** him **in the reign of Josiah** (627 B.C.; cf. 1:2; 25:3) until that day. This was the first formal compilation of Jeremiah's prophecies, and it was mentioned earlier (25:13). (See the chart "The Dating of Jeremiah's Prophecies," in the *Introduction*.) At least two additional stages of compilation are mentioned in the book (cf. 36:32; 51:64).

One purpose for recording these prophecies was so they could be read aloud to the people. The hope was that **the people** would **hear about every disaster** threatened by God and would **turn from** their **wicked way.** If the people would repent, God promised to **forgive their wickedness.**

36:4-7. Jeremiah summoned **Baruch,** his scribe (cf. 32:12-16; 36:26), and **dictated** to him **all the words.** It is not known whether Jeremiah recited all the prophecies from memory or if he read them from scrolls on which he had recorded them earlier. Both views allow for God's superintendence (cf. John 14:25-26). Jeremiah was **restricted,** or barred, from the **temple**—possibly because of his earlier unpopular addresses there (cf. Jer. 7:1-15; 26:1-19). Because of this restriction **Jeremiah told Baruch** to **go to the house of the LORD** in his place. **Baruch** was to go **on a day of fasting.** Prior to the fall of Jerusalem in 586 B.C. fast days were not specified but were called in times of emergency (cf. 36:9; 2 Chron. 20:3; Joel 1:14; 2:15). Only after the fall of Jerusalem were regular fast days instituted

(Zech. 7:3, 5; 8:19). **Jeremiah** hoped that as Baruch **read to the people from the scroll** they would repent of their sins.

(2) The reading of the scroll (36:8-19). **36:8-10.** Some time passed before a national emergency arose which prompted the leaders to call a fast. The scroll was written in Jehoiakim's fourth year (v. 1), but it was not **read** until **the ninth month of the fifth year.** This sounds like a gap of at least nine months, but because of the Hebrew method of dating it could have been a much shorter period of time. Assuming that **Jeremiah** employed the Tishri (September-October)-to-Tishri year for dating Judah's kings (see comments on 25:1), Jehoiakim's fourth year would have extended from October 7 (Tishri 1), 605 B.C. to September 25, 604 B.C. (not October 6 because of the lunar calendar); and his fifth year would have extended from September 26, 604 B.C. to October 14, 603 B.C. (including an intercalary month). However, when a specific month was given it was always reckoned by a Nisan (March-April)-to-Nisan year. Thus the "ninth month" was whatever ninth month from Nisan fell into the "fifth year" that began in Tishri. In the fifth year of Jehoiakim the ninth month extended from November 24, 604 B.C. through December 23, 604 B.C.—a date just three months after the end of Jehoiakim's fourth year. (For a more detailed discussion of these chronological problems see Edwin R. Thiele, *The Mysterious Numbers of the Hebrew Kings.* Rev. ed. Grand Rapids: Zondervan Publishing House, 1983; and Richard A. Parker and Waldo H. Dubberstein, *Babylonian Chronology: 626 B.C.–A.D. 75.* Providence, R.I.: Brown University Press, 1956.) The date was significant because the Babylonian Chronicle reports that at the same time Nebuchadnezzar was in Palestine collecting "vast tribute" from those nations he had conquered. In the same month the fast was called, Nebuchadnezzar captured the city of Ashkelon and plundered it (cf. Donald J. Wiseman, *Chronicles of Chaldean Kings (626–556 B.C.) in the British Museum.* London: Trustees of the British Museum, 1956, p. 69). It is possible that the fast was called to plead for deliverance from Babylon's harsh hand.

Baruch went to **the room of Gemariah son of Shaphan** (see the chart "The

Line of Shaphan," near 26:24) **which was in the upper courtyard** of the temple (cf. 26:10) **at the entrance of the New Gate.** Gemariah, like his brother Ahikam, supported Jeremiah's message and allowed **Baruch** to use his room from which he could **read** to **the people** gathered in the **temple** courtyard.

36:11-19. Gemariah did not remain in his room while Baruch read the scroll, but his son **Micaiah . . . heard all the words.** Micaiah **went to the royal palace** to report the contents of the scroll to **the officials.** Those gathered there included **Elishama the secretary** (cf. v. 21), **Delaiah son of Shemaiah** (cf. v. 25), and **Elnathan son of Acbor** (cf. v. 25). Though Acbor played a part in the recovery of the Law during the time of Josiah (2 Kings 22:12-14), his son Elnathan did not possess all his father's qualities. If he is the same Elnathan mentioned in 2 Kings 24:8, then he was King Jehoiakim's father-in-law. Though Elnathan did urge Jehoiakim not to burn Jeremiah's scroll (Jer. 36:25), he had also led an expedition to Egypt to extradite the Prophet Uriah back to Jerusalem to be executed (cf. 26:20-23). Also present in this meeting were **Gemariah** (36:10, 25), **Zedekiah son of Hananiah, and other officials.**

When **Micaiah** finished his report, **the officials sent Jehudi to Baruch** to summon him to appear before them. After **Baruch** entered the room they asked him to **sit down** and **read** the scroll **to** them. His reading caused the officials to look **at each other in fear** because they realized that they **must report all** its **words** to **King** Jehoiakim. They asked Baruch **how** the scroll was written, and he explained that **Jeremiah** had **dictated** the **words** and he **wrote them . . . on the scroll.**

Before the meeting adjourned, those present gave a word of warning **to Baruch.** Both he **and Jeremiah** were to **go and hide** and not **let anyone know where** they were. Jehoiakim's prior reaction against Uriah the prophet showed the wisdom of this advice (cf. 26:20-23).

(3) The burning of the scroll (36:20-26). **36:20-22.** Baruch's **scroll** was placed **in the room of Elishama,** and the officials **went to the king** and **reported** the incident **to** him. **Jehudi** was sent to retrieve **the scroll** and he **read it to the king** as

the officials watched. Jeremiah reemphasized that the events took place in **the ninth month** because that helped explain the story. The story happened between November 24 and December 23, 604 B.C.; the weather can be quite cold in Jerusalem during that time of year. Jehoiakim was **in his winter apartment,** which probably faced south to catch the winter sun, and he had **a fire burning in a firepot,** or brazier, to provide warmth.

36:23-26. The writing on **the scroll** was in vertical columns. After **Jehudi** would **read three or four columns,** Jehoiakim interrupted him to **cut** those columns **off** the scroll **with a scribe's knife.** He then **threw** those pieces **into the firepot until** he had burned **the entire scroll.** Jehoiakim, in contrast with his godly father Josiah (cf. 2 Kings 22:11-13), **showed no fear** of God's word of judgment **nor did** he and his counselors **tear their clothes** in a visible act of contrition or repentance. **Instead** Jehoiakim ordered the **arrest of Baruch and Jeremiah.** However, they were **hidden** by **the Lord** so the king's men could not find them.

(4) The rewriting of the scroll (36:27-32). **36:27-31.** Man can burn a **scroll,** but he cannot destroy the Word of God. Since Jehoiakim destroyed the first scroll, God told **Jeremiah** to **write** on **another scroll . . . all the words of the first** scroll. However, he was to include an additional word for King **Jehoiakim.** Because he had **burned** the **scroll** and refused to believe God's warning about the **king of Babylon,** God vowed to judge him. First, **no** descendant of his would permanently **sit on the throne** of David. Though his son, Jehoiachin, did follow him to the throne (cf. 2 Kings 24:8-17), he was deposed by Nebuchadnezzar after a reign of only three months. No other descendant of Jehoiakim ascended the throne (see comments on Jer. 22:24-30). Second, Jehoiakim would not receive a proper burial (cf. 22:18-19). Instead **his body** would **be thrown out** of the city and **exposed to** the elements. Third, Jehoiakim's **children and his attendants** would be judged **for their wickedness.** God would **bring** on them **every disaster** that He had **pronounced . . . because they** had **not listened.**

36:32. Jeremiah obeyed God's command and secured **another scroll.** He **dictated** while **Baruch wrote on** the new scroll all the words of the original scroll. Then Jeremiah added many similar words, most likely the contents of chapter 36 including the judgment on Jehoiakim.

2. DURING THE FALL (CHAPS. 37–39)

The events of chapters 37–39 are arranged chronologically. They trace Jeremiah's life and ministry during the final siege and fall of Jerusalem.

a. Jeremiah's message to Zedekiah (37:1-10)

37:1-2. The events in this section focus on Zedekiah, the last king of Judah, who was placed on the throne as a vassal king by Nebuchadnezzar (cf. 2 Kings 24:15-17). In these dark days Judah needed a strong and godly leader. Unfortunately Zedekiah possessed neither quality. From the king to the common people, no one paid any attention to Jeremiah's words of warning until it was too late.

37:3-10. But Zedekiah did send a delegation to Jeremiah asking him to pray to the LORD for Jerusalem. Jeremiah was . . . not yet . . . in prison, and Babylon had just lifted her siege of Jerusalem because Pharaoh's army had marched from Egypt. Perhaps Zedekiah hoped that Jeremiah's prayers would induce God to grant a victory to the Egyptians and force Babylon out of Palestine (cf. 21:1-7 for a similar request).

God's answer was not the one Zedekiah sought. The army of Egypt that had marched out to support Judah would be crushed by Babylon and forced to go back to its own land. Then the army of Babylon would return and attack Jerusalem. They would capture it and burn it down (cf. 21:10; 32:29; 34:2, 22; 37:10; 38:18, 23). Those who hoped for a Babylonian withdrawal were deceiving themselves. Even if only wounded men were in Nebuchadnezzar's army, God said that they still would burn Jerusalem down (cf. 37:8).

b. Jeremiah's imprisonment (37:11–38:28)

(1) Jeremiah's arrest and confinement in a dungeon. 37:11-16. The withdrawal of the Babylonian army to fight the Egyptians produced a period of relative calm in Judah. Jeremiah used this lull to leave the city for a short journey into the territory of Benjamin (cf. 1:1). The purpose of his trip was to get his share of some property belonging to his family. The word for "get his share" (hālaq) could also be translated "divide, share, apportion." Jeremiah was traveling to Anathoth to take care of personal business, either to secure some land or to divide up some land for sale to others. This land transaction probably does not relate to his purchase in chapter 32. By the time of the purchase in chapter 32 Jeremiah had already been arrested and confined to the courtyard of the guard (cf. 32:2). When he started toward Anathoth (chap. 37) he had not yet been arrested (cf. 37:4, 21; 38:13, 28). Therefore the events of chapter 37 took place before the events of chapter 32.

Just as Jeremiah started to leave, the captain of the guard seized him. Irijah . . . arrested Jeremiah and charged him with deserting to the enemy. Jeremiah denied the charge, but the captain would not listen. Instead . . . Jeremiah was taken to the officials who ordered him beaten and imprisoned. The prison was located in the house of Jonathan the secretary and was a vaulted cell in a dungeon (lit., "in the house of the cistern, in the vaulted rooms"). This was probably a complex of large, underground cisterns that had been converted into a prison. Jeremiah . . . remained there a long time.

(2) Jeremiah's first meeting with Zedekiah and transfer to the courtyard of the guard (37:17-21). 37:17-20. Babylon returned to Jerusalem and renewed her siege of the city. Zedekiah secretly sent for Jeremiah and brought him to the palace. Because of Jeremiah's unpopularity with the people (cf. 26:10-11; 37:11-15; 38:4) Zedekiah met with him privately to ask if he had any word from the LORD. Jeremiah's word from the Lord was unaffected by his imprisonment. Jerusalem would fall and Zedekiah would be handed over to the king of Babylon (cf. 21:3-7).

Jeremiah used the opportunity of this appearance before Zedekiah to protest his innocence. He demanded to know what crime he had committed. The other prophets had prophesied lies by declaring that the Babylonians would not attack. Jeremiah petitioned Zedekiah not to send him back to the prison where he had been confined. As a man who was probably in his 60s, Jeremiah was concerned for his health in that dank, dark dungeon. If he were taken back to that hole he might die there.

37:21. Granting Jeremiah's request, Zedekiah had him transferred from the underground vaulted cistern to the courtyard of the guard in the royal palace (cf. 32:2). Here Zedekiah could better protect Jeremiah from his enemies—though Zedekiah was a weak-willed protector (cf. 38:4-10). Zedekiah also arranged for Jeremiah to be given bread . . . each day so he would not starve. This continued until the siege depleted the supply of grain so that all the bread in the city was gone (cf. 52:6).

(3) Jeremiah's confinement in a cistern (38:1-6). **38:1-3.** By being confined to the courtyard of the guard (37:21) Jeremiah had some freedom to meet with people (cf. 32:1-2, 6). He used this time as an opportunity to deliver God's message to any who would listen. His message was overheard by four high-ranking officials: **Shephatiah son of Mattan** (not mentioned elsewhere), **Gedaliah son of Pashhur** (possibly a son of the Pashhur who beat Jeremiah, 20:1-3), **Jehucal son of Shelemiah** (sent by Zedekiah to inquire about the lifting of Babylon's siege, 37:3), and **Pashhur son of Malkijah** (sent by Zedekiah to inquire about Babylon's initial attack on Jerusalem, 21:1-2). These four powerful officials **heard** Jeremiah speaking to **all the people.**

The contents of Jeremiah's message are summarized in 38:2-3. The message was the same one that Jeremiah gave before (21:3-10). Those who remained in Jerusalem would **die by the sword, famine, or plague** (cf. comments on 14:12). Only those who deserted **to the Babylonians** would **live.** Jerusalem's only hope was to surrender. Any thought of withstanding Babylon's siege was futile since God had said the **city** would be **handed over to** Nebuchadnezzar **who** would **capture it.**

38:4-6. The officials went to Zedekiah and demanded that Jeremiah **be put to death** for his words. His "treasonous" remarks were **discouraging** both **the soldiers** and **all the people.** In their twisted nationalistic logic these officials believed that Jeremiah was **seeking the ruin** of his **people** when, in fact, Jeremiah wanted just the opposite (v. 2). Zedekiah's weakness was most evident in his response to these officials. Though earlier he had agreed to protect Jeremiah (37:18-21), Zedekiah now handed him over to those who sought his life. Zedekiah's lame excuse was that **the king could do nothing to oppose** them. Zedekiah was a political puppet, incapable of making strong, independent decisions. He was controlled either by Nebuchadnezzar (cf. 2 Kings 24:17) or by the city officials who urged him to rebel against Babylon and then influenced his decisions (Jer. 27:12-15; 38:5, 19, 24-28).

The officials **took Jeremiah** and **put him into** Malkijah's **cistern, in the courtyard of the guard.** A cistern was a large pit cut into rock and covered with plaster. It was used to gather rainwater in the winter for use during the dry summer (cf. 2:13). This **cistern** was so deep that they had to lower **Jeremiah** into it **by ropes.** Possibly because of the prolonged drought (cf. 14:1-4) the cistern **had no water in it.** All it contained was the **mud** that collected in the bottom of the pit from the dirt carried there by the rain. **Jeremiah** then **sank down into the mud.** His life was indeed threatened. Had the water or mud been deeper he would certainly have drowned or suffocated, and death by starvation was a near prospect. Also perhaps individuals threw stones at Jeremiah while he was in the cistern, hoping to kill him outright or to knock him unconscious so he would sink into the muddy water and die (cf. comments on Lam. 3:52-54).

(4) Jeremiah's rescue from the cistern (38:7-13). **38:7-9.** Many of Jeremiah's countrymen wanted him killed. The only official who cared enough to intercede on his behalf was **Ebed-Melech** (lit., "servant of the king") who was **a Cushite** from the area of upper Egypt (modern-day southern Egypt, Sudan, and northern Ethiopia). He was serving as **an official** (*sārîs*, lit., "a eunuch"; cf. comments on Dan. 1:7) **in the royal palace.** His exact position in the palace was not described, but he had access to the king.

Ebed-Melech went to the Benjamin Gate (cf. Jer. 20:2; 37:13) where **the king was sitting**—either conducting official business or supervising the strengthening of Jerusalem's defenses against the siege. His urgent message to **the king** was that the other officials had **acted wickedly** by throwing **Jeremiah . . . into**

a cistern where he would starve to death. Evidently Zedekiah had not known the officials' specific plan to kill Jeremiah or else he had not believed that they would carry it out. But now he knew Jeremiah's death was imminent.

38:10-13. Zedekiah ordered **Ebed-Melech** to **take 30 men from** there—possibly soldiers on duty at the gate—**and lift Jeremiah** from **the cistern before he** died. Thirty men would be needed to pull Jeremiah out of the mud and to stand guard against the officials who might oppose the rescue attempt. **Ebed-Melech** led the soldiers **to a room under the treasury in the palace** where the opening to the cistern was located. **Old rags and worn-out clothes** were passed down **to Jeremiah** to place **under his arms to pad the ropes.** Jeremiah was then **pulled . . . up with the ropes** and freed from **the cistern.** He was again put in **the courtyard of the guard** (cf. 37:21).

(5) Jeremiah's second meeting with Zedekiah (38:14-28). **38:14-16.** Zedekiah **sent for Jeremiah** again and met him in secret at **the third entrance to the temple.** This entrance, not mentioned elsewhere, may refer to a private entrance that connected the king's palace with the temple. Zedekiah wanted **to ask** Jeremiah **something,** and he told the prophet **not** to **hide anything from** him. Jeremiah voiced two objections. First, if he did **answer** with a message the king did not want to hear he had no guarantee that the king would **not kill** him. Second, any **counsel** Jeremiah gave was wasted because the king **would not listen to** him. Zedekiah answered the first objection but not the second. He promised that he would **neither kill** Jeremiah himself nor **hand** him **over to** people who were **seeking** his **life.** But the king made no promise to heed Jeremiah's message.

38:17-23. Jeremiah's message remained the same as before (cf. 21:1-10; 37:17; 38:1-3). If Zedekiah would **surrender** to the Babylonians his **life** would **be spared,** the **city** would **not be burned down,** and his **family** would **live.** However, if he would **not surrender,** the city would **be handed over to** the armies of Babylon who would **burn it down** (cf. 21:10; 32:29; 34:2, 22; 37:8, 10; 38:23); and Zedekiah would **not escape from their hands.**

Zedekiah refused to heed Jeremiah's advice because of fear. He was **afraid of the Jews** who had already **gone over to the Babylonians** because he thought **the Babylonians** would **hand** him **over to** those Jews who now opposed him. Given the opportunity, they would **mistreat** him for his past acts of cruelty to them. Jeremiah tried to assure Zedekiah that this would not happen. If he would **obey the LORD by** following Jeremiah's word, his **life** would **be spared. But if** he refused **to surrender** because of fear he would suffer the very ridicule and humiliation he sought to avoid. **The women** from his own **palace** (the royal harem) would scoff at Zedekiah as they were **brought out to the officials of . . . Babylon.** The theme of their song would be the gullibility of the king in trusting his advisers who had **misled** him while posing as his **trusted friends.** But when Zedekiah's **feet** had **sunk in the mud** of Babylon's pit (cf. 38:6) he would look around to discover that his **friends** who had brought him there had **deserted** him. If he refused to surrender to Babylon he would see his **wives and children** being led away (cf. 39:6). He himself would **be captured** and the **city** of Jerusalem would **be burned down** (cf. 38:18).

38:24-28. Zedekiah refused to follow Jeremiah's advice. Such a bold step was beyond the ability of this spineless monarch. Instead he warned Jeremiah **not** to **let anyone know about** their **conversation.** If word got out, the officials would try to kill Jeremiah. Palace spies were everywhere so Zedekiah gave Jeremiah an alibi in case he was questioned. **If the officials** asked Jeremiah **what** he **said to the king and what the king said to** him, he was to tell them that he **was pleading** with Zedekiah **not to send** him **back to** the dungeon in **Jonathan's house** (cf. 37:15). Jeremiah had indeed made such a request during his first meeting with Zedekiah (37:20).

Zedekiah's caution was well-founded because **the officials did** hear about the meeting and went **to Jeremiah to question** him. Jeremiah repeated the words Zedekiah told him **to say;** and since **no one had heard** the **conversation,** they accepted Jeremiah's story. **Jeremiah remained in the courtyard of the guard** (cf. 38:13) as a political prisoner till **Jerusalem was captured** by Nebuchadnezzar.

c. Jerusalem's destruction (chap. 39)

(1) The fate of the Jews (39:1-10).

39:1-4. Jeremiah's declarations of doom were ignored by the people of Jerusalem. His vindication came when God brought to pass Jerusalem's destruction just as he had predicted it. Jeremiah gave a detailed account of how Jerusalem was taken. The final conflict began in the 9th year of Zedekiah's reign in the 10th month. This event was so traumatic that it was recorded three other times in the Old Testament, even noting the day of the month (cf. 2 Kings 25:1; Jer. 52:4; Ezek. 24:1-2). The siege began on January 15, 588 B.C. and lasted until the ninth day of the 4th month of Zedekiah's 11th year. Using a Western method for reckoning of dates this would seem to give a siege of approximately 19 months (the last 3 months of the 9th year + the 12 months of the 10th year + the first 4 months of the 11th year). However, using the method for reckoning dates employed by the Hebrews, the length of the siege was much longer. For the *years* of the Hebrew kings were calculated on a Tishri (September-October)-to-Tishri calendar while the *months* of a year were calculated on a Nisan (March-April)-to-Nisan calendar (see comments on 36:9). Zedekiah's 11th year extended from October 18, 587 to October 6, 586. The 4th month from Nisan that coincided with his 11th year began on July 10, 586. The ninth day of that month was July 18, 586 B.C. Therefore the entire siege lasted just over 30 months, from January 15, 588 to July 18, 586 B.C.

After the 30-month siege the Babylonians broke through the city wall. The officials of . . . Babylon entered the city and took seats in the Middle Gate. The Middle Gate was probably on the north side of the city (where the Babylonians breached the walls) in the Central (or Tyropeon) Valley which separated the two quarters of the city. They "took seats" to establish their control over the city and to judge those taken captive (cf. comments on 38:7; Ezek. 11:1). One of these officials was **Nergal-Sharezer of Samgar** (also called Neriglissar) who was Nebuchadnezzar's son-in-law who ascended Babylon's throne in 560 B.C. after the death of Nebuchadnezzar's son, Evil-Merodach (cf. Jer. 52:31; also see the chart "Kings of the Neo-Babylonian Empire," in the *Introduction* to Dan.). The

other officials included **Nebo-Sarsekim** and **Nergal-Sharezer,** though the exact names and number of individuals listed are unclear (NIV marg.).

Zedekiah and his soldiers saw that the city had fallen. It would be only a matter of time till the Babylonians moved south through the city and captured them. In a desperate bid to escape **they fled** from the city at night. Their plan was to leave the city **by way of the king's garden,** located in the south near the Pool of Siloam (cf. Neh. 3:15). After passing **through the gate between the two walls,** the ragtag soldiers were in the steep ravine near where the Hinnom and Kidron Valleys unite. Climbing over the Mount of Olives the army **headed toward the Arabah,** probably hoping to cross the Jordan River and escape to Rabbah (modern Amman, Jordan), the capital of their allies, the Ammonites (cf. comments on Ezek. 21:18-23).

39:5-7. After waiting so long for this victory, the Babylonians were not about to let their prey escape. Pursuing **Zedekiah** and his soldiers, the Babylonians **overtook** them on the broad **plains of Jericho** just before the Jordan River. Zedekiah was **captured** and taken **to Nebuchadnezzar,** who had established his military headquarters **at Riblah in . . . Hamath** (see map "The World of Jeremiah and Ezekiel," in the *Introduction*). Nebuchadnezzar **pronounced sentence on** Zedekiah for rebelling against **Babylon. Zedekiah** was forced to watch as the Babylonians **slaughtered** his **sons . . . before his eyes** and killed **all the nobles of Judah.** To seal this sight of horror in Zedekiah's mind forever, Nebuchadnezzar **then . . . put out Zedekiah's eyes.** Finally he **bound** Zedekiah **with bronze shackles** to drag him in humiliation **to Babylon.** Zedekiah suffered the shame that he feared because he had ignored the warnings of the Lord (cf. 38:17-23).

39:8-10. Jerusalem too suffered the ignominious fate predicted by Jeremiah. The Babylonians **set fire** both to the magnificent **royal palace and the houses of the people** (cf. 21:10; 22:6-7; 32:29; 34:2, 22; 37:8-10; 38:18, 23). The soldiers also **broke down the walls of Jerusalem** so the city would remain defenseless (cf. Lam. 2:8-9; Neh. 1:3). **Nebuzaradan, commander of the imperial guard** (*raḇ-ṭabbāḥîm,* lit., "chief of the slaughterers";

cf. Gen. 37:36; Dan. 2:14), took as captives those who were still alive in the city (cf. Jer. 13:19; 15:2; Ezek. 5:8-12) along with the people who had defected (gone over to him) earlier (cf. Jer. 21:8-9; 38:1-4, 17-23). To insure loyalty, stability, and productivity, Babylon left behind a remnant of the extremely poor—people who owned nothing. He gave them vineyards and fields. No doubt he believed that those individuals would be grateful to the Babylonians for their newfound prosperity and would be unlikely to rebel. In return Babylon would receive income in the form of taxation on the produce of the land.

(2) The fate of Jeremiah (39:11-18). 39:11-14. Nebuchadnezzar had evidently heard of Jeremiah—possibly either through the letters the prophet had sent to Babylon (cf. chap. 29) or through the testimony of those who had defected to the Babylonians (21:8-9; 38:1-3). Nebuchadnezzar issued orders . . . through Nebuzaradan to his soldiers to take Jeremiah and look after him. They were not to harm him but were to do for him whatever he desired. Jeremiah was released from the courtyard of the guard (cf. 38:28) and turned . . . over to Judahite Gedaliah, who was the son of Ahikam and the grandson of Shaphan (see the chart "The Line of Shaphan," near 26:24). Gedaliah was appointed as governor of those who remained in the land (40:7). Some have thought that the account of Jeremiah's kind treatment in 39:11-14 contradicts the account of his being in chains in 40:1. However, the accounts can be easily harmonized. Jeremiah was rounded up with the other survivors of Jerusalem and then taken five miles north to Ramah for processing (cf. 31:15). It was there that the prophet of God was identified and released (40:4-5).

39:15-18. While Jeremiah had waited for the city to fall, God gave him a message for Ebed-Melech the Cushite (cf. 38:7-13). God's words against Jerusalem would be fulfilled before Ebed-Melech's eyes. God promised that when Jerusalem fell He would rescue Ebed-Melech so that he would not be executed with all the other officials (cf. 39:6; 52:10, 24-27). He would escape because he had demonstrated his trust in God by helping Jeremiah.

3. AFTER THE FALL (CHAPS. 40-45)

One would think that the fall of Jerusalem would have taught Judah a lesson she would never forget. However, by recording the events that happened after the fall of the city, Jeremiah demonstrated that the basic character of the people who remained in the land was unchanged. They still refused to trust in God or to submit to Babylon (cf. Ezek. 33:23-29).

a. Jeremiah's ministry to the remnant in Palestine (chaps. 40-42)

(1) The governorship of Gedaliah (40:1-12). 40:1-6. Jeremiah was released in Ramah where he had been taken bound in chains with the other captives. As Nebuzaradan let Jeremiah go he acknowledged his familiarity with Jeremiah's prophecies. No doubt some of those who had defected or who had been captured told the Babylonians about Jeremiah's messages. Nebuzaradan told Jeremiah that God brought disaster on Jerusalem as predicted because the people had sinned against Him. However, Nebuzaradan said he was freeing Jeremiah from his chains because he was innocent in Judah's revolt against Babylon.

Jeremiah was free to go wherever he wanted. If he went to Babylon with the other captives, Nebuzaradan promised to look after him (cf. 39:12). If he wished to stay in Judah, he could settle wherever he pleased. However, if he did stay in Judah Nebuzaradan suggested that he go . . . to Gedaliah and live with him. No doubt Governor Gedaliah could offer both the protection and the physical provisions that Jeremiah would need if he stayed. As Jeremiah left Ramah to make the three-mile journey to Mizpah—the administrative center for Judah after the destruction of Jerusalem—Nebuzaradan displayed his kindness by providing Jeremiah with provisions and a present.

40:7-12. As in many wars, scattered remnants of the army often still remain deployed in the field after the surrender of the main body of troops. The main forces of Judah, located in Jerusalem, Lachish, and Azekah, had been crushed; but groups of army officers and their men were still scattered in the open country. When these soldiers heard that Gedaliah was now governor over the land they came to him at Mizpah. Two of the leaders listed (v. 8) were worthy of special notice because of subsequent events. The one listed first was **Ishmael son of Nethaniah** (cf. vv. 14-15). He was from the royal line of David (cf. 41:1) and had served as one of King Zedekiah's officers. The second was **Johanan** who was one of two **sons of Kareah** (cf. 40:13-16). Nothing else is known about Johanan's background.

The commanders mentioned in verse 8 wanted to know what would happen if they would lay down their arms and surrender. Gedaliah reassured **them** that no harm would come to them if they surrendered. He encouraged them to **settle down in the land and serve . . . Babylon.** Gedaliah promised to **represent** them **before the Babylonians** while they concentrated on harvesting **the wine, summer fruit, and oil.** They would be free to **live in the towns** they had **taken over.**

In addition to reaching the scattered bands of Judah's resistance fighters, word of Gedaliah's appointment as governor also reached **the Jews in Moab, Ammon, Edom, and** elsewhere. These refugees **all came back to the land** to resettle, and helped in harvesting the **wine and summer fruit** (cf. v. 10).

(2) The assassination of Gedaliah (40:13–41:15). **40:13-16.** Judah's prospects looked bright. Peace and stability were returning to the land. The warring factions had submitted to Gedaliah's rule, and some refugees had returned. But just beneath the surface forces of intrigue and rebellion were churning and bubbling. It was only a matter of time before they broke to the surface.

The first report of trouble came from **Johanan son of Kareah** (cf. v. 8). He, along with **all the army officers,** reported to **Gedaliah** that **Baalis king of the Ammonites** had **sent Ishmael son of Nethaniah** (cf. v. 8) **to take** Gedaliah's **life.** Why would the king of Ammon conspire with Ishmael·to kill Gedaliah? The answer lies in understanding the relationship between Judah and Ammon. Both nations were vassals to Babylon and had participated in a secret meeting of nations in 593 B.C. to evaluate their prospects of uniting in rebellion against Babylon (cf. 27:1-11). That meeting did not produce any definite action; but in 588 B.C. Egypt's new Pharaoh (Hophra) per-suaded Judah, Ammon, and Tyre to revolt against Babylon. Nebuchadnezzar had to decide which nation to attack first, and God directed him to Judah instead of to Ammon (cf. Ezek. 21:18-23). Judah and Ammon were still allies when Jerusalem fell, and Zedekiah was probably heading for Ammon when he was captured (Jer. 39:4-5). But in spite of their union as allies, Judah and Ammon did not care for each other. Their union was a "marriage of convenience." Ammon rejoiced over Jerusalem's fall because she knew that if Nebuchadnezzar committed his army against Jerusalem he would not be able to attack Ammon (cf. comments on 49:1-6; Ezek. 25:1-7). Thus Gedaliah's commitment to Babylon was unsettling to Ammon. If Judah did submit to Babylon, then after Nebuchadnezzar finished his siege of Tyre (cf. Ezek. 29:17-18) he would probably attack Ammon next. But a destabilized Judah could force Nebuchadnezzar to commit large numbers of troops there to maintain order, which would improve Ammon's chances for survival. So it was to Ammon's advantage to replace pro-Babylonian Gedaliah with an anti-Babylonian leader like Ishmael.

Unfortunately **Gedaliah . . . did not believe** these officers. **Johanan** met **privately** with **Gedaliah** and offered to **kill Ishmael.** He planned to do it secretly so **no one** would **know** who was responsible. Johanan thought Ishmael should be eliminated for the good **of Judah.** If Ishmael were allowed to **take** Gedaliah's **life,** it could **cause all the Jews** in the land **to be scattered** and **to perish.** Gedaliah ordered **Johanan** not to **do such a thing** because he was certain that the rumors **about Ishmael** were **not true.** Gedaliah was an honorable man who made a fatal mistake when he misjudged Ishmael's character.

41:1-3. Ishmael came to Gedaliah **in the seventh month** (September-October). Though the month was given, the year was not, so the exact dating of the assassination is uncertain. It would be difficult for all of these events to have occurred in 586 B.C. because the army of Babylon was still in Jerusalem as late as August 17 of that year (52:12). This would allow less than two months for the Babylonians to deport the people, establish a government, allot the land, and withdraw the main body of their forces. So the assassination must have happened in a later year. But which year would fit best? One suggestion focuses on a little-known deportation in 583–582 B.C. (cf. Jer. 52:30). Why did Nebuchadnezzar make another excursion into the land at that time? A likely answer would be to restore order after the assassination of the governor and the small contingent of Babylonian troops stationed in Judah (cf. 41:2-3). If these events are related, then the "seventh month" when Gedaliah was assassinated began on October 4, 583 B.C.

Ishmael . . . came to Gedaliah **with 10 men** for a "peaceful" meeting. As they sat together **eating . . . Ishmael** and his cohorts **struck down Gedaliah.** They **also killed all the Jews** (probably those attending the banquet) **as well as the Babylonian soldiers who were** stationed **there** (cf. 2 Kings 25:25).

41:4-9. The assassinations probably took place in the evening. The plot had gone so well that early **the day after** the assassination nobody **knew about it.** On that day **80 men** in mourning (with **shaved . . . beards, torn . . . clothes,** and self-inflicted cuts; cf. comments on 16:6) were journeying to Jerusalem **from Shechem, Shiloh, and Samaria**—three cities that had been part of the Northern Kingdom of Israel. The fact that these men were from the Northern Kingdom implies that at least some of King Josiah's reforms (cf. 2 Kings 23:15-20; 2 Chron. 34:33) had a lasting impact. These men were carrying **grain offerings and incense** that they planned to offer at the temple. Though the temple had been destroyed (cf. Jer. 52:13, 17-23), people still worshiped at its site. No doubt these pilgrims were traveling to Jerusalem to celebrate one of the three feasts held during the seventh month (cf. Lev. 23:23-44).

Ishmael . . . went out to **meet** the pilgrims, **weeping as he went.** After feigning sympathy he invited them to **come to Gedaliah.** Certainly an offer to meet with the governor could not be refused so **they went into the city.** Once they were in the city **Ishmael** and his band of cutthroats **slaughtered** 70 of the 80 men and **threw** their bodies **into a cistern.** Why did Ishmael perform this savage act? Though not specifically stated, Jeremiah 41:8 implies that he intended to plunder his victims and seize their

provisions. Certainly a caravan of 80 pilgrims would carry a fair amount of food and money. **Ten of** the 80 managed to bargain for their lives by announcing that additional supplies of **wheat and barley, oil and honey were hidden in a field.** If he would spare them, they would show him the location of this cache. Ishmael's greed got the better of him so he **did not kill them.**

In a sidelight Jeremiah explained the historical significance of the site where the slaughter occurred (v. 9). **The cistern** in which **the bodies of the 70 men** and **Gedaliah** had been cast had been constructed nearly 300 years earlier by **King Asa.** It had served **as part of** Asa's **defense against Baasha** when the king of Judah sought to stem the advances of the **king of Israel** (cf. 1 Kings 15:16-22). The cistern that had once helped preserve life was now **filled . . . with the dead.**

41:10-15. Ishmael had killed only a select group of those living **in Mizpah** (v. 2). He **made captives of all the rest** who lived there. These included **the king's daughters** and **all the others who** had been assigned to **Gedaliah.** No doubt Jeremiah was included among the captives (cf. 40:6). The group **set out** from Mizpah to go to Ammon, Ishmael's ally (40:14).

The slaughter could not go undetected indefinitely. Someone either happened on the scene or escaped from the group and reported the matter to the other commanders. **When Johanan son of Kareah** and **the** other **army officers . . . heard about all the crimes . . . they** mobilized **all their men** and set off **to fight Ishmael.** The band of soldiers **caught up with** the slower group of captives **near the great pool in Gibeon** (cf. 2 Sam. 2:12-16). Those taken captive **were glad** when they spotted their rescuers, and in the surprise and confusion they **turned** away from Ishmael and **went over to Johanan. Ishmael** along with **8 of his men escaped** during the conflict and **fled to the Ammonites.** Two of Ishmael's 10 men must have been captured or killed (cf. Jer. 41:1).

(3) The leadership of Johanan (41:16–42:22). **41:16-18. Johanan . . . led away all the survivors** they had rescued **from Ishmael.** This group included **soldiers, women, children, and court officials.** But instead of returning to Mizpah

they went on. Their first place of rest was at **Geruth Kimham near Bethlehem,** a journey of about 13 miles from Gibeon. The group was **on** its **way to Egypt to escape the Babylonians** because **they were afraid** Babylon would retaliate for the death of **Gedaliah.**

42:1-6. Before continuing, **all the army officers,** including both **Johanan** and **Jezaniah** (called Azariah in 43:2) **son of Hoshaiah,** and **all the people** decided to ask God's guidance for their journey. They asked Jeremiah to **pray to . . . God** on their behalf. They wanted God to **tell** them **where** they **should go and what** they **should do.** They had already decided to flee Israel, but their destination remained uncertain (though 42:14 and 43:7 imply that they were already planning to go to Egypt).

Jeremiah agreed to **pray** for the people, and promised to **tell** them **everything** God said. Summoning **the LORD** as their **Witness** the people promised to **act in accordance with** whatever **God** commanded, **whether it** was **favorable or unfavorable.** After watching God destroy their nation because of disobedience they were careful to agree that they would **obey the LORD.**

42:7-12. Jeremiah prayed for the people, and **10 days later** God answered his request. Jeremiah **called together** the group and gave them God's answer. **If** they would **stay in the land,** God promised to **build** them **up.** They were **not to be afraid of the** Babylonians because God would **deliver** them from any harm **from** their **hands.** Indeed God vowed that Nebuchadnezzar would **have compassion** (*rāḥam,* "show tender concern"), a characteristic not usually associated with the Babylonians (cf. 6:23; 21:7). If the people submitted to the Babylonians, God promised that Nebuchadnezzar would **restore** them to their **land.**

42:13-18. Much like the blessings and cursings of Deuteronomy 28, Jeremiah followed his list of blessings for obedience with a list of judgments for disobedience. **If** the people refused to **stay in the land** and decided to **disobey . . . God** by going to **live in Egypt,** then they would experience God's judgment for violating their oath (Jer. 42:5-6). It is easy to understand their desire to move to **Egypt** where, in their understanding, they would no longer **see war or hear the**

trumpet announcing an impending attack (cf. 4:5, 19-21; 6:1). Also, in **Egypt** they would no longer **be hungry for bread** as they were during and after the siege of Jerusalem (cf. Lam. 1:11; 5:6, 9). Yet, warned Jeremiah, if they decided to disobey God and **settle in Egypt,** they would **die by the sword, famine,** or **plague** (cf. Jer. 14:12; 42:22). The very dangers they were wanting to avoid would come on them. No one would **escape the disaster,** and all those who left would **never see** the land of Israel **again.**

42:19-22. Jeremiah concluded his message by repeating God's command **not** to **go to Egypt.** God knew the people's hearts and warned them that they had **made a fatal mistake when** they asked Jeremiah to **pray** for them. For though they had vowed to do **everything** God said (cf. v. 6), when His word finally came they refused to obey it. Thus, Jeremiah warned them, the only thing they could **be sure** of was that they would **die by the sword, famine, and plague** (cf. v. 17) if they went to Egypt.

b. Jeremiah's ministry to the remnant in Egypt (chaps. 43–44)

(1) **The remnant's flight to Egypt (43:1-7). 43:1-3.** After **Jeremiah finished telling the people** God's answer to their request, both **Azariah** (called Jezaniah in 42:1) and **Johanan,** along with **all the arrogant men,** challenged his truthfulness. They said he was **lying** when he claimed **God** had said **not** to **go to Egypt,** and they accused **Baruch** of **inciting** Jeremiah to join a conspiracy **to hand** these former rebels **over to the Babylonians** who would then **kill** them or **carry** them **into exile.** It is not known why they singled out Baruch. But since he served as Jeremiah's confidant and companion, they might have assumed that he was responsible for Jeremiah's answer.

43:4-7. Instead of returning to Mizpah the group marched south from Geruth Kimham (41:17). In addition to **the army officers** and soldiers who had returned to Gedaliah (40:7-10) this band included **the remnant** who had returned **to Judah from all the nations** (41:11-12) and **the men, women, and children and the king's daughters** who had been entrusted to **Gedaliah.** The leaders also forced **Jeremiah** and **Baruch** to go along with them. They made their way to

Egypt and settled in **Tahpanhes,** a fortress city on the border of Lower (northern) Egypt (see the map "The World of Jeremiah and Ezekiel," in the *Introduction*).

(2) The prophecy of Nebuchadnezzar's invasion. 43:8-13. As the Jews watched, Jeremiah performed another symbolic act to gain their attention (cf. 13:1-11). He gathered **some large stones** and buried **them in clay** under **the brick pavement** that covered the large courtyard **at the entrance to Pharaoh's palace.** Since Pharaoh's main residence during this time was at Elephantine in Upper (southern) Egypt, the "palace" mentioned by Jeremiah was probably a government building that served as Pharaoh's residence when he visited the city of **Tahpanhes.**

The purpose of the **stones** was to mark the spot where **Nebuchadnezzar** would **set his throne** when God brought him to Egypt. The king of Babylon would **spread his royal canopy** over the place Jeremiah indicated when he came to **attack Egypt.** The specters of **death . . . captivity,** and **the sword** which these exiles were fleeing (cf. 42:13-17) would follow them into Egypt. Nebuchadnezzar would **set fire to the temples in Egypt** and **take** her **gods captive. He** would **wrap** up **Egypt** and carry her away captive as easily **as a shepherd wraps his garment around him.** In **the temple of the sun** (*bêṯ šemeš,* a possible reference to the city of Heliopolis, also called On), Egypt's worship was centered (see the map "The World of Jeremiah and Ezekiel," in the *Introduction*). This city that was full of **sacred pillars** (obelisks) and **temples** would be demolished.

When did Nebuchadnezzar's attack on Egypt occur? Because the Babylonian Chronicles that have been discovered go only through 594 B.C., there is a general lack of extrabiblical sources that supply any information. However, one fragmentary text has been found which implies an invasion of Egypt by Nebuchadnezzar in 568–567 B.C. This would harmonize well with the prophecy of Nebuchadnezzar's invasion of Egypt in Ezekiel 29:19. That prophecy, given on April 26, 571 B.C., indicated that the invasion was still future. Therefore Nebuchadnezzar's attack on Egypt probably occurred sometime between 571 and 567 B.C.

(3) The warning of God's judgment (chap. 44). 44:1-10. God's **word came to Jeremiah** a second time while he was in Egypt (cf. 43:8). This time the word concerned **all the Jews** who had traveled to Egypt. It applied to those in **Lower Egypt** which included the northern cities of **Migdol, Tahpanhes, and Memphis;** and it extended south to Upper **Egypt.** Jeremiah was using a figure of speech known as a merism in which, by listing the two extremes, he also included everything between them. Thus this message was for all Jews throughout the entire land of Egypt.

God reminded the Jews of the **disaster** He brought against Jerusalem and all Judah's **towns.** Their **ruins** stood as mute testimonies to God's judgment on **the evil they** had **done.** The particular sin to which God was referring was their worship of **other gods.** Though God had repeatedly warned the people through His **servants the prophets** to **turn from** their sin, they refused to **listen or pay attention.** God's **fierce anger** then **raged against . . . Judah** until only **desolate ruins** remained.

Jeremiah applied this "history lesson" to the Jews in Egypt. Instead of realizing the folly of idolatry they were **burning incense to other gods in** the land of **Egypt.** They were in danger of becoming **an object of cursing and reproach** (cf. comments on 24:9) by daring a holy God to judge them for their sin. It was as though they had **forgotten the wickedness** that both they and their ancestors had **committed** which had brought God's judgment. They had **not humbled themselves** before God or **followed** His **Law.** How quickly they seemed to have forgotten God's Word!

44:11-14. God would **bring disaster on the remnant in Egypt** for their sin just as He had the nation of **Judah. They** would **perish** by both **sword** and **famine** (cf. 42:22). This judgment would include nearly everyone. Those living **in Egypt** would experience the same judgments God used when He **punished Jerusalem.** Though these fugitives hoped to return home someday, God vowed that **none** would **return to the land of Judah.** All those who had fled to **Egypt** in violation of God's command would die there, **except** for **a few fugitives** whom God would allow to return.

44:15-19. Those who listened to Jeremiah's message refused to repent. The men, who knew that their wives were practicing idolatry, said they would continue to do everything just as they had in the past. These idolatrous practices included burning incense to the Queen of Heaven (see comments on 7:18). The widespread nature of that heathen practice is evident because it was done by the people, their ancestors (fathers), their kings, and their officials. In an ironic reversal of truth the people blamed their difficulties on their failure to continue these pagan rituals. As long as they sacrificed to the Queen of Heaven, so they said, they had plenty of food. They said that when they stopped burning incense they had nothing and began perishing by sword and famine. The people's hindsight was extremely myopic. They failed to remember that just the opposite was true in their history (cf. chap. 14; Hosea 2:5-9; Amos 4:4-12). Faithfulness and obedience to God brought blessing, and unfaithfulness and disobedience to God brought cursing (Lev. 26:1-45; Deut. 28). The women affirmed that their husbands knew (and evidently approved) of their idolatrous practices.

44:20-23. Jeremiah reminded the people that God knew about the idolatrous sacrifices that had been taking place. When He could no longer endure the sin, He judged the people and the land became an object of cursing and a desolate waste. Far from bringing blessing, Judah's worship of false gods had assured her doom. This failure to acknowledge and follow the Lord had produced the disaster in Judah which the remnant could see only too well.

44:24-28. The actions of the people revealed the sincerity of their pledge to continue worshiping the Queen of Heaven with incense and drink offerings (cf. v. 17). Since they were so determined to pursue their idolatry, God sarcastically told them to go ahead with the vows they had made to this false goddess. But as they worshiped her they were also to hear God's message of judgment. God took a solemn oath and swore by His great name that no Jew living anywhere in Egypt would ever again invoke His name or swear by Him in an oath. His judgment would pursue them till all were destroyed. Only a very few would

survive to return to Judah. They would then . . . know that only God's word would stand—a direct rebuke at their claim that idolatry brought prosperity (vv. 17-18).

44:29-30. God then gave a sign to validate the truth of His prophecy. The fulfillment of this sign would prove that God's threats of harm (cf. v. 27) against the idolatrous Jews in Egypt would stand. The sign was that Pharaoh Hophra would be handed over to his enemies . . . just as . . . Zedekiah was handed over to Nebuchadnezzar. According to historian Herodotus, Hophra lost his throne in 570 B.C. He sent Amasis, one of his generals, to quell a revolt among his army; but the army united behind Amasis and made him Pharaoh. Amasis defeated Hophra in battle and imprisoned him. Sometime later Amasis handed Hophra over to the Egyptians who were clamoring for Hophra's death, and they strangled him (Herodotus 2. 161-3, 169).

c. Jeremiah's ministry to Baruch (chap. 45)

45:1-3. This chapter was written in the fourth year of Jehoiakim (605-604 B.C.) after Baruch had recorded on a scroll the message Jeremiah was then dictating. The event in view was recorded in 36:1-8. Evidently Baruch was discouraged because of the content of the message. He felt that God had added sorrow to his pain. Much like Jeremiah earlier (cf. 8:21-9:2; 14:17-18; 15:10, 15-18), Baruch was worn out with groaning and could find no rest.

45:4-5. God's message to Baruch was intended to evoke a response of faith in the midst of judgment. God would indeed overthrow what He had built and uproot what He had planted (cf. 1:10). Baruch's discouragement came because the realities of judgment clashed with his personal aspirations of greatness. He was not to seek great things for himself because God was bringing disaster. Rather than being sad because God did not provide all he wanted, Baruch should have been thankful that God spared him. God did promise to let Baruch escape with his life despite the calamities happening all around. The response God expected of Baruch was the response of his contemporary, Habakkuk (cf. Hab. 3:16-19). The hope of a godly person in the midst of national judgment was to be fixed firmly on God. Probably Jeremiah placed this chapter last in his prophecies to Judah (Jer. 2–45) to emphasize the response that God wanted from godly Jews during the Exile.

III. Prophecies concerning the Nations (chaps. 46–51)

Jeremiah had been commissioned as a prophet to the nations (cf. 1:5; 46:1). He grouped his prophecies concerning the nation of Judah first (chaps. 2–45) because Judah was God's covenant nation and because she consumed the largest amount of Jeremiah's prophetic activity. Yet other nations did not escape his prophetic eye. If God would judge His own covenant people for their sin, how could the heathen nations around Judah hope to escape when their sin was even more pronounced? In chapters 46–51 the spotlight of God's judgment shifted from Judah to her heathen neighbors.

A. Prophecy against Egypt (chap. 46)

The first nation to be selected for judgment was Egypt, Judah's erstwhile ally. She had encouraged Judah's revolt against Babylon; but when it came time for Egypt to protect her partner in rebellion she proved incapable of meeting her commitments (cf. 37:4-10; Ezek. 29:6-7).

1. EGYPT TO BE DEFEATED AT CARCHEMISH (46:1-12)

46:1-6. Jeremiah's **message** was directed **against the army of Pharaoh Neco.** This **king of Egypt** killed King Josiah of Judah in 609 B.C. (2 Kings 23:29). **Jeremiah** penned his prophecy after the army of **Egypt** was **defeated at Carchemish** (see the map "The World of Jeremiah and Ezekiel," in the *Introduction*). This was the city **on the Euphrates River** where **Nebuchadnezzar** scored a major victory against the Egyptians. The battle took place in 605 B.C., **the fourth year of Jehoiakim.**

God sarcastically called the army of Egypt to **prepare** their **shields** and **march out for battle** against the Babylonians. **The horses** were to be harnessed and mounted, and infantry troops were to take their **positions** ready to fight. Their **spears** and **armor** were prepared, and the army of Egypt was poised for battle.

But the battle did not go Egypt's

way. Babylon's swift attack left the Egyptians **terrified** as **their warriors** were **defeated.** The panic-stricken soldiers fled **in haste.** In the ensuing confusion the fleeing soldiers hindered their own retreat so that the **swift** were not able to **flee nor** were the **strong** able to **escape.** Babylon overtook them and destroyed them. The Babylonian Chronicle confirms this picture of hopeless confusion and defeat. The Egyptian army "withdrew" before the Babylonians, but the Babylonians "overtook and defeated them so that not a single man escaped to his own country" (Donald J. Wiseman, *Chronicle of Chaldean Kings (626–556 B.C.) in the British Museum.* London: Trustees of the British Museum, 1956, pp. 67-9).

46:7-12. God asked **who** this nation was that was trying to imitate **the Nile** River with its **surging waters** that overflowed their banks and inundated the countryside. The answer was **Egypt.** She was trying to rise **like the Nile** and **cover the earth** with her conquests. The nation was trying to take on the characteristics of her life-giving river.

The surge of Egypt's armies with her **horses** and **charioteers** would resemble the rushing of a mighty river. Egypt's army contained mercenary soldiers from **Cush** (present-day southern Egypt, Sudan, and northern Ethiopia) and **Put** (modern-day Libya) who carried **shields** as infantrymen, and soldiers from **Lydia** (the west coast of Asia Minor) who were archers (drew **the bow**). Ezekiel named these same groups of mercenaries (Ezek. 30:5).

Though Egypt amassed a mighty army, the **day** of battle belonged to **the** LORD. God would bring **vengeance on** Egypt until she was destroyed. Only then would His **sword** of judgment be **satisfied.** God compared this slaughter to the offering of a **sacrifice** as He destroyed the Egyptians at Carchemish **by the River Euphrates.**

Even if the Egyptians went **to Gilead** to **get balm** for their wounds (see comments on Jer. 8:22), their **remedies** would be **in vain** because God would permit **no** healing for them. Surrounding **nations** would **hear of** Egypt's **shame** as her **cries** of anguish and pain filled **the earth.** The mighty warriors would **stumble over another** (cf. 46:6) as they would **fall down together** in defeat.

2. EGYPT TO BE INVADED AND EXILED (46:13-26)

46:13-19. Nebuchadnezzar defeated the Egyptians at Carchemish in 605 B.C., but he did not invade the land of Egypt until approximately 571–567 B.C. (see comments on 43:8-13). In this undated prophecy (46:13-26) God supplied additional details of the coming of Nebuchadnezzar . . . to attack Egypt. The warning of Nebuchadnezzar's approach was to be sounded in Migdol . . . Memphis, and Tahpanhes—the same three cities Jeremiah mentioned in 44:1 to describe Lower (northern) Egypt. This was the area where Nebuchadnezzar's forces were urged to take their positions on the fortifications and get ready.

Jeremiah asked why Egypt's warriors would be laid low (v. 15). There is a textual problem here because the Septuagint reads, "Wherefore has Apis fled. . . ?" (LXX, 26:15; the LXX has rearranged the order of several chapters in Jer. so that 46:15 in Heb. is 26:15 in Gr.) The Septuagint has divided the Hebrew verb for "laid low" (nishap) into two words (nis hap, "Haf (i.e., Apis) fled." Apis was the bull god of Egypt. The defeat of a people was often symbolized by the defeat of their god (cf. Isa. 46:1-2; Jer. 50:2; 51:44). If the Septuagint reading is accepted, then Jeremiah was pointing to the inability of Egypt's god Apis to protect them from the Lord. However, 46:15 seems to flow better if one accepts the Hebrew text's reading of verse 15a, "Why are the warriors laid low?" Jeremiah answered his own question. The warriors could not stand because God had pushed them down. As the mercenary army stumbled over one another in their effort to flee from Egypt they decided to return home to their own people and their native lands. Only by leaving Egypt could they escape the sword of the oppressor. Pharaoh Hophra had made bold claims about his ability to defeat the Babylonians, but these defeated soldiers realized now that his mighty words were only a loud noise. He could not deliver on his promises. He had already missed his opportunity to defeat Babylon.

God was sending someone to Egypt (i.e., Nebuchadnezzar) who towered above all others as Mount Tabor stood out among the mountains. This one would rise as impressively as Mount Carmel does by the sea. What Pharaoh Hophra could not accomplish, Nebuchadnezzar could. The Egyptians were to pack their belongings for exile (cf. Ezek. 29:9-16) because Nebuchadnezzar would attack Memphis (cf. Jer. 46:14) and leave it in ruins without inhabitant.

46:20-24. Jeremiah used several similes and metaphors to picture Egypt's fall to Babylon. First, he compared Egypt to a beautiful heifer. This metaphor is especially striking since Apis, one of Egypt's gods, was a bull. However, a gadfly . . . from the north (Babylon) was coming to bite her. Second, he compared the mercenaries (cf. vv. 9, 16) in Egypt's ranks of soldiers to fattened calves who had been prepared for their slaughter. They would turn and flee when the day of disaster came. Third, Jeremiah compared Egypt to a fleeing serpent that could do little more than hiss at her enemy as she slithered away to avoid the axes of these mighty woodcutters who had come to chop down her forest. Fourth, he compared the size of Babylon's army to a swarm of locusts which were too numerous to be counted. The point of every simile and metaphor was the same: Egypt would be put to shame (cf. v. 12) because God had handed her over to the people of the north.

46:25-26. God would spare neither the gods nor the kings of Egypt. He would bring punishment on Amon god of Thebes. Amon was the chief god of Thebes (or No) in Upper (southern) Egypt. Thus God's judgment which began in the north (cf. vv. 14, 19) would extend to the south. It would encompass Pharaoh, all Egypt's gods, and all the people who relied on Pharaoh. They would be handed over . . . to Nebuchadnezzar (cf. Ezek. 29:17-20). However, Egypt's destruction would not be permanent. God promised that later . . . Egypt would be inhabited as in times past. This could refer to the return of Egypt's exiles from Babylon (cf. Jer. 46:19; Ezek. 29:10-16). However, the association of Egypt's fortunes with the still-future restoration of Israel (Jer. 46:27-28) and the future focus in some of Jeremiah's other prophecies to the nations (cf. 48:47; 49:39) suggests that the ultimate fulfillment will come during the millennial reign of Christ when Egypt will again be in her land.

JEREMIAH

3. ISRAEL TO BE REGATHERED (46:27-28)

46:27-28. In contrast with Egypt, who would be taken into exile, Israel was **not** to **fear** or **be dismayed.** She could rejoice because God promised to return her people **from . . . exile.** Israel could look forward to a time when she would enjoy **peace and security.** Though she too went into exile, God vowed that He would **not completely destroy** her. A remnant would survive to again receive God's blessings (cf. 31:1-6).

B. Prophecy against Philistia (chap. 47)

47:1. Jeremiah's second prophetic broadside against the Gentile nations was directed toward **the Philistines.** Philistia occupied the coastal plain of Judah and had been a thorn in Israel's side since the time of the Conquest (cf. Jud. 3:1-4). Whenever the Philistines were strong, they tried to expand from the coastal plain into the hill country of Judah. These attempts were opposed by Shamgar (Jud. 3:31), Samson (Jud. 13-16), Samuel (1 Sam. 7:2-17), Saul (1 Sam. 13:1-14:23; 28:1-4; 29:1-2, 11; 31:1-10), and David (2 Sam. 5:17-25). David was finally able to subdue the Philistines (2 Sam. 8:1), and they remained a vassal of Israel through the reign of Solomon. During the time of the divided monarchy the balance of power shifted back and forth. Judah was in control during the reigns of Jehoshaphat (2 Chron. 17:10-11) and Uzziah, but Philistia regained dominion during the reigns of Jehoram (2 Chron. 21:16-17) and Ahaz (2 Chron. 28:16-18).

Jeremiah's message was delivered **before Pharaoh attacked Gaza.** The exact date for this event is uncertain though the two most likely times are either 609 B.C. when Pharaoh Neco marched north through Palestine to meet the Babylonians (2 Kings 23:29-30) or 601 B.C. when he defeated the armies of Babylon in a battle described only in the Babylonian Chronicle. Because of the reference to Ashkelon's still-future destruction, the 609 date is preferable. Ashkelon was destroyed by Nebuchadnezzar in late 604 B.C. (see comments on Jer. 36:9).

47:2-7. The Babylonians were pictured as **waters** that were **rising in the north.** They were about to **become an overflowing torrent** that would sweep away the Philistines. The Philistines would **cry out** in anguish as the swirl of **galloping steeds** and **enemy chariots** rushed through the land. **The people** would be so overcome by fear that **fathers** would **not** even **turn** back **to help their children.** Being destroyed, **the Philistines** would **not** be able to **help** their allies, **Tyre and Sidon** (cf. Ezek. 27-28).

The Philistines were **the remnant from the coasts of Caphtor,** that is, Crete (cf. Amos 9:7; Zeph. 2:5). They were one of the groups of sea peoples who made their way to the coast of Palestine (see the map "The World of Jeremiah and Ezekiel," in the Introduction). **Gaza** and **Ashkelon,** two of the five cities that formed the Philistine pentapolis (cf. Josh. 13:3; 1 Sam. 6:4, 18), were singled out for special mention. Gaza was attacked by the Egyptians (cf. Jer. 47:1), and Ashkelon was later destroyed by Nebuchadnezzar in November-December 604 B.C. (cf. comments on 36:9). God predicted that the Philistines would be caught in the middle of the struggle between Babylon and Egypt and would be destroyed. As a result, they were to **shave** their heads and **cut** themselves—both signs of mourning or grief (cf. comments on 16:6). God's **sword** of judgment would not **rest** till it had attacked **Ashkelon and the seacoast** and destroyed them (cf. Ezek. 25:15-17).

C. Prophecy against Moab (chap. 48)

The country of Moab was east of the Dead Sea. It was separated from Edom on the south by the Zered River and from Ammon on the north by the Arnon River. Jeremiah listed many of the Moabite cities that God would destroy. Much of the imagery used by Jeremiah was borrowed from Isaiah 16:6-12.

1. MOAB'S LAND TO BE DESTROYED (48:1-10)

48:1-5. Nebo, mentioned here by Jeremiah, was not the mountain of the same name on which Moses viewed the Promised Land and died (cf. Deut. 32:48-50). It was a city inhabited by the tribe of Reuben (cf. Num. 32:37-38) that was later captured by Moab. The city of **Kiriathaim** was also inhabited by the tribe of Reuben (Josh. 13:19) and later captured by Moab. God was now predicting that it would be **captured** from **Moab** by others. **The stronghold** could be translated "Misgab" (NIV marg.) and might refer to an as-yet unknown city or fortress that was **shat-**

182

tered by these invaders. Heshbon was the capital of Sihon, king of the Amorites, during the Exodus (Num. 21:25-30). It was given to the tribe of Reuben that rebuilt it (Num. 32:37; Josh. 13:17), though it was on the border of the tribe of Gad (Josh. 13:26). The Moabite Stone (now in the British Museum, London) implies that Heshbon was later occupied by individuals from the tribe of Gad. It was eventually taken by Moab. In a play on words Jeremiah indicated that in Heshbon (*b^eḥešbôn*) men will plot (*ḥāšbû*) Moab's downfall.

Jeremiah then described God's judgment on the town of Madmen which would be silenced. The cries from Horonaim (cf. 2 Sam. 13:34) would reverberate throughout the hills of Moab as the fugitives who fled up the way to Luhith wept bitterly and those traveling down to Horonaim shouted anguished cries over the destruction that confronted them.

48:6-10. The people of Moab would flee and run for their lives to escape the coming judgment. They would become like a bush in the desert—deserted and forlorn. It is possible to translate "like a bush" as "like Aroer" (*ka'ārô'ēr*), a city on the edge of the Arnon River gorge (cf. Deut. 2:36). The thought would be the same—the people of Moab would be like a deserted and forlorn city or a bush in the wilderness. Because Moab had trusted in her deeds and riches she too would be judged by being taken captive as was Judah. Her national god, Chemosh (cf. 1 Kings 11:7), would not be able to rescue her. Instead, he also would go into exile along with his priests and officials.

God's destruction would come on every town. The valley could refer to the many valleys in which the people lived, or it could refer to the Jordan Valley on Moab's western border. The plateau was the Transjordan highland where most of the cities of Moab were located. Moab's enemies would put salt on her land—a sign of destruction intended to show that the land was laid waste (cf. Jud. 9:45). God was so determined to assure Moab's destruction that He threatened to curse those nations appointed to destroy Moab who were lax in doing his work. These destroyers are not named, but Moab was destroyed by nomadic desert tribesmen from the East (cf. Ezek. 25:10).

2. MOAB'S COMPLACENCY TO BE SHATTERED (48:11-17)

48:11-13. Moab's history was one of relative peace. She had been at rest from her youth. Jeremiah compared her to wine left on its dregs that had not been poured from one jar to another. In making wine, first the grapes were stomped, then the juice was placed into bottles or skins and allowed to ferment. During this time the sediment, or dregs, would settle to the bottom. After 40 days the fermented wine was carefully poured into another container to separate it from the dregs. If the dregs were allowed to remain, the wine became too sweet and thick and was spoiled. This object lesson from nature was ultimately applied to people who had become too complacent (cf. Zeph. 1:12). Moab had never felt the harsh reality of exile so, like the unpoured wine, her aroma was unchanged.

God vowed that days were coming (cf. comments on Jer. 31:27), however, when He would arouse Moab from her complacency. He would send men to pour her out as wine that was no longer fit to drink. At that time Moab would be ashamed of Chemosh (cf. 48:7) just as Israel was ashamed when she had trusted in Bethel. Bethel was where one of the two golden calves was set up in the Northern Kingdom (cf. 1 Kings 12:26-30). Israel found out too late that her trust in the false god at Bethel could not prevent her destruction and deportation. Moab would learn the same lesson regarding her god.

48:14-17. Moab felt confident in her warriors who were valiant in battle. But these men would not be able to prevent her destruction. In fact they would go down in the slaughter which was at hand. Moab's calamity would come quickly. Jeremiah called for those nations surrounding Moab to come and console her at the time of her destruction. Together they could mourn the fact that her scepter (signifying her rule) had been broken.

3. MOAB'S CITIES TO EXPERIENCE CATASTROPHE (48:18-28)

48:18-25. The mighty city of Dibon was to humble herself because God vowed to come up against her. Those living in the remote city of Aroer (cf. comments on v. 6) were to stand by the road and ask the people fleeing past what had happened. They would be told that Moab had been disgraced and shattered. News of her fall would cause mourning even as far south as Aroer, by the Arnon River.

Jeremiah listed the cities of the Transjordan plateau that would be destroyed. Though the location of some is not certain, he seemed to follow a general movement from north to south. His point in naming these 11 cities was to show that all the towns of Moab, both far and near, would be destroyed.

Jeremiah used two symbols to show that Moab's power would be broken. First, he said Moab's horn would be cut off. An animal horn was a symbol of strength (cf. 1 Sam. 2:1, 10; Pss. 75:4-5; 89:17, 24; Micah 4:13; Zech. 1:19-21). Second, he said that Moab's arm, also a symbol of strength, would be broken (cf. comments on Ezek. 30:20-26).

48:26-28. Jeremiah pictured Moab's impending doom as someone becoming drunk (cf. 25:15-29). Because Moab had defied the LORD she would now wallow in her vomit and be ridiculed by others. She that had once treated Israel with the contempt of one caught among thieves would now experience the same scorn directed at her. She would be forced to abandon her towns and dwell among the rocks to hide from the invaders who sought her life.

4. MOAB'S PRIDE TO CEASE (48:29-39)

48:29-33. Moab's chief problem was her pride (cf. Isa. 16:6). Her physical security and history of relative peace had fed her arrogance. Unfortunately her insolence and boasts could do nothing to prevent her destruction. God expressed His concern for Moab as He mourned for Kir Hareseth (cf. Isa. 16:7, 11), another of her chief cities. Borrowing from Isaiah 16:9, Jeremiah indicated that God would weep along with the city of Jazer for the vines of Sibmah which had been destroyed. The country of Moab was known for its vineyards, and Jeremiah expanded the image to picture all Moab as a vineyard. Her branches had spread as far as the Dead Sea, but now the destroyer had fallen on her ripened fruit and grapes. Moab would be "harvested" much as a vine is plucked of its fruit. Orchards and fields would be devoid of

happiness, and the flow of wine from the presses would cease. When destruction came there would be shouts (cf. Jer. 48:3-5) but they would not be shouts of joy like those heard before.

48:34-39. The cries of Moab's mourners extended from Heshbon . . . Elealeh, and Jahaz in the northern part of the country to Zoar . . . Horonaim . . . Eglath Shelishiyah, and the waters of Nimrim in the southern part of the country. From north to south the land would be devastated. God would put an end to idolatrous practices at Moab's many high places where offerings were being made to their gods.

God raised a cry of lament for Moab that sounded like the high-pitched sound of a flute. The wealth that Moab had acquired was gone, and the people mourned their loss (cf. comments on 47:5). The once-proud country had become an object of ridicule and horror, that is, people mocked Moab and were also horrified at her desolate condition (cf. comments on 24:9).

5. MOAB'S DESTRUCTION TO BE COMPLETE (48:40-47)

48:40-44. Moab's enemies were like an eagle that would be swooping down and spreading its wings over her to seize her in its claws. The Moabites would be captured, and the warriors she depended on for protection (cf. v. 14) would be as fearful as a woman in labor (cf. 49:24; 50:43). Jeremiah repeated parts of 48:40-41 in 49:22 where he applied the message to Edom.

Lest Moab think her captivity was just accidental, God reminded her that her destruction would come because she defied Him. In view of her rebellion, none would escape; those who would try to flee God's terror would fall into a pit. Any who managed to get out of the pit would be caught in a snare (cf. Amos 5:18-20). God would make sure that all in Moab would take part in the year of her punishment.

48:45-47. Jeremiah ended his section on Moab by freely quoting an old song from Heshbon (cf. Num. 21:27-29). The fugitives who had escaped the destruction stood by helpless because God's fire of judgment had gone out into all Moab to burn those who had been boasters. Now the nation was destroyed, with her sons and daughters in captivity. Historically the people of Moab lost their national identity when they were overrun by the Arabians from the East (cf. Ezek. 25:10). Yet God still offered hope to Moab. He vowed to **restore the fortunes of Moab in days to come**. The use of "days to come" would imply that this restoration will occur during the millennial reign of Christ (cf. Deut. 4:30; Jer. 49:39; Dan. 2:28; 10:14).

D. Prophecy against Ammon (49:1-6)

The Ammonites were located east of the Jordan River and north of Moab. They were allied with Judah against Babylon during Judah's final revolt, but throughout the history of both nations they had been in conflict (see comments on 40:14).

49:1-3. By asking four questions (though questions one and two are parallel and three and four are parallel) Jeremiah focused on Ammon's main problem. The Northern Kingdom of Israel had been taken captive in 722 B.C.; and Ammon, assuming **Israel** had **no sons** or **heirs** who would return to the land, seized it for herself. **Molech** (which could be translated "their king"; cf. NIV marg.) was the national god of Ammon that had found its way into Judah (cf. 32:35). Ammon had **taken possession of** the territory belonging to the Israelite tribe of **Gad,** and Ammonites were living in **its towns**.

God announced that **days** were **coming** (cf. comments on 31:27) **when** an enemy would attack Ammon's capital city of **Rabbah**. Rabbah would **become** nothing but **ruins,** and Israel would **drive out** the Ammonites who had settled in her villages. **Heshbon,** on the border between Moab and Ammon, was controlled by different countries at different periods of time (cf. Jud. 11:12, 26; Jer. 48:34, 45). This **Ai** was not the city by the same name in Israel (cf. Josh. 7:2). It was a city in Ammon whose location is not known today. The people of **Rabbah** would **put on sackcloth** (see comments on Jer. 4:8) **and mourn** (cf. 48:37) because their god **Molech** (or their king; cf. comments on 49:1) would **go into exile**.

49:4-6. Ammon's problem, like that of Moab, was pride (cf. 48:29). Ammon boasted of her **valleys** that were **so fruitful**. She trusted in her **riches** and felt secure enough to question **who** would have the courage to **attack** her (cf. Ezek. 21:18-23). But God's judgment would shatter Ammon's complacency and pride when He brought His **terror on** her. Those who had been boasting of their security would be **driven away,** and **no** leader would be found to **gather the fugitives** to return and repossess their land. Yet in His grace God vowed that **afterward** He would **restore the fortunes of the Ammonites** (cf. Jer. 48:47; 49:39).

E. Prophecy against Edom (49:7-22)

The country of Edom was located south of Moab and east of the Dead Sea. It had a history of conflict with Judah and came to symbolize all the heathen nations that sought Judah's harm (cf. Ezek. 35; 36:5; Obad. 15-16). Much of the imagery Jeremiah used to describe Edom was seemingly borrowed from Obadiah, though there is considerable debate on when the Book of Obadiah was written (see comments under "Date" in the *Introduction* to Obad.).

49:7-13. The association of **wisdom** with the men of **Teman** was as old as the Book of Job which spoke of Eliphaz the Temanite (cf. Job 2:11). In fact all of **Edom** was known for its wise men (cf. Obad. 8). Teman was in central Edom about three miles from Sela, later known as Petra. **Dedan,** a city in the northern part of the Arabian peninsula southeast of Edom, was known for its trading (cf. Jer. 25:23; Ezek. 25:13). Those Dedanites living in Edom were warned to **turn and flee** from the **disaster** God was about to bring on Edom. Two images were used to show the thoroughness of God's judgment. His judgment would be more thorough than **grape pickers** who at least **leave a few grapes** on the vine when they are done (cf. Obad. 5c; Deut. 24:21). God's judgment would also be more thorough than **thieves . . . during the night** who **steal only as much as they** want (cf. Obad. 5). Even a thief leaves something behind, but God would **strip** Esau (Edom) **bare.** Only the helpless **orphans** and **widows** would be spared by God.

Edom had to be judged because of her many crimes. If God made **those who do not deserve to drink the cup** of His wrath (i.e., those nations "unrelated" to Judah who boasted over her fall) **drink it** (cf. Jer. 25:15-29) how could a nation with

185

close fraternal ties such as Edom's (cf. Deut. 23:7) hope to **go unpunished?** Sin against one's brother was a heinous crime. If nations unrelated to Judah were to be punished for their mistreatment of her, then nations closely related to Judah deserved greater condemnation (cf. Obad. 10). God would make the city of **Bozrah** in northern Edom **a ruin and an object of horror** (cf. comments on Jer. 24:9).

49:14-18. Borrowing language from international diplomacy used earlier by Obadiah (Obad. 1), Jeremiah pictured God sending **an envoy** to His allies among **the nations** asking them to **assemble** for an **attack** on Edom. Edom would become **small among the nations** and **despised** as God reduced her prestige and power (cf. Obad. 2). Edom's **pride** in her strong natural defenses made her feel secure, but God would **bring** her **down** (cf. Obad. 4) from her lofty perch and people would be horrified at her condition (cf. Jer. 49:13 and comments on 24:9). Edom would be destroyed **as** were **Sodom and Gomorrah** (cf. 50:40) so that no one would **dwell** there.

49:19-22. God would be as fierce as **a lion** when He rose up to **chase Edom from its land.** No one would be able to **challenge** God nor could a **shepherd . . . stand against** Him. The use of "shepherd" both continued the image of a shepherd trying to protect sheep from a marauding lion (cf. 1 Sam. 17:34-35) and implied God's judgment on the king who was the "shepherd" of the nation (cf. Jer. 23:1-4). God vowed to drag away **the young of the flock** and **destroy** the **pasture** of Edom. The **cry** of destruction would carry **to the Red** (Reed) **Sea**—the site of God's first destruction of a nation that threatened His Chosen People (cf. Ex. 14:21-31). God's prophet repeated (with slight modifications) Jeremiah 49:19-21 in 50:44-46 and applied the message to Babylon. Using an image He had earlier applied to Moab (48:40-41) God indicated that like **an eagle** He would **swoop down** in judgment **over Bozrah** in northern Edom. The **hearts of** the **warriors** on which Edom depended would be as afraid as **the heart of a woman in labor** (cf. 48:41; 49:24; 50:43). They would not be able to stop God's destruction.

Two points of interest may be noted. First, unlike Egypt, Moab, and Ammon (cf. 46:26; 48:47; 49:6), Edom was given no promise of future restoration. Second, this prophecy was fulfilled in the intertestamental period when desert tribesmen called the Nabateans drove the Edomites from their land. The people of Edom were forced to migrate into southern Judah where they were called Idumeans. In 125 B.C. John Hyrcanus I, a Maccabean, subjugated the Idumeans and made them accept Judaism (Josephus *Antiquities* 13. 9. 1; 15. 4). The Edomites thus ceased to be a distinct national group.

F. Prophecy against Damascus (49:23-27)

49:23-27. Three of the major cities of Syria—**Hamath . . . Arpad,** and **Damascus** (see the map "The World of Jeremiah and Ezekiel," in the *Introduction*)—were **dismayed** because of the **bad news** of Babylon's advance. Damascus' **pain** was **like that of a woman in labor** (cf. comments on 4:31). In Nebuchadnezzar's attack on Damascus the **soldiers** of Damascus were **silenced** (i.e., killed) and her fortifications burned (cf. Amos 1:4). God vowed to **consume the fortresses of Ben-Hadad.** "Ben-Hadad" (lit., "son of [the god] Hadad") was the name of the dynasty that ruled in Damascus in the ninth and eighth centuries B.C. (cf. 1 Kings 15:18, 20; 20:1-34; 2 Kings 6:24; 8:7; 13:3, 24; and see the chart "Kings of Aram in 1 and 2 Kings," near 1 Kings 11:23-25).

G. Prophecy against Kedar and Hazor (49:28-33)

Kedar was a nomadic tribe of Ishmaelites (cf. Gen. 25:13) in the Arabian desert known for her skills in archery (Isa. 21:16-17), her flocks of sheep (Isa. 60:7; Jer. 49:28-29), her extensive trade (Ezek. 27:21), and her warlike nature (Ps. 120:5-6). "The kingdoms of Hazor" do not refer to the city of Hazor in Israel just north of the Sea of Galilee. Rather it was some as-yet unknown place in the Arabian desert. Jeremiah 49:28b-29 seems to picture Nebuchadnezzar's destruction of Kedar, and verses 30-33 view his destruction of Hazor.

49:28-29. God summoned **Nebuchadnezzar** to **attack Kedar,** destroying **their** black, goat-hair **tents** (cf. Song 1:5) and seizing **their flocks** along **with all their goods and camels.** Then these nomads would experience **terror on every side.**

49:30-33. The people of **Hazor** were urged to **flee** and hide **in deep caves** because **Nebuchadnezzar** had plotted to go **against** them in battle. As God had done against Kedar (v. 28), so here He summoned Nebuchadnezzar to **arise and attack** Hazor. These Arabian people felt so secure in their remote desert location that they did not even have city **gates** or **bars** to protect against attack. Nebuchadnezzar would take **their camels** (cf. v. 29) **and their large herds** as booty. The inhabitants would be scattered **to the winds** and the city itself would **become a haunt of jackals . . . forever**—a symbol of desolation (cf. 9:11; 10:22; 51:37 for Jeremiah's other uses of this phrase).

H. Prophecy against Elam (49:34-39)

49:34-39. Elam was east of Babylon in what is today the country of Iran (see the map "The World of Jeremiah and Ezekiel," in the *Introduction*). This prophecy was given **early in the reign of Zedekiah,** about 597 B.C. God promised to **break the bow of Elam** which He called **the mainstay of their might.** This is significant because the Elamites were known for their archery skills (cf. Isa. 22:6). Her invaders would come from all directions (**the four winds** and **the four quarters of the heavens**) and would **scatter . . . Elam's exiles** throughout the earth.

Though there is some evidence that Nebuchadnezzar defeated the Elamites about 596 B.C., his subjugation at that time did not fulfill this message. Elam became a central part of the Persian Empire that later conquered Babylon (cf. Dan. 8:2). Jeremiah's statement about Elam's destruction seems to take on eschatological dimensions as God said He would **set** His **throne in Elam** to supervise her destruction. Yet Elam's destruction will not be total because God will **restore** her **fortunes . . . in days to come** (cf. Jer. 48:47; 49:6).

I. Prophecy against Babylon (chaps. 50–51)

1. THE ANNOUNCEMENT OF JUDGMENT (50:1-10)

50:1-5. Jeremiah was commanded to **announce** to **the nations** the public humiliation of **Babylon.** She would **be cap-**

tured and her protecting god **Bel** (cf. 51:44; Isa. 46:1; the storm god Enlil), also known as **Marduk,** the chief deity of Babylon, would, figuratively speaking, **be put to shame** (cf. Jer. 46:24) and **filled with terror** because of his inability to protect her. Babylon would be destroyed by **a nation from the north** (cf. 50:9). Many see this as a reference to Babylon's fall to the Medo-Persian Empire, but several points do not fit historically. First, the Persians were from the east of Babylon, not from the north. Second, when Cyrus took Babylon he did not **lay waste her land** or destroy the city so that **no one** would **live in it.** Several times Jeremiah repeated this fact about Babylon being without any inhabitants (cf. vv. 39b-40; 51:29, 37, 43, 62). The city was spared and made one of the ruling centers for the Persian Empire with Daniel serving there in an administrative position (cf. Dan. 5:30; 6:1-3). Third, no one fled the city when it fell to Medo-Persia. In fact Daniel, who had access to Jeremiah's prophecies (cf. Dan. 9:1-2), remained in the city during and after its fall (cf. Dan. 5:28, 30-31; 6:1-3). Fourth, the promise that **in those days** and **at that time . . . the people of Israel** and **Judah** would again unite as a nation, return **to Zion,** and **bind themselves to** God **in an everlasting covenant** (cf. Jer. 31:31; 32:40) was not fulfilled after Babylon's fall in 539 B.C.

Jeremiah's prophecy looked beyond the destruction of Babylon in 539 to an eschatological destruction that will reverse the fortunes of Israel and Judah. Possibly this prophecy represents a blending of the near and the far. That is, the fall of Babylon and the return of the captives under Zerubbabel merged in the prophetic picture with the still-future destruction of Babylon and the final restoration of Israel and Judah. The destruction of Babylon will be the climax of God's judgment on the Gentile powers that have oppressed His people and will open the way for the fulfilling of God's promises to Israel. Other portions of Scripture also point to this still-future rebuilding of Israel and destruction of Babylon (cf. Zech. 5:5-11; Rev. 17–18). The city of Babylon will be rebuilt only to be destroyed at the end of the Tribulation period before Christ returns to establish His millennial reign.

50:6-10. Verses 6-7 are an editorial

comment on the restoration of Israel and Judah, announced in verses 4-5. Israel and Judah will need to be restored because they **have been lost sheep** wandering **over mountain and hill** (cf. 23:1-2; Ezek. 36:5-6). They have been **devoured** by **their enemies** because they have **sinned against** God. God summoned His sheep to **flee out of Babylon** because of the **alliance of great nations** coming **from the . . . North** (cf. comments on Jer. 50:3) against her to **plunder her.**

2. THE FALL OF BABYLON (50:11-16)

50:11-13. Babylon sinned in proudly destroying Judah. God will judge any nation that can **rejoice and** be **glad** as it pillages His **inheritance** (cf. comments on Deut. 4:20), frolicking **like a heifer** and neighing **like stallions.** He vowed to disgrace Babylon by making it **a desert** uninhabited, and **completely desolate.** The once-great city will be so thoroughly destroyed that **all who pass** by **will be horrified and scoff** (cf. Lam. 2:15) at **her wounds** (i.e., her physical devastation; cf. comments on Jer. 6:14).

50:14-16. The battle was graphically portrayed as the enemy taking their **positions around** the city and shooting their **arrows** at her defenders. When the city finally **surrenders,** her **towers and walls** will be **torn down** and God's **vengeance** will be poured out **on** those who remain. Because of this coming **sword** God warned the foreigners living in Babylon to **flee to** their **own land.** Again, this scene was not fulfilled when Cyrus attacked Babylon in 539 B.C. It awaits a future fulfillment.

3. THE RESTORATION OF ISRAEL (50:17-20)

50:17-20. Israel, here representing both the Northern and Southern Kingdoms, had become like **scattered** sheep (cf. vv. 6-7). The Northern Kingdom had been conquered by **Assyria** in 722 B.C., and the Southern Kingdom was crushed by **Babylon** in 586 B.C. **God** vowed to reverse the situation. He will **punish the** kings of **Babylon** and **Assyria** for their destruction of His people, **but** He **will bring Israel back to** her land. The majestic summit of **Carmel** and the fertile plains of **Bashan** east of the Sea of Kinnereth (Galilee; see the map "The World of Jeremiah and Ezekiel," in the *Introduction*) will once again belong to

Israel as will **the hills of Ephraim and Gilead** on the western and eastern banks of the Jordan River. (Cf. Bashan and Gilead in Micah 7:14.) For the second time in this chapter (cf. Jer. 50:4) God indicated that **in those days** and **at that time** He will also bring about a spiritual renewal within His people. Though some will **search** for **Israel's guilt** and **the sins of Judah,** they will not find any because God **will forgive** His **remnant** (cf. comments on 31:31-34).

4. THE ATTACK ON BABYLON (50:21-40)

50:21-28. Using two wordplays, God ordered the **attack** on **the land of Merathaim and** on the people **in Pekod.** "Merathaim" was the region of *Mat Marratim* in southern Babylon where the Tigris and Euphrates Rivers enter the Persian Gulf. However, the word in Hebrew ($m^e r\bar{a}tayim$) means "double rebellion." "Pekod" referred to an Aramean tribe (*Pequdu*) in southern Babylon on the east bank of the Tigris River; but the word in Hebrew ($p^e q\hat{o}d$) means "to punish" or "punishment." Thus God was saying He would attack the land of double rebellion and inflict His punishment on it.

The **noise of battle** signaled the **destruction** of **Babylon.** She who like a **hammer** had been shattering others would find herself **broken and shattered.** God spoke of Himself as a hunter to indicate that He had **set a trap** in which **Babylon** unknowingly found herself **caught.** He then referred to Himself as a warrior to show that He was bringing **out** His **weapons of . . . wrath** against her.

Babylon's enemies would **come . . . from afar** to **break** her **open** as one would break open **granaries.** The bodies of her slain inhabitants would be piled up **like heaps of grain,** and her soldiers (the **young bulls**) would be slaughtered. Those **fugitives and refugees** who had escaped (cf. vv. 8, 16) would travel to **Zion** and declare there that Babylon's destruction was God's **vengeance** for her destruction of **His temple** (cf. 52:13).

50:29-32. Archers were summoned to **encamp . . . around** Babylon to insure that **no one** would **escape.** The city had to be destroyed because **she** had **defied the LORD** with her haughtiness. Verse 30 is almost identical to 49:26 where Jeremiah applied the same message to Damascus. God emphasized Babylon's haughtiness by calling her the **arrogant one** (50:31-32). She would **be punished** for her pride as God vowed to **kindle a fire** that would **consume** her (cf. 15:14; Lam. 4:11; Amos 1:4, 7, 10, 12, 14; 2:2, 5).

50:33-34. The people of Israel and Judah were being held by **captors** who refused **to let them go.** How were they then to return to their own land? (vv. 4-5, 8, 19) The answer was that **their Redeemer,** none other than **the LORD Almighty,** would guarantee their return. He vowed to **defend their cause** by giving them rest in **their** own **land** while giving **unrest** (i.e., judgment) **to those** living **in Babylon.**

50:35-38. The threat of "unrest" (v. 34) was explained in verses 35-38 as God's bringing of **a sword against. . . . Babylon.** The word **a sword** (ḥereḇ) is used five times, and is followed by the announcement of **a drought** (ḥōreḇ) in verse 38. This **sword** of judgment will be directed **against** the **officials and wise men,** the **false prophets,** and the **warriors.** It will also be used against the **horses . . . chariots,** and **foreigners** serving as mercenaries **in** Babylon's **ranks.** The **sword** of judgment will even attack **her treasures** which **will be plundered.** Also **her waters . . . will dry up;** Babylon will become poor and unproductive.

50:39-40. The bustling metropolis of Babylon, Jeremiah said, will become a deserted wilderness where **desert creatures . . . hyenas,** and owls will live. After this destruction Babylon will **never again be inhabited** (cf. comments on v. 3); her desolation will be as complete as that of **Sodom and Gomorrah** (cf. 49:18). This prediction has not yet been fulfilled. Babylon has been inhabited throughout her history, and the government of Iraq has begun restoring some portions of the ancient city. Iraq's plans to restore Babylon are published in a pamphlet, *Archaeological Survival of Babylon Is a Patriotic, National, and International Duty* (Baghdad: State Organization of Antiquities and Heritage, 1982). The prophecy about Babylon's complete ruin awaits a future fulfillment during the Tribulation period.

5. THE ANGUISH OF BABYLON (50:41-46)

50:41-46. God told Babylon to **look** at the **army** which will come **from the north** (cf. v. 3). It will not be the ill-equipped army of some vassal state trying to attack the might of Babylon. This army will come **from the ends of the earth. . . . armed with bows and spears** to attack. The character of this invading army will match that of the Babylonians (cf. 6:23). They will be **cruel and without mercy,** and the noise of the throng as it gallops to attack will **sound like the roaring sea.**

The **reports about** this approaching army will bring **anguish to the king of Babylon.** He will be as fearful as **a woman in labor** (cf. comments on 4:31). Jeremiah ended this section by applying to Babylon (50:44-46) the same judgment that he had earlier applied to Edom (49:19-21). **Like a lion** viciously and suddenly (**in an instant**) attacking lambs, God will attack **Babylon** (cf. 51:40). The rest of the world will **tremble** at His judgment of **Babylon.**

6. GOD'S VENGEANCE AGAINST BABYLON (51:1-14)

51:1-10. God will **stir up . . . a destroyer** and bring him **against Babylon** and **Leb Kamai.** "Leb Kamai" (lēḇ qāmāy) means "heart of my adversaries" but the expression is an *atbash* (see comments on 25:26) for Chaldea. The consonants for "heart of my adversary" (lbqmy), when reversed in the Hebrew alphabet, spell Chaldea (ksdym). **Foreigners** sent by God **to devastate her** will **completely destroy** Babylon's **army.**

God will destroy Babylon so that **Israel and Judah** will be free to return home (cf. 50:33-34). God called to His people to **flee from Babylon** to avoid being **destroyed** (cf. Rev. 18:4). **Babylon** had been God's **gold cup** of judgment from which He **made the whole earth** drink (cf. Jer. 25:15-29; Rev. 17:3-4; 18:6). However, **Babylon will** feel the sting of judgment. As she **suddenly** falls, her allies will try to find **balm for her pain** (cf. Jer. 8:22; 46:11) but they will search in vain for ways to heal her. She will not **be healed** so her allies will desert her to avoid the effects of **her judgment.** God's people, knowing that He **has vindicated** them, will raise a declarative song of praise in the temple **in Zion** to recount what He **has done.**

51:11-14. In an almost repetitive manner Jeremiah described the preparations of the armies poised to attack **Babylon.** This time he identified the attackers as **the kings of the Medes** (cf. v. 28). This could allude to the fall of Babylon in 539 B.C. to the Medo-Persians (cf. Dan. 5:31) or, more probably, it could indicate that one of the future kings who will invade Babylon will come from the area controlled by the Medes (i.e., what is today northern Iran). God will summon this army to **take vengeance** on **Babylon** for her having destroyed **His temple** (cf. 50:28). God **will carry out His purpose** to destroy the Babylonians (**who live by many waters;** i.e., near the Euphrates River) because He has taken an oath (**sworn by Himself**) that these invaders will completely cover **Babylon** like **a swarm of locusts** (cf. 51:27). God will personally assure Babylon's fall.

7. GOD'S SOVEREIGNTY OVER BABYLON (51:15-26)

51:15-19. Using language that is virtually synonymous with 10:12-16 (cf. comments there), Jeremiah stressed the sovereignty and power of the God who was guaranteeing Babylon's fall. God's **power** and **wisdom** were demonstrated in His Creation of the universe. Another visible demonstration of God's power is His control over a thunderstorm. In beautiful poetic language Jeremiah pictured the **clouds** with the **lightning** . . . **rain,** and **wind** as visible reminders of God's authority. In sorry contrast were the man-made **idols** (cf. comments on 2:5) that had **no breath in them.** Men made idols, but **the Portion of Jacob** (i.e., God, who in a sense is allotted to Israel; cf. 10:16) **is the Maker of all things, including** His Chosen People, **His inheritance** (cf. comments on Deut. 4:20).

51:20-26. Babylon had been God's **war club** used to **shatter** other **nations.** Jeremiah used the word **I shatter** nine times in verses 20-23 to indicate the extent to which God had used Babylon for judgment. (The form of the verb *nāpaṣ* means "to shatter to pieces.") Now, however, He said He will **repay Babylon** for **the wrong they** had **done in Zion.** God, being against the **mountain** (a symbol for a kingdom; cf. Dan. 2:35, 44-45) of Babylon, will make it **a burned-out mountain.** The judgment will be so complete that people will not even loot the ruins to find **a cornerstone** or a **stone for a foundation** to rebuild elsewhere. The ruins will lie **desolate forever.**

8. THE SUMMONS TO THE NATIONS AGAINST BABYLON (51:27-33)

51:27-33. For the third time God summoned the nations to **lift up** their **banner** and rally their troops **against** Babylon (cf. 50:2; 51:12). In addition to **the Medes,** mentioned both here (v. 28) and earlier (cf. v. 11), this invasion force will include the **kingdoms of Ararat, Minni, and Ashkenaz** (see the map "The World of Jeremiah and Ezekiel," in the *Introduction*). Ararat was located in present-day Armenia near Lake Van. Minni was located south of Lake Urmia in what is today western Iran, and Ashkenaz was located near Lake Urmia and Ararat. The people in all three areas were warlike.

God will send these invaders to accomplish His **purposes against Babylon,** namely, **to lay waste the land** and to remove its people (cf. comments on 50:3). Instead of offering resistance, the **warriors** of Babylon will stop **fighting** and withdraw to **their strongholds** (fortresses) for protection. The invaders will press their attack by setting Babylon's **dwellings . . . on fire.** Finally the **bars of her gates** holding out the attackers will be **broken.** Messengers will rush from the various quarters of the city **to announce to the** leader that the **entire city is captured.**

God then compared **Babylon** to a **threshing floor.** When an area for threshing was **trampled** down to prepare it for threshing and winnowing, then the people knew that **the time to harvest** would **soon come.** Likewise when the city of Babylon will be trampled down by these invaders, then the people will know that God's harvest of judgment has arrived.

9. GOD'S REVENGE ON BABYLON (51:34-44)

51:34-35. Jeremiah presented the complaint of the Jews against **Babylon.** Babylon had **devoured** them and set them aside like **an empty jar.** Or Nebuchadnezzar . . . **like a serpent,** had **swallowed** Judah whole. When **Babylon** was finished, she would vomit **out** the remains of the captives (i.e., release the exiles from captivity). The Jews called for God to act and to avenge **the violence** done to them. They wanted the **blood** (i.e., the guiltiness for their shed blood) to be required of **those who live in Babylonia.**

51:36-44. God answered Jerusalem's

request and vowed to **avenge** Judah. He will make **Babylon . . . a heap of ruins** and **a place where no one lives** (cf. comments on 50:3). And she will be scorned (cf. comments on 24:9). The Babylonians were fierce **like young lions. But** God **will** prepare **a feast for them to make them drunk.** As they drink from His cup of judgment they will fall asleep and never wake up (cf. 51:57). Using another figure, God compared the Babylonians to **lambs** (cf. 50:45) being led **to the slaughter.**

Sheshach was an *atbash* for Babylon (see comments on Sheshach in 25:26; also cf. 51:1). Babylon **will be captured** and destroyed. She will disappear as if **the sea** had risen **over** her to **cover her.** Or, to change images, **her towns will** become **desolate** (cf. comments on 50:3) like a **desert.** Swallowed by the sea or scorched by the sun, Jeremiah's point was that **Babylon** will be destroyed. God will **punish Bel,** a god of Babylon (cf. 50:2), by making **him spew out** the wealth he had **swallowed**—a direct answer to the complaint of the captives (51:34).

10. THE WARNING TO THE REMNANT IN BABYLON (51:45-48)

51:45-48. God ordered His people to **run for** their **lives** from **Babylon** to escape His **fierce anger.** They were not to **be afraid** of the many **rumors of** victory or **violence** floating through **the land.** Instead they were to remain confident that God **will surely** judge **Babylon.** At that time **heaven and earth . . . will shout for joy over** God's victory (cf. Rev. 18:20).

11. THE CERTAINTY OF BABYLON'S FALL (51:49-53)

51:49-50. God had ordained that **Babylon must fall because** she was responsible for killing many Israelites. God's promise to Abraham that those who cursed him would themselves be cursed (Gen. 12:2-3) was now applied to **Babylon.** When the Israelites escape from the future destruction of Babylon they should **not linger.** Instead they should **remember the L**ORD and **think on Jerusalem.** Babylon's destruction will be the catalyst God uses to bring the Jews home.

51:51-53. As the remnant still in exile thought of Jerusalem, they were **dis-**graced . . . insulted, and** full of **shame** because they remembered that **foreigners** had **entered the holy places of the** temple and desecrated it. God comforted these exiles by assuring them that **days are coming** when He **will** destroy Babylon's **idols** (cf. vv. 44, 47). No matter how exalted Babylon's position became or how much energy she devoted to fortifying her defenses, God still vowed to **send destroyers** (cf. v. 48) **against her** who would wipe her out.

12. GOD'S REPAYMENT OF BABYLON (51:54-58)

51:54-58. A sound of great destruction will be heard **from the land of** Babylon. The sound will come from **waves of** enemy soldiers attacking the city, the **roar of their voices** sounding forth over the other sounds of battle. These invaders will capture Babylon's **warriors** and destroy her military power (her **bows will be broken**). Every class of **officials** in **Babylon** will be forced to drink God's wine of judgment (cf. 25:15-29; 51:7-8) which will cause them to **sleep forever and not awake** (cf. v. 39). Again such wholesale destruction of Babylon's leaders and warriors did not occur when Babylon fell to Medo-Persia (cf. Dan. 5:29–6:2). It still awaits God's future fulfillment.

Jeremiah ended this message about Babylon's future fall by quoting a proverb (Jer. 51:58; also in Hab. 2:13) to show the futility of Babylon's attempts to resist God's judgment. Since God had already announced that **Babylon's . . . wall will be leveled and her . . . gates set on fire** (cf. Jer. 50:15; 51:30), any **labor** expended to prevent His judgment and shore up the defenses will only provide more **fuel** to feed **the flames** when they will finally come.

13. SERAIAH'S SYMBOLIC MISSION (51:59-64)

51:59. The capstone of Jeremiah's oracle against Babylon was a **message** he **gave to . . . Seraiah** who was a **staff officer** to . . . **the king.** By noting that Seraiah **was a son of Neriah, the son of Mahseiah** Jeremiah indicated that Seraiah was the brother of Baruch, his scribe (cf. 32:12). Seraiah **went to Babylon with Zedekiah . . . in the fourth year of** Zedekiah's **reign.** Why did Zedekiah make a trip to Babylon in 594–593 B.C.? William Shea offers strong evidence to suggest that Nebuchadnezzar summoned all his vassal kings to Babylon in 594 B.C. to insure their loyalty after an attempted revolt in Babylon a little less than a year earlier. Shea believes that this gathering was recorded in Daniel 3 (William H. Shea, "Daniel 3: Extra-Biblical Texts and the Convocation on the Plain of Dura," *Andrews University Seminary Studies* 20. Spring 1982:29-52). Whatever the exact cause, Zedekiah was forced to make an official trip to Babylon, and brought Baruch's brother, Seraiah.

51:60-64. Jeremiah compiled **on a scroll . . . all** the prophecies he had **recorded concerning Babylon.** Very likely this scroll was a copy of chapters 50–51 of the present book. He gave the scroll **to Seraiah** and told him to **read the words** aloud when he got **to Babylon.** After affirming God's intention to **destroy** that **place,** Seraiah was to **tie a stone to** the scroll and **throw it into the Euphrates.** As the scroll and stone sank beneath the water, Seraiah was to announce that **Babylon,** like the scroll, would **sink to rise no more** (cf. Rev. 18:21).

The final note, **the words of Jeremiah end here,** helps in understanding the process by which the Book of Jeremiah was compiled. This note was probably made by the person who later added chapter 52 to the already-compiled work of Jeremiah. Because chapter 52 was written approximately 25 years after the rest of the book (see the chart "The Dating of Jeremiah's Prophecies," in the *Introduction*), the later editor included this note to distinguish between the portion of the book that had been compiled by Jeremiah and the portion that was added later. Who was this man? No one knows for sure except to say that whoever wrote chapter 52 was also responsible for completing the Book of 2 Kings. (Tradition states that Jeremiah wrote 1 and 2 Kings except for the final chapter, 2 Kings 25.) Likely candidates for Jeremiah 52 include Baruch or some other disciple of Jeremiah who lived long enough to see the events of chapter 52 take place. Whoever the individual, obviously the Holy Spirit guided him to include the chapter as a fitting ending to the book.

IV. Conclusion (chap. 52)

Chapter 52 is nearly identical to 2 Kings 24:18–25:30 and was written

sometime after 561 B.C. when King Jehoiachin was released from prison in Babylon (Jer. 52:31). Much of the material is parallel to information recorded by Jeremiah in chapter 39. Why, then, was this chapter added to Jeremiah's prophecies? Most likely it was to show that Jeremiah's words of judgment against Jerusalem had been fulfilled and that his words about Judah's release from the Exile were about to be fulfilled. This final chapter served to vindicate the prophet and encourage the remnant still in captivity.

A. The fate of Jerusalem (52:1-23)

1. THE FALL OF ZEDEKIAH (52:1-11)

52:1-11. The history of Judah's final king is again summarized (cf. 39:1-7). Zedekiah . . . **became king** when he **was 21 years old,** and **he reigned** for **11 years.** He **rebelled against** Nebuchadnezzar, and in **the 9th year of** his **reign, on the 10th day of the 10th month** (Jan. 15, 588 B.C.; cf. 2 Kings 25:1; Jer. 39:1; Ezek. 24:1-2) Nebuchadnezzar began the final **siege** of **Jerusalem.** In **the 11th year of . . . Zedekiah** on **the 9th day of the 4th month** (July 18, 586 B.C.) **the famine . . . had become so severe that** the **food** ran out. All resistance was gone, and on that day the Babylonians made a breach in **the city wall.** Zedekiah and his soldiers tried to flee, but they were **captured** as Jeremiah had predicted (cf. Jer. 38:14-23). **Zedekiah** was **taken to** Nebuchadnezzar, forced to watch the execution of his **sons,** blinded, **bound . . . with shackles,** and taken **to Babylon where** he remained imprisoned until he died.

2. THE DESTRUCTION OF THE CITY (52:12-16)

52:12-16. The city of **Jerusalem** fared no better than her king. By **the 10th day of the fifth month** which was in Nebuchadnezzar's **19th year** (August 17, 586 B.C.) the city had been cleared of rebels and sacked and was put to the torch. There is a problem here because 2 Kings 25:8 indicates that Nebuzaradan came on "the **7th** day of the fifth month." Two possible answers have been suggested. Some think that one of the two dates is the result of a later scribal error in copying the text. However, there is no textual or manuscript evidence to support this position. Others believe that "the 7th" indicates the day Nebuzaradan arrived in Jerusalem and "the 10th" indicates the day he began burning the city. **Nebuzaradan. . . . set fire to the temple . . . the royal palace, and . . . the houses** as Jeremiah had predicted (cf. Jer. 22:7). **Every important building** was **burned down.** Those who survived the siege and **remained in the city** were **carried into exile.** Only **the poorest people** were left behind.

3. THE DESTRUCTION OF THE TEMPLE (52:17-23)

52:17-23. To understand this passage one must remember Jeremiah's conflict with the false prophet, Hananiah (cf. 27:16–28:17). Jeremiah had predicted that the furnishings still remaining in the temple would be taken to Babylon (27:19-22). Hananiah contradicted Jeremiah by promising that the furniture already taken to Babylon would be returned (28:3). Which prophet was correct? This additional chapter proves the truth of Jeremiah's prophecy. **The bronze pillars, the movable stands,** and the other furnishings named by Jeremiah were indeed **carried . . . to Babylon.** This was such an extensive undertaking that the author paused to explain the size of **the** bronze **pillars** which were removed (52:21).

B. The fate of certain people (52:24-34)

1. THE FATE OF THOSE IN THE CITY DURING ITS FALL (52:24-27)

52:24-27. All the city's leaders were rounded up by the Babylonians. These included **Seraiah the chief priest,** who was a grandson of Hilkiah, the high priest in King Josiah's time (1 Chron. 6:13-15), **Zephaniah the priest next in rank** (cf. Jer. 29:25-29; 37:3), **and the three doorkeepers** who were responsible for keeping order in the temple. Also captured were **the officer in charge of the fighting men** (secretary of defense), **seven royal advisers,** and the **chief officer** who was **in charge of conscripting the people** along with **60 of his men**—either lower officials or 60 conscripted soldiers. These were taken to **Riblah in the land of Hamath,** where Nebuchadnezzar had his headquarters (52:9), and **executed.**

2. THE FATE OF THE EXILES (52:28-30)

52:28-30. This section is not included in 2 Kings 25. The author added it here to show that other groups of exiles were taken to Babylon. The dates given for the first two deportations (Jer. 52:28-29) do not correspond with the dates of the two deportations given in 2 Kings 24:12-14; 25:8-12. Two possible solutions to this difficulty have been advanced. First, some have suggested that the deportations in 2 Kings and Jeremiah refer to the same events and should be harmonized. This is usually done by assuming that the writer of 2 Kings used a nonaccession-year method of dating the kings of Babylon while Jeremiah employed an accession-year method in Jeremiah 52:28-30 (see John Bright, A History of Israel. 3rd ed. Philadelphia: Westminster Press, 1981, p. 326, n. 45).

Second, others have suggested that the first two deportations listed in 52:28-30 were not the same as those in 2 Kings but were minor ones preceding the major deportations associated with Nebuchadnezzar's capture of the city in 597 and 586 B.C. Two arguments are said to support this second view. First, the years given (the **7th** and **18th** years of **Nebuchadnezzar**) are each one year earlier than the years given in 2 Kings for the two major assaults on Jerusalem by Babylon (the "8th," 2 Kings 24:12-14, and "19th," 2 Kings 25:8-12, years of Nebuchadnezzar). Second, the numbers of captives who were exiled in these deportations do not correspond with the numbers taken during the 597 and 586 deportations. In 597 about 10,000 people were taken (2 Kings 24:14), but Jeremiah 52:28 mentions only **3,023.** In 586 Nebuchadnezzar deported "the people who remained in the city, along with the rest of the populace and those who had gone over to the king" (2 Kings 25:11). The figure in Jeremiah 52:29 of **832** seems far too low to correspond to this final deportation. So according to this second view it seems reasonable to assume that these two deportations in verses 28-29 are secondary deportations. The author included them (along with a third minor deportation, v. 30) to show the full extent of Babylon's destruction of Judah. (See Alberto R. Green, "The Chronology of the Last Days of Judah: Two Apparent Discrepancies." Journal of Biblical Literature 101. 1982:57-73.)

The third deportation mentioned by Jeremiah possibly corresponds with Nebuchadnezzar's return to the land after Gedaliah's assassination (cf. chap. 41). Certainly such a threat to Babylon's control over Palestine did not go unnoticed. Perhaps Nebuchadnezzar sent a force to restore order and to remove anyone suspected of promoting rebellion. The small number of **745 Jews** would support the limited size of this action. The dates of these three deportations (based on a Tishri calendar) mentioned in 52:28-30 were then (a) **Nebuchadnezzar's** 7th year (598 B.C.), (b) his 18th year (587 B.C.), and (c) his **23rd year** (582 B.C.).

3. THE FATE OF JEHOIACHIN (52:31-34)

52:31-34. Jehoiachin became the "firstfruits" of those in captivity in Babylon. **In the 37th year of** Jehoiachin's **exile** (561–560 B.C.) **Evil-Merodach became king of Babylon.** As part of the festivities at the end of his accession year **he released Jehoiachin . . . from prison on the 25th day of the 12th month** (March 21, 560 B.C.). Jehoiachin was allowed to eat **regularly at the king's table.** Just as Jeremiah's prophecies of destruction had come true, so now his prophecies of future blessing were beginning. Jehoiachin's favor gave hope to the exiles that God's promised blessing and restoration would come.

BIBLIOGRAPHY

Bright, John. *Jeremiah: A New Translation with Introduction and Commentary.* The Anchor Bible. Garden City, N.Y.: Doubleday & Co., 1965.

Cunliffe-Jones, H. *The Book of Jeremiah: Introduction and Commentary.* New York: Macmillan Co., 1961.

Feinberg, Charles L. *Jeremiah: A Commentary.* Grand Rapids: Zondervan Publishing House, 1982.

Freeman, H. *Jeremiah.* London: Soncino Press, 1949.

Harrison, R.K. *Jeremiah and Lamentations.* The Tyndale Old Testament Commentaries. Downers Grove, Ill.: InterVarsity Press, 1973.

Huey, F.B., Jr. *Jeremiah: Bible Study Commentary.* Grand Rapids: Zondervan Publishing House, 1981.

Jensen, Irving L. *Jeremiah and Lamentations.* Everyman's Bible Commentary. Chicago: Moody Press, 1974.

Kinsler, F. Ross. *Inductive Study of the Book of Jeremiah.* South Pasadena, Calif.: William Carey Library, 1971.

Laetsch, Theo. *Jeremiah.* Bible Commentary. St. Louis: Concordia Publishing House, 1952.

Orelli, C. von. *The Prophecies of Jeremiah.* Translated by J.S. Banks. Reprint. Minneapolis: Klock & Klock Christian Publishers, 1977.

Thompson, J.A. *The Book of Jeremiah.* The New International Commentary on the Old Testament. Grand Rapids: Wm. B. Eerdmans Publishing Co., 1980.

LAMENTATIONS

Charles H. Dyer

INTRODUCTION

The Book of Lamentations is a mournful postscript to the Book of Jeremiah. Through the use of five dirges, or funeral laments, the author grieved over the fate of Jerusalem because of her sin. Yet the book contains more than just the backward glances of a vindicated prophet. "It is a mute reminder that sin, in spite of all its allurement and excitement, carries with it heavy weights of sorrow, grief, misery, barrenness, and pain. It is the other side of the 'eat, drink, and be merry' coin" (Charles R. Swindoll, *The Lamentations of Jeremiah*, "Introduction"). Lamentations both mourns the fall of the city and offers reproof, instruction, and hope to its survivors.

Title. The title of Lamentations is taken from the book's first word, *'ēkâh*. This word may be translated "Alas!" or "How" and was a characteristic cry of lament or exclamation (cf. 2 Sam. 1:19; Jer. 9:19). Rabbinic and Talmudic writers referred to the book by this title or by the name *qînôt* which means "dirges" or "laments."

The Septuagint translators converted the Rabbinic title *qînôt* into *thrēnoi*, the Greek word for "dirges." This title was also adopted by the Latin Vulgate which named the book *threni*, or "Lamentations." The translators of the English Bible followed the pattern established by the Septuagint and Vulgate translators and named the book "Lamentations" after a description of its contents. Many also followed the Jewish tradition of ascribing the work to Jeremiah. Thus the title of the book in English is either "The Lamentations of Jeremiah" (KJV, ASV, NASB, RSV) or "Lamentations" (JB, NIV).

Author and Date. The book does not name its author, but Jewish tradition attributes it to Jeremiah. The Septuagint

added the following words as an introduction to the book: "And it came to pass, after Israel was taken captive, and Jerusalem made desolate, that Jeremiah sat weeping, and lamented with this lamentation over Jerusalem, and said. . . ." The Aramaic Targum of Jonathan, the Babylonian Talmud, the Peshitta, and the Vulgate all made statements that attribute the work to Jeremiah.

Internal evidence also points to Jeremiah as the author. Several ideas used by Jeremiah in his prophecy reappear in Lamentations (cf. Jer. 30:14 with Lam. 1:2; and cf. Jer. 49:12 with Lam. 4:21). In both books the writer said his eyes flowed with tears (Jer. 9:1, 18; Lam. 1:16; 2:11); and in both the writer was an eyewitness of Jerusalem's fall to Babylon and pictured the atrocities that befell Jerusalem in her last days (Jer. 19:9; Lam. 2:20; 4:10).

Jeremiah's authorship of Lamentations was universally accepted till 1712 when Herman von der Hardt wrote a commentary which challenged this position. The objections raised by von der Hardt and others against Jeremiah's authorship have been answered (e.g., Gleason L. Archer, Jr., *A Survey of Old Testament Introduction.* Chicago: Moody Press, 1964, pp. 365-7; and Walter C. Kaiser, Jr., *A Biblical Approach to Personal Suffering*, pp. 24-30).

Assuming that Jeremiah was the author of the book, the book itself must have been composed within a narrow period of time. Jeremiah would have penned the poetic dirges after Jerusalem fell to Babylon in 586 B.C. (cf. 1:1-11) but before he was taken to Egypt after Gedaliah's assassination (ca. 583–582 B.C.; cf. Jer. 43:1-7). The vivid descriptions and deep emotions expressed in the Book of Lamentations argue for a composition shortly after the events occurred, possibly in late 586 B.C. or early 585 B.C.

Historical Background. From 588 to 586 B.C. the army of Babylon ground away at the defenses of Jerusalem (for comments on these dates see information at 2 Kings 25:1-10). So Judah's early flush of excitement and euphoria following her rebellion against Babylon was replaced with uncertainty and fear. Her ally, Egypt, had been vanquished in battle as she tried in vain to rescue Judah from Babylon's grasp. One by one the other cities in Judah were crushed (cf. Jer. 34:6-7) till only Jerusalem remained before the Babylonian hordes.

Within the city the ever-tightening siege by Babylon's armies began unraveling the fabric of society. Starving mothers ate their own children (Lam. 2:20; 4:10). Idolatry flourished as the people cried out to any and every god for deliverance. Paranoia gripped the people until they were willing to kill God's prophet as a traitor and spy just because he spoke the truth.

The long siege ended abruptly on July 18, 586 B.C. The walls were then breached and the Babylonian army began entering the city (2 Kings 25:2-4a). King Zedekiah and the remaining men in his army tried to flee, but were captured (2 Kings 25:4b-7). It took several weeks for Nebuchadnezzar to secure the city and strip it of its valuables, but by August 14, 586 B.C. the task was completed and the destruction of the city began (2 Kings 25:8-10). (For support of the dates July 18 and August 14, 586 B.C., see Edwin R. Thiele, *The Mysterious Numbers of the Hebrew Kings.* Rev. ed. Grand Rapids: Zondervan Publishing House, 1983, p. 190.) The armies of Babylon burned the temple, the king's palace, and all the other major buildings in the city; and they tore down the walls of the city which provided her protection. When the Babylonians finally finished their destruction and departed with their prisoners, they left a jumbled heap of smoldering rubble.

Jeremiah witnessed the desecration of the temple and the destruction of the city (cf. Jer. 39:1-14; 52:12-14). The once-proud capital had been trampled in the dust. Her people were now under the harsh hand of a cruel taskmaster. With all these events stamped vividly on his mind Jeremiah sat down to compose his series of laments.

Relationship to Deuteronomy 28. A crucial, though often overlooked, characteristic of the Book of Lamentations is its relationship to Deuteronomy 28. As John A. Martin has noted, "The author of the Book of Lamentations was attempting to show the fulfillment of the curses presented in Deuteronomy 28" ("The Contribution of the Book of Lamentations to Salvation History." Th.M. thesis, Dallas Theological Seminary, 1975, p. 44). The following chart shows many of the parallels between Lamentations and Deuteronomy 28.

All the heartaches and hardships experienced by Jerusalem in the Book of Lamentations had been predicted about 900 years earlier by Moses. God had warned of the fearful consequences of disobedience and, as Jeremiah carefully noted, God faithfully carried out those curses. Yet this characteristic makes the Book of Lamentations a book of hope for Israel. God was *faithful* in discharging every aspect of the covenant He had made. Israel was punished for disobedience, but she was not consumed because God's covenant was still in force. The same covenant that promised judgment for disobedience also promised restoration for repentance (cf. Deut. 30:1-10). Thus Jeremiah could offer hope in the midst of despair (Lam. 3:21-32). Jeremiah's message to the Israelites in captivity was to learn the lessons of Deuteronomy 28 and turn back to their Lord. The prayer of Lamentations 5:21-22 was not a doubting cry from a discouraged remnant. Rather it was the response of faith from those captives who had mastered the lessons of Deuteronomy 28 and the Book of Lamentations. They were calling on God to fulfill the final part of His covenant and to restore them as a nation from captivity.

Structure and Style. The Book of Lamentations has at least three major structural or stylistic distinctives:

1. Lament pattern. Lamentations is a series of five laments, or funeral dirges; each chapter is a separate lament. A lament was a funeral poem or song written and recited for someone who had just died (cf. 2 Sam. 1:17-27). The song usually emphasized the good qualities of the departed and the tragedy or loss felt by those mourning his death. Jeremiah was

Parallels between Lamentations and Deuteronomy

Lamentations		Deuteronomy	
1:3	She dwells among the nations; she finds no resting place.	28:65	Among those nations you will find no repose, no resting place for the sole of your foot.
1:5	Her foes have become her masters.	28:44	He will be the head, but you will be the tail.
1:5	Her children have gone into exile, captive before the foe.	28:32	Your sons and daughters will be given to another nation.
1:6	In weakness they have fled before the pursuer.	28:25	The LORD will cause you to be defeated before your enemies. You will come at them from one direction but flee from them in seven.
1:18	My young men and maidens have gone into exile.	28:41	You will have sons and daughters but you will not keep them, because they will go into captivity.
2:15	All who pass your way clap their hands at you; they scoff and shake their heads at the Daughter of Jerusalem.	28:37	You will become a thing of horror and an object of scorn and ridicule to all the nations where the LORD will drive you.
2:20	Should women eat their offspring, the children they have cared for?	28:53	Because of the suffering that your enemy will inflict on you during the siege, you will eat the fruit of the womb, the flesh of the sons and daughters the LORD your God has given you.
2:21	Young and old lie together in the dust of the streets.	28:50	. . . a fierce-looking nation without respect for the old or pity for the young.
4:10	With their own hands compassionate women have cooked their own children.	28:56–57	The most gentle and sensitive woman among you . . . will begrudge the husband she loves and her own son or daughter the afterbirth from her womb and the children she bears. For she intends to eat them secretly during the siege.
5:2	Our inheritance has been turned over to aliens, our homes to foreigners.	28:30	You will build a house, but you will not live in it.
5:5	We are weary and find no rest.	28:65	Among those nations you will find no repose.
5:10	Our skin is hot as an oven, feverish from hunger.	28:48	In hunger and thirst . . . you will serve the enemies the LORD sends against you.
5:11	Women have been ravished in Zion, and virgins in the towns of Judah.	28:30	You will be pledged to be married to a woman, but another will take her and ravish her.
5:12	Elders are shown no respect.	28:50	. . . a fierce-looking nation without respect for the old . . .
5:18	Mount Zion . . . lies desolate, with jackals prowling over it.	28:26	Your carcasses will be food for all the birds of the air and the beasts of the earth, and there will be no one to frighten them away.

lamenting the tragic "death" of the city of Jerusalem and the results of her demise which were being experienced by the people. Thus he used the form of a funeral lament to convey the feeling of sadness and loss being experienced by the survivors.

The lament pattern is emphasized by the use of two structural elements. The first is the repetition of the word "How" or "Alas" ('êkâh) to open three of the five chapters (cf. Lam. 1:1; 2:1; 4:1). As discussed earlier under "Title" the word 'êkâh conveyed the idea of strong exclamation or lament. The second element that emphasizes the lament pattern is the frequent use of the qînâh meter in chapters 1–4. In this rhythmic pattern the second half of a line of verse has one less beat than the first half of a line. This forms a 3 + 2 "limping meter" which conveys a hollow, incomplete feeling to the reader. Both of these elements lend an air of sadness to the dirges and heighten their emotional intensity.

2. *Acrostic arrangement.* One key stylistic element that defies translation is the acrostic arrangement of chapters 1–4. An acrostic is a composition in which the first word of each sentence or line, when taken in order, forms a word, a connected group of words, or the regular sequence of the letters of the alphabet. In the Book of Lamentations each of the first four chapters is arranged in an acrostic pattern. Thus verse 1 begins with the letter 'alep, verse 2 with bêt, etc. Chapters 1, 2, and 4 each have 22 verses which begin with the 22 letters of the Hebrew alphabet. Chapter 3, the heart of the book, has 66 verses. In this chapter the first three verses begin with 'alep, the next three begin with bêt, etc. Only chapter 5 is not arranged acrostically, though (like chaps. 1–2, and 4) it has 22 verses.

Before discussing the significance of the acrostics in the book, one variation should be noted. In each of chapters 2–4 two of the Hebrew letters are reversed. The normal order of the Hebrew alphabet for the 16th and 17th letters is 'ayin-pē (cf. Ps. 119). This is the order given in Lamentations 1. However, in Lamentations 2–4 this order is *reversed*, giving a pē-'ayin sequence. This reversal perplexed scholars for many years, but recent archeological discoveries have helped clear up the difficulty. Several Hebrew abecedaries (alphabets scratched on pieces of broken pottery by Hebrew children learning to write) have been found by archeologists. Some of these alphabetical lists are in the normal order for the Hebrew letters but others are in the reverse pē-'ayin order. Evidently both arrangements of the alphabet were acceptable. Thus the writer of Lamentations was merely employing two forms of the Hebrew alpha-

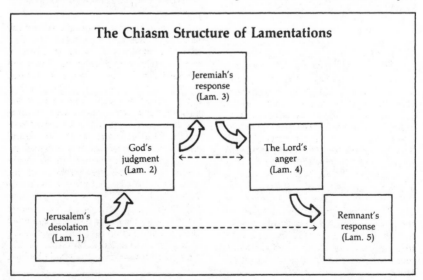

The Chiasm Structure of Lamentations

Jeremiah's response (Lam. 3)

God's judgment (Lam. 2)

The Lord's anger (Lam. 4)

Jerusalem's desolation (Lam. 1)

Remnant's response (Lam. 5)

bet, both of which were used in his time.

Why was the acrostic form used? One possible reason was to help readers remember the words of the lament. Most schoolchildren today remember the musical acronyms "face" and "every good boy does fine" by which they were taught the notes on the spaces and lines of the musical treble clef. In the same way the acrostic pattern would serve as a memory device so that the Israelites would not forget any of the important lessons written in the Book of Lamentations.

A second possible reason for using the acrostic pattern was to emphasize to the readers the complete nature of their suffering because of sin. The alphabet was used to remind the people that Jerusalem's judgment was "from A to Z." Possibly Jeremiah had both reasons in mind when he arranged chapters 1–4 as acrostics. He broke the pattern, though, in chapter 5.

3. Structural balance. The Book of Lamentations has a definite structural balance. Chapters 1–2 and 4–5 parallel each other and are arranged in a chiasm pattern. Thus chapters 1 and 5 focus on the people while chapters 2 and 4 focus on the Lord. Chapter 3 provides the pivot for the book, pointing to Jeremiah's response in the midst of affliction. The arrangement may be diagramed as on the preceding page.

The structural symmetry is balanced by a definite progression in the book. The first four chapters are acrostics; chapter 5 is not. The first four chapters frequently use the *qînâh,* or limping meter; chapter 5 does not. Three of the first four chapters begin with *'êkâh* (chap. 3 is the only exception among the acrostic chaps.); chapter 5 does not. In many ways chapter 5 "breaks the mold" established in the other chapters and offers a response to the suffering. It is no accident that the chapter begins and ends as a prayer ("Remember, O LORD," 5:1; "Restore us to Yourself, O LORD," v. 21). In chapter 5 Jeremiah presented the response that the remnant needed to make to God. It thus formed a fitting ending to the book. God's chastisement was intended to lead to repentance.

OUTLINE

COMMENTARY

I. First Dirge: Jerusalem's Desolation because of Her Sin (chap. 1)

Jeremiah's first dirge established the book's theme—the sorrow of sin. Five times in chapter 1 he noted that Jerusalem's cries for help after her fall went unanswered—"there is none to comfort her" (vv. 2, 9, 16-17, 21). The city had turned from the protective care of her God to pursue foreign alliances and lifeless idols; and now, at the time she needed the help of others most, she found herself alone—destitute and defenseless.

Jeremiah developed Jerusalem's plight by painting two pictures of the city. The first was that of an outside observer looking at the city (vv. 1-11). It is from the outside looking in. The second picture was that of Jerusalem personified calling out to those passing by to stop and observe her condition (vv. 12-22). This picture was from the inside looking out.

A. Jeremiah's lament over Jerusalem's desolation (1:1-11)

As Jeremiah stood surveying the scene of destruction that had once been a thriving city, he began his lament over her desolation. In verses 1-7 he vividly described the extent of her destruction, and in verses 8-11 he explained the cause for her destruction.

1:1. Jerusalem had experienced a catastrophic metamorphosis. Jeremiah listed three ways in which the city had changed. First, her population had been decimated. The once-bustling **city** was now **deserted.** Second, her economic position had changed. The city that had **once** been **great among the nations** was now reduced to the status of **a widow.** The concept of widowhood is used throughout the Old Testament to depict a position of helpless despair; it is often linked with aliens and orphans as individuals who could not protect themselves (cf. Ex. 22:22; Deut. 10:18; 24:19-21; 26:13; 27:19; Isa. 1:17). Jerusalem was now destitute and defenseless. Third, her social position had changed. The **queen . . . has now become a slave.** The city that used to rule other nations was now forced to serve the nation of Babylon.

1:2. As Jeremiah continued his personification of Jerusalem, he described her response to her desolation. While other nations enjoyed the peaceful benefits of sleep, Jerusalem found herself "crying in her pillow," bitterly lamenting her sad state. She needed the **comfort** of her **lovers** and **friends,** but it did not come. She had forsaken her true Lover and Friend Yahweh, for false gods and foreign alliances. But in her hour of need her fickle friends were not to be found. **They** had **become her enemies.** She had no one to help ease her misery.

1:3-6. In these verses Jeremiah amplified the calamity that had befallen Judah and Jerusalem. Instead of dwelling securely in her own land, **Judah** had **gone into exile.** The Babylonian Captivity, which lasted from 605 B.C. to 538 B.C., forced most of the people to leave their homes and live in a strange country as slaves. **The roads** and gates of Jerusalem that had once been filled with pilgrims coming to worship at the **appointed feasts** at the temple were now deserted. The temple itself lay desolate (cf. v. 10),

the **priests** groaned, and the feasts had been discontinued. The **foes** and **enemies** of God's people had triumphed. Jerusalem's **maidens** grieved (v. 4), **her children** were captured (v. 5), and her leaders (**princes**) fled **like** hunted **deer** (v. 6).

The word **Zion** (vv. 4, 6) referred originally to the hill in Jerusalem on which the city of David was built (cf. 2 Sam. 5:7; 1 Kings 8:1). Later with the temple's construction on Mount Moriah and the ark's transfer from the city of David to the temple (cf. 2 Chron. 5:2, 7), the hill on which the temple stood began to be called Mount Zion (cf. Pss. 20:2; 48:2; 78:68-69). The word eventually was applied to the entire city of Jerusalem, which included the city of David, the temple mount, and the western hill on which the city later expanded (cf. Jer. 51:35). The term "Zion" is often associated with God's dwelling place whether the temple proper or the city where the temple was located. (On the **Daughter of Zion** see comments on Lam. 2:1.) So in 1:4-6 Jeremiah emphasized the religious desolation in Jerusalem after the temple and its associated sacrifices and feasts, which symbolized God's presence and fellowship with His people, were destroyed.

1:7. As if the physical trauma were not enough, mental anguish also beset the people of Jerusalem. **Jerusalem** remembered **all the treasures that were hers in days of old.** Her present state of ruin and ridicule contrasted sharply with her former glory—and Jerusalem found no solace in remembering what once was hers. Falling **into enemy hands** (cf. vv. 2-3, 5-6), she was **laughed at.**

1:8-9. After describing *what* had befallen Jerusalem (vv. 1-7) Jeremiah explained *why* (vv. 8-11). **Jerusalem** had **sinned greatly** (cf. v. 5). The catastrophe that overtook Jerusalem was not an action of a heartless God against an innocent people. Jerusalem brought about her own destruction because of her sin. She reaped what she had sown. When she turned from God to pursue her own idolatrous ways, **she did not consider her future.** As is true of many individuals, Jerusalem did not seem to realize that sin leads only to death and destruction (Ezek. 18:4; Rom. 6:23).

1:10-11. Jeremiah briefly sketched

two of the results that Jerusalem received because of her sin. First, Jerusalem saw her temple become desecrated—pagan nations entered her sanctuary. The building the people had falsely relied on for their security (cf. Jer. 7:2-15; 26:2-11) was now defiled before their eyes by Gentiles who were not supposed to enter it. Evidently the Jews viewed their temple as a giant talisman or good luck charm. They felt that Jerusalem was safe because God's house was there. He might let other places be destroyed, they argued, but surely not His own house. The people learned too late that God does not hold stones in higher regard than obedience. Disobedience brings destruction.

Second, because of her sin, Jerusalem experienced famine. During and after the siege, food was scarce. People were forced to barter their treasures for food to keep themselves alive (cf. Lam. 1:19; 2:20; 4:10). The futility of materialism became evident for those who had more silver and gold than bread.

B. Jerusalem's plea for mercy (1:12-22)

The second half of this first lament now changed its focus. Instead of standing on the outside looking in, Jeremiah moved inside and looked out. Jerusalem herself called to those around to take note of her condition. Verses 12-19 contain Jerusalem's call to those who had observed her desolation. Verses 20-22 contain Jerusalem's call to the Lord.

1:12-13. Jerusalem called out to those passing by to stop and take note of her condition. First, she focused on God's judgment that had been poured out on her (vv. 12-17); then she explained that the judgment was deserved because of her sin (vv. 18-19).

Jerusalem's destruction was not a chance occurrence; it was a direct result of God's judgment. The LORD brought it (cf. 2:1-8; 4:11; 5:20). Jeremiah used four metaphors to describe God's work against Jerusalem. First, God's attack was like fire which He sent . . . down into Jerusalem's bones. This may refer to lightning bolts streaking down from the sky and striking people (cf. 1 Kings 18:38; 2 Kings 1:10, 12; Job 1:16; Ps. 18:12-14).

Second, God's attack was like that of a hunter who spread a net for Jerusalem's feet. Nets were used to trap numerous animals including birds (Prov.

1:17), fish (Ecc. 9:12), and antelope (Isa. 51:20). A net would entangle and trap an animal so that it could not escape.

1:14. Third, God's attack was like binding Jerusalem's sins . . . into a yoke which was placed over Jerusalem's neck. A yoke tied two draft animals together for pulling heavy loads. The heavy wooden crossbeam of the yoke referred metaphorically to slavery or to a burden or hardship someone had to bear (cf. Gen. 27:40; Lev. 26:13; Deut. 28:48; 2 Chron. 10:3-11; Isa. 9:4; 58:6, 9; Jer. 27:2, 6-11). Jerusalem's sins produced the yoke of judgment under which she was bound to serve Babylon. God sapped her strength and turned her over to her enemies.

1:15. Fourth, God's attack was compared to the treading of grapes. Like grapes, Jerusalem's young men were crushed. In His winepress the LORD has trampled the Virgin Daughter of Judah. Harvested grapes were placed in a winepress and trampled underfoot till the juice ran out into an adjoining pit. This action became associated with the thought of complete destruction (cf. Isa. 63:1-6; Joel 3:12-15; Rev. 14:17-20; 19:15). "The Virgin Daughter of Judah" referred to Jerusalem (cf. Lam. 2:2, 5) which felt the effects of God's judgment. God had summoned an army against her.

1:16-17. Jerusalem's explanation of God's judgment to those passing by ended in a cry of tragic despair. In a scene of touching sadness Jeremiah pictured Jerusalem as a broken, weeping widow (cf. v. 1) stretching out her hands to seek some condolence and aid. But no one was near to comfort; in fact there was no one at all to comfort her (cf. vv. 9, 21). The city was destitute and despised. Those neighbors to whom Jerusalem had turned for aid were now her foes (cf. v. 2) and viewed her as an unclean thing. The word used here (nidâh) referred to the ceremonial impurity associated with menstruation (cf. Lev. 15:19-20; Ezek. 18:6). Jerusalem was shunned and rejected by her erstwhile friends.

1:18-19. In Judah's confession of guilt, she acknowledged that judgment was caused by the righteous God disciplining an unrighteous people. The LORD is righteous, yet I rebelled against His command. God is not the author of evil nor is He a supreme sadist who delights in inflicting punishment on others (cf. Ezek. 33:11; 2 Peter 3:9). But God is righteous so He does not allow sin to continue unchecked. Sin exacts a horrible price from those who enjoy its temporary pleasures. Jerusalem abandoned her God to experience those "pleasures." Now Jerusalem was paying the cost—**suffering . . . exile** (cf. Lam. 1:3), betrayal by **allies,** and death by starvation.

1:20-22. Jerusalem had called to those passing by (vv. 12-19) but now she turned her cry to God. In baring her soul to the Lord, Jerusalem called on Him to notice her plight. **Outside, the sword bereaves; inside, there is only death.** While the city was under attack by Nebuchadnezzar's army, those who tried to escape to freedom by breaking through the siege were cut down by swords. Those who remained in the city died of starvation and plague.

After describing her plight, Jerusalem called on God to extend His judgment to her **enemies. May You bring the day You have announced so they may become like me.** The "day" was the "day of the LORD," which had already been announced by the prophets. This was the time when God's judgment would extend to all the earth to avenge injustice and bring about the Age of righteousness that had been promised (cf. comments on "the day of the LORD" under "Major Interpretive Problems," in the *Introduction* to Joel).

Jerusalem wanted God to judge the sins of her enemies as He had judged her sins: **deal with them as You have dealt with me because of all my sins** (cf. Lam. 4:21-22). This did not happen at that time, but God said He would judge all nations during and after the still-future Tribulation period (cf. Isa. 62:8–63:6; Ezek. 38–39; Joel 3:1-3, 9-21; Obad. 15-21; Micah 7:8-13; Zech. 14:1-9; Matt. 25:31-46; Rev. 16:12-16; 19:19-21.)

II. Second Dirge: God's Punishment of Jerusalem's Sin (chap. 2)

Charles Swindoll has appropriately titled this chapter "Words from the Woodshed." The focus of Jeremiah's attention moved from the personified city of Jerusalem to the punishment inflicted by God. The first 10 verses depict the

anger of God as He systematically dismantled the city in judgment. Verses 11-19 contain (a) Jeremiah's anguished cry as he wept over the destruction of the city he had loved and (b) his call for the people to cry out to God. Verses 20-22 give the people's response, in which Jerusalem again cried out for the Lord to see her plight.

A. God's anger (2:1-10)

The second dirge opens by focusing on the real cause for Jerusalem's calamity. God was the One who destroyed the city and its people. In these 10 verses Jeremiah hammered home the reality of God's judgment on Jerusalem because of her sin. The words Jeremiah used depict an image of God personally overseeing the dismantling of the city. The verb *bāla'* ("to swallow up" or "to engulf completely") was used four times (vv. 2, 5 [twice], 8 ["destroying"]), perhaps to picture the fire of God's judgment engulfing the city itself. Jeremiah used other vivid verbs as "hurled down" (v. 1), "torn down" (v. 2), "cut off" (v. 3), "burned" (v. 3), "destroyed" (vv. 5-6), "laid waste" (v. 6), "abandoned" (v. 7), "tear down" (v. 8), "broken and destroyed" (v. 9). These words describe the feeling of havoc and disarray in which Jerusalem found herself. God was the "one-man wrecking crew" responsible for the rubble.

2:1-5. Jeremiah explained that God's **anger** (vv. 1 [twice], 3; cf. 1:12; 2:6, 21-22; 3:43, 66; 4:11) and **wrath** (2:4; 3:1; 4:11) was directed against **the strongholds of the Daughter of Judah** (2:2). The "Daughter of Judah" referred specifically to the city of Jerusalem (cf. 1:15; 2:5). The city was also called the **Daughter of Zion** (1:6; 2:1, 4, 8, 10, 13, 18; 4:22) and the "Daughter of Jerusalem" (cf. 2:13, 15). This destruction included the physical **dwellings** (v. 2), **palaces** (v. 5; cf. v. 7), and **strongholds** (vv. 2, 5), but it also included the land's leaders. Thus God brought down **her kingdom and its princes** (v. 2). King Zedekiah and the royal family were ousted from their positions of leadership. The reference in verse 3 to **every horn of Israel** probably also meant the royal family. A "horn" was a symbol of strength; God removed all those to whom the people looked for guidance and leadership. Because of this destruction, in which God seemed to Judah like a **fire** (vv. 3-4) and **like an enemy** (vv. 4-5), the people were in **mourning and lamentation.**

2:6-7. God's anger was also directed against His temple: **He has laid waste His dwelling like a garden.** The word for "dwelling" (*śōk̄*) is a variant spelling of the word for "booth" (*sūkāh*). The thought expressed by Jeremiah is that God tore down His temple (**His place of meeting**) in the same way a farmer would tear down a temporary field hut or booth used to provide shade during a harvest. The **feasts,** Sabbath observances, all the sacrifices, and even the **altar** were affected by Jerusalem's fall. The **shout in the house of the LORD** was actually a wailing at the site of the destroyed temple.

2:8-10. Jeremiah again spoke of the leadership of Jerusalem which was devastated by Babylon. He pictured the leaders as being like a **wall around** Jerusalem which used to protect the people. But just as the physical **ramparts and walls** around Jerusalem were destroyed (vv. 8-9a), so her human wall of leadership was also dismantled (vv. 9b-10). The Davidic dynasty was ousted from its throne. The **king and her princes** (cf. v. 2) were **exiled among the nations.** Without the temple the function of the priests had been rendered ineffective (cf. v. 6) so that **the Law** was **no more.** Another group of leaders, the **prophets,** had been so corrupted by charlatans (cf. Jer. 23:9-32; 28; Ezek. 13) that they were **no longer** receiving communications (**visions**) from God or speaking in His name (cf. Lam. 2:14). Thus every group charged by God to lead the people—the king, the priests, and the prophets—was affected by Jerusalem's fall.

In response to their loss of leadership, the people mourned. The mourning extended from **the elders** to **the young women.** Possibly this is a figure of speech known as a merism, in which Jeremiah used two extremes (old men, young women) to show that *everyone*—young and old and all in between—was mourning the loss of leadership. In grief they were silent, sprinkling **dust on their heads,** and wearing **sackcloth,** both signs of sorrow and anguish (cf. Gen. 37:34; Job 2:12-13; Neh. 9:1). (On "sackcloth" see comments on Isa. 3:24, on "the Daughter of Zion" see comments on Lam. 2:1, and on "Zion" see comments on 1:6.)

B. Jeremiah's grief (2:11-19)

Jeremiah cried out in anguish at the scene he had been surveying. He sketched five portraits of Jerusalem's condition which prompted his cry.

2:11-12. The first sketch highlighted the starvation that had decimated Jerusalem during the siege. The saddest scenes in any war or conflict are the sufferings experienced by children. Jeremiah wept so much from inner **torment** that tears blinded his **eyes** (cf. 3:48-49). For his **heart** (lit., "liver") to be **poured out on the ground** meant that he was fully drained emotionally. He captured the pathos of the moment as he described **children and infants,** who were **faint** (cf. 2:19), calling out for food **as their lives** ebbed **away in their mothers' arms.** Parents who loved their children could not provide even the necessities of life.

2:13. The city's hopeless condition prompted Jeremiah to address her directly. His second sketch was of a man trying desperately to offer **comfort** to a grieving friend. Unfortunately the judgment's magnitude was so severe that no comfort could be given.

2:14. The third sketch Jeremiah drew was of false **prophets** hastening rather than hindering Jerusalem's downfall. God had threatened to destroy Jerusalem because of her **sin,** and the prophets were supposed to announce this impending disaster and exhort the people to repent. Unfortunately, though Jeremiah and Ezekiel were faithful prophets of God, others were tickling the people's ears with rosy predictions of peace and prosperity (cf. Jer. 28:1-4, 10-11; 29:29-32). Jerusalem chose to ignore the true prophets' warnings and to listen to the flattering and therefore **misleading** lies of the **false** prophets.

2:15-17. The fourth sketch pictured the victorious enemy mocking the vanquished people. The once-majestic and secure **city** of **Jerusalem** was now the object of scoffing and derision. People taunted her, poking fun at her former **beauty** and **joy,** which were now gone, and her **enemies** scoffingly rejoiced in their victory (cf. 3:46).

However, lest Jerusalem begin to believe her enemies' boasts, Jeremiah reminded the Jews again that the destruction was the work of *God:* **He has let the enemy gloat over you; He has exalted the horn of your foes.** The "horn" (i.e., "strength"; cf. 2:3) exhibited by Jerusalem's enemies in their destruction of the city was not their own. *God* gave them the ability to take Jerusalem; thus *He* was the One who overthrew them. And **He** did so **without pity** (cf. vv. 2, 21; 3:43) because of His people's sin.

2:18-19. Jeremiah's fifth sketch pictured the remnant **of the people** ceaselessly wailing to God in despair because of their calamity. The phrase **pour out your heart like water** referred to sincere prayer. The people were to unleash their innermost thoughts and emotions and share them with God (cf. Pss. 42:4; 62:8; 142:2). There is a similarity between Jeremiah's exhortation to the people here and his own response (recorded in Lam. 2:11). In both cases (a) they were weeping and in torment, (b) they poured out their feelings in prayer to God, and (c) the heartrending scene of starving **children** was the focus of their grief.

C. Jerusalem's pleas (2:20-22)

Jeremiah ended the expression of his personal grief (vv. 12-19) by calling on Jerusalem to respond to her calamity (v. 19) as he had. Then he recorded Jerusalem's plea to God.

2:20a-b. In a cry of pain and horror the city called on God to **look** and think about her calamity. The starving to death of children was a sickening twist. The siege against Jerusalem was so severe that all her inhabitants were in danger of starvation. In a shocking display of their self-preservation drive, some parents became cannibals and ate their own children. **Should women eat their offspring, the children they have cared for?** This action was predicted in graphic detail by Moses when he warned Israel of the consequences of disobedience to God's Law (cf. Lev. 26:27-29; Deut. 28:53-57). This reprehensible practice surfaced only during the most desperate times (cf. 2 Kings 6:24-31).

2:20c-21b. The slaughter moved beyond the children to encompass the religious leaders and people of all ages. **Priest and prophet** alike were slain inside the temple precincts as the Babylonian army rushed in for the conquest. As Jeremiah picked his way through the winding streets of Jerusalem, he saw bloated corpses strewn among the rubble: **young and old lay together in the dust of the streets.** When Babylon finally did break through Jerusalem's defenses, its soldiers were angry because Jerusalem had kept them at bay for 30 months. They made no distinction between age and sex; the bloodthirsty Babylonians butchered uncounted thousands.

2:21c-22. But lest anyone forget the ultimate Judge, Jeremiah again (cf. v. 17) reminded the people that God was the One wielding the sword of punishment. The Babylonians prevailed only because He let them prevail. God had warned Israel what He would do if she disobeyed Him (Lev. 26:14-39; Deut. 28:15-68) and He faithfully carried out His threat. Those whom He had loved were now **destroyed.**

III. Third Dirge: Jeremiah's Response (chap. 3)

Chapter 3 is the heart of Jeremiah's short book. This chapter gives the book a positive framework around which the other chapters revolve. The black velvet of sin and suffering in chapters 1–2 and 4–5 serves as a fitting backdrop to display the sparkling brilliance of God's loyal love in chapter 3.

The chapter itself differs markedly from the first two. Instead of 22 verses it has 66—3 verses for each letter of the Hebrew alphabet. The chapter also begins without the familiar "How" (*'ekâh*) that stands guard over chapters 1 and 2. Instead, a first-person narrative unfolds as the writer describes his personal reaction to the suffering he has experienced.

The identity of the subject in chapter 3 has been disputed. Some feel that "I," "me," and "my" refer to Jerusalem personified (cf. 1:12-22; 2:22). However, while parts of chapter 3 could refer to the city, other parts of the chapter must refer to an individual (cf. 3:14, 52-54). In fact the parallels between this individual and Jeremiah are remarkable. Both were hated by their countrymen (Jer. 1:18-19; Lam. 3:52), were ridiculed by those they tried to help (Jer. 20:7-8; Lam. 3:63), had plots made against their lives (Jer. 11:18-19; Lam. 3:60), were cast into watery pits (Jer. 38:4-13; Lam. 3:53-58), and wept over the people's destruction (Jer. 9:1;

13:17; 14:17; Lam. 3:48-49).

Therefore it is probable that the person in question is Jeremiah himself. Yet his description goes beyond just one person to include all the people. This is most obvious in his switch from the singular to the plural ("we," "us," "our") within the chapter (cf. vv. 22, 40-46). The best solution is to see the individual in chapter 3 as Jeremiah representing all Israelites. He used his own experiences because the things he suffered represented things that many Israelites had suffered.

The chapter may be divided into three sections. Jeremiah detailed his afflictions during the time of Jerusalem's fall (vv. 1-18). But his knowledge of God's ways in the midst of his affliction produced hope, not despair (vv. 19-40). So Jeremiah could lead Israel in prayer to God for deliverance, restoration, and vindication (vv. 41-66).

A. Jeremiah's afflictions (3:1-18)

3:1-3. In a long list of metaphors Jeremiah enumerated the many afflictions that he, as Judah's representative, suffered at the hand of God's **wrath** (cf. 2:2, 4; 4:11). Jeremiah was *confused* as he watched God seemingly reverse His past attitudes and actions. Instead of walking in the **light** of God's guidance he had been forced to stumble **in darkness** (cf. 3:6). God **turned His hand against** Jeremiah. This phrase is unique, but the concept of God's hand was known in the Old Testament (cf. 1 Sam. 5:6; Job 19:21). God's hand of favor had become a fist of adversity.

3:4-6. God's adversity resulted in *misery* for Jeremiah. God's afflictions had taken their toll on his health (cf. Ps. 38:2-3): his **skin** and **flesh** were **old** (probably wrinkled) and his **bones** were **broken** (figuratively speaking of his inner agony; cf. Ps. 42:10). These outward changes were matched by inner **bitterness** (cf. Lam. 3:15, 19). Jeremiah was broken in body and spirit.

3:7-9. Jeremiah could see no way out of his adversity. He was imprisoned and chained, so his freedom was gone. God refused to acknowledge his prayers **for help,** and all avenues of escape were blocked.

3:10-13. God's actions seemed designed to single out Jeremiah for punishment. God was **like a bear** or **lion in hiding** beside **the path** who attacked and mauled Jeremiah. Switching figures, Jeremiah said he felt like a **target** against which God was taking target practice (cf. Job 6:4; 7:20; 16:12-13). God had chosen him for adversity.

3:14-18. In a burst of vivid images Jeremiah concluded the description of his afflictions. He was mocked and laughed at by his compatriots, filled with bitterness (**bitter herbs** and **gall** [cf. v. 19], the most bitter-tasting plant in Judah), **trampled** underfoot, **deprived of peace** and **prosperity,** and led to despair.

B. Jeremiah's hope (3:19-40)

3:19-24. Jeremiah's condition paralleled that of Judah. His outward **affliction** (v. 19a; cf. vv. 1-4) and inward turmoil (v. 19b; cf. vv. 5, 13, 15) pushed him toward despair (**my soul is downcast,** v. 20). However, one thought (**this I call to mind**) crowded out the hopelessness that threatened to overwhelm him: **Because of the LORD's great love we are not consumed, for His compassions never fail.** Judah was down, but not out. God was punishing Judah for her sin, but did not reject her as His covenant people. The word for "great love" is *ḥeseḏ*, which has the idea of loyal love. God was sticking by the people He had chosen. The covenant made with Israel in Deuteronomy 28 (see *Introduction*) had not been abrogated. In fact God's loyal love could be seen in His faithfulness in carrying out the curses He had promised while at the same time preserving a remnant. The judgment itself was a witness to the fact that God had not abandoned His people. God's "compassions" (from *reḥem*, "womb," and in the pl. for intensity) showed His gentle feeling of concern for those who belonged to Him.

Could Judah push God so far that He would finally abandon her forever? Was God's supply of loyal love and compassion limited? Jeremiah's answer was no. God's "loving-kindnesses" (NASB) **are new every morning.** God offered a fresh supply of loyal love every day to His covenant people. Much like the manna in the wilderness, the supply could not be exhausted. This truth caused Jeremiah to call out in praise, **Great is Your faithfulness.** He was taken back by the limitless supply of God's grace offered to him. Because of this, Jeremiah resolved to **wait** for God to act, bringing about restoration and blessing. He could trust God despite his circumstances because he now understood how inexhaustible was God's supply of loyal love.

3:25-40. The God who brought the cursings spoken of in Deuteronomy 28 would also bring about the restoration promised in Deuteronomy 30. In the meantime God's people needed to develop the proper attitude toward their afflictions. Jeremiah wrote seven principles about the nature of Israel's affliction: (1) Affliction should be endured with **hope** in God's **salvation**, that is, ultimate restoration (Lam. 3:25-30). (2) Affliction is only temporary and is tempered by God's **compassion** and **love** (vv. 31-32). (3) God **does not** delight in **affliction** (v. 33). (4) If affliction comes because of injustice, God sees it and does not approve of it (vv. 34-36). (5) Affliction is always in relationship to God's sovereignty (vv. 37-38; cf. Job 2:10). (6) Affliction ultimately came because of Judah's **sins** (Lam. 3:39). (7) Affliction should accomplish the greater good of turning God's people back to Him (v. 40).

Jeremiah was able to place his (and Israel's) affliction in proper perspective by remembering how it related to God's character and His covenant with His people. Judah's afflictions were not cruel acts of a capricious God who delighted in inflicting pain on helpless people. Rather the afflictions came from a compassionate God who was being faithful to His covenant. He did not enjoy making others suffer, but He allowed the afflictions as temporary means to force Judah back to Himself. So Jeremiah ended this section by exhorting the people, **Let us examine our ways . .`. let us return to the LORD.** God's affliction was designed as a corrective measure to restore His wayward people (Deut. 28:15-68). It was designed to force the people to return to the Lord (Deut. 30:1-10).

C. *Jeremiah's prayer (3:41-66)*

The condition of the prophet (vv. 1-18) and the character of God (vv. 19-40) prompted Jeremiah to pray. This next section is in two parts. In the first part (vv. 41-47) the prophet exhorted the people to confess their sins to God because of their suffering. This section was written in the plural ("we," "us," "our"). In the second part (vv. 48-66) Jeremiah remembered God's personal deliverance after his cry; this prompted Jeremiah to call on God to judge his enemies. This section was written in the singular ("I," "me," "my"); it represented Jeremiah as the model for Judah. As God rescued Jeremiah and judged his enemies, so God would rescue Judah and judge her enemies if she would call on Him.

3:41-47. This prayer flows out of the exhortation in verse 40. Judah's return to the Lord would be accomplished through prayer. As she turned toward heaven she would acknowledge that she had **sinned and rebelled.** The nation's troubles—being under God's **anger** (cf. 2:1, 3, 6, 22; 3:43), having unanswered **prayer,** being rejected like **scum** by **the nations,** and being scoffed at (cf. 2:16)—stemmed from her disobedience **to God.** All her **terror and pitfalls, ruin and destruction** resulted from rebellion against God's covenant. When Judah would realize the awful consequences of her sin, she would finally admit her guilt.

3:48-51. In verse 48 Jeremiah abruptly shifted from the plural to the singular. Verses 48-51 provide a transition from the people's confession (vv. 41-47) to Jeremiah's example (vv. 52-66). As the people confessed their sin and then waited for God to respond, so Jeremiah continued to weep (cf. 2:11) and pray **until the LORD** would look **down from heaven and** see. God promised to restore Israel when she called on Him from her captivity (Deut. 30:2-3). So Jeremiah vowed to continue calling for God's restoration of His people till the event actually happened.

3:52-55. After vowing to pray for the people till God reversed their fortunes, Jeremiah related circumstances from his own life which were examples for them. As Judah was afflicted, Jeremiah was also afflicted. As she was to cry for relief, so Jeremiah had cried for relief. God's deliverance of Jeremiah was then a prelude to the deliverance He would bring the nation.

Jeremiah's ministry during Judah's final days created many **enemies.** The people from his own hometown plotted to kill him (Jer. 11:18-23), and everybody at the temple demanded that he be executed (Jer. 26:7-9). He was beaten and thrown into prison as a traitor (Jer. 37:11-16), and was later, near the end of Nebuchadnezzar's siege, lowered into a muddy cistern to starve to death (Jer. 38:1-6).

Jeremiah was probably referring to this last incident in Lamentations 3:53-55. He cried to God for deliverance from the **pit** where he was facing certain death. Some feel that the pit could also be a double reference to both the cistern and the grave or sheol (cf. 2 Sam. 22:5-6; Pss. 18:4-5; 69:1-2, 14-15; Jonah 2:5-6). Probably Jeremiah's experience in the physical **pit** brought to mind the Hebrew concept of the pit of death. One cannot push the metaphorical image too far, however, because the phrase **and threw stones at me** (Lam. 3:53) would be meaningless if the pit referred only to death. If one were sinking in the pit of death, why would he care if people were throwing stones at him? But if he were trapped in a physical cistern this could pose a real danger, as it did for Jeremiah.

3:56-58. Jeremiah's **plea** for deliverance from the pit was answered. **You came near when I called You.** God intervened on Jeremiah's behalf and rescued him from certain death in a muddy cistern (cf. Jer. 38:7-13). So Jeremiah was a living example to Judah of God's loyal love and faithfulness (cf. Lam. 3:22-23). God did deliver (**redeemed** here means "delivered") this man who called on Him for help.

3:59-66. Jeremiah then called on God to vindicate him before his **enemies,** those in Judah who opposed him. God had **seen . . . the wrong done to** Jeremiah—**their vengeance . . . their plots. . . . their insults,** and their mocking. Jeremiah also asked God to **pay them back what they deserve.** This was fulfilled historically when Nebuchadnezzar entered Jerusalem. The leaders responsible for rejecting and persecuting Jeremiah were punished by Babylon (cf. Jer. 39:4-7; 52:7-11, 24-27). The parallel to Jerusalem was obvious. She too was persecuted by her enemies (Lam. 3:46-47); but she could be confident that God would vindicate her before her enemies if she would turn to Him.

IV. Fourth Dirge: The Lord's Anger (chap. 4)

Chapter 4 parallels the judgment discussed in chapter 2. After describing the response of an individual in the midst of judgment (chap. 3), Jeremiah again returned to survey the scene of calamity in Jerusalem. He contrasted the conditions in Jerusalem before and after the siege (4:1-11), explained the causes for the siege, (vv. 12-20), and gave a call for vindication from Zion (vv. 21-22).

A. Contrasts before and after the siege (4:1-11)

The stark reality of Jerusalem's judgment was brought into sharp focus by comparing her present condition with that before the fall. Several scholars have seen a parallelism between verses 1-6 and 7-11 (see the chart). Both sections are written to point to the same conclusion—Jerusalem's present calamity is God's punishment for her sin (vv. 6, 11).

4:1-2. Jeremiah compared Jerusalem to dull gold and cast-off **gems.** Then he explained his figurative language. The "gold" and "gems" were the **precious sons of Zion,** the inhabitants of Jerusalem.

In their former glory they had been as precious as **gold,** but they were **now considered as pots of clay.** Clay was common in Palestine; nearly all vessels were made from it. Clay pots were abundant and their value was little. If one broke, it was thrown out and a new one replaced it. Similarly the people of Jerusalem, God's precious people, had become worthless.

Parallelism in Lamentations 4:1-11

4:1-6		4:7-11	
vv. 1-2	The value of the sons of Zion has become despised.	vv. 7-8	The value of the princes has become despised.
vv. 3-5	The little children and adults suffer.	vv. 9-10	The little children and adults suffer.
v. 6	Conclusion: The calamity is God's punishment.	v. 11	Conclusion: The calamity is God's punishment.

4:3-5. Jeremiah then turned from the people in general to the children in particular. The treatment of children by their mothers during the siege was worse than that expected of loathsome animals. **Jackals,** found throughout the Mediterranean area, traveled in packs. They were associated with areas of desolation and destruction (cf. Isa. 35:7; Jer. 9:11; 10:22; 49:33; 51:37; Mal. 1:3). Yet even jackals nourished their offspring while the cries of **the children** of Jerusalem **for bread** and water went unheeded by their parents. The people of Jerusalem had **become** as **heartless** as wild **ostriches.** Mother ostriches seem unconcerned about their young, for they lay their eggs in the sand where they may be trampled (see comments on Job 39:14-18).

Infants and children were dying **of thirst** and starvation (cf. Lam. 2:19). Another constant in the siege was that those who used to eat well were now **destitute,** and princes **(those nurtured in purple,** royal clothing) were lying in **ash heaps,** probably in sickness (cf. Job 2:8).

4:6. Jeremiah ended the first stanza of this fourth dirge by comparing Jerusalem to **Sodom.** But Jerusalem's **punishment** was worse than Sodom's because (a) Jerusalem's punishment was protracted while Sodom's was short **(in a moment),** and (b) Jerusalem's came despite assistance from Egypt while Sodom had no assistance **(without a hand . . . to help).**

4:7-9. Jeremiah's second stanza (vv. 7-11) paralleled his first (vv. 1-6), but the illustrations here are heightened and narrowed for effect. The "sons of Zion" (v. 2) are now called the **princes** (cf. 2:2, 9). The leaders of the city suffered the same fate as everyone else. Their fine complexions and healthy **bodies** did not escape the ravages of Babylon. They too saw their skin darken (become **blacker than soot)** and grow taut **(shriveled)** as their bodies became **racked** by **hunger** and emaciated (cf. 5:10).

4:10-11. The children who had been starving (vv. 4-5) were now victimized by their parents. The gnawing pangs of hunger (cf. 1:11, 19) finally drove **compassionate women** into cannibalizing **their own children** (cf. comments on 2:20).

Jeremiah concluded this second stanza by again pointing to **the LORD** as the source of Zion's punishment (cf. 1:12-17; 2:1-8; 5:20). Jerusalem was experiencing God's **wrath** (cf. 2:2, 4; 3:1) and **fierce anger** (cf. 1:12; 2:3, 6) for her sin. God's judgment was like **a fire** (cf. 2:3) that had raced out of control in Jerusalem, engulfing the entire city. Both the superstructure and foundations had been destroyed.

B. Causes for the siege (4:12-20)

4:12. Jerusalem was a mighty fortress that had seemed secure. The city had been entered by invading armies on a few occasions previously (cf. 1 Kings 14:25-28; 2 Kings 14:13-14; 2 Chron. 21:16-17). But its defenses had been rebuilt and strengthened (cf. 2 Chron. 32:2-5; 33:14), and a water supply into the city was established with the digging of Hezekiah's tunnel. So by Jeremiah's time **the kings** considered the city impregnable. Yet God allowed it to be captured.

4:13-16. One cause of Jerusalem's siege and fall was **the sins of her prophets and the iniquities of her priests.** The leaders who had been placed as mediators between God and people had become corrupt. Instead of promoting righteousness and stressing faithfulness to God's covenant, these men had **shed . . . the blood** of innocent people and therefore were **defiled with blood.** They were so polluted with sin that they were treated like lepers. Amazingly the prophets and priests were actually shunned as **unclean** lepers and were forced out of the covenant community (cf. Lev. 13:45-46). God **scattered** Jerusalem's leaders **(priests** and **elders)** because they had led the people into sin.

4:17-19. If the first cause of Jerusalem's siege was the sin of the prophets and priests (vv. 13-16), the second cause was the futility of foreign alliances. Instead of trusting in God, Jerusalem turned to Egypt for protection from Babylon. **In vain** she **watched for a nation that could not save** her. Both Jeremiah and Ezekiel had warned against the futility of trusting in Egypt for protection (Jer. 37:6-10; Ezek. 29:6-7). That false hope brought only bitter grief when Babylon's armies, **swifter than eagles** (cf. Hab. 1:8), finally captured Jerusalem, pursuing those who tried to escape, and the **end** came.

4:20. The third cause of Jerusalem's siege and fall was Zedekiah her king.

Zedekiah was the Lord's anointed. The word "anointed" (*māšîah*) was used of the kings of Israel because oil was poured on their heads to indicate that they were set apart for their task by God (cf. 1 Sam. 10:1; 16:1; 1 Kings 1:39-45; 2 Kings 11:12). When Jerusalem fell, Zedekiah tried to escape toward the Jordan River and Ammon (Jer. 39:2-7) but he was caught in the enemy's traps. His children were killed and he was carried away in chains. The leader Jerusalem looked to for security (her very life breath and her shadow) was powerless to protect her.

C. Call for vindication (4:21-22)

4:21-22. Because of God's covenant with Israel (Deut. 28–30) the people could hope for vindication. The last two verses in Lamentations 4 draw a contrast between Israel and her Gentile enemy Edom (see the chart).

Edom took an active role in promoting Jerusalem's fall to Babylon (cf. Ps. 137:7; Jer. 49:7-22; Ezek. 25:12-14; 35). (On **Uz** see comments on Job 1:1.) Edom's crimes against her "brother" Jacob (Deut. 23:7) represented the actions of all the nations that profited at Jerusalem's expense. God had noted their actions, and would punish those nations for their sin, exactly as He had said He would do (Deut. 30:7). Though Edom rejoiced and was glad over Jerusalem's calamity, the bitter cup would someday be passed to her (cf. Lam. 1:21-22). Drinking from a cup pictured being forced to undergo judgment (cf. Jer. 25:15-28). As God was judging Jerusalem in Jeremiah's day for her sin, so He would also judge Edom (and, by extension, all Gentile nations) for their sins. Jerusalem could look forward to restoration, but **Edom** could only expect judgment (cf. comments on Obad. 4, 15-18, 20-21).

V. Fifth Dirge: The Remnant's Response (chap. 5)

The prophet's final dirge breaks the pattern established in his earlier laments. The acrostic pattern and *qînâh* meter are not used. In fact the entire chapter is more properly a prayer than a lament. Chapters 1–3 each close with a prayer to the Lord (1:20-22; 2:20-22; 3:55-66) but no prayer is included in chapter 4. Therefore it is possible to see chapter 5 functioning as the prayer following chapter 4 and

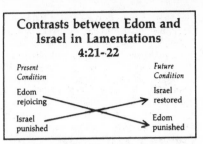

Contrasts between Edom and Israel in Lamentations 4:21-22

Present Condition		Future Condition
Edom rejoicing	→	Israel restored
Israel punished	→	Edom punished

serving as the book's concluding prayer.

The prayer itself is composed of two sections, each of which summarizes the response the remnant needed to make. The first response is a call for God to *remember* their condition (5:1-18). This section also includes a confession of sin. After the call for God to *remember* is a call for God to *restore* Judah (vv. 19-22). In context this is a call to restore both the land of Israel and the blessings of the covenant (Deut. 30:1-10).

A. The remnant's prayer for remembrance (5:1-18)

5:1. Verse 1 introduces the prayer. The remnant called on God to **remember** the indignities they had suffered and to **look** at their present **disgrace**. Jeremiah had already indicated that God notices such atrocities (3:34-36). Therefore the people's call was not just for God to **see** what had happened (for He sees everything: cf. Prov. 15:3), but rather that God see *and act* on their condition.

5:2. Through the use of the first person ("we," "us," "our") the people described (in vv. 2-10) the general conditions of suffering brought about by Babylon. The land of Judah had been parceled out **to foreigners**. Babylon assumed dominion over the land, and its occupying forces were stationed there (Jer. 40:10; 41:3). In addition, nations surrounding Judah appropriated or annexed some of her land for themselves (cf. Ezek. 35:10).

5:3. Besides losing their property, the people also lost their rights. Their new taskmasters were cruel despots who cared little for them. The men were as defenseless as the **orphans and fatherless** and the women were as vulnerable as **widows**. In Israel orphans and widows were the most helpless people in society (see comments on 1:1). They had no one to stand up for their rights or to insure that justice was done. Under Babylon's rule Judah had no rights or means of protection. She was the vanquished enemy, and Babylon her cruel overlord (cf. Hab. 1:6-11).

5:4-5. Babylon's rule over Judah was severe. The Jews now had to pay for the **water** they drank and the **wood** they used for cooking. Both in Judah and in Babylon the Jews found **no rest** from their pursuers. Persecution and fear dogged their every footstep (cf. Deut. 28:65-67; Ezek. 5:2, 12).

5:6-8. Still another reason accounted for Judah's calamity. She **submitted to Egypt and Assyria to get enough bread.** The words translated "submitted to" (*nāṯannû yāḏ*) literally mean "to give the hand to" or "to shake hands." The phrase implies the idea of establishing a pact or treaty (cf. 2 Kings 10:15) and often referred to one group surrendering or submitting to a more powerful group or person as part of a treaty (1 Chron. 29:24; 2 Chron 30:8; Jer. 50:15). Judah had pledged her allegiance both to Egypt and Assyria in her history, for the sake of national security (cf. Ezek. 16:26-28; 23:12, 21). Judah's past leaders (**fathers**) shifted their allegiance between countries, and their fickleness ultimately destroyed them. Their sin brought their death, and their survivors bore **their punishment.** The present generation was not claiming to be suffering unjustly for their forebears' sins (cf. Lam. 5:16), but saw their punishment as a logical conclusion to their ancestors' folly. Their forefathers' willing submission to godless nations was now bearing bitter fruit. Babylon appointed cruel taskmasters; men of low degree were exalted and the people of Judah were forced to submit to them: **Slaves rule over us.**

5:9-10. The severe conditions and scarcity of food prompted the people to take desperate means for survival. Probably **the sword** they had to brave was carried by the bands of roving **desert** nomads through whose area the people of Judah had to travel in order to buy **bread** (i.e., "food"). The Jews' **skin** was **feverish** because of their lack of adequate food (cf. 4:8).

5:11-14. In these verses the subject switches from the first person to the third person ("their"). After speaking of their general conditions of suffering (vv. 2-10), the people described its effects on different groups of individuals. No element of society escaped the ravages of judgment.

The first group mentioned who suffered the horrors of foreign occupation were the **women** of Jerusalem (**Zion**) and the **virgins . . . of Judah.** Women who survived the Babylonian assault on their cities were mercilessly raped by the sadistic soldiers. In a scene of savage brutality, repeated by many conquering armies throughout history, the victors went on a wanton spree of lustful revenge against defenseless women.

The city's leaders also felt the fury of the Babylonians. **Princes** were **hung up by their hands.** Those responsible for leading Judah's rebellion against Babylon were tortured to death in this cruel way. Possibly this was a form of crucifixion since hanging and impaling victims on stakes was the usual method of execution used during that time. **Elders** were also tortured.

The **young men** who survived the Babylonian attack were enslaved. Because of the shortage of domestic animals in Palestine (probably because most had been eaten during the 30-month siege), men were forced to perform tasks usually done by animals. Men turned **the millstones** (as Samson also was forced to do, Jud. 16:21) to grind grain, and **boys** were forced to carry large **loads of wood** needed in the city. Those who were Judah's hope had been reduced to the status of slaves.

Wisdom, justice, and happiness had departed from the city. **The city gate** where **the elders** used to gather was the place of justice and wisdom. Disputes between individuals were taken to the wise elders. But with the departure of the elders (cf. Lam. 5:12) the wisdom and justice normally available to the Jews was gone. Even the **music of the young men** had ceased. Music was associated with joy and happiness (cf. Ps. 95:1-2); and Judah had nothing to rejoice about now as her people suffered under the harsh hand of Babylon.

5:15-18. A veil of gloom hung over Jerusalem. The **joy** and revelry that had once been there was replaced by sadness and **mourning.** The bustling activity of a once-thriving city had given way to **desolate** ruins inhabited only by wild animals. **The crown** figuratively represented the

glory and majesty that had belonged to
Jerusalem. That glory was now gone. It
was lost because of sin. The people were
faint from hunger, and their **eyes** were
dim from tears (cf. 2:11; 3:48-49). Judah
had only herself to blame for her present
condition of desolation in which wild
jackals (cf. 4:3) prowled.

B. *The remnant's prayer for restoration
(5:19-22)*

5:19. After describing her condition
(vv. 1-18) Judah concluded her prayer by
calling on God to act (vv. 19-22). The
basis for this call was God's eternal sovereignty: **You, O Lord, reign forever.**
Judah was not suffering because her God
had been defeated by the stronger gods
of Babylon. Judah's God was the only
true God, and *He* had caused her calamity (cf. 1:12-17; 2:1-8; 4:11). Yet this same
God who brought about her destruction
also had the power to bring about her
restoration—if He chose to do so.

5:20. The knowledge of God's ability
to restore the nation prompted the people to ask two questions. Because of the
nature of Hebrew parallelism these two
questions should be viewed synony-
mously. To **forget** about Judah would be
to **forsake** her to her present condition of
suffering. The use of "forget" here is the
opposite of "remember" in verse 1. God
cannot "forget" anything. This figure of
speech means to forsake or abandon the
people *as though* He has forgotten them.
The people were asking God **why** He had
abandoned them for **so long.** Significantly Moses employed the figure of God
remembering His covenant if His people
would confess their sin (Lev. 26:40-42).
So the people of Judah were calling on
God to fulfill the remainder of His covenant promise.

5:21-22. The specific action the people requested was, **Restore us to Yourself . . . that we may return.** The people
wanted to be restored to the blessings of
God's covenant which included being restored to the land of Israel (Lev. 26:40-45;
Deut. 3:1-10). Their ultimate hope for restoration was God's faithfulness to His

covenant promises. **Unless** God had **utterly rejected** the nation (which He
vowed never to do; Lev. 26:44; Jer. 31:31-
37) the people could depend on Him to
answer their request.

Thus the Book of Lamentations ends
on a note of hope. In spite of severe
suffering because of her sin, Judah had
not been abandoned as a nation. God
was still sovereign, and His covenant
with Israel was still operative despite her
disobedience. The hope for the nation
was that if she would call on God and
confess her sin He would protect her
during her captivity (Lam. 3:21-30) and
would ultimately restore her as a nation
to covenant blessing (5:21).

BIBLIOGRAPHY

Cohen, Abraham. *The Five Megilloth.* London: Soncino Press, 1946.

Gottwald, Norman K. *Studies in the Book of
Lamentations.* London: SCM Press, 1962.

Harrison, R.K. *Jeremiah and Lamentations:
An Introduction and Commentary.* The Tyndale
Old Testament Commentaries. Downers
Grove, Ill.: InterVarsity Press, 1973.

Hillers, Delbert R. *Lamentations.* The Anchor Bible. Garden City, N.Y.: Doubleday &
Co., 1972.

Ironside, H.A. *Jeremiah: Prophecy & Lamentations.* New York: Loizeaux Brothers, 1950.

Jensen, Irving L. *Jeremiah and Lamentations.* Everyman's Bible Commentary. Chicago: Moody Press, 1974.

Kaiser, Walter C., Jr. *A Biblical Approach to
Personal Suffering.* Chicago: Moody Press,
1982.

Laetsch, Theo. *Jeremiah.* St. Louis, Mo.:
Concordia Publishing House, 1965.

Schaeffer, Francis A. *Death in the City.*
Downers Grove, Ill.: InterVarsity Press, 1969.

Swindoll, Charles R. *The Lamentations of
Jeremiah.* Bible Study Guide. Fullerton, Calif.:
Insight for Living, 1977.

EZEKIEL

Charles H. Dyer

INTRODUCTION

For the average reader of the Bible the Book of Ezekiel is mostly a perplexing maze of incoherent visions—a kaleidoscope of whirling wheels and dry bones that defy interpretation. This impression often causes readers to shy away from studying the book and to miss one of the great literary and spiritual portions of the Old Testament.

Authorship and Date. The author of this book is "Ezekiel the priest, the son of Buzi" (1:3). The name Ezekiel means "God will strengthen" or "God will harden."

Like Jeremiah (Jer. 1:1) and Zechariah (Zech. 1:1; cf. Neh. 12:4, 16), Ezekiel was a priest (Ezek. 1:3). Ezekiel's father Buzi is mentioned only in 1:3. Jeremiah, Zechariah, and Ezekiel were the only prophet-priests; and all three prophesied during the exilic or postexilic periods. Ezekiel's priestly background explains in part his emphasis on the temple in Jerusalem, the glory of the Lord, the actions of Jerusalem's priests, and God's future temple.

The date for Ezekiel's ministry can be determined by noting the chronological notations in his book (1:2; 8:1; 20:1; 24:1; 29:1, 17; 30:20; 31:1; 32:1, 17; 33:21; 40:1).

All Ezekiel's prophecies are arranged chronologically (starting with "the 5th year of the exile," 1:2, and ending with "the 25th year of our exile," 40:1, except the prophecies introduced in 29:1, 17). These two variations may be explained by the fact that they are grouped topically as part of the prophecies against Egypt in chapters 29–32.

Ezekiel's ministry began "in the fourth month on the fifth day" of "the fifth year of the exile of King Jehoiachin" (1:1-2). Jehoiachin came to the throne in December 597 B.C. after Jehoiakim died

(2 Kings 24:1-12). After a reign of only three months Jehoiachin was captured by Nebuchadnezzar and deported to Babylon. The fifth year of Jehoiachin's exile was 593 B.C., and the fourth month was the month Tammuz. According to Richard A. Parker and Waldo H. Dubberstein (*Babylonian Chronology: 626 B.C.–A.D. 75.* Providence, R.I.: Brown University Press, 1956) the exact meaning of this statement Tammuz (Akk., *Duzu*) began on July 27 in 593 B.C. Therefore Ezekiel began his ministry on July 31, 593 B.C. (the "fifth day" is inclusive, counting both July 27 and 31).

Ezekiel also said his ministry began "in the 30th year" (Ezek. 1:1). Scholars debate the exact meaning of this statement, but many feel it refers to Ezekiel's age. If so, he was commissioned as a prophet at the age he was qualified to enter the priesthood (cf. Num. 4:3).

The last dated prophecy in Ezekiel was "in the 27th year, in the first month on the first day" (Ezek. 29:17). Since Ezekiel began prophesying in 593 (the fifth year of Jehoiachin's exile, 1:2), this prophecy was 571 B.C. (March 26). So Ezekiel's prophetic activity spanned at least 22 years (593–571 B.C.), from age 30 to 52.

Till recently few Bible scholars had doubted the unity, authorship, or exilic date of Ezekiel. Arguments challenging these items have been satisfactorily answered by conservatives (e.g., Gleason L. Archer, Jr., *A Survey of Old Testament Introduction.* Rev. ed. Chicago: Moody Press, 1974, pp. 368-76; and John B. Taylor, *Ezekiel: An Introduction and Commentary*, pp. 13-20).

Historical Background. For a discussion of Judah's history in Ezekiel's time see "Historical Background" in the *Introduction* to Jeremiah.

The Book of Ezekiel was written during the time of Judah's bondage to Babylon under Nebuchadnezzar's rule. Ezekiel lived with a group of captives in Tel Aviv (not the modern-day city in Israel by that name), located beside the Kebar River (3:15) in Babylon. The exact site of this settlement is unknown, but the Kebar River has been identified with the Grand Canal (Akk., *naru kabaru*) in Babylon. This canal branched off from the Euphrates just above Babylon and flowed east of the city. It continued through the site of ancient Nippur and then reentered the Euphrates near Uruk (biblical Erech).

During these final years Ezekiel was ministering in Babylon, predicting the coming collapse of Jerusalem. His message fell on deaf ears till word of the city's destruction was received in Babylon. The fall of the city prompted a change in Ezekiel's prophetic message. Before Jerusalem fell, Ezekiel's message focused on Judah's forthcoming destruction because of her sin. After Jerusalem's fall, Ezekiel's message centered on Judah's future restoration.

Structure and Style. The structure and style of Ezekiel's book has at least four major characteristics.

1. Chronological arrangement. As noted earlier under "Authorship and Date" a definite chronological movement is evident within the book. Ezekiel is the only major prophet with such a precise chronological arrangement but the Books of Haggai and Zechariah have a similar arrangement.

2. Structural balance. In addition to its chronological arrangement Ezekiel's book also has a structural order and harmony. The first 24 chapters focus on the judgment of Judah; chapters 33–48 focus on the restoration of Judah. These two extremes are balanced by chapters 25–32 which deal with God's judgment on other nations. The glory of God departed from the temple in judgment (9:3; 10:4, 18-19; 11:22-25) and reappeared in the temple for blessing (43:1-5). Ezekiel was commissioned to deliver a message of judgment (chaps. 2–3) and later was recommissioned to give a message of deliverance (chap. 33).

3. Focus on the glory and character of God. Ezekiel emphasized the glory and character of God. Having received a vision of God's glory before he was commissioned, Ezekiel continued to refer to God's glory throughout the book (1:28;

3:12, 23; 8:4; 9:3; 10:4, 18-19; 11:22-23; 39:11, 21; 43:2-5; 44:4).

God's character determined His conduct throughout the book. Fifteen times God declared that He had acted for the sake of His name to keep it from being profaned (20:9, 14, 22, 39, 44; 36:20-23 [twice in v. 23]; 39:7 [twice], 25; 43:7-8). Over 60 times God said He had acted so that the people would "know that I am the LORD" (e.g., 6:7, 10, 13-14).

4. Use of literary devices. Ezekiel used unique literary devices to drive home his message to a "hardened and obstinate" people. These included proverbs (12:22-23; 16:44; 18:2-3); visions (chaps. 1–3; 8–11; 37; 40–48); parables (chap. 17; 24:1-14); symbolic acts (chaps. 4–5; 12; 24:15-27); and allegories (chaps. 16–17).

By these means Ezekiel presented his messages in dramatic and forceful ways, thus getting the people's attention so they would respond.

OUTLINE

COMMENTARY

I. Judgment on Judah (chaps. 1–24)

The first half of the Book of Ezekiel focuses on God's coming judgment of Judah. God's sword was poised to strike, and Ezekiel was commissioned with the task of explaining to people already in captivity *what* God's judgment entailed and *why* it was coming.

A. Ezekiel's preparation (chaps. 1–3)

The record of God's commissioning of Ezekiel is the longest such prophetic

call in the Bible (cf. Isa. 6; Jer. 1). Ezekiel, like Isaiah and Jeremiah, was prepared for his ministry by receiving a vision of the glory and majesty of God before he was called to serve the Lord.

1. INTRODUCTION (1:1-3)

1:1-2. When God appeared to Ezekiel to inaugurate his prophetic ministry, it was **in the 30th year, in the fourth month on the fifth day**; it was also **the 5th year of the exile of King Jehoiachin.** As noted under "Authorship and Date" in the *Introduction* this was July 31, 593 B.C. "The 30th year" probably referred to Ezekiel's age. As a priest (v. 3) this was the age he would normally have entered the Lord's service.

Ezekiel had been taken into captivity with King Jehoiachin in March of 597. He was one of **the exiles** who had been resettled **by the Kebar River**—a canal off the Euphrates River that flowed to the east of Babylon (see "Historical Backgound" in the *Introduction*).

I saw visions of God was Ezekiel's summary of the visions which he then described in detail in 1:4–2:7. This view of God's glory profoundly influenced him.

1:3. The word of the LORD points to the *source* of Ezekiel's message. Ezekiel was to receive the message *God* wanted him to deliver. He then elaborated on this (2:8–3:11). **The hand of the LORD** described Ezekiel's *mandate* for his ministry. He was not acting on his own initiative but was constrained by God to minister, a fact detailed later (3:12-27).

2. THE VISIONS FOR THE WORK (1:4–2:7)

In this section Ezekiel discussed in detail the visions he mentioned briefly in 1:1. The prophet described the visions (1:4-28) and then stated their purpose (2:1-7).

a. The four living beings (1:4-14)

1:4. As Ezekiel peered to **the north** he noticed an approaching thunderstorm. In the storm were a big **cloud,** strong winds, and **flashing lightning.** As the cloud approached, though, Ezekiel's gaze shifted from the darkness of the storm to the **light** emanating from its **center.** This light **looked like glowing metal** (*ḥašmāl*). This word occurs in the Old Testament only in Ezekiel (here and in v. 27; 8:2). It seems to refer to some shining substance. In the other two occurrences it describes God's glowing splendor.

1:5-8a. Ezekiel spotted **four living creatures** in the midst of **the fire.** These beings are identified in chapter 10 as cherubim, a special order of angelic beings. They have special access to God (cf. 28:14, 16) and are bearers of God's throne-chariot. On the tabernacle's ark of the covenant, gold images of cherubim, with outstretched wings, guarded the mercy seat where the glory of the Lord dwelt (Ex. 25:17-22; Num. 7:89). God was "enthroned between the cherubim" of the ark of the covenant (1 Sam. 4:4; 2 Sam. 6:2; Pss. 80:1; 99:1; Isa. 37:16). This place where God was enthroned was called "the chariot" (1 Chron. 28:18). Since the earthly tabernacle and temple were a copy of the heavenly reality (Heb. 8:5), Ezekiel's vision was of the actual throne-chariot of God, borne by cherubim.

The general **appearance** of the living beings was somewhat like **a man.** However, they would not be mistaken for humans. They **each** had **four faces and four wings.** (The prophet explained these features in detail, Ezek. 1:10-11.) The cherubim's **legs were straight,** which implies that they were standing upright, but **their feet** were calf-like instead of human, and were **like burnished** (highly polished) **bronze.** Ezekiel said the four cherubim also had human-like **hands.**

1:8b-9. Ezekiel then explained how the **four** creatures functioned as a unit. Two of the four **wings** of each creature were outstretched so that **their wings touched one another,** forming a connecting square. Having four **faces** on four sides of their heads and being connected in a square, they were able to travel **straight** in any direction and to change direction without turning. Thus **they did not turn as they moved.**

1:10. In recording more details of the cherubim (vv. 10-14), Ezekiel first described **their faces.** The front of each cherub was **the face of a man, and on the right side** was **the face of a lion. The left** side was **the face of an ox,** and **the face of an eagle** was apparently in the back. Some interpreters feel that these represent intelligence (man), power (lion), service (ox), and swiftness (eagle). How-

ever, it seems better to see the faces as representing the highest forms of life in God's created realm. Man was mentioned first because he was the acme of God's creative work. He was followed by the lion, "king" among wild beasts; the ox, one of the strongest of domestic animals; and the eagle, the "lord" of the birds.

1:11. Ezekiel then described the cherubim's **wings. Two** of the four **wings** on each cherub **were spread out upward,** or extended out above the cherub and were **touching a wing of** a cherub **on either side.** The effect was to form a large "box" with a cherub at each corner. The other **two wings** on each cherub were for **covering its body.** Because these creatures were ministering before God's holy presence, they covered their bodies in reverence (cf. Isa. 6:1-3).

1:12-14. The motion of the cherubim was always **straight ahead.** They could go in any direction **without turning** their faces. They were directed in their motion by **the spirit,** probably God's Spirit. These **creatures,** already described as "brilliant light. . . . glowing metal. . . . burnished bronze" (vv. 4, 7), were also said to look **like burning coals of fire or like torches.** The glowing embers were interspersed with **fire** that **moved back and forth among the creatures.** This seemed to presage Ezekiel's message of God's burning judgment on Judah.

b. The four wheels (1:15-21)

Looking below the cherubim, Ezekiel saw some wheels. He described the wheels generally (vv. 15-18) and then told how the wheels and the cherubim were related (vv. 19-21).

1:15-18. On the ground beside each cherub was **a wheel.** Each wheel **sparkled like chrysolite** (*taršîš*). This precious stone might be yellow jasper or some other gold-colored stone, or beryl which is commonly pale green, or chrysolite which is transparent yellow or green. The point is that the **wheels** sparkled with a yellow-green glow.

The two wheels for each cherub were unusual in shape; one **wheel** intersected another **wheel** at right angles. Thus they could roll in **four directions** without being turned and could move with the cherubim. Their great **awesome** (cf. v. 22) height added to their fearful design. This awesomeness was enhanced by the rims of the wheels being full of eyes all around. This unusual feature probably pictures divine omniscience (cf. 2 Chron. 16:9; Prov. 15:3), the eyes representing the all-seeing nature of the One who rides on this throne-chariot.

1:19-21. The statement, the spirit of the living creatures was in the wheels, may mean the wheels were like an extension of the cherubim on God's throne-chariot. Ezekiel envisioned the God of the universe on a mobile platform. As He directed the cherubim, the wheels responded and the chariot was propelled on its way.

c. The expanse (1:22-24)

1:22-24. The outstretched wings of the cherubim joined together. Above their wings was an area that Ezekiel said looked like an expanse (*rāqîaʿ*). This was not an empty space. This same word was used to describe the expanse created by God on the second day of Creation (Gen. 1:6-7). That "expanse" was pictured there as something solid (*rāqîaʿ* is from *rāqaʿ*, "to beat, stamp, beat out, spread out"), which supported the waters above it.

The shining brilliance of the expanse above the cherubim reminded Ezekiel of ice crystals sparkling in the light of the sun. Interestingly the Apostle John said the expanse around God's throne is "clear as crystal" (Rev. 4:6).

When the wings of the cherubim moved, their sound was like water rushing down a mountain stream, and was as intense as the voice of God (possibly an allusion to thunder which sometimes depicts God's voice, Job 37:4-5; 40:9; Pss. 18:13; 104:7). This cacophony reminded Ezekiel of the din of an army in battle. When the cherubim stopped, they lowered their wings.

d. The throne (1:25-28)

1:25-28. As the cherubim came to a halt and the sound of their wings stopped, Ezekiel became aware of another sound. It was a voice from above the expanse over their heads. This was the voice of God seated on the throne. As Ezekiel instinctively glanced upward in the direction of the voice, he saw above the expanse what looked like a throne of sapphire. "Sapphire" (*ʾeben-sappîr*) or,

more properly, *lapis lazuli* (NIV marg.) is an azure-blue stone, prized since ancient times. It is cut and polished for ornamental purposes.

Seated on this shining blue throne was Someone who looked like a man. Ezekiel's gaze was drawn first to the upper part of His body and then to the lower part. Though Ezekiel could describe the cherubim in detail, all he could say of God was that He looked like glowing metal and fire. The splendor of His glory was so bright that Ezekiel could see only His form before he was forced to look down. Ezekiel then noticed a radiance surrounding the vision. It looked like . . . a rainbow. The multisplendored colors of the rainbow were refracted from the blazing light of God's glory. The Apostle John described the same beauty in his vision of God's throne in heaven (Rev. 4:3).

Lest anyone doubt what Ezekiel saw, he stated clearly that it was the appearance of the likeness of the glory of the LORD. The Lord's glory is referred to 16 times in Ezekiel (1:28; 3:12, 23; 8:4; 9:3; 10:4, 18-19; 11:22-23; 39:21; 43:2 [twice], 4-5; 44:4; see comments under "Structure and Style" in the *Introduction*). Ezekiel had seen a theophany, as God had appeared to him in a visionary form. By using the terms "appearance" and "likeness" Ezekiel was pointing out that he had not seen God directly. That would have caused immediate death (cf. Ex. 33:18-23; John 1:18).

Ezekiel responded in humble submission; he fell facedown (cf. Ezek. 3:23). As he prostrated himself in awe before God's majesty, he heard God speak. This was probably the same voice mentioned in 1:25.

e. The task for Ezekiel (2:1-7)

As God spoke (1:28), He provided power for Ezekiel (2:1-2), told Ezekiel of his assignment (vv. 3-5), and challenged him to be faithful (vv. 6-7).

2:1-2. God told Ezekiel to rise and receive His message. Son of man (*ben-ʾāḏām*) occurs 93 times in the Book of Ezekiel to refer to that prophet. It emphasizes his humanity before God and seems to stress the distance that separates man from God. The word "son" expresses family and hereditary relationships, but often moves beyond the mere biological to denote association or identification with someone or something (cf. "sons of God," Gen. 6:2, 4; "son of the dawn," Isa. 14:12). By this title God was stressing Ezekiel's association with the human race.

When God told Ezekiel to stand, He also enabled him by the Holy Spirit to stand. In Old Testament times the Holy Spirit did not indwell all believers but indwelt selected persons temporarily for divine service (cf. Ex. 31:1-11; 1 Sam. 10:9-11; Ps. 51:11; Ezek. 3:24).

2:3-5. Ezekiel's assignment was difficult. His message was to be directed to a rebellious nation ("rebellious" occurs eight times in chaps. 2 and 3, and eight times elsewhere in Ezek.), people who were obstinate (cf. 3:7) and stubborn. Rather than acknowledging God's judgment and confessing their sins, the Jewish exiles viewed their time in Babylon as a temporary setback that would be alleviated by their soon return to Jerusalem. They refused to admit their sin or to believe the threat of impending judgment on their disobedient nation.

Ezekiel's task was to declare God's Word. Whether they responded was the people's own responsibility. But in the end (when the events did transpire), they (the rebellious house; cf. comments on 3:9) would know that a prophet had been in their midst.

As a prophet Ezekiel would be a channel for the Sovereign LORD ('ăḏōnāy Yahweh). Ezekiel used this title of God 217 times. Elsewhere in the Old Testament it occurs only 103 times (Theological Dictionary of the Old Testament. Grand Rapids: Wm. B. Eerdmans Publishing Co., s.v. 'āḏôn, 'ăḏōnāy, 1:62-3). This name stesses both God's sovereign authority and His covenant-keeping faithfulness.

2:6-7. Three times God told Ezekiel, Do not be afraid. He needed this encouragement because the task was difficult (briers and thorns are all around you) and even dangerous (you live among scorpions). Ezekiel learned his lesson well. Nowhere does the book hint that he cowered in fear or hesitated to proclaim God's message.

God said Ezekiel was to speak His words. Verses 7-8 are a bridge between two major sections. The first section (1:4–2:7) reports the visions for the work.

The next section (2:8–3:11) gives the message for the work. This One who gave Ezekiel the word is the Sovereign Lord whom Ezekiel had just seen in the vision.

3. THE MESSAGE FOR THE WORK (2:8–3:11)

Ezekiel's vision of God's glory provided the perspective and motivation for his task. But he also needed a message, the content of which came from the Lord (cf. the "word of the LORD," 1:3). The prophet was told to receive God's word (2:8–3:3) and then to deliver it (3:4-11).

a. The reception of God's word (2:8–3:3)

2:8. Israel had chafed under the bit of divine instruction and rebelled (v. 3) against God and His word. But Ezekiel was to open his mouth and eat what God gave him. He was to be receptive and responsive to God's words.

2:9-10. The specific word was then revealed to Ezekiel. A hand (probably God's) stretched out to him from His throne with a scroll. This is supported by the fact that the One speaking, God, also gave Ezekiel the scroll (3:2).

The scroll had writing on both sides. Scrolls were the common means for recording and preserving God's Word in Israel. Leather, papyrus, or parchment sheets were joined together in long rolls. The writing was in vertical columns, and very seldom was writing done on both sides of a scroll (but cf. Rev. 5:1). Many interpretations of why the scroll was written on both sides have been given, but the best explanation seems to be that God had much that He wanted Ezekiel to communicate to Israel.

The message consisted of words of lament and mourning and woe. This accurately summarizes the contents of Ezekiel 4–32. It does not, however, reflect the latter part of the book, in which the prophet spoke of Israel's restoration. This could explain, in part, why Ezekiel was recommissioned (chap. 33)—the content of his message was substantially changed after his message of woe was fulfilled.

3:1-3. God had already told the prophet to eat what He would give him (2:8). Now God repeated the order, specifically telling him to eat the scroll he had just received. The purpose was so he could then go and speak to the house of Israel (cf. comments on 3:4 about "Israel"). His task as a prophet was to deliver God's word to God's people.

As Ezekiel ate the scroll, **it tasted as sweet as honey.** Though his message was one of judgment, it was still God's word. The sweetness came from the source of the words (God) rather than the content of the words (judgment). This same thought was expressed by David (Ps. 19:10), Jeremiah (Jer. 15:16), and the Apostle John (Rev. 10:9-11).

b. *The delivery of God's word (3:4-11)*

3:4. After receiving God's word, Ezekiel was told to proclaim it. His hearers were to be **the house of Israel.** Does this refer to all Israel (including those still in Palestine) or only to those in exile in Babylon? The parallel command in verse 11 implies that only those Israelites "in exile" were in view. Yet the phrase "house of Israel" cannot be limited to them. In many of the 101 occurrences of this expression (or variations of it) in the Book of Ezekiel, more than Israelites in captivity were included (cf. 6:11; 8:11-12). Ezekiel's message was for the entire "house" (i.e., people) of Israel, though he specifically proclaimed it to a small portion of that household then in captivity.

God's specific task for Ezekiel was to **speak** God's **words to them** (Israel). At first these verses seem to repeat 2:3-7, but the focus of this passage is different. In 2:3-7 Ezekiel was commissioned as a prophet, and in 3:4-9 he was equipped for his task.

3:5-6. Ezekiel's task did not involve linguistic obstacles. He was **not being sent to a people of obscure speech and difficult language.** Obscure (lit., "deep") speech suggests words that are unfathomable or difficult to comprehend (e.g., the language of the Assyrians, Isa. 33:19). The words **difficult language** (lit., "heavy tongue") can denote speech that is thick or sluggish. Moses used this expression to describe his lack of eloquence (Ex. 4:10). In Ezekiel 3:5 it probably means **words** that are hard to **understand** because of a language barrier (v. 6). Ezekiel faced no such hurdle. His message was not for some distant land with an exotic language; it was for Israel. Though going to another culture and nation would have been difficult because of the language problem, the results elsewhere would have been more rewarding. Had

Ezekiel gone to another nation, **they would have listened to** him. Amazingly those who knew nothing of the true God of the universe would have been more responsive than those who claimed His name.

3:7. At the outset God warned Ezekiel not to expect dramatic results from his ministry (cf. Isa. 6:8-13; Jer. 1:11-19). In contrast with the open reception Ezekiel would receive from other nations, Israel was **not willing to listen to** him. She would reject him because she had rejected God. The people were not prepared to "listen to" or respond to Ezekiel **because they** were **not willing to listen to** God. Their spiritual deafness was acquired over long years of exposure to and rejection of God's word given by the prophets. Israel's response to God in the past was a harbinger of the response Ezekiel could expect.

The nation's malady extended to **the whole house of Israel.** This does not imply that every Israelite had rejected God, for Habakkuk, Jeremiah, Ezekiel, and Daniel were all ministering faithfully. God was referring to all parts of Israel rather than every Israelite. Rebellion had made its way into the royal household, the temple, the courts of justice, and into every city and town in the land. Though individuals here and there were still responding to the Lord, the nation as a whole had turned from Him.

3:8. Taking God's message of judgment to an unyielding people was a tough task. God encouraged Ezekiel by offering him the needed strength. The prophet need not worry about the weight of his assignment. God promised to **make** him **as unyielding and hardened as they** were. The word for "hardened" (*ḥāzāq*) is the same word that forms part of Ezekiel's name—*yᵉḥezqēʾl*, "God will strengthen" or "God will harden." When he heard his name he was reminded of God's promised strength.

3:9. God also said He would **make** Ezekiel's **forehead like the hardest stone, harder than flint.** Figuratively "forehead" expresses determination or defiance (cf. Isa. 48:4; 50:7, "face" is lit., "forehead"; Jer. 3:3, "the brazen look of a prostitute" is lit., "a harlot's forehead"; 48:45). Ezekiel's determination would not waver when beset by opposition. "Flint," the hardest stone in Palestine, was used by Israel for knives (cf. Josh. 5:2-3) and other implements. Ezekiel's God-given strength and determination would withstand any opposition (cf. Jer. 1:18).

Because of God's empowering of Ezekiel, He could command him **not to be afraid of them or terrified by them** (cf. Jer. 1:17). Though opposition was certain to come, Ezekiel had nothing to fear. God's power was more than adequate to overcome the expected resistance. **Rebellious house** is a term for Israel that Ezekiel used 12 times (Ezek. 2:5-6, 8; 3:9, 26-27; 12:3, 9, 25; 17:12; 24:3; 44:6), apparently to underscore the people's defiance against God.

3:10-11. To be an accurate channel of God's revelation Ezekiel was to **listen carefully and take to heart** God's word. The recipients of his message were his **countrymen in exile,** though the scope of his pronouncements went beyond that group to include all Israel.

Ezekiel was to proclaim to these exiles, **This is what the Sovereign LORD says.** In words that hearken back to 2:4-5 Ezekiel was reminded of his task. He was responsible to proclaim God's word accurately regardless of the response. Some would **listen,** that is, obey, and others would **fail to listen,** that is, refuse to obey (cf. 2:5).

4. THE MOTIVATION FOR THE WORK
(3:12-27)

Ezekiel's vision of God's glory had provided the needed *perspective* for his task (1:4–2:7). The *message* he was to deliver was provided by God (2:8–3:11). Then he needed *motivation* to direct him in the task. That motivation was provided by the "hand of the LORD" (cf. 1:3). He was first guided by the Spirit to his place of ministry (3:12-15); he was then formally appointed as God's watchman to Israel (vv. 16-21); then the Lord imposed several physical restraints on Ezekiel (vv. 22-27).

a. The leading of the Spirit (3:12-15)

3:12-14a. After seeing the vision of God, Ezekiel was transported back to Tel Aviv (v. 15) by the Holy Spirit. (See comments on Tel Aviv under "Historical Background" in the *Introduction*.) The movement began when the **Spirit lifted** him **up.** The "Spirit" who transported Ezekiel was the same One who had entered into him (2:2). This was the Holy Spirit who divinely enabled God's servants in Old Testament times. Several times the Holy Spirit transported Ezekiel (mentally rather than physically; cf. 8:3; 11:1, 24; 37:1; 43:5) to various places to give him information.

Ezekiel began to describe the movement by the Holy Spirit (3:12), but did not return to that subject till later (v. 14) because he was distracted by **a loud rushing sound.** After an interjection of praise (v. 12b) Ezekiel explained that the rushing sound was **of the wings of the** cherubim **brushing against each other and . . . of the wheels.** Ezekiel was transported by the Spirit on God's throne-chariot, and the sound generated by its movement startled him (cf. 1:24).

In describing his transport by God's Spirit, Ezekiel interjected, **May the glory of the LORD** (cf. comments on 1:28) **be praised in His dwelling place.** The "rushing sound" before his expression of praise was made by the cherubim's wings and wheels. Overcome by the sight and sound of God's glory, Ezekiel responded with this spontaneous note of praise to God.

3:14b-15. As Ezekiel was returned by the Holy **Spirit,** his own spirit was churning. He said, **I went in bitterness and in the anger of my spirit.** "Bitterness" (*mar*) carries the ideas of anguish (Gen. 27:34), discontentment (1 Sam. 22:2), and fierce anger (2 Sam. 17:8). Of these possible nuances, the parallelism with "anger (*ḥēmâh,* 'heat, rage') of my spirit" points to fierce anger as Ezekiel's emotion. As he associated himself with God he felt the same emotions toward Israel's sin as God did.

Ezekiel was guided in his mission by **the strong hand of the LORD.** "The hand of the LORD" is also mentioned in Ezekiel 1:3; 3:22; 8:1; 33:22; 37:1. The idea of "the hand of the LORD" (or "of God")—occurring nearly 190 times in the Old Testament—refers to God's power or authority.

Ezekiel returned **to the exiles . . . at Tel Aviv near the Kebar River** (cf. 1:3 and see "Historical Background" in the *Introduction*). He **sat among them for seven days—overwhelmed.** The character of the vision he had just seen and the awesomeness of the task before him left the prophet stunned. Ezekiel needed time to collect his thoughts and prepare himself for his ministry.

b. The appointment as a watchman (3:16-21)

3:16-19. After **seven days** of silence Ezekiel's solitude was shattered by God's words. God appointed him **a watchman for the house of Israel.** "Watchman" is used several times of prophets (cf. Isa. 56:10; Jer. 6:17; Hosea 9:8). Watchmen were stationed on city walls, hilltops, or specially designed watchtowers. A watchman was to be on the alert for approaching enemies and warn the city's people of any impending attack. This gave city dwellers outside the walls an opportunity to seek protection and gave the people time to secure the gates and man the defenses.

Similarly, as God's watchman, Ezekiel was responsible for sounding the **warning** of impending judgment to Israel. He was to warn both the **wicked** (Ezek. 3:18-19) and the righteous (vv. 20-21). **A wicked** person was to be warned **to turn from his evil ways in order to save his life.** Though both the Old and New Testaments clearly indicate the *spiritual* results of sin, the focus here is on the *physical* consequences. A wicked person who refuses to heed God's warnings **will die for his sin.** Since all are spiritually dead from birth, the obvious reference here is to physical death. As Nebuchadnezzar's armies approached, the **wicked** could expect death at the enemy's hands.

3:20-21. The **righteous man** also needed to be warned to prevent his turning **from his righteousness and** doing **evil.** If a righteous person had left the path of righteousness, he too was in danger of death. This is not referring to an individual losing his salvation. The "righteous" one described here was outwardly conforming to God's commandments, and the "death" spoken of here is physical death (cf. comments on vv. 18-19). The one obeying God's Law was to be protected during the approaching judgment, but those who broke the Law could expect death.

If Ezekiel failed to **warn** of approaching danger, God would **hold** him **accountable for** the **blood** of the people. The principle of blood accountability is expressed in Genesis 9:5-6. If Ezekiel did not **warn** the people, he would be held as responsible for their murder as if he had killed them himself. However, if Ezekiel fulfilled his responsibility, then he would **have saved** himself (Ezek. 3:19, 21). The word "saved" (*nāṣal*, "to deliver, snatch away, rescue") should be translated here "delivered," as it does not refer to eternal salvation. Rather, by giving warning, Ezekiel would have delivered himself from any responsibility for the coming calamity. People who refused to heed his warning had only themselves to blame.

c. The physical restraints of the Lord (3:22-27)

3:22-23. Ezekiel was called **out to the plain** to meet with God. "Plain" (*biq'âh*) means "valley" as it is translated in 37:1. The word refers to one of the many broad valleys or plains in the Mesopotamian basin (cf. Gen. 11:2). The location of the particular plain where Ezekiel went is unknown.

In the plain Ezekiel saw **the glory of the LORD** (cf. comments on Ezek. 1:28) for the second time. His response was again one of humble submission—he **fell facedown** (cf. 1:28).

3:24. The Spirit then **came into** him and made him stand up. In Old Testament times the Holy Spirit's indwelling was not continuous (cf. comments on 2:2). The Spirit again entered Ezekiel to give him strength for his ministry.

God then placed several restraints on the prophet. The first was a command to **shut** himself in his **house.** This does not imply that Ezekiel was never to leave his house (cf. 5:2; 12:3); instead he was to refrain from open fellowship with the people. Often the leaders came to him at his house to receive God's word (cf. 8:1; 14:1; 20:1).

3:25. The reason for Ezekiel's confinement was that if he did not stay in his house, people would **tie** him **with ropes . . . so that** he could not **go out among the people.** Some have suggested that God told Ezekiel to stay home out of concern for his physical safety, for those who opposed his ministry would physically try to keep him from proclaiming God's word. Yet there is no evidence that Ezekiel was ever physically bound or forcibly constrained. More likely this is a figure of speech. Ezekiel was **bound** from moving about among the people and was confined to his home because of their opposition to his message. It was a God-imposed restraint that would demonstrate to the people their rebellion.

3:26. God informed Ezekiel of another restriction: his **tongue** would **stick to the roof of** his mouth. Ezekiel experienced temporary dumbness so that he could not speak to the people. This dumbness, however, was not continuous (v. 27) or permanent (33:22). It was a sign to the **rebellious house** (cf. 3:27 and comments on 2:3 and 3:9) of their sin.

3:27. Some see a contradiction between Ezekiel's commission as a watchman (vv. 16-21) and his prohibition against speaking to the people (v. 26). The solution to the problem is in verse 27. Ezekiel's silence was placed on him as an individual. From then on, Ezekiel spoke only when God told him to. God said, **But when I speak to you, I will open your mouth.** When he was silent, it was because God had not spoken. When he spoke, it was because God had given him a message. As a watchman, he was to open his mouth to say, **This is what the Sovereign LORD says.**

The section closes, **Whoever will listen let him listen, and whoever will refuse let him refuse.** The first part of the sentence is literally, "Let the hearer hear" or "The one who hears will hear." The implication is that a person's reception or rejection of Ezekiel's message was determined by his openness or lack of it to God. One who was receptive to God would accept Ezekiel's message; one who rejected God would reject this message. These words are similar to Christ's words in His earthly ministry, "He who has ears, let him hear" (Matt. 11:15; 13:9, 43; Mark 4:9, 23; Luke 8:8; 14:35).

B. Ezekiel's prophecies against Judah and Jerusalem (chaps. 4–24)

Ezekiel's ministry began with a personal encounter with God. Then God appeared to Ezekiel and gave him His word of judgment for Israel. He appointed Ezekiel as the watchman who was responsible to sound the alarm. Chapters 4–24 include the watchman's cry.

In chapters 4–11 Ezekiel focused on the need for judgment because of the people's disobedience. The prophet then attacked the futility of false optimism

(chaps. 12–19). Next Ezekiel placed their present disobedience and future judgment in perspective by reviewing the history of Judah's corruption (chaps. 20–24).

1. THE NECESSITY OF JUDGMENT BECAUSE OF DISOBEDIENCE (CHAPS. 4–11)

Ezekiel's task was to confront Israel with her sin and warn her (cf. 3:17) of impending destruction. Ezekiel employed several means to focus on the people's need for judgment. These included signs (chaps. 4–5), sermons (chaps. 6–7), and visions (chaps. 8–11). In each case the emphasis was on sin and its ensuing suffering.

a. Four signs of coming judgment (chaps. 4–5)

Though Ezekiel was confined to his home (3:24), God still expected him to deliver His message of judgment. To arouse interest Ezekiel used objects and actions, possibly in his courtyard or at the entrance to his house. These were signs about the coming siege against Jerusalem.

(1) The sign of the brick (4:1-3). **4:1.** On a **clay tablet** Ezekiel drew an outline of **the city of Jerusalem.** The "clay tablet" (*lᵉḇēnâh*) could refer to a soft clay tablet used by the Babylonians for a writing pad, or it could refer to a large sun-baked brick, the major building material used in Babylon (cf. Gen. 11:3). It seems better to see the word used in its more normal sense of "brick." The shape of Jerusalem was distinctive so Ezekiel's sketch of it would be recognized immediately.

4:2. God then told Ezekiel to **lay siege** to the brick. Because Jerusalem was a well-fortified city, it would take Babylon months to capture it. The purpose of a siege was to starve out the enemies and wear them down by halting their flow of food, supplies, and weapons.

In depicting the attack on Jerusalem, Ezekiel may have used small wooden models or clods of dirt to represent the army of Babylon circling the city and laying siege to it. He first erected **siege works** (*dāyēq*) **against** his "city." These were earthen towers or walls of dirt erected all around Jerusalem (cf. 2 Kings 25:1; Jer. 52:4). They protected the offensive army from arrows fired from the wall and gave the attackers additional height from which to shoot arrows over the city wall.

Ezekiel was also to **build a ramp up to** the brick city. The ramp provided a relatively smooth incline up which siege towers and battering rams could be pushed. Also the ramp allowed the attackers to get above the bedrock and large foundation stones of the city so the smaller and more vulnerable upper stones could be reached by the battering rams.

To prevent reinforcements and supplies from coming in and to keep survivors from slipping out, an attacking army would **set up camps** around the besieged city. Ezekiel did the same on his small-scale model. Later Nebuchadnezzar's army surrounded Jerusalem during the siege and allowed the city no means of relief or escape. Once everything was positioned the **battering rams** were brought forward to begin their assault. Their constant hammering gradually weakened the city's walls.

4:3. As Nebuchadnezzar's **siege** (graphically pictured by Ezekiel) tightened its grip around Jerusalem, the people called to God for deliverance. Ezekiel pictured the futility of the people's cries by putting **an iron pan** like **an iron wall between** him and the city. The "pan" (*maḥăbaṭ*) probably referred to an iron plate or griddle used by the Israelites for baking their bread or cakes (cf. Lev. 2:5). Some scholars believe the iron pan was positioned to represent the severity or irresistible nature of the siege, but the vivid description of the siege (Ezek. 4:2) makes such an understanding unnecessary. More likely the pan represented an impregnable barrier between God and Jerusalem because of her sin (Isa. 59:2; Lam. 3:44). As the siege progressed, Jerusalem would cry out for deliverance, but God would not answer her prayers.

(2) The sign of Ezekiel's lying on his sides. **4:4-8.** This is the most difficult sign in the book to interpret, partly because of the ambiguity of the text and partly because of a textual problem.

God told Ezekiel to **lie on** his **left side and put the sin of the house of Israel** on himself. If Ezekiel prostrated himself with his head toward Jerusalem (cf. Dan. 6:10), he was facing north when he lay on his left side (and south when he lay on his right side, Ezek. 4:6). His fac-

ing north, which represented Israel, the Northern Kingdom, was to be **for 390 days.** Ezekiel did not remain in this position 24 hours a day, because the very next sign (vv. 9-17) includes some other actions Ezekiel was to do in that time. He probably remained in this position for a portion of each day.

After remaining on his left side for 390 days, he was to lie on his **right side, and bear the sin of the house of Judah.** His facing toward the south, representing Judah, the Southern Kingdom, was to last for **40 days.** To symbolize the confinement of the siege, God had Ezekiel tied **up with ropes** (v. 8). Apparently Ezekiel was tied up only during the time each day when he lay on his side.

The meaning of Ezekiel's actions is somewhat obscure. The Septuagint (Gr. trans. of the OT) causes even more confusion by substituting 190 days (vv. 5, 9) for 390. This emending of the text was probably done so it would make more sense. If so, the translators of the Septuagint also had difficulty interpreting the passage.

The first sign (vv. 1-3) visualized the coming siege, and the third and fourth signs (vv. 9-17 and chap. 5) focused on the results of the siege. Therefore this second sign also probably refers in some way to the siege of Jerusalem. In fact at least two factors clearly indicate that this is its point: (1) The 390 days and 40 days are called **the days of your siege** (4:8). (2) In the third sign Ezekiel rationed his food and water during the time he was lying on his side to depict the scarcity of food during the time of the siege (vv. 9, 16-17).

But why did the Lord choose the numbers 390 and 40? The days represent **the years of their sin** (v. 5), that is, each day corresponds to a year in Israel's and Judah's history. But were the years *past* or *future*? If they refer to the past, Ezekiel was showing the number of years Israel and Judah had sinned before this judgment. If they refer to the future, Ezekiel was indicating the number of years the nation would be oppressed by Gentiles after falling to Babylon.

Those who say the sign pointed to the future have tried to determine some historical point of fullfillment. Others interpret the numbers "symbolically" as indicating the end of the Babylonian Captivity, but the specific numbers and their association with both Israel and Judah make such a view unlikely.

Other scholars have said the numbers refer to 430 years of Gentile domination beginning with Jehoiachin's exile in 597 B.C., ending in 167 B.C., the year the Maccabean revolt began. This view has several problems. First, there is no indication that 597 should be used as a starting point instead of 592 (the year Ezekiel began prophesying) or instead of 586 (the year the city actually fell). Second, this view does not explain why 390 years were assigned to Israel. They had gone into captivity (to Assyria in 722 B.C.) 125 years before 597, when the time assigned to them actually began. Third, it is not clear that 167 B.C. actually was the year Israel was freed from the yoke of Syria. That year was only the beginning of the struggle.

Perhaps the best solution is to see the numbers as referring to the past. The 390 days corresponded to "the years of their sin" (v. 5), not the years of their chastisement. Yet no specific years can be determined with any certainty. But while the details are unclear, the message is obvious—Babylon would lay siege to Jerusalem because of her sin, and in some way the length of the siege would correspond to the years of her sin.

(3) The sign of the unclean food (4:9-17). **4:9-14.** Ezekiel's third sign emphasized the severity of the siege of Jerusalem. God told him to **take wheat and barley, beans and lentils, millet and spelt.** These were common grains in Israel's diet (cf. 2 Sam. 17:27-29). But the fact that Ezekiel was told to **put them in a container and make them into bread for** himself indicates a scarcity of food. Normally each of these foods was in abundance. During the siege, however, supplies were so scarce that several foods had to be combined to provide enough for a meal.

Ezekiel had **to eat** the mixture of foods **during the 390 days** he was lying **on** his left **side.** He was to **weigh out 20 shekels of food to eat each day . . . at set times.** This daily ration weighed about eight ounces (NIV marg.). He was also allowed to drink **a sixth of a hin,** two-thirds of a quart, **of water.**

The purpose of his eating and drinking these meager rations was to show the scarcity of food and water in Jerusalem during the siege (cf. Ezek. 4:16-17). This sign also showed the pollution and defilement the people would experience. Ezekiel was to **bake** his bread **in the sight of the people, using human excrement for fuel.** The use of dung as fuel was practiced throughout the Middle East because of the scarcity of wood. Dung was mixed with straw and allowed to dry. The dried dung burned slowly and gave off an unpleasant odor. No stigma was associated with the use of animal dung, but using human dung was considered repulsive.

Ezekiel understood the symbolism of the sign, but the action was personally distasteful to him. He could not bring himself to do it. He responded, **Not so, Sovereign LORD! I have never defiled myself.** Ezekiel had always kept God's dietary laws (Deut. 14). As a priest (Ezek. 1:3) he was careful to keep himself undefiled (cf. Lev. 22:8; Ezek. 44:31). Though the Law did not specifically prohibit the use of human dung for cooking, its guideline regarding the disposal of human excrement suggests that it was considered improper (cf. Deut. 23:12-14). The LORD explained the symbolism of using human dung: **The people of Israel will eat defiled food among the nations where I will drive them** (Ezek. 4:13). The siege (and subsequent captivity) would force the Israelites to eat defiled food and thus become ceremonially unclean.

4:15-17. God graciously granted Ezekiel's request. **I will let you bake your bread over cow manure instead of human excrement.** Less of a stigma was associated with the use of cow dung, so God let Ezekiel use it.

The scarcity of **food** and **water** during Babylon's siege of Jerusalem (cf. Lam. 1:11; 2:11-12, 19; 4:4-5, 9), and the people's accompanying **anxiety** (cf. Ezek. 12:19) and emaciation (cf. Lam. 4:8), was all **because of their sin** (cf. Lam. 4:13; 5:16).

(4) The sign of the shaved head and divided hair (chap. 5). This fourth sign visualized Jerusalem's fate. The sign was given in verses 1-4 and explained in verses 5-17. After Ezekiel represented the *fact* of the siege (first sign), the *length* of the siege (second sign), and its *severity* (third sign), he demonstrated the *results* of the siege (fourth sign). To accomplish

this sign Ezekiel journeyed from the confines of his house—certainly an action which in itself caught the people's attention. He went "inside the city" (v. 2a) and "all around the city" (v. 2b).

5:1. God told Ezekiel to shave his head and beard with a sharp sword. "Sword" (*ḥereb*) is the common word for the weapon used by ancient armies. Ezekiel used the word 83 times in his book to speak of the means by which Jerusalem (cf. 6:11), Edom (25:13), Tyre (26:6, 8), Egypt (29:8-9; 30:4), and Gog (38:21) would be destroyed. Shaving one's head (and beard) was a sign of mourning (Job 1:20; Isa. 15:2-3; Jer. 7:29; 48:37; Ezek. 7:18), humiliation (2 Sam. 10:4-5), and possibly repentance (Jer. 41:5). No doubt all these were implied in Ezekiel's actions.

After Ezekiel shaved, he was to use a set of scales for weighing his hair in three equal piles with a few strands left over. He did this possibly sometime near the end of his previous two signs. But he did nothing else till the 430 days of his symbolic siege had ended.

5:2. The hair that had been set aside earlier was now put to use. Ezekiel carried a third of his hair to the middle of the city and set it on fire. The purpose of this action, explained in verse 12, was to illustrate that a third of the people would die by the plague or by famine. When Nebuchadnezzar's army finally broke through the city's walls, they found a population decimated by famine. The food shortage was so severe that the people had resorted to cannibalism (v. 10). Such horrors had been predicted by Moses (Deut. 28:52-57) and were verified by Jeremiah (Lam. 2:20; 4:10).

Those who survived the famine had to face the sword. After burning the first third of his hair, Ezekiel went through the city with the second third and chopped it up with his sword. This action meant that a third of the Jerusalemites would die by the sword (Ezek. 5:12).

The one-third of the inhabitants of Jerusalem who would survive the siege would still be in jeopardy. This was illustrated by the prophet's scattering a third of his hair to the wind. Those who survived Jerusalem's fall to Babylon would be taken away in captivity and would live in fear.

5:3-4. After Ezekiel had burned, chopped, and scattered his hair, a few strands remained. God told Ezekiel to tuck them away in the folds of his garment. Hiding these few hairs represented God's preserving a remnant in the midst of judgment. The "garment" was the long robe or tunic men wore. It was secured at the waist by a belt or sash. The bottom was pulled up and tucked into the belt to form a pouch for carrying things. This was probably where Ezekiel put those few hairs.

The few hairs in Ezekiel's garment did not remain undisturbed, for he was to toss some of them in the fire. Some scholars feel that this refers to a purifying judgment that would refine the remnant in captivity (cf. 6:8-10). However, the fire (5:4) probably refers (as in v. 2) to the suffering and death awaiting these people. This judgment was for the whole house of Israel. Even the remnant in exile would not escape the flames of oppression.

5:5-7. God was not capriciously inflicting this punishment on Jerusalem. It came because of her rebellion. God set Jerusalem in the center of the nations, with countries all around her. Yet in spite of this exalted position (possibly also referring to her central position geographically in the Middle East), Israel rebelled (cf. 2:3) against God's laws and decrees more than the surrounding nations. Jerusalem was the recipient of His word, the dwelling place of His glory, and the object of His love. The splendor of His favor only magnified the blackness of her deeds. Instead of honoring her God she rebelled against Him. Amazingly Israel's conduct was lower than the standards of Gentile nations.

5:8-12. God's anger was directed at Jerusalem, the nation's capital, because of her sin. She would suffer judgment in the sight of the nations. The object of God's special favor would soon become the object of His special judgment.

5:13-17. In three short vignettes Ezekiel indicated that God's judgment would last till the fury of His anger was spent. Ezekiel stressed the divine source of each judgment as God announced, I the LORD have spoken (vv. 13, 15, 17). In the first statement (v. 13) Ezekiel indicated that God's judgment would cease and subside only after He had poured out His **wrath** on **them.**

The second statement (vv. 14-15) stressed the humiliation Jerusalem would feel because of God's judgment. Other **nations** would **reproach** and mock her (cf. Lam. 2:15). Yet those ridiculing nations would be horrified at what was happening to Jerusalem. In fact such carnage in the city would serve as **a warning** to them.

The third statement (Ezek. 5:16-17) pictured God as an attacking archer shooting His **destructive arrows** (cf. Deut. 32:23) against Jerusalem. God's "arrows" of judgment included **famine . . . wild beasts. . . . plague,** and **the sword**—calamities uniquely associated with divine judgment on God's disobedient nation (cf. Deut. 32:23-25; Ezek. 14:21).

b. Two messages of coming judgment (chaps. 6–7)

After giving his four dramatic signs, Ezekiel delivered two sermons, beginning the same way: "The word of the LORD came to me" (6:1; 7:1). God was the source of the words Ezekiel delivered. The first message (chap. 6) was on Israel's idolatry, the cause for judgment. The second message (chap. 7) depicted the nature of the judgment.

(1) Message on idolatry as the cause of judgment (chap. 6). **6:1-2.** God told the prophet to **set** his **face against the mountains of Israel.** The preposition "against" (*'el*) denotes movement toward something. The phrase "set your/his face toward" was used to denote direction (Gen. 31:21, "headed for"; Num. 24:1), determination or purpose (2 Kings 12:17, "turned to"), or hostile intentions (Lev. 17:10; 20:3, 5-6). Ezekiel used the phrase 14 times (Ezek. 4:3, 7; 6:2; 13:17; 14:8; 15:7 [twice]; 20:46; 21:2; 25:2; 28:21; 29:2; 35:2; 38:2). In each case the phrase means to turn one's face toward an object with hostile intentions. The instrument of God's judgment was being aimed at its intended target. Interestingly Ezekiel later prophesied to the "mountains of Israel" (36:1-15), but then he delivered a prophecy of coming blessing.

6:3-7. Ezekiel was also to speak against **Israel's ravines and valleys.** The significance of these words can be understood only in light of the Canaanite reli-gious practices that permeated Israel (cf. Jer. 2:20-28; 17:1-3; 32:35). Israel was supposed to worship only the God of heaven in His temple in Jerusalem, but she set up shrines to false gods throughout the land (cf. 2 Kings 21:2-6, 10-15). Thus by addressing his message to the land itself, Ezekiel was focusing on the people's immoral use of the land.

God's **sword** (cf. 5:1, 12) would **destroy** Israel's **high places.** A "high place" (*bāmâh*) was usually (though not always; cf. 2 Kings 23:8) a place of worship located on a hill or mountain. The elevated site supposedly brought worshipers closer to their gods. While a high place could include a temple (1 Kings 12:31), most high places had only altars for offering sacrifices.

High places were in Canaan before Israel arrived, and God commanded Israel to destroy them (Num. 33:52). Israel was to worship only at the tabernacle, placed at Shiloh (cf. Deut. 12:2-14; 1 Sam. 1:3). After the destruction of Shiloh (probably by the Philistines) and before the construction of the temple in Jerusalem, Israel had no central place of worship. The altar and tabernacle were relocated at Gibeon (2 Chron. 1:1-3) and the ark was taken to Kiriath Jearim (1 Sam. 6:21–7:1). The table for the bread of the Presence was apparently at Nob (1 Sam. 21:1-6). During this time God permitted the use of high places as temporary worship centers (cf. 1 Kings 3:2). Both Samuel (1 Sam. 9:12-14) and Solomon (1 Kings 3:3) worshiped the Lord at high places.

After the temple in Jerusalem was completed, worshiping at high places was once again discouraged. Most high places remaining in the land were dedicated to false gods (1 Kings 11:7-10). The conflict between true worship and false worship often centered on these high places. Those kings who followed God tried to destroy the high places (e.g., Hezekiah, 2 Kings 18:3-4; Josiah, 2 Kings 23:8-9), and kings who did not follow God rebuilt them (e.g., Manasseh, 2 Kings 21:1-6).

By Ezekiel's time the high places were again flourishing in Judah. They included **altars** for sacrificing animals to false gods, **incense altars** for offering incense to the gods, and **idols** which were physical representations of the gods

(Ezek. 6:4). Israel's pernicious idolatry was a cancer that had to be eradicated. God's judgment would be swift and sure. Both the false places of worship and those who built them and worshiped at them were to be destroyed. God vowed to intervene so that the **high places . . . altars . . . idols,** and **incense altars** would all be **wiped out.** Also **people** who built them would be killed, and their **dead bodies** would be strewn beside their crushed **idols** and **altars** (v. 5). Then the nation would realize that its gods were false. The people would **know,** God said, that **I am the LORD.** This phrase occurs 63 times in Ezekiel; by using Yahweh, God's covenant name, Ezekiel was focusing attention on the contrasting unfaithfulness and apostasy of the people.

6:8-10. In the midst of God's judgment came a promise of mercy. God vowed to **spare some** (cf. 5:3-5; 12:16). Not all Israelites would be destroyed, for **some** would **escape the sword when** Israel would be dispersed **among . . . nations.** The impending defeat of Judah by Babylon did not signal the end of God's covenant promise to Israel. God was not turning away from His promises.

Some Israelites in captivity would **remember** God. They would call to mind His character—**how** He **grieved** for them in their idolatry. The words **their adulterous hearts** refer to their involvement in idol-worship, an act of unfaithfulness as terrible as a spouse's unfaithfulness in adultery. They would also remember God's faithfulness to His promises, especially those in which He promised to punish disobedience.

Those in exile would **loathe themselves** because of **all their detestable practices.** The sad consequences of sin produced a belated but necessary repentance. In acknowledging their sin and the justness of their judgment, they were again brought back to God—**they will know that I am the LORD.** Their personal knowledge of God would result from the **calamity** of exile. God **did not** bring captivity on Israel **in vain.**

6:11-12. The last section (vv. 11-14) of this sermon begins with God instructing Ezekiel to **strike** his **hands together . . . stamp** his **feet, and cry out, Alas!** Striking hands together, clapping, was a sign of rejoicing (2 Kings 11:12; Ps. 98:8) or

derision (Job 27:23; Lam. 2:15; Ezek. 21:14, 17; 22:13; 25:6, "clapped your hands"; Nahum 3:19). The phrase here was probably a symbol of derision (cf. Ezek. 25:6).

Ezekiel was to demonstrate this derisive behavior **because of all the wicked and detestable practices of the house of Israel.** Destruction **by the sword, famine, and plague** summarized the judgment already enacted by the prophet's fourth sign (chap. 5). Those in Jerusalem who escaped one calamity would only find another waiting to strike them down (6:12).

6:13-14. The imagery in verses 1-7 was repeated here as God promised He would slay the **people . . . among . . . their altars, on every high hill and . . . under every spreading tree and every leafy oak.** Often on the high places where altars were built were luxuriant trees, which represented growth and possibly fertility (cf. Hosea 4:13). The "oak" (*'ēlâh*) was the terebinth tree. It is a deciduous tree common to Palestine and grows to a height of 35-40 feet. The Elah Valley, where David slew Goliath, probably received its name because of the abundance of these trees (1 Sam. 17:2, 19).

God had given Israel a land luxurious with "spreading" trees and "leafy" oaks, but the people corrupted His gift, using these displays of His bounty as **places** to offer **fragrant incense to all their idols.** Therefore God would reduce their rich land to rubble—**a desolate waste from the desert to Diblah.** Instead of "Diblah" some manuscripts read "Riblah" (NIV marg.), a town on the Orontes River in Syria. If this reading is correct, Ezekiel was referring to all the land, from the desert in the south to Riblah in the north. This seems likely for two reasons. First, there is no record of a city in Judah named Diblah. (Though this is an argument from silence, it seems strange that Ezekiel would use a little-known city to indicate the extent of God's judgment.) Second, the change from Diblah to Riblah can be explained by the similar shape of the Hebrew letters *d* (ד) and *r* (ר). A copyist could easily have misread the manuscript and mistakenly changed the letters.

For the third time in this chapter Ezekiel stated that as a result of the judgment Israel would come to **know that** He is **the** LORD (cf. Ezek. 6:7, 10, 14), that is, acknowledge His supreme authority.

(2) Message on the nature of judgment (chap. 7). **7:1-4.** This message began in the same way as the first one (cf. 6:1): **The word of the** LORD **came to me.** This time the focus was not on idolatry (as in chap. 6), but on **the land,** which meant the people living in the land.

Ezekiel's message was that **the end** had **come upon the four corners of the land.** The word "end" is used five times at the beginning of this sermon (7:2 [twice], 3, 6 [twice]). The Prophet Amos used that word in a similar way to describe the fall of the Northern Kingdom in 722 B.C. (Amos 8:2, "the end has come," NASB). Ezekiel repeated the same message for the Southern Kingdom. "The four corners of the land" indicate that no portion would escape God's judgment.

The events about to unfold on Israel would bring a new revelation of God's character; the people would realize that God, being righteous, punishes sin. God vowed to **unleash** His **anger against** Israel (Ezek. 7:3) without **pity** (v. 4). He would judge her according to her **conduct** (cf. vv. 4, 8-9, 27) and **repay** her for her **detestable practices** (cf. vv. 8-9). These judgments were repeated (vv. 3-4) for emphasis. **Then** she would **know that** God is **the** LORD. This clause appears again at the end of the sermon (v. 27).

7:5-6. The LORD was like a herald who had raced to the city to shout breathlessly the warning of approaching calamity (vv. 5-9). In Hebrew the phrases are short and choppy, and the words "coming" or "came" occur six times in verses 5-7. The watchman first proclaimed, **Disaster! An unheard-of disaster is coming.** What was about to come on Jerusalem had no historical parallel.

The exact nature of Jerusalem's disaster was implied by the repetition of the words **the end has come** (v. 6). In Hebrew the two words translated in the first clause, **the end has come** are reversed in the second clause. In a wordplay Ezekiel announced that the end had **roused itself against you.** The words "end" (*qēṣ* and *haqqēṣ*) and "roused" (*hēqîṣ*) in verse 6 sounded so much alike that they drew attention to themselves. Disaster had been predicted for Jerusa-

lem by Micah (Micah 3:12), but that prophecy had remained unfulfilled for over 100 years. Now Jerusalem's end was about to come.

7:7-9. Ezekiel described Jerusalem's coming destruction as a time of **doom** (*haṣṣpîrâh;* cf. v. 10). This word can mean "crown" or "diadem" (cf. Isa. 28:5), but not in this context. A similar word in Aramaic means "morning" which was the meaning adopted by the KJV translators. But neither does this fit because "morning" would imply blessing while the context speaks of disaster. Probably the word is related to the Akkadian *ṣabāru,* "destruction."

As the day of judgment would approach there would be **panic, not joy, upon the mountains.** Those who had been at ease in their idolatry on the high places (cf. comments on Ezek. 6:3) would be thrown into a state of apprehension when overtaken in judgment. Ezekiel repeated the theme of the impending calamity (7:8-9 is about the same as vv. 3-4). The destruction would come as predicted, so those affected would **know that . . . the** LORD had struck **the blow.** This is a variation of the other statements on knowing the Lord (6:7, 10, 14; 7:4, 27). Those who professed to know Him by other names (cf. Gen. 22:14; 33:20; Ex. 17:15) would now know Him by the name *Yahweh-makkeh,* "the LORD who strikes the blow."

7:10. The nearness of **the day** of judgment was compared to a budding rod. **Doom has burst forth, the rod has budded, arrogance has blossomed!** Ezekiel's imagery could be drawn from Aaron's rod that budded (Num. 17), or he could have been familiar with Jeremiah's picture of an almond tree in blossom (Jer. 1:11-12). If the allusion was to Aaron's rod, the point was that just as its budding indicated God had selected him for service, so the budding of Israel's rod of arrogance indicated God had selected Jerusalem for doom. If the prophet alluded to Jeremiah's almond tree in blossom, the point was that just as the budding of the almond tree indicated God's judgment was sure to follow so the budding of violence in Israel indicated God's judgment would follow.

7:11-14. In verse 10 the "rod" pictured the budding of Israel's wickedness, compared to the budding of a tree. But in verse 11 the rod became a rod of judgment used to flog the disobedient people: **a rod to punish wickedness.**

God's judgment would have economic consequences. When it struck, **none of the people** would **be left, none of that crowd** ("crowd," probably used derisively, occurs four times in vv. 11-14). **Nothing of value** would remain. Because of the Captivity, property and material possessions were worthless. Possessions would be confiscated and property owners torn from their land and carried to Babylon. Ezekiel exhorted, **Let not the buyer rejoice nor the seller grieve.** The buyer who normally rejoiced over a good business deal should not be happy because he would not be able to possess the land he had purchased. And one forced to sell his land should not grieve because he would have lost it anyway.

When land was sold in Israel, the transaction was always temporary. Every 50 years, during the Year of Jubilee, the property reverted to its original owners (Lev. 25:10, 13-17). However, God's coming judgment would prevent original owners from reclaiming their properties; they would be in exile along with the buyers.

No human effort could hinder God from accomplishing His plan. **Though they** would call soldiers to battle by **the trumpet, no one** would **go into battle.** Jerusalem would try to defend herself, but she would fall with little resistance.

7:15-16. Israel would find she had no defense *against* God's judgment and no escape *from* God's judgment. **Outside** would be **the sword, inside . . . plague and famine** (cf. 5:12). Those who sought **escape** outside Jerusalem's walls were hunted down and murdered by Babylon's armies. Those who sought protection within the city walls faced the dual enemies of famine and disease. The majority of the people would die, and even those who survived would pay a price. The pitiful wail of those hiding **in the mountains,** who were weeping over their **sins** and material losses, would sound like mourning **doves.**

7:17-18. Israel's response to God's onslaught is pictured in verses 17-19. Hands would **go limp, and** knees would **become as weak as water** (cf. similar words in 21:7; also cf. Jer. 6:24). The only

thing the defenders could do would be to lament their state (Ezek. 7:18) and remove the obstacle of materialism that had caused them to stumble (vv. 19-22). In their lament they would **put on sackcloth. . . . and their heads** would **be shaved.** "Sackcloth" was coarse cloth, woven from the long hair of goats or camels. Because of its dark color, sackcloth was considered appropriate for serious, somber occasions. To "put on sackcloth" was a sign of grief or mourning (Gen. 37:34; 1 Sam. 3:31; Job 16:15; Jer. 6:26) and repentance (Isa. 58:5; Dan. 9:3-4; Jonah 3:5-9; Matt. 11:21). Ezekiel was probably picturing the grief mixed with terror Israel would experience when the enemy destroyed her land. Shaving the head also pictured mourning, humiliation, and repentance (see comments on Ezek. 5:1).

7:19-20. In addition to lamenting their loss the people would remove the obstacles that had caused it (vv. 19-22). **They** would **throw their silver into the streets, and their gold** would **be an unclean thing.** Also their **idols** made from the metal of their **jewelry** would be **an unclean thing,** so items once deemed precious would be discarded. The word for "unclean thing" (*niddâh*) was used of the ceremonial impurity of menstruation (Lev. 15:19-33) and the touching of a corpse (Num. 19:13-21). It pictured the revulsion Israel would feel toward her wealth.

Why would the people suddenly loathe their material wealth? One reason was the inability of **silver and gold** to buy the security for which it was originally amassed. It would **not be able to save them.** God could not be "bought off." Another reason for the sudden revulsion of wealth was the inability of the silver and gold to buy food to **satisfy their hunger** in the famine.

7:21-22. Besides being useless as a means of deliverance, Israel's wealth was also temporary. All she had accumulated would be taken by Babylon; her wealth would be plundered by **foreigners.**

Even more disconcerting than the loss of wealth was God's pronouncement about the temple: **I will turn My face away from them, and they will desecrate My treasured place; robbers will enter it and desecrate it.** Many Israelites placed their hope of deliverance on God's temple in Jerusalem; they thought that surely He would not let His holy abode be destroyed (cf. Jer. 7:1-5). But Israel's sin was so serious that not even the temple would escape God's judgment (cf. Micah 3:12).

7:23-24. Chains would be used to carry into captivity the people, who were known for **bloodshed** and **violence** (cf. 8:17; 12:19). God's invasion plans were ready to be implemented: **I will bring the most wicked of the nations to take possession of their houses.** Babylon, a ruthless and cruel nation (cf. comments on 28:7), was selected by God to dispossess Israel (cf. Hab. 1:5-11). Israel's haughty **pride** and religious prostitution would be crushed under the heavy boot of Babylon's army.

7:25-26. Israel's response to the judgment portrayed the anguish, heartache, and despair that comes when sin is allowed to run its course. Israel felt she could never fall; but when she would finally realize the **terror** of her fate, it would be too late. Her desperate search for deliverance and **peace** would be in vain. God added, **Calamity upon calamity will come, and rumor upon rumor.** The blows of misfortune would pound relentlessly one after another without a break. The word for "calamity" (*hōwâh*), appearing only here and in Isaiah 47:11, conveys the idea of ruin or disaster. Like the catastrophes that hit Job (cf. Job 1:13-19), no sooner would one catastrophe be reported than word would come of another. Rumors spread through Jerusalem of alliances and deliverers and coups and reversals in Babylon—and each piece of gossip was eagerly received by a terrified people.

In addition to listening to the many false rumors racing through the city, the people would also seek out **the prophet . . . the priest,** and **the elders** to gain insight from God. But this too would be in vain. They had refused to heed the warnings from God's true spokesmen. So when they would desperately seek an answer, none would be available.

7:27. Because there would be no help from God, **the king,** Ezekiel said, would **mourn, the prince** would **be clothed with despair, and the hands of the people of the land** would **tremble.** Who are "the king" and "the prince"? Ezekiel generally used the word "prince" to refer to

Zedekiah (12:10, 12; 21:25), never giving him the title "king." The only Israelite Ezekiel called "king" was Jehoiachin, in captivity in Babylon (1:2).

"King" Jehoiachin was already in captivity mourning Jerusalem's certain fall, while "Prince" Zedekiah was in Jerusalem in despair over his plight. As a result the people were trembling in fear at their uncertain fate. God again said their punishment would be **according to their conduct** (a standard mentioned five times in chap. 7 [vv. 3-4, 8-9, 27]).

c. A vision of coming judgment (chaps. 8–11)

Ezekiel had repeatedly stated that the coming judgment was prompted by the people's sins. But what had the people of Jerusalem done to deserve such punishment? God took Ezekiel back to Jerusalem in a vision to show him the wickedness there (chaps. 8–11).

This vision occurred "in the sixth year" (of Jehoiachin's exile; cf. comments on 1:2) "in the sixth month on the fifth day" (8:1). This date was September 17, 592 B.C. This was exactly 14 months after Ezekiel's first vision (1:1-2). In the interim Ezekiel had received a vision of God (chaps. 1–3), had acted out four signs (chaps. 4–5), and had given two messages on judgment (chaps. 6–7). Now God gave him a new vision.

The vision recorded in chapters 8–11 is a single unit. Yet four specific sections are within it. Ezekiel was first confronted with the wickedness of the people in the temple (chap. 8); then he was shown the slaughter of the people of Jerusalem (chap. 9). Jerusalem was so wicked that God's glory departed from the temple (chap. 10), and as it left the city, judgment was pronounced on her rulers (chap. 11).

(1) The wickedness in the temple (chap. 8). **8:1.** Ezekiel mentioned the date (see comments two pars. earlier) to identify when **the hand of the Sovereign LORD came upon** him (cf. 1:3; 3:14, 22). It was when he was in his **house and the elders of Judah were sitting** there with him. Ezekiel's outside ministry was still limited (cf. 3:24), so the elders of the community had to come to his house. They had probably gone to seek his advice, possibly on the fate of Jerusalem. The vision was God's answer which Eze-

kiel then reported to them (cf. 11:24-25).

8:2-6. As Ezekiel sat before the elders he **saw a figure like that of a man.** The figure was a manifestation or theophany of God like the one recorded in 1:26. From His **waist down He was like fire, and from there up His appearance was as bright as glowing metal** (cf. 1:27). As in chapter 1, Ezekiel's description of the vision was deliberately vague. Lest he be accused of picturing God as just a glorified man, Ezekiel carefully phrased his description as he wrote under the Holy Spirit's inspiration. God does not have the body of a man; His appearance was merely "a figure like that of a man." God did not extend an actual human hand down to Ezekiel; **He stretched out what looked like a hand.**

What Ezekiel described in chapters 8–11 took place **in visions,** that is, it did not physically transpire. As Ezekiel was transported to Jerusalem (cf. 3:14; 11:1, 24; 37:1; 43:5) his physical body remained in Babylon. The elders seated before him did not see the theophany **of God.** As the vision passed from Ezekiel (11:24b), he described it to the elders.

In the vision Ezekiel was **lifted . . . up between earth and heaven** and transported **to Jerusalem.** "Flown" from Babylon to Jerusalem, the prophet landed at **the entrance to the north gate of the inner court** (see the sketch "Plan of Solomon's Temple" near 1 Kings 6). The north gate was one of three gates that opened from the outer court to the inner court. The other two were located on the east and south sides. Since Ezekiel was at the "entrance" to the north gate, he was probably standing in the outer court looking south toward the inner court.

Beside the north entrance to the inner court was **the idol that provokes to jealousy.** Ezekiel also called it the **idol of jealousy** (Ezek. 8:5), probably because he viewed it as an affront to God. This idol violated the second of the Ten Commandments (Ex. 20:4; cf. Deut. 4:23-24). God was being provoked to jealousy because a foreign god was receiving the homage that should have been His alone. The god or goddess represented by this idol is not named, but it may have been Asherah, the Canaanite goddess of fertility. King Manasseh had placed a carved image of Asherah in the temple during his reign (2 Kings 21:7; cf. Deut. 16:21),

but later he removed it (2 Chron. 33:13, 15). After Manasseh's death an Asherah pole found its way back into the temple, and Josiah removed it during his reforms (2 Kings 23:6). He burned it in the Kidron Valley outside Jerusalem in the hope of eradicating this idolatrous worship forever. Unfortunately after Josiah's untimely death the people returned to their idolatry. Evidently a new Asherah pole was made to replace the destroyed one.

As Ezekiel stared at this idol, beside him **was the glory of the God of Israel** (cf. comments on Ezek. 1:28). God's moral outrage was expressed in His rhetorical question to Ezekiel: **Do you see what they are doing . . . detestable things . . . that will drive Me far from My sanctuary? God** will not share His glory with an idol (cf. Isa. 42:8). If the idol inhabited the temple, God would leave.

The shock of seeing the idol in the Lord's house must have unnerved Ezekiel. Yet this was not all Israel had done to provoke her Lord. Ezekiel would **see things . . . even more detestable** (cf. Ezek. 8:13, 15).

8:7-13. Then God led Ezekiel through the gateway **to the entrance to the court,** probably the inner court. Ezekiel then **saw a hole in the wall** that surrounded the court. In his visionary state God told him to **dig** through **the wall.** When he did so, he **saw a doorway there.** As Ezekiel entered the chamber and gazed about, he **saw portrayed all over the walls all kinds of crawling things and detestable animals and all the idols of the house of Israel.** Some have suggested these were idols of Egypt, or Canaan, or Babylon. Perhaps *all* those countries were represented in this pantheon of idolatry.

Seventy elders . . . and Jaazaniah son of Shaphan were standing with **incense** censers before the portrayals on the wall. These 70 elders were not the Sanhedrin which ruled in Israel after the Babylonian Captivity, but they did represent the leading men of Jerusalem. When Moses appointed assistants to aid in leading the people, the number whom God consecrated was 70 (Num. 11:16-17). Perhaps this tradition continued and the 70 elders Ezekiel saw were men of the city who had some official leadership capacity. Among the 70 Ezekiel recognized Jaazaniah, a man whose relatives played important parts in the affairs of state during Judah's final years (see the chart "The Line of Shaphan" near Jer. 26:24). Jaazaniah's presence there surprised Ezekiel because everyone else in Jaazaniah's family had remained faithful to the Lord.

Sometimes incense was used to protect worshipers from the presence of God (cf. Lev. 16:12-13). In other instances incense represented worshipers' prayers being borne aloft to God (cf. Rev. 5:8). Whatever the exact purpose of the incense, these leaders of Israel had abandoned the true God and were worshiping idols—**each at the shrine of his own idol.** Evidently each elder had his own favorite god.

God, who knew their hearts, explained to Ezekiel that the elders sought to justify their sin by saying **The Lord does not see us; the Lord has forsaken the land.** The elders felt that what they did in their darkened chambers would escape God's notice. They thought He was only a petty god who had abandoned them. So they were courting other gods to protect them. These elders' attitude was soon transmitted to the people (cf. Ezek. 9:9).

The people's progression of idolatry went from open display of idols to secret worship of idols under the very shadow of the Almighty. Yet this was not the full extent of Israel's wickedness, for they were **doing things . . . even more detestable** (cf. 8:6, 15).

8:14-15. Ezekiel was taken out **to the entrance to the north gate of the** temple. This was probably the entrance to the temple's outer court. Beside this gate Ezekiel **saw women . . . mourning for Tammuz.** "Tammuz" is the Hebrew form of the name of the Sumerian god Dumuzi, the deity of spring vegetation. The apparent death of all vegetation in the Middle East during the hot, dry summer months was explained in mythology as caused by Tammuz's death and descent into the underworld. During that time his followers would weep, mourning his death. In the spring Tammuz would emerge victoriously from the underworld and bring with him the life-giving rains. The worship of Tammuz also involved fertility rites.

Worship of the true Giver of rain had been supplanted by the debased adoration of a pagan deity. The worship of the Creator was replaced by the worship of the cycles of creation He had established. And yet Ezekiel was to **see things . . . even more detestable than these** (cf. vv. 6, 13).

8:16. When God again led Ezekiel **into the inner court,** he saw **at the entrance to the temple, between the portico and the altar . . . about 25 men.** They were between the portico, or covered entrance, to the temple building (cf. 1 Kings 6:2-3) and the bronze altar in the middle of the courtyard on which the sacrifices were offered. This was where God's priests should have been weeping and crying out to God for mercy because of their sin (cf. Joel 2:17).

Who were these 25 men? Later they were called "elders" (Ezek. 9:6), a term that applied to both civil and religious leaders. Because of their location, these men were probably priests. The people were allowed to approach the altar, but the approach to God from the altar to the holy of holies was through the mediation of the priests.

These priests should have been acting as Israel's mediators, crying to God for mercy. But instead, **they were bowing down to the sun in the east.** The entrance to God's temple faced the east, so that when a person stood at the altar and faced the entrance he was looking west. But these priests were facing east! They had turned **their backs** on God and were bowing in submission and worship to the sun. This expressed contempt for the God of Israel and implied that they had disowned Him. This directly violated God's command (Deut. 4:19).

8:17-18. The horrors Ezekiel had **seen** in the temple of God were disturbing. But the evil was not confined there. The wickedness being practiced in the temple by the priests and the people had spread through the nation. **Violence** filled the nation, which **continually** provoked God **to anger.**

The people were even **putting the branch to their nose.** Some feel this refers to a ritual act associated with worship of other gods. No such ritual is actually known, though some pictorial designs discovered on Assyrian reliefs could imply its existence. Early Jewish commentators translated "branch" as "stench." Some scholars feel that "their" was a later scribal change for an original reading of "my." In this case the phrase would read "putting the stench to My nose," that is, idolatry is a putrid, offensive smell to God. One cannot be dogmatic on which interpretation is correct, but in either case the general sense is clear: the gesture was a gross insult to God.

God's response was decisive: **I will deal with them in anger** and not . . . **with pity.** God would not allow such open rebellion to continue. Even a last-minute desperate effort on their part to get God to hear their cries would do no good. The stage was set for judgment.

(2) The slaughter in Jerusalem (chap. 9). **9:1-2.** The second part of Ezekiel's vision portrayed the execution of God's judgment (announced in 8:18) on Jerusalem's inhabitants. God summoned **the guards of the city . . . each with a weapon in his hand.** "Guards" comes from the verb "to attend to, visit, muster, appoint." The RSV and NASB translate it "executioners" here, but this seems too strong. Ezekiel used it again in 44:11 ("having charge of") to refer to the Levites who will serve as gatekeepers in the millennial temple.

The "guards" in 9:1 were probably angelic beings posted by God around His city. **Each** guard carried **a deadly weapon**—possibly a sword or a club.

The guards came into the inner court **from the direction of the upper gate, which faces north.** To reach Ezekiel they passed the four groups mentioned in chapter 8. **With the six** guards **was a seventh man clothed in linen who had a writing kit.** The linen clothing suggested dignity, purity, or divine origin (cf. Dan. 10:5; 12:6-7; Rev. 15:6). The "writing kit" was literally, a "case for the scribe." "Case" is an Egyptian loanword, meaning a case for carrying reed pens with an inkhorn attached.

9:3-7. As the guards and the scribe came through the temple, the vision of God's **glory** (cf. comments on 1:28) **went up from above the cherubim, where it had been, and moved to the threshold of the temple.** Similar wording in 10:4 dramatically illustrated God's departure from Jerusalem. Because this was a vision, events could happen in an otherwise unusual sequence. Thus one minute

God was personally guiding Ezekiel through the temple while the next minute He was seated on the cherubim in the holy of holies or on His throne-chariot.

God told the scribe dressed **in linen, Go throughout . . . Jerusalem and put a mark on the foreheads of those who grieve and lament over the detestable things** in the city. God knew those who had remained faithful to Him, and would spare them in His judgment (cf. God's marking of the 144,000 for preservation during the Tribulation, Rev. 7:3-4).

God then told the guards to **follow** the scribe **through the city and kill, without showing pity.** Those not receiving **the mark** were to be destroyed. There was to be no distinction by age or sex; the judgment would come on the **old** and **young,** on **men . . . women, and children.**

Then God ordered the guards, **Begin at the sanctuary.** Significantly the judgment first began in the house of God (cf. 1 Peter 4:17). Since the evil had spread from the temple throughout the land (Ezek. 8), the judgment would follow the same course. So the guards **began with the elders,** the priests whose backs were turned to God (8:16). Their slaughter would **defile the temple and fill the courts with the slain,** but the temple had already been defiled with their idolatrous practices. The historical fulfillment of this is seen in 2 Chronicles 36:17-19.

9:8-10. Overwhelmed by the magnitude of this judgment Ezekiel cried out, **Are You going to destroy the entire remnant of Israel?** (cf. 11:13) Ezekiel was a man of compassion who cared for his nation (cf. Abraham's intercession for Sodom, Gen. 18:20-33; and Amos' praying for Israel, Amos 7:1-9).

Though Ezekiel's appeal revealed his concern, the nation's **sin** had progressed too far to avert disaster. God had given Israel and Judah ample time to repent of her sin, but the people had used the time to grow more perverse in their ways of **bloodshed** (cf. "violence," Ezek. 8:17) and **injustice,** all the while thinking **the** LORD no longer cared for them or saw them (cf. 8:12). Without **pity** (cf. 7:4, 9; 8:18; 24:14) He would give them what they deserved.

9:11. Then the angelic scribe returned with his report: **I have done as**

You commanded (cf. v. 4). Those who were righteous and whose hearts grieved over the nation's sin had received God's mark of protection. They would be spared. The unrighteous who had rejected God and embraced evil did not receive the mark of protection. They would be killed. Each person's destiny was determined by his character.

(3) The departure of God's glory from the temple (chap. 10). 10:1-2. God would not share His dwelling place with other "gods," and the sanctuary had been polluted with idolatry. God's worship center at Shiloh was removed shortly after His glory had departed from it (1 Sam. 4:1-4, 10-11, 19-23; Jer. 7:12-14); and the same fate awaited the Jerusalem temple.

Ezekiel, still standing beside the altar, looked at the sanctuary and saw the likeness of a throne of sapphire above the expanse that was over the heads of the cherubim. This was God's azure-blue throne on His throne-chariot (see comments on Ezek. 1:26). Though God was at the entrance to the sanctuary, His throne-chariot was "on the south side of the temple" (10:3).

God told the angelic scribe, Go in among the wheels beneath the cherubim and take burning coals . . . and scatter them over the city. The "burning coals" among the cherubim had been seen by Ezekiel earlier (1:13; cf. Isa. 6:6). Now God was going to use similar coals to purge His "holy" city.

10:3-5. Ezekiel's attention shifted back to God's throne-chariot beside the sanctuary. A cloud filled the inner court, signifying God's presence at the threshold of the sanctuary (cf. Ex. 33:9-10; 1 Kings 8:10-11; Isa. 6:1-4). Ezekiel repeated the fact that the glory of the Lord had moved from the throne-chariot to the threshold (Ezek. 10:4; cf. 9:3). As the cloud filled the temple . . . the court was full of the radiance of the glory (cf. comments on 1:28) of the Lord. The manifestation of God's glory pierced through the cloud to illuminate the plaza where Ezekiel stood. Along with this dazzling brightness was the sound of the cherubim's wings, so loud that it was heard in the outer court (cf. 1:24).

10:6-7. Ezekiel returned from his momentary digression to continue his account of the man in linen. The messenger approached God's throne-chariot and stood beside one of its four wheels and the cherubim (cf. 1:15-18). One of the cherubim then took some of the fire and put it into the hands of the man in linen, thus enacting the divine purification of Jerusalem.

God's judgment as a fire scattered on Jerusalem is interesting in light of her ultimate fate, for the Babylonian army destroyed her by fire (cf. 2 Kings 25:8-9). The man in linen took the fire and went out. Though Ezekiel did not write that the man scattered the fire over Jerusalem, it can be assumed. Possibly the prophet's eyes were still transfixed on God's throne-chariot.

10:8-13. Again Ezekiel described the cherubim and the wheels (vv. 8-11; cf. 1:15-21). However, Ezekiel noted some additional details (10:12-13). Their entire bodies . . . were completely full of eyes. Probably their eyes represent divine omniscience as did the eyes on the wheels (see comments on 1:15-18). The four creatures John saw surrounding God's throne were also covered with eyes (Rev. 4:8).

Then Ezekiel heard the wheels referred to as whirling wheels. "Whirling" (hagalgal) means rolling or revolving. Thus the wheels were named for their function: they set God's throne-chariot in motion by revolving. The naming of the wheels here seems to prepare the way for their departure (to be described in Ezek. 10:15-19). God's glory was about to whirl out of His temple on "the whirling wheels."

10:14. Ezekiel then described the faces of the cherubim a second time (see comments on 1:10). However, an apparent discrepancy exists between these two descriptions. In chapter 1 the cherubim had the faces of a man, a lion, an eagle, and an ox; but in chapter 10 they had the faces of a cherub . . . a man . . . a lion, and an eagle. Some have suggested that a later scribe mistakenly copied "a cherub" in place of "face of an ox." A second view is that the face of an ox was, in fact, the normal understanding of the face of a cherub. In Akkadian literature the kuribu (cognate of "cherub") appear to have nonhuman faces.

10:15-22. It was now time for God's glory to depart. Then the cherubim rose upward. God's throne ascended from the court of Israel into the air. Ezekiel's description of the movement of **the cherubim** and **wheels** (vv. 15-17) uses the same words he employed in chapter 1 (see comments on 1:19-20). God's **glory,** which had been standing at the entrance to the temple, **departed from over the threshold of the temple and stopped above the cherubim** (10:18). God was mounting His throne-chariot to ride out of His temple and city. The throne-chariot began moving toward the east; but as the cherubim approached the edge of the temple precincts, **they stopped at the entrance to the east gate of the LORD's house, and the glory** (cf. comments on 1:28) **of the God of Israel was above them.** These **creatures** (vv. 20-22) were unquestionably the same cherubim Ezekiel **had seen** earlier. Before **God** left both the temple and the city, there was a final pause. Once God passed from the gate, the inscription "Ichabod" ("the glory has departed") could be written over Jerusalem (cf. 1 Sam. 4:21-22). As if to delay this final movement in the departure of God's glory, Ezekiel inserted the story of 25 wicked rulers (Ezek. 11:1-21).

(4) The judgment on Jerusalem's rulers (chap. 11). This fourth portion of Ezekiel's vision completed his "tour" of the temple area in Jerusalem. Before God's glory departed from the city it stopped at the eastern gate and gave Ezekiel another glimpse of the sin of Jerusalem's inhabitants. Ezekiel received two messages from the Lord. The first emphasized judgment on the people who remained in Jerusalem (vv. 1-15), and the second emphasized the promised restoration of the people who were in captivity (vv. 16-21). Then Ezekiel recorded the final departure of God's glory (vv. 22-25).

11:1. As God's glory hovered over the eastern gate, **the Spirit lifted . . . up** (cf. 3:8, 14; 11:24; 37:1; 43:5) the prophet and took him **to the gate** facing **east** toward the Kidron Valley and the Mount of Olives. **At the entrance to the gate were 25 men,** not the same 25 who were worshiping the sun (8:16).

Among the 25 men at the entrance to the gate were **Jaazaniah son of Azzur and Pelatiah son of Benaiah.** The gate was the traditional place where the elders of a city sat to administer justice and oversee legal matters. It was a city's "courthouse" (cf. Gen. 23:10, 18; Deut.

21:19; Josh. 20:4; Ruth 4:1-2, 9, 11; Job 29:7, 14-17). "Jaazaniah son of Azzur" is not mentioned elsewhere in Scripture and should not be confused with three other Jaazaniahs living at the same time (cf. 2 Kings 25:23; Jer. 35:3; Ezek. 8:11). It is possible (though by no means certain) that this "Azzur" is the man named in Jeremiah 28:1. If so, then the Jaazaniah of Ezekiel 11 was a brother of Hananiah the false prophet who opposed Jeremiah and who delivered the same false message of hope just before Jerusalem's fall (cf. Jer. 28:1-4). Nothing else is known about Pelatiah. Both Jaazaniah and Pelatiah, **leaders of the people,** probably belonged to Israel's nobility.

11:2-3. These 25 were **plotting evil and giving wicked advice.** They should have been providing wise counsel and direction for Jerusalem, but instead were turning the people from the Lord.

Their wicked counsel was summarized for Ezekiel. **Will it not soon be time to build houses? This city is a cooking pot and we are the meat.** The elders were encouraging the Jerusalemites to forget the prophet's predictions of the coming Babylonian invasion. They were urging the people to build houses, a sign of peace and safety (28:26). After all, the people were safe in the city (Jerusalem) like meat in a kettle.

11:4-5. Because of this false optimism, God told Ezekiel to **prophesy against them.** The public statements of confidence only masked the people's underlying fears. They were seeking security from the ever-present danger of Babylon (by talking about building houses), but in their minds they feared such an attack and the consequences it would bring. God said He knew **what** they were thinking (vv. 5, 8).

11:6-12. Ezekiel then altered the elders' imagery of the meat and the pot. Those righteous men who had been murdered in the city (**you have killed many people in this city**) had been Jerusalem's hope for only they could have rescued the city. The elders thought they were safe as meat in a pot (v. 3). But the slain righteous were the "meat": **the bodies you have thrown there** (in the streets, v. 6) **are the meat and this city is the pot.** Though the elders felt secure within the "pot" of Jerusalem, God would **drive** them **out** and give them **over to foreign-**

ers. Instead of the city being a pot of safety with the people in it being "safe" like meat (v. 11) the city would be smashed and the people dragged away. God's judgment by the sword would be executed at the borders of Israel (vv. 10-11). This was fulfilled literally when the captives of Jerusalem were deported to Riblah in Syria and killed (cf. 2 Kings 25:18-21; Jer. 52:8-11, 24-27).

11:13-15. As Ezekiel prophesied against those elders and the city, **Pelatiah son of Benaiah died.** This was a confirmation of Ezekiel's message and foreshadowed the judgment that would soon destroy all Jerusalem's wicked leaders. Ezekiel, understanding the significance of that event, responded by again pleading to God for mercy (cf. 9:8): **Ah, Sovereign LORD! Will You completely destroy the remnant of Israel?**

God's response to Ezekiel was twofold. First, He showed Ezekiel that the remnant would not be destroyed. Those already in exile would be preserved. They were his **brothers,** his **blood relatives.** The phrase "your blood relatives" (gᵉʾullāṭekā) is translated "fellow exiles" in the Septuagint and Syriac texts (which has gālûṭekā). This makes better sense in the context. Ezekiel's brothers in exile were the true remnant.

The second part of God's response was to show Ezekiel the need for judgment on Jerusalem. Jerusalem's moral compass needle was bent. They felt that those in exile (whom God had just said were the true remnant) were **far away from the LORD.** They localized God and thought in terms of geographical rather than spiritual proximity. They also assumed that their right to the land was absolute since it was **given to** them as their **possession.** This was a correct but incomplete statement. God had given Israel the land, but He had also threatened to remove them from it for disobedience (cf. Deut. 28:36, 64-68). God would spare a remnant (Ezek. 6:8; 12:16), as Ezekiel asked, but it would not include the smug, self-righteous leaders of Jerusalem.

11:16. God had emphasized the coming judgment of the people who remained in Jerusalem (vv. 1-12). He assured the prophet that He would preserve a remnant, but it would be comprised of those in captivity, not those in

Jerusalem (vv. 13-15). As a sign of His faithfulness, God promised to restore the remnant to the land (vv. 16-21).

The proof of God's blessing on the remnant in captivity involved (a) what He had already done for them (v. 16) and (b) what He would do for them in the future (vv. 17-21). Though God had **sent** His people **far away among the nations,** He had not abandoned them. They had lost access to the "sanctuary," the temple in Jerusalem; but God Himself had been a **sanctuary for them in** those foreign **countries.** God was accessible to faithful Jews wherever they were geographically.

11:17. Yet there is to be a distinct future for Israel nationally. God promised, **I will gather you . . . from the countries where you have been scattered, and I will give you back the land of Israel again.** The remnant of Israel could look forward to a national restoration to the Promised Land. A partial restoration took place after the Babylonian Captivity (cf. Ezra; Neh.), but Ezekiel 11:17-21 goes beyond that return and points to a future gathering of Israel at the beginning of the Millennium (cf. 36:24-38; 37:11-28).

11:18-19. Israel's physical **return** will be accompanied by a spiritual renewal. When they come back to the land, **they will . . . remove all . . . vile images and detestable idols** (cf. v. 21). The land will be purged of idolatry, and the people will be purged too. For God said, **I will give them an undivided heart and put a new spirit in them.** Israel's external difficulties resulted from her internal condition. God promised to correct that.

Ezekiel's promise refers to the permanent indwelling of the Holy Spirit in Israel ("spirit" could read "Spirit"). Before the Church Age the Holy Spirit indwelt select individuals; this was generally a temporary enablement for a special task (see comments on 2:2). However, in the Millennium the Holy Spirit will indwell all believing Israelites (cf. 36:26-27; cf. Joel 2:28). The inauguration of the New Covenant, which includes this permanent indwelling (cf. Jer. 31:31-34), began with the death of Christ (cf. Matt. 26:28; Mark 14:24; Luke 22:20; Heb. 8:6-13; 9:15; 10:14-16; 12:24); but the ultimate fulfillment awaits the national regathering of Israel. The church today is participating in the *spiritual* (not the physical) benefits of the covenant through its association with Christ.

The results of the new "heart" (a **heart of flesh** instead of a **heart of stone**) for Israel will be new actions and a new relationship. **11:20-21.** In their actions the people of Israel will be obedient; **they will follow** God's **decrees and . . . keep His laws.** Their new internal condition will produce righteous actions. Also it will result in a new relationship with God: **They will be My people, and I will be their God** (cf. 14:11; 36:28; 37:23, 27; Hosea 2:23).

God ended this discourse by bringing Ezekiel back to the reality of sin. The remnant in captivity could look forward to restoration and blessing, but those in Jerusalem **devoted to their vile images and detestable idols** (cf. Ezek. 11:18) could expect only judgment for their sin. This reminded Ezekiel of the sinful actions he had just witnessed that caused God's glory to depart from His city (chaps. 8–11).

11:22-25. God's glory then continued its departure. **The glory of the LORD** (cf. comments on 1:28) **went up from within the city and stopped above the mountain east of it.** As God's **glory** left Jerusalem, it passed over the Kidron Valley to the Mount of Olives. This departure signaled Jerusalem's doom. The city would be devoid of God's blessing till the glory will return via the Mount of Olives (cf. 43:1-3). It is no coincidence that Christ ascended to heaven from the Mount of Olives (Acts 1:9-12) and promised to return to the same place (Acts 1:11; cf. Zech. 14:4).

Ezekiel's vision ended and he was transported by **the Spirit** (cf. 3:14; 8:3; 11:1; 37:1; 43:5) back to **the exiles in Babylonia.** As **the vision . . . went up from** him he **told the exiles everything the LORD had shown** him.

2. THE FUTILITY OF FALSE OPTIMISM (CHAPS. 12–19)

Ezekiel's task (chaps. 4–11) had been to show the necessity of Jerusalem's judgment because of her disobedience. He had demonstrated the fact of the siege through a series of signs, and then he explained the reason for the siege through two messages and an extended vision. However, the people were still not ready to accept the fact of Jerusalem's fall. Therefore Ezekiel gave a new series of signs and messages. Any optimism would be futile; Jerusalem's fate had been sealed.

Ezekiel used the clause, "The word of the LORD came to me," in introducing 10 of the 11 signs, sermons, and proverbs in chapters 12–19 (12:1, 17, 21; 13:1; 14:2, 12; 15:1; 16:1; 17:1; 18:1). The only variation is the final section (19:1), but this is a lament which seems to sum up the entire section's theme.

a. Two signs about impending captivity (12:1-20)

Ezekiel gave two more action-signs because of the people's unbelief. He said, "They have eyes to see but do not see and ears to hear but do not hear." Israel's blindness and deafness was willful. They had the faculties for receiving God's message, but they chose not to receive it because they were "a rebellious house" (v. 3; cf. comments on 3:9). Blindness and deafness often indicate disobedience or disbelief (cf. Deut. 29:1-4; Isa. 6:9-10; Jer. 5:21; Matt. 13:13-15; Acts 28:26-28).

(1) The sign of the baggage and the hole in the wall (12:1-16). **12:1-6.** Here Ezekiel's sign to Israel involved two separate actions. In the first action he packed his **belongings** and went **to another place** as the exiles watched him. The people recognized the meaning of that action because six years earlier they had made similar preparations for their own deportation to Babylon.

This first action **in the daytime** was followed by a second action **in the evening.** While the people watched, Ezekiel was to pretend he was being taken captive and was to **dig through the wall and take** his **belongings** (cf. v. 4) **out through** it, carrying them **on** his **shoulder.** As Ezekiel pantomimed before the **people** a furtive escape attempt he was also to **cover** his **face so that** he could not **see the land.**

12:7-11. Ezekiel performed the actions as he **was commanded.** Next **morning** God spoke to him again, this time asking him if the exiles inquired **what** he was **doing.** Evidently the people's curiosity was aroused. Once Ezekiel had their attention he could deliver God's message.

God explained that **this oracle** (message) concerned the prince in Jerusalem (i.e., King Zedekiah) and the whole house of Israel who were there (i.e., in Jerusalem, v. 10). This first part of Ezekiel's sign pictured the inevitability of the exile: they will go into exile as captives. Those at ease in Jerusalem would soon be exiles whose only possessions could be held in small sacks flung over their backs.

12:12-16. The second part of Ezekiel's sign (in vv. 5-6) pictured Zedekiah's vain escape attempt. He would try to escape at dusk from Jerusalem through a breach in the city wall. However, he would be caught in God's snare. Zedekiah's escape attempt would fail because God would make sure he was captured. The final destiny of Zedekiah was grim. I will bring him to Babylonia . . . but he will not see it, and there he will die. His troops who would try to escape with him would be pursued and killed by the sword.

All this was dramatically and accurately fulfilled in 586 B.C. After a futile escape attempt Zedekiah was taken to Nebuchadnezzar, forced to watch the enemy kill his sons, and then blinded and carried off to Babylon where he spent the rest of his life in prison (cf. 2 Kings 25:1-7; Jer. 52:4-11).

Those in Jerusalem would ultimately realize the sovereignty of God (Ezek. 12:15-16), but that knowledge would come only after they were dispersed among the nations. And yet, as God had said, He would spare a few of them (cf. 6:8).

(2) The sign of trembling while eating and drinking. 12:17-20. Ezekiel's second sign was briefer than the first, but it too was intended to convey a message about those living in Jerusalem and in the land of Israel (v. 19). Ezekiel was to tremble as he ate his food, and shudder . . . as he drank his water (v. 18).

Ezekiel's actions represented the terror Israel would experience. As he had said earlier (4:16) the people in Jerusalem would eat and drink in anxiety and in despair. The enemy would plunder the land, devastating the towns and making the land . . . desolate. Fear of the enemy would grip the people as they watched God's judgment decimate the land. Yet they brought the judgment on them-

selves by their violence (20:19; cf. 7:23; 8:17).

b. Five messages on the certainty of judgments (12:21–14:23)

Following Ezekiel's two signs (12:1-20), he delivered a series of five messages (12:21-25; 12:26-28; 13; 14:1-11; 14:12-23) to destroy the people's false optimism and to show the certainty of judgment.

(1) The first message on the certainty of judgment. 12:21-25. The first two messages were attacks on two popular proverbs the people were quoting. This message began with God asking Ezekiel about the proverb . . . The days go by and every vision comes to nothing. A "proverb" (māšāl) was a terse expression of a commonly held or self-evident truth. The point of this proverb was the belief that Ezekiel's (and other prophets') predictions of doom would not take place. It had the effect of labeling those prophets doomsayers thus allowing the people to ignore their messages.

God said He would keep the people from quoting that proverb any longer. The people's smug assurance would end when the judgments arrived. The past days had not invalidated the earlier predictions as the people supposed. Instead, they had decreased the time remaining till the prophecies would be accomplished. The days are near, God said.

False prophets had been contradicting the claims of God's true messengers in both Jerusalem (cf. Jer. 28:1-4) and Babylon (cf. Jer. 29:1, 8-9). Their optimistic predictions would cease as God hastened to fulfill His word. He would remove false visions and flattering divinations. Ezekiel's cries of doom were not distant rumblings of some still-future storm. The judgment was imminent: it shall be fulfilled without delay. God would fulfill whatever He predicted (cf. Ezek. 12:28).

(2) The second message on the certainty of God's judgment. 12:26-28. The first proverb attacked by Ezekiel expressed the people's doubts about the fact of God's judgment. The second proverb expressed their doubts about the imminency of God's judgment. This saying was not specifically called a proverb, but it was cast in the same mold as the first

proverb. It was another popular saying in Israel.

Even those Israelites who believed Ezekiel was a true prophet of God doubted the soon fulfillment of his oracles: **he prophesies about the distant future.** If God does act, their reasoning went, it will not be soon. Interestingly the Apostle Peter predicted that the same attitude would prevail in the last days regarding the second coming of Christ (2 Peter 3:3-10). God's delay is a sign of mercy, not uncertainty.

Ezekiel said the judgment was not distant; it was standing at Israel's very doorstep. God said, **None of My words will be delayed any longer** (cf. Ezek. 12:25). The second proverb, like the first, was giving false hope to a nation that needed a clear understanding of its dire condition.

(3) The third message on the certainty of judgment (chap. 13). Ezekiel's third message was directed against Israel's false prophets and prophetesses who were leading the nation astray. In a large measure they were responsible for the people's misplaced hope. Ezekiel denounced the prophets (vv. 1-16) and the prophetesses (vv. 17-23). For both groups he first condemned their sin and then pronounced judgment.

13:1-3. The message of the false prophets came from **their own imagination** (cf. v. 17), not from God. Ezekiel was challenging the source of their message. Since their message came from **their own spirit,** Ezekiel could rightfully claim that they had **seen nothing.**

13:4. Not only was the message of the false prophets untrue; it was also dangerous. The false **prophets** were **like jackals among ruins.** The word for "jackals" (*šú'ālîm*) may be rendered "foxes" (the normal Heb. word for jackal is *tan*). Though some feel Ezekiel emphasized the destructive nature of foxes, they are not generally known for their destruction. It is probably better to understand that Ezekiel was referring to the nature of the foxes' dwelling places. Just as foxes consider ruins to be a perfectly acceptable "home," so also the false prophets were able to flourish in a crumbling society.

13:5. The false prophets, Ezekiel said, had **not gone up to the breaks in the wall to repair it.** Israel's moral walls were ready to collapse, but the false prophets did nothing to help. **The day of the LORD** has an eschatological meaning in most Old Testament passages where it refers to the Tribulation period, the second coming of Christ, or the Millennium (cf. comments on "Major Interpretive Problems" in the *Introduction* to Joel). But in this passage it seems to refer to the coming judgment by the Babylonians.

13:6-9. The false prophets claimed to represent God, but He did not claim them. **Because of** their **false words and lying visions,** He was **against** them. Ezekiel mentioned three aspects of their judgment. First, **they** would **not belong to the council of** God's **people.** The false prophets had enjoyed favor among Israel's leaders. They were in positions of influence both in Jerusalem and in the exile; but after their prophecies were proved false, they would lose this favor. Second, besides losing their places on the council, they would also not **be listed in** Israel's **records** (i.e., their names would not be recorded in the city's list of citizens). To be excluded from the list would deprive an individual of the rights of citizenship (cf. Ezra 2:62). These false prophets would be excommunicated from the fellowship of Israel. Third, the false prophets would never again **enter the land of Israel.** They would die as captives in a foreign land.

13:10. The false prophets were **saying, Peace,** whereas Ezekiel was predicting destruction. Their deceptive ministry was like **a flimsy wall** covered **with whitewash.** Instead of calling Israel's attention to the serious cracks in its moral foundation (v. 5), these prophets were "dabbing plaster" to hide the deficiencies. A white paste, formed from the chalk deposits in Israel, was used to plaster over the rocks that formed the walls of most houses. This plaster hid uneven rocks under a smooth surface. The prophets were compounding Israel's difficulties by hiding problems that needed to be exposed.

13:11-12. Since the false prophets had deceived the people by plastering over an unsafe wall (v. 10), they would be blamed **when the wall** collapsed. God's judgment would break down the flimsy wall of Israel. Heavy **rain . . . hailstones . . . and violent winds** (cf. v. 13) would beat against the wall and it would collapse. Then the people would ask the prophets, **Where is the whitewash you covered it with?** The "whitewash" was their false prophecies; and when Jerusalem was destroyed, this would be revealed.

13:13-16. When **wind . . . hailstones . . . and . . . rain** would cause **the wall** of **Jerusalem** to **fall** (cf. v. 11), the prophets would **be destroyed in it**, for God's **wrath** would be **against** them.

13:17-19. Ezekiel turned from the false prophets (vv. 1-16) to address the false prophetesses (vv. 17-23). They were called **the daughters of your people who prophesy out of their own imagination** (cf. v. 2). True prophetesses ministered in both Old and New Testament times (Ex. 15:20; Jud. 4:4-5; 2 Kings 22:14; Acts 21:8-9). However, the "prophetesses" Ezekiel denounced were like mediums or sorceresses.

These prophetesses sewed **magic charms on all their wrists and** made **veils of various lengths for their heads.** The Hebrew word for "magic charms" occurs in the Old Testament only in this passage (Ezek. 13:18, 20). This practice probably came from Babylonian magic rituals, in which magical knots and bands were bound to various parts of the body to ward off evil spirits or to heal diseases. These "good-luck charms" supposedly had magical powers. The "veils" were long drapes that were placed on "their heads" and that covered the prophetesses' bodies, possibly to convey the impression of mystery.

The purpose for the magic charms and mysterious veils was **to ensnare people.** Especially in times of uncertainty and turmoil, frauds and charlatans seem to prey on the fears of the gullible. These sorceresses would "tell the future" or provide a "good-luck spell" **for a few handfuls of barley and scraps of bread,** either as payment for the divination or as a means employed for divination. In some cultures barley was used in occult practices either as an offering to the spirits or as a means of trying to determine the future. Whatever the case, these prophetesses were employing fraudulent practices as a hoax and were making a living off the fears of others. God said they were really **lying to My people** (v. 19).

The results of the prophetesses' work ran counter to Israel's best interests. **You have killed those who should not have died and have spared those who should not live.** The prophetesses should have exposed and denounced evil practices in Jerusalem (cf. 2 Kings 22:13-20). But instead they let the wicked ("those who should not live") go free.

13:20-21. God said His anger would be vented against the false prophetesses and that He would neutralize their **power.** He would **tear** their **magic charms . . . from** their **arms** and would **set free the people** they ensnared **like birds.** Also God would **tear off** their **veils and save** His **people from** their **hands.** These sorceresses would then be exposed as charlatans, and their gullible clients would desert them.

13:22-23. The prophetesses had **disheartened the righteous with** their **lies and encouraged the wicked not to turn from their evil ways.** This directly opposed God's purposes for the people.

When God would judge the prophetesses the people would then realize that these women had lied. And the prophetesses themselves would be forced to admit their sin. God would banish **false visions** and **divination** (see comments on Deut. 18:10) from Israel and **save** His **people from** their terrible deception.

(4) The fourth message on the certainty of judgment (14:1-11). **14:1-6.** Ezekiel's fourth message was a condemnation of idolatry. **Some of the elders of Israel** went to see Ezekiel. Though he was still confined to his house (3:24) these exiles recognized him as a prophet and came to him for advice (cf. 8:1). Presumably the elders wanted to receive a message from God about Jerusalem or the length of their exile.

As the elders **sat** before Ezekiel, God informed him that those **men** had **set up idols in their hearts and put wicked stumbling blocks before their faces.** The idolatry in Jerusalem was openly displayed (chap. 8), but the idolatry in Babylon was more subtle—it was internal rather than external. Like **stumbling blocks,** this idolatry would cause the people to fall. Several times Ezekiel spoke of a stumbling block (*mikšôl*) to show the effects of idolatry on the people (cf. 7:19, "stumble"; 14:3-4, 7; 18:30, "downfall"; 44:12, "fall"). In the Book of

Ezekiel Israel's idolatry was seen as the major cause for God's judgment on His people.

These hypocritical elders came to the true God for answers while having another "god" in their hearts. God asked Ezekiel, **Should I let them inquire of Me at all?** God was not obligated to answer them when they refused to acknowledge His sovereignty. So instead of giving these elders the information they *desired,* God instructed Ezekiel to give them the information they *needed*—God's attitude toward their **idolatry.**

God informed the elders that **when any Israelite** came to God while harboring idolatry **in his heart,** God would deal with the idolatry. God would do this for the ultimate benefit of the nation, **to recapture the hearts of the people.** The message Israel needed to hear was not some oracle about Jerusalem or the Captivity. The urgent message was, **Repent! Turn from your idols and renounce all your detestable practices!**

14:7-8. Ezekiel then widened the scope of his message. Verse 7 is identical to verse 4b except that in verse 7 the warning applied also to **any alien living in Israel.** The "alien" (*gēr*) was a resident alien in Israel who had accepted Israel's ways and was responsible to obey God's Law (Lev. 16:29-30; 17:12-16; 18:26; Num. 15:13-16; Isa. 56:3-8; Ezek. 47:22-23).

If an **Israelite** or an alien dared to presume on God while harboring idolatry, God would answer in judgment. **I the LORD will answer him Myself** (cf. 14:4) and **make him an example and a byword.** He would be a "byword" in the sense that people would know about him and talk about him (cf. 23:10; Job 17:6; 30:9; Ps. 44:14; Jer. 24:9; Joel 2:17). God would **cut him off from** His **people.** God would respond with actions, not words. He would move against that idolatrous person to kill him. This harsh action would be an example to others.

14:9-11. God said He would not respond through His prophet to an inquirer who was harboring idolatry in his heart. Therefore if a **prophet** *did* give an answer, it meant he was a false prophet. The clause, **I the LORD have persuaded that prophet,** is somewhat enigmatic and at first glance seems to indicate that God *did* prompt the prophet to speak. However, "persuaded" (from *pātâh*) is better

translated with a negative connotation such as "entice" or "deceive" (cf. Ex. 22:16, "seduces"; 2 Sam. 3:25; Jer. 20:7). The best illustration of Ezekiel's meaning is the story of God's letting false prophets deceive Ahab, to bring him to his death (1 Kings 22:19-23).

If a false prophet in Ezekiel's day received a word to give an idolater, it would be a deceptive word that would lead to the destruction of both (**the prophet will be as guilty as the one who consults him**). God would hold both individuals responsible for their sin and would punish them accordingly.

Then the people would return to Him and **no longer . . . defile themselves by their sins.** God would remove the stumbling block of idolatry that had brought the nation to ruin. Then, God said, **they will be My people and I will be their God** (cf. Ezek. 11:20; 36:28; 37:23, 27; Hosea 2:23). God ultimately will restore Israel to her place of fellowship with Him.

(5) The fifth message on the certainty of judgment (14:12-23). Ezekiel again pointed up the inevitability of judgment on Israel. If God would spare the wicked city of Sodom for the sake of 10 righteous people (Gen. 18:22-33), the Israelites in Ezekiel's day thought that surely He would spare Jerusalem because of its righteous individuals. But Ezekiel's fifth message made it clear that the righteous few would not prevent God's judgment on Jerusalem.

14:12-20. In the first section of his message Ezekiel gave four "hypothetical" cases of judgment. A particular **country sins against** God **by being unfaithful** and He stretches **out His hand against it.** Being just, God could (a) **cut off its food supply and send famine** (v. 13), (b) **send wild beasts through that country** (v. 15), (c) **bring a sword** (v. 17), and/or (d) **send a plague** (v. 19). God could use any of these four means to punish the land and kill its people (cf. 5:17). In fact all four will be used during the Tribulation when God pours His judgment on the whole earth for her sin (cf. Rev. 6:8).

In his four hypothetical cases Ezekiel interjected another element: what if three of the most righteous men who ever lived inhabited this land? God's answer was that it would make no difference.

Even if these three men—Noah, Daniel, and Job—were in it, they could save only themselves by their righteousness (cf. Ezek. 14:20). Both **Noah** and **Job** are understood by most scholars to refer to the biblical characters with the same names, but there is some question on the identity of **Daniel.** Ezekiel's spelling of the name differs slightly from the statesman-prophet who wrote the Book of Daniel. Many scholars feel that Ezekiel was referring to the mythical *Dan'el* in Ugaritic texts who, as a righteous ruler and judge, could not protect his sons from the wrath of the goddess Anat.

But this identification should probably be rejected. The minor difference in spelling could be explained by the common practice of multiple spellings of a given name (cf. "Azariah" = "Uzziah," 2 Kings 15:1; 2 Chron. 26:1; "Jehoram" = "Joram," 2 Kings 3:1; 8:16). The Prophet Daniel, well known in Babylon, would have been familiar to Ezekiel and his audience. There is no indication in the Old Testament that the mythical character *Dan'el* was known to the Jews or accepted as a model of righteousness. It was Ezekiel's purpose (Ezek. 14:1-11) to lambast idolatry. Would he use an idolatrous myth as a model of righteousness? By contrast, the biblical Daniel is the perfect example of a man who refused to compromise his beliefs.

God mentioned Noah, Daniel, and Job because of their similar characteristics. Each was a man of **righteousness** who overcame adversity. Righteous Noah was able to save only his immediate family from judgment (Gen. 6:8–7:1). Daniel was a righteous man in Ezekiel's day whom God used to save his friends from judgment (Dan. 2:12-24). Job was a righteous man who interceded for his three friends to save them from God's wrath after his own trials (Job 42:7-9).

Even if these three pillars of righteousness prayed together for mercy in a land under judgment, their praying for others in that case would be of no avail; they could save only themselves. (Cf. Jeremiah's words about the ineffectiveness of Moses' and Samuel's praying, Jer. 15:1.) This was made even more poignant when God declared, **they could not save their own sons or daughters. They alone would be saved** (Ezek. 14:18; cf. v. 20). Noah had "saved" his family and Job's

family was restored after his calamities; but when God's judgment would come on Israel, they would be able to rescue only themselves.

14:21-23. Having established this general principle (vv. 12-20), Ezekiel applied it to Jerusalem. **How much worse it will be when** God sends **against Jerusalem** His **four dreadful judgments— sword and famine and wild beasts and plague** (cf. 5:17). It would be worse for Jerusalem because she did not have three giants of righteousness to intercede for her. If those righteous leaders could not save a wicked land, how could Jerusalem hope to escape with her paucity of righteous individuals?

In the midst of announcing judgment God included a note of consolation. God's judgment would be vindicated by the exiles in captivity when they observed the evil character of those who survived Jerusalem's fall. **Yet there** would **be some survivors—sons and daughters who** would **be brought out of it,** that is, some would live through Jerusalem's destruction and be brought to Babylon as captives. As that group of exiles went to Babylon, the exiles already there (the ones addressed by Ezekiel) would **see their conduct and their actions,** and **be consoled regarding the disaster on Jerusalem.**

Some have felt that the "conduct and actions" Ezekiel was referring to were the righteous deeds of this remnant which prompted God to spare them. But Ezekiel was probably referring to the wicked ways of the captives. The word for "conduct" (*derek*) was used 35 times in Ezekiel's book to refer to the people's *evil* actions (cf. 3:18-19; 7:3-4, 8-9, 27; 11:21; 13:22; 14:22-23; 16:27, 43, 47 [twice], 61; 18:23, 25, 29-30; 20:30, 43-44; 22:31; 23:31; 24:14; 33:8-9, 11, 17, 20; 36:17, 19, 31-32). The word for "actions" (*ʿălîlôt*) is used 8 times in the book to refer to the *sinful* deeds of Israel (14:22-23; 20:43-44; 21:24; 24:14; 36:17, 19). These two words occur together 7 times, and in every occurrence the words convey sinful actions.

Those who questioned the severity of God's judgment would recognize its justice when they observed the evil character of the captives brought from Jerusalem. They would be forced to admit that these people did deserve to be punished and that God was not unjust.

c. Three parables on judgment (chaps. 15–17)

After his two signs (12:1-20) and five messages (12:21–14:23), Ezekiel delivered a series of three parables (chaps. 15–17) to show that there was no possibility of deliverance for Israel.

(1) The parable of the fruitless vine (chap. 15). **15:1-5.** God posed a question to Ezekiel. **Son of man, how is the wood of a vine better than that of a branch on any of the trees in the forest?** The obvious answer is that apart from its ability to bear fruit the wood of a tangled vine is inferior to the wood of a tree. God pressed His point by asking two additional questions. **Is wood ever taken from it to make anything useful? Do they make pegs from it to hang things on?** The wood of grapevines is useless as a building material. Its twisting, gnarled branches cannot even be fashioned into a stout peg for hanging objects.

If the vine by itself was nearly useless, how much more so would it be after it had been through **the fire?** The worthlessness of a **charred** branch with its crooked, blackened **ends** is obvious.

15:6-8. God then applied the parable to **Jerusalem.** She was the **vine** branch; since she had stopped bearing the fruit of righteousness, she was useless.

Israel thought of herself as the vine of God's blessing, but she had not produced the spiritual fruit God intended (cf. Ps. 80:8-18; Isa. 5:1-7; Jer. 2:21; Hosea 10:1). In fact Israel had become a wild vine of the forest that had tendrils expanding in all directions but with no fruit of any value. Its only use was as **fuel for the fire.** In the same way God would treat His **people** in Jerusalem.

God's judgment was certain: **I will set My face against them.** Jerusalem had surrendered to Babylon in 597 B.C.; and though they escaped total destruction then, God would bring Babylon back to finish the job. **Although they have come out of the fire, the fire will yet consume them.** There was no cause for optimism, for the judgment from Babylon had only been delayed.

(2) The parable of the adulterous wife (chap. 16). **16:1-5.** In this parable on Jerusalem's unfaithfulness Ezekiel pictured her as an unwanted child of a mixed union. **Your ancestry and birth were in the land of the Canaanites; your father was an Amorite and your mother a Hittite** (cf. v. 45). While Ezekiel had the *people* of Jerusalem in mind through most of this parable, this beginning seems to allude to the *city* of **Jerusalem** itself. Israel, of course, descended from Shem (Gen. 10:21-31); by contrast Jerusalem, before it was conquered by David (1 Chron. 11:4-9), was a Canaanite city (Canaan descended from Ham, not Shem, Gen. 10:6-20). The city's early inhabitants were called Jebusites (Jud. 19:10-12).

Why then did Ezekiel say that Jerusalem's father was an Amorite and mother a Hittite? Perhaps the pagan Jebusites were associated with and were apparently like the Amorites and Hittites. This association may be suggested in the Table of Nations, which lists the Jebusites *between* the Hittites and Amorites (Gen. 10:15-16; see comments on the Amorites in Gen. 14:13-16). A similar point of association but not actual blood relationship is evident in the reference to Sodom as a "sister" of Jerusalem (Ezek. 16:46).

The early beginnings of Jerusalem were like those of an unwanted child. Normally after a baby is **born** the umbilical **cord** is **cut.** In biblical times a newborn was then **washed** to remove the blood and vernix and was **rubbed with salt** to dry and firm the skin. Then the infant was **wrapped in cloth** for warmth and covering. But for Jerusalem these things were not done. **No one looked on her with pity or had compassion enough to do any of these things for** her.

Also the baby (Jerusalem) was **thrown out into the open field, for** she was **despised.** The cruel practice of infanticide was prevalent in the ancient world. Unwanted and deformed children were cast out at birth and left to die.

16:6-7. As God noticed the struggling infant wallowing helplessly (**kicking about in** her **blood**), He came to her aid. The life of the infant was hanging in the balance till God ordained her survival: **I said to you, Live!**

The child lived and **grew** to maturity **like a plant of the field.** The modern equivalent of that comparison is "She grew like a weed." As time went by, this baby grew into a young woman. Yet she was still **naked and bare,** in a destitute state.

16:8. God again passed by Jerusalem

and noticed that she was **old enough for love,** that is, of marriageable age. God then entered into a covenant of marriage with her. **I spread the corner of My garment over you and covered your nakedness. I gave you My solemn oath and entered into a covenant with you . . . and you became Mine.** The symbolic act of spreading the lower part of one's garment over another signified protection and betrothal (cf. Ruth 3:9). God pledged His fidelity to Jerusalem and took her as His own. The historical event to which this alludes could be the appointment of Jerusalem as Israel's capital and God's dwelling place.

16:9-14. God **clothed** His betrothed in splendor befitting a queen. The waif who had the stench of **blood** was **washed** and anointed with **ointments,** or expensive perfumes. The girl who was naked now received an **embroidered dress . . . leather sandals. . . . fine linen, and . . . costly garments.** God put **jewelry** on her, including **bracelets . . . a necklace,** a **ring** on her **nose, earrings,** and a **crown.** The "ring" was clipped to the outer part of a nostril and was worn as jewelry with bracelets and earrings (cf. Gen. 24:47; Isa. 3:21). All this suggests that under God's blessing during the reigns of David and Solomon Jerusalem became a magnificent city (cf. 1 Kings 10:4-5).

Besides receiving expensive jewelry and fine clothes Jerusalem also was given the choicest foods: **fine flour, honey, and olive oil.** Everything she could possibly need or want was lavished on her by her gracious, generous "Husband." Being **beautiful,** she became **a queen,** and her **beauty** was known throughout **the nations.**

Had Ezekiel's parable ended here, it would have been a beautiful rags-to-riches love story. But he added a bizarre twist to make the story correspond to the remainder of Jerusalem's history. He pictured the unfaithfulness of this woman who was made a queen (Ezek. 16:15-34).

16:15-19. Jerusalem's gaze turned from her Benefactor to her **beauty,** and she became proud (she **used** her **fame to become a prostitute**). Jerusalem forgot the One who had supplied her with her wealth, and turned away from Him (cf. Deut. 6:10-12; 8:10-20). Instead she basked in her **beauty** and prostituted herself to other gods. Beginning in Solo-

mon's reign (1 Kings 11:7-13), and continuing till her fall to Nebuchadnezzar, Jerusalem turned from God to idolatry. She had times of revival, but her general trend was downward.

The very blessings God had bestowed on the city were used to worship the false gods. She **took some of** her **garments to make gaudy high places,** false worship centers usually situated on high hills (see comments on Ezek. 6:3). God said, **You also took the fine jewelry I gave you** (cf. 16:11-13) **and you made for yourself male idols and engaged in prostitution with them.** Ezekiel used vivid imagery to drive home the truth of the vileness of Jerusalem's sin. He pictured her taking her jewelry to make a phallic image with which she engaged in sex. Similarly the people of Jerusalem took the material benefits given by God to make idols of false gods and committed spiritual adultery with them.

16:20-22. Jerusalem also offered up her own **sons and daughters** as human sacrifices (**as food**) to these false **idols.** The Canaanite practice of child sacrifice was forbidden to the Israelites (cf. Lev. 18:21; 20:2-5; Deut. 12:31). In Ammon, parents killed their **children** and offered them in fires to entreat the god Molech's favor. The practice crept into the nation of Israel, and by Ezekiel's time child sacrifice was practiced openly in Jerusalem (cf. 2 Kings 21:6; Jer. 7:30-31; 32:35). Jerusalem had strayed far from her "Husband"; she had forgotten all His blessings. In her pride she forgot who had saved her from her destitute state as a neglected newborn and had elevated her to her exalted position.

16:23-29. Jerusalem developed an ever-deepening lust for idols. Her harlotry moved from the "high places" to the highways as **shrines** to foreign gods were erected at every intersection (**in every public square**) and on **every street.** Her desire for idolatry drove her to seek out "lovers" promiscuously to satisfy her lust. Her whoredoms included Egypt (v. 26), Assyria (v. 28), and Babylon (v. 29). Mentioning these nations implies not only Jerusalem's desire for new foreign gods to worship but also her foreign intrigues and alliances.

God did not stand quietly by while His "wife" debased herself. He tried to curb her appetite by imposing judgment.

He **reduced** her **territory** (i.e., land governed by Jerusalem) and **gave** her **over to . . . the Philistines.** The Philistines attacked Judah and Jerusalem in the reigns of Jehoram (2 Chron. 21:16-17) and Ahaz (2 Chron. 28:16-19). Yet even the Philistines **were shocked by** Jerusalem's **lewd conduct.** The Philistines worshiped idols, but at least they remained faithful to their own gods.

16:30-34. Jerusalem was **like a brazen prostitute,** but with one major difference. A **prostitute** gets paid for her services, but Jerusalem **scorned payment.** She was an **adulterous wife** as well as a prostitute because she preferred **strangers to** her **own husband.** Jerusalem was a spiritual nymphomaniac. She had even resorted to paying bribes (rather than receiving **a** fee) to get the attention that earlier had been lavishly bestowed on her. Such a reversal was remarkably unusual, thus showing her debased commitment to idolatry and foreign alliances. As she departed from God, He then withheld His blessings that He had so freely given (cf. Deut. 28:15-23). Instead of realizing her sin and returning to the true God, she sought out still more gods and offered larger "bribes" to induce these other gods to bless her. Jerusalem was squandering her wealth on things that could not bless.

16:35-43. Jerusalem had degenerated from a queen to a tramp. Her beauty was gone; so she used her few remaining resources to try to bribe others into illicit relationships. God tried to stop her mad rush to destruction but she refused to heed His warnings. It was now time for Him to judge.

God's judgment on Jerusalem would fit her crime. She had **exposed** herself to all her **lovers;** now God would use her **lovers** to destroy her. He would bring the nations **against** her and **strip** her **in front of them,** so that they would all **see** her **nakedness.** Jerusalem would again be as defenseless before her enemies as she was before being espoused to the Lord (v. 8).

God said He would punish Jerusalem as **women** were punished **who commit adultery and who shed blood.** The sentence for adultery in the Old Testament was stoning (Lev. 20:10; cf. John 8:4-5). Jerusalem's "adultery" was her idolatry, and the punishment for idolatry

was the sword (Deut. 13:12-15). God actually employed both means of judgment—stoning and the sword—in Jerusalem's fall. **They will bring a mob against you, who will stone you and hack you to pieces with their swords** (cf. Ezek. 23:47). God had said that if a city in Israel became involved in idolatry its people were to be killed by the sword and the city was to be burned (Deut. 13:15-16). After Jerusalem's fall Babylon did in fact **burn down** her **houses and inflict punishment . . . in the sight of many women** (Ezek. 16:41).

God's judgment on Jerusalem would finally **put a stop to** her **prostitution.** Only after her destruction would His **wrath . . . subside.** God's **jealous anger** does not indicate pettiness or vindictiveness; instead it is an essential display of His holiness.

The root cause of Jerusalem's sin was her failure to **remember the days of** her **youth** (v. 43; cf. "you will remember" in vv. 61, 63). All her grandeur came as a result of the Lord's gracious favor. So when she turned from Him she was cutting herself off from the only true source of blessing and enraging the One who had raised her to greatness.

16:44-45. The first part of Ezekiel's parable (vv. 1-43) is an analogy between Jerusalem and an adulterous wife. The second part of the parable (vv. 44-63) is an analogy between Jerusalem and her **sisters** Samaria and Sodom. If Jerusalem's wicked sisters received judgment for their sin, how could Jerusalem, who was even more depraved, hope to escape?

Jerusalem had a proverb about her fate (see comments on 12:22), but God gave her a new **proverb: Like mother, like daughter.** This meant that the traits of the parents were seen in the **children.** Jerusalem's actions were characteristic of her family heritage. Her **mother** had **despised her husband and her children.**

For emphasis, Ezekiel repeated the ancestral background of Jerusalem, already stated in 16:3. The debauchery, petty rivalries, and heartless cruelties of the Canaanite tribes were well known. Jerusalem inherited these characteristics from her "parents" and displayed them in her abandoning God and in cruelly sacrificing her own children.

16:46-48. Ezekiel expanded his analogy by comparing Jerusalem to her sisters, both of whom had "despised their husbands and their children" (v. 45). These two sisters (**Samaria** and **Sodom**), who shared Jerusalem's family traits, were selected by Ezekiel to reinforce his point. Both cities—one **north** and one **south** of Jerusalem—were known for their gross sins and divine judgment.

Yet Jerusalem was even **more depraved than** both Samaria and Sodom. Not even **Sodom,** with its heinous sins, was guilty of some of Jerusalem's lewd ways! (v. 48)

16:49-52. Sodom's sin was her **haughty** unconcern for the needs of others in spite of their wealth. Also the Sodomites **did detestable things before** God. This could refer to their deviate sexual aberrations (cf. Gen. 19:4-5). The sin of Samaria, though not specifically stated, was her idolatry. But Jerusalem's sins were so vile that, in comparison, the sins of both **Sodom** and **Samaria** seemed almost like **righteous** deeds!

16:53-58. Having announced the sin of and judgment on Jerusalem, Ezekiel then offered consoling words for her. Verses 53-63 speak of the restoration of all three "sisters." **I will restore the fortunes** (blessings) **of Sodom . . . and of Samaria . . . and your fortunes along with them.** If God would restore Jerusalem, could He do any less for her more righteous sisters? Ezekiel was speaking of the national restoration of these cities in the Millennium. (Evidently Sodom will be rebuilt at that time.)

Once restored, Jerusalem will sense deep remorse. She will **bear** her **disgrace and be ashamed of all** she had **done in giving** Samaria and Sodom **comfort.** This statement is connected with verse 52. Jerusalem's shame would be deeper because the depths of her sins actually were a source of comfort to **Sodom** and **Samaria.** In other words, if God would restore (**return**) the wretched Jerusalem, certainly He would restore her **sisters.**

Jerusalem's sin became the subject of gossip. In her haughtiness, before her fall, she **would not even mention** the name of her "fallen" **sister Sodom.** However, after her exposure and sin Jerusalem would be the object of derision by surrounding nations, including **the daughters of Edom and all her neighbors and the daughters of the Philistines.**

Edom, south of the Dead Sea, was a constant rival of Judah (cf. 2 Kings 8:20-22; 2 Chron. 28:17; Obad.). Edom gloated over Judah's fall to Babylon and aided Babylon in her attack on Jerusalem (cf. Ps. 137:7; Ezek. 25:12-14; 35:5-6, 15). "The daughters" of Edom and Philistia probably were the cities located in those countries. Jerusalem would be restored—but she would first have to **bear the** shameful **consequences** of her sin.

16:59-63. Though Jerusalem's sin would be judged, God would restore her to fellowship with Him. Describing the certainty of Jerusalem's judgment, Ezekiel stressed that God was not abandoning His people forever. God had entered into a binding **covenant** with His people (cf. v. 8), and He would **remember** (i.e., keep) it. This **everlasting covenant** is the "New Covenant" spoken of by Jeremiah (Jer. 31:31-34) and Ezekiel (cf. Ezek. 11:18-20; 36:26-28; 37:26-28).

When this "everlasting covenant" is established, God will also change the relationship between Jerusalem and her restored **sisters.** They will become her **daughters,** that is, Jerusalem will assume responsibility for Samaria and Sodom when her kingdom is restored in the Millennium. God's **covenant** here (16:61) probably refers to the Mosaic Covenant established with Israel which she had broken (cf. vv. 59-60a).

In the Millennium, when God establishes the New Covenant and restores Jerusalem, she will **know that** God is **the LORD.** Jerusalem's problem had been her forgetting God's past deeds (v. 43). But God's final covenant will correct her problem of spiritual amnesia (v. 63). **Then,** God said, **when I make atonement for you . . . you will remember** (cf. v. 61) **and be ashamed** (cf. vv. 52, 54). God's judgment and subsequent restoration would have a humbling effect on the nation. Her problem of pride (v. 56) would be eliminated forever.

(3) The parable of the two eagles (chap. 17). This parable about two eagles pictures Zedekiah's rebellion against the king of Babylon and the judgment that would result.

17:1-2. God told Ezekiel to **set forth an allegory and tell the house of Israel a parable.** The Hebrew word for "allegory" (*ḥîḏâh*) refers to a riddle or an enigmatic saying that normally requires an explanation. It is used of the "riddle" Samson posed to the Philistines (Jud. 14:12-19) and the "hard questions" the Queen of Sheba asked Solomon (1 Kings 10:1; 2 Chron. 9:1). Ezekiel was told to deliver a discourse or extended riddle that would require an explanation. The word for parable is *māšāl*, which is normally translated "proverb," a short, pithy statement (cf. Ezek. 12:22; 18:1) but which can also refer to a longer work involving extensive comparison(s). Ezekiel's riddle or parable was stated in 17:3-10 and explained in verses 11-21.

17:3-4, 11-12. The first of two eagles, **with powerful wings, long feathers, and full plumage of varied colors, went to Lebanon.**

As Ezekiel explained later (v. 12), the eagle symbolized Nebuchadnezzar, and Lebanon stood for Jerusalem: **Do you not know what these things mean? The king of Babylon went to Jerusalem** (on the **rebellious house** see comments on 3:9).

Then Ezekiel explained why the "eagle" had gone "to Lebanon." The eagle clipped **the top** of a cedar tree and replanted the bough **in a city** known for trade. This referred to Nebuchadnezzar's attack on Jerusalem in 597 B.C. when he reestablished his control over the city and deposed King Jehoiachin. As Ezekiel explained, Nebuchadnezzar **carried off her king** (17:12), the top **shoot** of the tree, **and her nobles, bringing them back with him** (cf. 2 Kings 24:8-16) and replanted the "shoot" in **Babylon.**

17:5-6, 13-14. The "eagle," Nebuchadnezzar, was not totally heartless. **He took some of the seed of the land and . . . planted it like a willow by abundant water, and it sprouted and became a low, spreading vine.** Nebuchadnezzar weakened Jerusalem, but he did not destroy it at that time. Instead he set up Zedekiah as a vassal king. Jerusalem's military might was gone; but as long as she remained faithful to Nebuchadnezzar, her people could continue to live in peace. Zedekiah, **a member of the royal family,** by **a treaty** was put **under oath** (v. 13). Though Judah was **brought low,** weakened and humiliated, she could survive if she kept the **treaty** with Nebuchadnezzar.

17:7-8, 15. Another . . . eagle came along to "entice" **the vine** away from

where **it** had been **planted.** This new "eagle" was Egypt, which influenced Zedekiah to rebel against Babylon. Judah's **king** violated his oath of allegiance to Babylon and joined forces with Egypt, **sending . . . envoys to Egypt to get horses and a large army.** When Ezekiel penned this prophecy Zedekiah's final revolt had not yet happened. Assuming that the book was arranged chronologically, this prophetic parable was written sometime between 592 B.C. (8:1) and 591 B.C. (20:1). Zedekiah's final revolt against Babylon actually began in 588 B.C., so Ezekiel predicted Zedekiah's revolt about three years before it happened.

17:9-10, 16-21. The results for the "vine" (v. 8) would be disastrous. It would be **uprooted and stripped of its fruit** and wither. Because Zedekiah violated his **oath** to Nebuchadnezzar (an oath ordained by God; cf. Jer. 27), Nebuchadnezzar would not spare the city. As Ezekiel explained, this revolt meant that Zedekiah would **die in Babylon** for **Pharaoh** in Egypt would **be of no help.** In breaking his **oath** to Nebuchadnezzar, Zedekiah was also opposing God. **I will bring down on his head My oath that he despised and My covenant that he broke.** God would see that Zedekiah was caught by Nebuchadnezzar (in his **net** and **snare**) and brought **to Babylon,** with his **troops** killed **by the sword** (cf. 2 Kings 24:3-7).

17:22-24. Lest the people get overly discouraged about God's coming judgment, Ezekiel added an "addendum" to his prophecy against Jerusalem. Though not specifically calling God an "eagle," Ezekiel compared God's future actions to those of the two eagles (Babylon and Egypt) already mentioned. Neither of those eagles had been able to provide the security and prosperity Israel desperately longed for, but God would succeed where they had failed.

God said He (**I Myself) will take a shoot from the very top of a cedar and plant it.** The "shoot" was the Davidic line (cf. v. 4 with v. 12). God will replant a king from the line of David **on the mountain heights of Israel.** The kingdom will not be destroyed for God will restore it to the land of Israel. That kingdom **will produce branches and bear fruit and become a splendid cedar.** That is, it will prosper as it has never done before. Instead of plucking branches from it, **birds of every kind will nest in it.** This suggests that Israel will protect surrounding nations rather than being their pawn.

God's purpose in restoring Israel is to reveal His glory and plan for Israel to all nations. **All the trees . . . will know that I the LORD bring down the tall tree and make the low tree grow tall.** Israel's rise to prominence will be a catalyst to turn other nations to the Lord.

This prophecy was not fulfilled when Israel returned to the land after the Babylonian Captivity. The fulfillment of verses 22-24 awaits God's establishment of Israel in the Millennium under the Messiah, Jesus Christ. At that time God's kingdom will rule the world (cf. Dan. 2:44-45; Zech. 14:3-9, 16-17).

d. The message on individual responsibility (chap. 18)

Ezekiel had delivered three parables to convict the nation of her sin (chaps. 15–17). He then returned to the bluntness of a direct message to drive home the fact of Israel's guilt. The message in chapter 18 is similar to that in 12:21-28, for they both answered the people's proverbs that denied their coming judgment.

18:1-4. God asked Ezekiel about a **proverb** being circulated. This proverb— **The fathers eat sour grapes, and the children's teeth are set on edge**—must have been well known in Israel because Jeremiah also quoted it (cf. Jer. 31:29-30). The proverb's point was that children were suffering because of their parents' sins. True, Jerusalem was suffering, but as stated in the proverb the people thought they were suffering not because of *their* sins but because of their *parents'* sins. So these people were blaming God for punishing them unjustly (cf. Ezek. 18:25).

God saw that this false **proverb** had to be refuted. Yet, as with all false doctrines, a kernel of truth in the teaching made it seem plausible. In the Ten Commandments God indicated that He was "a jealous God, punishing the children for the sin of the fathers to the third and fourth generation of those who hate Me" (Ex. 20:5). This same threat was repeated in Exodus 34:6-7 and Deuteronomy 5:9. Even Ezekiel had traced God's coming judgment back to the people's past ac-

tions (cf. Ezek. 16:15-29). But the point of these passages was that the *effects* of sin are serious and long-lasting, not that God capriciously punishes the innocent for their ancestors' evil ways.

Blaming others for their misfortunes, the people were denying their own guilt. This was wrong because every individual is personally responsible to God. **For every living soul belongs to Me, the father as well as the son.** Those who are guilty will receive their own deserved punishment. **The soul who sins is the one who will die** (cf. 18:20). The people of Israel could not rightly charge God with injustice.

18:5-6a. Ezekiel then presented three "cases" to prove the principle of individual responsibility. Each hypothetical situation begins with **Suppose** (vv. 5, 10, 14). The cases are those of a righteous man who does right (vv. 5-9), a violent son of a righteous father (vv. 10-13), and a righteous son of a violent father (vv. 14-18). In each Ezekiel described the individual's actions and God's response.

The first hypothetical case was that of a **man** who was **righteous** and who followed God's Law with all his heart (vv. 5-9). He was not guilty of idolatry. **He** did **not eat at the mountain shrines** (cf. 8:12; 16:24-25, 31, 39; 18:15; 22:9) **or look to the idols.** The "mountain shrines" were the high places scattered throughout Israel where idolatry was practiced (see comments on 6:3-7). The "idols" were the foreign images being worshiped by the people (cf. chap. 8; 16:20-25).

18:6b-8a. The righteous man was also careful to keep the portions of the Law pertaining to his fellow Israelites. He kept himself morally pure. Both adultery (Ex. 20:14; Lev. 20:10) and intercourse during the menstrual **period** (Lev. 18:19) were prohibited by the Mosaic Law. The righteous man in Ezekiel's hypothetical case faithfully maintained sexual purity.

Ezekiel's model Israelite was also careful **not** to **oppress** his fellow Israelites. He would not keep collateral **for a loan** which the borrower needed (cf. Ex. 22:26; Deut. 24:6). He would never **commit robbery,** or forcibly take anything from a fellow Israelite (Ex. 20:15). He did the opposite; he gave **food** and **clothing** to the needy. His concern was how he could help others, not what he could get from them.

If this righteous man loaned something to a fellow Israelite, he did not try to profit on the deal by **usury** (an exorbitant interest rate). **Take excessive interest** could be translated "take interest" (NIV marg.) in light of the first part of the sentence. The Law prohibited any charging of interest on loans made to fellow Israelites (Deut. 23:19-20); this man carefully followed the Law. He put God's Law ahead of financial gain.

18:8b-9. This righteous person was compassionate (not **doing wrong**) and fair (**judging fairly between man and man**). He faithfully kept the highest standards of conduct demanded by God's **laws** for His covenant people.

The **righteous** Israelite would **surely live.** He would be spared from judgment (cf. 14:12-20) and would not suffer for the sins of others. The vast majority of Jerusalem's inhabitants were *not* righteous. Therefore the implication is that they would be punished for their sins.

18:10-13. Ezekiel moved to his second hypothetical situation. **Suppose** the righteous man **has a** rebellious (**violent**) son who commits sins his **father** had avoided (cf. vv. 11-13a with vv. 8-9).

God's verdict on this man was unfavorable. He would **be put to death and his blood** would **be on his own head.** The father's righteousness would not benefit his son (cf. 14:16, 18). This confirmed the fallacy of the people's proverb (18:2) and the truth of God's principle (v. 4).

18:14-20. Ezekiel's third case continued to follow this hypothetical family. **Suppose** (cf. "suppose" in vv. 5, 10) **this wicked son has a son who sees all the sins of his father** but **does not do such things** himself. Instead of following in the sin of his father, this son followed in the righteous path of his grandfather (cf. vv. 15-16 with vv. 6-9).

God's conclusion is obvious: **He will not die for his father's sin; he will surely live.** A righteous son will not be punished for his father's evil deeds. **But his father will die for his own sin.** The proverb being quoted (v. 2) was incorrect. When the people were judged, it was not for the sins of someone in a former generation. Only those who remained faithful to God would be delivered (v. 19). (By

the word **live** Ezekiel meant escaping punishment in this life. See comments on v. 24.) Ezekiel then repeated his point: **The soul who sins is the one who will die** (v. 20; cf. v. 4).

18:21-23. However, escape from judgment was possible. Sinners could avoid judgment if they repented of their **sins** by turning **from** them (cf. Prov. 28:13) and kept God's **decrees.** Ezekiel was not teaching salvation by works. First, he was speaking of a temporal deliverance from Babylon's armies rather than eternal deliverance from the second death (Ezek. 18:13). Second, he clearly indicated that these righteous works would spring only from a "new heart and a new spirit" (v. 31). Good works result from a changed life; they do not bring about such a change.

Why would God allow a sinner who repented to avoid judgment? The answer lies in God's character. He takes no **pleasure in the death of the wicked** (cf. v. 32). Instead, He is **pleased when they turn from their ways.** God is not a petty despot who holds grudges and longs to inflict punishment on those who wrong Him. As a God of grace He longs for people to forsake their wickedness and turn to His righteous ways.

18:24. Though God forgives the sins of those who turn to righteousness, He does not excuse the sins of someone who has been walking in **righteousness** and then **turns** to wickedness. **Will such a person live? None of the righteous things he has done will be remembered.** God was not saying that a saved Israelite would lose his salvation if he fell into sin. Both the blessing and the judgment in view here are temporal, not eternal. The judgment was physical death (cf. vv. 4, 20, 26), not eternal damnation. An Israelite who had followed God's Law but who later turned to idolatry or immorality could not expect his past righteousness to negate his present **sins.** God does not balance an individual's good deeds against his bad deeds to determine his fate. An individual's relationship with God when the judgment arrives determines whether he will live or **die.**

18:25-32. Israel had charged God with unrighteousness, but God now turned the tables. **Is My way unjust? Is it not your ways that are unjust?** (cf. v. 29; Job 40:8)

Ezekiel reminded Israel of the responsibility for sin borne by each member of the nation. **I will judge you, each one according to his ways.** If Israel fell, it would be for the sins of her own generation. Because of this, the nation needed to **repent** if she hoped to escape. Israel needed spiritual renewal. The people needed to get **rid . . . of** their **offenses** and **get a new heart and a new spirit** (cf. Ezek. 11:19; 36:26). The life or death of the people depended on their individual responses to God. Those who continued to rebel would **die;** those who repented and turned from sin would **live.**

e. The parable of lamentation for Israel's princes (chap. 19)

Ezekiel concluded this section on the futility of false optimism (chaps. 12–19) with a lament or dirge for Israel and her leaders. This is the first of five laments in the book (cf. 26:17-18; 27; 28:12-19; 32:1-16). Three of the other laments were directed against Tyre, and the fourth (32:1-16) was for Egypt. A "lament" was a funeral song usually recited in honor of a dead person. The song generally stressed the good qualities of the departed and the tragedy or loss engendered by his death (cf. 2 Sam. 1:17-27).

19:1-2. This **lament** was for **the princes of Israel.** "Princes" was the title Ezekiel gave the kings residing in Jerusalem (see comments on 7:27). At the time of this lament Zedekiah was king. The date was 592 B.C., five years before the fall of Jerusalem. Thus Ezekiel was taking up a funeral dirge even though the city's "death" was still in the future. Jerusalem's fall was so certain that Ezekiel considered it inevitable. Part of this dirge traces the fate of Jehoahaz and Jehoiachin—two of the three kings who preceded Zedekiah. The dirge was not over one individual; it was being sung for the Davidic dynasty and the "death" of its rule.

In Ezekiel's lament he recalled with fondness the lioness who had produced the fallen lions. **What a lioness was your mother among the lions!** Since the "lions" were the kings, some scholars feel that the "lioness" was Hamutual, wife of Josiah and mother of Jehoahaz and Zedekiah (cf. 2 Kings 23:31; 24:18). However, this seems unlikely for two reasons. First, the "king" in Ezekiel 19:5-9 seems to be

Jehoiachin; and his mother was Nehushta, another wife of Josiah (cf. 2 Kings 24:8). Second, the "mother" of the kings, referred to throughout Ezekiel 19, seems to depict more than a physical mother. In verses 10-14 the nation herself is the "mother" of the kings. Verse 13 seems to allude to Israel's captivity. Therefore the lioness/mother in this chapter is the nation Israel. She was the one who set up her kings but saw them destroyed, and she was the one who would go into captivity.

19:3-4. The lioness, Israel, **brought up one of her cubs, and he became a strong lion** (a king). This lion was Jehoahaz who came to the throne after Josiah's untimely death (see "Historical Background" in the *Introduction*). After a reign of only three months he was deposed by Pharaoh Neco II, who **led him with hooks** (probably literal hooks in his nose attached to a rope-leash; cf. v. 9) **to the land of Egypt.** In Egypt Jehoahaz died in captivity (cf. 2 Kings 23:31-34; Jer. 22:11-12).

19:5-9. The king after Jehoahaz was Jehoiakim, but Ezekiel did not refer to him in this chapter. Ezekiel emphasized that Zedekiah would be taken into captivity, so he mentioned only those kings who suffered a similar fate, Jehoahaz and Jehoiachin. Jehoiakim died in Jerusalem, so he was not included in this lament. (See the chart "The Last Five Kings of Judah," near 2 Kings 24.)

Jehoiachin, **another of** Israel's **cubs** who became **a strong lion,** reigned for only three months before he was deposed by Nebuchadnezzar. His brief reign (described in Ezek. 19:5-7) was a time of terror and destruction. With lionlike ferocity Jehoiachin wrought havoc, breaking **down their strongholds and . . . their towns. The land,** Israel, **and all who were in it were terrified by his roaring.** The "terror" was removed only when he was dethroned and deported by Nebuchadnezzar. **With hooks** (cf. v. 4) **they pulled him into a cage** (perhaps *sûgar,* "cage," means a neck yoke, based on the Akk. *šigāru*) **and brought him to the king of Babylon.** Nebuchadnezzar imprisoned Jehoiachin in Babylon because of the revolt his father Jehoiakim had begun (2 Kings 24:8-17). Jehoiachin remained in prison for 37 years till he was released when Evil-Merodach

(Amel-Marduk) succeeded his father Nebuchadnezzar on the throne in Babylon (2 Kings 25:27-30; Jer. 52:31-34). However, Jehoiachin remained in Babylon; he never returned to the land he had ravaged.

19:10-11. In verses 10-14 Ezekiel addressed King Zedekiah directly. He is the subject of the rest of the dirge. The **mother,** Israel, **was like a vine.** Since vines were common in Israel, the writers of Scripture often referred to Israel and others as vines (cf. Isa. 5:1-7; Ezek. 15; 17:5-10; Matt. 21:33-41; John 15:1-8). In her past glory, Israel **was,** figuratively speaking, **fruitful and full of branches.** It had prospered under the blessing of God, and had produced many rulers. **Its branches were strong, fit for a ruler's scepter.** The exact identification of the ruler(s) intended by Ezekiel's metaphor is unknown. Possibly Ezekiel was not pointing to specific rulers in Israel's past, but was merely showing that Israel's past was glorious and that it included **many** mighty leaders.

19:12-14. The vine's past glory contrasted sharply with its condition in Ezekiel's day. Israel the vine **was uprooted in fury and thrown to the ground.** It was shriveled and its **branches** were burned. Ezekiel did not explain the cause for this judgment, but in chapters 16-17 he had already stated why Israel went from blessing to disaster. The vine forgot that God was her source of blessing. Therefore God "uprooted" the nation, deporting her from the land.

The east wind would have conveyed a double meaning to Israel. The prevailing winds in Israel are from the west and bring moisture-laden air from the Mediterranean Sea. The east wind, known as the sirocco, blows on Israel from the desert in the east, bringing severe problems. It can wither vegetation (Gen. 41:6), destroy houses (Job 1:19), and cause severe distress (Jonah 4:8). However, Ezekiel's east wind referred to more than the sirocco. Babylon was also east of Israel; and when she "blew in" from the east, the nation shriveled under the heat of her oppression.

Ultimately Israel fell to Babylon. Ezekiel's statement, **Now it is planted in the desert, in a dry and thirsty land,** probably refers to Babylon's destruction of Israel. As the sirocco destroyed vegetation in

its path, so Israel would languish under Babylon's attacks. However, Ezekiel was possibly alluding to the Babylonian Captivity which the nation would soon face. The luxuriant vine of the nation would be uprooted from her homeland and cast down on foreign soil.

God's judgment would also affect the royal line. **No strong branch is left on it fit for a ruler's scepter.** The nation which had produced mighty rulers in the past (Ezek. 19:11) now would have no king. After Zedekiah was overthrown by Babylon, no king from the Davidic dynasty replaced him. Not till Christ returns will a "ruler's scepter" again arise in the line of David and reign as Israel's king.

3. THE HISTORY OF JUDAH'S CORRUPTION (CHAPS. 20–24)

These prophecies against Judah and Jerusalem focus on Judah's history. Ezekiel had presented that history in a parable (chap. 16), but in this section he gave a more direct presentation, especially in chapters 20 and 23. Chapter 21 contains a series of four messages on the sword that would smite Jerusalem, and chapter 22 has three additional prophecies of judgment on Jerusalem. The entire section closes in chapter 24 with two prophecies about the city's fall.

a. The message of Israel's past rebellion and restoration (20:1-44)

(1) Her past rebellion (20:1-31). **20:1-4.** This prophecy was given **in the seventh year, in the fifth month on the 10th day.** This was August 14, 591 B.C., almost 11 months after the last date given by Ezekiel (8:1). As in chapters 8 and 14, the message was given to Ezekiel when **some of the elders of Israel came to inquire of the LORD.** They again visited him to see if God had any new word for the nation.

The elders' question is not recorded, but it must have been inappropriate because God refused to respond: **I will not let you inquire of Me.** The answer God then gave was not a response to their question but a review of their history. To find an answer the people only needed to look into their past. The repetition of God's question **Will you judge them?** (20:4) conveyed His impatience with the people, and it has the force of a command, "Judge these people!" Ezekiel was to confront them regarding the detestable practices of their fathers. The court was to be opened and the evidence presented. Ezekiel was to act as the prosecuting attorney and present the evidence against the accused (cf. 22:2b).

20:5-9. When God sovereignly selected Israel to be His people He bound Himself to them as their God and Protector. The first evidence of His faithfulness was His self-revelation to them. He revealed Himself to them in Egypt and with uplifted hand He said to them, I am the LORD your God. This incident was at the burning bush when God appointed the people's deliverer (cf. Ex. 3:1-10). The uplifted hand (Ezek. 20:5 [twice], 15, 23, 42) was apparently a gesture used when one made an oath (cf. Ex. 6:8; Neh. 9:15; Ps. 106:26; Ezek. 36:7; 44:12; 47:14).

Why did God trace His selection of Israel only to the time of Moses? Was Ezekiel contradicting Genesis, which clearly indicates that God selected Israel when He made His covenant with Abraham? (cf. Gen. 12:1-3; 15; 17:1-8) No, Ezekiel was speaking of God's selection of Israel *as a nation*. When God made His covenant with Abraham, the patriarch did not even have an heir as the next recipient of the covenant. When the family of Joseph went into Egypt, they were only a small clan of nomadic herdsmen (cf. Gen. 46:1-27, 31-34). But in Moses' time Abraham's descendants had grown into a nation.

God also promised deliverance from bondage and provision for blessing. He assured Israel He would take her out of Egypt into a land . . . flowing with milk and honey, the most beautiful of all lands.

In His grace God asked the nation only to be faithful to Him, and to turn from the vile images and idols of Egypt. The Book of Exodus did not detail Israel's religious life before the Exodus, but Ezekiel implied that it was a time of apostasy.

But Israel refused to heed God's command. They did not remove the vile images . . . nor . . . forsake the idols of Egypt. This rebellion deserved judgment, so God was ready to pour out His wrath on them . . . in Egypt. Yet the wrath did not come; Israel was spared.

Israel's being spared from God's wrath was not because of any goodness on her part. It was only because of God's grace and mercy, for the sake of His name (cf. Ezek. 20:14, 22). The "name" of God expressed His revealed character. God's reputation among the nations was at stake in His covenant faithfulness to His people. Instead of giving them judgment, which they deserved, God gave deliverance.

20:10-12. Next Ezekiel traced Israel's history in the wilderness (vv. 10-26), discussing God's relationship to the first generation (vv. 10-17) and to the second generation (vv. 18-26).

The wilderness experience began with another outpouring of God's grace, by which He led them out of Egypt and . . . into the desert. Those listening to Ezekiel would remember hearing about the miracle at the Red Sea when God parted the waters for Israel and delivered them from Pharaoh's pursuing army. God did not rescue Israel only to abandon her in the heat of the desert. He saved her from Egypt so that He could set her apart to Himself as His special nation. The Books of Exodus and Leviticus contain God's Laws and statutes for His Chosen People.

God singled out one of His laws—the Sabbaths—as a visible manifestation of the Mosaic Covenant (cf. Isa. 56:1-8). It was a sign to the Israelites that they were God's special people and were obligated to keep His Law.

20:13-17. Instead of responding in obedience to God's gracious provision, the nation disobeyed and rebelled against His rule (cf. Num. 10:11–14:35) and kept on in idolatry (Ezek. 20:16).

God's response was the same as His response in Egypt. The people deserved to die, but for the sake of His name (cf. vv. 9, 22) He spared them. There was a temporal judgment, though. Those who had sinned were not allowed into the Promised Land (v. 15).

20:18-26. God repeated His opportunities of blessing to the second generation in the wilderness. But the same reaction developed. God gave the children the same orders He had given their parents (vv. 18-20; cf. vv. 11-12), but the children followed their parents in violating God's laws (v. 21a). Destruction was deserved, but once again God acted in grace for the sake of His name (vv. 21b-22; cf. vv. 9, 14).

God did not destroy the second generation of people for their sin, but He did impose some judgments on them. The first judgment was dispersion (v. 23). Just before Israel entered the land, God exhorted the people to obey His covenant. He delineated the blessings that would come through obedience and the problems that would result from disobedience (Deut. 28), including being scattered among the nations (Deut. 28:64-68).

God's second judgment was abandoning the people to their sin. He gave them over to statutes that were not good and laws they could not live by. Some have felt that God was referring here to the Mosaic Law, as if God imposed on the people stringent laws they could never keep. However, this view lowers the intrinsic quality of the Mosaic Law as an expression of God's righteousness. Paul declared that God's Law was "holy, righteous, and good" (Rom. 7:12). Even sinners must "agree that the Law is good" (Rom. 7:16). This view also neglects the chronology presented by Ezekiel. This judgment came *after* the second generation rebelled. The Mosaic Law was given to the first generation years earlier.

It is better to see the "statutes" and "laws" (Ezek. 20:25) as commandments of the pagan religions to which Israel had turned. These laws "required" the Israelites to offer the sacrifice of every firstborn (v. 26), a practice God strongly condemned (cf. Lev. 20:1-5).

God's "giving over" of the people to sin was His judicial act. Because they refused to follow His righteous ways, God would abandon them to the consequences of their actions. Paul expressed a similar judgment by God on the heathen (cf. Rom. 1:24, 26, 28).

20:27-29. Israel's new location in the land of promise did not change her sinful actions. In the land the people offered their sacrifices to idols on hills and under leafy trees, using the Promised Land as the setting for their idolatry. (On the "high place" see comments on 6:1-4.) With a wordplay Ezekiel emphasized the sin of the people by asking them, What is this high place (*mâh habāmâh*) you go to? (*habā'îm*) The similarity of these words underscored the point that Israel had turned to idol worship.

20:30-31. In Ezekiel's day Israel was still rebellious, just like her ancestors, and was involved in idolatry and child sacrifice. Therefore God refused to let them inquire of Him (cf. v. 3). He would not be a divine ouija board they could manipulate for an answer whenever they pleased.

(2) Her future restoration (20:32-44). **20:32-38.** After recounting Israel's past history of rebellion, God told of her future restoration. The people wanted to be like their idolatrous neighbors, but God would not let His people become totally divorced from Him: What you have in mind will never happen. He would remain their God, ruling over them with a mighty hand and an outstretched arm and with outpoured wrath (v. 33). The words "mighty hand" and "outstretched arm" would call to mind God's strength in delivering His people from Egypt (cf. Deut. 4:34; 5:15; 7:19; 11:2; Ps. 136:12; and cf. "outstretched arm" in Ex. 6:6 and "mighty hand" in Ex. 32:11). However, His hand and arm would now bring wrath, not deliverance.

Much as the Exodus brought Israel out of bondage into the wilderness, so God's new "Exodus" would bring Israel from the countries where she had been scattered. She would be brought into the wilderness, but this would be a desert of . . . judgment. In this "Exodus," like the one from Egypt, God repeated that He would use His mighty hand and . . . outstretched arm but in outpoured wrath (Ezek. 20:34).

As Israel gathered in the wilderness, God would begin the process of eliminating those who had rebelled. I will take note of you as you pass under My staff, and I will bring you into the bond of the covenant (v. 37). This pictures a shepherd holding out his rod and forcing the sheep to pass under it single file for counting (cf. Jer. 33:13). The shepherd would let those sheep that were actually his enter the fold, a place of protection. In this instance the fold was "the bond of the covenant." The "covenant" could refer to the Mosaic Covenant, which Israel had broken (cf. Ezek. 16:59), but this does not seem likely since Israel invalidated the Mosaic Covenant by her unbelief. Therefore God will make a New Covenant with her when He restores her to Himself (Jer. 31:31-33). Ezekiel seemed to make the same distinction (Ezek. 16:60) between the Old Covenant of Israel's "youth" and the "everlasting covenant" which will be enacted at the time of her restoration. God will again bring Israel into a covenant relationship with Him—but this covenant will be permanent.

As the sheep will pass under the rod of the Great Shepherd, those who do not belong to Him—unbelieving Israelites who **rebel against** God—will be removed. God will not allow those sheep to **enter** His land. God's process of purification will mean that only true sheep will enjoy the covenant of blessing.

This scene described by Ezekiel is yet future. At the end of the Tribulation God will regather Israel to the land of promise for the Millennium (cf. 36:14-38; 37:21-23). But first the Israelites will be required to stand before the Lord for judgment. Those who have placed their trust in Him will be allowed to enter the land and participate in His kingdom (cf. John 3:3). Those who are rebels will be judged for their sin and banished to everlasting punishment.

20:39-41. When Israel enters into the New Covenant she will really know the Lord (vv. 39-44). Though Israel was serving **idols** in Ezekiel's day (to her own defilement, vv. 25-26), in the future God will not permit such sin among His people (**you will . . . no longer profane My holy name**; cf. 39:7; 43:7).

God's ideal for Israel will finally be realized in the millennial kingdom. She will **serve** the Lord, He **will accept** her, and the people will offer Him their choicest **offerings . . . gifts,** and **sacrifices** in sincere worship. (For an explanation of sacrifices during the Millennium see the comments on 40:38-43.) As a result, God **will show** Himself holy. "Holy" (*qōḏēš*) means "set apart," the opposite of "profaned" or "made common." Israel had profaned her God by debasing her worship with sin and idolatry (20:39). In the future, however, she will set God apart so all **the nations** will sense God's holiness.

20:42-44. God's restoration of Israel will produce several changes: (1) The first change will be a new *realization* of her God. God said that Israel **will know that I am the LORD.** "LORD" (*Yahweh*) is God's personal name, revealed to **Israel** (cf. Ex.

3:13-15). It stresses God's self-existence and His covenant-keeping faithfulness. Israel will come to understand the true meaning of God's name (and character) when He brings her into Palestine. This promise does not depend on her faithfulness, for she had been extremely unfaithful. The promise, made by God, depends on *His* faithfulness. He will demonstrate His covenant loyalty by fulfilling it (cf. Ezek. 20:44).

(2) The second result of Israel's restoration will be her *repentance.* She **will remember** her **conduct** and **will loathe** herself **for all the evil** she has **done.** The shame **Israel** should have felt (but didn't) in Ezekiel's day will finally be manifested when God restores her.

b. The parable of the forest fire (20:45-49)

20:45-49. Ezekiel's long message (vv. 1-44) was followed by a short parable. In the Hebrew Bible 20:45 is actually the first verse of chapter 21, thus showing that this parable introduces the four messages in chapter 21. Ezekiel was to **face toward the south** (*têmānâh*) and **preach against the south** (*dārôm*) and **the southland** (*negeb*). The first of these three Hebrew words is literally "what is on the right hand" as an individual faces east. It was a poetic word, though when used as a proper name (Teman) it described a city in Edom, to Judah's south (cf. Amos 1:12; Jer. 49:7; Ezek. 25:13). Possibly the idea in 20:45 is that Ezekiel was to face toward Teman. The word *dārôm* was also poetic. Ezekiel used that word 12 other times, all in describing the millennial temple (cf. 40:24 [twice], 27 [twice], 28 [twice], 44-45; 41:11; 42:12-13, 18).

The third word used by Ezekiel (*negeb*, "southland" in the NIV) is also used as a proper name. Negev is the name of the southern portion of Palestine near Israel's border with Edom (cf. Josh. 15:21). Today the Negev is a semi-arid region with little rainfall and few sources of water. But since Ezekiel referred to the Negev **forest,** the land must have been more densely covered in those days. Major settlements in the Negev included Arad, Kadesh Barnea, and Beersheba.

In this prophecy against Judah, Ezekiel said God was going to devastate it by **fire** (probably a "fire" of judgment, not a literal fire).

The people saw Ezekiel's actions but

refused to understand them. Ezekiel complained to God that the people were saying he was **just telling parables,** or perplexing riddles. Though he was predicting Judah's destruction, the people were only confused by his words.

c. The four messages of the sword (chap. 21)

Since the people refused to understand Ezekiel's message about the fire on the southland (20:45-49), he gave four messages to expand his parable's meaning. In these messages Ezekiel changed the "fire" to a "sword" and the "Negev" to Judah and Jerusalem.

(1) The sword drawn (21:1-7). **21:1-5.** In the parable (20:45-49) Ezekiel had "set" his "face toward the south," but now God told him to **set his face against Jerusalem and preach against the sanctuary** and **prophesy against the land of Israel.** The object of God's judgment was His land, His Holy City, and His dwelling place.

God said that by a **sword** He would **cut off . . . both the righteous and the wicked.** This seems to contradict Ezekiel's earlier prophecy (18:1-24) that only the **wicked** would die and the **righteous** would live. This problem so perplexed the translators of the Septuagint that they changed "righteous" to "unrighteous." One possible solution is that "the righteous and the wicked" may be viewed from the people's perspective. As far as the people could tell the judgment was indiscriminate. It affected those who were in open idolatry as well as those who claimed to be followers of God. Yet in God's eyes only the wicked were being punished since He had promised to deliver those who were truly righteous. Another solution is that the phrase "cut off" may refer to captivity, not physical death. Whatever the exact meaning, Ezekiel was stressing the extent of the coming judgment.

The judgment would extend from **south** to **north** (already stated in 20:47). In case anyone failed to understand the parable of the forest fire, Ezekiel repeated this phrase to stress that all Judah would be judged. When judgment came, **then** the **people** would **know that . . . the** Lord had **drawn His sword** (cf. 21:3). Though the people refused to acknowledge the meaning of the parable (20:49),

they could not claim ignorance when God's slaughter would actually begin.

21:6-7. Ezekiel was instructed to act out the grief the people would feel when Jerusalem fell. As he sobbed in anguish, the people would **ask** what was wrong. He was to answer that it was **because of the news that** was **coming.** The awful realization of their country's demise would devastate them (cf. 7:17). Yet there was no doubt it would happen. **It will surely take place,** declared **the Sovereign Lord.**

(2) The sword sharpened (21:8-17). **21:8-10.** Ezekiel's second message about the sword was a poetic song of judgment. Its theme was that God's **sword** was **sharpened,** ready **for the slaughter.** The song is in three stanzas (vv. 8-10a, 11-12, 14-17). These sections were divided by two interludes, each focusing on "the rod" (vv. 10b, 13).

In the first stanza God's **sword** of judgment was **sharpened** with a whetstone to give it a keen cutting edge and **polished** and scoured to remove all rust and give the blade a gleam. Much like a soldier preparing for battle, God had honed His weapon so it would be effective.

The sword was coming because Israel had **despised the rod and all advice.** Some feel that "rod" refers to the king's scepter (cf. Gen. 49:9-10). If so, the people were rejecting God's threat of judgment and relying instead on His promise of a continued line of rulers for Judah. But this interpretation seems foreign to the passage. Perhaps "rod" refers to the chastisement God had used to try to curb Israel's sin and bring her back to Himself. A rod was often used for discipline (cf. Prov. 10:13; 13:24; 23:13), and God used "the rod" to discipline His own (cf. 2 Sam. 7:14; Job 9:34; 21:9). Israel had despised God's earlier attempts to use a rod to correct her, so He now used the sword. In this interpretation the **son** in Ezekiel 21:10 was not Ezekiel but Israel and her king.

21:11-13. The second stanza revealed the victims against whom the **sword** was drawn: God's **people** and all Israel's **princes.** The leaders had rejected God's advice and chastisement so all they could expect was the sword. Because of the massive destruction God told Ezekiel, **Cry out and wail.**

21:14-17. The third stanza stressed the work of the sword. In derision both the prophet and God would **strike** their **hands** (vv. 14, 17; cf. 6:11; 22:13). As **the sword** would move swiftly against the people and princes, it would **strike** and strike again (**twice, even three times**), seemingly coming **from every side.** In fear the people's **hearts** would **melt** (cf. 21:7). The judgment moved to all sides (**to the right, then to the left**) as it relentlessly pursued the people. It would stop only when the judgment was complete.

(3) The sword directed toward Jerusalem (21:18-27). **21:18-23.** Ezekiel's third message on the sword showed God's directing the sword of Babylon against Jerusalem. In symbolic actions Ezekiel pictured God supernaturally guiding Nebuchadnezzar to Jerusalem to overthrow the city.

God told Ezekiel to **mark out two roads for the sword of the king of Babylon to take.** When Jerusalem rebelled against Babylon in 588 B.C., she was one of three cities or countries seeking independence. The other two were Tyre and Ammon. Nebuchadnezzar led his forces north and west from Babylon along the Euphrates River. When he reached Riblah (north of Damascus in Syria) he had to decide which nation he would attack first. He could head due west toward the coast and attack Tyre, or he could go south along one of two "highways" leading to Judah and Ammon. Tyre was the most difficult of the three cities to attack (cf. chap. 26; 29:17-20), so Nebuchadnezzar decided not to make it his first objective. His choice then was whether to head down the coastal highway and attack **Judah and . . . Jerusalem** or to head down the Transjordanian highway and attack Ammon and **Rabbah.** "Rabbah" was the capital of Ammon and is identified with the modern city of Amman in Jordan.

The war council met at Riblah, **at the fork in the road,** to decide which course of action to take. Apparently Nebuchadnezzar and his generals could not agree on which direction to go, so they consulted their gods.

Nebuchadnezzar used three means to determine his course of action: casting **lots with arrows,** consulting **his idols,** and examining **the liver.** Casting lots

with arrows was probably similar to today's practice of drawing straws. Two arrows were placed in a quiver, each one inscribed with the name of one of the cities being considered for attack. The arrow drawn or cast out first was the one the gods indicated should be attacked. The consulting of "idols" ($t^e r \bar{a} p \hat{\imath} m$) involved the use of teraphim or household idols. The exact nature of this practice is unknown but perhaps the idols were used in an attempt to contact departed spirits and hear their advice. Examining the liver was a form of divination known as hepatoscopy. The shape and markings of the liver of a sacrificed animal were studied by soothsayers to see if a proposed plan was favorable or not.

These practices by themselves could do nothing, but God worked through them to accomplish His judgment. **Into** Nebuchadnezzar's **right hand** would **come the lot for Jerusalem.** As Nebuchadnezzar went through his procedures, God had all the signs point toward the coastal highway and Jerusalem. That would be where he decided to proceed.

The rulers of Judah had pledged **allegiance to** Babylon, but they had violated their oath by rebelling. Yet even as Nebuchadnezzar set up his **siege works** around the city, the people refused to believe he would succeed. They thought his **omen** was **false** and that he was doomed to failure—but they were wrong. Since they had broken their covenant with Nebuchadnezzar (cf. 17:11-21), he would **take them captive.**

21:24-27. God then pronounced judgment on the **people** (v. 24) and the prince (vv. 25-27). Because of **open rebellion,** Jerusalem's people would be **taken captive.** They felt secure in their city, but they would be forcibly torn from it and dragged in chains to Babylon.

The **profane and wicked prince of** Israel was King Zedekiah. Because he violated his oath of allegiance to Babylon, he would be deposed. Zedekiah was stripped of authority (his **turban** and **crown** were removed), blinded, and imprisoned for life in Babylon (2 Kings 25:4-7). The once-proud king was humbled (**the exalted will be brought low**). **The lowly** ("poorest people of the land," 2 Kings 25:12) who were allowed to remain took his place in managing the land for Babylon.

The right to rule in Israel was taken from Zedekiah, and the land was destroyed. Ezekiel's triple use of ruin stressed that Israel's throne was to be absolutely desolate. It will not be restored until He comes to whom it rightfully belongs; to Him I will give it. This prophecy recalls Genesis 49:10, which speaks of "the scepter" in the line of Judah. The line of David would not be restored till the righteous, God-appointed King would come. There were no valid claims till Christ rode into Jerusalem to claim His rightful rule (cf. Zech. 9:9; Matt. 21:1-11; Rev. 19:11-16; 20:4). Christ will fulfill Ezekiel's prophecy; *He* will be the King of Israel.

(4) The sword directed toward Ammon. 21:28-32. Ezekiel's fourth prophecy about the sword was directed against the Ammonites, who thought they had escaped Nebuchadnezzar's attack (cf. vv. 20-22). Ammon and Jerusalem, though enemies, had allied against Babylon. When Nebuchadnezzar decided to attack Jerusalem, Ammon was relieved and happy. They were thankful that Jerusalem would suffer in their place. In fact after Jerusalem's fall the Ammonites organized a coup that caused the death of Gedaliah, the governor of the land appointed by Nebuchadnezzar (Jer. 40:13–41:10). The Ammonites tried to set up another government in Israel that would be opposed to Babylon—probably so Nebuchadnezzar would again attack Judah instead of Ammon!

The sword that had been polished for Jerusalem (Ezek. 21:9, 11) would also reach Ammon. The Ammonites thought they had escaped Nebuchadnezzar's judgment but they would be punished. In God's wrath and fiery anger He would hand Ammon over to brutal men, men skilled in destruction. These invaders are identified in 25:4 as "people of the East" (cf. comments on Job 1:3)—possibly a reference to nomadic invaders. The fire of judgment directed against Judah (cf. 20:45-49) would also consume Ammon.

d. *The three messages on the defilement and judgment of Jerusalem (chap. 22)*

(1) The cause of judgment (22:1-16). 22:1-5. God asked Ezekiel, Will you judge her? Will you judge this city of bloodshed? This is similar to the questions God asked him at the beginning of this section on Jerusalem's sin (cf. 20:4). If Ezekiel was to function as a prosecuting attorney or judge, he had to declare the facts of the case. He needed to confront Jerusalem with all her detestable practices.

Then God gave Ezekiel two charges to present against the city: shedding blood and making idols. Ezekiel mentioned blood or bloodshed seven times in this message to drive home the city's sin of extreme violence (cf. "violence" in 7:23; 8:17; 12:19). These two sins opposed the Mosaic Law's standards for Israel's relationships with God and her fellow Israelites (cf. Matt. 22:34-40). Rather than loving God she had turned to idolatry; and her love for her fellow Israelites had been replaced by treachery.

Jerusalem's sin would be punished —the end of her years had come. When she fell, her neighbors would mock her. The pride of this infamous city would turn to shame as she would be exposed in her sin before others.

22:6-12. Ezekiel cited sins that specifically violated some of the Ten Commandments (cf. Ex. 20:1-17): social injustice (Ezek. 22:7), apostasy (v. 8), idolatry (v. 9), immorality (vv. 10-11), and greed (v. 12). The list concluded with another sin, the root problem behind the others: you have forgotten Me (cf. 23:35).

22:13-16. God would strike His hands together (cf. 6:11; 21:14, 17) in derision against Jerusalem. The proud and insolent people who treated God's commands lightly would not be able to dismiss His judgment. Their courage would vanish when God would disperse them among the nations. Moses had warned Israel that national disobedience would eventually lead to dispersion (cf. Lev. 26:27-39; Deut. 28:64-68). Israel had defiled God's Law; now she would be defiled in the eyes of the nations. After the nation was dispersed she would understand the character of the God she had scorned and forgotten: you will know that I am the LORD.

(2) The means of judgment (22:17-22). 22:17-19. Ezekiel's second message stressed that Jerusalem would become a furnace of affliction—a smelting furnace of judgment that would melt those who remained in it.

Israel had become worthless to God, for she was dross to Him—like the scum of copper, tin, iron, and lead left inside a furnace. Metallurgy was a developed science throughout the ancient Near East (cf. Job 28:1-11). When metals are heated in furnaces, the residue left after the pure metal is poured is the dross. To God, Israel was like dross—worthless because of her sin.

22:20-22. The dross was the by-product of smelting, but God was going to resmelt the dross. Much as metals are melted in a furnace, so God would gather the people inside the city and melt them. This thought is stated three times (vv. 20-22). Judah retreated to Jerusalem when Nebuchadnezzar invaded the land. The city became the crucible as God's fiery blasts of wrath and judgment blew on the people. God's judgment and destruction forced the people to acknowledge Him: And you will know that I the LORD have poured out My wrath upon you.

(3) The recipients of judgment (22:23-31). 22:23-24. This message names the recipients of the judgment: princes (v. 25), priests (vv. 26-27), prophets (v. 28), and people (v. 29).

In verse 24 the NIV has the Septuagint reading of rain instead of "cleansed" (see NIV marg.) because "rain" seems to match showers better than "cleansed." However, there is no compelling reason not to follow the Hebrew "cleansed." Because of her disobedience Israel had not experienced cleansing (from sin); she had not received rain (blessings) in the day God sent His wrath.

22:25. The sins of her princes (though possibly this should read "prophets," NIV marg.) were presented first. The "princes" probably referred to the royal family, including King Zedekiah (cf. 12:10-12; 19:1; 21:25). The leaders used their power for material gain, ravaging the people like a . . . lion (cf. 19:1-9). In their greed they took treasures and precious things; and they murdered, thus making many wives widows. Instead of being examples to the people, the leaders were corrupt despots.

22:26-27. The religious leaders were no better than the princes. Her priests do violence to My Law and profane My holy things (cf. Zeph. 3:4). They were not instructing the people in the ways of God, or enforcing the Law's statutes. They even shut their eyes to the keeping of God's Sabbaths (cf. Ezek. 20:16, 21, 24). Abandoning God's precepts, they let sin run rampant among the people.

Other government officials besides those in the royal family (princes, 22:25) were also guilty of unjust gain. Instead of equitably dispensing justice and upholding the rights of the disadvantaged, they were like wolves tearing their prey.

22:28-29. The prophets should have been God's spokesmen and denounced these wicked deeds; but (except for men like Ezekiel and Jeremiah) the prophets ignored those sins and gave the people false visions and lying divinations. They claimed to be speaking for God when the LORD had not spoken.

Then Ezekiel denounced the people, the commoners who followed their leaders' example. The populace too was involved in extortion and . . . robbery (cf. vv. 25, 27), and in oppression of the needy. So rulers oppressed the common people, and the common people oppressed the helpless.

22:30-31. The corruption was so complete that when God searched for a man who could stem the tide of national destruction (build up the wall and stand . . . in the gap), none could be found. No one in a position of authority in Israel had the moral qualities to lead the nation aright. Obviously Jeremiah had these qualities, but he lacked the authority to lead the nation from the brink of disaster.

Israel's extensive decay demanded justice. God concluded this message against Jerusalem by vowing to pour out His wrath and consume the people with His fiery anger (cf. 21:31).

Israel would suffer because of her sins. She had rebelled against God's grace; now she would feel God's wrath.

e. The parable of the two adulterous sisters (chap. 23)

Ezekiel presented another parable to illustrate Judah's unfaithfulness and the certainty of her punishment. Chapter 23 seems to be a restatement of the parable in chapter 16 since both chapters deal with Judah's unfaithfulness to God. However, in chapter 16 Ezekiel focused on Judah's idolatry, whereas in chapter 23 he stressed Judah's illicit foreign alliances in addition to her idolatry. In chapter 16 her trust was in other gods; in chapter 23 it was in other nations.

(1) The infidelity of the sisters (23:1-21). **23:1-3.** Two sisters shared the same moral degradation for **they became prostitutes in Egypt, engaging in prostitution from their youth.** Ezekiel's reference to Egypt would call to mind the origins of the nation Israel in Egypt (cf. 20:4-12). The two sisters were sexually promiscuous women.

23:4. After describing their character Ezekiel gave their names and identities. **The older was named Oholah, and her sister was Oholibah.** These names are based on the Hebrew word for "tent" (*'ōhel*). The first name means "her tent" and the second means "my tent is in her." Though one must be careful not to press a parable's details, probably these names have significance. The word "tent" implied a dwelling place or sanctuary. It was often used of God's sanctuary among Israel (cf. Ex. 29:4, 10-11, 30). The name Oholah ("her tent") could imply that the sanctuary associated with this sister was of her own making. By contrast, the name Oholibah ("my tent is in her") implies that God's sanctuary was in her midst.

Oholah represented **Samaria,** and **Oholibah** represented **Jerusalem.** These two "sisters," the capital cities of the kingdoms of Israel and Judah, represented the people of those two kingdoms.

Though God's covenant with these women was not explicitly stated, it was implied. **They were Mine and gave birth to sons and daughters.** The God of grace lavished His love on these undeserving sisters.

23:5-10. The sin of **Oholah,** the older sister, was her (Samaria's) association with **the Assyrians.** Samaria's alliance with Assyria ultimately led to her doom. Israel's relationships with Assyria are well documented. The Black Obelisk of the Assyrian king Shalmaneser III (dated ca. 841 B.C.) mentions "Jehu son of Omri" and pictures him bowing down to the Assyrian monarch. This is not mentioned in the Bible, but it probably resulted from the Syrian threat to Israel. Syria was expanding into Israel's land in the Transjordan during Jehu's reign (2 Kings 10:32-34). To counter that threat Jehu allied Israel with Assyria and submitted himself as a vassal. The obelisk pictures

Jehu and his servants bringing tribute to the Assyrian king. Menahem and Hoshea, two later kings of Israel, also paid tribute to Assyria (2 Kings 15:19-20; 17:3-4). The Prophet Hosea (ca. 760–720 B.C.) rebuked Israel for her dependence on Assyria instead of on the Lord (cf. Hosea 5:13-14; 7:11; 8:9; 12:1).

After Israel became Assyria's vassal she could not disentangle herself. When she finally tried to break away by forming a coalition with both Syria and Egypt (cf. 2 Kings 17:4; Isa. 7:1), she felt Assyria's wrath. The very nation to which Samaria had turned for assistance would destroy her. God gave all Israel, including Samaria, **over to her lovers, the Assyrians, for whom she lusted and who killed her with the sword.** In 722 B.C. Samaria fell to Assyria (cf. 2 Kings 17:5-6, 18-20).

23:11-18. The judgment of the older sister Oholah (Samaria) should have been a warning to the younger sister **Oholibah** (Jerusalem). Unfortunately she failed to heed the warning. In fact **she was more depraved than her sister.**

Jerusalem followed the immoral course charted by her sister: **she too lusted after the Assyrians.** Judah curried the favor of Assyria rather than relying on her God. Possibly Ezekiel had in mind the disastrous political move of King Ahaz of Judah who willingly made Judah Assyria's vassal. Israel and Syria had banded together to oppose Assyria, and they sought to bring Judah into the alliance. When Ahaz refused, they attacked Judah hoping to dethrone Ahaz and to replace him with a king who would support their uprising. Rather than trusting in God for deliverance (as Isaiah the prophet urged him to do), Ahaz sent to Assyria to enlist her aid and protection. With that act Judah became a vassal of Assyria for the next century (cf. 2 Kings 16:5-9; Isa. 7).

But Jerusalem's political intrigues did not stop there; **she carried her prostitution still further.** After appealing to Assyria, Jerusalem turned to Babylon. Ezekiel described in some detail the garb of the Babylonian soldiers Jerusalem lusted after (Ezek. 23:15).

Jerusalem **sent messengers to them in Chaldea. Then the Babylonians came to her, to the bed of love, and in their lust they defiled her.** Jerusalem's respite from Assyria's domination was short-lived. King Josiah established her independence, but he was killed in battle as he tried to thwart an Egyptian incursion through his country (cf. 2 Kings 23:29-30). Judah became a vassal of Egypt for four years. Probably during that time King Jehoiakim contacted Babylon to request her aid. When Babylon defeated the Egyptians at Carchemish in 605 B.C., Jehoiakim willingly switched allegiances and became Nebuchadnezzar's vassal (2 Kings 24:1).

But when Babylon came, Jerusalem found that the lovers for whom she had lusted were brutal. **After she had been defiled by them, she turned away from them in disgust.** Babylon became a harsher taskmaster than either Assyria or Egypt, and Jerusalem sought to escape Babylon's dominance.

While Jerusalem turned from Babylon, God turned from Jerusalem. Jerusalem continued in the ways of her sister and even surpassed Samaria's unfaithfulness. God had finally rejected Samaria for her actions, and He now rejected Jerusalem.

23:19-21. Jerusalem's faithlessness cost her the only true protection she ever had. Yet instead of repenting of her sin, she sought additional human help, becoming **more and more promiscuous.** Her cycle of sin brought her back to the very nation with which she had originally been defiled and which had enslaved her—**Egypt** (vv. 3, 19, 21).

To show his absolute disgust in this course of action, Ezekiel used coarse language (v. 20), not to be vulgar, but to portray graphically the utter spiritual degradation to which Judah had fallen.

In the last 14 years of Judah's history (600–586 B.C.) she attempted to elicit Egypt's help in her revolt against Babylon. King Jehoiakim rebelled against Babylon in 600 B.C. after Egypt defeated Babylon (2 Kings 24:1). Judah eagerly grasped Egypt's hollow promises of aid. Zedekiah's final revolt against Babylon in 588 B.C. came with Egypt's promise of assistance (2 Kings 25:1; Jer. 37:5-8; Ezek. 29:6-7).

(2) The punishment of the sisters (23:22-35). **23:22-27.** Here Ezekiel gave four oracles, each beginning with the words, **This is what the Sovereign Lord says** (vv. 22, 28, 32, 35). The oracles all focused on Jerusalem's judgment. Those Jerusalem despised would be the ones who would punish her. God would bring her **lovers against** her, including the **Babylonians . . . the men of Pekod and Shoa and Koa, and all the Assyrians.** Perhaps Pekod, Shoa, and Koa were three Aramean tribes (*Puqûdû, Sutû,* and *Qutû*), near the mouth of the Tigris River. These three tribes, along with the Assyrians, were part of the Babylonian Empire and were represented in Babylon's army. Ezekiel was saying that the combined army of Babylon and her allies would descend on Jerusalem.

When the Babylonians would attack Jerusalem with military **officers . . . weapons,** and well-protected soldiers the city would not escape. The **punishment** God would inflict on her in His **anger** through Babylon would be like a mutilation. **They will cut off your noses and your ears, and those . . . who are left will fall by the sword.** In Mesopotamia facial mutilation was a frequent punishment for adultery. A guilty woman would be rendered so grotesque that she would be forever undesirable to anyone else; she would be forced to bear her shame and guilt publicly. Similarly Jerusalem would be rendered unattractive to any more potential lovers.

Also some of Jerusalem's children would be carried away as slaves, others would be burned **by fire,** and her possessions (**clothes** and **jewelry**) would be stripped away. God's punishment would cure Judah's lust; she would no longer look to **Egypt** for help.

23:28-31. This second oracle repeats (for emphasis) several points stated in verses 22-27, and adds that when the Babylonians were done, Jerusalem would be left **naked and bare.** Though ashamed, this punishment would come because of her **promiscuity** in seeking aid from other **nations** and becoming perverted by their idols. Since she had sinned like her **sister,** she would be punished in a similar way (**I will put her up into your hand;** cf. comments on vv. 32-34)—by the sword and exile.

23:32-34. This third oracle of judgment against Jerusalem differs from the others because it is a poem. The point of the poem, which might be titled "The Cup of God's Judgment," is that Jerusalem was to take part in Samaria's judgment because she had taken part in Samaria's sin. God said, **You will drink your sister's cup** (cf. v. 31), **a cup large and deep; it will bring scorn and derision, for it holds so much.** The concept of imbibing a cup of judgment occurs throughout the Bible (cf. Ps. 75:8; Isa. 51:17-23; Jer. 25:15-19; 51:7; Hab. 2:16; Rev. 17:3-4; 18:6). The "contents" of the cup were the ruinous effects of sin—**sorrow . . . ruin, and desolation**—accumulated by the nation.

23:35. This fourth oracle presents the main reason Jerusalem was to be judged. She had **forgotten** God (cf. 22:12) **and thrust** Him **behind** her **back.** Jerusalem's illicit affairs with other nations came after she forgot her source of protection and openly rejected God. Because of this rejection, she **must bear the consequences of** her **lewdness.**

(3) Conclusion (23:36-49). In the final section of this chapter Ezekiel reviewed the sin and judgment of Samaria and Jerusalem. The history and judgment of both countries had been presented separately (vv. 1-35), but now they were combined for the sake of comparison. The sins of both nations were idolatry (vv. 36-39) and foreign alliances (vv. 40-44), and their judgments were the same (vv. 45-49).

23:36-39. Idolatry, though not the subject of verses 1-35, was common to Israel and Judah. The apex of their spiritual adultery was child sacrifice: **they even sacrificed their children, whom they bore to Me.** This, one of the most detestable practices of the Canaanite religions, had infiltrated both Israel and Judah (see comments on 16:20-22). The people were so hardened by sin that **on the very day they sacrificed their children to their idols, they entered** the temple with their children's blood on their hands and the smoky smell of burning flesh embedded in their clothes. Their very presence profaned and desecrated the **house** of God!

23:40-44. The spiritual adultery of the two nations was matched only by their political adultery. Both countries enticed foreign nations into illicit alliances. Ezekiel painted a vivid picture of the sisters preparing themselves for lovers (i.e., enticing other nations to help them). The harlot sisters **sent . . . for men** and **when they arrived** the girls

bathed themselves **for them, painted** their **eyes, and put on . . . jewelry** (cf. Prov. 7:6-21).

The enticements of the two sisters drew **a carefree crowd of Sabeans . . . from the desert** and **men from the rabble.** The word "Sabeans" (*sāḇā'îm*) may also be translated "drunkards" (from *sāḇā'*, "to imbibe, drink largely"; cf. NIV marg.). Perhaps Ezekiel deliberately chose the word because of its double meaning. The wild nomadic Sabeans may have behaved like drunkards. The reputation of the sisters was so well known that even the lower elements of society knew where to find them. Ezekiel also employed two similar-sounding words to draw attention to the baser elements being attracted to the women. They **brought** in (*mûḇā'îm*) "Sabeans/drunkards" (*sāḇā'îm*).

The sisters were using their charms to gain others' favors, so God reduced them to the status of prostitutes (cf. Ezek. 23:3). This appropriately pictures Israel and Judah turning to pagan nations for help and being molested by them.

23:45-49. God said that **righteous men** would **sentence them to the punishment** adulteresses deserved. Who were these "righteous men"? Certainly they were not the nations that ultimately destroyed the sisters, because those nations had previously committed adultery with them. Most likely the "righteous men" were the prophets of God raised up to denounce sin and pronounce judgment. They functioned like elders who decided the fate of someone accused of fornication (cf. Deut. 22:13-21).

The judgment for **adultery** was death (Lev. 20:10), generally by stoning (cf. Lev. 20:27; John 8:3-5); and the judgments for **idolatry** in a city were the sword and fire (Deut. 13:12-16). These judgments would be enacted against these "sisters." **The mob**—a derisive way of referring to the foreign nations—would **stone them and cut them down with . . . swords,** and flames would engulf **their houses.** These are the same judgments Ezekiel pronounced earlier (Ezek. 16:40-41). They would provide a **warning** to other nations.

f. The parable of the boiling pot (24:1-14)

Chapter 24 concludes the third series of judgments on Judah (chaps. 4–11; 12–

19; 20–24). Chapter 24 climaxes these prophecies with two additional messages that show the inevitability of judgment.

24:1-2. Ezekiel's final prophecies of doom against Jerusalem came **in the ninth year** (of King Jehoiachin's exile; cf. 1:2), **in the 10th month on the 10th day.** This was January 15, 588 B.C.—a day of national calamity for Jerusalem. **The king of Babylon besieged Jerusalem that very day.** This was the day Ezekiel had been pointing to for over four years. The date was so significant that it was also mentioned by the writer of 1 and 2 Kings (cf. 2 Kings 25:1) and by the Prophet Jeremiah (Jer. 39:1; 52:4).

24:3-5. Ezekiel told the **rebellious house** of Israel (cf. 3:9) **a parable** about a **cooking pot** being filled **with water** and **choice cuts of meat** being boiled. This was similar to his message in chapter 11, in which some leaders used the figure of a cooking pot to give Jerusalem false hope. The people thought that being in the pot (Jerusalem) would keep them safe; but here Ezekiel prophesied that the pot would be their place of destruction.

24:6-8. Ezekiel explained the parable through two similar statements (vv. 6-8, 9-14), each beginning with the words, **This is what the Sovereign LORD says: Woe to the city of bloodshed** (vv. 6, 9). These statements spoke of the city's blood-guiltiness (cf. 22:1-16).

Ezekiel said Jerusalem was like a **pot now encrusted, whose deposit will not go away!** "Encrusted" and "deposit" are from the Hebrew word *hel'âh* and could be translated "rusted" and "rust." In the fire of God's judgment Jerusalem's "impurities" floated to the surface. Her corruption could not be hidden. She was as unappealing as rusty scum floating on the surface of a meal being cooked.

The meal was ruined by the rusty scum, so the contents of the pot were dumped. People in Jerusalem who had felt secure from Babylon's onslaught would be dragged from the city into exile with no regard for their position in society (no **lots** would be cast **for them**).

The cause for the dispersion was repeated (24:7-8): bloodshed **poured** out openly on rocks, **not . . . where the dust would cover it.** Jerusalem had shed innocent blood and had not even bothered to hide her crimes. That blood was crying out, figuratively speaking, for vengeance (cf. Gen. 4:10; Lev. 17:13-14; Job 16:18). Because Jerusalem had openly shed the blood of others, God would openly shed **her blood on the bare rock.**

24:9-14. Ezekiel's second statement of judgment dealt specifically with the rusty pot. **The meat** in the pot was to be cooked "**well done,**" picturing the slaughter of the Jerusalemites by Babylon. But God's judgment would go beyond the inhabitants to encompass the city of Jerusalem itself. **The empty pot** (Jerusalem without its inhabitants) was to be **set . . . on the coals . . . its impurities** were **melted and its deposit,** or rust, **burned away.** The city itself had to be destroyed to remove its impurities.

God had **tried to cleanse** His people from their **impurities** but they resisted all such efforts. Therefore they would experience the purifying work of God's **wrath.** God's patience had run out; **the time** had **come** for Him to judge. He would **not hold back** or **have pity.** God's mercy prompts Him to withhold judgment as long as possible to enable people to repent (cf. 2 Peter 3:8-10), but He does not wait indefinitely. A time comes when God punishes wickedness.

g. The sign of the death of Ezekiel's wife (24:15-27)

24:15-17. Ezekiel acted out through his own heartbreaking experience the inner pain about to be felt by all those Israelites already in captivity.

God explained the sign to Ezekiel, possibly in a dream at night (v. 18). The tragedy of the death of Ezekiel's wife (**the delight of** his **eyes;** cf. v. 21) would normally produce an outpouring of grief and sadness. But God told him **not to lament or weep or shed any tears.** He was to **groan quietly** and **not mourn for the dead.** He had to keep his personal feelings of loss bottled up inside; he was not allowed to follow normal mourning procedures (v. 17b; cf. Jer. 16:5-7).

24:18-19. Next **morning** Ezekiel told **the people** about his vision, and that **evening** his **wife died. The next morning,** when his wife would have been buried, he followed God's instructions and did not mourn openly. Because the event had been explained to **the people** in advance, they realized that the action had some national significance. So they **asked** him to explain what it meant.

24:20-24. Ezekiel explained that the death of his wife symbolized the destruction of God's temple and the slaughter of the people of Jerusalem—people loved by those in exile. Ezekiel had lost the "delight" of his "eyes" (v. 16) and the exiles would lose Jerusalem, **the delight** of their **eyes** (cf. v. 25), to Babylon. Just as Ezekiel had experienced a great personal tragedy, so those already in captivity would feel the tragedy when they heard about Jerusalem's fall and the massacre of their loved ones (**sons and daughters**) there.

The Jews in captivity would be devastated by the news of Jerusalem's fall, and the magnitude of destruction would render all grief inadequate. Normally when a personal tragedy occurs, friends and relatives gather to share in the grief of the one affected and to support him in his time of anguish and loss. But when Jerusalem fell everyone was in anguish because everyone was affected. The tragedy would be so awesome that any public expression of grief would seem insignificant. The Jews already in Babylon were to avoid all public display of grief just as **Ezekiel** had **done.** They would simply **waste away because of** their **sins** while groaning **among** themselves. The catastrophe would send all the exiles into a state of shock and would force them to acknowledge their Lord: **When this happens, you will know that I am the Sovereign** LORD.

24:25-27. When **the news** of Jerusalem's fall reached the exiles, the prophet's **mouth** would **be opened;** he would no **longer be silent.** Ezekiel had been commanded to remain silent before his fellow exiles except to pronounce the prophecies God gave him (cf. 3:25-27). His part-time dumbness would end when the prophecies he had delivered were confirmed (cf. 33:21-22).

II. Judgment on Gentile Nations (chaps. 25–32)

The siege of Jerusalem had begun; it was only a matter of time till her destruction would be complete. So Ezekiel turned from Jerusalem to give messages against those nations surrounding it. If God would not spare His own people because of their sin, how could the nations around her hope to escape His judgment? God's judgment began in Is-

rael (chaps. 4–24), but it would extend from there to other nations (chaps. 25–32).

God's judgment on these nations is based on the Abrahamic Covenant (cf. Gen. 12:1-3; 15). Those who bless the descendants of Abraham will be blessed, and those who curse the descendants of Abraham will be cursed. Ezekiel pronounced God's curse on seven countries that contributed to Judah's downfall.

The first three—Ammon, Moab, Edom—formed the eastern boundary of Judah; the fourth nation, Philistia, was on her western boundary. Tyre and Sidon, cities of Phoenicia, were the principal powers north of Judah; Egypt was the major power to the southwest. God's judgment would extend out from Judah in all directions.

Ezekiel's first four prophecies (against Ammon, Moab, Edom, and Philistia) each cited the sin that prompted God's judgment and then described that judgment. These two parts form a "because/therefore" pattern. "Because" (*ya'an*) the nation had sinned against God's people, "therefore" (*lākēn*) God would punish them. Each prophecy closes with a statement of the result of its judgment: then "they will know that I am the LORD."

A. Judgment on Ammon (25:1-7)

25:1-2. Ezekiel had already pronounced judgment on Ammon (21:28-32). Now Ammon was singled out to head the list of nations that would feel the sting of divine judgment.

Ammon and Israel had been in conflict since the time of Jephthah during the period of the Judges (Jud. 10:6–11:33). Saul fought with the Ammonites to rescue Jabesh Gilead (1 Sam. 11:1-11), and David conquered Ammon (1 Chron. 19:1–20:3). Sometime after the death of Solomon the Ammonites regained their independence and renewed their hostilities with Judah. During Jehoshaphat's reign the Ammonites joined the Moabites and Edomites in an unsuccessful attack on Judah (2 Chron. 20:1-30). Ammon tried to expand her territory at Israel's expense (cf. Jer. 49:1), and she even sided initially with Nebuchadnezzar in an attempt to gain additional territory after Jehoiakim's revolt, about 600–597 B.C. (cf. 2 Kings 24:1-2).

In 593 B.C. Ammon joined a secret meeting of other potential conspirators to consider rebelling against Babylon (cf. Jer. 27:1-7). That plan did not materialize, but in 588 B.C. she did unite with Judah and Tyre against Babylon. So two ancient enemies, Judah and Ammon, were joined against a common foe.

When Nebuchadnezzar decided to attack Judah instead of Ammon (cf. Ezek. 21:18-27), Ammon was relieved that she had been spared. Instead of coming to Judah's aid, she rejoiced over Judah's misfortune, hoping to profit territorially from Judah's destruction.

25:3-7. Against this background Ezekiel gave this prophecy. Twice he repeated his "because/therefore/you will know" formula to show the destruction of Ammon (vv. 3-5, 6-8). Ammon rejoiced over the destruction of the temple (mockingly saying **Aha!**) and the decimation and exile of **the people of Judah.** The Ammonites gloated over Judah's misfortune (v. 6).

God's judgment would fit Ammon's sin. They rejoiced over Judah's downfall so *they* would fall. God would send them **to the people of the East,** nomadic desert tribesmen, **as a possession.** These nomads would overrun the Ammonites, turning **Rabbah,** Ammon's capital city, **into a pasture for camels and Ammon into a resting place for sheep.** Because of Ammon's **malice** against **Israel,** Ammon would be plundered by other **nations** and destroyed (**cut . . . off**).

B. Judgment on Moab (25:8-11)

The hostility between Moab and Israel began when Balak, king of Moab, tried to oppose Israel as Moses was leading them to Palestine (cf. Num. 22–24). During the time of the Judges, Israel was oppressed by Eglon, king of Moab (Jud. 3:12-30). Relations between the countries improved slightly after that, and some Israelites went to Moab during a famine. Through this contact Ruth the Moabitess entered Israel's history and the royal line of David.

The relationship between Moab and Israel again deteriorated during Saul's reign (cf. 1 Sam. 14:47). David conquered Moab and made it a vassal of Israel (2 Sam. 8:2); it remained under Israel's control through Solomon's reign. Moab rebelled against Israel years after Israel and Judah split, during Jehoshaphat's regime (cf. 2 Kings 3:4-27). Moab united with Ammon and Edom in an ill-fated attempt to defeat Judah also during Jehoshaphat's reign (2 Chron. 20:1-23). Later Moab supported Babylon and attacked Judah after Jehoiakim's revolt, possibly hoping to gain additional territory (cf. 2 Kings 24:2). Moab then joined other nations and considered revolting from Babylon in 593 B.C. (cf. Jer. 27:1-7), but no evidence indicates that she ever did.

25:8-11. Moab's sin, Ezekiel said, was her contempt for God's people. **Moab and Seir said, Look, the house of Judah has become like all the other nations.** Seir was the name of the mountain range south of the Dead Sea that encompassed the country of Edom. The word became synonymous with the land of Edom (cf. 2 Chron. 20:10 with Num. 20:14-21). Edom was included here with Moab (though her own judgment comes next) because she was guilty of the same sin of envy and contempt. In their scorn Moab and Edom were denying God's promises to Israel. By minimizing Judah's position of centrality among the nations, they were profaning the name of God who had promised Judah that position.

Because **Moab** treated Judah with contempt, God would remove Moab's **glory** by exposing its northern **flank** to attack. He would destroy three towns: **Beth Jeshimoth, Baal Meon, and Kiriathaim.** Beth Jeshimoth guarded the ascent to the Medeba Plateau from the Plains of Moab by the Jordan River. Baal Meon and Kiriathaim were important fortresses on the Medeba Plateau.

In addition to losing her defenses Moab would also lose her freedom. God said He would **give Moab . . . to the people of the East,** the same fate as Ammon (cf. v. 4). The nomadic desert tribesmen who would overrun Ammon would also overrun **Moab.**

C. Judgment on Edom (25:12-14)

Like Ammon and Moab, Edom was involved in a long series of conflicts with Israel. The strife actually began when Edom refused to let Israel cross her territory during the time of the wilderness wanderings (cf. Num. 20:14-21). Saul fought the Edomites (1 Sam. 14:47), and David finally captured Edom and made it a vassal state to Israel (2 Sam. 8:13-14). Solomon further exploited Edom and established Elath in Edom as Israel's seaport (cf. 1 Kings 9:26-28); but Edom opposed Solomon during the latter part of his reign (1 Kings 11:14-18). The nation continued as a vassal state after Israel and Judah split, and it was controlled by a governor from Judah till after the time of Jehoshaphat (1 Kings 22:47-48).

In the days of Jehoram (ca. 845 B.C.) Edom successfully rebelled against Judah (2 Kings 8:20-22a) and regained her freedom. Thereafter Judah and Edom struggled to see who would control the vital caravan and shipping routes at the southern end of the Transjordanian highway. Both Amaziah (2 Kings 14:7) and Uzziah (or Azariah, 2 Kings 14:21-22) regained territory that had been lost to Edom, but Edom counterattacked during Ahaz's reign and inflicted a major loss on Judah (2 Chron. 28:17).

Edom became a vassal of Babylon after Nebuchadnezzar's stunning defeat of Egypt in 605 B.C. Then in 593 B.C. Edom joined the other conspirators in planning to revolt against Babylon (cf. Jer. 27:1-7), but did not carry out the plan. When Judah revolted in 588 B.C., Edom sided with Babylon and aided Babylon in her assaults on Judah (cf. Ps. 137:7; Jer. 49:7-22).

25:12-14. Ezekiel said Edom's sin was that she **took revenge on the house of Judah.** Edom saw in Judah's conflict with Babylon an opportunity to oppose her rival. If her foe were destroyed then Edom could achieve a place of power at the southern end of the Dead Sea.

Because Edom had aided in Judah's destruction, God said He would aid in her destruction. He would **kill** Edom's **men and their animals . . . from Teman to Dedan.** Teman was a city in central Edom about three miles from Sela, later known as Petra. Dedan was southeast of Edom in northern Arabia. Perhaps Dedan was mentioned here because some Edomites were living there. Edom was conquered by the Nabateans during the intertestamental period. The remnant of the Edomites (also called Idumeans) moved west to the Negev. Later they were forced to become Jewish converts (Josephus *The Antiquities of the Jews* 13. 9. 1). Thus the Edomites lost both their country and their national identity.

God said **Israel** would bring His **vengeance** against the Edomites. As a result the Edomites would come to **know** (experience) His **vengeance.** This differs from what He had said about Ammon and Moab (vv. 7, 11).

D. Judgment on Philistia (25:15-17)

The Philistines had been Israel's enemy from the time of the Conquest. Israel had failed to take all the Promised Land because she disobeyed God and because of the Philistines' military superiority on the coastal plain (cf. Jud. 3:1-4). Then the Philistines moved into the hill country in an attempt to control all the territory of Israel. They were opposed by the judges Shamgar (Jud. 3:31), Samson (Jud. 13-16), and Samuel (1 Sam. 7:2-17). Saul's major battles in Israel were designed to check the Philistines' advances on the central Benjamin plateau (1 Sam. 13:1-14:23) and in the Jezreel Valley (1 Sam. 28:1-4; 29:1-2, 11; 31:1-3, 7-10).

David finally subdued the Philistines. After a series of battles early in his reign blunted a Philistine challenge to his kingdom (2 Sam. 5:17-25), David was able to go on the offensive and defeat the Philistines (2 Sam. 8:1). Philistia remained a vassal country through the reign of Solomon and into the divided monarchy.

The battle between Philistia and Judah was renewed during the divided monarchy as each country tried to control the other. Jehoshaphat was able to dominate Philistia as a vassal state (2 Chron. 17:10-11), but she revolted against his son Jehoram and sacked Judah and Jerusalem (2 Chron. 21:16-17). Uzziah reestablished Judah's control over Philistia (2 Chron. 26:6-7), but Philistia again gained the upper hand in Ahaz's reign (2 Chron 28:16-18).

The feud between Philistia and Judah was halted by Babylon's intervention. Nebuchadnezzar established control over both countries. Yet the rivalry remained. Philistia waited for an opportunity to try again to conquer Judah.

25:15-17. Ezekiel placed his finger on Philistia's underlying sin. She **acted in vengeance and took revenge** (cf. v. 12) **with malice** (cf. v. 6), **and with ancient hostility** she **sought to destroy Judah.** Philistia's history included a string of attacks on God's Chosen People as they tried to dispossess Israel of the Promised Land.

Because Philistia had tried to destroy Judah, God would destroy her. He would **stretch out His hand** (cf. v. 13) **against the Philistines, and** would **cut off the Kerethites and destroy those remaining along the seacoast.** "Kerethites" (*kᵉrēṯîm*) was a synonym for the Philistines (cf. 1 Sam. 30:1-14; Zeph. 2:5). The word might have come from "Crete" which was known as "Caphtor" in Old Testament times (cf. Amos 9:7). Ezekiel used "Kerethites" here instead of "Philistines" to produce an interesting wordplay: God would "cut off" (*hiḵraṯî*) the "Kerethites" (*kᵉrēṯîm*).

During the intertestamental period the Philistines disappeared as a nation. This nation that had tried to usurp God's people discovered God's true character (**they will know that I am the LORD;** cf. Ezek. 25:7, 11) when He judged them for their sin.

E. Judgment on Tyre (26:1–28:19)

After four short prophecies against the nations east and west of Israel (chap. 25) Ezekiel delivered a long prophecy against the city/nation of Tyre to the north of Israel. This section is actually four separate oracles, each beginning with "The word of the LORD came to me" (26:1; 27:1; 28:1, 11). The first oracle (26:2-21) was a direct prophecy of Tyre's destruction; the second prophecy (chap. 27) was a lament or funeral dirge for the fallen city. The third and fourth messages were directed against the "ruler" of Tyre (28:1-10) and the "king" of Tyre (28:11-19).

1. DESTRUCTION OF THE CITY (CHAP. 26)

26:1-2. All but the first of four divisions in this chapter are introduced with the clause, "This is what the Sovereign LORD says" (vv. 7, 15, 19). This prophecy was given **in the 11th year, on the first day of the month.** The 11th year of Jehoiakim's exile was the year 587–586 B.C., but Ezekiel did not state which month. Since Jerusalem fell to Babylon on July 18, 586 B.C., possibly Ezekiel's prophecy against Tyre was prompted by Jerusalem's imminent collapse.

In verses 1-6 Ezekiel followed the "Because/therefore/then you will know" format he used in chapter 25. Tyre's sin was her greedy rejoicing over Jerusalem's fall, saying **Aha!** (cf. 25:3) Now that **Jerusalem** was destroyed, her **doors** would be swung open to **Tyre,** and Tyre would **prosper.** Both Tyre and Jerusalem had vied for the lucrative trade routes between Egypt and the rest of the Middle East. Tyre dominated the sea routes, but Jerusalem controlled the caravan routes. Tyre responded to Jerusalem's fall like a greedy merchant gloating over a rival's catastrophe. Without Jerusalem being able to secure the overland caravan routes, more products would be shipped by sea. So Tyre saw Jerusalem's fall as an opportunity to "corner the market" for trade.

26:3-6. God's judgment against **Tyre** fit her crime. He said, **I will bring many nations against you, like the sea casting up its waves.** Tyre's pride was her seagoing prowess. She knew the Mediterranean Sea better than most nations. So Ezekiel used the image of a violent ocean storm to picture God's punishment. Like ocean **waves,** invading nations would pound against Tyre's defenses, smashing her **walls** and **towers.** God added that He would **scrape away her rubble and make her a bare rock.** In an interesting wordplay Ezekiel described Tyre's fate. "Tyre" (*ṣōr*) means "rock" or a "hard pebble." God would make the "rock" (*ṣōr*) a barren crag (*sela'*). No longer being the central city of commerce, she would **become a place to spread fishnets.** Fishermen generally spread out their nets to dry on barren rocks, to keep them from becoming tangled in trees or bushes. Tyre would be so decimated that the once-bustling city would be barren enough to use as a drying place for nets.

The city of **Tyre** included the mainland and an island about a half mile off the coast. The main city was supported by many satellite communities or suburbs around it. People in these **settlements** (*bᵉnôṯèhā,* lit., "her daughters") **on the mainland** would **be ravaged by the sword.**

26:7-14. God said He would bring **from the north . . . Nebuchadnezzar.** Tyre's gloating over Jerusalem's fall would be short-lived. The **king** who destroyed Jerusalem would also attack **Tyre.** After defeating Jerusalem, Nebuchadnezzar moved his army north to Tyre in 585 B.C. and besieged the city for

13 years till all **settlements on the mainland** were destroyed. Tyre could hold out for all those years because her navy brought in supplies that would otherwise have been depleted. Nebuchadnezzar destroyed mainland Tyre (depicted graphically by Ezekiel, vv. 8-12), but not the island stronghold. However, other evidence indicates that the island surrendered to Nebuchadnezzar in 573–572 B.C. That year Baal II succeeded Ethbaal III to the throne of Tyre. Most likely this was a political move by Nebuchadnezzar to remove the rebellious king and install a loyal vassal king. Some think Ethbaal III was deported to Babylon, but 28:8-9 seems to indicate that Nebuchadnezzar assassinated him.

Ezekiel switched from the singular **he** to the plural **they** (26:12). Probably this shift pointed to the "nations" (v. 3) that followed Nebuchadnezzar in attacking Tyre, completing the destruction he began. Alexander the Great devastated the city in 332 B.C. when it refused to submit to his advancing forces. Alexander destroyed the mainland city and then built a causeway out to the island fortress which he destroyed. In doing this, he threw **stones, timber, and rubble into the sea.** Though Tyre recovered from Nebuchadnezzar's and Alexander's onslaughts, she never regained the power she held before these attacks.

The final destruction of Tyre would be complete, for God predicted the city **will never be rebuilt.** Today this once-great commercial center lies in ruins. Though the surrounding area has been rebuilt, the original site is a mute testimony to God's awesome judgment.

26:15-18. The third section of this prophecy discusses the response of Tyre's neighbors to her **fall.** These coastal powers, dependent on Tyre for their trade and commerce, would be dismayed at Tyre's fall. Tyre's fall would send shock waves throughout the maritime community (**the coastlands** would **tremble**). **The princes of the seacoast** would remove their trappings of luxury (**robes** and **garments**) and **sit** in mourning, **trembling** and **appalled at** the unbelievable fate of their chief benefactor. Sitting in mourning was a common way to express grief for a loved one or friend (cf. Job 2:11-13). As Tyre's allies came to sit and

mourn her passing, they also sang a funeral **lament,** contrasting her present condition with her former glory. **Tyre** had been a formidable **power on the seas,** reigning supremely on the eastern Mediterranean shores. Her fall sent **terror** rippling to every shore she had touched. With their source of supplies gone, those nations would suffer great economic loss.

26:19-21. In Tyre's demise she would descend into the underworld never to rise again. Ezekiel had said Tyre's fate was like an ocean sweeping over it (v. 3). Now again he said **the ocean depths** would sweep **over** Tyre. The most fearful prospect facing ancient mariners was to be caught in a storm and be "lost at sea." Tyre would drown in the ocean and all traces of her would be lost. This same point was made again in 27:26-35.

Ezekiel then changed the imagery slightly. Instead of descending into the ocean depths, Tyre would **go down to the pit** (*bôr*), a figurative way of expressing death. "Pit" is synonymous with "sheol" or "the grave" (Prov. 1:12; Isa. 14:15, 19; 38:18). In Old Testament times death was a fearful event. Though the saints had some idea of resurrection (cf. Heb. 11:17-19), most viewed the grave as a place of no return. Ezekiel expressed this thought about Tyre: she would enter the place of the departed dead and never be able to **return** to **the land of the living.** People would long for her, but she would **never again be found.**

2. DIRGE OVER THE CITY (CHAP. 27)

27:1-4. Ezekiel's second message against **Tyre** was a lament over the city's fall (cf. comments on chap. 19 about a funeral lament). Tyre's destruction was so certain (chap. 26) that the funeral dirge could begin. Chapter 27, in which **Tyre** is compared to a ship, could be called "The Sinking of Tyre's Ship of State." The first section (vv. 1-9), written in poetry, pictures Tyre's former glory by describing her, appropriately, as a beautiful ship. The second section (vv. 10-25), in both poetry and prose, enumerates Tyre's many trading partners. The third section (vv. 26-36), again in poetry, describes Tyre's catastrophic shipwreck. This chapter focuses on the many countries and cities associated commercially with Tyre (see the map "The World of

Jeremiah and Ezekiel" in the *Introduction to Jer.*).

Ezekiel was told to recite his lament to **Tyre,** the city **situated at the gateway to the sea, merchant of peoples on many coasts.** The lament centered on Tyre's reputation as a major seaport and merchant power. Tyre was like a proud ocean vessel: **Your domain was on the high seas; your builders brought your beauty to perfection.** Focusing on Tyre's pride at the beginning of the lament (vv. 3-4) intimates that this was the reason for her downfall (cf. 28:2-10).

27:5-9. The materials used in constructing Tyre's "Ship of State" emphasized the city's sound construction. Her connections with other nations supposedly guaranteed her security. The **timbers** (probably for the ship's hull) had been selected from the finest **pine trees from Senir,** the Amorite name for Mount Hermon (Deut. 3:9) north of the Sea of Chinnereth, later named the Sea of Galilee. The ship's **mast** was made from **a cedar from Lebanon.** The Lebanon cedar trees, prized for their height and strength, were exported for use in construction (cf. 1 Kings 4:33; 5:6; 1 Chron. 17:1-6; Ezra 3:7; Isa. 2:13). The sturdy **oars** for the ship were crafted **of oaks from Bashan,** the area east of the Sea of Chinnereth, famous for its oak forests (cf. Isa. 2:13; Zech. 11:2).

The **deck** of the ship was made **of cypress wood from . . . Cyprus** and was **inlaid with ivory.** So Tyre used four kinds of wood: pine, cedar, oak, and cypress.

The **sail** of this vessel was sewn from **fine embroidered linen from Egypt.** Egypt was known for its fine linen cloth (cf. Gen. 41:42; Prov. 7:16). The **awnings,** colored with **blue and purple** dye **from the coasts of Elishah,** were possibly tent-like canopies that helped protect crewmen from bad weather. The location of Elishah is unknown though some scholars identify it with Alashia, the ancient name for Cyprus. Other suggestions are that Elishah was in Greece, Italy, or Syria. The dye industry was common throughout the Mediterranean.

The crewmen of the ship were the best available. **Men of Sidon and Arvad** (Ezek. 27:8) manned the oars and **men** of **Tyre** were the **seamen.** Sidon, another seaport 20 miles north of Tyre (cf. 28:20-

23), was one of the oldest maritime powers (cf. Gen. 10:15-19). Arvad was an island off the coast of Syria. Both cities were known for their shipping. The earliest Phoenician ships each had 50 oarsmen and were quite fast. The later commercial ships were much longer and had a crew of up to 200 with two or three banks of oars on each side.

Also **on board** the ship were experienced repairmen, **veteran craftsmen of Gebal.** Because the **ships** were wooden-hulled, the **seams** between the wood were caulked with pitch to help make the vessel watertight (cf. Gen. 6:14). The friction of the ocean could work the caulking loose and let water seep into the hold, so **shipwrights** were on board to make necessary repairs. Gebal was the name of the modern city of Jebeil, located on Syria's Mediterranean coast. The craftsmen of Gebal were famous builders (cf. 1 Kings 5:18).

Ezekiel pictured Tyre as a strong, seaworthy vessel. She was the pride of the fleet, built with the best materials and manned by the best crews. **All the ships of the sea** (i.e., other countries) **and their sailors came alongside to trade for** her **wares.**

27:10-11. Ezekiel then described the military and commercial activity of this mighty city (vv. 10-25). Tyre was protected by the best mercenary army that could be mustered. The **soldiers** included **men** from **Persia, Lydia, and Put.** Persia, east of Babylon, ultimately defeated the Babylonians in 539 B.C. Lydia, on the west coast of Asia Minor, is sometimes translated Lud. The country of Put has sometimes been associated with "Punt" (Somalia) in East Africa, but the connection is tenuous. It is better to associate Put with the area of present-day Libya. Both Lydia and Put supplied mercenary soldiers for the Egyptian army (cf. Jer. 46:8-9). These mercenaries were joined by men from **Arvad** (cf. Ezek. 27:8), **Helech,** and **Gammad.** Helech was the Akkadian name for the region of Cilicia (where the city of Tarsus, Paul's birthplace, was located) in southeastern Asia Minor. The location of "Gammad" is unknown.

27:12-25. Tyre's partners in commerce (see the chart "Tyre's Trading Partners") spanned the limits of the then-known world, and their products represented numerous kinds of merchandise.

Tyre's Trading Partners
Ezekiel 27:12-25

Name	Location	Merchandise
1. Tarshish	Spain (?)	Silver, iron, tin, lead
2. Greece	Modern Greece	Slaves, bronze implements
3. Tubal	Eastern Turkey	Slaves, bronze implements
4. Meshech	Central Turkey	Slaves, bronze implements
5. Beth Togarmah	Eastern Turkey	Work horses, war horses, mules
6. Rhodes*	Modern Rhodes	Ivory tusks, ebony
7. Aram (or Edom)†	Syria (or Jordan)	Turquoise, purple fabric, embroidered work, fine linen, coral, rubies
8. Judah	Palestine	Wheat, olive oil, balm, confections, honey
9. Israel	Palestine	Wheat, olive oil, balm, confections, honey
10. Damascus	Syria	Wine, wool
11. Danites‡	Aden(?)	Wrought iron, cassia (a bark for perfume), calamus (an herb)
12. Greeks§ from Uzal	Yemen (or southeastern Turkey)	Wrought iron, cassia, calamus
13. Dedan	Arabia	Saddle blankets
14. Arabia	Arabia	Lambs, rams, goats
15. Kedar	Arabia	Lambs, rams, goats
16. Sheba	Southern Arabia	Spices, precious stones, gold
17. Raamah	Southern Arabia	Spices, precious stones, gold
18.-23. Haran, Canneh, Eden, Sheba, Asshur, Kilmad	Mesopotamia	Blue fabric, embroidered work, multicolored rugs

*The Hebrew has "Dedan" (*d⁼dān*) while the Septuagint has "Rhodes" (*rōdān*). The difference in the Hebrew consonants is between a "d" (ד) and an "r" (ר). Since "Dedan" occurs again in verse 20, it is better to see "Rhodes" here.

†Most Hebrew manuscripts have "Aram" (*'ārām*) but some Hebrew manuscripts and the Syriac read "Edom" (*'ĕdōm*), and the Septuagint reads "men" (*'āḏām*). The difference in the Hebrew consonants is between an "r" (ר) and a "d" (ד).

‡The "Danites" are not the tribe of Dan which had already been taken into captivity. The NASB translates the word as "Vedan." The best conjecture is that it should be associated with the city of Aden on the Persian Gulf.

§"Greeks" is the translation of "Javan" (cf. v. 13), but the Javan in verse 19 must be different from that of verse 13. "Javan" could be referring to a tribe by that name in Yemen, or "Uzal" could refer to the city of Izalla in the Anatolian foothills of Asia Minor.

The fact that Tyre traded with about two dozen nations and cities shows her vast influence and commercial expertise. Tyre's trading was so brisk that **the ships of Tarshish** were the **carriers for** Tyre's **wares** (v. 25). Tarshish does not refer to the origin of the ships. "Ships of Tarshish" probably referred to large vessels carrying **cargo** on the open **sea.** This was the kind of ship Hiram and Solomon built to bring cargo to Israel (2 Chron. 9:21; cf. 2 Chron. 20:36-37; Isa. 2:16).

27:26-27. Ezekiel was building to a climax. He had described the beautiful construction of the ship (vv. 1-9) and its successful commerce (vv. 10-25). Then in a lament he described the ship's catastrophic sinking (vv. 26-36). Ezekiel reverted to poetry to accentuate the tragedy.

Tyre's destruction came in the element where she was most at home—the open sea. In **the high seas . . . the east wind** would **break** the ship **to pieces.** Most ships tried to stay close to the shore to avoid the rough storms. But Tyre's ship of state, venturing in her commercialism on "the high seas," was caught in a violent storm. During the fall and winter, weather on the Mediterranean becomes unpredictable and travel is hazardous (cf. Acts 27:9-26). A storm from the east or northeast would blow a ship away from the coast and out into the ocean where there was little chance of its survival. Ezekiel was again using the "east wind" in a dual meaning (cf. comments on Ezek. 19:12). Here the violent storm from the east referred to Babylon, east of Tyre. Tyre's ship of state was about to go down with the loss of all her people and her **wealth.** She would **sink into the heart of the sea.**

27:28-32. The surrounding countries would mourn the loss of Tyre. **They** would **cry . . . sprinkle dust on their heads, and roll in ashes.** Also they would **shave their heads** and **put on sackcloth.** These were signs of intense grief associated with personal loss (cf. Es. 4:1-3; Job 1:20; 2:8; Jer. 6:26). These people would bemoan their loss by taking **up a lament concerning . . . Tyre.** Ezekiel recorded a second lament within his larger lament: **Who was ever silenced like Tyre, surrounded by the sea?** Those who traded with the once-bustling city of Tyre would be appalled at her sudden loss and silence.

27:33-36. Tyre's commercial activity had enriched others. She had **satisfied many nations** and had **enriched . . . kings.** Having benefited immensely from her trade, those other countries would feel the loss. Those who had profited from her would be **appalled** and **their kings** would **shudder with horror** and **fear.** These rulers were fearful because if the great city of Tyre could be detroyed by the Babylonians, their hope of escape was dim. **The merchants** would also whistle through their teeth (**hiss**) in shock at Tyre's demise. This action does not necessarily indicate derision or scorn (cf. 1 Kings 9:8, where "scoff" is incorrectly substituted for "hiss"; Jer. 49:17; 50:13). It more often expressed astonishment. The businessmen would be astonished because the "pride of the fleet" had **come to a horrible end.**

3. DOWNFALL OF THE PRINCE OF THE CITY (28:1-19)

28:1-5. Ezekiel's third message against Tyre was directed specifically **to the ruler of Tyre.** "Ruler" (*nāgîd*) means "the man at the top" (cf. 1 Sam. 9:16; 10:1; 13:14; 2 Sam. 7:8). Ezekiel had prophesied against the whole city; he was now singling out the city's leader for

a special **word** from God. This ruler then was Ethbaal III, who ruled from 591-590 B.C. to 573-572 B.C.

The underlying sin of Tyre's king was his **pride,** which prompted him to view himself as **a god.** His claim to deity is referred to again in Ezekiel 28:6, 9. Evidently in Ezekiel's day the kings of Tyre believed they were divine.

The king's claims to deity were false. God said, **You are a man and not a god.** Ethbaal III was only a mortal. Evidently he felt he had wisdom that only a god could possess. In a statement dripping with irony Ezekiel asked the king, **Are you wiser than Daniel? Is no secret hidden from you?** The "Daniel" in view was probably the Prophet Daniel (see comments on 14:14, 20). He had already achieved a reputation for his wisdom in the courts of Nebuchadnezzar (cf. Dan. 1:19-20; 2:46-49). The irony was that Ethbaal III felt his wisdom exceeded that of even Daniel who served the country that would ultimately defeat Tyre. Daniel, who attributed all his wisdom to God (cf. Dan. 2:27-28), was much wiser than Ethbaal III, who claimed to be a god.

Ethbaal III had been able to use his **wisdom** and **skill** to acquire material possessions. His lucrative trade had produced great **wealth,** including **gold and silver,** but it also increased his pride (his **heart** had **grown proud**).

28:6-10. God would not let the pride (vv. 2, 5) of Tyre's ruler go unchallenged. The **foreigners** whom God would **bring against** Tyre had already been identified as the Babylonians (26:7-11). Babylon was **ruthless** (*'ārîs,* "terror-striking") in her treatment of others (cf. 30:11; 31:12; 32:12). Unimpressed with Ethbaal's **beauty and wisdom,** Babylon would destroy him in a **violent** way **in the heart of the seas** (cf. 27:26). When slain by his enemies, it would be evident that he was no **god.** Ethbaal III was removed from his throne by Nebuchadnezzar in 573-572 B.C. and Baal II was put in his place. Ethbaal III paid a high price for rebelling against Nebuchadnezzar. In fact Ethbaal would **die the death of the uncircumcised at the hands of foreigners.** While the Phoenicians practiced circumcision, Ezekiel's words conveyed a meaning that went beyond this cultural practice. To "die the death of the uncircumcised" meant to die in shame (cf. 32:30; 1 Sam.

17:26, 36). This king who claimed to be a god would suffer an ignoble death as a man.

28:11-19. Ezekiel's final prophecy against Tyre was **a lament concerning the king of Tyre.** The use of "king" (*melek*) instead of "ruler" (v. 2) was significant. Ezekiel used the word "king" sparingly. Apart from King Jehoiachin (1:2) he did not use the title "king" of any of Israel's monarchs.

The change from "ruler" to "king" was also significant in light of the content of these two prophecies. In 28:1-10 Ezekiel rebuked the *ruler* for claiming to be a god though he was just a man. But in verses 11-19 Ezekiel described the *king* in terms that could not apply to a mere man. This "king" had appeared in the Garden of Eden (v. 13), had been a guardian cherub (v. 14a), had possessed free access to God's holy mountain (v. 14b), and had been sinless from the time he was **created** (v. 15).

Some think Ezekiel was describing Ethbaal III in highly poetic language, comparing him with Adam (both had great potential, but sinned; both were judged, etc.). But some of the language does not apply to Adam. For example, Adam was not a guardian cherub and did not have free access to the mountain of God. Also the descriptions in verses 13 and 16 do not fit the first man in the Garden of Eden. When Adam sinned he was not cast from the mountain **of God** to the earth (vv. 16-17), and no **nations** existed to be **appalled** at his fall (v. 19).

Other scholars have held that Ezekiel was describing the "god" behind the king of Tyre (perhaps Baal). God judged the ruler of Tyre (vv. 1-10) and the god of the city who empowered the ruler (vv. 11-19). But it seems incongruous that Ezekiel would give credence to a mythological tale of a god supporting the ruler of Tyre when much in his book showed the falsehood of pagan beliefs. Also Ezekiel's imagery was drawn from the biblical account of Creation, not from pagan mythologies.

Ezekiel was not describing an ideal man or a false god in verses 11-26. But his switch from "ruler" to "king" and his allusions to the Garden of Eden do imply that the individual being described was more than human. The best explanation is that Ezekiel was describing Satan who

was the true "king" of Tyre, the one motivating the human "ruler" of Tyre. Satan was in the Garden of Eden (Gen. 3:1-7), and his chief sin was pride (1 Tim. 3:6). He also had access to God's presence (cf. Job 1:6-12). Speaking of God's judging the human "ruler" of Tyre for his pride (Ezek. 28:1-10), the prophet lamented the satanic "king" of Tyre who was also judged for his pride (vv. 11-19). Tyre was motivated by the same sin as Satan, and would suffer the same fate.

Ezekiel described the beauty and perfection of Satan as God originally created him (vv. 12-15a). He was **the model of perfection, full of wisdom, and perfect in beauty.** God did not create Satan as some prime minister of evil. As with all God's Creation, Satan was a perfectly created being—one of the crowning achievements in God's angelic realm.

Satan was given an exalted place; he was **in Eden, the garden of God.** Eden was the epitome of God's beautiful Creation on earth (cf. Gen. 2:8-14). Satan's beauty matched that of Eden: **every precious stone adorned** him. Ezekiel listed nine gemstones in describing Satan's beauty. These were 9 of the 12 kinds of stones worn in the breastplate of Israel's high priest (cf. Ex. 28:15-20; 39:10-13). The precious stones probably symbolized Satan's beauty and high position.

God had **anointed** Satan **as a guardian cherub** (Ezek. 28:14). The cherubim (pl. of cherub) were the "inner circle" of angels who had the closest access to God and guarded His holiness (cf. 10:1-14). Satan also had free access to God's **holy mount** (28:14), heaven, and he **walked among the fiery stones** (cf. v. 16). Some associate "the fiery stones" with the precious gems (v. 13), but the stones there were part of Satan's attire whereas the stones in verses 14 and 16 were part of the abode where Satan dwelt. Others have identified the "fiery stones" with God's fiery wall of protection (cf. Zech. 2:5). They see Satan dwelling *inside* or *behind* God's outer defenses in the "inner courts" of heaven itself. This view is possible, and the word translated "among" (*mitôk*) can have the idea of "between" or "inside." Whatever the exact identification, Ezekiel was stating that Satan had access to God's presence.

As originally created by God, Satan

was **blameless . . . till wickedness was found in** him (Ezek. 28:15) **and he sinned** (v. 16). The sin that corrupted Satan was self-generated. Created blameless, his sin was pride (1 Tim. 3:6) because of his **beauty.** Satan spoiled his **wisdom because of** his **splendor** (cf. Ethbaal's similar problem, Ezek. 28:1-2, 5, 7). Satan's pride led to his fall and judgment.

Though Ezekiel presented the fall of Satan as a single act, it actually occurred in stages. Satan's initial judgment was his expulsion from the position of God's anointed cherub before His throne. God expelled him **from the mount of God** (heaven, v. 16; cf. v. 14). Satan was cast from God's government in heaven (cf. Luke 10:18) but was still allowed access to God (cf. Job 1:6-12; Zech. 3:1-2). In the Tribulation Satan will be cast from heaven and restricted to the earth (Rev. 12:7-13); in the Millennium he will be in the bottomless pit (Rev. 20:1-3); and after his brief release at the end of the Millennium (Rev. 20:7-9) he will be cast into the lake of fire forever (Rev. 20:10).

One of the elements of Satan's sin was his widespread **dishonest trade.** The word for trade comes from the verb *rākal* which means "to go about from one to another." Ezekiel had used that noun in speaking of Tyre's commercial activities (Ezek. 28:5). Does this mean Satan was operating a business? Obviously not. Instead, Ezekiel was comparing the human "prince" of Tyre and his satanic "king." So Ezekiel used a word that could convey a broad meaning. Satan's position in heaven involved broad contact with many elements of God's creation much as the prince of Tyre's position enabled him to contact many nations.

Though Ezekiel was describing the "ultimate" ruler of Tyre, Satan, the purpose of the lament was to speak of the city's destruction. So he began to blend the characteristics of the satanic king with the human ruler. Satan would be cast **to the earth** (v. 17), and the king of Tyre would also be cast down **before** other **kings,** his enemies. Satan's ultimate destiny will be the lake of fire (cf. Rev. 21:10), and the defeat and death of the human ruler of Tyre was pictured as being **consumed** by **fire** (Ezek. 28:18). Both Satan's and Tyre's defeats would shock those nations who had followed them. They would be appalled because of

Satan's and Tyre's **horrible end** (cf. 27:35-36).

F. Judgment on Sidon (28:20-26)

28:20-24. This judgment **against Sidon** begins the same way as the oracles against Tyre. **The word of the LORD came to me** (cf. 26:1; 27:1; 28:1, 11). Sidon, a sister city of Tyre (cf. Jer. 25:22; 47:4; Joel 3:4; Zech. 9:2; Luke 6:17; 10:13-14), was 20 miles farther up the Mediterranean coast. Because of their close association, Ezekiel may have used this same introductory formula to link the two cities in judgment. Sidon was so closely allied with Tyre that perhaps Ezekiel felt it unnecessary to cite the same sins. She had violated God's holy character and He would not allow her sin to remain unpunished. He would **gain glory within** Sidon and **show** Himself **holy.** God's judgment would be by **a plague** and **the sword.**

The judgment on Sidon would have two results: (1) It would force the Sidonians to acknowledge God's righteous character—**They will know that I am the LORD** (stated in Ezek. 28:22, repeated in v. 23). (2) The judgment would remove an obstacle to Israel's walk with God. Their **malicious neighbors** with their wicked influence on Israel had been like a pain in Israel's side (painful **briers and sharp thorns**). The sinful practices of Baal worship had entered Israel through "Jezebel daughter of Ethbaal king of the Sidonians" (1 Kings 16:31).

28:25-26. The second part of Ezekiel's prophecy against Sidon focused on the results of the destruction for **Israel.** As God would reveal His holiness by destroying Sidon (v. 22), so He would reveal His holiness by rescuing Israel **from the nations.** Several times in the Book of Ezekiel God said, **I will show Myself holy** (20:41; 28:22, 25; 36:23; 38:16; 39:27). God punished Israel for her sin, but He has not abandoned her. She is unique among all **nations** because God had established His covenant with her. Though all nations would be punished, only Israel was promised a restoration of fellowship. The land promise made to Abraham (Gen. 13:14-17; 15:17-21) and renewed to Jacob (Gen. 35:11-13) has not been revoked. Israel **will live in** her **own land,** because God has given it to **Jacob.** Restored to her land, Israel will enjoy God's blessings, including **safety** and prosperity. This promise, made through Ezekiel, has never been literally fulfilled; it awaits fulfillment in the millennial kingdom. After the Babylonian Captivity, some Israelites did go back to the land (cf. Neh. 1:3) but they did not **live there in safety.** When God finally punishes Israel's enemies and blesses His Chosen People, they will recognize their Lord: **they will know that** He is **the** LORD **their God.**

G. Judgment on Egypt (chaps. 29–32)

The seventh and final nation Ezekiel prophesied against was Egypt. This prophecy was actually a series of seven oracles directed against Egypt and its Pharaoh. Each oracle is introduced by the clause, "The word of the LORD came to me"; and six of the seven oracles are dated (29:1, 17; 30:1 [undated], 20; 31:1; 32:1, 17). Though 29:1; 30:20; 31:1; 32:1; and 32:17 are in chronological order, 29:17 (the second oracle) is dated later than the others. This departure from his usual chronological arrangement is probably because Ezekiel wanted to arrange the oracles in a logical progression. He possibly placed 29:17-21 where he did to clarify his first prophecy (29:1-16). After predicting that the Pharaoh and Egypt would be destroyed (29:1-16), he then specified who would destroy them (29:17-21).

1. THE SIN OF EGYPT (29:1-16)

This prophecy includes three sections, each of which closes with the words seen so often in Ezekiel, "then they will know that I am the LORD" (vv. 6a, 9, 16).

29:1-6a. This first of seven prophecies against Egypt was given **in the 10th year, in the 10th month on the 12th day.** That day, January 5, 587 B.C., was almost a year after the siege of Jerusalem began (cf. 24:1-2).

The **Pharaoh** in **Egypt** at that time was Hophra who reigned from 589 to 570 B.C. His promises of assistance prompted Judah to break with Babylon. Both Egypt and her leader were singled out for judgment.

Ezekiel compared **Pharaoh** to a **great monster** in Egypt's **streams.** "Monster" (*tannîm*, a variant spelling of *tannîn*) described reptiles, from large snakes (Ex.

7:9-10) to giant sea monsters (Gen. 1:21). It probably included crocodiles. This word was also used in Semitic mythology to describe the chaos-monster who was destroyed when the world was created. Possibly Ezekiel had both ideas in mind. Reptiles in the Nile (especially crocodiles) symbolized Egypt's strength and ferocity. Egyptians believed that Pharaoh could conquer the chaos-monster; but here, ironically, God called Pharaoh the monster! Pharaoh was considered a god; therefore he thought of himself as having created **the Nile** (cf. Ezek. 29:9). Pharaoh, however, would soon learn he was no match for the true Creator-God. God said He would drag Egypt away from her place of protection in the Nile and **leave** her **in the desert.** This depicts God's subduing a crocodile (or the mythological "god" who lived in the water) and dragging him to a barren place where he would soon perish. God would defeat **Egypt** despite her great strength.

29:6b-9. The second section of this prophecy deals with Egypt's basic sin: she had **been a staff of reeds for the house of Israel.** A "staff" was used as a cane or walking stick for support on the rough terrain in Israel (cf. Zech. 8:4; Mark 6:8; Heb. 11:21). Israel leaned on Egypt for support in her revolt against Babylon, but Egypt's support was as fragile as the reeds which grew abundantly on the Nile River's shores. When the pressure came, the reed snapped, and Israel found herself unable to stand. Possibly Ezekiel was quoting a proverb commonly applied to Egypt which had a reputation as an unreliable ally (cf. 2 Kings 18:20-21).

The time of this prophecy probably coincided with Egypt's halfhearted attempt to aid Jerusalem during Nebuchadnezzar's siege (cf. Jer. 37:4-8). Egypt backed out and Jerusalem suffered the consequences. Jerusalem learned too late that a slender reed could not give support. When she leaned on Egypt for deliverance from Babylon, Egypt let her down (like a reed, she **splintered** and **broke**).

Because of Egypt's false promises of support to Judah, God said He would punish the Egyptians by the **sword** and Egypt would **become a desolate wasteland.**

29:10-16. This portion of Ezekiel's

prophecy discusses the extent of God's judgment on **Egypt**. The desolation would extend **from Migdol to Aswan, as far as the border of Cush.** "Migdol" was in the Delta region in northern (lower) Egypt and "Aswan" (or "Syene") was at the first cataract in southern (upper) Egypt and was the southern boundary between Egypt and Cush. Cush corresponds to present-day southern Egypt, Sudan, and northern Ethiopia.

God's total devastation of **Egypt** would last **for 40 years.** Judah had been destroyed because she relied on Egypt; Egypt would suffer the same fate. God would **disperse** Egypt **among the nations;** she would also be carried into **captivity.**

No archeological finding has yet confirmed an Egyptian deportation similar to the one experienced by Israel. However, it is unwise to dismiss a clear statement of Scripture on the basis of incomplete archeological data. Nebuchadnezzar did attack Egypt (29:17-21; cf. Jer. 43:8-13; 46:1-25). Assuming that he conquered the country, one would expect him to deport people to Babylon as he did others he conquered. Presumably, then, the Egyptian captives would have been allowed to return home in the reign of Cyrus of Persia, who defeated Babylon in 539 B.C. (ca. 33 years after Nebuchadnezzar's attack). Allowing seven additional years for the people to return and rebuild, a 40-year period of desolation was entirely possible.

God would then take the Egyptians **back . . . to Pathros, the land of their ancestry.** "Pathros" (cf. 30:14) was a geographic region located in southern (upper) Egypt. Some feel that this was the traditional birthplace of the nation of Egypt. Perhaps "Pathros" was used here to represent the entire land of Egypt.

Though God would let **the Egyptians** return to their land, Egypt would not achieve the place of power she once held. Instead she would be **the lowliest of kingdoms.** After Persia's rise to power, Egypt never again in biblical times became a major international power. She tried to exert herself during the intertestamental period, but she was held in check by Greece, Syria, and Rome. Egypt's political weakness would be a continual object lesson to **Israel.** She would look at **Egypt** and remember her

folly of depending on men instead of God.

2. THE DEFEAT OF EGYPT BY BABYLON (29:17-21)

29:17-21. Ezekiel's second prophecy against Egypt came **in the 27th year, in the first month on the first day.** This is the latest dated prophecy in the Book of Ezekiel. The date was April 26, 571 B.C. As stated earlier, Ezekiel probably placed this prophecy out of chronological order to draw attention to his logical progression. He had just described Egypt's coming judgment (vv. 1-16); he placed verses 17-21 afterward to indicate who would bring the judgment. **Nebuchadnezzar** himself would attack Egypt.

This prophecy was written shortly after Tyre's surrender to Babylon in 572 B.C. For 13 years Nebuchadnezzar had besieged the city of Tyre (585-572 B.C.). The picture of heads **rubbed bare** because of the prolonged wearing of helmets and of shoulders that were **raw** from carrying wood and stone for building siege mounds is graphic. Nebuchadnezzar had worked hard for meager results. **Yet he . . . got no reward from** that **campaign . . . against Tyre.** Tyre surrendered to Nebuchadnezzar, but there were no vast spoils of war to distribute as booty to his army. Evidently Tyre shipped off her wealth before she surrendered.

Nebuchadnezzar needed money to pay his soldiers for their labor so he turned to **Egypt.** Prompted by economic necessity, Babylon attacked Egypt and plundered **its wealth to pay . . . his army.** Yet it was really God who was "paying" Babylon to attack Egypt: **I have given him Egypt as a reward for his efforts.**

Ezekiel's second prophecy against Egypt ended with a promise to Israel. **That day** is interpreted in various ways. Some see a reference to a still future day of the Lord when God will restore Israel to her land and judge the nations around her. However, such a jump seems foreign to the text. The "day" in question was probably the time when God would judge Egypt through Babylon and then restore Egypt to her land.

When God finally restored the nations of Israel and Egypt, He would **make a horn grow for . . . Israel.** A horn symbolized strength (cf. 1 Sam. 2:1; 2 Sam. 22:3; 1 Kings 22:11; Jer. 48:25) and was applied in an ultimate sense to the strength of the Messiah, Christ, who would deliver Israel (cf. Luke 1:69). However, here the "horn" probably refers to Israel's strength which Nebuchadnezzar had destroyed. When Egypt was restored, Israel would also be restored as a nation.

When Israel's strength as a nation was renewed, God said He would open Ezekiel's **mouth among them.** This cannot refer to the ending of Ezekiel's divine dumbness (cf. Ezek. 3:26) for two reasons: (1) Ezekiel's dumbness had already ended in the 12th year of Jehoiachin's exile (33:21-22), and this prophecy came in the 27th year (29:17). (2) This prophecy would take place **after** Israel was restored from captivity. Ezekiel was 30 years old in 592 B.C. (1:1-2), so he would have been 83 when Cyrus' edict to let Israel return to her land was issued. Perhaps an 83-year-old might not have survived such an arduous journey from Babylon to Israel. None of the postexilic records refer to Ezekiel returning to Israel. The best explanation is that Ezekiel's spoken prophecies which had perplexed the people would become clear when they were fulfilled. Israel would recognize God's character as He faithfully accomplished His promise.

3. THE DESTRUCTION OF EGYPT AND HER ALLIES (30:1-19)

30:1-5. Unlike Ezekiel's other prophecies against Egypt, he did not date this one, which stressed Babylon's judgment on Egypt and her allies. It has four sections, each beginning with **This is what the "Lord"** (or **Sovereign Lord**) **says** (vv. 2, 6, 10, 13).

In verses 2-5 Ezekiel discussed the day of the Lord. **Wail and say, Alas for that day! For the day is near, the day of the Lord is near—a day of clouds, a time of doom for the nations.** Clouds often pictured doom (cf. v. 18; 32:7-8; 34:12; Joel 2:2; Zeph. 1:15). Though some think this refers to the future day of the Lord when God will judge the world for her sin, that view divorces the phrase from its context. True, "the day of the Lord" usually refers to God's future judgment on the earth (cf. Isa. 13:6-16; 34:8; Mal. 4). It will be a time when Israel and the nations will be judged and when Israel will be restored to her place of national blessing. However, the "day" of the Lord can refer to any time God comes in judgment (cf. Lam. 2:21-22 and see comments under "Major Interpretive Problems" in the *Introduction* to Joel). Both Israel and Judah experienced a "day" of God's judgment when they were punished for their sins (cf. Ezek. 7:1-14, esp. vv. 7, 10, 12). Now God's "day" of judgment would extend to **Egypt,** who would be defeated by Babylon (cf. 30:10-12).

God's judgment—"a time of doom" —would lead to death and destruction. The **sword** drawn **against** Israel (21:1-17) would also overtake Egypt, and **anguish** would extend to **Cush,** adjoining Egypt on the south, out of fear that she would be attacked next (cf. 30:9). Egypt's people would be killed and her treasuries looted.

Egypt's allies would also be caught in her judgment. Egypt had many mercenary soldiers in her army (Jer. 46:8-9, 20-21). **Cush,** as stated earlier, refers to present-day southern Egypt, Sudan, and northern Ethiopia (Es. 1:1; Jer. 46:9; Ezek. 27:10). **Put** is modern-day Libya (Isa. 66:19; Jer. 46:9; Ezek. 27:10), and **Lydia** was on the west coast of Asia Minor (cf. 27:10). The words **all Arabia** could read "all the mixed people." Only one vowel in these Hebrew words makes this difference. Jeremiah used these same words to refer to all the foreigners residing in Egypt (cf. Jer. 25:20).

The Hebrew word translated **Libya** is actually "Cub" (*kûb,* NIV marg.). The normal Hebrew word for Libya is *lûb,* as in Nahum 3:9. No manuscript evidence warrants a change from *kûb* to *lûb.* It seems better to read "Cub" and to admit that the exact location of this nation is unknown. **The people of the covenant land** probably refers to those Israelites who fled to **Egypt** to avoid Nebuchadnezzar's attacks against Judah (cf. Jer. 42:19-22; 44:1-14).

30:6-9. Ezekiel continued to discuss the defeat of Egypt's mercenary **allies** within Egypt's borders. Throughout the land, **from Migdol to Aswan** (the northern and southern extremities of Egypt [see the map in the *Introduction* to Jer.]; cf. Ezek. 29:10). These allies would be crushed and the **cities** where they had settled would be ruined. The destruction would force these nations to acknowledge the God who predicted their downfall: **Then they will know that I am the Lord.**

The news of **Egypt's** destruction would spread rapidly, causing panic among her allies. **Messengers** would travel in ships up the Nile River south to **Cush** to announce Egypt's defeat. The news would cause panic in Cush because they, having sided with Egypt against Babylon, would now be vulnerable to attack. **Anguish** would **take hold of them** (cf. 30:4). "The day of the Lord" (v. 3) was now explained as **the day of Egypt's doom.** God's day of judgment on **Egypt** would surely take place.

30:10-12. The third section of this prophecy again zeroed in on the means of destruction against **the hordes of Egypt.** "Hordes" was mentioned 14 times in chapters 30–32 by Ezekiel, apparently to stress that proud nation's teeming populace. Egypt's judgment would come **by the hand of Nebuchadnezzar** (cf. 29:17-21). God selected Babylon, **the most ruthless of nations** (cf. 28:7; 30:10-11; 32:12), to accomplish His judgment. Babylon treated her captives cruelly. After King Zedekiah of Judah rebelled, Nebuchadnezzar forced him to watch soldiers kill all his sons. Then Zedekiah's eyes were put out so the last thing he ever saw was his sons' deaths (2 Kings 25:7). Ezekiel said that Babylon, after defeating Judah, would turn her cruel war machine against Egypt, killing the Egyptians with **swords** (cf. Ezek. 30:4).

In describing Babylon's attack, Ezekiel carefully pointed up the ultimate Source of destruction. Three times in verses 10-12 God said "I will" do this. Babylon was only a tool God used to accomplish His judgment. God declared that **by the hand of foreigners I will lay waste the land.** For the fifth time in this book God called the Babylonians "foreigners" (7:21; 11:9; 28:7, 10; 30:12).

30:13-19. In this fourth section of the prophecy Ezekiel enumerated the many places in Egypt that would be destroyed. No major city there would escape God's wrath. First, God said He would **destroy the idols and . . . put an end to the images in Memphis** (cf. v. 16). According to legend, Memphis was the first capital of united Egypt (ca. 3200 b.c.). But later, when Memphis was no longer the capi-

tal, the city still was important as a religious center. Numerous temples were built there. A colony of Jews had settled in Memphis (cf. Jer. 44:1).

Other cities would also feel the sting of judgment. **Pathros** was an area about midway between Cairo and Aswan. "Pathros" was a synonym for upper Egypt (cf. Jer. 44:1) and possibly for all Egypt (cf. Ezek. 29:14). **Zoan** was a royal residence in the Delta region (cf. Ps. 78:12, 43; Isa. 19:11, 13). Later Zoan was called Tanis by the Greeks. **Thebes** (or No), mentioned three times in this passage (Ezek. 30:14-16), was in southern (upper) Egypt about 400 miles south of Cairo at the site of modern Karnak and Luxor. For a long time it was the country's capital. The city was destroyed by the Assyrians in 663 b.c. (cf. Nahum 3:8-10) but was rebuilt. Jeremiah also predicted Thebes' destruction (cf. Jer. 46:25). **The hordes of** people there would be slain and the city would be **taken** suddenly **by storm.**

Pelusium would receive God's **wrath** (Ezek. 30:15), and when **fire** would spread through **Egypt, Pelusium** would **writhe in agony** (v. 16). Pelusium (or Sin) was in the Delta about a mile from the Mediterranean Sea. The city was a major military center and guarded the northern entrance to Egypt. Appropriately Ezekiel called it **the stronghold of Egypt.**

Ezekiel named the last three of the eight cities of Egypt in verses 17-18: **Heliopolis . . . Bubastis,** and **Tahpanhes.** Heliopolis (or On) was in northern (lower) Egypt just south of the Delta region. It was a major religious center during much of Egypt's ancient history. Possibly Jeremiah had Heliopolis in mind when he predicted the destruction of "the temple of the sun in Egypt" (cf. Jer. 43:13). Bubastis (or Pi Beseth) was northeast of the modern city of Cairo, in northern (lower) Egypt. Bubastis served briefly as a capital of Egypt, and it too was an important religious center. Tahpanhes was near the present Suez Canal. In Jeremiah's day Pharaoh had a palace in that city (Jer. 43:9) which may be why Ezekiel mentioned it last—for climactic effect. Jeremiah condemned that city along with Memphis (cf. Jer. 2:16). He was forced to go there after Gedaliah was assassinated (Jer. 43:7-8).

By naming Egypt's major cities God

was saying that the **strength** of the entire nation would be ended, like the breaking of a **yoke. She** would **be covered with clouds,** a figurative way to express doom and judgment (cf. Ezek. 30:3; 32:7-8; 34:12; cf. Joel 2:2; Zeph. 1:15). As gathering clouds herald an approaching storm, so covering Egypt with clouds would herald her coming judgment. Major cities would be destroyed, and people in the **villages** would be taken **into captivity.**

4. THE SCATTERING OF EGYPT (30:20-26)

30:20-26. Ezekiel's fourth of seven prophecies against Egypt was given **in the 11th year, in the first month on the seventh day.** That date was April 29, 587 B.C., almost four months after Ezekiel's first prophecy against Egypt (29:1). The first prophecy signified the time when the forces of Egypt went out to "rescue" Israel from Babylon (cf. Jer. 37:4-5); the fourth prophecy was recorded after the Babylonians defeated Egypt. The theme of the prophecy was Egypt's defeat by God: **I have broken the arm of Pharaoh king of Egypt.** This Pharaoh was Hophra, who ruled Egypt from 589 to 570 B.C. Possibly the days between the first and fourth prophecies were approximately the length of time the siege on Jerusalem was lifted as Babylon repositioned its army to meet the Egyptian attack.

Nebuchadnezzar broke the "arm" of Egypt so she was unable to defend Judah. In fact the damage done to Egypt was irreparable. Egypt's arm, symbolizing strength, was not even **put in a splint so as to become strong enough to hold a sword.**

Egypt "broke her arm" in her feeble attempt to rescue Israel, but this was only a prelude to God's full judgment. God said He would **break both** of Egypt's **arms, the good arm as well as the broken one.** In other words God would totally destroy Egypt's strength. Her ability to protect both others and herself would be eliminated.

Though God would destroy the power of Egypt, He would strengthen the power of Egypt's chief foe, **Babylon.** Nebuchadnezzar's **arms** would be strengthened by God, and **Pharaoh,** groaning **like a mortally wounded man,** would be utterly defenseless before the Babylonians.

Ezekiel's point was to contrast the recent defeat suffered by Egypt (her one "broken arm") with the still greater defeat she would suffer. She had been disarmed when she tried to intervene in Babylon's attack on Jerusalem, but she would later be destroyed by **Babylon.** When Nebuchadnezzar attacked **Egypt** herself, she would fall to him (cf. Ezek. 29:1-20). God would then **disperse** Egypt **among the nations** (a fact stated twice for emphasis; 30:23, 26; cf. 29:12). Egypt would follow Judah into exile.

5. THE SIMILARITY OF EGYPT AND ASSYRIA (CHAP. 31)

Ezekiel's fifth prophecy against Egypt is an allegory on Pharaoh's fall.

a. The allegory of Assyria as a cedar tree (31:1-9)

31:1-9. This prophecy was given **in the 11th year, in the third month on the first day.** This was June 21, 587 B.C., less than two months after the prophecy recorded in 30:20-26. Ezekiel addressed his message **to Pharaoh king of Egypt and to his hordes.** He ended it with the same words (31:18). This ruler (Hophra) and his mighty army obviously felt so secure in their military might and ability that Ezekiel responded rhetorically, **Who can be compared with you in majesty?** Obviously Egypt thought she was in a class by herself.

Ezekiel offered an example against whom Egypt could compare herself: **Consider Assyria.** Some scholars think that "Assyria" (*'aššûr*) should be emended to read "cypress tree" (or "pine tree") (*te'aššûr*) because of the difficulty in understanding why Ezekiel would mention Assyria in his prophecies against Egypt. However, there is no need to alter the text. Assyria would have had great significance to Egypt for two reasons. First, Assyria had been the only Mesopotamian nation to invade Egypt. In 633 B.C. Assyria had entered Egypt and destroyed the capital of Thebes (cf. Nahum 3:8-10). So the only nation that could be "compared" with Egypt was Assyria. Second, Assyria had been destroyed by Babylon, the same nation Ezekiel said would enter Egypt and destroy *it.*

Ezekiel compared Assyria to **a cedar in Lebanon.** (A lofty cedar also depicted the leaders of Israel; cf. Ezek. 17.) At the apex of her power Assyria dominated the Middle East, towering like a cedar **higher than all the trees of the field** (31:5). Several key cities of Assyria were situated at or near the Tigris River, which provided much-needed water. Thus situated, Assyria grew like a cedar nourished by **waters . . . deep springs** (v. 4), and **abundant waters** (vv. 5, 7). **Birds** in the cedar's **branches** and animals under its shade (v. 6; cf. vv. 12, 17) speak of Assyria, like a tall tree, overshadowing and protecting all her neighbors.

In a hyperbole Ezekiel stressed Assyria's grandeur: **The cedars in the garden of God** (Eden; cf. 28:13) **could not rival it.** This "tree" was unmatched by any of God's other "trees." In fact this tree was **the envy of all the trees of Eden.**

In Assyria's former exalted position, she had attained power and influence that far exceeded Egypt's. She was the perfect example to show Egypt the effects of God's judgment.

b. The downfall of Assyria (31:10-14)

31:10-14. Assyria fell because of her pride. God judged the nation **because,** like a cedar, **it towered on high, lifting its top above the thick foliage, and because it was proud of its height.** Judah (16:56), Tyre (27:3; 28:2), and Egypt (30:6) would all be judged for their pride.

God judged Assyria by handing **it over to the ruler of the nations.** He was Nebuchadnezzar who, following in his father's footsteps, continued to expand the borders of Babylon at Assyria's expense. God ordained Assyria's fall (cf. Nahum). The city of Nineveh fell to Nabopolassar (Nebuchadnezzar's father) in 612 B.C., and the rest of the Assyrian army was crushed by Nebuchadnezzar in 609 B.C. at Haran (see "Historical Background" in the *Introduction* to Jer.).

The most ruthless of foreign nations (i.e., Babylon; cf. 28:7; 30:11; 32:12) **cut . . . down** Assyria, like felling a large tree. Then those who had sought protection **under** Assyria's **shade** (cf. 31:6, 17) abandoned her.

Assyria's fall was an object lesson to other nations. **No other trees so well-watered are ever to reach such a height** (v. 14). Egypt's desire to become a lasting great power in the Middle East was destined to failure. She and all other nations were **destined for** the grave **(death** and **the pit)** instead of glory. (The "pit" is the place of the departed dead; see comments on 26:20-21.) No nation should exalt itself highly over others because they will all suffer Assyria's fate.

c. The descent of Assyria into the grave (31:15-18)

31:15-18. Having mentioned death (v. 14), Ezekiel expanded and applied that fact by focusing on the reaction of other nations to Assyria's fall (vv. 15-18). The nations mourned her (the **springs** were held back by their **mourning)** and were alarmed **(the nations tremble)** that one as strong and mighty as Assyria could ever **fall.** If the strong "cedar" could fall, then how could any lesser "trees" (nations) hope to remain standing?

While the nations were alarmed, those that had already been destroyed **(all the trees of Eden)** were comforted and **consoled in the earth below** (in the grave). The lesser nations, their **allies** who had **lived in** Assyria's **shade** (cf. vv. 6, 12) and were now in the **grave,** could comfort themselves that even Assyria had descended to where they were. All were equal in death.

Assyria's "allies among the nations" brought the circle back to Egypt because she was Assyria's chief ally when Assyria fell to Babylon. Ezekiel drove home the point of his allegory (v. 18): **Which of the trees of Eden can be compared with you in splendor and majesty?** This was similar to the question in verse 2, but the answer was now obvious. Egypt, who was similar to Assyria, would suffer the same fate. She too would be **brought down with the trees of Eden to the earth below.** Egypt's end would be one of shame like that of **the uncircumcised** (see comments on 28:10; 32:19). And her fall would be fatal, **by the sword.** For emphasis Ezekiel repeated the subject of his story: **This is Pharaoh and all his hordes** (cf. 31:2).

6. THE LAMENT FOR PHARAOH (32:1-16)

32:1-2a. Ezekiel's sixth prophecy against Egypt was given **in the 12th year, in the 12th month on the first day.** That was March 3, 585 B.C.—two months after the news of Jerusalem's fall reached the captives in Babylon (cf. 33:21). The fall of

Egypt was now so certain that Ezekiel was told to **take up a lament concerning Pharaoh king of Egypt.** A lament, or funeral dirge, was usually delivered when one was buried. (For an explanation of a lament see the comments on chap. 19.) Ezekiel had already written laments for Judah (chap. 19), the city of Tyre (26:17-18; 27), and the king of Tyre (28:12-19). The lament against Egypt is in three parts (32:2b, 3-10, 11-16). The second and third sections each begin with, "This is what the Sovereign LORD says" (vv. 3, 11).

32:2b. Ezekiel said Pharaoh (Hophra), in his fierce power, was **like a lion** (cf. Judah's kings, 19:2-9) **among the nations** and **a monster in the seas** (cf. 29:2-5). The "monster" could refer to a crocodile or to the mythological chaos-monster, to picture Pharaoh's ferocity and seeming invulnerability. Possibly the crocodile is suggested as Ezekiel said Pharaoh was **churning** up the normally placid **water** (cf. Job 41:31-32). Pharaoh's actions were disturbing the international scene as he tried to blunt Babylon's power.

32:3-10. Ezekiel then spoke of Pharaoh's judgment. If Pharaoh were a crocodile, God would lead Pharaoh's enemies on a "crocodile hunt." **With a great throng of people I will cast My net over you, and they will haul you up in My net** (cf. 29:3-5). Pharaoh would be trapped by his enemies and removed from his sphere of power. This was an amazing statement, for in Egypt the Pharaoh supposedly could defeat a crocodile! (Cf. comments on Job 41.) God would drag Pharaoh from his place of power and **throw** him **on the land and hurl** him **on the open field.** Pharaoh's power would be broken and his people scattered.

The destruction of Pharaoh and Egypt was couched in terms that conjured up images of Egypt's judgment at the time of the Exodus. God said He would **drench the land with** Egypt's **flowing blood** (Ezek. 32:6). This recalled the first plague on Egypt in which the water turned to blood (Ex. 7:20-24). But this time, the blood would come from the slain in Egypt. God also said He would **darken** the **stars . . . sun,** and **moon,** bringing **darkness over the land** (Ezek. 32:7-8). Though these cataclysmic signs are similar to those that will accompany

the day of the Lord (Joel 2:30-31; 3:15), it seems Ezekiel was alluding here to the darkness of the ninth plague (Ex. 10:21-29).

In response to Egypt's fall the surrounding nations would **be appalled** (cf. Ezek. 26:16; 27:35; 28:19) **and their kings** would **shudder with horror.** God's revealing His holy character through Egypt's judgment would have a profound effect on other nations. If mighty Egypt could be destroyed, so could they.

32:11-16. This third section of Ezekiel's lament drops the figurative description of destruction (vv. 3-8) and portrays Egypt's fall to Babylon literally. **The sword of the king of Babylon will come against you.** Pharaoh's army would be crushed by the ruthless Babylonians (cf. 29:17-21; 30:10-12, 24) and the land of **Egypt** would be decimated. Egypt's **pride** would be shattered, **her hordes . . . overthrown** (cf. comments on "hordes" in 30:10), and **her cattle** by the Nile and streams destroyed. Both man and beast would be affected by the coming attack.

The waters that were once **stirred by the foot of man** and **muddied by the hoofs of cattle** would now be stilled. Figuratively Pharaoh had "muddied the waters" with his international intrigue (32:2); literally the Nile was muddied through the daily activities of man and beast (v. 13). But now the streams and rivers would **settle** because those activities would be curtailed through death and deportation. The **streams** would **flow like oil,** smoothly, undisturbed.

Like professional "chanters" the surrounding nations (**daughters of the nations;** cf. v. 18) would be "hired" as mourners to **chant** a dirge over Egypt's fall.

7. THE DESCENT OF EGYPT INTO SHEOL
   (32:17-32)

32:17-21. Ezekiel's last of seven prophecies against Egypt came **in the 12th year, on the 15th day of the month.** The month was not named, but many interpreters assume it was the same month as the previous prophecy (v. 1). If so, the date of this message was March 17, 585 B.C., exactly two weeks after the preceding message. The message's theme was the consignment of the hosts of **Egypt** to sheol. Since the language is highly poetic, Ezekiel's purpose was not to give a precise description of the afterlife. However, he did indicate that after death a person has no opportunity to change his destiny.

In his own funeral dirge for Egypt, Ezekiel assigned her to sheol with her surrounding nations (**the daughters of mighty nations**; cf. v. 18), **with those who go down to the pit.** (On the "pit" as a figure for death see the comments on 26:19-21.) God's word of judgment was so sure that Egypt's appointment to the grave was already made.

Ezekiel derided both Pharaoh and his nation. **Are you more favored than others? Go down and be laid among the uncircumcised.** Egypt's pride would be shattered when her people were destroyed. She would be forced to take her place in death with "the uncircumcised." This phrase, used 10 times in chapter 32 (vv. 19, 21, 24-30, 32), described a death of shame and defeat (cf. comments on 28:10; 31:18). Every time Ezekiel used this phrase for death he associated it with defeat by **the sword** at the hands of one's enemies.

The descent of Egypt's defeated army **and her allies** into sheol would be derided by the military men already there. They would observe that she had **come down** to lie with the uncircumcised, with those killed by the sword. Egypt exulted in her military prowess, but would be humbled in death, taking her place with other defeated nations.

32:22-32. Ezekiel described the nations that Egypt would join in sheol. The descriptions are similar, for he spoke of each nation's being **slain . . . by the sword** and being in the grave. All (except Edom) were said to have caused **terror** among those they attacked. **Assyria is there with her whole army** (v. 22; cf. v. 23). Assyria had already been used as an object lesson by Ezekiel (chap. 31). All Assyria's soldiers killed in battle were buried **around her.**

The second country mentioned by Ezekiel was **Elam . . . with all her hordes around her grave** (32:24-25). Elam, east of Babylon, was a warlike nation (cf. Gen. 14:1-17). Though subdued by Assyria and conquered by Nebuchadnezzar (Jer. 49:34-39), Elam regained power and later became a major part of the Persian Empire. But Ezekiel was referring only to the defeated Elamites of

the past who were already in the **grave.**

The third group awaiting Egypt in the grave were the nations of **Meshech and Tubal** (Ezek. 32:26-27). "Meshech and Tubal," mentioned earlier (27:13), were probably located on the northern fringe of what is now eastern and central Turkey. They appear again in chapters 38-39 as Gog's allies. Aggressive Meshech and Tubal had carried on a long battle with the Assyrians for control of the area south of the Black Sea. **Do they not lie with the other uncircumcised warriors who have fallen?** Some scholars see this statement as a further judgment on Meshech and Tubal and translate it as an assertion ("they do not lie with . . . "). However, it seems better to view it as the NIV renders it. Meshech and Tubal are not being singled out from the other countries but are included with them in judgment. The once-awesome might **of these warriors** had vanished, and they were now suffering the judgment due their sin.

Ezekiel paused to state why he spoke of the grave. **You too, O Pharaoh, will be broken and will lie among the uncircumcised, with those killed by the sword** (32:28). The fate of these other nations was an object lesson to Egypt. Like those once-powerful nations that were now in the grave, Pharaoh and his powerful army could expect the same fate.

Then Ezekiel resumed listing other nations. **Edom is there, her kings and all her princes** (v. 29). Edom had already received notice of God's judgment (cf. 25:12-14). Her leaders who had died were in sheol awaiting Egypt's arrival.

The final group in the grave was **all the princes of the north and all the Sidonians** (32:30). These "princes of the north," connected with Sidon, were probably the Phoenician city-states. All these mighty maritime powers suffered the same humiliating fate: **slain in disgrace despite the terror caused by their power.** Their past exploits could not save them from the specter of death. They too were awaiting Egypt's appearance in sheol.

Ezekiel again mentioned Egypt's fate (vv. 31-32). **Pharaoh** would have a perverted sense of comfort (**be consoled**) when he and his hordes would finally arrive in sheol because **he** would **see that** he was not alone in his shame and humiliation.

III. Blessings on Israel (chaps. 33–48)

This last major division of the book focuses on the restoration of Israel's blessing. Israel would be judged for her sin (chaps. 1–24) as would the surrounding nations (chaps. 25–32). But Israel will not remain under judgment forever. God had set her apart as His special people, and He will fulfill His promises to her.

A. New life for Israel (chaps. 33–39)

The first step in Israel's restoration will be national renewal. Israel as a nation "died" when she went into captivity. Her homeland was gone, her temple destroyed, and her kings dethroned. Israel's enemies had triumphed. Her false leaders within had led the people astray, and her neighbors without had plundered and decimated the land. For Israel to experience God's blessing she will need to be "reborn" as a nation. The false leaders will be replaced with a true shepherd who will guide the people (chap. 34). The external enemies of Israel will be judged (chap. 35). The people will be restored both to the land and to their God (chaps. 36–37), and their security will be guaranteed by God Himself (chaps. 38–39).

1. WATCHMAN EZEKIEL REAPPOINTED (CHAP. 33)

a. Ezekiel's duties as a watchman (33:1-20)

33:1-20. Ezekiel had been named God's **watchman** to warn. . . . **Israel** of coming judgment (see comments on 3:16-27). Ezekiel's first commissioning was to a ministry of judgment, but that ministry was now completed. God then appointed Ezekiel as a **watchman** for a second time, but this message was different. The focus was still on individual accountability and responsibility, but the message's thrust was God's restoration of **Israel**.

b. The opening of Ezekiel's mouth (33:21-33)

33:21-22. Ezekiel was primed for his new ministry, inaugurated when news of Jerusalem's fall reached the captives in Babylon. **In the 12th year of** their **exile, in the 10th month on the fifth day,** that is, on January 9, 585 B.C., news of the fall was delivered by one of Jerusalem's sur-

vivors, who had traveled several months and several hundred miles to tell Ezekiel. Only then did the awful reality of Ezekiel's prophecies strike home. Now that Ezekiel's message was confirmed, there was no need for him to be silent. **So** his **mouth was opened** the night **before the** messenger **arrived.** Ezekiel had remained **silent** for seven years, only speaking to utter God's judgments (cf. 3:26-27).

33:23-29. In the rest of chapter 33 Ezekiel addressed two groups of people. First he condemned those Israelites who remained **in the land of Israel** and expected a soon end to the Babylonian Captivity (vv. 23-29). Then he rebuked those who gathered to hear him in Babylon (vv. 30-33).

The people who remained in Israel after Jerusalem's fall refused to acknowledge God's judgment. Comparing themselves to **Abraham,** they claimed to be the remnant left by God to possess His Promised Land. If the *one* man, Abraham, had a right to the land, certainly, they reasoned, the *many* Israelites remaining there had a right to it.

But there was one big difference between Abraham and those in **the land.** Abraham was righteous and they were wicked. They ate **meat with the blood still in** it (cf. Lev. 17:10-14), worshiped **idols** (Ex. 20:4-6), and **shed blood** (cf. Ex. 20:13). The right to **possess the land** depended on spiritual obedience, not numerical strength. Because of their sins these people had forfeited their rights to the Promised Land.

Those who felt a smug arrogance in their possession of **the land** would soon experience the pains of judgment. Those in the city's **ruins** would **fall by the sword,** those who fled to the countryside would be eaten by **wild animals,** and those who hid **in strongholds and caves** would **die of a plague.** Strikingly those were the same judgments the people of Jerusalem had experienced earlier (cf. Ezek. 5:17; 14:21). In addition, **the land** (Judah) would be **desolate.**

33:30-33. Ezekiel then spoke to the exiles in Babylon. He had developed a popular following among the people who recognized him as a prophet. They frequently gathered to **hear** his messages. The people liked to hear God's word, but neglected to obey it (cf. James 1:22-25):

they did not put the prophet's words into practice. They were paying lip service to God, but still harbored sin in their hearts. With their mouths they were expressing devotion, but their hearts were greedy. Ezekiel's words tantalized the people's ears much as beautiful love songs would do; but his message never penetrated their hearts.

But a day of reckoning would come. When all his words of prophecy would come true . . . then they would know that he was a prophet. Ezekiel was not referring to his prophecies about Jerusalem's fall because those had already "come true" (Ezek. 33:21). Some suggest he was referring to his prophecy against the remnant in Judah (vv. 23-29), but it is doubtful that a message of judgment on the remnant would have had any greater impact on those in captivity than the fall of the city. Therefore Ezekiel was probably referring to the fact of individual responsibility and judgment that God imposes on all people (cf. vv. 12-20). Each person would be held accountable for his actions and his responses to God's word. When their day of accountability came, then those "hearers of the Word" (James 1:22, KJV) would be forced to acknowledge the prophetic nature—and thus the truth—of Ezekiel's message.

2. THE PRESENT FALSE SHEPHERDS CONTRASTED WITH THE FUTURE TRUE SHEPHERD (CHAP. 34)

a. The present false shepherds (34:1-10)

34:1-6. God charged the prophet to **prophesy against the shepherds of Israel.** The rulers of the people were often called shepherds (cf. Ps. 78:70-72; Isa. 44:28; 63:11; Jer. 23:1-4; 25:34-38). They were to be strong, caring leaders who guarded their nation like a flock. Ezekiel first explained the sins of the shepherds (Ezek. 34:1-6), then pronounced judgment on them (vv. 7-10).

Israel's leaders did not serve their **flock.** Their first error was to put their own interests above those of the people (vv. 2-3). **Woe to the shepherds of Israel who only take care of themselves!** Israel's kings had added to their wealth at the expense of the common people. They viewed **the flock** as a source of wealth to be exploited rather than a trust to be protected.

The second error of the leaders was their harsh treatment of the people. A shepherd was to lead his sheep to food, protect them from attack, nurse to health the **injured** sheep, and search for any that strayed and got **lost.** However, Israel's shepherds did not gently nurture the people. They **ruled . . . harshly and brutally.**

The third error of the rulers was their flagrant disregard for the people, letting them be **scattered** without looking **for them** (vv. 5-6). Three times in verses 5-6 Ezekiel mentioned that the sheep were **scattered.** The chief job of a **shepherd** was to prevent such a catastrophe. Ezekiel was probably alluding to the Assyrian and Babylonian captivities which had scattered Israel and Judah among the nations. The **shepherds** had been unable to prevent the very thing they were appointed to guard against.

34:7-10. The **shepherds** had neglected their task, and the sheep were scattered. It was now time to call the shepherds to judgment for their actions. Holding **the shepherds . . . accountable** for His **flock,** God would judge the rulers and **remove them from** their positions of power. They would no longer have opportunities to profit at the people's expense. God said, **I will rescue My flock from their mouths, and it will no longer be food for them,** in the sense of the leaders taking advantage of the people. This statement was a bridge to the next section. The false **shepherds** had brought Israel to ruin. So God Himself would intercede and rescue His people.

b. The future true shepherd (34:11-31)

What the false shepherds failed to accomplish because of their greed (vv. 1-10), God would bring to pass. He would care for His flock (vv. 11-16), judge between His sheep (vv. 17-24), and establish a covenant of peace (vv. 25-31).

34:11-16. The **flock** was **scattered** because of cruel and indifferent shepherds (vv. 2-6). If the sheep were to be rescued and restored, the Great Shepherd would need to rescue them Himself. **I Myself will search for My sheep and look after them.** God would intervene personally on Israel's behalf.

God's first action would be to restore **Israel** to her land **from the nations** and to **pasture** her like sheep in **good grazing land.** God will do what the false shepherds had failed to do—**tend. . . . search . . . bring back. . . . strengthen,** and **shepherd . . . with justice.** This prophecy was not fulfilled when Israel returned to her land after the Babylonian Captivity. It still awaits future fulfillment in the Millennium.

34:17-24. In exercising His justice God said He would begin by judging between the individual sheep: **I will judge between one sheep and another, and between rams and goats.** Before the millennial kingdom begins, God will sort out the righteous from the unrighteous (cf. Matt. 25:31-46) and allow only the righteous into the Millennium.

But how will God differentiate one from the other? The character of the sheep is seen in their conduct (Ezek. 34:17-21). The wicked sheep are those that follow the conduct of the shepherds, oppressing the weaker sheep. They **trampled** the pasturelands and even **muddied** the streams so that other sheep were left with less-than-desirable vegetation and drinking water. These **fat sheep** were successful in brutalizing the **lean sheep.** The wicked sheep even butted **all the weak sheep with** their **horns,** to drive **them away.** God will not permit these wicked practices to continue. Instead He will rescue the oppressed and will judge the aggressors. He **will judge between one sheep and another** (v. 22; cf. v. 17).

After judging the individual sheep, God will exercise His leadership by appointing a new **shepherd** (vv. 23-24). This shepherd, God stated, will be His **servant David.** Many see this as an allusion to Christ, the Good Shepherd (cf. John 10:11-18), who descended from the line of David to be the King of Israel (cf. Matt. 1:1). However, nothing in Ezekiel 34:23 *demands* that Ezekiel was not referring to the literal King David who will be resurrected to serve as Israel's righteous prince. David is referred to by name elsewhere in passages that look to the future restoration of Israel (cf. Jer. 30:9; Ezek. 37:24-25; Hosea 3:5). Also Ezekiel indicated that **David will be** the **prince** (*nāśî*) of the restored people (Ezek. 34:24; 37:25). This same "prince" will then offer sin offerings for himself during the millennial period (45:22; 46:4). Such actions would hardly be appropriate for the sinless Son of God, but they would be for David. So it seems this is a literal refer-

ence to a resurrected David. In place of the false shepherds God will resurrect a true **shepherd** to tend his **sheep.**

34:25-31. God's care and protection will result in peace for His people. **I will make a covenant of peace with them.** The peace that Israel has always longed for will be experienced. The uncertainties associated with desolate **places, wild animals,** other **nations,** and unpredictable weather will be alleviated. The **land** will enjoy peace and prosperity. **Trees** will bear **fruit and the ground will yield its crops,** and **the people will be secure in their land,** living **in safety.**

God's "covenant of peace" looks forward to the blessings **Israel** will experience in the Millennium. This covenant will establish Israel in her land permanently with David as her shepherd. Later Ezekiel stated that the covenant of peace will also involve the rebuilding of God's temple as a visible reminder of His presence (37:26-28).

God will restore Israel because of her unique relationship to Him. **You My sheep, the sheep of My pasture, are** My **people, and I am your God.**

3. THE ENEMY (EDOM) DESTROYED (CHAP. 35)

Why did Ezekiel devote a second prophecy to Edom (cf. 25:12-14), and why was it placed in this section on Israel's restoration? Most likely Edom was listed here to represent the judgment God would inflict on all nations who oppose Israel. Edom was the prototype of all Israel's later foes. The destruction of Edom would signal the beginning of God's judgment on the whole earth based on that nation's treatment of Israel (cf. Gen. 12:3).

The prophecy against Edom is in three parts, each ending with Ezekiel's common expression, "Then you/they will know that I am the LORD" (Ezek. 35:4, 9, 15).

35:1-4 In a direct statement of judgment on Edom, God said, **I am against you, Mount Seir.** Seir, Edom's geographical name, was the mountain range east of the Wadi Arabah south of the Dead Sea. This was the mountainous homeland where the Edomites lived. God would **make** that people as **desolate** as their land.

35:5-9. Ezekiel's second section followed the "because/therefore" format (used in 25:1-17) in explaining why Edom would be judged. Edom's sin was her enmity against Israel. She had **harbored an ancient hostility and delivered the Israelites over to the sword** (cf. Obad. 10, 14). Edom hoped to profit from Israel's loss, and she abetted Israel's collapse.

Because Edom had assisted in Israel's slaughter, God would assist in her slaughter. Four times (in Heb.) in Ezekiel 35:6 God referred to **bloodshed** (*dām*, lit., "blood"). This may be a wordplay on Edom's name ('*ĕdōm;* from '*ādōm*, "to be red"). Edom, with its red mountains, was now red with blood. **Since you did not hate bloodshed, bloodshed will pursue you.** Edom would suffer the same fate she had tried to inflict on Israel (see comments on Obad.). Many people would be **slain** and her **towns** would become **desolate,** no longer **inhabited.**

35:10-15. Ezekiel again used the "because/therefore" formula. Edom also sinned in her desire to possess the land God had promised to Judah and Israel. Edom had said those **two nations** would become her **possession.** God severely chastised Israel and Judah for their sin, but He never abrogated His promises made to Abraham and his descendants. Edom was trying to usurp Israel's title deed to the land which had been guaranteed by God.

God's judgment corresponded to Edom's guilt: **I will treat you in accordance with the anger and jealousy you showed in your hatred of them** (v. 11). Edom had dared plot **against** God's Chosen People, so she would now experience the consequences. In her boast **against** God (v. 13) Edom **rejoiced when . . . Israel became desolate.** Therefore God would make Edom **desolate.** Her treatment of Israel determined her own fate.

Edom became an object lesson for all nations. When God restores Israel's fortunes in the future, He will judge the world's other nations based on their treatment of Israel (cf. Matt. 25:31-46). They will be measured by their actions toward Israel.

4. THE PEOPLE BLESSED (CHAP. 36)

Chapter 36 is set in antithesis to chapter 35. When God intervenes on Israel's behalf, the "mountains" of Israel's enemies will be judged (35:1-3, 8) but the "mountains of Israel" (cf. 35:12) will be blessed (36:1). In verses 1-7 Edom is again pictured as representing all nations who seek Israel's harm (cf. vv. 5, 7). The first section of the prophecy (vv. 1-15) uses the "because/therefore" format to compare the judgment on the nations with Israel's restoration. The second section of the prophecy (vv. 16-38) moves from the mountains of Israel to the people of Israel who will be the personal recipients of God's blessing.

The fact of Israel's future restoration seemed so remote after her fall to Babylon that God put great emphasis on His personal character (rather than external circumstances) as the basis for the fulfillment. Ten times the prophet stated, "This is what the Sovereign LORD says" (vv. 2-7, 13, 22, 33, 37).

a. Israel's mountains to prosper (36:1-15)

Ezekiel contrasted Israel's present humiliation before her enemies with her future glorification.

36:1-7. God promised to punish Israel's enemies for their sin in hounding, slandering (v. 3), plundering (vv. 4-5), rejoicing over, and having **malice** against Israel. **Therefore** God swore **with uplifted hand** (a gesture accompanying an oath; cf. 20:5, 15, 23; 47:14) **that the nations** who had scorned her (36:6) **will also suffer scorn.** Surrounding **nations** seemed to have triumphed, but their victory was merely temporary. They would suffer for their sin.

36:8-12. In contrast with the judgment about to be inflicted on Israel's enemies, Israel herself could look forward to restoration and blessing. In a reversal of the catastrophe that God had earlier called against the **mountains of Israel** (6:1-7), He said the mountains **will produce branches and fruit for** His **people . . . will soon come home.** God will restore the land so that it can provide for the restored remnant.

God's blessing will involve numerical growth, for **the number of people** will be multiplied. The nation that had been decimated in the land (6:3, 5-7) will replenish it. Israel's latter state will be far superior to her former. When God finally restores the **people** to the land He will **prosper** the land; He guarantees the permanence of this arrangement. Once Israel is restored to the land her **inheritance** will be secure. The land **will never again**

deprive Israel of her **children.** Rather than being a cruel wilderness with drought, famine, and death (cf. Lev. 26:18-22; Num. 13:32; Deut. 28:20-24), it will be a place of blessing. This will take place when Israel possesses her land during Christ's millennial reign.

36:13-15. Besides punishing Israel's enemies (vv. 1-7) and restoring Israel's land (vv. 8-12), God will also remove Israel's reproach (vv. 13-15). The mockery and humiliation (**taunts** and **scorn**) Israel had been forced to endure (vv. 3-6) will cease (cf. 16:57-58). She will once again be restored to her position of prestige as God's Chosen People (cf. Deut. 28:13; Zech. 8:13, 20-23).

b. Israel's people to be regathered (36:16-38)

After discussing Israel's sinful past (vv. 16-21), Ezekiel discussed (in three parts, each beginning with "This is what the Sovereign LORD says," vv. 22, 33, 37) the nation's future restoration.

36:16-21. Before dwelling on Israel's future cleansing, Ezekiel reminded the exiles of their past sin which caused their judgment. **When** they **were . . . in the land, they defiled it by their conduct** and **actions** (cf. v. 19). This profaning was like a menstrual discharge that rendered a woman ceremonially unclean and defiled everything she touched (cf. Lev. 15:19-23). How did the people defile the land? By bloodshed and idolatry (cf. Ezek. 33:25). As a result God removed them from the defiled land. Yet even when **scattered** among other **nations,** they **profaned** God's **holy name.**

36:22-23. Other nations viewed the **sovereign** God through the actions **of Israel,** thus besmirching His holy name. Therefore God said He would restore **Israel . . . not for** her **sake . . . but for the sake of** His **holy name.** Israel had no intrinsic value which prompted God to act on her behalf. He would restore the nation because His character was at stake. He would **show the holiness of** His **great name** (cf. 20:41; 28:22, 25; 38:16; 39:27). God had shown His justice when He punished Israel for her sin; He will show His grace and faithfulness when He restores her and renews His covenant promises.

36:24-32. The means God will use to show His holiness are explained in these verses. He will first restore the nation physically: He **will gather** her **from all the countries and bring** her **back into** her **own land** (v. 24). Headlining God's future program will be the restored nation of Israel.

However, Israel's restoration will be more than physical. God promised, **I will sprinkle clean water on you and you will be clean; I will cleanse you from all your impurities and from all your idols.** This did not refer to water baptism. In Old Testament times sprinkling or washing with water pictured cleansing from ceremonial defilement (cf. Lev. 15:21-22; Num. 19:17-19). Since Israel's sin was like the ceremonial impurity of menstruation (Ezek. 36:17) her cleansing was now compared to the ceremonial act of purification. The point is that God will purify Israel from her sins. This cleansing will be followed by the impartation of new life. God will give the converted nation **a new heart and . . . a new spirit.** In place of a **heart of stone** He will **give** Israel **a heart of flesh** (cf. 11:19). With God's **Spirit** indwelling them (cf. 37:14), they will be motivated to obey His **decrees** and **laws** (cf. 37:24). God's restoration will not simply be an undoing of Israel's sin to bring her to a state of neutrality. Rather it will involve the positive implanting of a new nature in Israel's people that will make them righteous. Jeremiah called this work of God the "New Covenant" (cf. comments on Jer. 31:31-33).

Implanting God's Spirit in believing Israelites will produce a new relationship between Israel and her God: **You will be My people, and I will be your God** (cf. Ezek. 11:20; 14:11; 37:23, 27). God will extend all His graciousness to His people. Being delivered from their sin, they will experience the bountiful provision of the land including **grain . . . fruit,** and **crops** (cf. 34:27) without **famine** (cf. 34:29).

When Israel reflects on God's grace and her former character (her **evil ways and wicked deeds**), she will realize she does not deserve His favor. In fact she **will loathe** herself because of her **detestable practices,** looking back in horror at them. The blackness of her past actions will contrast starkly with the light of God's grace. In the future, when Israel recalls her past actions, she will recognize that God had **not** saved her because of her merit. God will be **doing this** not **for** her **sake,** but to magnify His own name.

36:33-36. When Israel is restored and the **land . . . cultivated,** people will note that this wasteland will be **like the Garden of Eden.** Israel's **cities,** formerly **in ruins,** will be **fortified and inhabited.** To the surrounding nations Israel will become an object lesson of God's grace. They will be forced to acknowledge God's sovereign power in restoring His people: **they will know that I the LORD have rebuilt what was destroyed.**

36:37-38. God will also cause the nation to increase numerically. This was considered a sign of God's blessing (cf. Gen. 12:2; 15:1-6; 1 Sam. 1:5-6; 2:1-11; Zech. 8:4-5). Ezekiel, a priest, compared the swelling population of Israel to the **numerous . . . flocks** of sacrificial animals gathered for the **feasts in Jerusalem.** As tightly packed herds jostle for space because of their vast numbers, so Israel's **ruined cities,** then empty and desolate, will **be filled with flocks of people.**

5. THE NATION RESTORED (CHAP. 37)

Chapter 37 vividly illustrates the promise of chapter 36. God had just announced that Israel will be restored to her land in blessing under the leadership of David her king. However, this seemed remote in light of Israel's present condition. She was "dead" as a nation—deprived of her land, her king, and her temple. She had been divided and dispersed for so long that unification and restoration seemed impossible. So God gave two signs (37:1-14 and vv. 15-28) to Ezekiel to illustrate the fact of restoration and confirm the promises just made.

a. The vision of the dry bones revived (37:1-14)

Most Israelites may have doubted God's promise of restoration. Their present condition militated against the possibility of that being fulfilled. So God stressed the fact of His sovereign power and ability to carry out these remarkable promises. Their fulfillment depended on Him, not on circumstances. Ezekiel reported the vision (vv. 1-10) and then interpreted it (vv. 11-14).

37:1-10. God transported Ezekiel **by the Spirit** (cf. 3:14; 8:3; 11:1, 24; 43:5) to a **valley . . . full of bones.** There he noticed that the **bones . . . were very dry,** bleached and baked under the hot sun.

God asked the prophet a remarkable question: **Son of man, can these bones live?** Was there potential for life in these lifeless frames? Ezekiel knew that humanly speaking it was impossible, so his answer was somewhat guarded. **O Sovereign LORD, You alone know.** Only God can accomplish such a feat.

God then directed Ezekiel to **prophesy to these bones.** The content of his message was God's promised restoration: **I will make breath enter you, and you will come to life.** "Breath" (*rûaḥ*) could also be translated "wind" or "spirit." In 37:14 the same word is translated "Spirit." Possibly God had in mind Genesis 2:7. In creating man, He transformed Adam into a living being by breathing into his nostrils "the breath of life." Whether God was referring to wind, physical breath, the principle of life, or the Holy Spirit is uncertain. However, the results were obvious. God gave life to these dead bones. As Ezekiel was giving this prophecy, he saw a remarkable thing. **The bones came together** (Ezek. 37:7), **flesh** developed, **skin covered them** (v. 8), **breath entered them,** and they **stood up** (v. 10).

37:11-14. To what did this vision refer? God said it was about the nation of Israel (**the whole house of Israel**) that was then in captivity. Like unburied skeletons, the people were pining away and saw no end to their judgment: **Our hope is gone; we are cut off.** The surviving Israelites felt their national hopes had been dashed. Israel had "died" in the flames of Babylon's attack, and had no hope of resurrection.

The reviving of the dry bones signified Israel's national restoration. The vision showed that Israel's new life depended on God's power, not outward circumstances: **I will open your graves . . . I will bring you back to the land of Israel.** Also when God restores Israel nationally, He will renew them spiritually. He **will put** His **Spirit** in Israel. The breath of life the corpses received symbolized the Holy Spirit, promised in Israel's New Covenant (cf. 36:24-28).

The Israelites residing in Palestine today are not the fulfillment of this prophecy. But it will be fulfilled when God regathers believing Israelites to the land (Jer. 31:33; 33:14-16), when Christ returns to establish His kingdom (cf. Matt. 24:30-31).

b. The sign of the two sticks united (37:15-28)

Ezekiel's second sign in this chapter visualized God's restoration of the nation. First the sign was given (vv. 15-17), then explained (vv. 18-28).

37:15-17. Ezekiel was told to **take** two sticks **of wood** and to **write on** one of them the name of **Judah** and on the other the names of Ephraim and **Joseph**. Ezekiel was then to hold **them together** like **one stick.**

Some have claimed that the two sticks represent the Bible (the stick of Judah) and the Book of Mormon (the stick of Joseph). However, this assertion ignores the clear interpretation in verses 18-28 and seeks to impose a foreign meaning on the sticks.

After Solomon died the nation of Israel split asunder, in 931 B.C. The Southern Kingdom was known as Judah because Judah was its larger tribe and because the country was ruled by a king from that tribe (cf. 1 Kings 12:22-24). The Northern Kingdom was called Israel, or sometimes Ephraim (e.g., Hosea 5:3, 5, 11-14) either because Ephraim was the strongest and most influential tribe or because the first king of Israel, Jeroboam I, was an Ephraimite (1 Kings 11:26). Israel was taken into captivity by Assyria in 722 B.C., and Judah was taken into exile by Babylon in 605, 597, and 586 B.C.

37:18-28. The uniting of **the sticks** pictured God's restoring *and* reuniting His people in the **land** as a single nation (cf. Hosea 1:11). Cleansed from their **backsliding . . . they will be My people,** God said, **and I will be their God** (cf. Ezek. 11:20; 14:11; 36:28; 37:27).

When united, **Israel** will be led by King **David** himself (see comments on 34:23-24). As God's **servant,** he will be their **one shepherd.**

Then God repeated the blessings to be bestowed on the people **in the land.** They will have an eternal inheritance there and **David . . . will be their prince.** God's **covenant of peace** (cf. 36:15; Isa. 54:10) will be established **with them,** and His presence will remain with them **forever** (in contrast with the departing of His glory, Ezek. 9–11). The visible reminder of God's presence will be His **sanctuary,** His **dwelling place.** Then again God added, **I will be their God, and they will be My people** (cf. 11:20; 14:11; 36:28; 37:23). These promises anticipate the detailed plans for God's new sanctuary (chaps. 40–43). This literal structure will serve as a visual object lesson to Israel and **the nations** of God's presence in the midst of His people.

6. THE ATTACK BY GOG REPULSED (CHAPS. 38–39)

Israel has been trampled underfoot by her enemies, but God will intervene in the future to insure her safety. He will defend His people and judge her enemies in distant countries (judgment on the nearby countries had already been cited, chaps. 25–32).

Some of the countries mentioned in Ezekiel 38 and 39 had already been identified as trading partners with Tyre. See the map "The World of Jeremiah and Ezekiel" in the *Introduction* to Jeremiah for the location of the places mentioned in Ezekiel 38:2-6.

Besides those place names another possible name must be considered. The NIV translates the word rō'š in 38:2 as "chief." However, other translations have taken the word as a proper noun and translated it "Rosh." Should the Hebrew word, which means "head," be taken as an adjective ("head prince," i.e., "chief prince") or as a proper noun ("Rosh")? The evidence seems to favor taking it as an adjective. "Rosh" never appears as a nation in any other biblical list of place names while all the other names are well attested (cf. Gen. 10:1-7; 1 Chron. 1:5-7; Ezek. 27:13-24; 32:26). One possible exception might be Isaiah 66:19 (NASB) but this is doubtful (see NIV).

Should these names be connected with the Soviet Union? One must first identify the areas against which Ezekiel prophesied and then determine the countries that occupy those land areas today. Ezekiel's rō'š does not point to "Russia" merely because the words sound similar. Neither should one identify "Meshech" with "Moscow" or "Tubal" with "Tobolsk." Ezekiel had historical places in mind (not modern-day names) and these areas must be located in Ezekiel's time. However, while one must avoid dogmatic assertions, three reasons suggest including the Soviet Union within Ezekiel's prophecy: (1) Some of the countries named by Ezekiel were located in what is now Russia. (2) The armies are said to come "from the far north" (Ezek. 38:6, 15; 39:2). This probably includes the land bridge between the Black and Caspian Seas, now part of the Soviet Union. (3) Ezekiel spoke of a coalition of several nations, many of whom are today aligned with or under the influence of the Soviet Union. These include Iran ("Persia"), Sudan and northern Ethiopia ("Cush"), Libya ("Put"), and Turkey ("Meshech," "Tubal," "Gomer," and "Beth Togarmah"). All these nations (see 38:2-3, 5-6), possibly led by the Soviet Union, will unite to attack Israel.

When will this prophecy be fulfilled? No past historical events match this prophecy, so it still awaits a future fulfillment. Some think this attack on Israel should be identified with the attack of Gog and Magog at the end of Christ's millennial reign (Rev. 20:7-9), but this identification has several flaws: (1) The results of Ezekiel's battle do not coincide with the events that follow the battle in Revelation 20. Why bury the dead for seven months after the battle (Ezek. 39:12-13) when the next prophetic event is the resurrection of the unsaved dead? (Rev. 20:11-13) Why would the people remain on earth after the battle to burn the weapons of war for seven years (Ezek. 39:9-10) instead of entering immediately into eternity? (Rev. 21:1-4) The events after each battle are so different that two separate battles must be assumed (see comments on Rev. 20:7-9). (2) The effect on the people is different. In Ezekiel the battle is the catalyst God will use to draw Israel to Himself (cf. Ezek. 39:7, 22-29) and to end her captivity. But the battle in Revelation 20 will occur after Israel has been faithful to her God and has enjoyed His blessings for 1,000 years.

If the battle of Ezekiel 38–39 is not at the end of the Millennium, could it be at the beginning of the Millennium? This also seems extremely doubtful. Everyone who enters the Millennium will be a believer (John 3:3), and will have demonstrated his faith by protecting God's Chosen People (cf. comments on Matt. 25:31-46). At the beginning of the Millennium all weapons of war will be destroyed (Micah 4:1-4). Thus it seems difficult to see a war occurring when the unsaved warriors have been eliminated and their weapons destroyed.

It seems best to place Ezekiel's battle of Gog and Magog in the Tribulation period. Other internal markers indicate that it should be placed in the first three and one-half years of the seven-year period. The attack will come when Israel is at peace (Ezek. 38:8, 11). When Israel's covenant with the Antichrist is in effect at the beginning of Daniel's 70th Week (Dan. 9:27a), she will be at peace. But after the covenant is broken at the middle of the seven-year period, the nation will suffer tremendous persecution (Dan. 9:27b; Matt. 24:15-22). This will provide the time needed to bury the dead (Ezek. 39:12-13) and to burn the weapons of war (39:9-10). So the battle described by Ezekiel may take place sometime during the first three and one-half years of the seven-year period before Christ's second coming. Possibly the battle will occur just before the midpoint of the seven-year period (see the "Outline of End-Time Events Predicted in the Bible," between Ezek. and Dan., point I.D.).

Ezekiel was describing a battle that will involve Israel's remotest neighbors. They will sense their opportunity to attack when Israel feels secure under the false protection of her covenant with the Antichrist sometime at the beginning of the seven-year period. The nations involved in the attack will include the Soviet Union, Turkey, Iran, Sudan, Ethiopia, and Libya. Ezekiel first pictured the invasion by Gog and his allies (38:1-16), and then described the judgment of Gog and his allies (38:17–39:29).

a. The invasion by Gog (38:1-16)

38:1-6. On the identification of the proper names in these verses see the preceding paragraphs under "6. The Attack by Gog Repulsed (chaps. 38–39)." Gog's attack on Israel will actually be orchestrated by God. The LORD said, **I will turn you around, put hooks in your jaws, and bring you out with your whole army— your horses . . . horsemen . . . a great horde with . . . shields** and **swords.** On whether the horses and weapons are literal, see the comments on 39:9. God will use **Gog** and all his allies as pawns in His larger plans for Israel. Yet the idea for attacking Israel also will originate with

Gog. Gog will act freely to accomplish his own evil goals. He "will devise an evil scheme," 38:10.

38:7-9. This attack will be against Israel, whose people will be gathered from many nations and will be living in safety. Gog and his allies will go against Israel in massive strength, advancing like a storm and a cloud (cf. v. 16).

38:10-13. Gog's purpose in the attack will be to plunder and loot unwalled and unsuspecting Israel, which will be rich in livestock and goods, living at the center of the land. Israel's importance geographically, politically, and economically will be noticed. She will be a strategic target for any power wanting to control commerce between Asia and Africa.

38:14-16. Gog's attack against Israel will come from all sides. Gog will come from the far north. With him will come his allies from the east (Persia = Iran), the south (Cush = Sudan, southern Egypt, and northern Ethiopia), and the west (Put = Libya). They will advance against ... Israel like a cloud (cf. v. 9) that covers the land. This awesome army will overrun all obstacles as effortlessly as a cloud sailing across the sky.

This attack will be another means of God's displaying to the nations His holy character and sovereign power. In going against Israel, the nations will come to know God for He will show Himself holy (cf. 20:41; 28:22, 25; 36:23; 39:27). As a result of the unsuccessful attack Israel will be delivered and God glorified.

b. The judgment of Gog (38:17–39:29)

(1) The defeat of Gog (38:17–39:8). **38:17-23.** Gog's attack will be crushed by God Himself. God asked Gog, **Are you not the one I spoke of in former days by My servants the prophets of Israel?** This has caused some confusion among interpreters because no direct reference to Gog is made by any of the previous writing prophets. Perhaps this means earlier prophets had predicted the coming of invading armies against Israel in the last days, which Ezekiel now associated specifically with Gog (cf. Joel 3:9-14; Zeph. 3:15-20).

When the armies reach Israel, God's anger will be aroused against them. He will cause a massive earthquake in ... Israel that will interrupt Gog's invasion plans and spread fear and confusion throughout the ranks of the invading forces.

In the pandemonium, communication between the four invading armies will break down and they will begin attacking each other. Every man's sword will be against his brother (Ezek. 38:21). Fear and panic will sweep through the forces so each army will shoot indiscriminately at the others.

The slaughter of the armies will be aided by additional "natural" catastrophes, including torrents of rain, hailstones, and burning sulphur (v. 22). The rain will combine with dirt and debris from the earthquake to produce massive mud slides and floods. Large hailstones will pelt the survivors, killing many (cf. Josh. 10:11). The "burning sulphur" might be volcanic ash.

39:1-8. The invading armies will be totally destroyed by God. Having brought them against the mountains of Israel (v. 2; cf. 38:8), God will weaken them (39:3) and strike them down on the mountains of Israel. This once-mighty army will then be food for birds and ... wild animals.

God will also punish the homelands of the invaders: I will send fire on Magog and on those who live in safety in the coastlands. Sending fire implies destruction and military devastation (30:8, 14, 16; cf. Hosea 8:14; Amos 1:4, 7, 10, 14; 2:2, 5). The nation that will spawn the invasion will herself be destroyed. The "coastlands," already mentioned several times by Ezekiel (cf. Ezek. 26:15, 18; 27:3, 6-7, 15, 35), imply the farthest reaches of the known world. Through all this God will teach Israel that He is holy and is not to be profaned by their sins (cf. 36:22). Also the nations will see that He is the Holy One in Israel.

(2) The aftermath of the battle (39:9-20). **39:9-11.** Those who will come to plunder Israel (38:12) will themselves be plundered. Israelites will use the fallen soldiers' weapons for fuel. . . . for seven years. Should the weapons of war—horses, swords, shields . . . bows . . . arrows . . . clubs . . . and spears (38:4-5; 39:9)—be understood literally or do they refer figuratively to modern-day weaponry? The text itself can allow for both interpretations, but the normal meaning of the words would lead one to see Ezekiel referring to literal horses, etc. With the

other worldwide catastrophes evident during the first three and one-half years of Daniel's 70th Week (Matt. 24:6-8; Rev. 6), a reversion to more primitive methods of warfare might become possible.

Throughout the remainder of the Tribulation period and into the beginning of the Millennium, as Israel will be burning those weapons, she will not need to cut down trees. This will be an amazing reversal of Gog's fortunes. Israel will plunder those who plundered her and loot those who looted her.

After the battle Israel will also bury Gog's dead. The burials will take place in the valley of those who travel east toward the Sea. This translation is somewhat confusing as "toward" was supplied by the translators, and the "east" (qidmat) should be translated "on the east of" (cf. Gen. 2:14; 1 Sam. 13:5). The valley where Gog's army will be buried is "on the east side of" the Dead Sea (NIV marg.) in what is today Jordan. The phrase "those who travel east" (hā'ōḇ'rîm) could be taken as a proper name. It might refer to the "mountains of Abarim" (hā'ăḇārîm) east of the Dead Sea that Israel traversed on her way to the Promised Land (cf. Num. 33:48). If so, Gog's burial will be in the Valley of Abarim just across the Dead Sea from Israel proper in the land of Moab. Yet the burial will be in Israel because Israel controlled that area during some periods of her history (cf. 2 Sam. 8:2; Ps. 60:8).

The number of corpses will be so great that the way of travelers will be blocked. "The way of travelers" could again be translated "Abarim." The valley will be clogged with the bodies of soldiers. The name of the valley will be changed to the Valley of Hamon Gog, meaning "the Valley of the hordes of Gog."

39:12-16. The number of soldiers killed will be so great that for seven months the house of Israel will be burying them. Even after the initial cleanup, squads of men will be employed to search the land for additional remains. As they go through the land and one of them sees a human bone, he will set up a marker beside it. Then as gravediggers see the markers they will take the remains to the Valley of Hamon Gog for burial. The operation will be so vast that a town will be set up in the valley at the

gravesites to accommodate those cleansing the land. It will be named Hamonah —a form of the word "hordes."

39:17-20. Another result of Gog's defeat will be a feast for the wild animals. (These vv. expand v. 4 where God announced that the corpses of those who fall will be food for birds and beasts.) God will reverse the roles of animals and people. Usually people slaughtered and ate sacrificed animals. Here, however, the men of Gog's armies will be sacrifices; they will be eaten by animals. In addressing the birds and animals God said that at this great sacrifice they will eat flesh and drink blood . . . as if they were . . . fattened animals from Bashan. Bashan, east and northeast of the Sea of Kinnereth (later the Sea of Galilee) was known for its fertile land and fat cows (cf. Amos 4:1). At God's table the animals will eat their fill of horses and riders, mighty men and soldiers of every kind.

(3) The effects of the battle on Israel (39:21-29). **39:21-24.** Two results will come from the battle: (a) the nations will see God's glory (cf. comments on 1:28) and (b) Israel will turn back to her God (39:22; cf. v. 7). God's stunning defeat of Gog will force Israel to acknowledge His power.

39:25-29. The defeat of Gog will also hasten God's plans to restore the other Israelites from other nations. Verses 25-29 look ahead to the end of the Tribulation when God will restore the nation from her final dispersion. God will . . . bring Jacob back from captivity and will have compassion on all the people of Israel. God will show Himself holy through them (cf. 20:41; 28:22, 25; 36:23; 38:16), acknowledging them as His people. Also He will pour out His Spirit on the house of Israel (cf. 36:27; 37:14; Joel 2:28). The ultimate result of the battle with Gog will be Israel's national repentance and spiritual restoration. This will be fulfilled in the millennial kingdom.

B. New order for Israel (chaps. 40–48)

Chapters 33–39 dealt with the new life Israel will experience when she is gathered back into her land and restored to fellowship with God. The last nine chapters of the book explain how Israel's new order will be established. A new temple will be built as a sign of God's presence among His people (chaps.

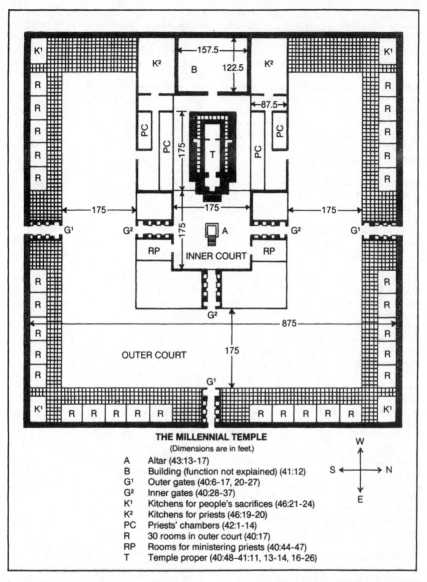

THE MILLENNIAL TEMPLE
(Dimensions are in feet.)

A	Altar (43:13-17)
B	Building (function not explained) (41:12)
G¹	Outer gates (40:6-17, 20-27)
G²	Inner gates (40:28-37)
K¹	Kitchens for people's sacrifices (46:21-24)
K²	Kitchens for priests (46:19-20)
PC	Priests' chambers (42:1-14)
R	30 rooms in outer court (40:17)
RP	Rooms for ministering priests (40:44-47)
T	Temple proper (40:48–41:11, 13-14, 16-26)

40–43), and a new service of worship will be established so the people will have access to their God (chaps. 44–46). Then a new division of the land will be made for the people (chaps. 47–48).

1. A NEW TEMPLE (CHAPS. 40–43)

God had promised to rebuild His sanctuary among His people (37:26-28); chapters 44–46 give the plans for the tem-

ple to be rebuilt. Three interpretations of chapters 40–43 are held by Bible students: (1) Ezekiel predicted a rebuilding of Solomon's temple after the Babylonian Captivity. (2) Ezekiel was prophesying about the church in a figurative sense; he did not have a literal temple in mind. (3) A still-future literal temple will be built during the millennial kingdom. The first view must be eliminated because it suggests that Ezekiel was mistaken when he wrote. No prophet speaking under God's authority ever uttered a false prediction (Deut. 18:21-22; cf. Matt. 5:17-18). Also the remnant that returned to Israel after the Exile did not follow Ezekiel's specifications. The second view must also be eliminated because it violates the normal meaning of Ezekiel's words. Those who hold this view are inconsistent for they interpret Ezekiel's earlier, now-fulfilled prophecies literally, yet interpret his yet-unfulfilled prophecies symbolically.

Why did Ezekiel take so much space to describe the millennial temple? Here are two reasons: (1) The sanctuary was the visible symbol of God's presence among His people. The prelude to Israel's judgment began when God's glory departed from Solomon's temple in Jerusalem (Ezek. 8–11). The climax to her restoration as a nation will come when God's glory reenters the new temple in Jerusalem (43:1-5). (2) The new temple will become the visible reminder of Israel's relationship to God through His New Covenant. Since God gave detailed instructions for building the tabernacle to accompany His inauguration of the Mosaic Covenant (cf. Ex. 25–40), it is not unusual that He would also supply detailed plans for His new center of worship, to accompany the implementation of the New Covenant. This temple will be the focal point for the visible manifestation of Israel's new relationship with her God.

a. Introduction (40:1-4)

40:1-4. The vision of the new temple came to Ezekiel **in the 25th year of . . . exile, at the beginning of the year, on the 10th of the month, in the 14th year after the fall of the city.** The date was sometime in 573 B.C. The phrase "the beginning of the year" poses some problems. The Israelite religious new year began in Nisan (April-May) and was established at the time of the Exodus (Ex. 12:1-2). However, in Israel's later history the seventh month, Tishri (October-November), became established as the first month of Israel's civil or regnal year. So the date would be either April 28, 573 B.C. or October 22, 573 B.C. The October date was also the Day of Atonement (cf. Lev. 23:27).

On that very day. . . . God . . . took Ezekiel back to Jerusalem in a vision (cf. Ezek. 8:1-3). Jerusalem was then vastly different from what it was before. Ezekiel was led on a "tour" of the future temple which he recorded in remarkable detail (see the sketch "The Millennial Temple," on the previous page). This tour was given by **a man,** probably an angel, **whose appearance was like bronze.**

b. The outer court (40:5-27)

40:5. The angelic being with Ezekiel had a **measuring rod . . . six long cubits, each of which was a cubit and a handbreadth.** A common cubit was about 18 inches long and a long cubit (probably the one used in Ezek.) was about 21 inches long. So the measuring rod was about 10½ feet in length. **The wall** surrounding the temple was 10½ feet (**one . . . rod) thick** and 10½ feet (**one rod) high.**

40:6-16. Ezekiel passed into the outer court through **the gate facing east.** This was one of three gates leading into the outer court. Since it faced east, it was the most important gate (cf. comments on 44:1-3). He described the gate in detail, with **its steps . . . threshold,** guards' **alcoves. . . . portico facing the temple. . . . with palm trees** (40:16) along **the projecting walls** (see the sketch "The Gate to the Millennial Temple").

40:17-19. Entering **the outer court,** Ezekiel **saw . . . a pavement . . . all around the court** with **30 rooms along the pavement.** These rooms were probably spaced in even numbers along the north, east, and south walls of the temple (see the sketch "The Millennial Temple"). The use of these rooms was not stated, but they may have been storage rooms or meeting rooms for the people when they celebrated their feasts (cf. Jer. 35:2). **The distance from the inside of the lower gateway** (i.e., the east gate) **to the outside of the inner court** (i.e., to the threshold of the gate leading to the inner court) **was 175 feet (100 cubits).**

40:20-27. Ezekiel was then led from the **east** gate of **the outer court** to the **north** gate (vv. 20-23) and to the **south** gate (vv. 24-27). The design and dimensions of both gates were identical to those of the gate facing **east.**

c. The inner court (40:28-47)

40:28-37. After measuring the outer court the angel measured **the inner court.**

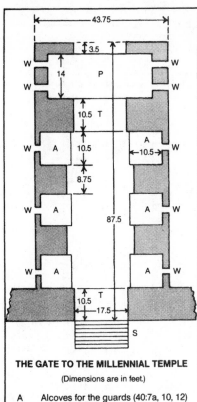

THE GATE TO THE MILLENNIAL TEMPLE

(Dimensions are in feet.)

A	Alcoves for the guards (40:7a, 10, 12)
P	Portico (40:8-9)
S	Steps (40:6a)
T	Thresholds (40:6b, 7b)
W	Windows (41:16)

He went from the south gate of the outer court **through the south gate** of the inner court. This gate **had the same measurements as the others**. The **south gate** (vv. 28-31), **east** gate (vv. 32-34), and **north gate** (vv. 35-37) of the inner court were identical and were also the same as the three gates of the outer court except that the porticos of the inner gates **faced the outer court**. The **portico** or vestibule was reversed on these gates (see the sketch "The Millennial Temple").

40:38-43. At the sides of **the inner** gates **tables** were set up for slaughtering the sacrifices. **Four tables** were **on one side of the** gate and four on the other—**eight tables in all**. The sacrifices prepared on these tables would then be offered on the altar in the inner court.

Many have objected to the thought of animal sacrifices being reinstituted during the Millennium. Since these sacrifices, it is argued, revert back to the Levitical sacrificial system, they would seem to be out of place in the Millennium. This has caused some to take the passage symbolically rather than literally. However, no difficulty exists if one understands the proper function of these sacrifices. First, animal sacrifices *never* took away human sin; only the sacrifice of Christ can do that (Heb. 10:1-4, 10). In Old Testament times Israelites were saved by grace through faith, and the sacrifices helped restore a believer's fellowship with God. Second, even after the church began, Jewish believers did not hesitate to take part in the temple worship (Acts 2:46; 3:1; 5:42) and even to offer sacrifices (Acts 21:26). They could do this because they viewed the sacrifices as memorials of Christ's death.

Levitical sacrifices were connected with Israel's worship of God. When the church supplanted Israel in God's program (cf. Rom. 11:11-24) a new economy or dispensation began. The Levitical sacrificial system, which looked forward to Christ, was replaced by the Lord's Supper, which looked back to His death and forward to His second coming (1 Cor. 11:24, 26).

At Christ's second coming Israel will again assume her place of prominence in God's kingdom program (cf. Rom. 11:25-27). The Lord's Supper will be eliminated, because Christ will have returned. It will be replaced by animal sacrifices, which will be memorials or object lessons of the supreme sacrifice made by the Lamb of God. The slaughtering of these animals will be vivid reminders of the Messiah's suffering and death.

The millennial sacrifices will differ from the Levitical sacrifices though there are some similarities (see comments on Ezek. 45:18-25). Other passages also refer to a sacrificial system in the Millennium (Isa. 56:7; 66:20-23; Jer. 33:18; Zech. 14:16-21; Mal. 3:3-4).

40:44-47. As Ezekiel entered **the inner court** he again noticed **two rooms, one at the side of the north gate and facing south and another at the side of the south gate facing north** (see rooms designated "RP" in the sketch "The Millennial Temple"). **The room on the north** side was the one **facing south** (i.e., its

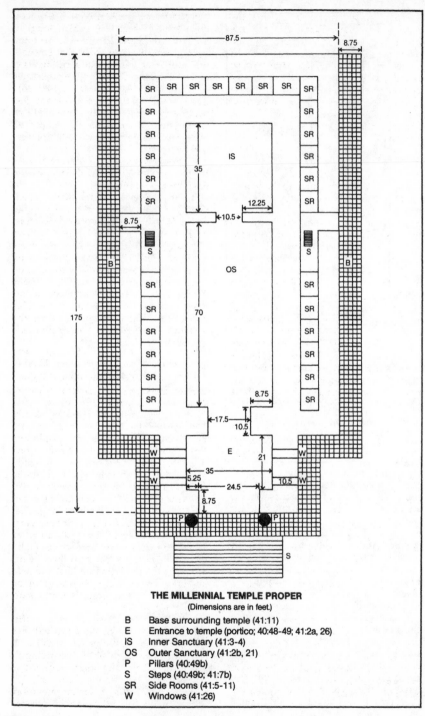

THE MILLENNIAL TEMPLE PROPER
(Dimensions are in feet.)

B	Base surrounding temple (41:11)
E	Entrance to temple (portico; 40:48-49; 41:2a, 26)
IS	Inner Sanctuary (41:3-4)
OS	Outer Sanctuary (41:2b, 21)
P	Pillars (40:49b)
S	Steps (40:49b; 41:7b)
SR	Side Rooms (41:5-11)
W	Windows (41:26)

entrance opened to the south into the inner court). This room was **for the priests in charge of the temple,** and the room on the south side was **for the priests** in charge of the altar. These rooms probably will serve as utility rooms and rest areas for the priests on duty. These priests will be descended from **Zadok** (cf. 43:19; 44:15; 48:11), the high priest in Solomon's day (1 Kings 1:26-27).

d. The temple building (40:48–41:26)

40:48–41:4. Standing in the inner court, Ezekiel's gaze shifted to the temple building itself (see the sketch "The Millennial Temple Proper"). He described the structure in great detail as he was led through it. Ezekiel went first **to the portico** or entrance to **the temple** (40:48-49). This was the porch-like vestibule on the front of the temple. **A flight of stairs** led up to **the portico** and **pillars** were **on each side of the jambs.**

Ezekiel climbed the stairs and entered through the vestibule into **the outer sanctuary** (41:1). As one enters the building each gate or doorway is narrower than the one before it. Possibly this reflects God's restricting man's access into His holy presence. Ezekiel entered the outer sanctuary but not **the most holy place,** the inner sanctuary. Instead the angel **went into the inner sanctuary** to measure it. As a priest (1:3), Ezekiel was allowed into the outer sanctuary, but was barred from the most holy place (cf. Lev. 16; Heb. 9:6-7).

41:5-11. Surrounding **the temple** were **three levels** of **side rooms . . . one above another, 30 on each level** (see the rooms "SR" in the sketch "The Millennial Temple Proper"). These rooms were probably storerooms for the temple equipment and storage chambers for the people's tithes and offerings (cf. Mal. 3:8-10). These rooms were similar to those in Solomon's temple (cf. 1 Kings 6:5-10).

41:12-26. Ezekiel then recorded the overall dimensions of **the temple** proper (vv. 12-15) and described its decorations and furnishings (vv. 16-26). Immediately west of the temple was a structure described as **the building facing the temple courtyard on the west side** (v. 12). The function of this building (designated "B" in the sketch "The Millennial Temple") is not explained. The temple was 87½ feet wide and 175 feet **(100 cubits) long.**

Carved cherubim and palm trees were etched into the **wood** that covered the interior of the temple **building.** The carved cherubim represent the guardians of God's dwelling place (cf. 1:4-28; 10). Possibly the palm trees represent the fruitfulness and blessing provided by God. These decorations are similar to those Solomon included in his temple (cf. 1 Kings 6:29).

The only piece of furniture in the temple proper Ezekiel described **was a wooden altar three cubits (5¼ feet) high and two cubits (3½ feet) square,** called **the table that is before the LORD** (Ezek. 41:22). Was this the altar of incense in the holy place (cf. Ex. 30:1-3; 1 Kings 7:48) or the table that held the bread of the Presence? (Ex. 25:23-30) The proportions of the piece are closer to those of the altar of incense (cf. Ex. 25:23; 30:1-2). **Double doors** led to **the outer sanctuary** of the temple and to **the most holy place.** The doors to the outer sanctuary had **cherubim and palm trees . . . carved** on them (cf. Ezek. 41:17-20).

e. The chambers in the inner court (42:1-14)

42:1-12. Leaving **the temple** proper, Ezekiel then described several adjacent structures for use by the priests (see rooms designated "PC" in the sketch "The Millennial Temple," near 40:1-4). This complex of rooms was connected with **the inner court,** with entrances from **the outer court.** There were two buildings on **the north side** with a common corridor 17½ feet **(10 cubits) wide** (v. 4). **The row of rooms . . . next to the outer court was** 87½ feet **(50 cubits) long.** The other **row** of rooms next to **the sanctuary** was twice as **long,** 175 feet **(100 cubits,** v. 8). These rooms were **three** stories high, with the rooms on the third level being **narrower** than those on the first and second floors (vv. 3-6). An identical group of **rooms** was on the temple's **south side** (vv. 10-12).

42:13-14. In those **rooms . . . the priests who approach the LORD will eat the most holy offerings** (cf. 46:20) and store their **garments** (44:19). According to the Mosaic Law the priests received a portion of some offerings (Lev. 2:3, 10; 6:16, 26-30; 7:7-10). A similar provision will be made for the millennial priests.

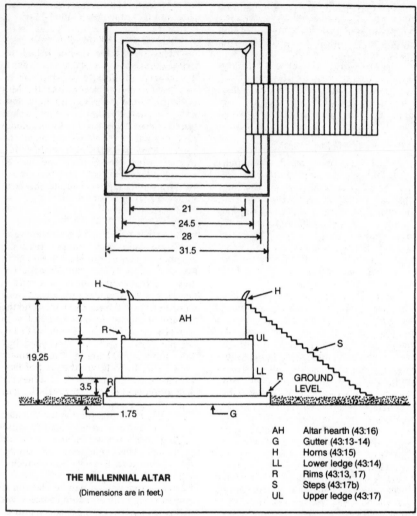

AH	Altar hearth (43:16)
G	Gutter (43:13-14)
H	Horns (43:15)
LL	Lower ledge (43:14)
R	Rims (43:13, 17)
S	Steps (43:17b)
UL	Upper ledge (43:17)

THE MILLENNIAL ALTAR

(Dimensions are in feet.)

f. The outer walls of the temple (42:15-20)

42:15-20. After the angel measured everything within **the temple** complex, **he led** Ezekiel outside to record the external dimensions of the temple. The complex was a square measuring 875 feet (**500 cubits**) on each side. The total area occupied by this temple area was 765,625 square feet—enough square feet for more than 13 football fields!

g. The return of the Lord's glory (43:1-12)

43:1-5. In a dramatic reversal of the departure of the Lord's glory (chaps. 10–11) Ezekiel saw **the glory of . . . God** returning **from the east** to dwell once again in His nation. **The glory of the LORD** (cf. comments on 1:28) **entered the temple through the gate facing east. Then the Spirit lifted** Ezekiel **up** (cf. 3:14; 8:3; 11:1, 24; 37:1) **and brought** him **into the inner court** in front of the temple proper, **and the glory of the LORD filled the temple.**

43:6-9. God said the new temple is to be **the place** of His **throne . . . the place. . . . where** He **will live among the Israelites forever** (v. 7; cf. v. 9). **The temple** will serve as God's earthly dwelling place among His people. God assured

Ezekiel that this home would be permanent. **Never again** would Israel **defile His holy name** (cf. 20:39; 39:7) by worshiping **lifeless idols**, bringing destruction on the nation (43:7-8).

43:10-12. The man (an angel, v. 6; cf. 40:3) standing next to Ezekiel told him to **describe the temple to the people of Israel, that they may be ashamed of their sins.** A clear vision of God's ideal **plan** would remind the people of the sins that had led to the destruction of the old temple. Another reason in sharing the **design** with the nation was to motivate the people to return to God and rebuild the temple: **so that they may be faithful to its design and follow all its regulations.** Though this prophecy was not fulfilled after the return from the Babylonian Captivity (and thus awaits a future fulfillment), the potentiality for fulfillment was there.

h. The altar of burnt offering (43:13-27)

When the millennial temple is established and God is enthroned in it, daily services will begin. Ezekiel was given a description of the altar (vv. 13-17) and regulations for consecrating it (vv. 18-27).

43:13-17. The height of **the altar** was 19¼ feet (11 **long cubits;** see the sketch "The Millennial Altar"), but part of this was below ground. The height of the altar above the ground (10 cubits) corresponds to the altar constructed by Solomon (2 Chron. 4:1). However, since Solomon used the shorter 18-inch cubit (2 Chron. 3:3), the total height of his altar was only 15 feet compared with an above-ground height of 17½ feet for the millennial altar. **The altar hearth,** 21 feet **square,** was reached by a flight of **steps** facing **east.**

43:18-27. A seven-day ritual will be employed by **the priests . . . of Zadok** (cf. 40:46) to set **the altar** apart to the **Lord.** This consecration service will be similar in some ways to the services followed by Moses (Ex. 40:10, 29) and Solomon (2 Chron. 7:8-9) to sanctify their houses of worship to God. After **seven days** of **offering** bulls, goats, and rams **the priests** will **present** the people's **burnt offerings and fellowship offerings on the altar.** This process will mark the full resumption of God's fellowship with His people, as then God **will accept** them. These sacrifices will point Israelites

to Christ who will have given them access to the Father (Heb. 10:19-25).

2. A NEW SERVICE OF WORSHIP (CHAPS. 44-46)

After the temple was described, its daily operation was explained to Ezekiel. A new way of life and worship will be practiced by the people during the Millennium. Yet in describing the holy standards in Israel's future worship, Ezekiel asked the people of his day to reevaluate their present practices. He explained the duties of the temple ministers (chap. 44), described the allocation of land for the temple priests (45:1-12), and then spoke of the offerings to be made to the Lord (45:13—46:24).

a. The temple ministers (chap. 44)

44:1-3. Ezekiel had been standing in the inner court of the temple, receiving instructions about the altar there (43:5). Now he was led out of the inner court to the **east** gate of **the outer** court, **and it was shut. This gate** at the outer court opened toward the Kidron Valley and the Mount of Olives. Ezekiel had just seen **the Lord** enter it on His return to His temple (43:4). God's presence had hallowed the gate. Therefore **it is to remain shut because the Lord, the God of Israel, has entered through it.** No one else will be allowed to tread through the gate which God Himself had entered.

Some have thought that the "Golden Gate" of Jerusalem, now sealed, is the gate spoken of here. However, the dimensions of the "Golden Gate" do not correspond with Ezekiel's gate, which is still future.

Only one person will be allowed to enter through the east gate complex: **the prince himself** (cf. 46:2). This "prince" has already been identified as King David (cf. 34:24; 37:24-25). He will be allowed **to eat in** the gate, possibly referring to the fellowship offerings which the worshipers will eat after offering them to the Lord (cf. Lev. 7:15-21). **The portico** (vestibule) faces the outer court (see the eastern G¹ in the sketch "The Millennial Temple," near Ezek. 40:1-4), so David, going east, will enter the gate complex from the outer court.

44:4-9. As Ezekiel went back into the inner court **by way of the north gate,** he **saw the glory of the Lord** (cf. comments on 1:28) **filling the temple of the Lord.**

Because of God's holiness Ezekiel told the nation, a **rebellious house** (cf. 2:5-6, 8; 3:9, 26-27; 12:3, 9, 25; 17:12; 24:3), that God said, **Enough of your detestable practices, O house of Israel!** God demanded holiness from His people, and a turning from the practice of allowing **un- circumcised** foreigners into the **temple** (44:9; cf. v. 7). The Jews who returned from the Babylonian Captivity stressed this prohibition (cf. Ezra 4:1-3; Neh. 13:1- 9; cf. Acts 21:27-32).

44:10-14. The duties of **the Levites** for the new **temple** were explained to Ezekiel. Because of their sinful practices before Israel's fall to Babylon, their posi- tion will be downgraded in the new tem- ple from ministers to servants. They will be allowed to **serve** as gatekeepers, slay- ers of the **sacrifices,** and to help the wor- shipers. However, they will not be al- lowed **to serve** the Lord **as priests or come near any of** His **holy things or . . . offerings.** The tasks of the Levites in Sol- omon's temple were more extensive (cf. 1 Chron. 15:16; 16:4; 23:28-31).

44:15-19. Then Ezekiel discussed the duties of **the priests . . . of Zadok.** The line of Zadok was one branch of the priestly line, a limited group of Levites. Zadok was appointed chief priest during Solomon's reign (and hence over the first temple) because he faithfully supported Solomon as king (cf. 1 Kings 1:32-35; 2:26-27, 35). Though the people had sinned, the priests in Zadok's line had remained faithful to God. So they will be restored to their position of honor. **They are . . . to offer sacrifices** (Ezek. 44:15) and **they alone are to enter** the **sanctuary** and **minister** there. These priests will serve as mediators between Israel and her God in much the same way as did the priests in Old Testament times.

Several Mosaic laws governing the priests were repeated by the Lord. The priestly vestments are to be made of **lin- en** (cf. Ex. 28:39-41). Linen is lighter than wool, which was not permitted because the priests **must not wear anything that makes them perspire.** Before the priests **go** among the **people** in **the outer court,** they will change from the vestments they wear in **ministering** before the Lord. This will help people distinguish between the holy and the common.

44:20-23. The priests **must not shave their heads or let their hair grow long.**

Completely shaving one's head or letting one's hair go unkempt were signs of mourning (cf. Lev. 10:6; 21:5, 10). The priests will be prohibited from drinking **wine** before ministering lest they become drunk and not perform their duties prop- erly (cf. Lev. 10:8-9). Also restrictions will be placed on whom they can **marry** (cf. Lev. 21:7, 13-15). These actions, designed to promote holiness, will help the **people** see **the difference between the holy and the common.**

44:24-27. The priests will **serve as judges,** and will follow God's regulations regarding the **feasts** and **Sabbaths.** Also the priests will avoid ritual defilement, by not **going near a dead person** (cf. Lev. 21:1-4). Even though death will be un- common during the Millennium (cf. Isa. 65:20), provision was made for those in- stances when it will occur. An exception was made for close family members, but the priest will have to **wait seven days** and then **offer a sin offering** before reen- tering the temple service.

44:28-31. To emphasize the priests' position as the Lord's ministers, God will not let them possess land in Israel out- side the allotment surrounding the tem- ple (cf. 45:4). The reason is that He will **be the only inheritance the priests have.** He **will be their possession.** God will take care of those who minister before Him (cf. Deut. 18:1-5), by having them live off the sacrifices the people will bring to the temple.

*b. The land of the temple priests
(45:1-12)*

Because Ezekiel had been speaking extensively about the priests and Levites (44:10-31), he then included their inheri- tance in the land (cf. 48:9-12). They will not have inheritances as will people in the other tribes (44:28). (The land for the priests is shown in the inset in the map "The Division of the Land during the Millennium" near 47:13-23.)

45:1-6. In the division of the land Israel is **to present to the Lord a portion of the land as a sacred district, 25,000 cubits** (about 8.3 miles) **long and 20,000 cubits** (about 6.6 miles) **wide.** Within this land **area** will be the temple complex Eze- kiel had just described (chaps. 40–43). This rectangle of land will be divided into two equal portions, each about 8.3 miles long and about 3.3 miles wide. The first portion, in which will be located **the sanctuary,** will be allotted to **the priests. . . . for their houses as well as a holy place for the sanctuary.** The second portion will be allotted **to the Levites, who serve in the temple, as their possession for towns to live in.** Instead of being scattered throughout Israel as they were earlier (Josh. 21:1-42) the priests and Levites will reside near their place of ministry.

The rectangle formed by the priests' and Levites' portions was converted into a square with the addition of land for the city of Jerusalem itself. **The city is to cover an area 5,000 cubits** (about 1.7 miles) **wide and 25,000 cubits** (about 8.3 miles) **long, adjoining the sacred portion.** This will then be subdivided into the city proper, grazing land, and farmland (cf. Ezek. 48:15-18).

45:7-8. This square of land, 8.3 miles in each of its four dimensions, will be located at the present site of Jerusalem. A band of land will extend from the city to the east and west. **The prince** (i.e., David; cf. comments on 34:24) **will have the land bordering each side of the area formed by the sacred district and the property of the city.** This strip of land will extend on the east to the Jordan River and on the west to the Mediterranean Sea.

45:9-12. Ezekiel used the reality of God's promised future blessings as a springboard to exhort the princes in his day to repentance. **You have gone far enough, O princes of Israel!** (cf. 44:6) **Give up your violence and oppression and do what is just and right.** Israel's civil leaders had callously disregarded the rights of those they were to protect (cf. 19:1-9; 22:25; 34:1-10). Their basic problem was greed. So Ezekiel exhorted them to **use accurate scales, an accurate ephah, and an accurate bath.** An **ephah** was a measure of dry capacity and a **bath** was a **measure** of liquid capacity. They were each equivalent to approximately five gallons (see "Biblical Weights and Measures" before the commentary on Gen.). Each of these was **a 10th of a homer.** A **homer** was approximately 50 gallons or about 6 bushels. The Hebrew word ḥōmer, possibly related to ḥămôr ("donkey"), suggests that this was a "donkey load."

Ezekiel also defined the measure of weight (in addition to the measures of capacity): **the shekel is to consist of 20 gerahs.** A "shekel" weighed just under 11½ grams or about 2/5 of an ounce. The "gerah" was Israel's smallest unit of weight; it took 20 gerahs to make one shekel (cf. Ex. 30:13; Lev. 27:25; Num. 3:47). Ezekiel stated that 60 **shekels** (20 + 25 + 15) **equal one mina.** Some have felt that this was a deviation from the usual standard of 50 shekels to a mina, as in Ugaritic texts. However, there is evidence that the standard, at least in Babylon, was 60 shekels to a mina. This would make the mina about 24 ounces or 1½ pounds.

Weights found from Old Testament times vary to some extent. Apparently people used weights of differing sizes to cheat others. Ezekiel was exhorting Israel's leaders to establish honest standards for all Israelites.

c. The offerings (45:13–46:24)

Having chastised the princes of Israel for using unjust weights, Ezekiel returned to discussing the Millennium, in which the future prince will use just weights to receive and offer gifts to God (45:13-17). This mention of offerings caused Ezekiel to describe briefly the future sacrificial system (45:18–46:24) before returning to the subject of the division of the land.

45:13-17. Ezekiel listed specific amounts of produce the people will give the prince (David; see comments on 34:24). **The prescribed portion** is to be proportionate to each individual's wealth or lack of it. They are each to give a 60th of their **wheat and . . . barley** (45:13), one percent of their olive **oil** (v. 14), and **1 sheep . . . from every . . . 200** of their flocks (v. 15). This tithe or tax will be required of **all the people** for use by **the prince in Israel.** As the people's representative, he will collect their gifts and use them to maintain the temple sacrifices, including **burnt offerings, grain offerings, and drink offerings at the festivals, the New Moons, and the Sabbaths.** (For a discussion on the use of sacrifices during the Millennium see the comments on 40:38-43.)

45:18-25. The festivals where the offerings will be given will include the New Year feast (vv. 18-20), the Passover/Unleavened Bread feast (vv. 21-24), and the seven-day Feast of Tabernacles (v. 25). The New Year's day celebration, on Nisan 1 (mid-April), will be to purify the sanctuary (v. 18). If someone sins unintentionally, a second purification will be offered on the seventh day of the month (v. 20). This offering and ceremonial cleansing possibly will replace the Day of Atonement (in the seventh month, Lev. 23:26-32).

This time of cleansing will be followed by the celebration of the Passover (Ezek. 45:21-24)/Unleavened Bread festival. The Passover will last seven days, during which the people will eat bread made without yeast. The prince will provide the sacrifices for that period (vv. 22-24). The fact that the prince is to make a sin offering for himself shows that he is not Christ.

The third feast will begin in the seventh month on the 15th day. This is the Festival of Tabernacles, also a seven-day celebration (Lev. 23:33-44), the last feast in Israel's yearly calendar.

Why did Ezekiel omit Israel's other national feasts, the Feast of Pentecost, the Feast of Trumpets, and the Day of Atonement? Two explanations may be given. First, he may have been signaling a change in God's program for Israel. The inauguration of the New Covenant and the fulfillment of Israel's kingdom promises may render those three feasts unnecessary. Thus only three of the six annual feasts under the Levitical system (cf. Lev. 23:4-44) will be followed: two feasts celebrating national cleansing (Passover and Unleavened Bread combined as one feast; see the chart "Calendrical Offerings," near Num. 28:1-8), which will point back to Christ's death, and the Feast of Tabernacles that will symbolize Israel's new position in God's millennial kingdom. Second, perhaps Ezekiel employed a figure of speech known as a merism to include all the feasts. By naming the first two feasts in Israel's festal calendar (Passover and Unleavened Bread) and the last one (Tabernacles), maybe he implied that all Israel's feasts would be reinstituted.

46:1-10. After speaking of selected feasts in Israel's religious year, Ezekiel provided information on the daily aspects of Israel's worship. He gave regulations for the Sabbath and New Moon sacrifices (vv. 1-10) and for the conduct and offerings of the people in the temple (vv. 11-15).

The east gate from the outer court to the inner court will be closed six days of the week, but on the Sabbath Day and on the day of the New Moon it is to be opened. The prince, David, will be allowed to stand at the gatepost of the east gate during these days as the sacrifice he brought on behalf of the people will be offered (cf. 44:3). He will also provide the sacrifices for the people on the Sabbaths and New Moons as well as on the major feast days.

The worshipers at the temple are given regulations to aid in their orderly assembly before the LORD. There is no entrance to the temple on the west, and the east gate will be permanently shut (cf. 44:1-2). Thus access into the temple will be from the north and the south. To avoid confusion the worshipers will be directed through the temple according to predesignated routes so that whoever enters by the north gate to worship is to go out the south gate; and whoever enters by the south gate is to go out the north gate. God is a God of order, and He wants orderliness to prevail in worship.

46:11-15. If the prince desires to make a freewill offering to the LORD . . . the gate facing east is to be opened for him. The regulation concerning the closing of the east gate to the inner court (cf. v. 1) will be suspended for this special offering. But after the prince leaves, the gate is to be closed again. Then Ezekiel mentioned the morning sacrifice, but not the evening sacrifice (cf. Ex. 29:38-41). This omission could be explained by the fact that he was giving only the highlights of the sacrificial system. So by listing the morning sacrifices he may have assumed that his readers would apply the same regulations to the evening sacrifice.

46:16-18. Another topic related to freewill gifts is the Year of Jubilee. Every 50 years property was to revert to its original owners (Lev. 25:10-13). Ezekiel posed two hypothetical cases based on the generosity of the prince to show that the Year of Jubilee will be in force during the Millennium. If the prince will give part of his estate to one of his sons, it will also belong to his descendants. Property given to a family member will not be returned in the Year of Jubilee.

However . . . a gift made to a servant will not be permanent; the servant may keep it until the year of freedom; then it will revert to the prince. Because the land will belong to God, He will apportion it to Israel as His stewards. This regulation assures that no one individual will gain permanent control of the land.

The prince will not be allowed to claim any land outside his allotted inheritance. In contrast with evil princes in Ezekiel's day (Ezek. 45:8-9), the prince during the Millennium will not oppress the people or take their property.

46:19-24. Ezekiel's angelic guide led him to the kitchens in the temple complex. He first described the priests' kitchens (vv. 19-20), then the kitchens for the people's sacrifices (vv. 21-24).

The kitchens for the priests are to be at the west end of the priests' chambers adjacent to the temple proper (see the sketch "The Millennial Temple," near 40:1-4). There the priests will cook the guilt offering and the sin offering . . . to avoid bringing them into the outer court. The priests will be allowed to eat a portion of the sacrifices brought to the temple.

The kitchens for the sacrifices of the people will be in the four corners of the outer court. When the people offer fellowship offerings to the Lord, they will be allowed to eat part of the sacrifice in a fellowship meal (cf. Lev. 7:15-18). Evidently at these four kitchens the priests will cook the people's sacrifices. This magnificent temple will be a place of fellowship as well as worship.

3. A NEW LAND (CHAPS. 47-48)

a. The river from the temple (47:1-12)

One feature in the Millennium will be a life-giving river flowing from the temple. Many think this refers *only* symbolically to the blessings that flow from God's presence. But nothing in the passage suggests that Ezekiel had anything in mind other than a literal river. The inclusion of details such as the fishermen (v. 10) and the salty swamps and marshes (v. 11) lend a touch of realism to the passage. These details become meaningless if the passage is only symbolic of spiritual blessing. Joel had mentioned this river before Ezekiel's time (cf. Joel 3:18), and Zechariah spoke of it after Israel returned from the Babylonian Captivi-

ty (cf. Zech. 14:8). In the Millennium this river will be another visible reminder of God's presence and blessing.

47:1-6a. Ezekiel was led from the kitchens in the temple's outer court back into the inner court to the entrance of the temple proper. There he saw water coming out from under the threshold of the temple toward the east. That stream of water, flowing out from God's presence, went eastward and passed south of the altar. Ezekiel left the temple complex by way of the north gate and saw the water . . . flowing out of the temple on the south side of the east gate into the Kidron Valley.

Zechariah recorded that the water flowing from Jerusalem will divide, with half flowing east toward the Dead Sea and half flowing west toward the Mediterranean (Zech. 14:8). Ezekiel followed only the branch that went toward east.

The angelic being led Ezekiel toward the east along the riverbank. After 1,750 feet (1000 cubits) the water . . . was ankle-deep; in another 1,750 feet the river was knee-deep. The angel measured another 1,750 feet and the water reached Ezekiel's waist. A fourth measurement of 1,750 feet farther to the east revealed that the water had risen and was deep enough to swim in—a river that no one could walk across. Perhaps this rise in depth will come from additional streams feeding into this river, though Ezekiel did not mention them.

47:6b-12. Ezekiel went back to the bank of the river and saw many trees on each side of the river. These waters will produce beautiful vegetation along their banks.

The millennial river will flow toward the eastern region and will go down into the Arabah, where it will enter the Sea. The "Arabah" is the Jordan Valley running south from the Sea of Galilee to the Dead Sea and ultimately to the Gulf of Aqabah. The millennial river will merge with the Jordan River at the northern mouth of the Dead Sea.

As this new river enters the Dead Sea, the water there will become fresh. The Dead Sea, now some six times saltier than the ocean, will become completely salt-free—truly a miracle of God! This now-lifeless body of water will then support life so that where the river flows

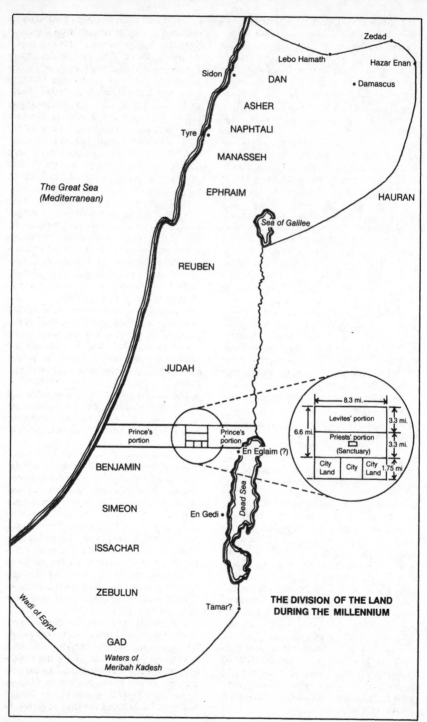

THE DIVISION OF THE LAND
DURING THE MILLENNIUM

everything will live. Fishermen will crowd the shores from En Gedi to En Eglaim (see the map "The Division of the Land during the Millennium") to catch many kinds of fish there. "En Gedi" is a settlement about midway down the western shore of the Dead Sea. The location of "En Eglaim" (lit., "Spring of the Two Calves") is uncertain. Suggested locations have included the southwestern shore of the Dead Sea near Zoar and an area on the northwestern shore south of Khirbet Qumran. Because of Ezekiel's focus on the water entering the Dead Sea at the northern end, the site near Qumran seems a possibility.

While the Dead Sea itself will be made fresh, the swamps and marshes will not become fresh; they will be left for salt. The lowlands near the Dead Sea will remain salt-crusted. Salt is essential to life, and the Dead Sea area is Israel's chief source of salt. God will provide for all of Israel's needs.

Another way God will provide for Israel is by the trees on the riverbanks that will bear fruit year-round. The fruit will provide food and their leaves will provide healing. How healing will come from the leaves is not clear, but sickness will be virtually eliminated. God will use these trees to meet people's physical needs.

b. *The boundaries of the land (47:13-23)*

47:13-14. God promised Abraham (cf. Gen. 13:14-17; 15:17-21) and his descendants the land of Palestine, and that promise has never been rescinded. Israel's experiencing blessing in the land was conditioned on her obedience (Deut. 28), but her right to possess the land has never been revoked. When God inaugurates His New Covenant with Israel in the future, she will be restored to her place of blessing in the land (cf. Ezek. 36-37). To prepare the people for this new occupation, God defined the boundaries of the country. He said, Because I swore with uplifted hand (a gesture that often accompanied oath-taking; cf. Ex. 6:8; Neh. 9:15; Ps. 106:26; Ezek. 20:5, 15, 23, 42; 36:7; 44:12) to give it to your forefathers, this land will become your inheritance. Israel's borders during the Millennium will be similar to those promised her during the time of Moses (cf. Num. 34:1-12).

47:15-17. The northern boundary of the land . . . will run east from the Great Sea, the Mediterranean, starting somewhere north of Tyre and Sidon (more precisely, "Mount Hor," Num. 34:7). The boundary line will go by the Hethlon road past Lebo Hamath to Zedad, Berothah, and Sibraim . . . as far as Hazer Hatticon . . . on the border of Hauran. The location of Hethlon is unknown, but many associate it with the modern town of Heitela, northeast of Tripoli in modern Lebanon. Lebo Hamath has sometimes been identified with the city of Hamath on the Orontes River in modern Syria. The word "Lebo" is then taken to mean "by the way of" rather than as a proper name. However, this identification is problematic because Hamath is about 100 miles farther north than the other cities mentioned by Ezekiel. It is better to take "Lebo" as a proper name and to identify Lebo Hamath with the modern town of Al-Labwah in the Biqa Valley.

Zedad should probably be identified with the town of Sadad about 25 miles north of Damascus. The locations of the towns of Berothah and Sibraim are not known, but are said to lie on the border between Damascus and Hamath. Hamath (not the same as Lebo Hamath) is north of Damascus. So these cities are north of Damascus on the border between the territories held by Damascus and Hamath, probably near the town of Zedad.

Hazer Hatticon (Ezek. 47:16) is probably another name for Hazer Enan (v. 17). It is located on the border between Syrian Damascus and the province of Hauran. Hauran may possibly be identified with a district east of the Sea of Galilee north of the Yarmuk River. Some say Hazer Enan is modern-day Al-Qaryatayn, an important desert oasis northeast of Damascus. So the northern border will stretch east from the Mediterranean Sea north of the modern city of Tripoli and will include what was then the northern border of Syria.

47:18. The eastern border will extend between Hauran and Damascus. The edge of Israel's territory will arch back from Hazar Enan along the southern border of Syria till it reaches the Jordan River south of the Sea of Galilee. From there it will go along the Jordan between Gilead and the land of Israel, to the eastern sea and as far as Tamar. The eastern border will be the Jordan River and the Dead Sea. Gilead and the Transjordan area to the east of the Jordan will not be included in Israel's future inheritance. The exact location of Tamar, to which the eastern boundary will continue, is uncertain, but it may be south of the Dead Sea.

47:19. The southern border of Israel's millennial kingdom will extend from Tamar as far as the waters of Meribah Kadesh, then along the Wadi of Egypt to the Great Sea. Since "the waters of Meribah Kadesh" were at Kadesh Barnea (cf. Num. 27:14), the southern border will stretch southwestward from Tamar to Kadesh Barnea. From there it will go to the "Wadi of Egypt." This is probably the Wadi el-Arish (cf. Num. 34:5), not the Nile River. The words "of Egypt," not in the Hebrew, are supplied as an explanatory addition.

47:20. The western border of the Promised Land will be the Great Sea, the Mediterranean. The border will go along the shoreline from the Wadi el-Arish in the south to a point opposite Lebo Hamath in the north.

47:21-23. The land will be distributed according to the tribes of Israel. This is the prelude to the division of the land (chap. 48). Ezekiel also included regulations for allotting land to resident aliens who will want to associate with Israel. Being considered native-born Israelites . . . they are to be allotted an inheritance among the tribes of Israel. Though foreigners had always been allowed to live in Israel (cf. Lev. 24:22; Num. 15:29), in the Millennium they will be allowed to enjoy other privileges previously granted only to Israelites (cf. Isa. 56:3-8). Though the Millennial Age will be a time of blessing for believing Israel, believing Gentiles will also enjoy God's blessing.

c. The division of the land (48:1-29)

48:1-7. In dividing the millennial land among the people, God will give seven tribes portions in the northern part of the land. Proceeding from the north these tribes will be Dan (v. 1), Asher (v. 2), Naphtali (v. 3), Manasseh (v. 4), Ephraim (v. 5), Reuben (v. 6), and Judah (v. 7).

48:8-22. The central band of land was allotted to the prince (David, v. 21;

cf. 34:24), the priests, and the Levites (see comments on 45:1-8). That central portion will also include the city of Jerusalem and its suburbs. The city will be laid out as a square 7,875 feet (4,500 cubits) on each side and will cover approximately 2.2 square miles (48:16). Jerusalem will be surrounded by a band of land 437½ feet (250 cubits) wide, which will serve as pastureland for flocks and herds belonging to people living in the city (v. 17). On either side of the city proper will be two portions of land 3.3 miles (10,000 cubits) long (v. 18) and 1.65 miles (5,000 cubits) wide (cf. v. 15). This farmland will be cultivated to supply food for the workers of the city.

48:23-29. The lower part of the land will be allotted to the five remaining tribes. Proceeding southward these will be Benjamin (v. 23), Simeon (v. 24), Issachar (v. 25), Zebulun (v. 26), and Gad (v. 27). The locations of all 12 tribes will differ from their locations during Joshua's time to the captivities (Josh. 13-19).

d. The gates of the city (48:30-35)

In describing the gates of the new city of Jerusalem, Ezekiel brought the city "full circle" from what it was at the beginning of his book. The city doomed for destruction will be restored to glory.

48:30-31. The new city of Jerusalem will have 12 gates, 3 on each side. Why these gates are grouped as they are is obscure. The three gates on the north side (closest to the sanctuary) will be named for Reuben . . . Judah, and Levi. Perhaps these three were listed first because of their preeminent positions among the tribes. Reuben was the firstborn of Jacob's 12 sons, Judah was the royal tribe, and Levi was the tribe of the priesthood. Also all three were children of Jacob's first wife Leah (cf. Gen. 29:31-35).

48:32. On the east side of Jerusalem the gates will be named for Joseph . . . Benjamin, and Dan. Because Levi was given a gate (v. 31) the tribes of Ephraim and Manasseh were combined as the one tribe of Joseph (cf. Gen. 48:1). Joseph and Benjamin were both sons of Rachel (Gen. 30:22-24; 35:16-18), and Dan was the first son of Rachel's servant Bilhah, who became Jacob's concubine (Gen. 30:4-6).

48:33. The gates on the south were named after Simeon . . . Issachar, and

Zebulun. These three were also born to Leah (Gen. 29:33; 30:17-20). Since each of these tribes was relocated in the southern portion of the land (cf. 48:24-26), the **gates** faced their inheritances.

48:34. The gates **on the west side** were named for **Gad . . . Asher,** and **Naphtali.** These three tribes descended from sons of Jacob's concubines. Gad and Asher were born to Zilpah (Gen. 30:9-13), and Naphtali was born to Bilhah (Gen. 30:7-8).

48:35. The most remarkable aspect of **the** new **city** of Jerusalem will be the presence of the Lord. God's glory had departed from the city as a prelude to its judgment (cf. chaps. 10–11), and His return will signal Jerusalem's blessing. This fact so impressed Ezekiel that he wrote that the city will be given a new name: THE LORD IS THERE. As the Prophet Ezekiel had stated repeatedly, God will return to dwell with His people. No longer worshiping lifeless idols and engaged in detestable practices, Israel will enjoy the Lord's holy presence in the Millennium.

BIBLIOGRAPHY

Alexander, Ralph. *Ezekiel.* Everyman's Bible Commentary. Chicago: Moody Press, 1976.

Cooke, G.A. *A Critical and Exegetical Commentary on the Book of Ezekiel.* The International Critical Commentary. Edinburgh: T. & T. Clark, 1936.

Craigie, Peter C. *Ezekiel.* The Daily Study Bible (Old Testament). Philadelphia: Westminster Press, 1983.

Eichrodt, Walther. *Ezekiel.* The Old Testament Library. Philadelphia: Westminster Press, 1970.

Feinberg, Charles Lee. *The Prophecy of Ezekiel.* Chicago: Moody Press, 1969.

Fisch, S. *Ezekiel.* London: Soncino Press, 1950.

Greenberg, Moshe. *Ezekiel 1–20.* The Anchor Bible. Garden City, N.Y.: Doubleday & Co., 1983.

Hengstenberg, E.W. *The Prophecies of the Prophet Ezekiel Elucidated.* Translated by A.C. Murphy and J.G. Murphy. Edinburgh: T. & T. Clark, 1869. Reprint. Minneapolis: James Publications, 1976.

Keil, C.F. "Ezekiel." In *Commentary on the Old Testament in Ten Volumes.* Vol. 9. Reprint (25 vols. in 10). Grand Rapids: Wm. B. Eerdmans Publishing Co., 1982.

Tatford, Frederick A. *Dead Bones Live: An Exposition of the Prophecy of Ezekiel.* Eastbourne, East Sussex: Prophetic Witness Publishing House, 1977.

Taylor, John B. *Ezekiel: An Introduction and Commentary.* The Tyndale Old Testament Commentaries. Downers Grove, Ill.: InterVarsity Press, 1969.

Wevers, John W. *Ezekiel.* The New Century Bible Commentary. Grand Rapids: Wm. B. Eerdmans Publishing Co., 1969.

Zimmerli, Walther. *Ezekiel 1.* Translated by Ronald E. Clements. Philadelphia: Fortress Press, 1979.

_____. *Ezekiel 2.* Translated by James D. Martin. Philadelphia: Fortress Press, 1983.

Outline of End-Time Events Predicted in the Bible

I. Events Before, During, and After the Seven-Year End-Time Period (This seven-year period is the 70th "seven" of Daniel, Dan. 9:27.)
A. Events immediately before the seven-year period
1. Church raptured (John 14:1-3; 1 Cor. 15:51-52; 1 Thes. 4:16-18; Rev. 3:10)
2. Restrainer removed (2 Thes. 2:7)
3. Judgment seat of Christ (in heaven, 1 Cor. 3:12-15; 2 Cor. 5:10)
4. Antichrist rises to power over the Roman confederacy (Dan. 7:20, 24)[1]
B. Event at the beginning of the seven-year period
Antichrist (the coming "ruler") makes a covenant with Israel (Dan. 9:26-27)
C. Events in the first half of the seven-year period
1. Israel living in peace in the land (Ezek. 38:8)
2. Temple sacrifices instituted (Rev. 11:1-2)
3. World church dominates religion and the Antichrist (Rev. 17)
D. Events perhaps just before the middle of the seven-year period
1. Gog and his allies invade Palestine from the north (Ezek. 38:2, 5-6, 22)[2]
2. Gog and his allies destroyed by God (Ezek. 38:17-23)[2]
E. Events at the middle of the seven-year period
1. Satan cast down from heaven and energizes the Antichrist (Rev. 12:12-17)
2. Antichrist breaks his covenant with Israel, causing her sacrifices to cease (Dan. 9:27)
3. The 10 kings under the Antichrist destroy the world church (Rev. 17:16-18)
4. The 144,000 Israelites saved and sealed (Rev. 7:1-8)[3]
F. Events of the second half of the seven-year period
These three-and-one-half years are called "the Great Tribulation" (Rev. 7:14; cf. "great distress," Matt. 24:21; "time of distress," Dan. 12:1; and "a time of trouble for Jacob," Jer. 30:7)
1. Rebellion (apostasy) against the truth in the professing church (Matt. 24:12; 2 Thes. 2:3)[4]
2. Antichrist becomes a world ruler (1st seal,[5] Rev. 6:1-2) with support of the Western confederacy (Rev. 13:5, 7; 17:12-13)
3. Antichrist revealed as "the man of lawlessness," "the lawless one" (2 Thes. 2:3, 8-9)
4. War, famine, and death (2nd, 3rd, and 4th seals,[5] Rev. 6:3-8)
5. Converted multitudes from every nation martyred (5th seal,[5] Rev. 6:9-11; 7:9-14; Matt. 24:9)
6. Natural disturbances and worldwide fear of divine wrath (6th seal,[5] Rev. 6:12-17)
7. Antichrist's image (an "abomination") set up for worship (Dan. 9:27; Matt. 24:15; 2 Thes. 2:4; Rev. 13:14-15)
8. Two witnesses begin their ministry (Rev. 11:3)[6]
9. The false prophet promotes the Antichrist, who is worshiped by nations and unbelieving Israel (Matt. 24:11-12; 2 Thes. 2:11; Rev. 13:4, 11-15)
10. Mark of the beast used to promote worship of the Antichrist (Rev. 13:16-18)
11. Israel scattered because of the anger of Satan (Rev. 12:6, 13-17) and because of the "abomination" (Antichrist's image) in the temple (Matt. 24:15-26)
12. Jerusalem overrun by

---

*Though premillenarians differ on the order of some of these events (see notes at the end of this outline) they do include all these events in the pattern of the end times.

Gentiles (Luke 21:24; Rev. 11:2)
13. Antichrist and false prophets deceive many people (Matt. 24:11; 2 Thes. 2:9-11)
14. The gospel of the kingdom proclaimed (Matt. 24:14)
15. Israel persecuted by the Antichrist (Jer. 30:5-7; Dan. 12:1; Zech. 13:8; Matt. 24:21-22)
16. Trumpet judgments (Rev. 8–9) and bowl judgments (Rev. 16) poured out by God on Antichrist's empire
17. Blasphemy increases as the judgments intensify (Rev. 16:8-11)

G. Events concluding the seven-year period
1. Two witnesses slain by the Antichrist (Rev. 11:7)[7]
2. Two witnesses resurrected (Rev. 11:11-12)[7]
3. The king of the South (Egypt) and the king of the North fight against the Antichrist (Dan. 11:40a)[8]
4. Antichrist enters Palestine and defeats Egypt, Libya, and Ethiopia (Dan. 11:40a-43)[8]
5. Armies from the East and the North move toward Palestine (Dan. 11:44; Rev. 16:12)
6. Jerusalem is ravaged (Zech. 14:1-4)
7. Commercial Babylon is destroyed (Rev. 16:19; 18:1-3, 21-24)
8. Signs appear in the earth and sky (Isa. 13:10; Joel 2:10, 30-31; 3:15; Matt. 24:29)
9. Christ returns with the armies of heaven (Matt. 24:27-31; Rev. 19:11-16)
10. Jews flee Jerusalem facilitated by topographical changes (Zech. 14:5)
11. Armies unite at Armageddon against Christ and the armies of heaven (Joel 3:9-11; Rev. 16:16; 19:17-19)[8]
12. Armies are destroyed by Christ (Rev. 19:19, 21)[8]
13. The "beast" (Antichrist) and the false prophet are thrown

into the lake of fire (Rev. 19:20)

H. Events following the seven-year period
1. Final regathering of Israel (Isa. 11:11-12; Jer. 30:3; Ezek. 36:24; 37:1-14; Amos 9:14-15; Micah 4:6-7; Matt. 24:31)
2. A remnant of Israelites turn to the Lord and are forgiven and cleansed (Hosea 14:1-5; Zech. 12:10; 13:1)
3. National deliverance of Israel from the Antichrist (Dan. 12:1b; Zech. 12:10; 13:1; Rom. 11:26-27)
4. Judgment of living Israel (Ezek. 20:33-38; Matt. 25:1-30)
5. Judgment of living Gentiles (Matt. 25:31-46)
6. Satan cast into the abyss (Rev. 20:1-3)
7. Old Testament saints resurrected (Isa. 26:19; Dan. 12:1-3)
8. Tribulation saints resurrected (Rev. 20:4-6)
9. Daniel 9:24 fulfilled
10. Marriage supper of the Lamb (Rev. 19:7-9)
11. Christ begins His reign on earth (Ps. 72:8; Isa. 9:6-7; Dan. 2:14-35, 44; 7:13-14; Zech. 9:10; Rev. 20:4)

II. Characteristics and Events of the Millennium
A. Physical characteristics
1. Topography and geography of the earth changed (Isa. 2:2; Ezek. 47:1-12; 48:8-20; Zech. 14:4, 8, 10)
2. Wild animals tamed (Isa. 11:6-9; 35:9; Ezek. 34:25)
3. Crops abundant (Isa. 27:6; 35:1-2, 6-7; Amos 9:13; Zech. 14:8)
4. Human longevity increased (Isa. 65:20-23)

B. Spiritual and religious characteristics and events
1. Satan confined in the abyss (Rev. 20:1-3)
2. Millennial temple built (Ezek. 40:5–43:27)
3. Animal sacrifices offered as memorials to Christ's death (Isa. 56:7; 66:20-23;

Jer. 33:17-18;
Ezek. 43:18-27; 45:13–46:24;
Mal. 3:3-4)
4. Feasts of the New Year,
Passover, and Tabernacles
reinstituted (Ezek. 45:18-25;
Zech. 14:16-21)
5. Nations worship in Jerusalem
(Isa. 2:2-4; Micah 4:2; 7:12;
Zech. 8:20-23; 14:16-21)
6. Worldwide knowledge of God
(Isa. 11:9; Jer. 31:34; Micah 4:5;
Hab. 2:14)
7. Unparalleled filling of and
empowerment by the Holy
Spirit on Israel
(Isa. 32:15; 44:3; Ezek. 36:24-29;
39:29; Joel 2:28-29)
8. New Covenant with Israel
fulfilled (Jer. 31:31-34;
Ezek. 11:19-20; 36:25-32)
9. Righteousness and justice
prevails (Isa. 9:7; 11:4; 42:1-4;
Jer. 23:5)
C. Political characteristics and events
1. Israel reunited as a nation
(Jer. 3:18; Ezek. 37:15-23)
2. Israel at peace in the land
(Deut. 30:1-10; Isa. 32:18;
Hosea 14:5, 7; Amos 9:15;
Micah 4:4; 5:4-5a; Zech. 3:10;
14:11)
3. Abrahamic Covenant land-
grant boundaries established
(Gen. 15:18-21;
Ezek. 47:13–48:8, 23-27)
4. Christ in Jerusalem rules over
Israel (Isa. 40:11;
Micah 4:7; 5:2b)
5. Davidic Covenant fulfilled
(Christ on the throne of
David, 2 Sam. 7:11-16;
Isa. 9:6-7; Jer. 33:17-26;
Amos 9:11-12; Luke 1:32-33)
6. Christ rules over and judges
the nations (Isa. 11:3-5;
Micah 4:2-3a; Zech. 14:9;
Rev. 19:15)
7. Resurrected saints reign with
Christ (Matt. 19:28;
2 Tim. 2:12; Rev. 5:10; 20:6)
8. Universal peace prevails
(Isa. 2:4; 32:17-18; 60:18;
Hosea 2:18; Micah 4:2-4; 5:4;
Zech. 9:10)
9. Jerusalem made the world's
capital (Jer. 3:17;
Ezek. 48:30-35; Joel 3:16-17;

Micah 4:1, 6-8; Zech. 8:2-3)
10. Israel exalted above the
Gentiles (Isa. 14:1-2; 49:22-23;
60:14-17; 61:5-9)
11. The world blessed through
Israel (Micah 5:7)
D. Events following the Millennium
1. Satan released from the abyss
(Rev. 20:7)
2. Satan deceives the nations
(Rev. 20:8)
3. Global armies besiege
Jerusalem (Rev. 20:9a)
4. Global armies destroyed by
fire (Rev. 20:9b)
5. Satan cast into the lake of fire
(Rev. 20:10)
6. Evil angels judged (1 Cor. 6:3)
7. The wicked dead resurrected
(Dan. 12:2b; John 5:29b)
8. The wicked judged at the
Great White Throne
(Rev. 20:11-14)
9. The wicked cast into the lake
of fire (Rev. 20:14-15; 21:8)
III. Eternity
A. Christ delivers the mediatorial
(millennial) kingdom to God the
Father (1 Cor. 15:24)
B. Present heavens and earth
demolished (Rev. 21:1)
C. New heavens and new earth
created (2 Peter 3:10; Rev. 21:1)
D. New Jerusalem descends to the
new earth (Rev. 21:2, 10-27)
E. Christ rules forever in the eternal
kingdom (Isa. 9:6-7;
Ezek. 37:24-28; Dan. 7:13-14;
Luke 1:32-33; Rev. 11:15)

Notes

1. Some identify Antichrist's initial rise
to power with the first seal judgment
(Rev. 6:1-2)
2. Some place the battle of Gog and his
allies at the very middle of the seven-
year period; others place it later.
3. Some say the 144,000 will be saved
and sealed in the first half of the
seven-year period.
4. According to some, this apostasy will
begin in the first half of the seven-year
period.
5. Many premillenarians place the seal
judgments in the first half of
the seven-year period.
6. Some Bible scholars say the work of
the two witnesses will be in the
first half of the seven-year period.

7. Some suggest that the two witnesses will be slain and resurrected in the first half of the seven-year period.

8. Some equate these events with the battle of Gog and his allies.

DANIEL

J. Dwight Pentecost

INTRODUCTION

Though the Book of Daniel is placed after the Prophet Ezekiel in English Bibles (as well as in the LXX and the Vulgate), the prophecy of Daniel is in a different place in the Hebrew Scriptures. The Hebrew Bible is divided into three portions. the first division is the Law, containing the five Books of Moses. The second is the Prophets, which includes Joshua, Judges, 1 and 2 Samuel (in Heb. 1 and 2 Sam. are one book), 1 and 2 Kings (also counted as one book), Isaiah, Jeremiah, Ezekiel, and the 12 Minor Prophets (which are counted as one book). The third classification is called the Writings. It contains 12 books: Psalms, Proverbs, Job, Song of Solomon, Ruth, Lamentations, Ecclesiastes, Esther, Daniel, Ezra, Nehemiah, 1 and 2 Chronicles (the latter two counted as one book). Thus the Book of Daniel is not included among the Prophets, the second major division. Nor is the man Daniel referred to in his book as a prophet. Also God did not deliver a message through Daniel *publicly* to the nation Israel. Yet Jesus called Daniel a prophet (Matt. 24:15). Certainly he was God's messenger with God's message to reveal truths God had disclosed to him.

Author. This book bears the simple title, "Daniel," not only because he is one of the chief characters portrayed in the book but more so because it follows a custom (though not a consistent one) of affixing the name of the author to the book he wrote. Little is known of Daniel's family background. From the testimony of his contemporaries he was known for his righteousness (Ezek. 14:14, 20) and his wisdom (Ezek. 28:3). He is mentioned in these passages with Noah and Job, who were historical people, so Daniel was also a historical person, not a fictional character.

Daniel was born into the royal family and was of noble birth (Dan. 1:3, 6). He was physically attractive and mentally sharp (1:4). He lived at least until the third year of Cyrus, that is, till 536 B.C. (10:1). Therefore he must have been a young man when he was taken captive by Nebuchadnezzar in 605 B.C. (In 1:4 Daniel was one of the "young" men of Israel.) If he were 16 when captured, he was 85 in Cyrus' third year.

Literary Form. The prophecy of Daniel is the first great book of apocalyptic literature in the Bible. The Greek word *apokalypsis,* from which comes the English "apocalypse," means an unveiling, a disclosing, or a revelation. Though all Scripture is revelation from God, certain portions are unique in the form by which their revelations were given and in the means by which they were transmitted.

Apocalyptic literature in the Bible has several characteristics: (1) In apocalyptic literature a person who received God's truths in visions recorded what he saw. (2) Apocalyptic literature makes extensive use of symbols or signs. (3) Such literature normally gives revelation concerning God's program for the future of His people Israel. (4) Prose was usually employed in apocalyptic literature, rather than the poetic style which was normal in most prophetic literature.

In addition to Daniel and Revelation, apocalyptic literature is found in Ezekiel 37–48 and Zechariah 1:7–7:8. In interpreting visions, symbols, and signs in apocalyptic literature, one is seldom left to his own ingenuity to discover the truth. In most instances an examination of the context or a comparison with a parallel biblical passage provides the Scriptures' own interpretation of the visions or the symbols employed. Apocalyptic literature then demands a careful comparison of Scripture with Scripture to arrrive at a correct understanding of the revelation being given.

DANIEL

Languages. The Book of Daniel is unusual in that it is written in two languages: 1:1–2:4a and chapters 8–12 are in Hebrew, and 2:4b–7:28 is in Aramaic, the lingua franca of the prophet's day. Hebrew was the language of God's covenant people Israel, and Aramaic was the language of the Gentile world.

Though the Book of Daniel is a single literary work, it has two major emphases. One has to do with God's program for the Gentile nations. This is contained in 2:4b–7:28. It was fitting that this prophecy concerning the Gentiles should be in their language. Hence the prophet used Aramaic in that portion of the book.

The second major emphasis is on the nation Israel and the influence or effect of the Gentiles on Israel. This theme is developed in 1:1–2:4a and chapters 8–12. Therefore it was fitting that Daniel wrote those portions in Hebrew, the language of the Jews.

Unity. Some scholars have questioned the unity of the Book of Daniel. They point out that chapters 1–6 record historical incidents in Daniel's lifetime, and that chapters 7–12 record prophetic visions given to Daniel. This observation, coupled with Daniel's use of two languages, has led some to infer a multiplicity of authors.

However, those observations do not support such a conclusion. As already pointed out, Daniel had reasons for employing two languages. Ancient literature often used different literary forms to heighten a contrast. The Book of Job, for instance, is mostly poetic but the prologue (chaps. 1–2) and epilogue (42:7-17) are in prose. Thus nothing in the literary style of the Book of Daniel demands more than one author.

The unity of Daniel's book is further supported by noting the interdependence of its two portions. The revelation in chapter 2 parallels closely the revelation in chapter 7. Further, some of the terms and theological concepts in the first half are similar to those in the second half. "Dream(s) and visions" are mentioned in 1:17; 2:28; 7:1. Lying "on (in) . . . bed" is referred to in 2:28; 4:10; 7:1. That God's "kingdom" is eternal is spoken of four times in the first half (2:44; 4:3, 34; 6:26) and three times in the second half (7:14, 18, 27). God's eternal "dominion" is extolled in 4:3, 34; 6:26; 7:14. And God is called "the Most High" or "the Most High God" nine times in the first half (3:26; 4:2, 17, 24-25, 32, 34; 5:18, 21) and four times in the second half (7:18, 22, 25, 27).

Also Daniel has a significant and unifying role in both portions of the book. Furthermore the message of the book is the same in both halves of the book. God is sovereign, rules over the nations, and controls them so that they fulfill His will. He is sovereignly preserving the nation Israel and bringing her to the fulfillment of the covenant He made with Abraham.

Date and Authorship. According to the contents of the Book of Daniel, it was written in the sixth century B.C. by Daniel who lived during its events. Daniel is referred to many times as the recipient of God's revelation. And he took part in many of the historical events recorded in the book. The Lord Himself attributed the authorship of the book to Daniel (Matt. 24:15). Daniel's familiarity with the individuals spoken of in the book and with the historical events and customs mentioned in the book necessitates a sixth-century date for the book.

The minute details included in the book could hardly have been retained accurately by oral tradition for some 400 years, as suggested by those who postulate a late date for the book. The fact that manuscript fragments from the Book of Daniel were found in Qumran, written perhaps in the second century B.C., preclude the notion that Daniel was written in 165 B.C., as many critics suggest. Not enough time would have been available for the book to have reached the Essene community in Qumran and for it to have been copied there. Also the fact that the Book of Daniel was accepted by the Jews into the canon of Scripture bears witness to its authenticity.

Critics reject an early date for the writing of Daniel mainly because they reject predictive prophecy. The book unfolds details concerning the history of Babylon, Medo-Persia, Greece, and Rome. Details recorded in Daniel 11:5-35 were fulfilled in the fourth to the second centuries B.C. Skeptics insist that Daniel could not have foreknown those details but must have written them *after* the events transpired and cast them in the form of prophecy to give credence to his writing. (Or they maintain that someone other than the Prophet Daniel wrote the book in the second century B.C. and used his name.) Such a view of course denies the power of God to reveal what He has predetermined.

A number of other objections have been raised against the early date for the book. For example, some argue that the several Persian and Greek words in the book indicate that it must have been written much later than the sixth century B.C. However, archeology has revealed that commerce existed between Greece and Babylon even *before* Daniel's day. This would explain the presence of Greek words. And the Persian words in the book were from an official or literary form of the Persian language which was in wide use throughout the Near East. (Cf. D.J. Wiseman et al., *Notes on Some Problems in the Book of Daniel*, pp. 23-7, 35-50.)

A further objection is based on the apocalyptic literature found in the book. Such literature appeared prolifically in Israel in the later time of the Maccabees (literature that is not part of the biblical canon); therefore many scholars infer that the book must have been written in that period (168–134 B.C.). However, as already noted (see "Literary Form"), apocalyptic literature is found in the Book of Ezekiel and he, like Daniel, was a sixth-century prophet.

Further objection is made to an early date because of the advanced theology in the book. Critics claim that frequent references to angels and a reference to the resurrection of the dead (12:2) necessitates a late postexilic date for the book. This, however, overlooks the fact that angels are frequently referred to throughout Israel's long history and that resurrection is mentioned in passages such as Psalm 16:10 and Isaiah 26:19, which certainly predate the time of Daniel.

Some have objected to Daniel's sixth-century date on the grounds that the book is included in the Writings, the third section of the Hebrew Bible, rather than among the Prophets, the second division. The last prophetic book (Malachi) was written in the fifth century B.C. Those arguing for a late date for Daniel allege that if his book were written in the sixth century, it would have been included in the second division (the Prophets) rather than relegated to the third (the Writings). However, as previously noted, the prophets were set apart by God as His messengers with a special ministry to the nation Israel. Since Daniel was counted by his contemporaries as a governmental leader rather than a prophet, his writings were included in the third division rather than in the second. Thus the status of the author rather than the date of his book determined the division in which his book was included in the Hebrew Bible.

Some critics hold that since God's name Yahweh is not used by Daniel and since the name was commonly used in Daniel's day by others, the book must have been written at a later time. However, this objection fails to note that in chapter 9 this name *is* used eight times (Dan. 9:2, 4, 8, 10, 13-14 [thrice], 20). The name for God an author used in a given passage was determined by his content, not by popular custom.

Some have objected to Daniel's authorship because of supposed historical errors found in the book. Some have asserted, for instance, that Nebuchadnezzar was not the father of Belshazzar, as indicated in Daniel 5:2, 11, 13, 18 (cf. v. 22). They argue that if Daniel had written the book, he would not have made such an error. However, it has been demonstrated that a royal successor to the throne was called a "son" (5:22) even if he had no blood relationship to an earlier king. (See the chart "Kings of the Neo-Babylonian Empire.")

Again objection is made to Daniel's authorship because the writer refers in 1:21 to the time of Daniel's death. However, 1:21 does not state when Daniel died; it states that he "remained there" (in Babylon) till Cyrus' first year. Cyrus' decree liberated the Jews from their exile in Babylon, thus bringing the 70-year Captivity to a near end. Daniel 1:21 is simply pointing out that Daniel lived through the span of the Captivity. The verse does not specify the time of his death. In fact he lived on into at least Cyrus' third year (10:1).

Historical Background. Nineveh, the Assyrian capital, fell before the assault of

Kings of the Neo-Babylonian Empire

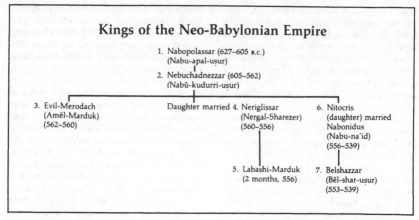

1. Nabopolassar (627–605 B.C.)
   (Nabu-apal-uṣur)

2. Nebuchadnezzar (605–562)
   (Nabū-kudurri-uṣur)

3. Evil-Merodach
   (Amēl-Marduk)
   (562–560)

Daughter married 4. Neriglissar
   (Nergal-Sharezer)
   (560–556)

6. Nitocris
   (daughter) married
   Nabonidus
   (Nabu-na'id)
   (556–539)

5. Labashi-Marduk
   (2 months, 556)

7. Belshazzar
   (Bēl-shar-uṣur)
   (553–539)

the forces of Babylon and Media in 612 B.C. Under the leadership of Ashur-uballiṭ some Assyrians fled westward to Haran, from which they claimed authority over all of Assyria. Nabopolassar, the king of Babylon, moved in 611 B.C. against the Assyrian forces in Haran. The next year, 610 B.C., Babylon, allied with Media, attacked the Assyrians in Haran. Assyria withdrew from Haran westward beyond the Euphrates River and left Haran to the Babylonians.

In 609 B.C. the Assyrians sought the help of Egypt, and Pharaoh Neco II led an army from Egypt to join Assyria. Josiah, the king of Judah, hoping to incur favor with the Babylonians, sought to prevent the Egyptians from joining Assyria and met the Egyptian army at Megiddo. Josiah's army was defeated and he was killed in this attempt (2 Kings 23:28-30; 2 Chron. 35:24).

Pharaoh Neco proceeded to join the Assyrians and together they assaulted Babylon at Haran but were unsuccessful. Assyria seems to have passed from the scene at that time, but conflict continued between Egypt and Babylon.

In 605 B.C. Nebuchadnezzar led Babylon against Egypt in the Battle of Carchemish. Egypt was defeated, and Carchemish was destroyed by the Babylonians in May-June of that year. While pursuing the defeated Egyptians Nebuchadnezzar expanded his territorial conquests southward into Syria and toward Palestine. Learning of the death of his father Nabopolassar, Nebuchadnezzar returned from Riblah to Babylon in August 605 to receive the crown. Then he

returned to Palestine and attacked Jerusalem in September 605. It was on this occasion that Daniel and his companions were taken to Babylon as captives. Perhaps Nebuchadnezzar considered them hostages to warn the people in Judah against rebellion. Or the young men may have been taken to Babylon to prepare them for positions of administrative leadership there if Nebuchadnezzar should have to return to subjugate Judah. Returning to Babylon, Nebuchadnezzar reigned for 43 years (605–562).

Nebuchadnezzar returned to Judah a second time in 597 B.C. in response to Jehoiachin's rebellion. In this incursion Jerusalem was brought in subjection to Babylon, and 10,000 captives were taken to Babylon, among whom was the Prophet Ezekiel (Ezek. 1:1-3; 2 Kings 24:8-20; 2 Chron. 36:6-10).

Nebuchadnezzar returned to Judah a third time in 588 B.C. After a long siege against Jerusalem the city walls were breached, the city destroyed, and the temple burned in the year 586. Most of the Jews who were not killed in this assault were deported to Babylon (2 Kings 25:1-7; Jer. 34:1-7; 39:1-7; 52:2-11).

The restoration of the Jews back to their land was made possible when in 539 B.C. Cyrus overthrew Babylon and established the Medo-Persian Empire. Having a policy to restore displaced peoples to their lands, Cyrus issued a decree in 538 that permitted the Jews who so desired to return to Jerusalem (2 Chron. 36:22-23; Ezra 1:1-4). About 50,000 Jewish exiles returned to the land and began to rebuild the temple. This was in keeping with Daniel's prayer (Dan. 9:4-19). The temple was completed in 515 B.C. (Ezra 6:15). (See the chart "The Three Returns from Exile," in the *Introduction* to Ezra.) From the first subjugation of Jerusalem (605 B.C.) until the Jews returned and rebuilt the temple foundation (536) was approximately 70 years. From the destruction of the temple (586) until the temple was rebuilt (515) was also about 70 years. So Jeremiah's prophecy about the 70-year duration of the Babylon Exile was literally fulfilled (Jer. 25:11-12).

Purposes. The purposes of the book can be deduced from its contents:

1. Daniel's personal dedication to God (Dan. 1) would have been an example to the deportees on how they should live in a heathen society. Daniel served as an outstanding example of godliness to the exiles.

2. The book emphasizes God's sovereign authority over Gentile nations, how He establishes and deposes kings and empires to serve His purpose. It was this great truth that Nebuchadnezzar came to understand (4:35).

3. The book gives an example of God's faithfulness to His covenant people in protecting and preserving them even though they were under divine discipline for their disobedience. God does not cast off His covenant people; He deals patiently with them to bring them to blessing.

4. The book was also written to outline graphically the prophetic period known as "the times of the Gentiles" (Luke 21:24). The Book of Daniel marks the course of Gentile history through that extended period in which Israel was and is being disciplined by Gentiles. Also the consummation of God's program for the Gentiles will come to its conclusion in the coming Tribulation period. The book carefully and in detail shows the effect the Gentile nations will have on Israel while she is waiting for God's covenants to her to be fulfilled under the Messiah's reign.

5. Daniel's book also reveals Israel's future deliverance and the blessings she will enjoy in the coming Millennial Age. As God covenanted with Abraham, his descendants will occupy the land God promised them. Even though the nation must be disciplined because of her dis-

obedience, she will be brought to repentance, confession, and restoration. God remains faithful. He preserves His covenant people and guarantees them ultimate blessing in their covenanted kingdom on this earth.

Importance of the Book. The Book of Daniel is important historically. It bridges the gap between Israel's historical books and the New Testament. It records certain events in Israel's history in the 70-year Babylonian Captivity which are recorded nowhere else in Scripture (except for snatches of information in Ezek.). Daniel outlines the history of the times of the Gentiles and describes past and future empires that occupy Palestine and rule over Israel until the Messiah returns.

The prophecies in the book concerning God's program for the Gentiles, for the land of Palestine, and for the people of Israel, lay the foundation for His eschatological program. Some of the themes introduced in the Book of Daniel, with its emphasis on the Gentiles, are paralleled in the Book of Zechariah. And the themes introduced in these books come to their ultimate consummation in the Book of Revelation. To understand fully the culmination of God's program revealed to the Apostle John in Revelation, it is necessary to understand the inception of His program revealed to Daniel.

OUTLINE

COMMENTARY

I. Personal History of Daniel (chap. 1)

A. Daniel's deportation (1:1-7)

1:1-2a. The first two verses of the Book of Daniel state when and how the prophet was taken to Babylon. The events in the book began **in the third year of the reign of Jehoiakim king of Judah.** This seems to conflict with Jeremiah's statement that the first year of Nebuchadnezzar, king of Babylon, was in the *fourth* year of Jehoiakim's reign (Jer. 25:1). At least two explanations may be given for this apparent discrepancy. The first is the difference between Jewish and Babylonian reckoning. The Jewish calendar began the year in Tishri (September-October) while the Babylonian calendar began in the spring in the month of Nisan (March-April). If Babylonian reckoning were used, the year Nebuchadnezzar besieged Jerusalem was the fourth year of Jehoiakim's reign. But if the Jewish reckoning were used it was Jehoiakim's third year. Daniel, a Jew, may well have adopted the familiar Jewish calendar.

A second explanation is based on the Babylonian method of reckoning the dates of a king's reign. The portion of a king's reign that preceded the beginning of a new year in the month Nisan, that is, the year of accession, was called the first year even if it was of short duration. If Jeremiah followed that method of reckoning, he counted Jehoiakim's year of accession (which was only part of a full year) as the first year. And if Daniel used the Jewish method of reckoning (which did *not* count the first months of a king's reign before the new year) he then counted only the three full years of Jehoiakim's reign. The year was 605 B.C.

Daniel referred to **Nebuchadnezzar** (whose name means "Nabu has protected my inheritance") as **king of Babylon**. At that time (605) Nabopolassar was king in Babylon, and Nebuchadnezzar had not yet acceded to the throne. However, Nebuchadnezzar, while in battle, heard of the death of his father and hastened to Babylon to be enthroned (see "Historical Background" in the *Introduction*). Writing at a later date, Daniel referred to Nebuchadnezzar as king in anticipation of his occupation of the throne.

Nebuchadnezzar's besieging of **Jerusalem** took place during the reign of **Jehoiakim**, the 17th **king of Judah** and eldest son of Josiah (cf. 2 Chron. 36:2 with 2 Chron. 36:5). Jehoiakim's younger brother Jehoahaz had been placed on Judah's throne after Pharaoh Neco killed King Josiah in 609 B.C. (See the chart "The Last Five Kings of Judah," near 2 Kings 23:31-35.) But Neco dethroned Jehoahaz and placed Jehoiakim on the throne (2 Chron. 36:3-4).

Jeremiah had warned Jehoiakim of impending invasion by Babylon. And Jehoiakim had heard of the prophet's instruction to God's people to submit to Babylon without resistance. So when Nebuchadnezzar besieged the city, little or no resistance was offered, and Jehoiakim was captured and taken to Babylon. Thus Judah came under Nebuchadnezzar's authority.

With this incursion by Nebuchadnezzar an important prophetic time period —the times of the Gentiles (Luke 21:24)—began. The times of the Gentiles is that extended period of time in which the land given in covenant by God to Abraham and his descendants is occupied by Gentile powers and the Davidic throne is empty of any rightful heir in the Davidic line. The times of the Gentiles, beginning with Nebuchadnezzar's invasion of Jerusalem in 605 B.C., will continue till the Messiah returns. Then Christ will subdue nations, deliver the land of Israel from its Gentile occupants, and bring the nation Israel into her covenanted blessings in the millennial kingdom.

God had made a covenant with Israel in Moab (Deut. 28–30) just before she entered the land (Deut. 29:1). In this covenant God set forth the principle by which He would deal with His people. Their obedience to Him would bring blessing (Deut. 28:1-14) but disobedience to Him would bring discipline (Deut. 28:15-68). In this second portion God outlined the disciplines He would use to correct the people when their walk was out of line with His revealed Law. These disciplines would seek to conform them to His demands so they would be eligible for His blessings. The ultimate discipline He would use to correct His people was the invasion of Gentile nations who would subjugate them to their authority and disperse them from their land (Deut. 28:49-68).

Moses then stated when Israel would come under God's discipline, that discipline would not be lifted until the people forsook their sin, turned in faith to God, and obeyed His requirements (Deut. 30:1-10). The Northern Kingdom of Israel had gone into captivity to Assyria in 722 B.C. This was the outworking of the principles of Deuteronomy 28. From time to time (though not consistently) the Southern Kingdom (Judah), in light of the fall of the Northern Kingdom, had heeded the prophets' admonitions and turned to God. The Southern Kingdom continued for more than a century longer because of her repentance and obedience under her godly kings.

That condition, however, did not last. Judah also ignored God's covenant, neglected the Sabbath Day and the sabbatical year (Jer. 34:12-22), and went into idolatry (Jer. 7:30-31). Therefore, because of the covenant in Deuteronomy 28, judgment had to fall on Judah. God chose Nebuchadnezzar as the instrument to inflict discipline on God's disobedient people (cf. Jer. 27:6; Hab. 1:6).

1:2b-3. When Nebuchadnezzar returned to Babylon from this invasion of Judah, he brought spoils to signify Judah's submission to Babylon. First, he brought some valuable **articles from the temple** in Jerusalem which he placed in **the temple of his god in Babylonia** (cf. 2 Chron. 36:7). "His god" may have been Bel, also called Marduk, the chief god of the Babylonians (cf. comments on Dan. 4:8). (In Heb. the word rendered Babylonia is Shinar, NIV marg., an ancient name for that land; cf. Gen. 10:10; 11:2; 14:1;

DANIEL

Isa. 11:11, NIV marg.; Zech. 5:11, NIV marg.) This would signify the conquest of the God of Judah by the Babylonian deities.

Second, Nebuchadnezzar brought with him **some of the Israelites** (Jews) **from the royal family and the nobility.** As stated in the *Introduction*, these royal princes may have been considered hostages, to help assure Judah's continued submission to Babylon. Or they may have been taken to Babylon to prepare them to fulfill positions of administrative leadership there if Nebuchadnezzar should have to return to subjugate Judah. **Ashpenaz was chief of the court officials.** He is mentioned by name only here in the Old Testament but is called "the official" or "the chief official" six times (Dan. 1:7-11, 18). It is not clear whether the word for "official" (*sārîs*) means a eunuch or simply a courtier or court officer. Kitchen suggests it meant eunuch in Daniel's time (Kenneth A. Kitchen, *Ancient Orient and Old Testament.* Downers Grove, Ill.: InterVarsity Press, 1966, pp. 165-6).

1:4-5. These captives were choice **young men** both physically and mentally and as such, they could be an asset to **the king's palace.** An attempt was made to assimilate them into the culture of the court for they were compelled to learn both **the language and** the **literature** of the people among whom they now dwelt. They were to undergo a rigorous **three**-year course of training **after** which **they were to enter the king's service.** That educational program probably included a study of agriculture, architecture, astrology, astronomy, law, mathematics, and the difficult Akkadian language.

1:6-7. No mention was made of how many captives were taken but four are mentioned here by name because of their later significant role in Babylon. Because all four bore names that honored Yahweh, the God of Israel, their names were changed. *El* means God and *-iah* (or *-yah*) is an abbreviation for Yahweh, thus suggesting that the young men's parents were God-fearing people who gave them names that included references to God. **Daniel,** whose name means "God has judged" (or "God is my Judge"), was given the name **Belteshazzar** (*Bēlet-šar-uṣur* in Akk.), which means "Lady, pro-

tect the king." Eight of the 10 times "Belteshazzar" occurs in the Old Testament are in the Aramaic section of the Book of Daniel (2:26; 4:8-9, 18-19 [3 times]; 5:12). The other 2 occurrences are in 1:7 and 10:1.

Hananiah ("Yahweh has been gracious") became **Shadrach** probably from the Akkadian verb form *šādurāku,* meaning "I am fearful (of a god)."

Mishael ("Who is what God is?") was given the name **Meshach,** which possibly was from the Akkadian verb *mēšāku,* meaning "I am despised, contemptible, humbled (before my god)."

Azariah ("Yahweh has helped") was named **Abednego,** "Servant of Nebo" (Nego being a Heb. variation of the Babylonian name of the god Nebo). Nebo (cf. Isa. 46:1), son of Bel, was the Babylonian god of writing and vegetation. He was also known as Nabu (cf. comments on Dan. 1:1 on Nebuchadnezzar's name).

Thus **the chief** court **official** (Ashpenaz, v. 3) seemed determined to obliterate any testimony to the God of Israel from the Babylonian court. The names he gave the four men signified that they were to be subject to Babylon's gods.

B. Daniel's devotion to God (1:8-16)

1. THE REQUEST (1:8)

1:8. Nebuchadnezzar had made abundant provision for the captives. Theirs was a life of luxury, not deprivation, for they were given a portion of **food and wine** daily from the king's own table. However, this food did not conform to the requirements of the Mosaic Law. The fact that it was prepared by Gentiles rendered it unclean. Also no doubt many things forbidden by the Law were served on the king's table, so to partake of such food would defile the Jewish youths. Further, without doubt this royal food had been sacrificed and offered to pagan gods before it was offered to the king. To partake of such food would be contrary to Exodus 34:15, where the Jews were forbidden to eat flesh sacrificed to pagan gods.

Similar problems would arise in drinking the wine. To abstain from the Old Testament prohibition against "strong drink" (e.g., Prov. 20:1, KJV; Isa. 5:11, "drinks"), Jews customarily diluted wine with water. Some added 3 parts of water to wine, others 6 parts, and some as much as 10 parts of water to 1 part of wine. The Babylonians did not dilute their wine. So both the food and the drink would have defiled these Jewish young men. **Daniel** knew the requirements of the Law governing what he should and should not eat and drink.

Daniel's desire was to please God in all he did. So he **resolved** that even though he was not in his own land but in a culture that did not follow God's laws, he would consider himself under the Law. He therefore **asked the chief** court **official** to be excused from eating and drinking the food and wine generously supplied by the king. Daniel was courageous, determined, and obedient to God.

2. THE REQUEST GRANTED (1:9-14)

1:9-10. The chief official's reticence to grant Daniel's request is understandable. He was responsible to oversee the young captives' physical and mental development so they would become prepared for the roles **the king** had in mind for them. Evidently these youths held a strategic place in the king's plans, so he wanted them well trained. If the men had been of little consequence to **the king,** their physical conditions would not have mattered and Ashpenaz would not have risked the loss of his life.

Daniel had trusted his situation to God who intervened on Daniel's behalf to move the official's heart **to show favor** (*ḥesed*, "loyal love") **and sympathy** (*raḥămîm*, "compassion") **to Daniel.**

1:11-14. When Daniel's request seemed to have been denied by **the chief official** . . . **Daniel** approached **the guard whom** Ashpenaz placed over the four youths and requested a **10-day** trial period in which **Daniel** and his companions would be given only **vegetables . . . and water.** (The Heb. word for vegetables, meaning "sown things," may also include grains.) Since the Mosaic Law designated no vegetables as unclean, Daniel could eat any vegetables put before him without defiling himself. In so short a time (**10 days**) there could have been no marked deterioration that would jeopardize the life of anyone in authority. In fact Daniel hinted that their **appearance** would be better than that of the others who were on the king's diet.

Since the guard was under the chief official's authority he must have acted not on his own but with permission from Ashpenaz. This indicates that God intervenes on behalf of those who trust Him, and protects and preserves those who obey Him, even under pagan rule.

3. THE RESULT (1:15-16)

1:15-16. At the conclusion **of the 10 days,** the four who had lived on vegetables appeared **healthier** than those who had dined on the king's **food.** Since the four looked better—and not worse than the others, as Ashpenaz had feared (v. 10)—he did not object to the diet Daniel had requested for himself and his friends. So they were allowed to continue on a diet of **vegetables.**

Though God did not prohibit eating meat altogether (cf. Gen. 9:3; Rom. 14:14; 1 Cor. 10:25-26), the vegetable diet was superior to the king's food. Also this shows that God blesses those who obey His commands and prospers those who trust Him. This incident would have been a lesson for the nation Israel. God had demanded obedience to the Law. Punishment came because of disobedience but even during a time of discipline, God protects and sustains those who obey Him and trust Him for their sustenance.

C. Daniel's appointment (1:17-21)

1:17. These four . . . men being prepared by Nebuchadnezzar for positions of responsibility in the royal court were actually being prepared by God. For **God gave** them **knowledge and understanding** in many realms. "Knowledge" has to do with reasoning skills and thought processes. They were able to think clearly and logically. "Understanding" has to do with insight. This points up their ability to discern the nature of things clearly and to interpret them in their true light. The **literature and learning** in which God gave them ability was broad (cf. comments on v. 4). By divine enablement and through his years of instruction under able teachers, **Daniel** gained a wide knowledge of arts and sciences.

Though the knowledge of others in Babylon in those subjects may have equaled that of Daniel, he was superior to them all in one area: he had the God-given ability to **understand visions and dreams.** People have always been curious about the future and have sought to predict coming events. For example, after Israel entered the land of Canaan, they encountered many who attempted to prognosticate the future by various means. But Israel was forbidden to follow any of these practices (Deut. 18:9-13), which were also prevalent in Babylon.

1:18-21. At the end of the time set by the king (i.e., at the end of the three years' training; cf. v. 5), **the king** examined **Daniel** and his three companions and **found** that **none** equaled them. In fact they were **10 times better than all** who practiced the arts of divination. (On **magicians** and **enchanters,** see comments on v. 17.) "Ten times" is an idiom meaning "many times" (cf. Gen. 31:7, 41; Num. 14:22; Job 19:3).

The king consulted magicians, enchanters, sorcerers, astrologers, wise men, and diviners. "Magicians" (*ḥarṭummîm*, Dan. 1:20; 2:2) was a general word referring to men who practiced the occult. (This word is also used in Gen. 41:8, 24; Ex. 7:11, 22; 8:7, 18-19; 9:11.) "Enchanters" (*'aššāpîm*, used only twice in the OT, Dan. 1:20; 2:21) may refer to those who used incantations in exorcisms. The word "sorcerers" (*mᵉkaššᵉpîm*, 2:2) probably is from the Akkadian verb *kašāpu*, "to bewitch, to cast a spell." (This participial noun, rendered "sorcerers," used only here in Dan., occurs only four other times in the OT: Ex. 7:11; 22:18; Deut. 18:10; Mal. 3:5.) "Astrologers" (Heb., *kaśdîm*, Dan. 2:2, 4; Aram., *kaśdāʾîn*, 2:5, 10 [twice]; 3:8; 5:7, 11) seems to refer to a priestly class in the Babylonian religion (misleadingly rendered "Chaldeans" in the KJV) who depended on revelation through the stars, which were objects of worship. "Diviners" (*gāzᵉrîn*, 2:27; 4:7; 5:7, 11) may be those who sought to ascertain or decree the fate of others.

The practices of these five groups may have overlapped extensively. Several times Daniel referred to these men under the general rubric of "wise men" (2:12-14, 18, 24 [twice], 48; 4:6, 18; 5:7-8, 15).

Daniel's ministry in the royal court of Babylon continued until the overthrow of the Babylonian Empire by **Cyrus** in 539 B.C. God had said, "Those who honor Me, I will honor" (1 Sam. 2:30). **Daniel** determined to honor God even though

he was living where people did not have the high standards God demanded. And God honored Daniel's obedience to the Law and promoted him in the king's court. This incident would have reminded Israel that obedience brings blessing and that righteousness is a prerequisite for enjoying the covenanted blessings.

The fact that God gave Daniel the ability to understand and interpret visions and dreams (Dan. 1:17) meant that throughout Nebuchadnezzar's long reign he depended on Daniel for understanding future events, revealed through dreams and visions. This anticipated the ministry Israel will one day fulfill. God had set Israel apart to be a kingdom of priests (Ex. 19:6). As such they were God's light to the world (Isa. 42:6; 49:6). They were to receive God's revelation and communicate it to nations that were ignorant of God. They were continually reminded of their role by the lampstand erected in the tabernacle. Daniel, during his tenure in the royal court in Babylon, fulfilled that function as God's spokesman to the Gentiles. When Israel will enter her millennial blessing under the reign of the Messiah, she will fulfill the role for which she was set apart by God and will then communicate God's truth to the Gentiles (Zech. 8:21-23).

II. Prophetic History of the Gentiles during the Times of the Gentiles (chaps. 2–7)

A. The dream of Nebuchadnezzar (chap. 2)

1. THE DREAM OF THE KING (2:1-16)

a. The dream (2:1-3)

2:1. Soon after Nebuchadnezzar's accession to the throne, he was plagued with a recurring dream. Since Daniel recalled and interpreted only a single dream (cf. vv. 24-26), the use of the plural here (**dreams**) seems to indicate a recurrence of the same dream. This dream evidently was perceived by **Nebuchadnezzar** as having great significance, for he **was troubled** (cf. v. 3) by the dream and so agitated that he was unable to **sleep.**

2:2-3. The king summoned the wise men of his realm. They professed to be able to foretell the future by one means or another (cf. comments on 1:17). If the method used by one failed to produce the desired result, hopefully the method employed by another would reveal the dream's significance. They were called collectively to exercise their enchantments in order to give the king an interpretation that would placate him. The king challenged the wise men, saying, I want to know what it means.

b. The desperation of the wise men (2:4-11)

2:4. Evidently the request to interpret a dream (v. 3) had been made of the wise men on other occasions for they were not surprised. (As stated under "Languages" in the Introduction, 1:1–2:4a is in Heb., and beginning with the words O king in verse 4b the language is Aramaic through 7:28.) The wise men confidently asserted that when the king revealed the dream to them, they would interpret it to him. They were confident that with their collective wisdom, they could satisfy the king with an interpretation.

2:5-6. Though the king may have made such a demand on the wise men previously and been satisfied with their answers, he evidently had never asked them to interpret a dream that he discerned had such significance. So he decided to test them. If they could predict the future by interpreting dreams, they should be able to reconstruct the past and recall the king's dream. So he refused to share his dream with them. This does not mean he had forgotten it. Had he done so, the wise men, to save themselves from death, could easily have fabricated a dream and then interpreted it. The king reasoned that if they could not recall the past, their predictions concerning the future could not be trusted.

The king promised rewards and honor for the wise men's recalling and interpreting the dream. But he put them under a death penalty (they would be cut into pieces) and their houses would be burned to rubble if they proved to be false prognosticators who could not recall the dream.

2:7-9. Again the wise men (cf. v. 4) asked that the king share the dream with them, promising then to interpret it. The king complained that they were stalling for time. He again referred to the penalty (cf. v. 5) for failure to tell him the dream. He felt that the only way he could trust

their interpretation of the future was by having them first recall his dream. Otherwise he would conclude that they were conspiring to tell him misleading and wicked things. Also Nebuchadnezzar may have become impatient with the wise men who were presumably older than he as he had inherited them from his father. Another reason for the test may have been that he was suspicious of their claims to wisdom.

2:10-11. To defend themselves, the wise men asserted that the king was making an unreasonable request, one never asked by any other potentate. They attested that the future belongs to the gods, not to men. Interestingly this was an admission that they had deceived the king in their past interpretations, a startling revelation from those held in high esteem in the court.

c. The decree of the king (2:12-13)

2:12-13. After the wise men revealed that they were unable to satisfy the king's demands, the king was angry and furious (cf. 3:13, 19). He issued an order for the execution of all the wise men of Babylon. The decree was not only for those currently serving the king's court, but on all who professed to be able to reveal the future. Since Daniel and his three friends were classified as wise men, the judgment also fell on them.

d. The declaration of Daniel (2:14-16)

2:14-16. What had transpired in the royal court was unknown to Daniel. Perhaps he had refused to answer the king's summons (v. 2) to avoid contact with the pagan leaders. When word came that he was under a death sentence, he tactfully asked Arioch, the commander of the king's guard, for the reason. Arioch . . . explained the incident that had exposed the wise men's deception of the king.

Daniel boldly approached the king with the request that the executions be stayed for a while so that he might interpret the king's dream. This took boldness because the king had already accused the wise men of wanting more time (v. 8).

Daniel was evidently held in high esteem by the king because he was permitted access to the king's presence and was able to petition the king directly.

Though not recorded, Daniel had possibly interpreted dreams previously, though not necessarily for the king. So he was sure he could recall the dream and interpret it.

2. THE DREAM REVEALED TO DANIEL (2:17-23)

a. The petition (2:17-18)

2:17-18. In this time of testing **Daniel** was calm. He **returned to his house,** sought out his three **friends,** and together they prayed **for mercy from the God of heaven.** ("God of heaven" is a title used of God six times in Dan.: 2:18-19, 28, 37, 44; 5:23, nine times in Ezra, and four times in Neh. Elsewhere in the OT it occurs only in Gen. 24:3, 7; Ps. 136:26; Jonah 1:9.)

Mercy is God's response to a person's need. Daniel recognized his own inability in the circumstances and turned to God in confidence, expecting the Lord to meet his need.

b. The revelation (2:19a)

2:19a. In response to the prayer of the four, the dream **was revealed to Daniel,** evidently that same **night.**

c. The praise (2:19b-23)

2:19b-23. Daniel responded appropriately by offering praise to **God.** He acknowledged that God is a God of **wisdom,** knowing the end from the beginning, and a God of **power,** for whatever He determines, He can do. Daniel began and concluded His prayer speaking of God's **wisdom and power** (cf. v. 23).

Evidences of His *power* are seen in His control of events (**He changes times and seasons**) and of the destiny of nations (**He sets up kings and deposes them**). Nebuchadnezzar was on the throne because God determined to use him there to fulfill His will.

Evidences of God's *wisdom* are seen in His imparting **wisdom to the wise** (v. 21b) and in His revealing **deep** and dark **things** (v. 22). **Light dwells with** God in the sense that all things are clear to Him though people are surrounded by **darkness.** God knows and can reveal the future. God, not Daniel's insight, gave him **the dream** and its interpretation. Daniel's prayer of praise closed with thanks that **God** had revealed the king's dream to the four who had trusted Him.

3. THE DREAM EXPLAINED TO NEBUCHADNEZZAR (2:24-45A)

a. The explanation by Daniel (2:24-30)

2:24-25. Receiving from God the knowledge of the **dream** and its interpretation (v. 19) **Daniel went to Arioch,** the king's executioner (cf. v. 14), and informed him that he was ready to **interpret** the king's **dream.** Evidently the royal court knew of the king's agitation for **Arioch took Daniel . . . at once to the king.** Officer Arioch wrongly claimed credit for having **found** an interpreter for the king's dream. Actually it was Daniel who "went to Arioch." Arioch evidently expected to be highly rewardly for finding someone who could alleviate the king's agitation.

2:26-28. The king inquired whether **Daniel** was **able to tell** him **what** he had dreamed and then to **interpret it.** Daniel was subjected to the same test of his veracity the king had demanded of the wise men. They had previously said that only the gods could reveal the future to man (v. 11). Now **Daniel** asserted that what the wise men of Babylon could not do (v. 27) by consorting with their false deities, Daniel was able to do because **there is a God in heaven** (cf. comments on v. 18) **who reveals mysteries** (v. 28; cf. v. 47). Daniel took no credit to himself (cf. v. 23).

2:29-30. Daniel asserted at the outset that the king's dream was prophetic (cf. v. 45, "what will take place in the future"), about **things to come** and **what was going to happen.** Nebuchadnezzar's dream covered the prophetic panorama of Gentile history from his time till the forthcoming subjugation of Gentile powers to Israel's Messiah. This time period is called "the times of the Gentiles" (Luke 21:24). This dream was given to Nebuchadnezzar, the first of many Gentile rulers who would exert power by divine appointment during the times of the Gentiles. God was not revealing spiritual truth to Nebuchadnezzar but facts concerning the political dominion that Gentiles would exercise. Everything in the dream would be readily understandable to Nebuchadnezzar.

Again Daniel humbly affirmed that the **mystery** was not **revealed to** him **because** he was wiser than others (cf. Dan. 2:27-28).

b. The recitation of the dream (2:31-35)

2:31-33. The king's dream was relatively simple. Daniel reported that the **king** had seen an enormously **large statue.** Its size and **appearance** were **awesome.** It made the king appear insignificant when he stood before it. The **statue** was **dazzling** because of the metals of which it was made. **The head of the** image was fashioned **of pure gold,** the **chest and arms** were **of silver, the belly and thighs of bronze,** and the **legs** were **of iron,** with **its feet partly . . . iron and partly . . . baked clay.** A casual glance would reveal the various parts of the statue.

2:34-35. The statue was not permanent; it was **struck on the feet** by **a rock (cut . . . not by human hands)** which reduced the whole statue to **chaff** that was blown away. Chaff was the light, unedible portion of grain stalks which blew away when the broken stalks were winnowed (tossed up in the air) on a windy **summer** day. **The rock that** destroyed **the statue** grew into **a huge mountain** that **filled the whole earth.** The dream itself was simple. It was the meaning of the dream that agitated the king.

c. The interpretation of the dream (2:36-45a)

2:36-38. Daniel's interpretation makes it clear that the image revealed the course of Gentile kingdoms which in turn would rule over the land of Palestine and the people of Israel. Nebuchadnezzar, head of the Babylonian Empire, was represented by the **head of gold** (v. 38). His father had come to power in Babylon by military conquest, but Nebuchadnezzar received his **dominion and power and might and glory** from God (who sets up kings and deposes them, v. 21). (On **the God of heaven** see comments on v. 18.)

Nebuchadnezzar's rule was viewed as a worldwide empire, in which he ruled over all **mankind** as well as over **beasts** and **birds.** At the time of Creation the right to rule over the earth was given man who was to have dominion over it and all the creatures in it (Gen. 1:26). Here Nebuchadnezzar by divine appointment was helping fulfill what God had planned for man.

2:39. The second portion of the statue, the chest and arms of silver, represented the rise of the Medes and Persians (cf. 5:28; 6:8; also cf. 5:31). The Medo-Persians conquered the Babylonians in 539 B.C. The arms of silver evidently represent the two nations of Media and Persia that together defeated Babylon. Though that **kingdom** lasted over 200 years (539–330 B.C.),longer than the Neo-Babylonian Empire of 87 years (626–539), the Medo-Persian Empire was **inferior to** it, as silver compared with gold.

The belly and thighs **of bronze** represented the third kingdom to arise. This was the Grecian Empire (cf. 8:20-21). Alexander the Great conquered the Medo-Persians between 334 and 330 B.C. and assumed authority over its peoples and territory. By Alexander's conquests he extended the Greek Empire as far east as the northwestern portion of India—an extensive empire that seemingly was **over the whole earth.**

2:40. The legs of **iron** represent the Roman Empire. This fourth kingdom conquered the Greek Empire in 63 B.C. Though the Roman Empire was divided into two legs and culminated in a mixture of iron and clay, it was one empire. This empire was characterized by its strength, as **iron** is stronger than bronze, silver, and gold. The Roman Empire was stronger than any of the previous empires. It crushed **all the** empires that had preceded it. Rome in its cruel conquest swallowed up the lands and peoples that had been parts of the three previous empires and assimilated those lands and peoples into itself.

2:41-43. The empire that began as **iron** regressed to a state of **clay** mixed with **iron.** This mixture speaks of progressive weakness and deterioration. Two metals together form an alloy which may be stronger than either of the metals individually. But **iron** and **clay** cannot be mixed. If iron and clay are put into a crucible, heated to the melting point, and poured into a mold, when the pour has cooled the iron and clay remain separate. The clay can be broken out which leaves a weak casting.

The Roman Empire was characterized by division (it was **a divided kingdom**) and deterioration (it was **partly strong and partly brittle**). Though Rome succeeded in conquering the territories that came under its influence, it never could unite the peoples to form a united empire. In that sense **the people** were a mixture and were not **united**. (Other views of this mixture of strength and weakness are suggested: [a] the empire was strong organizationally but weak morally; [b] imperialism and democracy were united unsuccessfully; [c] government was intruded by the masses, i.e., mob rule; [d] the empire was a mixture of numerous races and cultures.)

2:44-45a. Daniel then focused on the overthrow of those kingdoms. **The time of those kings** may refer to the four empires or, more likely, it refers to the time of the 10 toes (v. 42) since the first four kingdoms were not in existence at the same time as apparently the toes will be (cf. comments on the 10 horns of the fourth beast, 7:24). Nebuchadnezzar had seen a **rock** hit and smash the image (2:34). The statue was destroyed by the rock, **not by human hands.** In Scripture a rock often refers to Jesus Christ, Israel's Messiah (e.g., Ps. 118:22; Isa. 8:14; 28:16; 1 Peter 2:6-8). God, who had enthroned Nebuchadnezzar and would transfer authority from Babylon to Medo-Persia, then to Greece, and ultimately to Rome, will one day invest political power in a King who will rule over the earth, subduing it to His authority, thus culminating God's original destiny for man (Gen. 1:27).

In Nebuchadnezzar's dream the smiting rock became **a mountain** that filled the whole earth (Dan. 2:35). In Scripture a mountain is often a symbol for a kingdom. So Daniel explained that the four empires which would rule over the land and the people of Israel would not be destroyed by human means, but rather by the coming of the Lord Jesus Christ, the striking Stone. When He comes He will establish the messianic kingdom promised to Israel through David (2 Sam. 7:16). At His return He will subjugate **all . . . kingdoms** to Himself, thus bringing **them to an end** (cf. Rev. 11:15; 19:11-20). Then He will rule **forever** in the Millennium and in the eternal state.

Amillennialists hold that this kingdom was established by Christ at His *First* Advent and that now the church is that kingdom. They argue that: (a) Christianity, like the growing mountain, began to grow and spread geographically and is still doing so; (b) Christ came in the days of the Roman Empire; (c) the Roman Empire fell into the hands of 10 kingdoms (10 toes); (d) Christ is the chief Cornerstone (Eph. 2:20).

Premillenarians, however, hold that the kingdom to be established by Christ on earth is yet future. At least six points favor that view: (1) The stone will become a mountain suddenly, not gradually. Christianity did not suddenly fill "the whole earth" (Dan. 2:35) at Christ's First Advent. (2) Though Christ came in the days of the Roman Empire, He did not destroy it. (3) During Christ's time on earth the Roman Empire did not have 10 kings at once. Yet Nebuchadnezzar's statue suggests that when Christ comes to establish His kingdom, 10 rulers will be in existence and will be destroyed by Him. (4) Though Christ is now the chief Cornerstone to the church (Eph. 2:20) and "a stone that causes [unbelievers] to stumble" (1 Peter 2:8), He is not yet a smiting Stone as He will be when He comes again. (5) The Stone (Messiah) will crush and end all the kingdoms of the world. But the church has not and will not conquer the world's kingdoms. (6) The church is not a kingdom with a political realm, but the future Millennium will be. Thus Nebuchadnezzar's dream clearly teaches premillennialism, that Christ will return to earth to establish His rule on the earth, thereby subduing all nations. The church is not that kingdom.

4. DANIEL HONORED (2:45B-49)

2:45b. Daniel had validated his interpretation by first recalling **the dream** (vv. 31-35) and had certified that **the interpretation** (vv. 36-45a) was **trustworthy** because it had come from **God** (cf. vv. 19, 23, 28, 30), who holds the destiny of nations in His own power. He knows **what will take place in the future** (cf. vv. 28-29).

2:46-47. The **king** was so moved at Daniel's interpretation that he prostrated himself **before Daniel** and **ordered that an offering** be made to **Daniel,** an honor that would normally have been given only to the gods of Babylon. Such was Nebuchadnezzar's recognition of Daniel's divine authority. Through Daniel's revelation and interpretation of the dream, Nebuchadnezzar was led to confess that Daniel's **God** is superior to all the **gods** of Babylon and that He is **Lord** over the earth's **kings.** Daniel's **God** was exalted in the eyes of **Nebuchadnezzar** because He through Daniel revealed the course of forthcoming history. God is, the king said, **a Revealer of mysteries,** as Daniel had said (cf. v. 28). Nebuchadnezzar apparently accepted the fact of his own appointment to power by Daniel's God (cf. vv. 37-38) and recognized His authority.

2:48-49. Nebuchadnezzar appointed **Daniel** to a **position** of responsibility in the government and rewarded him materially with royal gifts. Babylon was divided into many provinces, each one under the leadership of a satrap (3:2). Daniel was evidently made a satrap over the province in which the royal court was located (**the province of** [the city of] **Babylon**). Daniel did not forget his friends but asked that they be promoted too. So **the king** made **Shadrach** (Hananiah), **Meshach** (Mishael), and **Abednego** (Azariah) **administrators** to serve under Daniel in the same **province.** Daniel was able to remain in **the royal court,** perhaps as an adviser to Nebuchadnezzar.

In a remarkable way God elevated Daniel to a position in the royal court so that he could serve as a mediator between the king and the exiles from Judah who would shortly (in 597 and 586) be brought to Babylon.

B. The image of Nebuchadnezzar (chap. 3)

1. THE ERECTION OF THE IMAGE (3:1-7)

3:1. The effect of the revelation given to **Nebuchadnezzar** about his significant role in Gentile history (2:37-38) is discerned from his response in the events recorded in chapter 3. Identified as the head of gold (2:38), Nebuchadnezzar then caused **an image of gold** to be erected! (3:1) When he erected this image is not known. It had to follow the events recorded in chapter 2 because Daniel's three companions were in a position of authority (3:12) to which they had been appointed (2:49).

The Septuagint adds in 3:1 that this event occurred in Nebuchadnezzar's 18th year (587), one year before the fall of Jerusalem (cf. 2 Kings 25:8). Since the final destruction of Jerusalem was the culmination of Nebuchadnezzar's conquests, that inference may well be true. However, a consideration of Daniel 3

seems to indicate that the events recorded there took place nearer the beginning of Nebuchadnezzar's long reign. The events associated with the king's erecting the image suggest that he wanted to unify his empire and consolidate his authority as ruler. The image was to become the unifying center of Nebuchadnezzar's kingdom.

The Aramaic word translated "image" ($s^e l\bar{e}m$) is related to the Hebrew word for image ($selem$). A general term, it allows for the image to have been in a human form (perhaps like the statue the king saw in his dream), though it does not require it. Perhaps sometime earlier Nebuchadnezzar had seen an Egyptian obelisk, on which were recorded the exploits of one of the pharaohs, and wanted to record his own conquests that way. The dimensions of the image would be fitting for an obelisk, for it was **90 feet high** (about the height of a present-day eight-story building) and only **9 feet wide.** This 10-to-1 ratio of height to width does not fit an image in human form, for it would be too slender. However, the Babylonians often distorted the human figure in constructing their images. Or perhaps the image was in proper human proportions but was set on a pedestal to make it more imposing.

Regardless of the image's form, it was an awesome sight (cf. 2:31), both because of its height and because of the gold of which it was constructed. The size and weight of the image seem to preclude that the image was of solid gold. It must have been overlaid with gold. Without doubt the use of gold in this image was inspired by Daniel's interpretation of the king's dream (2:32, 38).

The image was **set up . . . on the plain of Dura in the province of Babylon.** Dura was a common name in Mesopotamia for any place that was enclosed by mountains or a wall. "The province of Babylon" (cf. 2:48) seems to require a location close to the city of Babylon itself from which Nebuchadnezzar ruled his kingdom. Archeologists have uncovered a large square made of brick some six miles southeast of Babylon, which may have been the base for this image. Since this base is in the center of a wide plain, the image's height would have been impressive. Also its proximity to Babylon would have served as a suitable rallying point for the king's officials.

3:2-3. Nebuchadnezzar **summoned** eight classes of officials **to the dedication of the image.** This may suggest that the image was intended to symbolize the empire and its unity under Nebuchadnezzar's authority. The officers referred to in verse 2 are listed again in verse 3 and four of them in verse 27, thus emphasizing the political implications of this incident.

The **satraps** were chief representatives of the king, the **prefects** were military commanders, and the **governors** were civil administrators. The **advisers** were counselors to those in governmental authority. The **treasurers** administered the funds of the kingdom, the **judges** were administrators of the law, and the **magistrates** passed judgment in keeping with the law. The **other provincial officials** were probably subordinates of the satraps. This list of officers probably included all who served in any official capacity under **Nebuchadnezzar.**

On the possibility that Zedekiah, Judah's last king, was summoned to Babylon for this occasion see comments on Jeremiah 51:59.

To see so many officials stand before the image in Dura in Nebuchadnezzar's presence to swear their allegiance to him must have been impressive.

3:4-6. In demanding that these officials **fall down** before **the image of gold . . . Nebuchadnezzar** was demanding a public display of recognition and submission to his absolute authority in the kingdom.

The fact that the officials were commanded not only to fall down before the image, but also to **worship** it, indicates that the image had religious as well as political significance. Since no specific god is mentioned, it may be inferred that Nebuchadnezzar was not honoring one of the gods of Babylon, but rather was instituting a new form of religious worship with this image as the center. Nebuchadnezzar purposed to establish a unified government and also a unified religion. The king constituted himself as both head of state and head of religion. All who served under him were to recognize both his political and religious authority.

The officials summoned by Nebuchadnezzar to assemble in the plains of Dura had not been told why they were called. When they were all assembled, the king's **herald** then announced that the officials were to recognize Nebuchadnezzar's political and religious power. The herald addressed the officials as **peoples, nations, and men of every language** (cf. v. 7; 4:1; 5:19; 6:25; 7:14), apparently considering the officials as representatives of the peoples over whom they ruled. So the officials' act of obedience signified submission not only by the officials themselves, but also by those peoples they ruled.

Elaborate preparations in the construction of the image of gold made the occasion aesthetically appealing. To this was added musical accompaniment to make the occasion emotionally moving. The orchestra included wind instruments (the **horn** and **pipes**; cf. 3:10, 15), a reed instrument (the **flute**), and stringed instruments (**zither, lyre, harp**). Some critics argue that since the names of some of these instruments were Greek, the book was written later, in the time of the Grecian Empire. But communication between Greece and the Near East had been carried on for years before the Greek conquest by Alexander (see comments under "Date and Authorship" in the *Introduction*).

Failure to comply to the command to worship the image was penalized by sudden death, being **thrown into a blazing furnace.** The severity of the penalty indicates that submission on the part of every official was obligatory.

3:7. Overwhelmed by the king's command, the awesomeness of the image, and the sound of the **music**, the assembled officials **fell down and worshiped the image of gold.** In this way the officials and the peoples they represented recognized the political and religious authority of **Nebuchadnezzar.**

2. THE ACCUSATION AGAINST THE JEWS (3:8-12)

3:8-12. No indication is given of the size of the multitude that assembled on this occasion. But because it included all the kingdom's officials (vv. 2-3) it must have been huge. **Some** court advisers (**astrologers**; cf. comments on 1:17) were quick to bring an accusation against **the Jews.** The word translated **denounced** is strong, meaning "to tear in pieces." The accusation was severe, intended to destroy the accused. The accusers were evidently motivated by jealousy for they referred to the fact that **Nebuchadnezzar** had set **some Jews . . . over the affairs of the province of Babylon** (3:12; cf. 2:49). The jealousy evidently sprang from the king's recognition of the unusual ability of these men (1:20). Subjugated peoples, such as the Jewish captives, were normally relegated to positions of servitude, not elevated to authority in a realm. So the high positions of "some Jews" were resented.

The counselors evidently sought to curry favor from the **king** by contrasting the three Jews' refusal to bow to **the image** with their own **worship** of it. Interestingly they accused Daniel's three friends—**Shadrach, Meshach, and Abednego**—but not Daniel. Since Daniel was appointed to a higher office (2:48) he may not have been required to attend (cf. comments on 4:8) or perhaps he may have been elsewhere in the empire carrying out his duties. Or maybe the astrologers did not dare accuse Daniel, who was present but like the other three did not bow. Whatever the reason for his not being mentioned, Daniel's dedication to his God and submission to the Law certainly precluded his bowing before the image.

3. THE FAITH OF THE ACCUSED (3:13-18)

3:13-15. How significant this event was to **Nebuchadnezzar** is seen by his response to the astrologers' accusation of the three noncompliant Jews (vv. 9-12). When he heard that the three refused to bow, he became **furious with rage** (cf. v. 19; 2:12). The high esteem with which these men had previously been held by Nebuchadnezzar (1:20) did not exempt them from submission to his authority. Nebuchadnezzar did not pass an immediate judgment on the three but asked them if the accusation against them were **true**. He gave them another opportunity to bow before **the image**. By doing so they could prove the falsehood of the accusation (or show a changed attitude).

The king impressed on them the importance of such submission, warning them that the penalty for rebellion (being **thrown . . . into a blazing furnace**; cf. 3:6) would be carried out **immediately**.

Nebuchadnezzar considered himself above all gods, for he asked, **What god will be able to rescue you from my hand?** Again this shows that he claimed absolute authority in both political and religious realms. He was challenging any god to circumvent his authority. The matter then became a conflict between Nebuchadnezzar and Yahweh, the God of Daniel's companions.

3:16-18. The three showed absolute confidence in God, stating that their God was greater than **Nebuchadnezzar** and was **able to** deliver them from Nebuchadnezzar's judgment in a display of His superior power. Their words, **the God we serve** (cf. 6:16, 20), show they recognized that God's authority was greater than the authority claimed by Nebuchadnezzar. Though they were employed by Nebuchadnezzar (2:49), they "served" Yahweh.

Their God demanded implicit obedience and had forbidden them to worship any other gods. One who obeys God is not presuming when he expects God to protect and deliver him. Obeying God was more important than life to these three, so if God chose **not** to deliver them, they would still obey Him. Therefore they refused to **serve** Nebuchadnezzar's **gods** (or **worship the image** he made, possibly meaning to worship *him* as god) even if it meant they would die.

4. THE DELIVERANCE BY GOD (3:19-30)

3:19. In spite of the high regard with which **Nebuchadnezzar** had held these three (1:20), he determined to demonstrate his authority by ordering their immediate execution. This would serve as a lesson to any others who might consider rebelling against his political and religious authority. In a fit of anger (cf. 2:12; 3:13) Nebuchadnezzar had **the furnace heated seven times hotter than usual.** A low fire would have increased their torture by extending the duration of the punishment. A hotter fire would be expected to kill them instantly. Nebuchadnezzar wanted to display publicly the cost of rebelling against his authority.

3:20-23. The king ordered **some of** his **strongest soldiers . . . to tie up** the three **and throw them into the blazing furnace.** The furnace was probably constructed with an opening in the top, through which fuel could be fed, and an opening in the lower side from which ashes could be taken. **Soldiers** threw or lowered the **three** . . . **into the blazing furnace**. It was customary to remove the clothing of those being executed, but because of the haste in which the king wanted his command carried out (**the king's command was . . . urgent**) this practice was not followed this time. **The flames** leaping through the top opening of the furnace **killed the men who** had **thrown the three** into the fire.

3:24-26a. **Nebuchadnezzar** was watching the proceedings intently from a safe distance. As he peered into the furnace, probably through the lower opening, what he saw amazed him. The men who had been **tied up** were **walking around in the** furnace, **unbound.** And instead of seeing **three men** in the furnace, he saw **four,** and he said **the fourth** was **like a son of the gods.** This One was probably the preincarnate Christ (cf. comments on Gen. 16:13). Though Nebuchadnezzar did not know of the Son of God, he did recognize that the Person appearing with the three looked supernatural.

Nebuchadnezzar . . . approached as near as he dared to **the opening of the . . . furnace** so that his command could be heard. He ordered the three to **come out** of the furnace and to approach him. In giving this order he called them **servants of the Most High God.** Thus Nebuchadnezzar recognized that the God these three faithfully served (cf. Dan. 3:17) is truly God. The term "the Most High (lit., the Highest) God" or "the Most High" occurs 13 times in Daniel, more than in any other book except Psalms. Of those 13 occurrences 7 pertain to Nebuchadnezzar (3:26; 4:2, 17, 24-25, 32, 34) and 2 to Belshazzar (5:18, 21). The other 4 are in chapter 7 (7:18, 22, 25, 27).

This was a remarkable admission by Nebuchadnezzar. Up to then he had believed that his Babylonian gods were superior to Yahweh (though he had once acknowledged the greatness of Yahweh, 2:47). After all, he had taken captives from Judah and vessels from the Jews' temple. But his gods could not deliver anyone alive from a furnace! (cf. 3:29) As the three had predicted, their God (Yahweh) was able to deliver them from the furnace (v. 17). Though the king recognized the unusual nature of Yahweh, he

did not acknowledge Him as *his* God.

3:26b-27. When the three walked **out of the fire** and were carefully examined, Nebuchadnezzar's officials (cf. comments on v. 2) saw that the **bodies** of the three men were unharmed, their clothing unaffected, and that the **smell of fire** was not even on their clothes.

3:28-30. In view of the evidence presented to him, **Nebuchadnezzar** declared that this was an act of **the God of Shadrach, Meshach, and Abednego who** had **sent His angel** (cf. v. 25) to rescue the three who served this God (cf. v. 17). Nebuchadnezzar was moved by the devotion of the three to their **God** (he knew **they trusted in Him**), even though it entailed their disobeying the king and jeopardizing **their** own lives.

As a result the king decreed that **the God** of the three young men was to be held in honor and that anyone who dishonored this God would lose his life (he would **be cut in pieces** and his house would be burned to **rubble**; cf. 2:5). **The king** then honored **Shadrach, Meshach, and Abednego** by promoting them to positions of greater honor and power in the kingdom.

This historical incident seems to have prophetic significance as well. In the coming Tribulation a Gentile ruler (7:8) will demand for himself the worship that belongs to God (2 Thes. 2:4; Rev. 13:8). Any who refuse to acknowledge his right to receive worship will be killed (Rev. 13:15). Assuming political and religious power, he will oppress Israel (Rev. 13:7). Most of the people in the world, including many in Israel, will submit to and worship him. But a small remnant in Israel, like the three in Daniel's day, will refuse. Many who will not worship the Antichrist will be severely punished; some will be martyred for their faithfulness to Jesus Christ. But a few will be delivered from those persecutions by the Lord Jesus Christ at His second coming.

In the forthcoming Tribulation period God will do for this believing remnant what He did for Daniel's three companions. They withstood the decree of the king, and though they were not exempted from suffering and oppression they were delivered out of it by the God they trusted. No doubt the remnant of believing Jews in that coming day will find great comfort, consolation, and instruction from this incident in the lives of Daniel's three companions, as those in Daniel's day must have found as they were living under Gentile rule.

C. The second dream of Nebuchadnezzar (chap. 4)

1. THE KING'S PROCLAMATION (4:1-3)

Apparently a number of years transpired between the experience of Daniel's three friends in chapter 3 and Nebuchadnezzar's dream and period of insanity in chapter 4. Nebuchadnezzar reigned for 43 years (605–562 B.C.). His insanity lasted seven years and he returned to the throne for a short time afterward before he died. His last years did not take place until he had time to conclude his extensive building operations (v. 30). Thus this incident may have taken place about the 35th year of Nebuchadnezzar's rule, or about 570. This would be some 30 years after the experience of the three men in the fiery furnace, about the 50th year of Daniel's life.

4:1-3. Daniel recorded an official proclamation made by **Nebuchadnezzar** which was circulated throughout his realm. Daniel was led by the Holy Spirit's inspiration to include this official proclamation. God had shown the king that He is able to deliver and preserve those who trust and obey Him. But God's revelation of Himself to Nebuchadnezzar did not conclude there. For God further revealed Himself to the king through the circumstances recorded in this chapter. And in his proclamation to all the people in his empire (**peoples, nations, and men of every language;** cf. comments on 3:4), Nebuchadnezzar declared that through God's **miraculous signs** he had learned of His power and that **God (the Most High;** cf. comments on 3:26) is sovereign and exerts His will in **His . . . eternal kingdom.** Whereas earlier Nebuchadnezzar believed it was his own power and wisdom that had consolidated the kingdom under his authority, he learned that it is *God* who rules according to His will and uses those He chooses as His instruments.

2. THE KING'S TREE VISION (4:4-18)

a. The request for interpretation by the wise men (4:4-7)

4:4-7. For the second time a revelation was given to **Nebuchadnezzar** through **a dream** (cf. 2:1, 27-29). This dream, like the one years before, **terrified** the king (cf. 2:1, 3). Though **contented and prosperous,** he was **afraid.** So he sought an interpretation of **the dream to** allay his fears. Though **all the wise men of Babylon** had been discredited previously because of their inability to interpret the king's first dream (2:10-12), counselors had been retained by the king. He summoned **the magicians, enchanters, astrologers, and diviners** (see comments on 1:17) and ordered them **to interpret the dream** which he revealed to **them.** However, they were unable to do so.

b. The dream explained to Daniel (4:8-18)

4:8. Then the king **told . . . the dream** to Daniel. Unable once again to be helped by his own conjurers, he had to consult one who worshiped Yahweh. However, the king still acknowledged his own **god** (perhaps Bel, alias Marduk) as he referred to Daniel by his Babylonian name (**Belteshazzar;** cf. comments on 1:7) which included Bel's name. The word **finally** suggests that some time passed before Daniel went **into** the king's **presence.** Obviously Daniel was not among the wise men who had first been summoned to interpret the dream (4:6). Apparently Daniel was in a position of significant governmental authority and not serving as a counselor to the king (cf. comments on 3:12). That would explain why he was not included in the invitation given previously to the wise men.

Because of the impression made on Nebuchadnezzar through Daniel's previous interpretation (cf. 2:46) it is not likely that the king had forgotten about Daniel's ability to interpret dreams. Possibly the king suspected the ominous message contained in his dream and hoped that the wise men could soften the message when they intepreted it to him. The king thought that Daniel operated by **the spirit of the holy gods** (cf. 4:9, 18; 5:11, 14) and that through Daniel the message would be unveiled. Obviously Nebuchadnezzar was still a polytheist though he had acknowledged Yahweh's sovereignty years before (2:47; 3:28-29).

4:9-12. Nebuchadnezzar referred to Daniel as **chief of the magicians,** not because he was in authority over the wise men but because he was wiser than all of them, capable of understanding and interpreting dreams. The king implored Daniel to interpret his dream for him. Nebuchadnezzar's dream was a simple one. He was perplexed not by what he had seen, but by his inability to understand its meaning.

Previously Nebuchadnezzar had traveled to Lebanon to watch the felling of the great cedars to provide timber for his construction projects in Babylon. So he had witnessed the felling of mighty trees. The tree he saw in his dream was significant because of its size (vv. 10-11), its beauty (v. 12), and its fruit (v. 12). It provided food and shelter for all the animals and birds who lived under it or in it.

4:13-14. The king then explained that he saw a messenger, a holy one. This holy messenger, unknown to Nebuchadnezzar, would have been known to the Jewish people as an angel sent from heaven with an announcement. The messenger said that the tree was to be cut down, the branches trimmed from the trunk, the leaves stripped off, and the fruit scattered. The animals and birds that found shelter under and in its branches were to scatter.

4:15-16. However, the stump was not to be removed but secured with bands of iron and bronze. The first part of the vision of the tree (vv. 10-12) probably would have caused Nebuchadnezzar no concern. It may have even produced pride as he recognized himself in the tree as the one who provided bountifully for the subjects in his realm. But this second part of the vision (vv. 13-15a), that the tree was to be cut down, must have greatly disturbed him.

The third part of the vision (vv. 15b-16) must have been even more terrifying—if Nebuchadnezzar recognized himself as represented by the tree—for sanity was to leave him and he would become demented, living among the animals. He would have no more mental ability than an animal. This condition would continue for an extended period of time (till seven times pass by; cf. vv. 23, 25, 32). The "seven times" were probably seven years because (a) seven days or months would have been inadequate for his hair to have grown to the length of feathers (v. 33), and (b) "times" in 7:25 means years (cf. comments there).

4:17-18. Several messengers (holy ones) announced the lesson to be learned through the vision: so that the living may know that the Most High (cf. comments on 3:26) is sovereign over the kingdoms of men and gives them to anyone He wishes and sets over them the lowliest of men. This vision was designed to be a part of God's revelation of Himself and His authority over Nebuchadnezzar who in pride had exalted himself above God. The king again (cf. 4:9) asked Daniel (Belteshazzar; cf. comments on v. 8) to tell him the meaning of the dream.

3. THE VISION INTERPRETED (4:19-27)

4:19. Whereas Daniel had had no reticence about interpreting Nebuchadnezzar's first dream to him (2:27-45), he now was reluctant to interpret this second dream. The first dream exalted Nebuchadnezzar; he was the head of gold (2:38). But this second dream debased him. When the king saw Daniel's reluctance, he encouraged Daniel not to be alarmed but to share its meaning with him. Daniel respectfully stated that he wished the dream pertained to the king's enemies.

4:20-22. Daniel repeated the description of the greatness of the tree (vv. 20-21) and then explained that the tree represented Nebuchadnezzar (v. 22). Daniel tactfully gave the good news first! Like the tree, Nebuchadnezzar had become great and strong, and his kingdom had been expanded and consolidated under his rule. His kingdom had become greater than any kingdom up to that time.

4:23-25. Then came the bad news. The cutting down of the tree—a decree from the Most High—meant that Nebuchadnezzar would be removed from his position of authority in the kingdom. He would be turned out of the palace (driven away from people) and would live like an animal among the wild animals until seven times (v. 23) would pass by. The word "times" is used again in 7:25 where it also means a year (cf. comments there). Thus Daniel predicted that Nebuchadnezzar would live in a demented state for seven years.

In the mental illness known as zoanthropy (an illness observed in modern times) a person thinks of himself as an animal and acts like one. This may have been the disease Nebuchadnezzar had. Daniel then referred to the purpose of this experience, which the messengers had announced in the dream (4:17). Through this illness Nebuchadnezzar would come to **acknowledge that the Most High is sovereign over the kingdoms of men and gives them to anyone He wishes.**

4:26-27. The fact that **the stump** was not to be uprooted (but was to be secured and left in the field, v. 15) indicates that **the king** would **be restored** to the throne. However, that restoration would not take place till Nebuchadnezzar acknowledged God's sovereign right to rule (**that heaven rules**).

Daniel concluded by exhorting the king to **renounce** his **sins.** This points out the principle that any announced judgment may be averted if there is repentance (cf. the Book of Jonah). Daniel urged Nebuchadnezzar to turn from his sinful pride and produce fruits of righteousness (**doing what is right** and **being kind to the oppressed**)—acts which stem from a heart that is submissive to God. Had Nebuchadnezzar done so, he would have averted his seven years of insanity.

4. THE VISION FULFILLED (4:28-33)

4:28-33. The revelation given **to . . . Nebuchadnezzar** through Daniel's interpretation was soon forgotten and Daniel's exhortation was ignored. Nebuchadnezzar continued in his sinful pride. He did not repent as Daniel had advised him to do (v. 27). The **king** was controlled by his great egotism. He considered the city of **Babylon** itself as his personal possession and as a reflection of his **power** and **glory** (v. 30).

God endured Nebuchadnezzar's pride for **12 months.** This may have been a period of grace in which God was giving Nebuchadnezzar an opportunity to turn to Him in repentance. But when Nebuchadnezzar ignored Daniel's exhortation God, who had given Nebuchadnezzar his authority, announced the interruption of his rule.

What had been predicted was no longer postponed and judgment came on **Nebuchadnezzar,** in keeping with Daniel's interpretation. As the king was boasting of his accomplishments while **walking on the roof** (apparently a flat roof, common in those days) **of** his **royal palace** (v. 29), **a voice . . . from heaven** (v. 31) announced his judgment.

As predicted, the king lived like an animal in the field, eating **grass like cattle.** (Later Daniel added that the king lived with wild donkeys, 5:21.) **His body was drenched with . . . dew . . . his hair grew** long like an eagle's **feathers . . . and his nails** grew **like** a bird's **claws.** He gave no attention to his bodily appearance. Perhaps, because of his royal position, Nebuchadnezzar was hidden in a secluded park so his true condition could be hidden from the populace. Also in the king's absence Daniel may have played a major role in preserving the kingdom and possibly in preventing anyone from killing the king.

5. THE KING'S RESTORATION (4:34-37)

4:34-35. When the seven years (cf. comments on v. 23) had transpired (**at the end of that time) Nebuchadnezzar** with his **sanity . . . restored . . . praised the Most High** (cf. comments on 3:26). The king who had sought honor and glory for himself now acknowledged that the Most High **lives forever.** The king confessed that God's **dominion is . . . eternal,** that **His kingdom endures** (cf. 6:26; 7:14, 27). Thus he acknowledged God's sovereign authority.

Nebuchadnezzar also acknowledged God's irresistible will: **He does as He pleases with the powers of heaven and the peoples of the earth.** Also the king confessed that man is answerable to God, not God to man, for no one can stop God and **no one** has a right to question Him (cf. Job 33:12b-13; Isa. 29:16; 45:9; Rom. 9:19-20).

4:36-37. The king's acknowledgment of God's right to rule (vv. 34-35) brought about the restoration of the king's **sanity** (cf. v. 34) and a restoration to his **throne.** Having been humbled before God, Nebuchadnezzar rose to **greater** heights of honor than he had known when he walked in pride. He said he praised, exalted, and glorified **the King of heaven** (cf. "honored" and "glorified" in v. 34). These verbs indicate continued action, suggesting that Nebuchadnezzar did these things habitually. These verbs embody the ideas of reverence, respect, honor, admiration, and worship.

Since Nebuchadnezzar said that these attitudes characterized his life, many have concluded that he experienced regeneration, becoming a child of God. Nebuchadnezzar did confess that what God had done in dealing with him was **right** and **just**. This is certainly not acknowledged by one who continues in rebellion against God. The king also admitted that he had walked in **pride** (cf. 5:20) but had been humbled by his experience. This too would testify to a transformation in Nebuchadnezzar's character through a newfound knowledge of God.

There seems to be prophetic significance in this incident as well as in the one in chapter 3. Even though God has appointed Gentiles to a place of prominence in His program during the times of the Gentiles, yet most nations and people walk in rebellion against God. This attitude is graphically described in Psalm 2:1-3. God will deal with the nations to humble them and bring them into subjection to Himself. One purpose of the Tribulation, which will immediately precede Christ's second coming, will be to humble the nations and bring them to the point of subjection to Christ's authority. At the conclusion of God's judgments, described in Revelation 6–19, Jesus Christ, the victorious Rider on the white horse, will descend from heaven and smite the nations. Then an angel will announce that "the kingdom of the world has become the kingdom of our Lord and of His Christ and He will reign forever and ever" (Rev. 11:15). God's judgment on Nebuchadnezzar, designed to subject him to God's authority, seems to prefigure God's judgment on the nations to subject them to the authority of the One who has been given the right to rule.

D. The feast of Belshazzar (chap. 5)

1. THE REVELRY OF THE KING (5:1-4)

The events recorded in Daniel 1–4 pertained to the reign of Nebuchadnezzar, who expanded and united the Babylonian Empire. Nebuchadnezzar died in 562 B.C. after ruling 43 years. The ensuing years of Babylonian history till its overthrow by Cyrus in 539 B.C. were marked by progressive deterioration, intrigue, and murder. Nebuchadnezzar was succeeded by his son Evil-Merodach who ruled for two years (562–560 B.C., 2 Kings 25:27-30; Jer. 52:31-34). Evil-Merodach was murdered in August 560 by

Neriglissar, Nebuchadnezzar's son-in-law and Evil-Merodach's own brother-in-law. Neriglissar then ruled four years (560–556 B.C.). He is the Nergal-Sharezer mentioned in Jeremiah 39:3, 13. At his death, he was succeeded by his young son Labashi-Marduk, who ruled only two months (May and June 556) before he was assassinated and succeeded by Nabonidus, who reigned 17 years (556–539 B.C.). See the chart "Kings of the Neo-Babylonian Empire," in the *Introduction.*

Nabonidus did much to restore the glory that had belonged to Babylon under the reign of Nebuchadnezzar. Nabonidus' mother was the high priestess of the moon god at Haran. Perhaps because of her influence, he had great interest in restoring and expanding the Babylonian religion and did much to restore abandoned temples. He was absent from Babylon for 10 of his 17 years, from 554 through 545. In Haran he restored the temple of the moon god Sin, and then he attacked Edom and conquered parts of Arabia where he then lived for some time.

Belshazzar was Nabonidus' eldest son and was appointed by his father as his coregent. (Nebuchadnezzar is referred to as Belshazzar's father [Dan. 5:2, 11, 13, 18; cf. v. 22] in the sense that he was his ancestor or predecessor.) This coregency explains why Belshazzar was called king (v. 1) and why he exercised kingly authority even though Nabonidus actually held the throne.

5:1. Babylon was being besieged by the Persian army, led by Ugbaru, governor of Gutium, while **Belshazzar,** inside the city, was giving a **great banquet for 1,000 of his nobles.** Belshazzar's name means "Bel (another name for the god Marduk) has protected the king." Perhaps the banquet was given to show Belshazzar's contempt for the Persians and to allay his people's fears. Archeologists have excavated a large hall in Babylon 55 feet wide and 165 feet long that had plastered walls. Such a room would have been sufficient to house a gathering of this size. Belshazzar considered his city secure from assault because of its massive walls. Within the city were supplies that would sustain it for 20 years. Therefore the **king** felt he had little cause for concern.

5:2-4. The banquet itself showed Belshazzar's contempt for the power of men. Then, to show his contempt for the power of the true **God,** he ordered that **the gold and silver goblets that Nebuchadnezzar . . . had taken from the temple in Jerusalem** (cf. 1:1-2) be brought to the banquet hall so the assembled revelers **might drink from them.** In drinking, the people honored **the gods** of Babylon—idols made **of gold . . . silver . . . bronze, iron, wood, and stone.** Nabonidus, Belshazzar's father, had attempted to strengthen the Babylonian religion. In keeping with that, this act by his son may have been an attempt to undo the influence of Nebuchadnezzar's honoring the God of Israel (4:34-35). The polygamous king's **wives** and **concubines** were there too.

2. THE REVELATION TO THE KING (5:5-12)

5:5-7. Suddenly the hilarity of the revelry gave way to hushed fear. **Near** one of the lampstands that illuminated the banquet hall, **fingers of a human hand** were seen writing **on the plastered wall.** The terrified **king** (cf. 4:5) **watched** as **the hand . . . wrote** a message. The king had evidently arisen from the chair in which he had been seated to lead the festivities and stood to watch. **He** became **so frightened that . . . his legs gave way** and he fell to the floor. As was the custom (cf. 2:2; 4:6-7) Belshazzar summoned **the** wise men, **enchanters, astrologers, and diviners** (cf. comments on 1:17) and promised to reward **whoever** would interpret the meaning of this strange phenomenon.

The reward was great. The interpreter would **be clothed in purple** (cf. Mordecai's purple robe, Es. 8:15), that is, he would be given royal authority. Also he would receive **a gold chain** (cf. Gen. 41:42), which no doubt had great monetary value. And he would be **made the third highest ruler in the kingdom.** Since Nabonidus was king and Belshazzar his coregent, the highest office to be conferred was that of the third highest ruler. The king's offer shows the extremity of his fear.

5:8-12. The **wise men** were unable to **read** or interpret **the writing** on the wall. This fact produced even greater fear in **the king.** Their inability to interpret the message made it even more ominous.

Then all the guests who like the king had seen the writing on the wall were thrown into utter confusion (**his nobles were baffled**). The sound of confusion in the banquet hall came to the ears of **the queen.** Evidently she was not a wife of Belshazzar for his wives were with him in the hall (vv. 2-3). She was the king's mother, or perhaps even his grandmother. Her familiarity with both **Nebuchadnezzar** and **Daniel** seems to suggest that she was the king's grandmother. She evidently had previous contact with Daniel, **a man . . . who,** she said, **has the spirit of the holy gods** (cf. 4:8-9, 18; 5:14). She knew of his **insight . . . intelligence . . . wisdom** (v. 11), **knowledge . . . understanding and . . . ability to interpret dreams** (v. 12). (On Daniel's position as "chief of the magicians" and others, see comments on 4:9.) So she counseled Belshazzar to summon **Daniel** and let him interpret **the writing** on the plaster.

3. THE REQUEST OF THE KING (5:13-16)

5:13-16. Following the queen's suggestion, Belshazzar had **Daniel . . . brought** in **before** him. **The king** seemingly belittled Daniel, referring to him as **one of the exiles . . . from Judah.** He was from the same land whose God Belshazzar was holding in contempt! (vv. 2-3) The king told Daniel what he had **heard** from the queen (vv. 11-12) about Daniel's ability to do what **the wise men and enchanters** were unable to do. He promised Daniel the same rich rewards he had promised the wise men (v. 16; cf. v. 7) if Daniel could **read** the **writing** on the wall and interpret it. Though written in Aramaic, it was difficult to read, perhaps because it was in an unusual script.

4. THE REPLY BY DANIEL (5:17-28)

a. The humbling of Nebuchadnezzar (5:17-21)

5:17-19. In his reply **Daniel** summarized God's dealing with Belshazzar's predecessor Nebuchadnezzar. He related lessons that Nebuchadnezzar had learned from God's dealings with him. God is sovereign and rules over nations and appoints kings according to His own will; Nebuchadnezzar was brought to his position of power in the Babylonian Empire by divine appointment. (**The Most High God**; cf. comments on 3:26, **gave . . . Nebuchadnezzar sovereignty.**) His authority was widely recognized (by **peoples and nations and men of every language**; cf. 3:4, 7; 4:1; 6:25; 7:14), and his decrees were unchangeable (5:19).

5:20-21. When Nebuchadnezzar failed to recognize that the power was God's and not his own, he **became arrogant** and proud (cf. 4:30). God then humbled him and **stripped** him of **his . . . throne** while he lived like **an animal . . . with the wild donkeys.** Through this discipline Nebuchadnezzar came to recognize the greatness of God's authority (4:34-35). Though the facts of Nebuchadnezzar's seven-year insanity may have been hidden from the populace, they were known by the royal family (cf. 5:22).

b. *The pride of Belshazzar (5:22-24)*

5:22-24. Belshazzar . . . knew what his predecessor had experienced, and should have learned from it. However, Belshazzar had not done so; in fact he had openly challenged **the Lord of heaven** (cf. "the King of heaven," 4:37) by drinking wine from the **goblets** taken **from the temple** in Jerusalem (5:2-3) and by praising man-made **gods** (v. 4). They have no life, but by contrast the true **God** not only *has* **life**, but held *Belshazzar's* life **in His hand.** Perhaps Daniel intended an interesting wordplay by adding that God, who held Belshazzar's life in His *hand*, **sent** a *hand* to write him a message. Belshazzar, knowing about God, failed to **honor** Him.

c. *The judgment by God (5:25-28)*

5:25. As God had judged Nebuchadnezzar's pride by removing him from the throne, so He would judge Belshazzar's pride by taking the kingdom from him and giving it to another people. **This** judgment **was written** in the words that appeared on the plaster. First Daniel read **the inscription** which the wise men were unable to read. It was brief, containing only three words with the first word repeated. *MENE* (*mᵉnēʾ*) is an Aramaic noun referring to a weight of 50 shekels (a mina, equal to 1¼ pounds). It is from the verb *mᵉnâh*, "to number, to reckon." *TEKEL* (*tᵉqēl*) is a noun referring to a shekel (2/5 of an ounce). It is from the verb *tᵉqāl*, "to weigh." *PARSIN* (*parsîn*) is a noun meaning a half-mina (25 shekels, or about ⅔ of a pound). It is from the verb

pᵉras, "to break in two, to divide." The word on the wall was actually *Ūparsîn*, which means "and Parsin" (NIV marg.).

Even if the wise men could have read the words (which they couldn't), they could not have interpreted them for they had no point of reference as to what had been numbered, weighed, and divided.

5:26-27. Then Daniel proceeded to interpret the meaning of **these words.** He explained that *MENE* meant that **God** had **numbered** (*mᵉnâh*) the duration of **the days of** Belshazzar's kingdom and was about to bring **it to an end.** *TEKEL* meant that Belshazzar had **been** evaluated by God, **weighed** (*tᵉqîltâh*, from *tᵉqāl*) in a balance and had been **found wanting,** that is, he was too light. A balance was the normal device used in weighing payments. A payment was to meet a certain standard so if it did not meet that standard, it was rejected as unacceptable. Belshazzar's moral and spiritual character did not measure up to the standard of God's righteousness so he was rejected. "By Him [God] deeds are weighed" (1 Sam. 2:3).

5:28. In interpreting the third word Daniel changed the plural *parsîn* (v. 25) to the singular *PERES* (*pᵉrēs*). Belshazzar's **kingdom** was to be broken up (**divided,** *pᵉrîsat*) **and given to the Medes and Persians.** Apparently Daniel intended a play on words for a change in the vowels in *pᵉrēs* gives the word "Persian" (*Pāras*). Thus the message was that because of the moral and spiritual degradation of the king and his kingdom, God would terminate the Babylonian Empire and give it to the Medes and Persians.

5. THE REVELATION FULFILLED (5:29-31)

5:29-31. One might have expected **Belshazzar's** wrath to fall on **Daniel** because of the message he brought. But instead the king, faithful to his word (cf. v. 16), rewarded Daniel. However, Daniel's enjoyment of those honors and the position to which he had been promoted was short-lived for **that very night Belshazzar** was killed **and Darius the Mede took over the kingdom.** (On the identity of Darius the Mede see comments on 6:1.)

The city had been under assault by Cyrus. In anticipation of a long siege the city had stored supplies to last for 20 years. The Euphrates River ran through the city from north to south, so the residents had an ample water supply. Belshazzar had a false sense of security, because the Persian army, led by Ugbaru, was outside Babylon's city walls. Their army was divided; part was stationed where the river entered the city at the north and the other part was positioned where the river exited from the city at the south. The army diverted the water north of the city by digging a canal from the river to a nearby lake.

With the water diverted, its level receded and the soldiers were able to enter the city by going under the sluice gate. Since the walls were unguarded the Persians, once inside the city, were able to conquer it without a fight. Significantly the defeat of Babylon fulfilled not only the prophecy Daniel made earlier that same night (5:28) but also a prophecy by Isaiah (Isa. 47:1-5). The overthrow of Babylon took place the night of the 16th of Tishri (October 12, 539 B.C.).

The rule of the Medes and Persians was the second phase of the times of the Gentiles (the silver chest and arms of the image in Dan. 2). The events in chapter 5 illustrate that God is sovereign and moves according to His predetermined plans. Those events also anticipate the final overthrow of all Gentile world powers that rebel against God and are characterized by moral and spiritual corruption. Such a judgment, anticipated in Psalm 2:4-6 and Revelation 19:15-16, will be fulfilled at the Second Advent of Jesus Christ to this earth.

E. The edict of Darius (chap. 6)

1. THE PROMINENCE OF DANIEL (6:1-3)

6:1a. Critics have long questioned the historicity of Daniel. They challenge Daniel's reference to the accession of **Darius** (vv. 1, 28; 9:1; called Darius the Mede in 5:31) because there is no historical evidence outside the Bible for his reign. However, several explanations are possible: (1) Darius may have been another name for Cyrus. Daniel 6:28 may be translated, "So Daniel prospered during the reign of Darius, even the reign of Cyrus the Persian." It was common for ancient rulers to use different names in various parts of their realms. Thus Darius may have been a localized name for Cyrus. (This is the view of D.J. Wiseman,

"Some Historical Problems in the Book of Daniel," in *Notes on Some Problems in the Book of Daniel,* pp. 12-14.)

(2) A second explanation is that Darius was appointed by Cyrus to rule over Babylon, a comparatively small portion of the vast Medo-Persian Empire. According to Daniel 9:1 Darius "was *made* ruler over the Babylonian Kingdom." This suggests that he ruled by appointment, rather than by conquest and thus would have been subordinate to Cyrus, who appointed him. The historical situation leading to this appointment, based on the Nabonidus Chronicle, was that Babylon was conquered by Ugbaru, governor of Gutium, who entered the city of Babylon the night of Belshazzar's feast. After Ugbaru conquered Babylon on October 12, 539 B.C., Cyrus entered the conquered city on October 29 of that same year. Ugbaru was then appointed by Cyrus to rule on his behalf in Babylon. Eight days after Cyrus' arrival (Nov. 6) Ugbaru died. If Darius the Mede is another name for Ugbaru, as is entirely possible, the problem is solved. Since Darius was 62 years old when he took over Babylon (5:31), his death a few weeks later would not be unusual. According to this view (presented by William H. Shea, "Darius the Mede: An Update," *Andrews University Seminary Studies* 20. Autumn 1982, pp. 229-47), Gubaru is another spelling for Ugbaru, with the name Gobryas being a Greek form of the same name and appearing in Xenophon's *Cyropaedia* 4. 6. 1-9; 7. 5. 7-34.

(3) A third explanation is that Ugbaru, governor of Gutium, conquered Babylon, and that Gubaru, alias Darius, was the man Cyrus appointed to rule over Babylon. (This is the view of John C. Whitcomb, Jr., *Darius the Mede.* Nutley, N.J.: Presbyterian & Reformed Publishing Co., 1974.)

(4) Still others suggest Darius the Mede should be identified with Cambyses, Cyrus' son, who ruled Persia 530–522 B.C. (This view is held by Charles Boutflower, *In and Around the Book of Daniel.* Reprint. Grand Rapids: Kregel Publishing Co., 1977, pp. 142-55.) Any of these four views may be correct, but perhaps the second one is preferable.

6:1b-3. One of Darius' first responsibilities was to reorganize the newly conquered kingdom of Babylon. He appointed **120 satraps** (cf. 3:2) **to rule** over the **kingdom** of Babylon, and put them under **three administrators . . . one of whom was Daniel. The satraps were** responsible to the three administrators (perhaps 40 satraps to each administrator) **so that the king** was greatly aided in his administrative responsibilities. Daniel was an exceptional administrator, partly because of his extensive experience under Nebuchadnezzar (2:48) for about 39 years. So **the king planned to** make Daniel responsible for the administration of **the** entire **kingdom.** This of course created friction between Daniel and the other administrators and 120 satraps.

2. THE PLOT OF THE LEADERS (6:4-9)

6:4-5. The two **administrators** and 120 **satraps** sought some basis on which to accuse **Daniel in his** administrative work. They were probably jealous of his position and resented him because he was a Judean (cf. comments on 3:12). But they found that Daniel was not **corrupt;** he was **trustworthy** and diligent in discharging his responsibilities. They decided that they would have to find some **basis** for accusation in his religious practices, which obviously were well known to them.

6:6-9. So the 122 leaders devised a plot. (Daniel was certainly outnumbered!) They suggested to **King Darius** that he, **the king,** be made the sole object of worship for **30 days.** Either the 122 got others to agree to the plan (including **prefects . . . advisers, and governors**) or the 122 merely *said* the others agreed. Saying that they **all agreed** (v. 7) was wrong for they certainly had not discussed this with Daniel. All prayer was to be addressed to the **king** in recognition of his power in the religious realm. The penalty for rebelling against his religious authority was to be death by being **thrown into** a den of lions. **Darius,** no doubt flattered by the adulation he would receive, consented to the plot and signed it into law, which according to Medo-Persian custom was irrevocable.

3. THE PRAYER OF DANIEL (6:10-11)

6:10-11. The **decree** signed into law by Darius became public knowledge. But **Daniel,** knowing of the decree, followed his customary practice (**just as he had done before**) of going to his own **upstairs** room. . . . **three times** each **day** to pray to . . . **God** (cf. Ps. 55:17). He prayed **toward Jerusalem** (cf. Ps. 5:7; 2 Chron. 6:21, 34, 38).

Daniel's prayer was first a prayer of thanksgiving (Dan. 6:10) as he acknowledged God's goodnesses to him. His prayer was also a prayer for guidance and **help** (v. 11). Doubtless the responsibility of high office rested heavily on **Daniel** and he sought God's wisdom in the decisions he had to make. Daniel was more than 80 years old at this time (539 B.C.); he was about 16 when he was taken captive 66 years earlier (605 B.C.). So because of his years he may have also sought **God** for physical strength to carry on his heavy duties. Daniel made no attempt to hide his devotion to or his dependence on God, even though it now meant disobeying a governmental decree (cf. Acts 5:29). Daniel would not and could not look to Darius for the guidance and strength he knew God alone could supply. Apparently his opponents knew where and when he prayed, so they **went** (lit., rushed) to his room at the time and, as expected, **found** him **praying.**

4. THE PROSECUTION OF DANIEL (6:12-18)

6:12. Accusation was soon made against Daniel by his opponents before Darius who had issued the **decree.** Darius found himself bound by his own law; he said, **the decree stands.** Nebuchadnezzar the Babylonian was above law, whereas Darius the Mede was bound by law. This was intimated in the contrast between the gold and the silver in the image in Nebuchadnezzar's dream (2:32, 39).

6:13-16. Hearing their accusation against **Daniel,** whom they derisively belittled as **one of the exiles from Judah** (as Arioch and Belshazzar had done; cf. 2:25; 5:13), Darius **was greatly distressed.** Interestingly three kings in the Book of Daniel were distressed (cf. 2:1; 3:13; 5:6, 9).

Though Darius knew he was bound by the law he had made, he sought some way **to rescue Daniel** from the penalty the law incurred. But finding it impossible to do so, he **gave the order** that **Dan**iel be thrown **into the lions' den.**

As he was thrown in—to what seemed to be certain death—**the king said . . . May your God, whom you** serve continually (cf. 6:20; 3:17), rescue you. Whether Darius knew about God's deliverance of Daniel's three friends from the fiery furnace in Nebuchadnezzar's day is not known. Yet Darius' statement expressed a desire that Daniel be spared. He certainly *wanted* him spared, for he obviously appreciated his administrative abilities (cf. 6:2-3). Perhaps he had been impressed with Daniel's confidence in God.

6:17-18. So that Daniel could not escape from the lions' den, **a stone was . . . placed over the mouth of the den,** which was then **sealed** with a royal seal. Besides the side opening to the den (perhaps an underground cave) there may have been an opening at the top (cf. vv. 23-24). The seal, an impression made in clay by an image on a **ring,** would inform others that the stone was not to be tampered with in an effort to free Daniel. Reluctantly **the king** confined Daniel to the den.

The king was deeply agitated that he had been tricked by his administrators and satraps and that he was subject to his own laws. So he spent a sleepless **night** (cf. Xerxes' sleepless night, Es. 6:1).

5. THE PRESERVATION OF DANIEL (6:19-24)

6:19-22. At **dawn the king,** after a sleepless night (v. 18), **hurried to the lions' den.** In anguish over probably finding **Daniel** consumed, Darius hoped against hope (cf. v. 16) that the elderly statesman might have been rescued by **God, whom** he served (cf. 3:17; 6:16).

Daniel replied that **God** had in fact kept him unharmed because of his flawless life (v. 22) and **because he . . . trusted in . . . God** (v. 23). God's **Angel,** Daniel said, had kept the lions' **mouths** shut. Perhaps this Angel, like the One in the fiery furnace with the three young men (3:25), was the preincarnate Christ.

6:23. Discovering that **Daniel** was still alive, Darius **was overjoyed** and had him **lifted from the den** (cf. comments on v. 17). This experience illustrated for Darius the validity of faith in God and His power to control circumstances and deliver those who trust in Him. For 30 days Darius was addressed as God by the people in his realm (cf. v. 7). But **Daniel** served the true God, who did what Darius could never do: shut the mouths of lions to protect one who depended on Him.

6:24. Then the king ordered that Daniel's accusers and their families be **thrown into the . . . den.** The attempt by false accusation to exterminate this Jewish captive-turned-executive boomeranged (cf. Haman's similar fate, Es. 7:9-10). The accusers had persuaded Darius to put in effect a decree that was intended to eliminate **Daniel,** but ironically they could not dissuade **the king** from eliminating them!

6. THE PRONOUNCEMENT OF THE KING (6:25-28)

6:25-28. The one who by his **decree** was being revered for a month as god (v. 7) now made a proclamation that all subjects of his nation (**all the peoples, nations, and men of every language;** cf. 3:4; 7; 4:1; 5:19; 7:14) **must fear and reverence** Daniel's **God.** This was an amazing turnaround on Darius' part! The reason for this, **Darius wrote,** is that Daniel's God lives (**He is the living God;** cf. 6:20) whereas the gods of the Medes and Persians were dead idols. This God is eternal, **His kingdom** is indestructible (cf. 7:14), and He intervenes in people's affairs and delivers those who trust Him. He works by miraculous power (**signs and wonders;** cf. 4:2-3) to perform His will, including the miraculous delivery of **Daniel.** Such a God is truly to be reverenced and worshiped. In spite of the opposition of the satraps and administrators, **Daniel** was honored and lived **during** the reigns **of Darius** and **Cyrus.**

F. The vision of the four beasts (chap. 7)

1. THE VISION (7:1-14)

a. The four beasts (7:1-8)

7:1. The vision recorded by the Prophet **Daniel** in this chapter was revealed to him **in the first year of** Belshazzar's reign, 553 B.C., when **Belshazzar** was made coregent with Nabonidus. Daniel's dream predated by 14 years his experience in the lions' den (chap. 6) which occurred in or soon after 539. When the **dream** came Daniel was about 68 years of age, for he was taken captive (at about the age of 16) 52 years earlier in 605 B.C.

The revelation was given Daniel in **a dream** through **visions** (cf. 2:28; 4:5, 10).

In referring to the experience as "a dream" (sing.) Daniel was emphasizing the unity of the revelation and in referring to it as "visions" (pl.) he emphasized the successive stages in which the revelation was given. (Five times in chap. 7 he said "looked" [vv. 2, 6-7, 13] and once "I kept looking" [v. 11].) The dream refers to his being asleep, and the visions refer to what he saw while dreaming. Sometimes, however, a person had a vision while he was awake (cf., e.g., 9:23). Because of the great significance of Daniel's dream, he immediately wrote down a summary of it.

Daniel had been the interpreter of two dreams by Nebuchadnezzar (chaps. 2; 4). Then the prophet-statesman became the recipient of four dreams or visions (chaps. 7; 8; 9:20-27; 10:1–12:5).

7:2. In the first six chapters, Daniel wrote in the third person; in the last six chapters he wrote in the first person. In his **vision** Daniel first saw **the great sea** churned by the action of **four winds.** The word translated "winds" may also be rendered "spirits," that is, angels. Elsewhere in Scripture this word is used to refer to God's providential actions in the affairs of men through angels (Jer. 23:19; 49:36; 51:1; Zech. 6:1-6; 7:14; Rev. 7:1-3). Throughout the Old Testament the Mediterranean Sea is referred to as the Great Sea (Num. 34:6-7; Josh. 1:4; 9:1; 15:12, 47; 23:4; Ezek. 47:10, 15, 20; 48:28). This vision then related specifically to the Mediterranean world.

7:3-4. The second thing Daniel saw in the vision was **four great beasts** emerging from **the** agitated **sea.** As explained to Daniel later (v. 17) the four beasts represented four kingdoms. **The first** beast **was like a lion,** an animal symbolizing power and strength. This lion had eagle **wings,** which speak of swiftness. Interestingly the lion and eagle were both symbols of Babylon (cf. Jer. 4:7, 13; Ezek. 17:3). The violent wrenching of the **wings** from the lion would deprive it of its great mobility. This could refer to Nebuchadnezzar's insanity or to his empire's deterioration after his death. The lion's rising up on **two feet** (its hind legs) made it look more **like a man.** The fact that it got a man's **heart** suggests that the animal lost its beastly nature and showed compassion. The lion's rising on its hind legs and

may refer to Nebuchadnezzar's humanitarian interests.

7:5. The **second beast** was **like a bear,** an animal of formidable strength (1 Sam. 17:34; Amos 5:19; Hosea 13:8). This represents Medo-Persia, the empire that followed Babylon. The Medo-Persian army was strong and fierce (Isa. 13:15-18). Unlike the grace of the manlike lion, the bear was ponderous and ungainly. It was evidently reclining with **one** side higher than the other. This suggests that though Persia rose later than Media, Persia soon overshadowed the Medes in their united kingdom. The **three ribs** in the bear's **mouth** may represent the kingdoms of Egypt, Assyria, and Babylon, which had preceded the empire represented by the bear. Or they may represent Babylon, Lydia, and Egypt, three nations conquered by the Medes and Persians. The bear **was told** to devour **flesh.** This command suggests that kingdoms operate by divine appointment, not their own authority. In devouring other kingdoms and extending its territory into a vast empire, the bear was fulfilling God's purpose.

7:6. The third **beast** Daniel saw was **like a leopard,** an animal noted for its swiftness (Hab. 1:8), cunning, and agility (Jer. 5:6; Hosea 13:7). This beast **had four wings like . . . a bird,** stressing a swiftness beyond its natural capacity. An additional feature of **this beast** is that it **had four heads.** Also **authority to rule** was **given** it. The kingdom that conquered Medo-Persia was Greece, which did so with great speed, conquering the entire empire between 334 and 330 B.C. A few years after Alexander died his kingdom was divided into four parts (cf. Dan. 8:8, 22).

7:7a. Daniel now described **a fourth beast.** Instead of likening it to some known animal Daniel simply called it a beast. Apparently it was a mongrel composed of parts of a lion, bear, and leopard (cf. the beast in Rev. 13:2). This fourth beast was more **terrifying** and **powerful** than the three preceding beasts, which were all ferocious and destructive. This beast **had large iron teeth** with which it was able to crush and devour its prey. The empire represented by this mongrel beast had **crushed** and assimilated into itself the three previous empires described by the lion, the bear, and the leopard (it **trampled underfoot whatever was left**; cf. Dan. 7:19).

7:7b-8. A significant feature of this fourth and **different** beast was that **it had 10 horns.** According to verse 24 they represent 10 kings. As Daniel focused his attention on **the horns,** he saw **another horn** begin to emerge among the 10. This **little** horn had an insignificant beginning but in its growth it was able to uproot **three of the** existing **horns.** This little horn was noted for its intelligence (it had **the eyes of a man**) and its blasphemous claims (it had **a mouth that spoke boastfully;** cf. vv. 11, 20, 25). (See vv. 19-26 for comments on the identity of this fourth beast and its little horn.)

b. The Ancient of Days (7:9-12)

7:9-10. In this portion (vv. 9-12) of the vision Daniel saw **thrones** of judgment **set** up. One throne was occupied by **the Ancient of Days.** This is the sovereign God (cf. Isa. 43:13; 57:15a) who exercises control over men and nations. His white **clothing** and **hair** speak of His holiness (Rev. 1:14). Daniel's description of the glory surrounding the One seated on the flaming **throne** with **wheels** recalls the description of the glory of God which Ezekiel saw (Ezek. 1:4-28). The **thousands** who surrounded the throne were God's servants, angels who execute His will. When Daniel saw God the Judge take His seat, **the court** (cf. Dan. 7:26) was convened, **and the books were opened.** (Interestingly, as stated earlier, Daniel's name means "God has judged" or "God is my Judge"; cf. 1:7. Here Daniel saw God as the world's Judge.) In Revelation 20:12 the opening of books refers to a review and judging of one's stewardship. Thus God, who assigns power to kingdoms, will judge those kingdoms.

7:11-12. As Daniel was watching the little **horn** because of its boasting (cf. v. 8) he saw that the fourth **beast was slain** and consigned to **blazing fire.** This event will terminate "the times of the Gentiles" (Luke 21:24, 27). The kingdoms represented by the three preceding **beasts had** already **been stripped of their** power by military conquest. But the fourth beast will be relieved of its power not by being conquered militarily, but by divine judgment (cf. Dan. 9:27; Rev. 11:15; 19:15). Each of the three, however, had been

allowed to live for a short time. This may mean that the cultures of each of the first three conquered empires were assimilated into the conquering nations.

c. The Son of Man (7:13-14)

7:13-14. In the third major portion of this **vision** Daniel saw the **Son of Man** approaching **the Ancient of Days.** Jesus Christ, taking the title "Son of Man" from this prophecy, frequently used it to refer to Himself (as recorded in the Gospels; cf. comments on Mark 8:31; John 1:51). When the Son of Man was brought **into** the **presence** of the Ancient of Days, all the **authority, glory, and sovereign power** that had been exercised by rulers in the four kingdoms over **all peoples, nations, and men of every language** (cf. Dan. 3:4, 7; 4:1; 5:19; 6:25) was conferred on Him and those peoples **worshiped Him.** This is in keeping with the Father's promise to the Son in Psalm 2:6-9, and will be fulfilled at Christ's Second Advent (Matt. 24:30; 25:31; Rev. 11:15).

The Son of Man will establish **an everlasting dominion** or kingdom (cf. Dan. 4:34; 7:27). That kingdom will **never be** conquered by another (cf. 6:26). His reign will be established on earth (Rev. 20:1-6). At the expiration of the 1,000 years of the Lord's millennial reign, He will surrender the kingdom to God the Father, after which Christ will be appointed as Ruler over God's eternal kingdom forever (1 Cor. 15:24-28).

2. THE INTERPRETATION (7:15-28)

a. The four beasts explained (7:15-17)

7:15-17. Like Nebuchadnezzar before him (cf. 2:1; 4:4-5), **Daniel** was **disturbed** by his dream (cf. 7:28). Though he had demonstrated the ability to interpret dreams on previous occasions (chaps. 2; 4), he could not interpret this one or his next one (8:15). So he called on **one of those standing** nearby, apparently the angel later identified as Gabriel (8:16; 9:21), to interpret the vision to him. It was explained that **the four great beasts** represent **four kingdoms.** As stated earlier, the four kingdoms are Babylon, represented by the lion; Medo-Persia, represented by the bear raised up on one side; Greece, represented by the winged leopard with four heads; and Rome, represented by the mongrel beast. (See the maps of these four empires.)

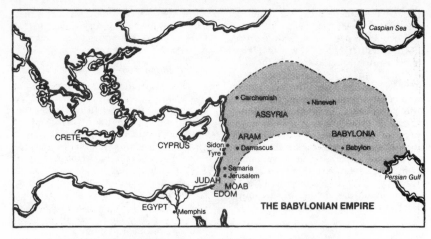

THE BABYLONIAN EMPIRE

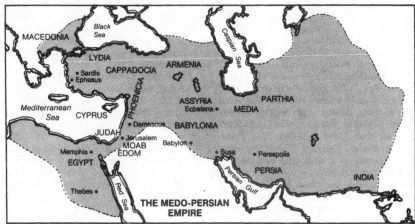

THE MEDO-PERSIAN EMPIRE

b. The promise to Israel (7:18)

7:18. After the destruction of the fourth beast at the Second Advent, **the saints of the Most High** (cf. comments on "the Most High" at 3:26) **will receive the kingdom** (cf. 7:22, 27). The "saints" refer to the believing Jews (cf. comments on v. 25), not to believers of the Church Age. The existence of the church in the present Age was nowhere revealed in the Old Testament. The nation Israel has been set aside by divine discipline in the present "times of the Gentiles," which began with Nebuchadnezzar. During the "times of the Gentiles" four empires, Daniel was told, would rise and rule over the land and people of Israel. Yet God's covenant to David (2 Sam. 7:16; Ps. 89:1-4) stands and will ultimately be fulfilled.

The "saints" (believing Jews when Christ returns to earth) will enjoy the kingdom, the fulfillment of God's promise to Israel.

c. The details of the fourth kingdom (7:19-28)

(1) The request. **7:19-20.** Daniel seems to have had no difficulty in interpreting the significance of the first three beasts. It was **the fourth beast** that caused him consternation, and he asked the angel (probably Gabriel; cf. 8:16; 9:21) to interpret the **meaning** of **the beast** and its **10 horns** and **the other horn that came up** among the 10 and was so **imposing.** What is represented by the 10 horns and particularly the little **horn** is of great significance. For from this point on to the end of the prophecy, Daniel concerned

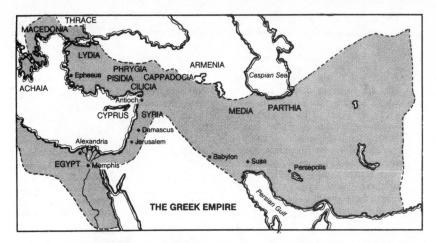

THE GREEK EMPIRE

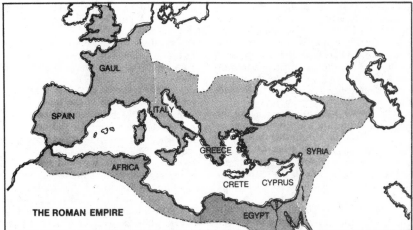

THE ROMAN EMPIRE

himself with the revelation about the person and work of the individual represented by this little horn.

(2) The judgment on the beast. **7:21-22.** Several facts about **this** little **horn** had already been revealed to Daniel (v. 8): (1) It came after the 10 horns (kings; cf. v. 24) were in existence and then was contemporaneous with them. (2) It uprooted 3 of the 10 horns (kings). (3) It was intelligent (it had the eyes of a man). (4) It was arrogant and boastful (cf. v. 11).

Now (vv. 21-22) three additional facts are given: (5) He will persecute **the saints of the Most High** (cf. v. 25; on "the Most High" see comments on 3:26). Obviously the horn represents a person. In 7:24 he is said to be a king. As in verse 18, **the saints** refer to the nation Israel.

His persecution of Israel will take place in the Tribulation. (6) He will overcome (he **was defeating**) the nation Israel and will bring that nation under his authority (Rev. 12:13-17; 17:7). (7) He will be judged by God (cf. Rev. 19:19-20), and Israel, no longer under the rule of the little horn, will enter into her covenanted blessings in **the kingdom** (cf. Dan. 7:18).

(3) The scope of the beast's kingdom. **7:23.** Though historically the sphere of **the fourth beast,** though greater than the extent of each of the previous three kingdoms, was limited, the sphere of this coming ruler in the **fourth kingdom** will be worldwide. Daniel was told that this empire **will devour the whole earth** (cf. Rev. 13:7). And it will be a ferocious conquest, in which that kingdom will tram-

341

ple and crush those who oppose it. This anticipates a coming one-world government under a worldwide dictator.

(4) The ten horns and the little horn (7:24-25). **7:24.** The angel then interpreted the meaning of **the 10 horns,** stating that they **are 10 kings in this kingdom.** The fourth empire, in spite of its great power (vv. 7, 23), will be characterized by progressive weakness, deterioration, and division (cf. comments on 2:41-43 on iron and clay in the fourth part of Nebuchadnezzar's image). When the hordes from the north conquered the Roman Empire in the fifth century A.D., they did not unite to form another empire. Instead individual nations emerged out of the old Roman Empire. Some of those nations and others stemming from them have continued till the present day. The present Age, then, is the 10-horned era of the fourth beast. (Other premillenarians, however, hold that the time of the 10 horns is yet future, that the present Church Age is not seen in this vision, and that 10 kings will coexist over a future revived [or realigned] Roman Empire.)

Sometime after the rise of the 10 horns—and no clue was given Daniel as to how much later—**another king** (the little horn, 7:8, 20) **will arise.** In his rise to power **he will subdue 3 kings** (called 3 horns in v. 8), that is, he will bring 3 of the 10 nations under his authority in his initial rise to power.

7:25. Besides several facts already given about this coming king (see comments on vv. 21-22), three additional ones are now revealed: (1) He will oppose God's authority. **He will speak against the Most High** (cf. Rev. 13:6). On "the Most High" see comments on Daniel 3:26. (2) He will **oppress His saints** (i.e., Israel; cf. comments on 7:21). (3) He will introduce an entirely new era in which he will abandon all previous **laws** and institute his own system. As in 9:27a, he will appear as Israel's friend, but will become Israel's persecutor (**the saints will be handed over to him**) and he will occupy Jerusalem as the capital of his empire (11:45) for three and one-half years (Rev. 12:6; 13:5). **A time, times, and half a time** (cf. Dan. 12:7; Rev. 12:14) refer to the three and one-half years of the Great Tribulation, with "a time" meaning one year, "times" two

years, and "half a time" six months. This equals the 1,260 days in Revelation 12:6 and the 42 months in Revelation 11:2; 13:5. (Cf. comments on "times" in Dan. 4:16.)

(5) The promise to Israel. **7:26-27.** When the Judge, God the Father, convenes **the court** (cf. v. 10), that is, when He judges the little horn, his **power will be** removed and he will be **destroyed** (cf. v. 11; 2 Thes. 2:8; Rev. 19:20). This will occur at the Second Advent of Christ. At the beginning of the Millennium the Son of Man will be given authority to rule (cf. Dan. 7:14), and He will rule over **the saints, the people of the Most High** (cf. comments on 3:26), that is, the nation Israel (cf. 7:18, 22), which has been bound to God by God's covenant with Abraham (Gen. 12:1-6; 13:14-17; 15:18-21). This **kingdom** will not be overthrown and superseded by another. It will continue in the Millennium and on forever (cf. Dan. 4:34; 6:26; 7:14). **All peoples and kings will worship and obey Him.**

(6) The response of Daniel. **7:28.** This prophetic panorama of the times of the Gentiles was so awesome to **Daniel** that he **was deeply** moved. He did not share the vision with anyone at the time. But later when he wrote the prophecies that bear his name, he recorded what had been revealed to him in the vision.

One cannot escape the parallels between the truths revealed to Daniel on this occasion and what was revealed to Nebuchadnezzar early in his reign (chap. 2). Both cover the span of the times of the Gentiles. Both dreams indicate that Israel and her land will be ruled over by four successive world empires. The first was Babylon, represented by the head of gold and the winged lion. The second was the Medo-Persian Empire, represented by the chest and arms of silver and the bear raised up on one side. The third was the Grecian Empire, represented by the belly and thighs of bronze and the four-headed winged leopard. The fourth was the Roman Empire, represented by the legs of iron with feet mixed with clay and by the mongrel beast. The iron-like strength of the fourth empire is seen in the iron legs (2:40) and the beast's iron teeth (7:7). Sovereignty passed from Assyria to Babylon in 609 B.C., from Babylon to Persia in 539 B.C., from Persia to Greece in 330

B.C., and from Greece to Rome in the first century B.C.

Toward the end of the times of the Gentiles, worldwide authority will be exercised by one called "a little horn" who will seek to prevent Christ's rule on the earth by destroying God's covenant people. His short reign of seven years (see comments on "one 'seven' " in 9:27) will be terminated by the Second Advent of Christ. At His coming Christ will establish His millennial kingdom on earth in fulfillment of God's covenant with Israel.

The amillenarian view that the "little horn" has already appeared sometime in the past (but since Christ's First Advent) is wrong because: (a) no such ruler has attained worldwide status (7:23), (b) no such ruler has subdued 3 of 10 kings who were ruling at once (v. 24), (c) no such ruler has persecuted Israel (v. 21) for three and one-half years (v. 25), and (d) no such ruler has been destroyed forever (v. 26) by Christ's return. Nor could this "little horn" be the Roman Catholic papacy because: (a) the "little horn" is a king, not a pope, (b) the papacy's power has not been limited to three and one-half years, (c) the papacy has not concentrated on persecuting the nation Israel, and (d) the papacy has not been destroyed by the return of Christ to the earth.

III. The Prophetic History of Israel during the Times of the Gentiles (chaps. 8–12)

A. The vision of the ram and the goat (chap. 8)

Chapters 8–12 (and 1:1–2:4a) are written in Hebrew, whereas 2:4b–7:28 are in Aramaic. For the significance of this, see "Languages" in the *Introduction.*

1. THE VISION (8:1-14)

a. The preparation (8:1-2)

8:1-2. The vision recorded by **Daniel** in chapter 8 came to him two years after the vision of chapter 7 (cf. Belshazzar's **third year,** 8:1, with his "first year," 7:1). In his **vision** Daniel **saw** himself **in the** palace in **Susa,** one of the Persian royal cities, more than 200 miles east of Babylon on **the Ulai Canal** (see map "The World of Jeremiah and Ezekiel" in the *Introduction* to Jer.). A century later the Persian king Xerxes built a magnificent palace there, which was where the

events recorded in the Book of Esther took place (cf. Es. 1:2). And Nehemiah was King Artaxerxes' cupbearer in the Susa palace (Neh. 1:1).

b. The vision of the ram (8:3-4)

8:3-4. In his vision Daniel saw **a ram with two** long **horns** near the **canal.** The significant thing was that **one** horn **was longer than the other.** The horns did not arise simultaneously; the longer one arose after (**grew up later** than) the shorter one. The disparity between the ram's two horns recalls the bear raised up on one side (7:5). **The ram** that had been standing by the canal began to charge **toward the west . . . north and . . . south.** His charge was irresistible; **none could** escape his onslaught. Doing **as he** wished, the ram dominated all the territory against which he moved **and became great.**

c. The vision of the goat (8:5-14)

8:5-8. Daniel then saw **a goat with a** powerful single **horn** arise **suddenly . . . from the west.** His speed was so great that his feet did not touch **the ground.** The goat, determined to destroy **the two-horned ram,** went **at him in great rage . . . furiously** and broke the ram's **two horns.**

The ram was powerless to defend himself and the goat subjugated the ram. The greatness that had characterized **the ram** now belonged to **the goat.** Previously none could escape from the ram's power (v. 4); now **none could** escape from the goat (v. 7). As soon as **the goat** was elevated to great **power,** his **large** single **horn was broken off, and** its **place** was taken by **four prominent horns.**

The description of this goat is somewhat parallel to the third beast in 7:6, the leopard with wings. Both were rapid, and the leopard had four heads whereas the goat had four horns. The goat's horns probably represented kings (just as the horns on the fourth beast represented kings, 7:24).

8:9-12. Out of one of the four horns **came another horn.** It had an insignificant beginning but it exerted **power** southward and eastward **and toward the Beautiful Land,** that is, the land of Israel. He became a great persecutor of the people of Israel (**the host of the heaven;** cf. "host" in v. 13) and he subjugated that

A Comparison of Daniel 2; 7; and 8

Daniel 2 Metals	Daniel 7 Animals	Daniel 8 Animals	Nations
Gold	Winged lion	—	Babylon
Silver	Bear	Ram	Medo-Persia
Bronze	Winged leopard	Goat	Greece
Iron (and iron and clay)	Beast	—	Rome

nation (**trampled on them**). He **set** himself **up** as Israel's king, calling himself **the Prince of the host.** He compelled the nation to worship him, as suggested by the fact that he prohibited Israel from following her religious practices (removing **the daily sacrifice**) and desecrated the temple (**brought** the **sanctuary . . . low**). The nation Israel (**the saints**; cf. comments on 7:18) acceded to this individual's wishes because of his rebellious attitude (cf. "rebellion" in 8:13). He **prospered** and so despised the truth contained in God's Word that **truth was** said to be **thrown to the ground.**

This part of the vision anticipated the rise of a ruler in the Greek Empire who subjugated the people and land of Israel, desecrated her temple, interrupted her worship, and demanded for himself the authority and worship that belongs to God.

8:13-14. For Daniel's benefit an angel (**a holy one**; cf. "holy ones" in 4:17) addressed the revealing angel (**another holy one**) and asked, **How long will it take for the vision to be fulfilled?** The answer was, **It will take 2,300 evenings and mornings.** (For the meaning of the "2,300 evenings and mornings" see the comments on 8:23-25.) At the conclusion of that time, **the sanctuary** that had been defiled would be cleansed and restored (**reconsecrated**) to its rightful place in the nation's life.

2. THE INTERPRETATION (8:15-27)

a. Gabriel's intervention (8:15-18)

8:15-18. Once again **Daniel,** though able to interpret Nebuchadnezzar's dreams (chaps. 2; 4), could not interpret this dream (cf. 7:16). **Gabriel** was sent to interpret **the meaning of the vision** to Daniel. Understandably Daniel **was terrified** (cf. 7:15) by the appearance of the glorious messenger **and fell prostrate** before him. Referring to Daniel as a **son of man** (cf. comments on Ezek. 2:1; not to be confused with Christ, the Son of Man), Gabriel explained that **the vision** pertained to **the time of the end** (cf. Dan. 8:19), that is, events future from Daniel's day, events concerning the nation Israel under the Greek Empire.

b. Gabriel's interpretation (8:19-26)

8:19. Gabriel stated that **the vision** pertained to events beyond Daniel's time (**what will happen later,** and **the appointed time of the end;** cf. v. 17). Significantly this later time, within the times of the Gentiles, was called **the time of wrath.** As stated earlier (chap. 2) the times of the Gentiles is the period from Nebuchadnezzar's reign to the second coming of Christ during which Israel is undergoing divine discipline. Her acts of disobedience brought forth God's disciplinary wrath on the nation.

8:20-21. Gabriel first interpreted the meaning of **the two-horned ram** (cf. vv. 3-7). This beast represented **Media and Persia,** the same empire represented by the bear raised up on one side (7:5). Though Persia rose later than Media (559 B.C. for Persia compared with centuries earlier for Media) the Persians overshadowed the Medes. So the second horn on the ram was larger than the first horn. Persia extended its empire to the west, north, and south with a vast army of more than 2 million soldiers.

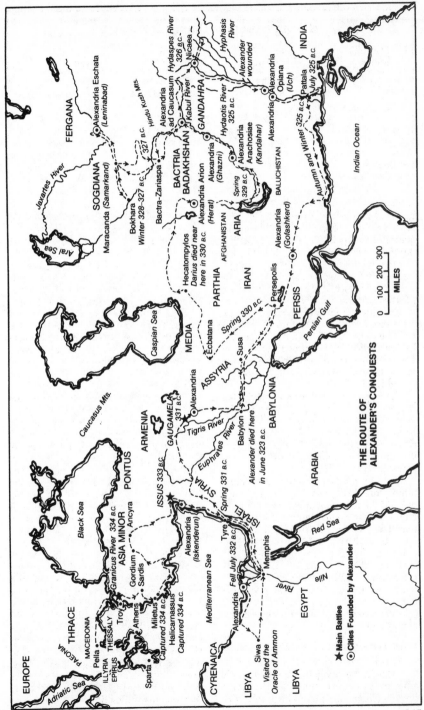

THE ROUTE OF ALEXANDER'S CONQUESTS

The angel then gave the meaning of **the shaggy goat** with **the large horn between his eyes.** The goat represented **the king** (or kingdom) **of Greece,** who in 7:6 was depicted by the winged leopard. (See the chart on p. 1356, "A Comparison of Daniel 2; 7; and 8.") The single horn represented Greece's **first king,** Alexander (cf. 11:3). Though his father Philip II of Macedonia had united all the Greek city-states except Sparta, Alexander is considered Greece's first king.

Alexander the Great (the prominent horn, 8:5) came from the west with a small but fast army. He was enraged (v. 6) at the Persians for having attacked them many years before at the Battle of Marathon (490 B.C.) and the Battle of Salamis (481), Greek cities near Athens. He quickly conquered Asia Minor, Syria, Egypt, and Mesopotamia in a few years, beginning in 334 B.C. The Persians were helpless to resist him (v. 7). (See the map on p. 1357, "The Route of Alexander's Conquests.") Alexander died of malaria and complications from alcoholism in 323 B.C. at the age of 32 in Babylon. At the height of his power he was cut off (v. 8).

8:22. Since Alexander had no heirs to succeed him, the kingdom was divided several years later among his four generals, represented here by **the four horns** (cf. v. 8; cf. 11:4). But the divided kingdom of Greece never had **the same power** Greece had enjoyed under Alexander. To Ptolemy was given Egypt and parts of Asia Minor. Cassander was given the territory of Macedonia and Greece. Lysimachus was given Thrace and parts of Asia Minor (western Bithynia, Phrygia, Mycia, and Lydia). Seleucus was given the remainder of Alexander's empire which included Syria, Israel, and Mesopotamia.

8:23-25. Years later from among one of the four horns (kings) there would **arise,** Gabriel said, a severe (**stern-faced**) and cunning **king** (**a master of intrigue;** cf. **deceit,** v. 25). A powerful ruler, he would devastate property and **destroy** people in order to expand his kingdom. **The holy people,** the nation Israel (cf. "saints," 7:18, 22, 27), would be a special target of his oppression. In subjugating Israel, **many** would lose their lives just when they thought they were safe. His antagonism against Israel would also be **against** her God, **the Prince of princes.**

Yet this mighty conqueror himself would **be destroyed** by supernatural **power.** His rise was not his own doing (8:24) and his downfall was **not by human** means (he died insane in Persia in 163 B.C.).

The king referred to here is known as Antiochus IV Epiphanes. After murdering his brother, who had inherited the throne in the Seleucid dynasty, he came to power in 175 B.C. In 170 B.C. Ptolemy VI of Egypt sought to recover territory then ruled over by Antiochus. So Antiochus invaded Egypt and defeated Ptolemy VI and proclaimed himself king in Egypt. This was his growth "in power to the south" (v. 9). On his return from this conquest, trouble broke out in Jerusalem so he decided to subdue Jerusalem ("the Beautiful Land," v. 9; cf. 11:16, 41). The people were subjugated, the temple desecrated, and the temple treasury plundered.

From this conquest Antiochus returned to Egypt in 168 but was forced by Rome to evacuate Egypt. On his return he determined to make the land of Israel a buffer state between himself and Egypt. He attacked and burned Jerusalem, killing multitudes (cf. 8:10). The Jews were forbidden to follow the Mosaic Law in observing the Sabbath, their annual feasts, and traditional sacrifices, and circumcision of children (cf. v. 11). Altars to idols were set up in Jerusalem and on December 16, 167 B.C. the Jews were ordered to offer unclean sacrifices and to eat swine's flesh or be penalized by death. (Though his friends called him *Epiphanes* ["the Illustrious One"] no wonder the Jews called him *Epimanes* ["the Madman"].) (For more on the role of Antiochus IV Epiphanes see comments on 11:21-35.)

Antiochus' desecration of the temple was to last 2,300 evenings and mornings before its cleansing (8:14). Some take the 2,300 evenings and mornings to mean 2,300 days, that is, a little more than six years. In this interpretation, the six years were from Antiochus' first incursion into Jerusalem (170 B.C.) to the refurbishing and restoring of the temple by Judas Maccabeus in late 164. A second interpretation seems preferable. Rather than each evening and each morning representing a day, the reference may be to evening and morning sacrifices, which were interrupted by Antiochus' desecration (cf.

"the daily sacrifice," vv. 11-21). With two sacrifices made daily, the 2,300 offerings would cover 1,150 days or three years (of 360 days each) plus 70 days. This is the time from Antiochus' desecration of the temple (December 16, 167 B.C.) to the refurbishing and restoring of the temple by Judas Maccabeus in late 164 and on into 163 B.C. when all the Jewish sacrifices were fully restored and religious independence gained for Judah. Whichever interpretation it is that one accepts, the figure of 2,300 was a literal one and so the time period was literally fulfilled.

There is no question among expositors that Antiochus is in view in this prophecy. What was prophesied was fulfilled literally through him. However, the prophecy looks beyond Antiochus to a future person (the Antichrist) of whom Antiochus is only a foreshadowing. This coming one is said to "stand against the Prince of princes" (v. 25). This can be none other than the Lord Jesus Christ. Thus the prophecy must go beyond Antiochus and look forward to the coming of one whose ministry will parallel that of Antiochus.

From Antiochus certain facts can be learned about the forthcoming desecrator: (1) He will achieve great power by subduing others (v. 24). (2) He will rise to power by promising false security (v. 25). (3) He will be intelligent and persuasive (v. 23). (4) He will be controlled by another (v. 24), that is, Satan. (5) He will be an adversary of Israel and subjugate Israel to his authority (vv. 24-25). (6) He will rise up in opposition to the Prince of princes, the Lord Jesus Christ (v. 25). (7) His rule will be terminated by divine judgment (v. 25). So it may be concluded that there is a dual reference in this striking prophecy. It reveals Israel's history under the Seleucids and particularly under Antiochus during the time of Greek domination, but it also looks forward to Israel's experiences under Antichrist, whom Antiochus foreshadows.

8:26. Daniel was told to **seal up the vision** in the sense of concluding it, not in the sense of keeping it secret, because it needed to be preserved for the **future.** He kept it in his mind and later preserved it in writing when he wrote it down under the Holy Spirit's inspiration.

c. Daniel's response (8:27)

8:27. Daniel was completely overcome (**exhausted and . . . ill**) by the interpretation of this **vision. For several days** he was unable to carry on his official **business.**

B. The vision of the 70 "sevens" (chap. 9)

1. THE OCCASION OF THE VISION (9:1-2)

9:1-2. It was now **the first year** of the reign **of Darius** the Mede. (On the identity of this Darius see comments on 6:1.) This was 539 B.C., 66 years after Daniel had been exiled.

The overthrow of **the Babylonian Kingdom** by the Medo-Persians was indeed a momentous event. It had been revealed to Belshazzar through Daniel's interpretation of the writing on the wall (5:25-28, 30). The Babylonian overthrow prepared the way for liberation of the Jews who had been in exile since Nebuchadnezzar's first invasion **of Jerusalem** in 605 B.C. Besides predicting the overthrow of the people **Jeremiah** had also predicted that Israel's sojourn in Babylon was to **last 70 years** (Jer. 25:11-12).

Evidently moved by Darius' victory **Daniel** searched **the Scriptures** to understand the events of which he was a vital part. He **understood** Darius' victory meant that the termination of the 70-year Captivity was near. Thus these significant events became even more momentous for Daniel.

2. THE PRAYER OF DANIEL (9:3-19)

a. Confession (9:3-14)

9:3-6. Daniel's study of the Scriptures led him to turn to **God** and to pray a **prayer** of confession (vv. 3-14) and **petition** (vv. 15-19), with **fasting.** Wearing **sackcloth and/or ashes** was evidence of mourning in grief or repentance (cf. Gen. 37:34; Neh. 9:1; Es. 4:1, 3; Isa. 58:5; Jer. 49:3; Ezek. 7:18; Joel 1:8; Matt. 11:21).

Moses revealed the principle on which God would deal with His covenant people: obedience would bring blessing, and disobedience would bring discipline. One form of discipline was that Israel would be subjugated to Gentile powers (Deut. 28:48-57, 64-68). Israel's experience in Babylon was the outworking of this principle.

Then Moses revealed the basis on which the discipline would be lifted and the nation would be restored to blessing (Deut. 30). She would have to return to God and obey His voice; then **God** would turn back her Captivity and restore the people to the land from which they had been dispersed and shower blessings on them.

Daniel evidently was fully aware that the years in Babylon were a divine discipline on Israel. Knowing that confession was one requisite to restoration, he **confessed** the sin of his people, identifying himself with their sin as though he were personally responsible for it.

Daniel noted that blessing depends on obedience, for **God . . . keeps His covenant of love** (hesed, "loyal love") **with all who love Him and obey** Him. Even a covenant people cannot be blessed if they disobey. Four times Daniel acknowledged that his people had **sinned** (Dan. 9:5, 8, 11, 15). Their sin was a sin of rebellion (cf. v. 9) against God and in turning **away** (cf. v. 11) **from the** Word of God (His **laws**; cf. vv 10-11) which they knew. God in grace had sent **prophets** (cf. v. 10) to exhort the people to return to Him but they had refused to heed their messages (**we have not listened**). **Kings** and **people** alike stood guilty before God.

9:7-11a. Daniel then acknowledged that God is **righteous** (cf. vv. 14, 16) and just in disciplining Israel for her **unfaithfulness,** for which she was **covered with shame** (vv. 7-8) and dispersed (**scattered**) into foreign **countries.** God's discipline did not mean that He had withheld mercy (cf. v. 18) and forgiveness from His people, but it meant that He, being righteous, must punish people's rebellion and disobedience (v. 10). They refused to keep God's **laws** (v. 10; cf. v. 5) for they **transgressed** His **Law** (v. 11) and **turned** from God (cf. v. 5), being obstinate in their disobedience (**refusing to obey**).

9:11b-14. Because of her rebellion and disobedience Israel was experiencing **the curses and . . . judgments written** by **Moses** (cf. v. 13) in Deuteronomy 28:15-68. In spite of the severity of the discipline, including **great** national **disaster** (Dan. 9:12), the nation was not **turning from** her **sins** and submitting to the authority of **the Law,** God's **truth. This disaster,** the fall of Jerusalem, was because **God is righteous** (cf. vv. 7, 16) and Israel had **not obeyed** Him (cf. vv. 10-11).

b. Petition (9:15-19)

9:15-16. Daniel began his petition (v. 15) by mentioning two of the same things with which he began his confession (vv. 4-5): God's greatness and the people's sin. Daniel spoke of God's delivering Israel **out of Egypt** by His great power (**with a mighty hand**). God was glorified through the deliverance of His people. But because the nation had **sinned** (Daniel's fourth time to state that his people had sinned; cf. vv. 5, 8, 11) she had become **an object of scorn to** those nations **around** her. In prayer that God, **in keeping with** His **righteous acts** (cf. vv. 7, 14), would **turn away** His **anger and . . . wrath from Jerusalem,** Daniel was asking that God's discipline might be lifted and the people freed from their present bondage. (Jerusalem is God's **city;** cf. v. 24, and His **holy hill;** cf. v. 20; Joel 2:1; 3:17; Zeph. 3:11.)

Once again Daniel attributed the nation's present status to her past sin, the **sins and . . . iniquities of our fathers** (cf. Dan. 9:6, 8).

9:17-19. Having prayed for the negative, the removal of God's wrath (vv. 15-16), the prophet now prayed for the positive, God's favor, mercy, and forgiveness (vv. 17-19). Daniel asked that **God** would **hear** his **prayers** and restore (**look with favor on**) the **sanctuary** (the temple in Jerusalem) for His **sake** (cf. v. 19). And he wanted God to **hear** his request (**give ear**) and to **see** (**open Your eyes**) the city's **desolation.** Interestingly Daniel did not specify what God should do; he only asked that God "look" on the sanctuary and "see" the city, both in desolation for many years.

Daniel based his requests on God's **great mercy** (cf. v. 9), not on the nation's righteousness for she had none. But because God is merciful and forgiving, he prayed, **O Lord, listen! O Lord, forgive!** Concerned for God's reputation, Daniel wanted the Lord to **act** quickly (**do not delay**) on behalf of the **city** and **people** that bore His **name.** All this would bring glory to God for it was **for** His **sake** (cf. v. 17).

3. THE RESPONSE OF THE LORD (9:20-27)

a. The message of Gabriel (9:20-23)

9:20-21. Daniel's prayer included confession of his **sin and the sin of** his **people,** and his **request** that God restore

Jerusalem (God's **holy hill**). The answer to Daniel's **prayer** was not delayed (cf. "do not delay," v. 19). For he was interrupted by the appearance of **Gabriel,** who had come to him **earlier** to interpret his **vision** of the ram and the goat (8:15-16). Gabriel **came** swiftly **about the time of the evening sacrifice.** This was one of the two daily sacrifices required in the Law (Ex. 19:38-39; Num. 28:3-4; cf. "evenings and mornings" in Dan. 8:14). Even though the temple was destroyed so the sacrifices could not be offered for those 66 years, Daniel still observed that time of day as an appointed time of worship. Perhaps this was one of the three times he prayed daily (6:10).

9:22-23. Though **Daniel** did not refer to it in his prayer, he was evidently concerned about God's program for Israel from that point on (cf. v. 2). Jeremiah's prophecy (Jer. 25:11-12) had revealed God's plan for the nation only up to the end of the 70-year Babylonian Captivity. Daniel wanted to know what would transpire after that. Daniel's previous two visions (Dan. 7–8) of forthcoming events dealt primarily with Gentile nations that would rise beginning with Babylon. So Gabriel was dispatched by God to satisfy Daniel's desire and to reveal God's program for His people until its consummation in the covenanted kingdom under Israel's Messiah. Gabriel would **give** Daniel **insight into** God's purposes for His people. Because the prophet was **highly esteemed** (cf. 10:11, 19) by God, Gabriel had received **an answer** for Daniel **as soon as** Daniel **began to pray.**

b. The program in the 70 "sevens" (9:24)

9:24. Daniel was first informed that God's program would be consummated in **70 "sevens."** Since Daniel had been thinking of God's program in terms of years (v. 1; cf. Jer. 25:11-12; 2 Chron. 36:21), it would be most natural for him to understand these "sevens" as years. Whereas people today think in units of tens (e.g., decades), Daniel's **people** thought in terms of sevens (heptads). Seven days are in one week. Every seventh year was a sabbath rest year (Lev. 25:1-7). Seven "sevens" brought them to the Year of Jubilee (Lev. 25:8-12). Seventy "sevens," then, is a span of 490 years. The 490 could not designate *days* (about 1⅓ years) for that would not be enough

time for the events prophesied in Daniel 9:24-27 to occur. The same is true of 490 weeks of seven days each (i.e., 3,430 days, about 9½ years). Also if days were intended one would expect Daniel to have added "of days" after "70 sevens" for in 10:2-3 he wrote literally, "three sevens of days" (NIV, "three weeks").

Also since Israel and Judah had failed to keep the sabbatical years (every seventh year the land was to lie fallow, Lev. 25:1-7) throughout her history, the Lord enforced on the land 70 "sabbaths" (cf. Lev. 26:34-35). Thus 490 years would be required to complete 70 sabbatical years with one occurring every seventh year.

This span of time was decreed for Daniel's people (cf. "your people" in Dan. 10:14; 11:14) and the Holy City (cf. 9:16, 24). This prophecy, then, is concerned not with world history or church history, but with the history of Israel and the city of Jerusalem. By the time these 490 years run their course, God will have completed six things for Israel. The first three have to do with sin, and the second three with the kingdom. The basis for the first three was provided in the work of Christ on the cross, but all six will be realized by Israel at the Second Advent of Christ.

1. At the end of the 490 years God will **finish** the **transgression** of Israel. The verb "to finish" (*kālā'*) means "to bring something to an end." Israel's sin of disobedience will be brought to an end at Christ's second coming when she repents and turns to Him as her Messiah and Savior. Then she will be restored to the land and blessed, in answer to Daniel's prayer.

In Old Testament days the highpoint in Israel's festival calendar was the Day of Atonement (Lev. 16). On that day the nation assembled before God, acknowledged her sin, and offered blood sacrifices to cover that sin. Though that sacrifice covered Israel's sin for 12 months, it did not permanently remove that sin (Heb. 10:1-3). It was necessary that a sacrifice be offered God that would permanently remove all the accumulated sins. This sacrifice was offered by Jesus Christ who by His death made payment for all sins that had not been removed in the past (cf. Rom. 3:25). So His atoning work on the cross has made possible His future "finishing" of Israel's transgression.

2. God will **put an end to sin.** The verb *ḥāṭam* has the idea of sealing up. Here the thought is sealing something up with a view to punishment (cf. Deut. 32:34; Job 14:17). This emphasized that Israel's sin which had gone unpunished would be punished—in or through Jesus Christ, her Substitute, who would bear the sins of the world on the cross. Then at Christ's second coming He will remove Israel's sin (Ezek. 37:23; Rom. 11:20-27).

3. God will **atone for wickedness.** The verb "to atone" (*kāpar*) means "to cover or expiate." This too relates to God's final atonement of Israel when she repents at Christ's second coming, as the provision for that atonement has already been made at the Cross. Israel's Day of Atonement should be kept in view here too, as in the first of these six accomplishments. On that day God provided a just basis on which He would deal with a guilty people. The blood applied to the mercy seat ("the atonement cover," Lev. 16:14) over the ark of the covenant enabled Him to dwell among His sinful people. Similarly Daniel's prophecy promised that because of Christ's blood shed on the cross God would deal with sinners, and here in particular, with sinners in Israel.

Being propitiated (i.e., satisfied) by Christ's blood, God can atone for or expiate sin. The Greek words for "atonement cover" (*hilasmos*; KJV, "mercy seat") and "propitiate" (*hilaskomai*) are related.

4. The second three accomplishments deal with positive aspects of God's program. Being satisfied by the death of Christ, God will **bring in everlasting righteousness.** The form of the verb "bring in" here means "to cause to come in." The word "everlasting" (here pl. in Heb.) means ages. Thus this phrase (lit., "to bring in righteousness of ages") is a prophecy that God will establish an age characterized by righteousness. This is a reference to the millennial kingdom (Isa. 60:21; Jer. 23:5-6).

5. God will **seal up vision and prophecy.** All that God through the prophets said He would do in fulfilling His covenant with Israel will be fully realized in the millennial kingdom. Until they are fulfilled, prophecies are "unsealed." ("Seal" translates the same verb,

ḥāṭam, used in the second of these six accomplishments.)

6. God will **anoint the Most Holy.** This may refer to the dedication of the most holy place in the millennial temple, described in Ezekiel 41–46. Or it may refer not to a holy place, but to the Holy One, Christ. If so, this speaks of the enthronement of Christ, "the Anointed One" (Dan. 7:25-27) as King of kings and Lord of lords in the Millennium.

These six accomplishments, then, anticipate the establishment of Israel's covenanted millennial kingdom under the authority of her promised King. The six summarize God's whole program to bring the nation Israel the blessings He promised through His covenants (Gen. 15:18-21; 2 Sam. 7:16; Jer. 31:31-34).

c. The divisions of the 70 "sevens" (9:25-27)

9:25. Important revelation was then given Daniel about the inception of this important time period and its divisions. The 70 "sevens" would begin, Gabriel said, with **the issuing of the decree to restore and rebuild Jerusalem.** This decree was the fourth of four decrees made by Persian rulers in reference to the Jews. The first was Cyrus' decree in 538 B.C. (2 Chron. 36:22-23; Ezra 1:1-4; 5:13). The second was the decree of Darius I (522–486) in 520 B.C. (Ezra 6:1, 6-12). This decree actually was a confirmation of the first decree. The third was the decree of Artaxerxes Longimanus (464–424) in 458 B.C. (Ezra 7:11-26). The first two decrees pertain to the rebuilding of the temple in Jerusalem and the third relates to finances for animal sacrifices at the temple. These three say nothing about the rebuilding of the city itself. Since an unwalled city was no threat to a military power, a religious temple could be rebuilt without jeopardizing the military authority of those granting permission to rebuild it. No one of these three decrees, then, was the decree that formed the beginning of the 70 sevens.

The fourth decree was also by Artaxerxes Longimanus, issued on March 5, 444 B.C. (Neh. 2:1-8). On that occasion Artaxerxes granted the Jews permission to rebuild Jerusalem's city walls. This decree is the one referred to in Daniel 9:25. The end or goal of the prophecy is the appearance of **the Anointed One, the**

The 483 Years in the Jewish and Gregorian Calendars

Jewish Calendar (360 days per year*)	Gregorian Calendar (365 days a year)

Jewish Calendar
(360 days per year*)

$(7 \times 7) + (62 \times 7)$ years = 483 years

```
    483 years
×   360 days
  173,880 days
```

Gregorian Calendar
(365 days a year)

444 B.C. to A.D. 33 = 476 years†

```
    476 years
×   365 days
  173,740 days
+     116 days in leap years‡
+      24 days (March 5–March 30)
  173,880 days
```

*See comments on Daniel 9:27b for confirmation of this 360-day year.
†Since only one year expired between 1 B.C. and A.D. 1, the total is 476, not 477.
‡A total of 476 years divided by four (a leap year every four years) gives 119 additional days. But three days must be subtracted from 119 because centennial years are not leap years, though every 400th year is a leap year.

Ruler. This refers to Christ Himself. God the Father anointed Christ with the Spirit at the time of His water baptism (Acts 10:38), but the anointing referred to here is the anointing of Christ as the Ruler in His kingdom (cf. comments on "anoint the Most Holy" in Dan. 9:24). This prophecy of the 70 sevens, then, ends not with the First Advent of Christ, as some suggest, but rather with the Second Advent and the establishing of the millennial kingdom.

This 490-year period is divided into three segments; (a) 7 "sevens" (49 years), (b) 62 "sevens" (434 years), and (c) 1 "seven" (v. 27; 7 years). The first period of 49 years may refer to the time in which the rebuilding of the city of Jerusalem, permitted by Artexerxes' decree, was completed (444–395 B.C.). Though Nehemiah's wall construction project took only 52 days, many years may have been needed to remove the city's debris (after being desolate for many decades), to build adequate housing, and to rebuild the **streets and a trench.**

9:26a. The 62 "sevens" (434 years) extend up to the introduction of the Messiah to the nation Israel. This second period concluded on the day of the Triumphal Entry just before Christ was **cut off,** that is, crucified. In His Triumphal Entry, Christ, in fulfillment of Zechariah 9:9, officially presented Himself to the nation of Israel as the Messiah. He was

evidently familiar with Daniel's prophecy when on that occasion He said, "If you, even you, had only known on this day what would bring you peace—but now it is hidden from your eyes" (Luke 19:42).

Thus the first two segments of the important time period—the 7 sevens (49 years) and the 62 sevens (434 years)—ran consecutively with no time between them. They totaled 483 years and extended from March 5, 444 B.C. to March 30, A.D. 33. How can 444 B.C. to A.D. 33 equal 483 years? For an answer see the chart "The 483 Years in the Jewish and Gregorian Calendars." (For more details see Harold W. Hoehner, *Chronological Aspects of the Life of Christ.* Grand Rapids: Zondervan Publishing House, 1977, and Alva J. McClain, *Daniel's Prophecy of the Seventy Weeks.* Grand Rapids: Zondervan Publishing House, 1969.)

According to Daniel 9:26 **the Anointed One** was not "cut off" *in* the 70th "seven"; He was cut off **after** the 7 and 62 "sevens" had run their course. This means that there is an interval between the 69th and 70th "sevens." Christ's crucifixion, then, was in that interval, right after His Triumphal Entry, which concluded the 69th "seven." This interval was anticipated by Christ when He prophesied the establishing of the church (Matt. 16:18). This necessitated the setting aside of the nation Israel for a season in order that His new program for the church might be instituted. Christ predicted the setting aside of the nation (Matt. 21:42-43). The present Church Age is the interval between the 69th and 70th "sevens."

Amillenarians teach that Christ's First Advent ministry was in the 70th "seven," that there was no interval between the 69th and 70th "sevens," and that the six actions predicted in Daniel 9:24 are being fulfilled today in the church. This view, however, (a) ignores the fact that verse 26 says *"after* the 62 'sevens,'" not *"in* the 70th 'seven,'" (b) overlooks the fact that Christ's ministry on earth was three and one-half years in length, not seven, and (c) ignores the fact that God's six actions pertain to Daniel's "people" (Israel) and His "Holy City" (Jerusalem), not the church.

When the Anointed One would be cut off, Daniel was told, he would **have nothing.** The word translated "cut off" is used of executing the death penalty on a criminal. Thus the prophecy clearly points to the crucifixion of Christ. At His crucifixion He would "have nothing" in the sense that Israel had rejected Him and the kingdom could not be instituted at that time. Therefore He did not then receive the royal glory as the King on David's throne over Israel. John referred to this when he wrote, "He came to that which was His own [i.e., the throne to which He had been appointed by the Father] but His own [i.e., His own people] did not receive Him" (John 1:11). Daniel's prophecy, then, anticipated Christ's offer of Himself to the nation Israel as her Messiah, the nation's rejection of Him as Messiah, and His crucifixion.

9:26b. The prophecy continues with a description of the judgment that would **come** on the generation that rejected the Messiah. **The city** which contains **the sanctuary,** that is, Jerusalem, would be destroyed by **the people of the ruler who will come.** The ruler who will come is that final head of the Roman Empire, the little horn of 7:8. It is significant that the *people* of the ruler, not the ruler himself, will destroy Jerusalem. Since he will be the final Roman ruler, the people of that ruler must be the Romans themselves. This, then, is a prophecy of the destruction of Jerusalem about which Christ spoke in His ministry.

When the leaders of the nation registered their rejection of Christ by attributing His power to Beelzebub, the prince of the demons (Matt. 12:24), Christ warned that if they persisted in that view they would be guilty of sin for which there would be no forgiveness (Matt. 12:31-32). He also warned the nation that Jerusalem would be destroyed by Gentiles (Luke 21:24), that it would be desolate (Matt. 23:38), and that the destruction would be so complete that not one stone would be left on another (Matt. 24:2). This destruction was accomplished by Titus in A.D. 70 when he destroyed the city of Jerusalem and killed thousands of Jews. But that invasion, awesome as it was, did not end the nation's sufferings, for **war,** Gabriel said, would **continue until the end.** Even though Israel was to be set aside, she would continue to suffer until the prophecies of the 70 "sevens" were completely fulfilled. Her sufferings span the entire period from the destruction of Jerusalem in A.D. 70 to Jerusalem's deliverance from Gentile dominion at the Second Advent of Christ.

9:27a. This verse unveils what will occur in the 70th seven years. This seven-year period will begin after the Rapture of the church (which will consummate God's program in this present Age). The 70th **"seven"** will continue till the return of Jesus Christ to the earth. Because Jesus said this will be a time of "great distress" (Matt. 24:21), this period is often called the Tribulation.

A significant event that will mark the beginning of this seven-year period is the confirming of **a covenant.** This covenant will be made **with many,** that is, with Daniel's people, the nation Israel. "The ruler who will come" (Dan. 9:26) will be this covenant-maker, for that person is the antecedent of the word **he** in verse 27. As a yet-future ruler he will be the final head of the fourth empire (the little horn of the fourth beast, 7:8).

The covenant he will make will evidently be a peace covenant, in which he will guarantee Israel's safety in the land. This suggests that Israel will be in her land but will be unable to defend herself for she will have lost any support she may have had previously. Therefore she will need and welcome the peacemaking role of this head of the confederation of 10 European (Roman) nations. In offering this covenant, this ruler will pose as a prince of peace, and Israel will accept his authority. **But** then **in the middle of that "seven,"** after three and one-half years, **he will** break the covenant. According to 11:45, he will then move from Europe into the land of Israel.

This ruler will **end . . . sacrifice and offering.** This expression refers to the entire Levitical system, which suggests that Israel will have restored that system in the first half of the 70th "seven." After this ruler gains worldwide political power, he will assume power in the religious realm as well and will cause the world to worship him (2 Thes. 2:4; Rev. 13:8). To receive such worship, he will terminate all organized religions. Posing as the world's rightful king and god and as Israel's prince of peace, he will then turn against Israel and become her destroyer and defiler.

9:27b. Daniel was told that "the ruler who will come" (v. 26) **will place abominations on a wing of the temple.** Christ referred to this incident: "You [will] see standing in the holy place the abomination that causes desolation" (Matt. 24:15). John wrote that the false prophet will set up an image to this ruler and that the world will be compelled to worship it (Rev. 13:14-15). But then his end will come **(the end that is decreed is poured out on him).** With his false prophet he will be cast into the lake of fire when Christ returns to the earth (Rev. 19:20; cf. Dan. 7:11, 26).

This covenant could not have been made or confirmed by Christ at His First Advent, as amillenarians teach, because: (a) His ministry did not last seven years, (b) His death did not stop sacrifices and offerings, (c) He did not set up "the abomination that causes desolation" (Matt. 24:15). Amillenarians suggest that Christ confirmed (in the sense of fulfilling) the Abrahamic Covenant but the Gospels give no indication He did that in His First Advent.

As stated, the Antichrist will break his covenant with Israel at the beginning of the second half of the 70th "seven," that is, it will be broken for three and one-half years. This is called "a time, times, and half a time" (Dan. 7:25; 12:7; Rev. 12:14). The fact that this is the same as the three and one-half years, which in turn are equated with 1,260 days (Rev.

11:3; 12:6) and with 42 months (Rev. 11:2; 13:5), means that in Jewish reckoning each month has 30 days and each year 360 days. This confirms the 360-day Jewish year used in the calculations in the chart, "The 483 Years in the Jewish and Gregorian Calendars" (near Dan. 9:26a). Since the events in the 69 sevens (vv. 24-26) were fulfilled literally, the 70th "seven," yet unfulfilled, must likewise be fulfilled literally.

C. The final vision (chaps. 10–12)

1. THE PREPARATION OF THE PROPHET (10:1–11:1)

a. The occasion of the vision (10:1-3)

10:1-3. The final vision **given to Daniel** came **in the third year** of the reign of Cyrus which was 536 B.C. Exiles had returned from Babylon and had begun rebuilding the temple. (Perhaps Daniel had not returned with the exiles because of his age.) Israel's captivity had ended. Jerusalem was being reoccupied, and the nation seemed to be at peace. The **revelation** in the vision given to Daniel on this occasion shattered any hope the prophet might have had that Israel would enjoy her new freedom and peace for long. For God revealed that the nation would be involved in many conflicts (**a great war**). **Understanding** the significance of the **vision,** Daniel fasted **for three weeks** (lit., "three sevens of days"; cf. comments on 9:25). During this time of mourning he abstained from **choice** foods and apparently waited on God in prayer (cf. 10:12) concerning his people's destiny.

b. The heavenly messenger (10:4-11)

10:4-11. After three weeks (cf. v. 3) Daniel was visited by a messenger as the prophet **was standing** by the **Tigris** River (cf. 12:5). The messenger was an angel from heaven, not a human being. He was **dressed in linen** (cf. 12:7) and had a dazzlingly bright appearance. Since Gabriel previously had been sent by God to reveal truth to Daniel (8:16), probably Gabriel was also the visitor on this occasion. Angels, who dwell in the presence of God who is light, are themselves clothed with light, and Daniel saw something of heaven's glory reflected in this one who visited him (10:5-6).

Some Bible students say that the **man** was the preincarnate Christ because of (a) the similarity of the description here to that of Christ in Revelation 1:13-16, (b) the response of Daniel and his friends (Dan. 10:7-8), and (c) the fact that this "Man" may be the same as the "Son of Man" in 7:13 and the "Man" in 8:16. On the other hand, in favor of this messenger being an angel is the improbability of Christ being hindered by a prince (demon) of Persia (10:13) and needing the help of the angel Michael, and the fact that the person is giving a message from heaven.

Daniel's companions evidently **saw** the brilliance of the light without seeing the visitor and **they fled** to hide from its shining. Daniel remained **alone** in the angel's presence and, being weak, Daniel prostrated himself before the messenger. In that position Daniel **fell asleep.** He was then aroused from his **sleep** by the angel so he might receive the revelation the angel had come to deliver. The angel, calling the prophet **highly esteemed** (cf. 9:23; 10:19), declared, **I have now been sent to you** by God, who had heard Daniel's request for understanding.

c. The explanation by the heavenly messenger (10:12-14)

10:12-14. Encouraging Daniel **not to be afraid** (cf. v. 8), Gabriel explained the reason for the delay in God's answer to Daniel's prayer. When Daniel first began fasting and mourning in response to the vision of a great war (vv. 1-2), **God** had dispatched Gabriel with a message for him, but Gabriel was hindered by **the prince of the Persian kingdom** (cf. "the prince of Persia," v. 20). Since men cannot fight with angels (Jacob's wrestling was with God, not an angel; cf. comments on Gen. 32:22-32), the prince referred to here must have been a satanic adversary.

God has arranged the angelic realm in differing ranks referred to as "rule, authority, power, and dominion" (Eph. 1:21). Gabriel and Michael have been assigned authority over angels who administer God's affairs for the nation Israel (cf. Michael in Dan. 10:21; 12:1; Jude 9). In imitation Satan has also apparently assigned high-ranking demons to positions of authority over each kingdom. The prince of the Persian kingdom was a satanic representative assigned to Persia.

To seek to prevent Gabriel's message from getting to Daniel, the demonic prince attacked Gabriel as he embarked on his mission. This gives insight into the nature of the warfare fought in the heavenlies between God's angels and Satan's demons to which Paul referred (Eph. 6:12): "Our struggle is not against flesh and blood but against the rulers, against the authorities, against the powers of the dark world, and against spiritual forces of evil in heavenly realms."

The battle between Gabriel and the prince (demon) of Persia continued for three weeks until **Michael, one of the chief princes** of the angelic realm (cf. Dan. 10:21; 12:1), **came to** Gabriel's assistance. Such angelic-demonic conflict indicates something of Satan's power. While **the king of Persia** was fighting Michael, Gabriel was able to bring a message to Daniel concerning **the future** of Israel, Daniel's **people** (cf. "your people," 9:24). It was to be a revelation of the warfare (10:1) between Israel and her neighbors until Israel is given peace by the coming Prince of peace. This vision contains the most detailed prophetic revelation in the Book of Daniel.

d. The strengthening of the prophet (10:15–11:1)

10:15-19. Daniel had been weakened at the appearance of the messenger (v. 8; cf. 7:15; 8:27). Now he was also overwhelmed (**speechless,** 10:15) at learning of the angelic-demonic conflict that delayed the answer to his prayer. Moreover, he was **overcome with anguish** (v. 16) at the content of **the vision** of Israel's coming sufferings. He was left totally debilitated (cf. v. 8) and gasping for breath.

In addressing the messenger as **my lord** (cf. v. 19; 12:8) Daniel was using a title of respect something like the modern-day "Sir."

To meet the prophet's need, the angel first quieted the alarm in Daniel's heart (**Do not be afraid;** cf. 10:12, **O man highly esteemed;** cf. 9:23; 10:11), and **strengthened** him physically and emotionally. Daniel was then ready to receive the details of the message.

10:20–11:1. The messenger then stated that when he returned **to fight against the prince of Persia** (cf. "the prince of the Persian kingdom," 10:13),

The Ptolemies and the Seleucids in Daniel 11:5-35

Ptolemies (Kings "of the South," Egypt)		Seleucids (Kings "of the North," Syria)	
Daniel 11:5	Ptolemy I Soter (323–285 B.C.)*	Daniel 11:5	Seleucus I Nicator (312–281 B.C.)
11:6	Ptolemy II Philadelphus (285–246)		Antiochus I Soter† (281–262)
		11:6	Antiochus II Theos (262–246)
11:7-8	Ptolemy III Euergetes (246–221)	11:7-9	Seleucus II Callinicus (246–227)
		11:10	Seleucus III Soter (227–223)
11:11-12, 14-15	Ptolemy IV Philopator (221–204)	11:10-11, 13, 15-19	Antiochus III the Great (223–187)
11:17	Ptolemy V Epiphanes (204–181)		
		11:20	Seleucus IV Philopator (187–176)
11:25	Ptolemy VI Philometer (181–145)	11:21-32	Antiochus IV Epiphanes (175–163)

*The years designate the rulers' reigns.
†Not referred to in Daniel 11:5-35.

the prince of Greece would come. These princes, as stated earlier (see comments on vv. 11-14), were demons, Satan's representatives assigned to nations to oppose godly forces. Persia and Greece were two major nations discussed in detail in chapter 11 (Persia, vv. 2-4; Greece, vv. 5-35).

What is **the Book of truth?** It was probably "God's record of truth in general, of which the Bible is one expression" (John F. Walvoord, *Daniel: The Key to Prophetic Revelation,* p. 250). The messenger was about to tell Daniel God's plans for Israel under Persia and Greece (11:2-35) and later in the Tribulation (vv. 36-45) and the Millennium (12:1-4).

The messenger told Daniel he was supported by **Michael** in his struggle with demons (cf. 10:13). Michael is **your** (Daniel's) **prince** in the sense that he has a special relationship to Israel (cf. 12:1), Daniel's people. When **Darius the Mede** (11:1; see comments on 6:1a; cf. 9:1) began his rule over Babylon, the messenger supported Darius in some way. Or if **him** refers to Michael then the thought is that the messenger supported Michael in return for Michael supporting the messenger.

2. THE DETAILS OF ISRAEL'S HISTORY UNDER THE SECOND AND THIRD EMPIRES (11:2-35)

a. History under Persia (11:2)

11:2. The angel informed Daniel that the present leadership in the Persian Empire would be succeeded by four rulers. The first was Cambyses, Cyrus' son, who came to the throne in 530 B.C. He was followed by Pseudo-Smerdis, who reigned a short period in 522 B.C. He was succeeded by Darius I Hystaspes who ruled from 521 to 486 B.C. He in turn was succeeded by Xerxes, known in the Book of Esther as Ahasuerus, who ruled from 485 to 465 B.C. (See the chart "Chronology of the Postexilic Period," near Ezra 1:1.) Xerxes was the most powerful, influential, and wealthy of the four. During his reign he fought wars against Greece.

b. History under Greece (11:3-35)

(1) The rise of Alexander (11:3-4). **11:3.** The **mighty king** was Alexander whose rise had been foreshadowed by (a) the bronze belly and thighs of Nebuchadnezzar's image (2:32, 39b), (b) the winged leopard (7:6), and (c) the prominent horn of the goat (8:5-8). Between 334 and 330

355

B.C. Alexander conquered Asia Minor, Syria, Egypt, and the land of the Medo-Persian Empire. His conquests extended as far as India (see the map "The Route of Alexander's Conquests," near 8:20-21) before Alexander's death at the age of 32 in 323 B.C. from malaria with complications from alcoholism.

11:4. A few years after Alexander's death, his kingdom was divided among his four generals (cf. 8:22): Seleucus (over Syria and Mesopotamia), Ptolemy (over Egypt), Lysimacus (over Thrace and portions of Asia Minor), and Cassander (over Macedonia and Greece). This division was anticipated through the four heads of the leopard (7:6) and the four prominent horns on the goat (8:8). Alexander founded no dynasty of rulers; since he had no heirs, his kingdom was divided and the **empire** was marked by division and weakness.

(2) The conflict between the Ptolemies and the Seleucids (11:5-20). The Ptolemies who ruled over Egypt, were called the kings "of the South." The Seleucids, ruling over Syria, north of Israel, were called the kings "of the North." This section (vv. 5-20) gives many details of the continuous conflict between the Ptolemies and the Seleucids during which the land of Israel was invaded first by one power and then by the other.

11:5. The strong **king of the South** was Ptolemy I Soter, a general who served under Alexander. He was given authority over Egypt in 323 B.C. and proclaimed king of Egypt in 304. The commander referred to in verse 5 was Seleucus I Nicator, also a general under Alexander, who was given authority to rule in Babylon in 321. But in 316 when Babylon came under attack by Antigonus, another general, Seleucus sought help from Ptolemy I Soter in Egypt. After Antigonus' defeat in 312, Seleucus returned to Babylon greatly strengthened. He ruled over Babylonia, Media, and Syria, and assumed the title of king in 305. Thus Seleucus I Nicator's **rule** was over far more territory than Ptolemy I Soter's.

11:6. Ptolemy I Soter died in 285 B.C. and Ptolemy II Philadelphus, Ptolemy's son, ruled in Egypt (285-246). Meanwhile Seleucus was murdered in 281 and his son Antiochus I Soter ruled till 262. Then Seleucus' grandson Antiochus II Theos ruled in Syria (262-246). Ptolemy II and Antiochus II were bitter enemies but finally (**after some years**) they entered into an alliance in about 250. This alliance was sealed by the marriage of Ptolemy II's **daughter** Berenice to Antiochus II. This marriage, however, did **not last,** for Laodice, whom Antiochus had divorced in order to marry Berenice, had Berenice killed (she was **handed over**). Laodice then poisoned Antiochus II and made her son, Seleucus II Callinicus, king (246-227).

11:7-8. Berenice's brother, Ptolemy III Euergetes (246-221), succeeded his father and set out to avenge the death of his sister Berenice. He was **victorious** over the Syrian army (**the king of the North**), put Laodice to death, and returned **to Egypt** with many spoils.

11:9-10. After this humiliating defeat, Seleucus II Callinicus (**the king of the North**) sought to **invade** Egypt but was unsuccessful. After his death (by a fall from his horse) he was succeeded by his son, Seleucus II Soter (227-223 B.C.), who was killed by conspirators while on a military campaign in Asia Minor. Seleucus III's brother, Antiochus III the Great, became the ruler in 223 at 18 years of age and reigned for 36 years (till 187).

The two **sons** (Seleucus III and Antiochus III) had sought to restore Syria's lost prestige by military conquest, the older son by invading Asia Minor and the younger son by attacking Egypt. Egypt had controlled all the territory north to the borders of Syria which included the land of Israel. Antiochus III succeeded in driving the Egyptians back to the southern borders of Israel in his campaign in 219-217.

11:11-13. The **king of the South** in this verse was Ptolemy IV Philopator (221-204 B.C.). He was the one driven back by Antiochus III the Great (cf. comments on v. 10). Ptolemy IV came to meet Antiochus III at the southern borders of Israel. Ptolemy IV was initially successful in delaying the invasion of Antiochus (Ptolemy slaughtered **many thousands**). But after a brief interruption Antiochus returned with **another army** (much larger) and turned back **the king of the South.**

11:14-17. Syria was not Egypt's only enemy, for Philip V of Macedonia joined with Antiochus III against Egypt. Many

Jews (**your own people**, i.e., Daniel's people, the Jews; cf. "your people" in 9:24; 10:14) also joined Antiochus against Egypt. Perhaps the Jews hoped to gain independence from both Egypt and Syria by joining the conflict, **but** their hopes were not realized.

Antiochus then sought to consolidate control over Israel from which he had expelled the Egyptians. The **fortified city** seems to refer to Sidon which Antiochus captured in 203 B.C. Antiochus III continued his occupation and by 199 had established **himself in the Beautiful Land** (cf. 8:9; 11:41). Antiochus sought to bring peace between Egypt and Syria by giving his daughter to marry Ptolemy V Epiphanes of Egypt. But this attempt to bring a peaceful alliance between the two nations did not succeed (v. 17).

11:18-19. Antiochus III **then** turned **his attention** to Asia Minor in 197 B.C. and Greece in 192. However, Antiochus did not succeed because Cornelius Scipio (**a commander**) was dispatched from Rome to **turn** Antiochus **back.** Antiochus returned to **his own country** in 188 and died a year later. Antiochus III the Great had carried on the most vigorous military campaigns of any of Alexander's successors, **but** his dream of reuniting Alexander's empire under his authority was never realized.

11:20. Antiochus III's son Seleucus IV Philopator (187–176 B.C.) heavily taxed his people to pay Rome, but he was poisoned (**destroyed . . . not in . . . battle)** by his treasurer Heliodorus.

(3) Invasion by Antiochus IV Epiphanes (11:21-35). These verses describe Antiochus IV Epiphanes, a son of Antiochus III the Great. This one Seleucid who ruled from 175–163 B.C. is given as much attention as all the others before him combined. He is the little horn of Daniel 8:9-12, 23-25. A long section (11:21-35) is devoted to him not only because of the effects of his invasion on the land of Israel, but more so because he foreshadows the little horn (king) of 7:8 who in a future day will desecrate and destroy the land of Israel.

11:21-22. Antiochus IV is introduced as **a contemptible person.** He took to himself the name Epiphanes which means "the Illustrious One." But he was considered so untrustworthy that he was nicknamed Epimanes which means "the

Madman." The throne rightly belonged to Demetrius Soter, a son of Seleucus IV Philopator, but Antiochus IV Epiphanes seized the throne and had himself proclaimed king. Thus he did not come to the throne by rightful succession; he seized **it through intrigue.** He was accepted as ruler because he was able to turn aside an invading **army,** perhaps the Egyptians. He also deposed Onias III, the high priest, called here **a prince of the covenant.**

11:23-24. **After** his military victories, Antiochus Epiphanes' prestige and **power** rose with the help of a comparatively small number of **people.** He evidently sought to bring peace to his realm by redistributing **wealth,** taking from the rich and giving to **his followers.**

11:25-27. After Antiochus consolidated his kingdom, **he** moved **against** Egypt, **the king of the South,** in 170. Antiochus was able to move his army from his homeland to the very border of Egypt before he was met by the Egyptian army at Pelusium near the Nile Delta. In this battle the Egyptians had a **large . . . army but** were defeated and Antiochus professed friendship with Egypt. The victor and the vanquished sat at a **table** together as though friendship had been established, but the goal of both to establish peace was never realized for they both were deceptive.

11:28. Antiochus carried **great wealth** back to his homeland from his conquest. On his return he passed through the land of Israel. After his disappointment in Egypt (he had hoped to take all of Egypt but failed) he took out his frustrations on the Jews by desecrating the temple in Jerusalem. Evidently he opposed (set **his heart . . . against**) the entire Mosaic system (**the holy covenant**). After desecrating the temple, he returned **to his own country.**

11:29-30a. Two years later (in 168) Antiochus moved against Egypt (**the South**) **again.** As he moved into Egypt, he was opposed by the Romans who had come to Egypt in **ships** from **the western coastlands** (lit., "ships of Kittim"; cf. NIV marg., i.e., Cyprus). From the Roman senate Popillius Laenas took to Antiochus a letter forbidding him to engage in war with Egypt. When Antiochus asked for time to consider, the emissary drew a circle in the sand around Antiochus and demanded that he give his answer before he stepped out of the circle. Antiochus submitted to Rome's demands for to resist would be to declare war on Rome. This was a humiliating defeat for Antiochus Epiphanes (**he will lose heart**) but he had no alternative but to return to his own land.

11:30b-32. For a second time (cf. v. 28) Antiochus took out his frustration on the Jews, the city of Jerusalem, and their temple. He vented **his fury against the holy covenant,** the entire Mosaic system (cf. v. 28), favoring any renegade Jews who turned to help him (cf. v. 32). He desecrated **the temple** and abolished **the daily sacrifice.** Antiochus sent his general Apollonius with 22,000 soldiers into Jerusalem on what was purported to be a peace mission. But they attacked Jerusalem on the Sabbath, killed many people, took many women and children as slaves, and plundered and burned the city.

In seeking to exterminate Judaism and to Hellenize the Jews, he forbade the Jews to follow their religious practices (including their festivals and circumcision), and commanded that copies of the Law be burned. Then he **set up the abomination that causes desolation.** In this culminating act he erected on December 16, 167 B.C. an altar to Zeus on the altar of burnt offering outside the temple, and had a pig offered on the altar. The Jews were compelled to offer a pig on the 25th of each month to celebrate Antiochus Epiphanes' birthday. Antiochus promised apostate Jews (**those who . . . violated the covenant;** cf. v. 30) great reward if they would set aside the God of Israel and worship Zeus, the god of Greece. Many in Israel were persuaded by his promises (**flattery**) and worshiped the false god. However, a small remnant remained faithful to **God,** refusing to engage in those abominable practices. Antiochus IV died insane in Persia in 163 B.C. (Cf. comments on this Antiochus in 8:23-25.)

11:33-35. The Jews who refused to submit to Antiochus' false religious system were persecuted and martyred for their faith. The word **fall** (vv. 33-34), literally "stumble" (*kāšal*), refers to severe suffering on the part of many and death for others. This has in view the rise of the Maccabean revolt. Mattathias, a priest,

was the father of five sons. (One of them, Judas, became well known for refurbishing and restoring the temple in late 164 B.C. He was called Judas Maccabeus, "the Hammerer.") In 166, Mattathias refused to submit to this false religious system. He and his sons fled from Jerusalem to the mountains and began the Maccabean revolt. At first only a few Jews joined them. But as their movement became popular, **many** joined them, some out of **sincere** motives and some from false motives. The suffering that the faithful endured served to refine and purify them. This time of persecution was of short duration. It had previously been revealed to Daniel that the temple would be desecrated for 1,150 days (8:14; see comments on 8:23-25). Here Daniel was assured that this persecution would run its course and then be lifted, for its end **will still come at the appointed time.**

3. THE PROPHETIC HISTORY OF THE 70TH SEVEN (11:36–12:3)

a. The king described (11:36-39)

All the events described thus far in chapter 11 are past. The intricate details of the conflicts between the Seleucids and the Ptolemies were fulfilled literally, exactly as Daniel had predicted. So detailed are the facts that skeptics have denied that the book was written by Daniel in the sixth century B.C. They conclude that the book must have been written during the time of the Maccabees (168–134 B.C.) *after* the events took place. However, the God who knows the end from the beginning, was able to reveal details of forthcoming history to Daniel.

In verses 36-45 a leader is described who is introduced simply as "the king." Some suggest that this is Antiochus IV Epiphanes and that the verses describe additional incursions of his into Israel. However, the details given in these verses were not fulfilled by Antiochus. True, Antiochus was a foreshadowing of a king who will come (cf. comments on 8:25). But the two are not the same. One is past and the other is future. The coming king (the little "horn" of 7:8 and "the ruler" of 9:26) will be the final ruler in the Roman world. His rise to prominence by satanic power is described in Revelation 13:1-8 where he is called a "beast." According to John (Rev. 17:12-13), he will gain authority not by military conquest but by the consent of the 10 kings who will submit to him. Starting with Daniel 11:36 the prophecy moves from the "near" to the "far." The events recorded in verses 36-45 will occur during the final seven years of the 70 sevens (9:24).

11:36. This coming **king** will be independent of any authority apart from himself (he **will do as he pleases**). Midway during his seven-year reign he will exercise the political power given him by the 10 kings who will have elected him (Rev. 17:12-13). He will also take to himself absolute power in the religious realm, magnifying **himself above** all gods and defying and speaking blasphemously **against the God of gods.** "He opposes and exalts himself over everything that is called God or is worshiped, and even sets himself up in God's temple, proclaiming himself to be God" (2 Thes. 2:4). "He will speak against the Most High" (Dan. 7:25). The world will be persuaded to worship him as god by the miracles the false prophet will perform in his name (Rev. 13:11-15). He will succeed in spreading his influence around the world, both politically and religiously (Rev. 13:7-8).

The duration of this king's rule **has been determined** by God. **He will be successful** as the world ruler during **the time of wrath,** the three and one-half years of the Great Tribulation, but at the end of that period the judgment determined by God will be meted out to him (cf. Dan. 7:11, 26; 9:27; Rev. 19:19-20).

11:37. Because of the reference to **the gods** (or God, 'ĕlōhîm) **of his fathers,** some have concluded that this ruler will be a Jew, since the Old Testament frequently uses the phrase "the God of your fathers" to refer to the God of Abraham, Isaac, and Jacob (e.g., Ex. 3:15). However, since this individual will be the final ruler in the Roman world, the little horn of the fourth beast (Dan. 7:8, 24b), he must be a Gentile. His showing **no regard** for the gods of his fathers means that in order to gain absolute power in the religious realm, this king will have no respect for his religious heritage. He will set aside all organized religion (**nor will he regard any god**) and will set himself up (**exalt himself**) as the sole object of worship. Instead of depending on gods, he will depend on his own power (received from Satan, Rev. 13:2) and by that

power he will demand worship of himself.

The fact that he has no regard **for the one desired by women** suggests he repudiates the messianic hope of Israel. Perhaps many an Israelite woman had longingly wondered if she would become the mother of the coming Messiah, the nation's Savior and King.

11:38-39. The Antichrist **will honor a god of fortresses,** that is, he will promote military strength. And because of his political and religious power he will be able to accumulate vast wealth. The **god unknown to his fathers** (ancestors), who will give him strength, may be Satan. Though this king will come to power offering peace through a covenant with Israel (cf. 9:27) he will not hesitate to use military power to expand his dominion. And he will be helped by **a foreign god.** Those who submit to his authority will be put in positions of power (he **will greatly honor** them), and his ability to dispense favors (**distribute the land at a** [reduced?] **price**) will gain him a great following.

b. The king attacked (11:40-45)

11:40a. The events in verses 40-45 will transpire **at the time of the end,** that is, they will occur in the second half of the 70th "seven" of years. **Him** refers back to the king introduced in verse 36. In verses 40-45 every occurrence of "he" (seven times), "him" (four times), and "his" (three times) refers to this coming king. He will have entered into a covenant with the people of Israel, binding that nation as a part of his domain (9:27). Any attack, then, against the land of Israel will be an attack against him with whom Israel will be joined by covenant.

The king of the South will attack Israel. Some suggest that this will occur at the middle of the 70th "seven" of years; more likely it will take place toward the end of the second half of that seven-year period. Since "the king of the South" in 11:5-35 referred to a king of Egypt, there seems to be no reason to relate *this* king of the South (v. 40) to some other nation. In fact Egypt is mentioned twice in verses 42-43. In this invasion Egypt will not come alone but will be joined by the Libyans and Nubians (v. 43). These nations, referred to elsewhere as Put and Cush, may be nations in Africa. However, it is more likely that Put refers to Arab nations in the Sinai area and Cush to nations in the Persian Gulf region (cf. Gen. 2:13 and comments there).

Simultaneous with the invasion of Israel by the king of the South (Egypt) will be an invasion by **the king of the North.** Some Bible scholars equate this invasion with the one by Gog and Magog, for Gog will "come from . . . the far north" (Ezek. 38:15). Others say the battle of Gog and Magog will occur in the first half of the 70th "seven" and thus *before* this two-pronged invasion in Daniel 11:40. They suggest that the battle of Gog and Magog will occur when Israel is at peace (Ezek. 38:11, 14). According to that view, a difference is made between Gog who will come from "the far north" (Ezek. 38:15) and a later invasion which will be headed by "the king of the North" (Dan. 11:40). Either way the king of the North in verse 40 is certainly not one of the *Seleucid* kings of the North in verses 5-35. This invasion has no correspondence to historical facts; it is yet future.

The king of the South and the king of the North will fight against the Antichrist. Israel will be occupied and many Jews will flee, seeking refuge among the Gentile nations (see comments on Rev. 12:14-16).

11:40b-43. When the Antichrist hears of this invasion, he will move his army from Europe into the Middle East, sweeping through **many countries . . . like a flood** (v. 40). He will move quickly into the land of Israel, **the Beautiful Land** (v. 41; cf. v. 16; 8:9). His first strike will be against **Egypt** (11:42-43a), for Egypt and her Arab allies (**Libyans and Nubians,** v. 43) are the ones who will initiate the invasion on Israel. On this occasion the king will not conquer the territory of **Edom, Moab, and . . . Ammon** (v. 41), now included in the present kingdom of Jordan. But he will gain control over "many countries."

11:44-45. Then the Antichrist will hear alarming reports **from the east** (probably referring to an invasion by a massive army of 200 million soldiers from east of the Euphrates River, Rev. 9:16) and from **the north** (perhaps another attack by the king of the North; cf. Dan. 11:40). Enraged, the Antichrist will set out to **destroy . . . many** of the invaders.

Then he will occupy Israel and **will pitch his royal tents between the seas,** that is, between the Dead Sea and the Mediterranean Sea, **at the beautiful holy mountain,** probably Jerusalem. Posing as Christ, the Antichrist will set up his headquarters in Jerusalem, the same city from which Christ will rule the world in the Millennium (Zech. 14:4, 17). The Antichrist will also pose as Christ by introducing a one-world government with himself as the ruler and a one-world religion in which he is worshiped as god. But God will destroy the kingdom of this king (**he will come to his end**; cf. Dan. 7:11, 26) at the personal appearance of Jesus Christ to this earth (Rev. 19:19-20).

c. Israel delivered (12:1-3)

12:1. No doubt when the revelation contained in chapter 12 was given Daniel, he was concerned about his people's destiny. Now at the conclusion of this vision, the angel consoled Daniel by revealing two facts (vv. 1-3). First, the people of Israel (**your people**; cf. 9:24; 10:14) **will be delivered** by the intervention of **Michael** the angelic **prince** (cf. 10:13, 21), **who** is Israel's defender. In the Great Tribulation Satan will attempt to exterminate every descendant of Abraham (see comments on Rev. 12:15). This **will be a time of** great unprecedented **distress** for Israel (cf. Matt. 24:21). Satan's attack against the people of the kingdom will be part of his effort to prevent the return and reign of Christ.

The deliverance of Israel, Daniel's "people," refers not to individual salvation, though a remnant will be saved, but rather to national deliverance from subjugation to the Gentiles (cf. comments on "all Israel will be saved" in Rom. 11:26).

12:2-3. The second fact that consoled Daniel is the promise that those who sleep will be resurrected. Many Jews will lose their lives at the hands of Gentiles in the events revealed in chapter 11 (cf. Rev. 20:4). To **sleep in the dust of the earth** (cf. Ps. 7:5) does not mean unconscious existence in death. It simply means that a dead person *appears* to be asleep. The body is "asleep," not the soul (cf. comments on 1 Thes. 4:13). Unbelieving Jews will be resurrected **to shame and everlasting contempt** and will not partake in the covenanted blessings. Jews, however, who believe the Messiah will be resurrected bodily **to everlasting life** and to positions of honor in Christ's millennial kingdom. Being glorified in the kingdom, they **will shine like the brightness of the heavens.** (Cf. Matt. 13:43, "Then the righteous will shine like the sun in the kingdom of their Father.") They will be **wise,** for they will trust in the Messiah even though it will result in their suffering.

This message that God will remember His covenant and will fulfill all He promised to Israel (in spite of her sufferings at the hands of the Gentiles) will be a consolation that will in turn cause them to **lead** others **to righteousness** (cf. the "wise" in Dan. 12:10). No righteousness of God's people ever goes unrewarded so those who are faithful under persecution will shine **like the stars forever and ever.**

The resurrection of believers martyred in the Tribulation will occur at the second coming of Christ (cf. Rev. 20:4, "they came to life and reigned with Christ 1,000 years"). The unbelieving dead, however, will be resurrected to "everlasting contempt" and torment at the end of the 1,000-year reign of Christ (cf. Rev. 20:5; John 5:28-29).

4. CONCLUSION (12:4-13)

a. Sealing of the book (12:4)

12:4. Understandably **Daniel** and his immediate readers could not have comprehended all the details of the prophecies given in this book (cf. v. 8). Not until history continued to unfold would many be able to understand these prophetic revelations. But God indicated that an increased understanding of what Daniel had written would come. People today, looking back over history, can see the significance of much of what Daniel predicted. And in **the time of the end** (cf. v. 9, and note " the end" and "the end of the days" in v. 13) the words of this book that have been sealed (kept intact) will be understood by **many** who will seek to gain **knowledge** from it. This will be in the Tribulation (cf. 11:40, "the time of the end"). Even though Daniel's people may not have fully understood this book's prophecies, the predictions did comfort them. They were assured that God will ultimately deliver Israel from the Gentiles

and bring her into His covenanted promises.

b. Questions concerning the Great Tribulation (12:5-13)

12:5-6. This section (vv. 5-13) includes two requests (one by an angel and one by **Daniel**) and two angelic replies. The first request is in verses 5-6, and the first answer is in verse 7. The second question is in verse 8, and the second reply is in verses 9-13. Evidently **two** angels had attended the angelic messenger, who was probably Gabriel (cf. comments on 10:5). **One of** the angels across **the river** (the Tigris; cf. 10:4) called to an angel standing by Gabriel (the one **clothed in linen;** cf. 10:5) and asked, **How long will it be before these astonishing things are fulfilled?** "These astonishing things" probably refer to the events recorded in 11:36-45, which pertain to Israel's final occupation by the coming Gentile ruler.

12:7. Gabriel answered the inquiring angel that those events will be fulfilled in **a time, times, and half a time,** that is, in three and one-half years (cf. comments on 7:25). Though this final ruler will reign for seven years, the first half will be a time of comparative peace for Israel. They will be enjoying the benefits of the covenant this king will make with them (9:27). Israel will be "a land of unwalled villages," a land in which the people will be "without walls and without gates and bars" (Ezek. 38:11). But the Antichrist will break that covenant (Dan. 9:27) near the middle of the 70th "seven" of years. Then the king of the South and the king of the North will invade Israel (11:40). After destroying these two armies, this Gentile king (the Antichrist) will move into Israel, occupy the land, and set up his political and religious headquarters in Jerusalem (11:41, 45). He will reign in Jerusalem as king and god and will become the greatest persecutor Israel has ever known (Rev. 13:5-7). Israel's **power** will be **broken** by his ruthless power, and then at the end of the Tribulation **all these things** (the events in 11:40-45) **will be completed.**

12:8. Then Daniel addressed a question to Gabriel, whom he called **My lord** (a term of respect like "Sir"; cf. 10:16-17, 19). Daniel asked, **What will the outcome of all this be?** He wanted to know God's program for Israel beyond the Tribulation period. Little information about Israel's blessings in the millennial reign following the Second Advent of Christ had been given to Daniel, though he did know that God's eternal kingdom will be established (2:44; 7:14, 22, 27) and the saints will possess (rule in) that kingdom. Many such prophecies had been given through the prophets and more would be given through prophets who were yet to come (Haggai, Zechariah, Malachi).

12:9-10. As the angel already stated (v. 4), **the words are** to be **closed up and sealed** (kept intact and thus made available) **until the time of the end** (the second half of the 70th "seven" of years; cf. v. 7; also note "end" in vv. 4, 13). In that period of time **many** Jews will turn to the Savior (cf. v. 3), and as a result (**will be** spiritually **purified . . . spotless and refined. But the wicked will continue** in their ways, following and worshiping the Antichrist, the world ruler. What God revealed to Daniel will continue to be osbcure to them (cf. 1 Cor. 2:14), but **the wise** (i.e., the righteous; cf. "wise" and "righteousness" in Dan. 12:3) **will understand.**

12:11. The angel said that **1,290 days** will be measured off **from the time that the daily sacrifice is abolished** (cf. 9:27, "he will put an end to sacrifice") **and the abomination that causes desolation is set up** (cf. 9:27, "one who causes desolation will place abominations on a wing of the temple"). The last half of the 70th "seven" of years is "a time, times, and half a time" (7:25; Rev. 12:14), which is three and one-half years. It is also designated as 42 months (Rev. 11:2) or 1,260 days (Rev. 11:3). How then can the variance of 30 days (1,290 compared with 1,260) be explained? Some suggest that the 30 days will extend beyond the end of the Tribulation, allowing for the judgment of Israel and the judgment of the nations. Another possibility is that the 1,290 days will begin 30 days before the middle of the 70th "seven" of years when the world ruler will set up "the abomination that causes desolation" (Matt. 24:15). The 1,290 days could begin with an announcement (about the abomination) made 30 days before the abomination is introduced. This abomination, as stated earlier, will be an image of himself (Rev.

13:14-15) and will be the symbol of this religious system.

12:12-13. Blessing is pronounced on **one who waits for and** lives to see **the end of the 1,335 days.** This is an additional 45 days beyond the 1,290 days (v. 11). Forty-five days after the end of the Tribulation Israel's long-awaited blessings will be realized. This may mark the blessing of the Millennium; or it may be when Christ, who will have appeared in the *heavens* (Matt. 24:30) 45 days earlier, will actually descend to the *earth,* His feet touching down on the Mount of Olives (cf. Acts 1:11). For believers Christ's coming is a blessing and a glorious hope.

Daniel did not live to see many of his prophecies fulfilled. He, the angel said, would **rest,** that is, in death (cf. v. 2). But he will be resurrected (**you will rise at the end of the days**), and he will receive his **allotted inheritance** in the Millennium. Because of Daniel's faith in God he led a life of faithful service for Him, and for that faith and that obedience he will receive a glorious reward. All who like Daniel trust the Lord will share in the blessings of His millennial kingdom.

BIBLIOGRAPHY

Anderson, Robert. *The Coming Prince.* London: Hodder & Stoughton, 1881. Reprint. Grand Rapids: Kregel Publications, 1975.

Baldwin, Joyce G. *Daniel: An Introduction and Commentary.* The Tyndale Old Testament Commentaries. Downers Grove, Ill.: Inter-Varsity Press, 1978.

Campbell, Donald K. *Daniel: Decoder of Dreams.* Wheaton, Ill.: SP Publications, Victor Books, 1977.

Culver, Robert D. *Daniel and the Latter Days.* Rev. ed. Chicago: Moody Press, 1977.

———. *The Histories and Prophecies of Daniel.* Winona Lake, Ind.: BMH Books, 1980.

McDowell, Josh. *Daniel in the Critic's Den.* San Bernardino, Calif.: Here's Life Publishers, 1979.

Price, Walter K. *In the Final Days.* Chicago: Moody Press, 1977.

Walvoord, John F. *Daniel: The Key to Prophetic Revelation.* Chicago: Moody Press, 1971.

Wilson, Robert Dick. *Studies in the Book of Daniel.* Grand Rapids: Baker Book House, 1979.

Wiseman, D.J., et al. *Notes on Some Problems in the Book of Daniel.* London: Tyndale Press, 1965.

Wood, Leon. *A Commentary on Daniel.* Grand Rapids: Zondervan Publishing House, 1973.

_____. *Daniel: A Study Guide.* Grand Rapids: Zondervan Publishing House, 1975.

At David C Cook, we equip the local church around the corner and around the globe to make disciples. Come see how we are working together—go to **www.davidccook.com**. Thank you!

transforming lives together